For Reference

Not to be taken from this room

SHORT STORIES
for Students

Advisors

Jayne M. Burton is a teacher of English, a member of the Delta Kappa Gamma International Society for Key Women Educators, and currently a master's degree candidate in the Interdisciplinary Study of Curriculum and Instruction and English at Angelo State University.

Tom Shilts is the youth librarian at the Okemos branch of Capital Area District Library in Okemos, Michigan. He holds an MSLS degree from Clarion University of Pennsylvania and an MA in U.S. History from the University of North Dakota.

Amy Spade Silverman has taught at independent schools in California, Texas, Michigan, and New York. She holdsa bachelor of arts degree from the University of Michigan and a master of fine arts degree from the University of Houston. She is a member of the National Council of Teachers of English and Teachers and Writers. She is an exam reader for Advanced Placement Literature and Composition. She is also a poet, published in *North American Review*, *Nimrod*, and *Michigan Quarterly Review*, among others.

SHORT STORIES
for Students

**Presenting Analysis, Context, and Criticism
on Commonly Studied Short Stories**

VOLUME 39

Matthew Derda, Project Editor

Foreword by Thomas E. Barden

GALE
CENGAGE Learning

Farmington Hills, Mich • San Francisco • New York • Waterville, Maine
Meriden, Conn • Mason, Ohio • Chicago

Short Stories for Students, Volume 39

Project Editor: Matthew Derda

Rights Acquisition and Management:
Lynn Vagg

Composition: Evi Abou-El-Seoud

Manufacturing: Rhonda A. Dover

Imaging: John Watkins

Product Design: Pamela A. E. Galbreath,
Jennifer Wahi

Digital Content Production: Kevin Duffy

Product Manager: Meggin Condino

For product information and technology assistance, contact us at
Gale Customer Support, 1-800-877-4253.
For permission to use material from this text or product,
submit all requests online at **www.cengage.com/permissions.**
Further permissions questions can be emailed to
permissionrequest@cengage.com

While every effort has been made to ensure the reliability of the information presented in this publication, Gale, a part of Cengage Learning, does not guarantee the accuracy of the data contained herein. Gale accepts no payment for listing; and inclusion in the publication of any organization, agency, institution, publication, service, or individual does not imply endorsement of the editors or publisher. Errors brought to the attention of the publisher and verified to the satisfaction of the publisher will be corrected in future editions.

Gale
27500 Drake Rd.
Farmington Hills, MI, 48331-3535

ISBN-13: 978-1-4144-9526-2

ISSN 1092-7735

This title is also available as an e-book.
ISBN-13: 978-1-4144-9283-4
Contact your Gale, a part of Cengage Learning sales representative for ordering information.

Printed in Mexico
1 2 3 4 5 6 7 18 17 16 15 14

Table of Contents

Why Study Literature At All?

Short Stories for Students is designed to provide readers with information and discussion about a wide range of important contemporary and historical works of short fiction, and it does that job very well. However, I want to use this guest foreword to address a question that it does *not* take up. It is a fundamental question that is often ignored in high school and college English classes as well as research texts, and one that causes frustration among students at all levels, namely why study literature at all? Isn't it enough to read a story, enjoy it, and go about one's business? My answer (to be expected from a literary professional, I suppose) is no. It is not enough. It is a start; but it is not enough. Here's why.

First, literature is the only part of the educational curriculum that deals directly with the actual world of lived experience. The philosopher Edmund Husserl used the apt German term *die Lebenswelt*, "the living world," to denote this realm. All the other content areas of the modern American educational system avoid the subjective, present reality of everyday life. Science (both the natural and the social varieties) objectifies, the fine arts create and/or perform, history reconstructs. Only literary study persists in posing those questions we all asked before our schooling taught us to give up on them. Only literature gives credibility to personal perceptions, feelings, dreams, and the "stream of consciousness" that is our inner voice. Literature wonders about infinity, wonders why God permits evil, wonders

what will happen to us after we die. Literature admits that we get our hearts broken, that people sometimes cheat and get away with it, that the world is a strange and probably incomprehensible place. Literature, in other words, takes on all the big and small issues of what it means to be human. So my first answer is that of the humanist we should read literature and study it and take it seriously because it enriches us as human beings. We develop our moral imagination, our capacity to sympathize with other people, and our ability to understand our existence through the experience of fiction.

My second answer is more practical. By studying literature we can learn how to explore and analyze texts. Fiction may be about *die Lebenswelt*, but it is a construct of words put together in a certain order by an artist using the medium of language. By examining and studying those constructions, we can learn about language as a medium. We can become more sophisticated about word associations and connotations, about the manipulation of symbols, and about style and atmosphere. We can grasp how ambiguous language is and how important context and texture is to meaning. In our first encounter with a work of literature, of course, we are not supposed to catch all of these things. We are spellbound, just as the writer wanted us to be. It is as serious students of the writer's art that we begin to see how the tricks are done.

Seeing the tricks, which is another way of saying "developing analytical and close reading skills," is important above and beyond its intrinsic literary educational value. These skills transfer to other fields and enhance critical thinking of any kind. Understanding how language is used to construct texts is powerful knowledge. It makes engineers better problem solvers, lawyers better advocates and courtroom practitioners, politicians better rhetoricians, marketing and advertising agents better sellers, and citizens more aware consumers as well as better participants in democracy. This last point is especially important, because rhetorical skill works both ways when we learn how language is manipulated in the making of texts the result is that we become less susceptible when language is used to manipulate us.

My third reason is related to the second. When we begin to see literature as created artifacts of language, we become more sensitive to good writing in general. We get a stronger sense of the importance of individual words, even the sounds of words and word combinations. We begin to understand Mark Twain's delicious proverb "The difference between the right word and the almost right word is the difference between lightning and a lightning bug." Getting beyond the "enjoyment only" stage of literature gets us closer to becoming makers of word art ourselves. I am not saying that studying fiction will turn every student into a Faulkner or a Shakespeare. But it will make us more adaptable and effective writers, even if our art form ends up being the office memo or the corporate annual report.

Studying short stories, then, can help students become better readers, better writers, and even better human beings. But I want to close with a warning. If your study and exploration of the craft, history, context, symbolism, or anything else about a story starts to rob it of the magic you felt when you first read it, it is time to stop. Take a break, study another subject, shoot some hoops, or go for a run. Love of reading is too important to be ruined by school. The early twentieth century writer Willa Cather, in her novel *My Antonia*, has her narrator Jack Burden tell a story that he and Antonia heard from two old Russian immigrants when they were teenagers. These immigrants, Pavel and Peter, told about an incident from their youth back in Russia that the narrator could recall in vivid detail thirty years later. It was a harrowing story of a wedding party starting home in sleds and being chased by starving wolves. Hundreds of wolves attacked the group's sleds one by one as they sped across the snow trying to reach their village. In a horrible revelation, the old Russians revealed that the groom eventually threw his own bride to the wolves to save himself. There was even a hint that one of the old immigrants might have been the groom mentioned in the story. Cather has her narrator conclude with his feelings about the story. "We did not tell Pavel's secret to anyone, but guarded it jealously as if the wolves of the Ukraine had gathered that night long ago, and the wedding party had been sacrificed, just to give us a painful and peculiar pleasure." That feeling, that painful and peculiar pleasure, is the most important thing about literature. Study and research should enhance that feeling and never be allowed to overwhelm it.

Thomas E. Barden
Professor of English and Director of
Graduate English Studies, The
University of Toledo

Introduction

Purpose of the Book

The purpose of *Short Stories for Students* (*SSfS*) is to provide readers with a guide to understanding, enjoying, and studying short stories by giving them easy access to information about the work. Part of Gale's "For Students" Literature line, *SSfS* is specifically designed to meet the curricular needs of high school and undergraduate college students and their teachers, as well as the interests of general readers and researchers considering specific short fiction. While each volume contains entries on "classic" stories frequently studied in classrooms, there are also entries containing hard-to-find information on contemporary stories, including works by multicultural, international, and women writers.

The information covered in each entry includes an introduction to the story and the story's author; a plot summary, to help readers unravel and understand the events in the work; descriptions of important characters, including explanation of a given character's role in the narrative as well as discussion about that character's relationship to other characters in the story; analysis of important themes in the story; and an explanation of important literary techniques and movements as they are demonstrated in the work.

In addition to this material, which helps the readers analyze the story itself, students are also provided with important information on the literary and historical background informing each work. This includes a historical context essay, a box comparing the time or place the story was written to modern Western culture, a critical overview essay, and excerpts from critical essays on the story or author. A unique feature of *SSfS* is a specially commissioned critical essay on each story, targeted toward the student reader.

To further help today's student in studying and enjoying each story, information on audiobooks and other media adaptations is provided (if available), as well as reading suggestions for works of fiction and nonfiction on similar themes and topics. Classroom aids include ideas for research papers and lists of critical and reference sources that provide additional material on the work.

Selection Criteria

The titles for each volume of *SSfS* were selected by surveying numerous sources on teaching literature and analyzing course curricula for various school districts. Some of the sources surveyed include: literature anthologies, *Reading Lists for College-Bound Students: The Books Most Recommended by America's Top Colleges*; *Teaching the Short Story: A Guide to Using Stories from around the World*, by the National Council of Teachers of English (NCTE); and "A Study of High School Literature Anthologies," conducted by Arthur Applebee at the Center for the Learning and Teaching of Literature and sponsored by the National Endowment for the

Arts and the Office of Educational Research and Improvement.

Input was also solicited from our advisory board, as well as educators from various areas. From these discussions, it was determined that each volume should have a mix of "classic" stories (those works commonly taught in literature classes) and contemporary stories for which information is often hard to find. Because of the interest in expanding the canon of literature, an emphasis was also placed on including works by international, multicultural, and women authors. Our advisory board members—educational professionals— helped pare down the list for each volume. Works not selected for the present volume were noted as possibilities for future volumes. As always, the editor welcomes suggestions for titles to be included in future volumes.

How Each Entry Is Organized

Each entry, or chapter, in *SSfS* focuses on one story. Each entry heading lists the title of the story, the author's name, and the date of the story's publication. The following elements are contained in each entry:

Introduction: a brief overview of the story which provides information about its first appearance, its literary standing, any controversies surrounding the work, and major conflicts or themes within the work.

Author Biography: this section includes basic facts about the author's life, and focuses on events and times in the author's life that may have inspired the story in question.

Plot Summary: a description of the events in the story. Lengthy summaries are broken down with subheads.

Characters: an alphabetical listing of the characters who appear in the story. Each character name is followed by a brief to an extensive description of the character's role in the story, as well as discussion of the character's actions, relationships, and possible motivation.

Characters are listed alphabetically by last name. If a character is unnamed—for instance, the narrator in "The Eatonville Anthology"—the character is listed as "The Narrator" and alphabetized as "Narrator." If a character's first name is the only one given, the name will appear alphabetically by that name.

Themes: a thorough overview of how the topics, themes, and issues are addressed within the story. Each theme discussed appears in a separate subhead.

Style: this section addresses important style elements of the story, such as setting, point of view, and narration; important literary devices used, such as imagery, foreshadowing, symbolism; and, if applicable, genres to which the work might have belonged, such as Gothicism or Romanticism. Literary terms are explained within the entry, but can also be found in the Glossary.

Historical Context: this section outlines the social, political, and cultural climate in which the author lived and the work was created. This section may include descriptions of related historical events, pertinent aspects of daily life in the culture, and the artistic and literary sensibilities of the time in which the work was written. If the story is historical in nature, information regarding the time in which the story is set is also included. Long sections are broken down with helpful subheads.

Critical Overview: this section provides background on the critical reputation of the author and the story, including bannings or any other public controversies surrounding the work. For older works, this section may include a history of how the story was first received and how perceptions of it may have changed over the years; for more recent works, direct quotes from early reviews may also be included.

Criticism: an essay commissioned by *SSfS* which specifically deals with the story and is written specifically for the student audience, as well as excerpts from previously published criticism on the work (if available).

Sources: an alphabetical list of critical material used in compiling the entry, with bibliographical information.

Further Reading: an alphabetical list of other critical sources which may prove useful for the student. Includes full bibliographical information and a brief annotation.

Suggested Search Terms: a list of search terms and phrases to jumpstart students' further information seeking. Terms include not just titles and author names but also terms and topics related to the historical and literary context of the works.

In addition, each entry contains the following highlighted sections, set apart from the main text as sidebars:

Media Adaptations: if available, a list of audio-books and important film and television adaptations of the story, including source information. The list also includes stage adaptations, musical adaptations, etc.

Topics for Further Study: a list of potential study questions or research topics dealing with the story. This section includes questions related to other disciplines the student may be studying, such as American history, world history, science, math, government, business, geography, economics, psychology, etc.

Compare and Contrast: an "at-a-glance" comparison of the cultural and historical differences between the author's time and culture and late twentieth century or early twenty-first century Western culture. This box includes pertinent parallels between the major scientific, political, and cultural movements of the time or place the story was written, the time or place the story was set (if a historical work), and modern Western culture. Works written after 1990 may not have this box.

What Do I Read Next?: a list of works that might give a reader points of entry into a classic work (e.g., YA or multicultural titles) and/or complement the featured story or serve as a contrast to it. This includes works by the same author and others, works from various genres, YA works, and works from various cultures and eras.

Other Features

SSfS includes "Why Study Literature At All?," a foreword by Thomas E. Barden, Professor of English and Director of Graduate English Studies at the University of Toledo. This essay provides a number of very fundamental reasons for studying literature and, therefore, reasons why a book such as *SSfS*, designed to facilitate the study of literature, is useful.

A Cumulative Author/Title Index lists the authors and titles covered in each volume of the *SSfS* series.

A Cumulative Nationality/Ethnicity Index breaks down the authors and titles covered in each volume of the *SSfS* series by nationality and ethnicity.

A Subject/Theme Index, specific to each volume, provides easy reference for users who may be studying a particular subject or theme rather than a single work. Significant subjects from events to broad themes are included.

Each entry may include illustrations, including photo of the author, stills from film adaptations (if available), maps, and/or photos of key historical events.

Citing Short Stories for Students

When writing papers, students who quote directly from any volume of *SSfS* may use the following general forms to document their source. These examples are based on MLA style; teachers may request that students adhere to a different style, thus, the following examples may be adapted as needed.

When citing text from *SSfS* that is not attributed to a particular author (for example, the Themes, Style, Historical Context sections, etc.), the following format may be used:

> "How I Met My Husband." *Short Stories for Students*. Ed. Sara Constantakis. Vol. 36. Detroit: Gale, Cengage Learning, 2013. 73–95. Print.

When quoting the specially commissioned essay from *SSfS* (usually the first essay under the Criticism subhead), the following format may be used:

> Dominic, Catherine. Critical Essay on "How I Met My Husband." *Short Stories for Students*. Ed. Sara Constantakis. Vol. 36. Detroit: Gale, Cengage Learning, 2013. 84–87. Print.

When quoting a journal or newspaper essay that is reprinted in a volume of *SSfS*, the following form may be used:

> Ditsky, John. "The Figure in the Linoleum: The Fictions of Alice Munro." *Hollins Critic* 22.3 (1985): 1–10. Rpt. in *Short Stories for Students*. Vol. 36. Ed. Sara Constantakis. Detroit: Gale, Cengage Learning, 2013. 92–94. Print.

When quoting material from a book that is reprinted in a volume of *SSfS*, the following form may be used:

> Cooke, John. "Alice Munro." *The Influence of Painting on Five Canadian Writers*. Lewiston, NY: Edwin Mellen Press, 1996. 69–85. Rpt. in *Short Stories for Students*. Vol. 36. Ed. Sara Constantakis. Detroit: Gale, Cengage Learning, 2013. 89–92. Print.

We Welcome Your Suggestions

The editorial staff of *Short Stories for Students* welcomes your comments and ideas. Readers who wish to suggest short stories to appear in future volumes, or who have other suggestions, are cordially invited to contact the editor. You may contact the editor via E-mail at: **ForStudentsEditors@cengage.com.** Or write to the editor at:

Editor, *Short Stories for Students*
Gale
27500 Drake Road
Farmington Hills, MI 48331-3535

Literary Chronology

1850: Guy de Maupassant is born on August 5 in Château de Miromesnil in Normandy, France.

1857: Joseph Conrad is born on December 3 in Berdichev, Ukraine.

1875: Thomas Mann is born on June 6 in Lübeck, Germany.

1881: Lu Xun is born on September 25 in Shaoxing, China.

1883: Guy de Maupassant's "La ficelle" is published in *Le Gaulois*. It is later published in English as "The Piece of String" in *Best Short Stories of Guy de Maupassant* in 1944.

1888: Katherine Mansfield is born on October 14 in Wellington, New Zealand.

1892: Pearl S. Buck is born on June 26 in Hillsboro, West Virginia.

1893: Guy de Maupassant Maupassant dies of syphilis on July 6 in Passay, Paris.

1897: Joseph Conrad's "The Lagoon" is published in *Cornhill Magazine*.

1903: Thomas Mann's "Das Wunderkind" is published in *Neue Freie Presse*. It is published in English as "The Infant Prodigy" in *Stories of Three Decades* in 1936.

1908: João Guimarães Rosa is born on June 27 in Cordisburgo, Brazil.

1915: W. C. Heinz is born on January 11 in Mount Vernon, New York.

1922: Katherine Mansfield's "A Cup of Tea" is published in *The Story-Teller*.

1923: Katherine Mansfield dies of a pulmonary hemorrhage on January 9 in Fountainebleau, France.

1924: Joseph Conrad dies of heart failure on August 3 in Canterbury, England.

1924: Lu Xun's "The New-Year Sacrifice" is published in *Dongfang Zazhi*. It is later published in English in *The New-Year Sacrifice and Other Stories* in 2002.

1929: Barbara Kimenye is born on December 19 in Halifax, West Yorkshire.

1929: Thomas Mann is awarded the Nobel Prize for Literature.

1932: Pearl S. Buck is awarded the Pulitzer Prize for *The Good Earth*.

1936: Lu Xun dies of tuberculosis on October 19 in Shanghai, China.

1938: Pearl S. Buck is awarded the Nobel Prize for Literature.

1939: Toni Cade Bambara is born on March 25 in New York, New York.

1941: Anne Tyler is born on October 25 in Minneapolis, Minnesota.

1942: Sue Ellen Bridgers is born on September 20 in Winterville, North Carolina.

1950: W. C. Heinz's "One Throw" is published in *Collier's Weekly*.

1954: Sandra Cisneros is born on December 20 in Chicago, Illinois.

1955: Thomas Mann dies of atherosclerosis on August 12 in Zurich, Switzerland.

1955: Pearl S. Buck's "Christmas Day in the Morning" is published in *Collier's*.

1959: Ben Okri is born on March 15 in Minna, Nigeria.

1962: João Guimarães Rosa's "A terceira margem do rio" is published in *Primeiras estórias*. It is published in English as "The Third Bank of the River" in *The Third Bank of the River and Other Stories* in 1968.

1965: Barbara Kimenye's "The Winner" is published in *Kalasanda*.

1967: João Guimarães Rosa dies of a heart attack on November 19 in Rio de Janeiro, Brazil.

1973: Pearl S. Buck dies of lung cancer on March 6 in Danbury, Vermont.

1983: Anne Tyler's "Teenage Wasteland" is published in *Seventeen* magazine.

1986: Anne Tyler is awarded the Pulitzer Prize for *Fiction for Breathing Lessons*.

1987: Sue Ellen Bridgers's "The Beginning of Something" is published in *Visions: Nineteen Short Stories by Outstanding Writers for Young Adults*.

1991: Sandra Cisneros's "Barbie-Q" is published in *Woman Hollering Creek and Other Stories*.

1993: Ben Okri's "A Prayer from the Living" is published in *New York Times*.

1996: Toni Cade Bambara's "The War of the Wall" is published in *Deep Sightings and Rescue Missions: Fiction, Essays, and Conversations*.

1995: Toni Cade Bambara dies of colon cancer on December 9 in Germantown, Pennsylvania.

2008: W. C. Heinz dies of natural causes on February 27 in Bennington, Vermont.

2012: Barbara Kimenye dies on August 12 in London, England.

Acknowledgements

The editors wish to thank the copyright holders of the excerpted criticism included in this volume and the permissions managers of many book and magazine publishing companies for assisting us in securing reproduction rights. We are also grateful to the staffs of the Detroit Public Library, the Library of Congress, the University of Detroit Mercy Library, Wayne State University Purdy/Kresge Library Complex, and the University of Michigan Libraries for making their resources available to us. Following is a list of the copyright holders who have granted us permission to reproduce material in this volume of *SSfS*. Every effort has been made to trace copyright, but if omissions have been made, please let us know.

COPYRIGHTED EXCERPTS IN SSfS, VOLUME 39, WERE REPRODUCED FROM THE FOLLOWING SOURCES:

ALAN Review, 27.1, fall, 1999. Copyright © 1999 by *ALAN Review*. Reproduced by permission of the publisher.—*Appalachian Journal*, 26.4, summer, 1999. Copyright © 1999 by *Appalachian Journal*. Reproduced by permission of the publisher.—Billy, Ted. From *A Wilderness of Words: Closure and Disclosure in Conrad's Short Fiction*. Texas Tech University Press, 1997. Copyright © 1997, Texas Tech University Press. Reproduced by permission of the publisher.—*Booklist*, 99.4, October 15, 2002. Copyright © 2002 by *Booklist*. Reproduced by permission of the publisher.—

Butler-Evans, Elliott. From ***Race, Gender, and Desire: Narrative Strategies in the Fiction of Toni Cade Bambara, Toni Morrison, and Alice Walker***. Temple University Press, 1989. Copyright © 1989, Temple University Press. Reproduced by permission of the publisher.—Doyle, Paul A. From ***Pearl S. Buck***. Twayne Publishers, 1965. Copyright © 1965, Cengage Learning. Reproduced by permission of Gale, a part of Cengage Learning.—Evans, Elizabeth. From ***Anne Tyler***. Twayne Publishers, 1993. Copyright © 1993, Cengage Learning. Reproduced by permission of Gale, a part of Cengage Learning.—Gregorio, Laurence A. From ***Maupassant's Fiction and the Darwinian View of Life***. Peter Lang, 2005. Copyright © 2005, Peter Lang. Reproduced by permission of the publisher.—***Guardian*** (London, England), October 22, 2012. Copyright © 2012 by ***Guardian***. Reproduced by permission of the publisher.—Hipple, Ted. From ***Presenting Sue Ellen Bridgers***. Twayne Publishers, 1990. Copyright © 1990, Cengage Learning. Reproduced by permission of Gale, a part of Cengage Learning.—***Kirkus Reviews***, 70.21, November 1, 2002. Copyright © 2002 by ***Kirkus Reviews***. Reproduced by permission of the publisher.—Lesér, Esther H. From ***Thomas Mann's Short Fiction: An Intellectual Biography***. Edited by Mitzi Brunsdale. Fairleigh Dickinson University Press, 1989. Copyright © 1989, Fairleigh Dickinson University Press. Reproduced by permission of the publisher.—Le V. Harris, Trevor A. From

Maupassant in the Hall of Mirrors: Ironies of Repetition in the Work of Guy de Maupassant. St. Martin's Press, 1990. Copyright © 1990, St. Martin's Press. Reproduced by permission of the publisher.—Liao, Kang. From *Pearl S. Buck: A Cultural Bridge Across the Pacific*. Greenwood Press, 1997. Copyright © 1997, Greenwood Press. Reproduced by permission of the publisher.—*Library Journal*, 126.10, June 1, 2001; 127.11, June 15, 2002. Copyright © 2001, 2002 by *Library Journal*. Reproduced by permission of the publisher.—Lim, David C.L. From *The Infinite Longing for Home: Desire and the Nation in Selected Writings of Ben Okri and K. S. Maniam*. Rodopi, 2005. Copyright © 2005, Rodopi. Reproduced by permission of the publisher.—May, Charles E. From *Reference Guide to Short Fiction*, 2nd ed. Edited by Thomas Riggs. St. James Press, 1999. Copyright © 1999, St. James Press. Reproduced by permission of the publisher.—*Military Review*, 84.1, January–February, 2004. Copyright © 2004 by *Military Review*. Reproduced by permission of the publisher.—Nathan, Rhoda B. From *Critical Essays on Katherine Mansfield*. Edited by Rhoda B. Nathan. G.K. Hall, 1993. Copyright © 1993, G.K. Hall. Reproduced by permission of the publisher.—Petry, Alice Hall. From *Understanding Anne Tyler*. University of South Carolina Press, 1990. Copyright © 1990, University of South Carolina Press. Reproduced by permission of the publisher.—Rebolledo, Tey Diana. From *The Chronicles of Panchita Villa and Other Guerrillas*. University of Texas Press, 2005. Copyright © 2005, University of Texas Press. Reproduced by permission of the publisher.—Tokarczyk, Michelle M. From *Class Definitions: On the Lives and Writings of Maxine Hong Kingston, Sandra Cisneros, and Dorothy Allison*. Susquehanna University Press, 2008. Copyright © 2008, Susquehanna University Press. Reproduced by permission of the publisher.—Vincent, Jon S. From *João Guimarães Rosa*. Twayne Publishers, 1978. Copyright © 1978, Cengage Learning. Reproduced by permission of Gale, a part of Cengage Learning.—von Kowallis, Jon Eugene. From *The Lyrical Lu Xun: A Study of Classical-Style Verse*. University of Hawai'i Press, 1996. Copyright © 1996, University of Hawai'i Press. Reproduced by permission of the publisher.—Wagenknecht, Edward. From *The Critical Response to Katherine Mansfield*. Edited by Jan Pilditch. Greenwood Press, 1996. Copyright © 1996, Greenwood Press. Reproduced by permission of the publisher.—Wilentz, Gay. From *Healing Narratives: Women Writers Curing Cultural Dis-ease*. Rutgers University Press, 2000. Copyright © 2000, Rutgers University Press. Reproduced by permission of the publisher.

Contributors

Susan K. Andersen: Andersen holds a PhD in English. Entry on "Barbie-Q." Original essay on "Barbie-Q."

Bryan Aubrey: Aubrey holds a PhD in English. Entry on "The War of the Wall." Original essay on "The War of the Wall."

Rita M. Brown: Brown is an English professor. Entry on "Teenage Wasteland." Original essay on "Teenage Wasteland."

Catherine Dominic: Dominic is a novelist and a freelance writer and editor. Entries on "A Cup of Tea" and "A Prayer from the Living." Original essays on "A Cup of Tea" and "A Prayer from the Living."

Kristen Sarlin Greenberg: Greenberg is a freelance writer and editor with a background in literature and philosophy. Entry on "The Beginning of Something." Original essay on "The Beginning of Something."

Michael Allen Holmes: Holmes is a writer with existential interests. Entries on "One Throw" and "The Third Bank of the River." Original essays on "One Throw" and "The Third Bank of the River."

Sheri Metzger Karmiol: Karmiol teaches literature and drama at the University of New Mexico, where she is an adjunct professor in the University Honors College. Entry on "The Piece of String." Original essay on "The Piece of String."

David Kelly: Kelly is an instructor of literature and creative writing. Entry on "Christmas Day in the Morning." Original essay on "Christmas Day in the Morning."

Amy Lynn Miller: Miller is a graduate of the University of Cincinnati and currently resides in New Orleans, Louisiana. Entry on "The New-Year Sacrifice." Original essay on "The New-Year Sacrifice."

Michael J. O'Neal: O'Neal holds a PhD in English. Entry on "The Lagoon." Original essay on "The Lagoon."

April Paris: Paris is a freelance writer with an extensive background writing literary and educational materials. Entry on "The Winner." Original essay on "The Winner."

Bradley Skeen: Skeen is a classicist. Entry on "The Infant Prodigy." Original essay on "The Infant Prodigy."

Barbie-Q

SANDRA CISNEROS

1991

Sandra Cisneros is one of the founding voices of Chicano literature, focusing especially on Chicana feminist themes. By the time Cisneros published *Woman Hollering Creek and Other Stories*, which includes the short story "Barbie-Q," in 1991, she had already made a breakthrough as the first mainstream Chicana author in the United States with *The House on Mango Street* (1984). The main character in *The House on Mango Street*, Esperanza, is like the narrator of "Barbie-Q," a child who tells of growing up in a poor Latino neighborhood in Chicago. Cisneros has continued to use that innocent voice as a reflector of the contradictory experiences of Mexican Americans, with their bicultural, bilingual legacy.

The little girls in "Barbie-Q" are both Mexican and American, but a Mexican American girl is going to have a different experience playing with a Barbie doll than does an Anglo-American girl. Cisneros does not tell the reader what the difference is; she lets the details speak for themselves. From the descriptions of Chicago and the Barbie dolls, the story appears to take place in the 1960s, when Cisneros herself would have been growing up there. The story is very short because the author, also a poet, writes impressionistic vignettes in a poetic prose so that the reader can see and feel what the characters are experiencing. She allows readers to form their own conclusions.

Sandra Cisneros (© *AP Images | Eric Gay*)

AUTHOR BIOGRAPHY

Sandra Cisneros was born in Chicago, Illinois, on December 20, 1954, to Alfredo Cisneros Del Moral and Elvira Cordero Anguiano. She was the only girl in a family of six sons. Alfredo had come from a once-wealthy family in Mexico City who sent him to college to be an accountant. He failed in the first year and ran away to the United States rather than face his father's anger. In Chicago, he met and married Elvira and lived in poverty while raising his family and working as an upholsterer. Elvira came from a poor Mexican Indian family that came to Chicago to work on the railroads. Alfredo constantly moved his family back and forth between Chicago and Mexico City, making Sandra feel insecure and homeless as a child, although she later appreciated her intimacy with Mexican culture. Each time the family returned to Chicago, they had to find a new home and a new school.

Elvira did not finish high school but had a sharp intellect and read constantly, and she passed these traits on to her daughter, allowing her time to herself to read in her room instead of doing housework. When she was eleven, the family had enough money to buy their first shabby house in a Puerto Rican neighborhood called Humboldt Park in Chicago, the background for her book *The House on Mango Street*. Cisneros wrote poems from the age of ten, and at Loyola University, where she majored in English, she took a creative writing class. She was encouraged by teachers to apply to the University of Iowa Writers' Workshop and was accepted, studying under Donald Justice, Marvin Bell, and Mark Strand.

The workshop had turned out famous writers like Flannery O'Connor and Robert Bly. But Cisneros and other minority students, such as her friend Native American poet Joy Harjo, did not feel as if they fit in. Cisneros finally had a revelation about her life work there—to write about her own unique Chicana experience. She got her MFA in 1978 and taught for three years at the Latino Youth Alternative High School in Chicago while writing *The House on Mango Street*, which was published in 1984. Her volume of poetry *My Wicked Wicked Ways* was received enthusiastically in 1987. *Woman Hollering Creek and Other Stories*, her collection of short stories including "Barbie-Q," came out in 1991. *Loose Woman*, a book of poems, followed in 1994; the novel *Caramelo* was published in 2002; and *Have You Seen Marie?* came out in 2012. Cisneros is considered an important author in the Chicano Renaissance and has taught in college creative writing programs at the University of California at Berkeley and the University of Michigan. She is part of the local arts community and engages in Latino social activism in San Antonio, Texas, where she makes her home.

Cisneros remains known as one of the important founders of the Chicano literary movement, but she is equally famous for her double-minority stance as a feminist from an ethnic culture. She has received fellowships from the National Endowment for the Arts, a MacArthur Fellowship, the Texas Medal of the Arts, an honorary doctorate from the State University of New York–Purchase, the PEN Center West Award, and the Lannan Foundation Literary Award for *Woman Hollering Creek*, as well as numerous other awards.

PLOT SUMMARY

"Barbie-Q" is a short, first-person narrative told by a little Chicana girl to her friend, Licha, the name given in the dedication under the title. The speaker addresses her friend in the second person throughout, as "you," and speaks in the present tense, as though they are at play with their Barbie dolls. The narrator seems to be the leader or recorder of their play. The time period implied is the 1960s, when the dolls mentioned and their clothing styles were popular.

The first paragraph describes each girl's Barbie doll and their outfits in detail. They have only been able to afford one doll and one extra outfit apiece. Each Barbie is wearing a swimsuit, and the narrator describes her friend's extra outfit for Barbie by the manufacturer's brand name for the ensemble, with its A-line coatdress and Jackie Kennedy hat, while her own doll's outfit is a strapless evening dress with long gloves and a chiffon scarf. Some of the black glitter has worn off the evening dress from their dressing and undressing the doll. In addition, they have designed their own Barbie dress from an old sock. It is apparent that the girls are poor, but judging from the way they speak the manufacturer's language, they have adopted the whole Barbie-doll culture. The reader may gather from the context that these are Chicana girls playing with Anglo-looking dolls.

The narrator sounds slightly bored by their Barbie play. She says they always play the same story. The two Barbies are roommates, and the narrator's Barbie invites in her boyfriend, Ken, whom the other Barbie steals and kisses. Then the two Barbies fight and call each other names. A problem is that their Ken doll is invisible because they cannot afford one and would rather wait to ask for new Barbie outfits next Christmas instead of wasting money on a boy doll. The story sounds like a soap opera, marked by jealous and competitive fighting over a man, probably suggested by the many comics, books, and accompanying Barbie materials.

The next Sunday the girls are walking through the Maxwell Street Market, a famous flea market in the Latino district of Chicago, and they spy among diverse bargains two Mattel boxes, one with a "Career Gal" business suit outfit and the other with a nightgown set. The girls say please over and over until they are given the outfits by their parents. The precise

MEDIA ADAPTATIONS

- *Loose Woman* (poetry) and *Woman Hollering Creek* (short stories), written and read by Sandra Cisneros, are available as an unabridged audiobook download from Random House Audio, 2005.

commercial descriptions of these Barbie outfits, with long lists of accessories, spoken by the little Chicana girls, is humorous on the one hand, but on the other, they imply a glamorous white middle-class lifestyle that is beyond the reach of the poor. The reader understands this dramatic irony and social commentary while the child characters are just innocently enjoying the dolls. The Barbie-doll appearance and clothes are the unrealistic stereotypes of a mainstream Anglo female life they are imbibing in their play but will never experience in adult life. Though Mattel later made ethnic Barbie dolls, this seems to be from a time when only white Barbies are available to the Chicana girls.

The girls are skipping with joy at their new purchases, but at the next stand they find even greater treasure—more Barbie dolls! These are Ken, Skipper (Barbie's sister), Tutti and Todd (the twins), Midge (Barbie's friend), Scooter and Ricky (Skipper's friends), Alan (Ken's friend), Francie (Barbie's cousin), and Bendable Legs Barbie. The girls are beside themselves to find the whole Barbie doll family. The language of excitement allows the reader to picture the girls jumping up and down at this important find.

Then comes the realization of why the bargains are available—all the dolls are water and smoke damaged from the fire in the toy warehouse on Halsted Street across the Dan Ryan Expressway. It is a fire sale for today only. They can still see the smoke rising from the warehouse blocks away. The street and expressway names contribute to the picture of Chicago's poorer urban district, home to a Latino flea market visited by thousands every Sunday for bargains.

The child narrator tries to be happy with the new family of dolls bought on Maxwell Street even if they still smell like smoke after being washed. The prettiest doll is Francie, and who cares that her left foot is melted? If she wears the prom dress with the gold belt and one does not lift the dress, one will never know. This last paragraph emphasizes that Barbie-doll play encourages children to focus on appearance as the most important thing in a woman's life. From an early age, an American female learns to hide her physical flaws so she can look acceptable, like everyone else. It also makes clear that these are disadvantaged children trying to fit into the mainstream image and culture without the money or heritage to do so. They take merchandise no one else wants, and the hidden message is that they might always be stuck with second best.

CHARACTERS

Alan

Alan Sherwood is a doll, Ken's best friend from 1964. He dated and married Midge in 1991 in the Barbie stories. He and the family of damaged Barbie dolls mentioned in the story were found and purchased by the narrator and her friend at the Maxwell Street Market during a fire sale.

Barbie

Barbie is the original doll from 1959, a teen fashion doll, whose name, according to the Barbie books, is Barbie Millicent Roberts, daughter of George and Margaret Roberts from Willows, Wisconsin. Barbie is shown as a teenager with pets and cars and friends but is also marketed as a career girl, doctor, stewardess, astronaut, and airplane pilot, as well as other occupations.

Bendable Legs Barbie

Introduced in 1965, Bendable Legs Barbie could bend and had a pageboy hairdo. She is now a collector's item, like the other vintage dolls from the 1950s and 1960s.

Francie

Francie was available from 1966 to 1977 as Barbie's modern cousin, with rooted eyelashes and a more modern look than the older dolls.

Ken

Ken Carson has been Barbie's boyfriend doll from 1959 except during their fictional break-ups, when she would date someone else temporarily.

Licha

Licha is the real little girl playmate of the narrator. The story is addressed to her in the second person, as though the two girls are currently playing with their Barbie dolls. Licha seems to be more passive, allowing the narrator to shape the play.

Midge

Midge Hadley has been Barbie's best friend doll from the 1960s to the present.

Narrator

The little Chicana girl narrator of the story uses the second person, *you*, to address her friend Licha as they play with their Barbie dolls. The narrator is the imaginative leader of the play, enthusiastic about finding the dolls and their outfits and trying to figure out how to collect them when they do not have any money. She is clever and makes a dress for Barbie out of a sock. The two girls are poor and living in Latino Chicago, probably in the 1960s, judging from the descriptions of the dolls.

Ricky

Ricky is the doll who is Skipper's friend, the boy next door, introduced in 1965.

Scooter

Scooter is Skipper's friend, and a friend of Ricky's, introduced in 1965.

Skipper

Skipper was added in 1964 as Barbie's younger sister.

Tutti and Todd

Added in 1965 for a few years, Tutti and Todd were smaller-sized twins and younger siblings of Barbie and Skipper.

THEMES

Mexican American Culture

Unlike many of the stories in *Woman Hollering Creek*, "Barbie-Q" contains no Spanish words or specific references to Chicana lifestyle. The reader knows that the narrator and her friend are Chicana from the context in the book and from the neighborhood references to Chicago. The scene might well have come from Cisneros's childhood memories of living on the north side of Chicago in Puerto Rican Humboldt Park, near the Latino Maxwell Street Market, where many Mexican Americans made their living selling items. Like the historic moment when the United States took over northern Mexico in 1848, incorporating the Mexicans there as US citizens, these little Chicana girls are surrounded and enfolded by American culture. They do not speak Spanish but seem to parrot commercial phrases in English.

Cisneros explores the theme of the borderland in almost all of the stories in this volume. Characters live near the US-Mexican border, or they carry a borderland in their awareness, having to negotiate both their Mexican heritage and their American lifestyle. They do not know how to balance both worlds. In the short story "Mericans," for instance, some tourists in a Mexican border town ask in Spanish if they can take a picture of a boy. The boy then speaks in English, and when the tourists are surprised, he explains that he is American. The boy and his siblings are Mexican Americans visiting their grandmother in Mexico. They play Flash Gordon while waiting outside the Mexican church. Cisneros and her family crossed and recrossed the border, living in both Mexico and the United States, like many Mexican Americans who are bilingual and bicultural.

Many of the stories in *Woman Hollering Creek* are about the mixture of values in the lives of Mexican American women, who are torn between traditional and modern lifestyles. As evidenced in "Barbie-Q," Cisneros shows the difficulty of maintaining an authentic identity in what is essentially a foreign culture, even though the Mexican Americans may be citizens of the United States. The little Chicana girls are fascinated by the high-fashion Barbie dolls, though they have little relevance to their own lives. They cannot afford the doll clothes, let alone the lifestyle Barbie represents, and from the ironic tone

TOPICS FOR FURTHER STUDY

- How does a child's filtering of the surroundings and behaviors of others differ from that of an adult? Write a scene, a sketch, or a short story from the point of view and in the voice of a child who does not really understand the implications of what he/she is seeing or saying.

- Is there a difference between a tale with a child narrator and children's literature? Compare and contrast the purpose of "Barbie-Q" with a story about Christopher Robin in the Winnie-the-Pooh books, or some other children's story. Write a paper showing the differing purposes and effects; be sure to give examples.

- As a class, do research on the history of the southwestern United States. Give PowerPoint presentations on cross-cultural views of the Southwest, highlighting differing histories and perspectives of the area, using excerpts from multicultural writers such as Simon J. Ortiz (Native American), Edward Abbey (environmentalist), Barbara Kingsolver (Anglo fiction writer), Jimmy Santiago Baca (Chicano poet), or Joyce Carol Thomas (African American children's author of *Marked by Fire*) to illustrate.

- Read the young-adult novel *Obasan* (1993), by Joy Kogawa, about the evacuation and relocation of Canadian citizens with Japanese ancestry during World War II. In class, compare the experience in this novel to the fiction of Sandra Cisneros, who shows in "Barbie-Q" and other stories what it feels like to be a foreigner from a different tradition in one's own country. Then interview people from different ethnic backgrounds living in the United States, and post your interviews on a class blog, discussing the difficulties and advantages of living on the border of two or more cultures.

The sisters in "Barbie-Q" are close — bickering and playing together. (© Tracy Whiteside / Shutterstock.com)

of the story, Cisneros is suggesting that Barbie is not going to help them know their own worth.

Americanization

The Barbie doll is part of the American ideal of beauty, fashion, wealth, and glamour. In this story, the dolls represent the process of Americanization that people of foreign or traditional cultures face when they live in a country with a predominantly Anglo population. Their own culture is marginalized in favor of popular culture and dominant values. If this story takes place in the 1960s, as is suggested, there would have been few mainstream references to Chicano culture, so the children want to be accepted as Americans. The little girls have already been turned into American consumers driven with a desire for the dolls and their extensive wardrobes. The children nag until the parents give in. They learn to want things they cannot have or cannot easily get since they are poor. They must take the compromised leftover dolls after the toy warehouse burns down. Mexican Americans without education or connections, like Cisneros's father, are often forced to take low-wage jobs in the United States and live in ghettos or barrios, ethnic neighborhoods where they face violence and poverty. This situation fosters a desire to be like more privileged Americans and live an affluent life rather than turning to one's own ethnic heritage. Pride in ethnic identity is lost, along with those cultural values.

Stereotypes

Another one of Cisneros's major themes concerns the construction of gender stereotypes. Women face the issues of acceptable female appearance which the Barbie doll raises as a role model. There have been many controversies over the implied message of Barbie, who is so thin as to look emaciated. The fear of being fat has led to many suffering from bulimia and anorexia. This can be a racial issue as well, since genes and standards of other ethnic groups may differ from Anglo bodies and standards. The original Barbie had a visible bust but no hips and sticklike legs, looking like many contemporary fashion models. There is a whole culture surrounding the doll, with movies, books, and other spin-offs that promote a certain commercialized lifestyle of popularity, cars, fashion, boyfriends, and money. In the story "Never Marry a Mexican" in *Woman Hollering Creek*, Clemencia is in love with an Anglo man but is thrown over for a Barbie-doll type who marries him and has a perfect house with Italian clothes and Estée Lauder cosmetics. Chicana Clemencia, however, being a mestiza artist, is very earthy and angry and passionate. She remakes her lover and herself in her paintings. She lives her own hybrid lifestyle, refusing to marry or yield to mainstream stereotypes.

The Barbie doll has been accused of representing certain patriarchal views of female beauty and identity, thus being a way to control female sexuality. For all their glamour, the Barbies do not evoke the kind of powerful sexuality that Cisneros attributes to her Mexican American characters in *Woman Hollering Creek*. There is Inez, for example, the sorceress common-law wife of the Mexican hero Zapata in "The Eyes of Zapata," who is sexually seductive and possessive but also a warrior and survivor.

STYLE

Chicano Literature

Literature written by Mexican Americans in the United States dates mostly from the time after 1848 when the United States annexed what was northern Mexico. These authors tend to radiate *chicanismo*, or Chicano identity, speech, culture, and ways of seeing. Because Chicanos, like Native Americans, were part of a conquest of territory, they were stranded within a larger foreign culture, having to develop their own culture, neither Mexican nor American but a hybrid.

Cisneros was the first major Chicana writer to be accepted by the mainstream literary world. *The House on Mango Street* was her breakthrough work, accepted by Vintage Press in 1989 after being published by the Latino Arte Público Press in 1984. Previously, only Chicano authors like Gary Soto had been recognized.

Many Chicano authors focus on borderland identity, as in "Barbie-Q," where the Chicana girls in Chicago are becoming Americanized. Other examples include Chicano poet Luis Omar Salinas, whose *Crazy Gypsy* (1970) is a seminal work in Chicano literature. Lorna Dee Cervantes is a major poet who founded the literary journal *MANGO*, which first published Cisneros and other Chicano writers. Cervantes published *Ciento: 100 100-Word Love Poems* in 2011. Poet Tino Villanueva (*Hay Otra Voz Poems*, 1972) is the founder of *Imagine: International Chicano Poetry Journal*. Tomás Rivera is known for his 1972 novella *This Migrant Earth*, as well as for being the first Chicano chancellor at the University of California, Riverside. Daniel Olivas is a short-story writer whose stories in *Devil Talk* (2004) are examples of magical realism. Luis Valdez, American playwright, actor, and film director, is best known for his 1978 play *Zoot Suit* and for his film *La Bamba*, about rock star Ritchie Valens.

Chicana Feminism

When the feminist movement in the United States was gaining momentum in the 1960s, women of color found that, although they had some issues that were similar to those of Anglo women, they had many concerns that were different. All women were dealing with sexism, but in addition, African American, Native American, and Latino women were dealing with racism and conditions within their own cultures. In Latin America, for instance, women had been historically treated by the men in their family as childbearers and homemakers without any voice or decision-making power. The double standard in Latin American sexual behavior condoned men's being unfaithful in marriage while women would be condemned. In addition, domestic violence was common and accepted. Women were frequently without voice, rights, or protection, even within their own families. These conditions come out clearly in *Woman Hollering Creek*.

Some well-known Chicana feminists are Cherríe Moraga, Gloria Anzaldúa, and Ana Castillo, who have spread Chicana feminism through theory and their literary works. Denise Chavez's 1986 collection of short stories *The Last of the Menu Girls* won many prizes. Like other Chicana feminists, Chavez combines writing with social activism. Author Norma Alarcón, a friend who encouraged Cisneros to publish, is also the founder of Third Woman Press.

Cisneros's feminism is a central theme in *Woman Hollering Creek*. The stories take place in Mexico, in Texas, and in Chicago and highlight Chicana narrators and characters. Often she uses an innocent child narrator to record what an adult would find distressing. The child, however, is too young to comment on the violence or poverty around her, so it is left to the reader to get the point. Other stories use a first-person female adult narrator, thus showing a Chicana finding her voice. The women suffer almost insurmountable hardships as a result of poverty, sexism, and racism, yet they manage to survive and grow, establishing their own identities.

Postmodern/Postcolonial Short Story

Realism is commonly seen as characteristic of modern fiction before World War II. In the last half of the twentieth century, postmodernist authors felt free to use a variety of techniques to portray the worlds of people living in an age of cultural diversity. For instance, the short stories of ethnic writers often use surrealism or magical realism, including magic, ritual, poetry, song, and dream sequences (as in, for example, Cisneros's "The Eyes of Zapata"). Postmodern fiction frequently lacks the narrative arc of the classic short story of beginning, middle, and end, as tightly structured to produce a single and often surprise effect. Postmodern short stories may seem to ramble and lack clear endings by comparison. The moral may not be easy to draw because moral judgment itself is dependent on the viewpoint of the observer. "Barbie-Q" consists of a few vivid paragraphs from the point of view of a Chicana girl that do not preach or come to a conclusion but imply much more than is stated.

Postcolonial fiction probes the political, psychological, and historical confusion of people who are both traditional and modern at the same time. They are in this condition because of the centuries of conquest and domination by European powers over indigenous cultures. Postcolonial literature deals with racial inequality, poverty, and modernization. In "Barbie-Q" as well as in the other stories in *Woman Hollering Creek*, the characters are a minority race having to create their lives as a hybrid identity out of two languages and two cultures. Cisneros uses impressionistic poetic vignettes or sketches to express this condition, rather than a long, connected realistic narrative. She mixes genres with a short story that is really a sketch told in poetic prose. The narrator weaves in details that are telling but, as in poetry, not necessarily sequential. There is a movement of feeling in "Barbie-Q" but not a developed plot. Instead there is a flow of consciousness with lists of items and long strings of adjectives. Cisneros is also postcolonial in her frequent use of Spanish words and Chicano terms.

HISTORICAL CONTEXT

The US-Mexican Border and Immigration

When the United States annexed Texas in 1846, it caused a war with Mexico (the Mexican-American War, 1846–1848). The Spanish had been colonizing what is now the southwestern United States since the sixteenth century. After the Mexican-American War, the Treaty of Guadalupe Hidalgo forced Mexico to cede all of its northern territory, including Texas, New Mexico, Arizona, Nevada, Utah, California, and parts of Colorado and Wyoming, to the United States. The Rio Grande became Mexico's northern border. Mexico's people were of Spanish descent or of mixed Spanish and Indian descent (mestizo). Suddenly, the northern part of Mexico was within the borders of the United States, and all the people became US citizens.

During the Mexican Revolution (1910–1920), many more Mexicans fled to the southwestern United States to find jobs. They worked in industries such as railroads and mining, construction and agriculture, restaurants and meatpacking. Until the 1960s most lived near the border in Texas or California, but there were also large Mexican communities in Chicago, Kansas City, Denver, San Francisco, and Salt Lake City. The immigrants remained mostly in low-wage jobs. The Mexican-American border was open in the beginning, and the United States accepted immigrants and refugees.

During the Great Depression, however, thousands of Mexican immigrants were forced back to Mexico by the US government to leave more jobs open for other Americans. In 1935 a federal court ruling upheld the federal law that Mexican immigrants could not become citizens because they were not white. Franklin Roosevelt challenged this by asking federal agencies to classify all Mexicans as white. During World War II, the labor shortage in the United States was addressed by the bracero program, contracting Mexicans to do certain jobs, collect their money, and go home. They were not allowed to bring their families and settle in the United States, and they had no civil rights.

COMPARE
&
CONTRAST

- **1960s:** Barbie dolls are all white with Anglo lifestyle and fashions.

  1991: Though ethnic Barbie dolls, including Hispanic Teresa, are available with brown or black skin, the facial features are not realistic, and the tiny waist remains.

  Today: The ethnic Barbie dolls have more distinct racial features and a larger waist. The Mexico Barbie doll, dressed in a long, flouncy dress, carrying a Chihuahua dog and a passport, creates controversy for some Mexicans, as though pointing out that many Mexicans cross the border illegally, without passports, although Mattel claims it includes passports with other international dolls as well.

- **1960s:** The Chicano movement begins during the African American civil rights movement.

  1991: There is a resurgence of student activism in the early 1990s on California campuses to keep up funding for Chicano/ Chicana studies departments that are being defunded.

  Today: Chicana/Chicano studies programs are growing in universities across the country because of the increasing numbers of Latinos in the United States.

- **1960s:** Chicano immigrants are drawn to the United States because of its higher standard of living. Many, like the Cisneros family, return frequently to Mexico to reconnect with family and traditional culture.

  1991: Immigration, legal and illegal, from Mexico to the United States grows rapidly in the 1980s and 1990s, despite strict quotas.

  Today: A reversal in immigration from the United States back to Mexico is taking place because of the difficulties Chicanos experience in getting jobs, increased deportations, and the criminalization of illegal entry, as well as better conditions for Chicanos in Mexico and stricter border control after September 11, 2001.

In 1954, Operation Wetback and the US Border Patrol began to deport Mexicans who were in the United States illegally. By 1965 Mexican quotas were smaller than the number wanting to get in, thus increasing illegal entry. In 1986, the Immigration Reform and Control Act allowed undocumented people who had come before 1982 to become citizens while clamping down harder on current illegal immigrants by imposing criminal penalties on employers who hired them. Yet Mexican immigration continued to increase in the 1980s and 1990s. After the terrorist attacks on September 11, 2001, border security became tighter, and it became even more dangerous to cross illegally. Immigration policy continues to be hotly debated, and Mexican Americans without legal documentation are often deported.

Chicano Movement

Mexicans who live in the United States are called Chicanos/Chicanas (sometimes spelled Xicano or Xicana). In Mexico, *Chicano* meant someone of the lower class, but it became a term of ethnic pride in the United States. Chicanos are also referred to as Mexican Americans, Latinos/Latinas, or Hispanics, although Hispanic and Latino are more general terms for people with Spanish and Latin American origin, respectively. The term *Hispanic*, as a category used by the census, is less favored by Chicanos themselves. In the 1960s and 1970s Chicanos, like other ethnic groups, began working for civil rights. Radical student groups even advocated nationalism and withdrawal from the United States by taking back the territory Mexico had lost as a result of the Treaty

The girls are thrilled to find fire-damaged Barbie dolls at a flea market. (© Luisa Fumi / Shutterstock.com)

of Guadalupe Hidalgo. They called the American Southwest Aztlán, a legendary Aztec paradise and their true home, contending that the Southwest had been taken from them. They called themselves La Raza, "the Race." *Mestizo* is a term referring to the mixed race of Spanish and indigenous people. In California, Mexican American children had to attend segregated schools. This policy became unconstitutional in 1947, the first step toward ending all racial segregation in education, which finally occurred with *Brown v. Board of Education* in 1954.

Some famous activists in the 1960s were Rodolfo Gonzales in Denver and Reies Tijerina, who was a proponent of nationalism, in New Mexico. La Causa, the great cause, however, was fought by the United Farm Workers and César Chavez in California for the rights of seasonal agricultural laborers. Mexican Americans sought political power through La Raza Unida Party, based in Texas and founded by Willie Velásquez. Students demanded and got Chicano studies programs on campuses.

Chicanos in Chicago

In Chicago, where "Barbie-Q" is set, Chicanos are the largest Latino group, with Puerto Ricans second. These immigrants came from Mexico in waves after 1910, and Chicago has the largest number of Chicanos/Chicanas in the United States outside the Southwest. Latinos live in certain neighborhoods. Pilsen, on the lower southwest side, is where newer immigrants arrive. Puerto Ricans settled on the near northwest side in Humboldt Park, where Sandra Cisneros grew up. The Maxwell Street Market mentioned in the story is still there but is more multicultural now, with shops, restaurants, and festivals. Latinos continue to move out from these older neighborhoods and to Aurora, Illinois, forty miles west of Chicago, which boasts a complete Chicano culture. The Chicano movement helped to start political activity in Chicago, with many local Mexican Americans now in office.

The Barbie Doll Industry

Barbie is a fashion doll manufactured by the Mattel Toy Company. She was invented by Ruth Handler, whose husband was a Mattel executive. Dolls for girls were generally baby dolls, so when Handler saw an adult doll called Bild Lilli in Germany, she got the idea for Barbie. Barbie had her own fashion designer at Mattel and was launched in March 1959 with a swimsuit and a ponytail. Fashions and accessories sold separately. Over the next fifty years, she changed her shape and clothing styles, adding family member dolls and other spin-offs like books and video games about her teen life and friends. She is known around the world and appeared as a character in the animated films *Toy Story 2* and *Toy Story 3*.

There have been many controversies about this doll, which Cisneros takes advantage of in the story. For many feminists, Barbie has been a symbol of the false and unhealthy brand of femininity sold to young women. Barbie seems to be a role model for perfect outer appearance and social acceptance. Though Mattel has tried to update Barbie's image as, for example, a career woman who can fly planes, for years she was seen as a somewhat empty-headed conformist interested in shallow things like fashions and dating and her popularity. Cisneros and other feminists refer to a Barbie-doll type as someone who has bought into this stereotype of the perfect female body dressed fashionably for show. It has been pointed out that Barbie looks anorexic and encourages girls to be too thin. No one can really attain her body proportions and remain healthy. The manufacturers finally gave her a bigger waist in 1997.

Barbie was also an inappropriate and unattainable model for girls of other races. Mattel finally introduced ethnic Barbie dolls, but at first their features and lifestyles were still Caucasian, though their skin was black or brown. The ethnic Barbies now have distinctive facial features. The Barbie craze has been charged with turning girls into consumers at a young age. The Chicana girls are aware of their poverty because they cannot afford the products.

CRITICAL OVERVIEW

Cisneros originally thought of herself as a poet. Her writing, however, is a mixture of genres, using poetic prose and prosaic poetry, as poet Gary Soto notes in his review of her 1988 volume of poems, *My Wicked Wicked Ways*, in the *Bloomsbury Review*. Whatever the genre, he claims Cisneros "is foremost a storyteller." This is also true of her 1991 book of poetic short stories, *Woman Hollering Creek*.

In a review of *Woman Hollering Creek and Other Stories* for the *New York Times Book Review* in 1991, Bebe Moore Campbell finds that the stories are not balanced in their view of faithless Latino men, but they use male chauvinism to focus on "women struggling to take control of their lives" and "invite us into the souls of characters as unforgettable as a first kiss." Campbell mentions that the little Chicana girls in "Barbie-Q" have "tempered enthusiasm" for their Barbie dolls because they have learned how "to make do" with what they can salvage in their world.

How does a Chicana woman find her authentic self? Jeff Thomson, in an article for *Studies in Short Fiction* in 1994, asserts that "Barbie-Q" is about the stereotypes that are forced on Chicana women in mainstream culture, while the stories in *Woman Hollering Creek* as a whole succeed in "establishing aspects of an archetypal Chicana female identity." This identity is obviously in a completely opposite direction from the values of the Barbie consumer image, shown as Chicana women search for their own roots.

Harryette Mullen in a 1996 article for *MELUS*, "A Silence between Us like a Language: The Untranslatability of Experience in Sandra Cisneros's *Woman Hollering Creek*," sees that the short stories, like much of Cisneros's work, concern "the silenced and marginalized, including children, homosexuals, and working class and immigrant Chicanos and Mexicanos, whose stories have been untold or untranslated."

Critic Trinna S. Frever compares and contrasts uses of the doll in "'Oh! You Beautiful Doll!' Icon, Image, and Culture in Works by Alvarez, Cisneros, and Morrison" for a 2009 issue of *Tulsa Studies in Women's Literature*. She points out that "Barbie-Q" works through creating a tension between the uncritical joy of the Chicana girls over their damaged Barbie dolls and the author's implied sympathy for the poverty of the young girls, who are subjected to a foreign culture they cannot understand or master.

CRITICISM

Susan K. Andersen

Andersen has a PhD in literature. In the following essay, she considers "Barbie-Q" within the context of the whole collection Woman Hollering Creek and Other Stories *and its definition of a mestiza, or a mixed-race Mexican American woman.*

Sandra Cisneros's book *Woman Hollering Creek and Other Stories*, including the story "Barbie-Q," explores the lives of Chicana women and children. Some stories take place in Mexico, some in San Antonio, Texas, where Cisneros now lives, and some in Chicago, where she grew up. The stories illustrate living on the border—the physical border between Mexico and the United States, or the cultural border of American/Mexican, or the psychological border of being of mixed race. The race (often referred to as La Raza by Chicanos) resulting from the interbreeding of Spanish and indigenous Indians in Mexico is called *mestizo/ mestiza*. In *Border Crossings and Beyond*, Carmen Haydée Rivera shows that Cisneros tries to portray a distinctive mestiza image for the modern world. She asserts that Cisneros's fiction creates what Chicana feminist Gloria Anzaldúa has coined a *mestiza consciousness*—that of a mixed-race woman who has to negotiate two cultures and live with contradiction. Cisneros's mestiza characters are passionate and imaginative, finding their own way around in patriarchal and foreign landscapes, trying to be themselves despite all odds.

Woman Hollering Creek has three groups of short stories. The first group is about mestiza children and includes "Barbie-Q." The second part is about teenagers. The third and longest part includes stories about mestiza women. The children's stories are told from the innocent point of view that Cisneros developed in *The House on Mango Street* with the voice of Esperanza. This is an effective technique for letting a child show the details of barrio life without bitterness or criticism. "My Friend Lucy Who

> CISNEROS'S MESTIZA CHARACTERS ARE PASSIONATE AND IMAGINATIVE, FINDING THEIR OWN WAY AROUND IN PATRIARCHAL AND FOREIGN LANDSCAPES, TRYING TO BE THEMSELVES DESPITE ALL ODDS."

Smells like Corn," for instance, is written in a poetic and childlike diction describing the young narrator's love for her friend Lucy Anguiano, who lives in her poor neighborhood in Texas. Like the narrator in "Barbie-Q," this little Chicana narrator is excited about everything she sees around her and does not seem to know that she and her friend Lucy are disadvantaged. Children play with what they have. The narrator and Lucy play with paper dolls and marbles but also dare each other to put their feet under the porch where rats live; they slam the screen door that does not have a screen; they share three M&Ms they have been saving; and they wear each other's clothes. The child narrator thinks it would be fun to live in a big family of nine girls, like Lucy's, instead of being an only child who sleeps alone in a fold-out chair in her living room. She thinks Lucy is adventuresome for trying to eat dog food, but perhaps Lucy is only hungry. The details tell the depressing conditions of poverty the children live in, but Esperanza, Lucy, and the narrators of "My Friend Lucy" and "Barbie-Q" are full of an unquenchable spirit. They create their own world of beauty and love out of almost nothing.

The child narrator of "Barbie-Q" is not quite as effervescent as the "Lucy" narrator, but she still tries to find what she can in the foreign culture of Barbie dolls to be happy about. She and her friend learn to put up with disappointment, such as the fact that they cannot have new, undamaged dolls. The narrator says "so what" to the fact that the Francie doll smells like smoke and has a melted left foot. They can pretend these things away.

The narrator is a young girl already using the commercial language of the Mattel Toy Company and the fashion industry to describe the Barbie outfits. This kind of detail indicts

WHAT DO I READ NEXT?

- The 1991 novel by Dominican American writer Julia Alvarez *How the García Girls Lost Their Accents* tells the story of four sisters forced to flee to New York with their family from the Dominican Republic because of the dictator Rafael Trujillo. The novel begins in their adult lives and goes back to their childhood in the Dominican Republic, showing their hardships in adapting to a new culture and their confusion of identity.

- Influential Chicana feminist and author Gloria Anzaldúa's *Borderlands/La Frontera: The New Mestiza* (1987) is in the form of a journal written by a mestiza who is discovering her identity out of her many languages and cultures. She weaves together poetry and prose using design and color that suggest Aztec art. Anzaldúa is the writer who identified mestiza consciousness as a special borderland point of view.

- Sandra Cisneros's *The House on Mango Street* (1984) is a coming-of-age story that brought Cisneros into literary prominence. It tells the story of a Latina girl, Esperanza Cordero, growing up in a poor Latino neighborhood in Chicago.

- Native American poet Joy Harjo was a friend of Cisneros's at the Iowa Writers' Workshop in the late 1970s, where they felt out of place as women of color. Joy Harjo's prose poem "Grace," in *In Mad Love and War* (1990), records a moment at the workshop where, like Cisneros, she had a revelation of her ethnic identity and solidarity in the middle of Anglo America.

- Rohinton Mistry's *Swimming Lessons and Other Stories from Firozsha Baag* (1987), is a collection of eleven short stories, including the much anthologized "Swimming Les-

sons," illustrating the double lives of Indian Parsi immigrants in Toronto.

- *Chicanas of 18th Street: Narratives of a Movement from Latino Chicago* (2011), by Leonard G. Ramírez, records the testimonies of six Pilsen neighborhood Chicana activists for social change in Chicago. They speak of immigration, religion, identity, gender, and education during the 1960s and 1970s and tell how the Chicano movement grew.

- *Chicano! The History of the Mexican American Civil Rights Movement* (1996), by F. Arturo Rosales, covers the Chicano movement from 1965 to 1975. Rosales discusses background history from the Mexican-American War and the Mexican Revolution as well as connecting the details of the Chicano movement to the larger civil rights movement of the 1960s and 1970s.

- Gary Soto's young-adult book *Baseball in April and Other Stories* (1990) is by a Mexican American poet and writer remembering his childhood growing up in California. The book won the ALA Best Book for Young Adults award. Soto's stories include references to Barbie dolls as well as to Little League baseball. A glossary of Spanish terms is included.

- *Breadgivers* (1925), by Anzia Yezierska, records the coming of age of Sara Smolinsky, who leads a life similar to that of Cisneros's Chicanas growing up in Chicago. Yezierska grew up in a patriarchal Polish Jewish immigrant family on the Lower East Side of Manhattan. She describes the pressures of patriarchy, poverty, and racial prejudice, which her main character overcomes by getting an education and becoming independent.

American culture as commercial and materialistic, trying to foist consumer values on children. Cisneros's originality with this theme is to show

further how such an advertising culture impacts a child from an ethnic group with little money and different values. Mexican American tradition values extended family, children, festivals, and social gatherings with food and eating, spirituality and religion, a relationship with the earth, colorful handmade textiles and embroidered clothing of native design, music and the arts; in addition, Mexican American body types look nothing like an Anglo Barbie doll. There is nothing in the surroundings of these Chicago Chicana children to remind them of their heritage or to bring out their identity. They will grow up labeled as disadvantaged in a foreign culture.

The saving grace, however, is in the voice of this child narrator. She may try to be like American children collecting her Barbie dolls, but at the same time, she cannot repress her own point of view. The Barbie play is shallow and repetitive to her. The Barbies are hostile to one another. The emphasis on physical appearance seems to end in a competition for a man's attention. The game is won by the Barbie doll most ruthless in stealing Ken from the other. The girls trade insults, and the game does not further any human values or friendship. By contrast, in "My Friend Lucy" the girls are poor but share everything, even their last M&Ms.

The narrator of "Barbie-Q" likes finding the extra dolls on Maxwell Street because they make a family. She can accept the melted left foot of Francie because she is a member of Barbie's family. Competition is thus transcended. There is a subtle shift in the story from focus on the single Barbie and her career-girl image to the family of Barbie dolls with siblings and cousins and friends, much more similar to the Mexican American pattern of family. There is a hint in this that the Chicana girls may make the Barbie dolls into something closer to their own hybrid culture.

Other Chicano children in the stories of *Woman Hollering Creek* are not as happy. "Salvador Late or Early" describes a motherless boy who must take care of numerous younger siblings rather than have his own childhood. "Eleven" tells the story of a poor Chicana girl ashamed of the ugly oversized sweater she has to wear to school. She tries to disown it.

When the stories move to teenaged Chicanas, they become more serious and depressing, including sexual abuse and early pregnancy. Some of the celebrated stories in the adult section include "Woman Hollering Creek," "Never Marry a Mexican," "The Eyes of Zapata," "Little Miracles, Kept Promises," and "*Bien* Pretty."

In these tales, Cisneros shows trapped women trying to escape their Mexican American limitations. As in her own case, she wants to see these characters turn *mestiza* into a positive and distinctive image where women find their voices and their strength. To do this, the Anglo culture of Barbie beauty must be discarded for more authentic images derived from Mexican American storytelling. The Chicana womanhood Cisneros fashions in *Woman Hollering Creek* reimagines the archetypes of the Virgin Mary, La Malinche, and La Llorona, as Shannon Wilson explains in "The Chicana Trinity: Materna Mestiza Consciousness in *Woman Hollering Creek and Other Stories*."

The Virgen de Guadalupe—a Mexican identity of Mary—is a type of the good and holy mother. She appeared to a mestizo man, Juan Diego, in colonial times, asking for a church to be built to her at Tepeyac, where previously Aztec goddesses had been worshipped. Mexicans sometimes see her as an attempt to replace their own Aztec mother goddesses, such as Tonantzín or Coatlicue, who were not passive and virginal like Mary, but fierce earth goddesses. Like the essentially asexual Barbie doll, the chaste and passive Mary divorces sexuality from women, making those women who are sexy, bad. In the story "Little Miracles, Kept Promises," letters are left at the altar of the Virgen de Guadalupe asking for or giving thanks for miracles of healing. One letter from a young mestiza named Chayo thanks the Virgen that she is not pregnant after having sex because she wants her independence. She has never liked the Virgen before this favor was granted to her; she blamed the Virgen for teaching women to suffer in silence. Chayo now sees the Virgen as bare-breasted and holding snakes, like the Aztec goddesses. She believes in the Virgen because Mary understands that a woman wants to control her own fertility, like Tonantzín. Cisneros thus reverses the patriarchal idea of the Virgen with a powerful image of a pagan goddess that returns sexuality to mestizas.

Another archetype is *La Malinche*. La Malinche is a historical figure, a Nahuatl noblewoman sold into slavery and given to the Spanish explorer Hernán Cortés. She was a skillful translator, thus allowing him to learn secrets to subdue the indigenous people of Mexico. She had a son by Cortés who was, according to legend, the first mestizo. Ever since, La Malinche has been

The Barbie doll has become such a cultural icon that the toy was honored with a stamp from the United States Postal Service. (© catwalker / Shutterstock.com)

known as a type of the traitor-whore who destroys her own people and race. In reality, the woman was a slave, but collaboration with the enemy is the meaning of her name to Chicanos. In "Never Marry a Mexican" Cisneros depicts a romance between a white man and a Chicana woman. The American man playfully calls her La Malinche, pretending he is Cortés. In this version of the story, however, La Malinche gets her revenge when the white man will not marry her. She undermines his marriage to a woman who looks like a Barbie doll and

seduces his son. This Chicana is not nice but shows that she is not to be walked over like the historical Indian princess.

In "Woman Hollering Creek," a third archetype is depicted, called *La Llorona*, the Weeping Woman. Cleófilas is a Mexican bride taken from her father's house in Mexico to her Chicano husband's house in Texas. She thinks her life will be like a fairy tale, because she watches *telenovelas*, Mexican soap operas. Instead, she ends up as a victim of domestic violence when her husband gets drunk and beats her and neglects her. She is so shocked that she becomes passive and withdrawn. She sees the creek behind the house and thinks of La Llorona, the legendary woman who was so depressed she drowned her children and then cast herself into the river, becoming a ghost, forever weeping for her lost children. Cleófilas begins to have dark thoughts of suicide too. A woman physician examining her during her second pregnancy sees that she has been beaten and arranges for a woman friend to help Cleófilas return to her father's house. As they cross the creek, the women holler jubilantly, and the creek becomes *La Gritona*, the Woman Hollering Creek of freedom. Cisneros shows a woman casting victimhood aside. The Weeping Woman, La Llorona, becomes the Hollering Woman, La Gritona.

From Barbie to La Gritona is a large imaginative journey that Cisneros allows her readers to take in *Woman Hollering Creek*. Carmen Haydée Rivera notes that Cisneros's characters are realistic people, not pictured as simply nice or perfect, but offering alternatives for Chicanas and giving them the message that they can change themselves and their circumstances, rather than being victims or consumers of someone else's culture.

Source: Susan K. Andersen, Critical Essay on "Barbie-Q," in *Short Stories for Students*, Gale, Cengage Learning, 2014.

Michelle M. Tokarczyk

In the following excerpt, Tokarczyk characterizes Cisneros as an outspoken, working-class feminist.

. . . The young Cisneros was something of an *hocicona* or outspoken persona—someone who would buy a "menstruation red" pickup truck. As she has gotten older and embraced Buddhism, she has become less angry, more preoccupied with understanding—although she can still get angry. As a writer, she is reserved. She guards her privacy and her writing time, feeling somewhat on display in San Antonio. Being accessible and non-threatening, she reflected in conversation, has the drawback of inviting too many visitors. In interviews she has stated that she would like to have more contact with some women writers, such as Julia Alvarez and Dorothy Allison, but that writers do not interrupt one another while they are working. She feels a kinship with Allison, she explains to Kevane and Heredia, because they are similar in many ways. Each has worked in her community, and each

> AN AUTOGRAPHIC WRITER, CISNEROS IS ACUTELY AWARE THAT HER WORK AND HER LIFE ARE CONTINUALLY EVOLVING. HER COMMITMENT TO CHANGING THE WORLD FOR MEN AS WELL AS WOMEN, IF EVER SO SLIGHTLY, REFLECTS HER EVOLUTION FROM FEMINISM TO WOMANISM."

values the erotic element in her writing, having what Cisneros, in words echoing Lorde, describes as a fascination with sexual power and creativity. Furthermore, each writes stories of people who barely escape with their lives—"survivors, a great segment of the American population that has not been allowed to tell their stories" (Kevane and Heredia, "Home in the Heart," 56). Again Cisneros, like Esperanza, left the barrio not just physically and psychically intact but enriched. She uses her experience and observations to represent people who barely have their lives. Her role is not that of a traditional anthropologist or historian recording notes, but rather, like Zora Neale Hurston, of a creative writer who artfully renders stories that have remained untold.

Sandra Cisneros identifies herself as a border writer who blends English, Spanish, and indigenous Mexican elements in her work; she calls herself a translator or amphibian negotiating two worlds, that of the United States and Mexico (Kevane and Heredia, "Home in the Heart," 18). (And, I would add, between the lower and upper classes.) For her, the nature of this "translation" differs with the genre. In prose she finds an implicit political agenda that is missing in poetry, and thus prose is more suited to more public, less autobiographical subject matter. Political or social content, however, is never an excuse for compromising prose style. Often Cisneros questions herself or finally a professional editor as to whether she is being too heavy handed (Zumwalt, "A House of My Own").

Interestingly, when queried by Dorothy Allison as to what she feared, Cisneros said giving birth. When Allison clarified that she wondered about Cisneros's writerly fears, Cisneros replied that she has the same fear of "giving birth." For Sandra Cisneros, collecting stories and titles is fun. Much of the early writing is fun, as she maintains everything she writes is for pleasure. What is difficult, however, is that actual creation—choosing which stories to tell and crafting them. Cisneros admits she was terrified while writing *Caramelo*. The only thing that comforted her, at the time, was the knowledge that she had been just as terrified when writing *Woman Hollering Creek*. Each time she writes, Cisneros confronts her own anxieties, her imposter syndrome, and her resultant fear that she will disappoint herself and her community. The process of writing is thus similar to the process of coming to terms with sexuality; one must realize that the fear is a fear of power as well as a fear of failure and work to capture the power.

Although Cisneros identifies with working-class feminists such as Dorothy Allison, she finds it more difficult to communicate with upper-class feminists, unless they make an effort to learn about her culture. The move to Texas deepened Cisneros's resentment toward some whites whom she saw as indifferent to Chicanos/Chicanas. In San Antonio, she had been working in the barrio with Chicano art, and she found that whites did not come to see it or learn about it. She, in turn, had no time to travel to white neighborhoods and educate them about Chicana/Chicano art; her commitment was to her neighborhood and her small press projects. (In the 1980s, she was on the advisory board for Third Woman Press.) Although she appreciates the exposure major presses offer writers, she is often more interested in the work of small presses because they take more chances. Aside from Dorothy Allison and Julia Alvarez, Cisneros cites many working-class writers as her favorites. She "loves" Maxine Hong Kingston, in whose innovative hybrid *The Woman Warrior* Cisneros found permission to write the nonlinear *The House on Mango Street*. She is less interested in writers who tell linear narratives or write traditional novels. Explaining that *Caramelo* is her first actual novel as opposed to the mosaic *The House on Mango Street*, she offers a developmental analogy. "We're [Latinas] young writers, and you don't start by building a house if you haven't learned to build a room" (Dasenbrock and Jussawalla, *Interviews with Writers*, 5).

As a person, Sandra Cisneros can appear alternately as forceful and outspoken, vulnerable and soft. When she reads, she can sound like a child, or like an innocent puzzled woman. She has learned to use this childlike quality to her advantage not only in telling stories, but also in finding the sources for them. Well into her thirties she noted that when she was washing clothes at the Laundromat, for example, people often saw her as a girl. The "little voice" she once hated turned into an asset, disarming others and allowing Cisneros the writer to infiltrate their lives (Sagel, "PW Interviews," 74). Yet Cisneros's life has been anything but girlish; it has been a struggle to become an independent woman and working writer without class or gender models. In her twenties, she tried to imitate successful male writers by drinking, carousing, and traveling. These were very bold steps for a Mexican-American woman, because even Mexican-American men often did not choose to live alone. As Richard Rodriguez notes in his essay "The Achievement of Desire," it is hard for a scholar/writer to find solitude in a large, close-knit Latino family. The desire to be alone is viewed at best as peculiar, at worse as antisocial. For women, the judgment is even harsher. Cisneros was perceived as rejecting her gender, her culture, her family. Her father could not believe that she made a living as a writer until she bought her Nissan pickup with her writing money. Then her father knew the writing was serious (Bray, "Interview with Sandra Cisneros"). Still, her family did support her; she lived with her brother Alfred and her sister-in-law for a time while writing *Woman Hollering Creek and Other Stories*, and her parents repeatedly offered financial assistance. However, Cisneros's career and lifestyle choices puzzled her loved ones. It took her mother a long time to read *Woman Hollering Creek and Other Stories* because, although she may have been more freethinking than some Chicana women, she was nonetheless embarrassed by the sexuality in many of the stories ("Sandra Cisneros," video). (Cisneros's father read only Spanish, and probably would not have read any of her writing if it had been translated. He just wasn't fond of reading.)

Currently Cisneros lives in San Antonio with a filmmaker whom she has been seeing for some time. They share the house with three dogs (two are strays), three cats, and a parrot. With the completion of *Caramelo*, Cisneros is able to spend more time outside San Antonio. Her financial independence has allowed her to stop offering writing workshops at colleges and community centers and instead offer them at home, for free, as a gift. Writing *Caramelo* required her to stop work at the Guadalupe Arts Center, and she eventually stopped working with the MacArturos to devote more time to her masters level writing workshop, Macondo. This workshop is given in her home during the summer. At first, a few people whose work she admired were invited; now there is a formal application process, with some funding available. Participants must be writers who are not just interested in getting published, but rather are committed to making their writing truly excellent. Each participant must contribute something to the group—cooking, teaching yoga, and so forth. Cisneros hopes the group commitment and critical, yet supportive, atmosphere will enhance writing as many formal creative writing programs cannot. In the Macondo workshop, Cisneros has found what Kingston found in the veterans' writing workshop: a way to combine writing, spirituality, and practice.

The blossoming of Latina/Latino literature in this nation has been compared to that of Jewish-American literature in the 1960s when Jewish writers began to gain recognition for their representation of their American experience. Moreover, interest in many Latin artists—musicians and painters, as well as writers—is burgeoning. Latinos/Latinas are the fastest growing ethnic group in our nation today. Many of these Latinas/Latinos are laborers; many are Chicanos/Chicanas who identify as Mexicano/Mexicana and as working class. As a Chicana writer, Sandra Cisneros gives voice and shape to varieties of Mexican working-class experience in the United States. She highlights the stories of its women who have been ignored and casts a spotlight on gender inequity. She is a writer and a person with a sense of humor; her stories delight. In her interview with Elliott, Cisneros says that she knows she is telling a good story when people stop what they are doing to listen—that is, when those who are serving food and the like—stop, for Cisneros cares about reaching all people, not just the presumed literati. During a conversation with me, Elliott speculated that some people operate in an "economy of lack" in which praise, love, and success are limited commodities one shares at peril. In contrast, the "economy of plenty" enriches one who shares. The latter is what Cisneros embraces. Cisneros says a line from Dorothy Allison's *Two or Three Things I Know for Sure* has been an inspiration to her. "In the world as I remade it, nothing was forbidden, everything was possible." These words not only reminded Cisneros that she could remake *Caramelo* many times over, but also that she writes to change the world. An autographic writer, Cisneros is acutely aware that her work and her life are continually evolving. Her commitment to changing the world for men as well as women, if ever so slightly, reflects her evolution from feminism to womanism....

Source: Michelle M. Tokarczyk, "The Voice of the Voiceless: Sandra Cisneros," in *Class Definitions: On the Lives and Writings of Maxine Hong Kingston, Sandra Cisneros, and Dorothy Allison*, Susquehanna University Press, 2008, pp. 141–45.

Tey Diana Rebolledo

In the following excerpt, Rebolledo examines the image that has been cultivated for Cisneros as a writer.

. . . In this essay I am not going to analyze Cisneros's writing. As you may know, Cisneros is the author of *Bad Boys* (1980), *The House on Mango Street* (1983), *My Wicked Wicked Ways* (1987), *Woman Hollering Creek* (1991), and *Loose Woman* (1994), as well as many essays and interviews. I very much admire Cisneros as a writer. When I first read *The House on Mango Street* many years ago, I found it a fresh and innovative work, a distinct voice. The works that have followed and her many poems and essays have continued to prove Cisneros an original. But there are many writers, also fresh and original, who have not been elevated to the same status as Cisneros. I want to examine why.

To begin, the sales of Cisneros's books have been phenomenal. *The House on Mango Street* had sold over half a million copies by May of 1996, and her other books have been equally well received. I want to analyze not the academic examination of her writing but rather how she is seen in the popular press, the book reviews in newspapers and book trade journals, her images in popular magazines such as the *New Yorker*, *Glamour*, *Vanity Fair*, and *Ms.*, and how she is viewed abroad, as her books are increasingly translated into other languages. For much of this information I am indebted to Sandra herself, as she has sent me much of the material to be archived.

In addition to her own creative voice, Cisneros has been part of the tidal wave of interest

" PART OF THE CISNEROS MYSTIQUE IS THE
FACT THAT SHE IS AN ETHNIC WOMAN OF WORKING-
CLASS BACKGROUND (HER FATHER WAS AN
UPHOLSTERER, HER MOTHER A FACTORY WORKER);
THIS MYSTIQUE ALLOWS CHILDREN TO SEE A MODEL
FOR THEIR OWN DREAMS."

in women's literature and minority literature. In the last fifteen years there has been extraordinary interest in Latino/a writing. The sales of books by Laura Esquivel, Julia Alvarez, Isabel Allende, and Rosario Ferré have been excellent. Indeed one headline in the press says, "Book publishers say 'hola' to US Hispanic Market" (Campbell, 9). Along with this interest there is a particular emphasis on the women writing. The group solidarity that the women show for and with each other has made it into the popular press as "Las Girlfriends." Although the designation can encompass any of the Latinas writing today, the picture that was published in *Vanity Fair* in 1994 shows Ana Castillo, Denise Chávez, Julia Alvarez, and Sandra Cisneros. They are attractive, appealing, and eminently photogenic.

From the beginning, as seen in her book *My Wicked Wicked Ways*, Cisneros has written about her rich cultural heritage and traditions, and she has not been afraid to tackle taboo subjects. Moreover, she has maintained a healthy sense of self and of life's ironies. Many of her poems and stories are self-reflexive as well as self-referential. At times her ironic voice is misunderstood, as irony often is. She states,

> I am the woman of myth and bullshit.
> (True. I authored some of it.)
> I built my little house of ill repute.
> Brick by brick. Labored,
> loved and masoned it.
> (Loose Woman, 113)

When interviewed by the popular press, Cisneros says what she thinks. Thus she admits that she has self-consciously aided in the creation of her own media image. Because she finds herself in the public eye, what she thinks has an impact. She is often in the thick of things, talking about

the problems in Sarajevo, involved in the campaign against AIDS, discussing racism and prejudice, and making controversial statements, such as in the recent documentary on Selena where Cisneros said she did not think Selena was a good role model for young Latinas. She becomes a public spokesperson for Chicana feminists, for Latinos, for women. Often she is treated kindly by the press, at times not. Over the years I am sure she has learned when to speak out, bracing herself for the consequences when others do not agree with her views. Thus she can be seen as the woman and the writer who is effective in raising Chicana/Mexicana consciousness, empowering students, and filling the literary landscape. One critic writes, "Writer Cisneros Lends Power to Chicanas" (Walsh, E4), and another says her "tales speak to the hearts of women" (Nakao, C1). On the other hand, she has been seen as an "intellectual shock jock" (Allen). That she stirs the emotions with her writing and her comments cannot fail to interest us. Caroline Pierce states, "Cisneros scattershoots with wicked wit. Rebellious Mexican-American writer spares no one with her acerbic humor." Later she adds, "Sandra Cisneros is a wicked, wicked woman [playing off Cisneros's title]," and ends, "And whatever else you do, never repent.... The world needs you the way you are" (Pierce, E7).

The press in the United States delights in seeing Cisneros as a "bad girl," and Cisneros images herself as that at times....

Part of the Cisneros mystique is the fact that she is an ethnic woman of working-class background (her father was an upholsterer, her mother a factory worker); this mystique allows children to see a model for their own dreams. Cisneros always credits her mother for teaching her how to be different and for giving her the space to read. Because of this, one of her greatest causes has been the support of public libraries. As stated in *Library Journal*, "For the writer who grew up feeling that 'being good was never good enough,' the public library was a special refuge. Now Cisneros is concerned that libraries are closing down, effectively closing out youngsters like herself who need that refuge. Chicago may have a sparkling new central library, but the branch in her mother's neighborhood—which has been located in a former menswear store— has burned down" ("Sandra Cisneros: Giving Back," 55).

Cisneros often gets high marks for her work with schoolchildren. In 1992 while in Chicago she was invited to give a talk to a class of eighth-grade girls at Seward School, where 95 percent of the students are Latino. Cisneros held up her fifth-grade report card full of C's and D's as proof that bad grades don't necessarily mean a bad mind. In the public press there are often stories of how children have been affected by Cisneros's writing, from *Hairs/Pelitos* to *The House on Mango Street*. Seeing themselves for once reflected in the literature they read has a positive impact on them.

Moreover, her public call to a friend in war-torn Sarajevo, "Who wants stories now?" published in the *New York Times*, was a call to remember the personal elements in those strife-ridden war zones. Cisneros said, "A woman I know is in there.... Something must be done! ...I don't know what to do!" (17). This was not merely a dramatic call, abstractly thought out for Cisneros. She had lived for some time in Sarajevo and has close friends there. The war impacted her personally.

Headlines of articles give us some insight into Cisneros's public persona: "Sandra Cisneros: 'Cuando me pedían que hablara de cisnes, hablaba de ratas'" (When they asked me to write about swans, I wrote about rats) ("Sandra Cisneros: Cuando me pedían," 22); "Municiones envueltas en papel picado" (Arms wrapped in delicate cut paper) (Joysmith, 7), a statement reminiscent of what surrealist André Breton said about Frida Kahlo—that she was a bum dressed as a butterfly; "Sandra Cisneros: 'Beware, Honey'" (Bacharach, 4); and "En mi literatura creo mi Frankestein, donde un personaje es diversos cuerpos" (In my literature I create a Frankenstein where a character is many bodies) (Molina, 26). Over the years Cisneros, born and raised in Chicago, has had a problematic relationship with the press in that town. Though she was at first dismissed as a writer by the press, Chicago's attitude toward her is changing. As one reviewer wrote:

> Sandra Cisneros has come a long way from the loose-limbed woman featured on the cover of the very first *Third Woman* magazine in 1980. Back then she had a hopeful, girl-next-door quality about her.... Friday night reading at the Duncan YMCA ...Cisneros was something else entirely. First, she came back as an out of towner, wryly noting that she gets more support now than when she lived here. Second,

she came back a hero, with two books of poetry and two of fiction under her belt, all of them critically praised and door openers for other Latino writers.... But more significant on Friday night, perhaps, was the change to the highly stylized and cool persona Cisneros now shows her public. Dressing almost exclusively in vintage Mexican wear, Cisneros seemed to banter easily from the stage. (OBEJAS, 124)

Another reviewer, Kim Berez, said that night, "Both Sandra and Angela [Jackson] have strong stage personalities befitting entertainers." She went on to say, "If you've read Sandra but never heard her, from the strength of voice in print you might be surprised at how small and high and staid her voice is" (Berez, 8).

The decorative aspect of Cisneros, her striking looks and her beauty as well as her costumes and her voice are very much commented on in the press: "Cisneros in horn-rimmed glasses purchased in a Chicago airport looks like a cross between a 1950s librarian and a go-go dancer, with a punchy delivery and an unerring sense for the 'healthy' lie. She writes and speaks in bilingualese, always from her 'corazón'—of fibers and filaments, abandoned daughters, fathers too late appreciated" (Meyers, B1). When Cisneros read at the Poetry Center, Dina Lee Fisher observed: "In walks Sandra Cisneros, just on time. Cisneros, a fiercely passionate woman, has a lot to be thankful for and a lot to be angry about. Born and raised in Chicago, she writes about the dreams, yearnings and realities of lives lived amongst the tenement houses and streets she grew up in.... Standing with a black velvet sash crisscrossing her chest in a giant X, arms akimbo and legs planted firmly apart, Cisneros struck me as a modern day bandit making nighttime raids on a wealthy border town" (Meyers and Fisher, 2)....

Source: Tey Diana Rebolledo, "The Chicana Bandera: Sandra Cisneros in the Public Press; Constructing a Cultural Icon (1996–1999)," in *The Chronicles of Panchita Villa and Other Guerrillas*, University of Texas Press, 2005, pp. 125–30.

SOURCES

Campbell, Bebe Moore, "Crossing Borders," in *New York Times Book Review*, May 26, 1991, p. 6.

Cisneros, Sandra, "Barbie-Q," in *Woman Hollering Creek and Other Stories*, Random House, 1991, pp. 14–16.

Comfort, Mary S., "Reading the Puns in 'Barbie-Q,'" in *Sandra Cisneros's "Woman Hollering Creek,"* edited by Cecilia Donohue, Rodopi, 2010, pp. 79–87.

Frever, Trinna S., "'Oh! You Beautiful Doll!' Icon, Image, and Culture in Works by Alvarez, Cisneros, and Morrison," in *Tulsa Studies in Women's Literature*, Vol. 28, No. 1, Spring 2009, pp. 121–39.

Mullen, Harryette, "A Silence between Us like a Language: The Untranslatability of Experience in Sandra Cisneros's *Woman Hollering Creek*," in *MELUS*, Vol. 21, No. 2, Summer 1996, pp. 3–20.

Rivera, Carmen Haydée, *Border Crossings and Beyond: The Life and Works of Sandra Cisneros*, Women Writers of Color Series, Praeger, 2009, pp. 3, 6–10, 15, 28, 35–36, 43, 48–50.

Soto, Gary, "Voices of Sadness & Science," in *Bloomsbury Review*, Vol. 8, No. 4, July–August 1988, p. 21.

Thomson, Jeff, "What Is Called Heaven: Identity in Sandra Cisneros's *Woman Hollering Creek*," in *Studies in Short Fiction*, Vol. 31, No. 3, Summer 1994, pp. 415–24.

Wilson, Shannon, "The Chicana Trinity: Maternal Mestiza Consciousness in *Woman Hollering Creek and Other Stories*," in *Sandra Cisneros's "Woman Hollering Creek,"* edited by Cecilia Donohue, Rodopi, 2010, pp. 31–52.

FURTHER READING

Acuña, Rodolfo, *Occupied America: A History of Chicanos*, 7th ed., Pearson, 2010.
Acuña is a historian and activist, the winner of awards for his books on Mexican American history, and a founder of Chicano studies. He gives an alternative historical account of the southwestern United States from the Chicano viewpoint.

Arredondo, Gabriela F., Aída Hurtado, Norma Klahn, Olga Nájera-Ramírez, and Patricia Zavella, eds., *Chicana Feminisms: A Critical Reader*, University Press Books, 2003.
This book includes recent statements on Chicana feminism by creative writers, scholars, anthropologists, folklorists, psychologists, and others, concerning such issues as bilingualism, living on the US-Mexican border, sexuality, and the Chicano movement of the 1960s.

Castillo, Ana, *So Far from God*, W. W. Norton, 1993.
A surreal, magical, and mystical novel about Sofia (wisdom) and her daughters Fe (Faith), Esperanza (Hope), Caridad (Charity), and La Loca (Madwoman) who suffer all the miseries of Chicana womanhood in New Mexico but eventually triumph.

Romo, Leticia I., "Sandra Cisneros' 'Barbie-Q': A Subversive or Hegemonic Popular Text?," in *Studies in Latin American Popular Culture*, Vol. 24, 2005, pp. 127–37.
Romo discusses the ideology behind the Barbie doll and how Cisneros uses the doll's image in the story.

Vigil, James Diego, *From Indians to Chicanos: The Dynamics of Mexican-American Culture*, 3rd ed., Waveland Press, 2011.
An anthropologist gives an ethnohistorical overview of Mexican American history from pre-Columbian days to the present.

SUGGESTED SEARCH TERMS

Sandra Cisneros

Woman Hollering Creek and Other Stories

Barbie-Q AND Cisneros

Chicana OR Chicano

Chicano movement

Mexican American AND border

Mexican AND immigration

Chicanos AND Chicago

Barbie doll AND history

mestizo OR mestiza

The Beginning of Something

SUE ELLEN BRIDGERS

1987

Sue Ellen Bridgers is best known as an author of young-adult literature, but she insists that her books and stories are not only for children or teens. She bristles at people who dismiss young-adult literature because of its label. "People who are denigrating toward young adult literature usually haven't read any and assume that because it is not written for adult readers, it's substandard in some way," explained Bridgers in an interview with Nancy Carol Joyner. She continued, "A lot of young adult literature is better written than most adult literature. It's just that the subject matter is chosen for its appeal to the young reader. Older readers usually enjoy it too, when they get a chance at it."

Bridgers's short story "The Beginning of Something" (1987) is a perfect example of young-adult literature that proves her point. It is a story about teenage characters struggling with issues that are important and interesting to teens—the first brush with romance, in the midst of a family funeral—but such issues are universal. Also, Bridgers's careful writing, with its attention to detail and distinctive character voices, makes the story equally rewarding for adult readers. In "The Beginning of Something," the young narrator loses her childish selfishness and begins to think more of others than of herself. "The Beginning of Something" is available in *Visions: Nineteen Short Stories by Outstanding Writers for Young Adults* (1987).

Melissa hides under the covers because she does not want to face the day. (© Sergey Peterman | Shutterstock.com)

AUTHOR BIOGRAPHY

Bridgers was born Sue Ellen Hunsucker on September 20, 1942, in Winterville, North Carolina. Her father, Wayland, was a tobacco farmer, and her mother, Elizabeth, was a homemaker. Bridgers had one older sister and one younger brother. Sickly as a child, Bridgers was diagnosed with rheumatic fever. This meant that she spent a lot of time indoors, sometimes spending days in bed. She believes her frequent confinement inside influenced her as a writer, because she read a lot and listened to the adult conversations of her extended family. Bridgers started writing poetry in first grade. By the time she was in high school, she had some poems published in a newspaper in Raleigh, North Carolina.

In 1960 Bridgers enrolled at East Carolina State College, but she did not finish college at that time. During her junior year, she married Ben Bridgers. They moved to Mississippi, where he was stationed in the US Air Force. The couple had three children: Elizabeth, Jane, and Sean. The family moved to Sylva, North Carolina, in 1971. Bridgers began to send short stories to magazines and was able to get a few published. In 1975 she went back to college at Western Carolina University, and she graduated with honors in 1976.

Also in 1976, Bridgers published her first book, *Home before Dark*, which is about a family of migrant workers. She thereafter published six other novels: *All Together Now* (1979), *Notes for Another Life* (1981), *Sara Will* (1985), *Permanent Connections* (1987), *Keeping Christina* (1993), and *All We Know of Heaven* (1996). Bridgers has also taught young-adult literature classes and published several essays and short stories, including "The Beginning of Something," which was included in the anthology of short stories for young adults titled *Visions* (1987).

In 1985, Bridgers received the ALAN Award for outstanding contributions to the field of young-adult literature. Several times her novels have been selected as one of the best books of the year for young adults by the American Library Association. As of 2013, Bridgers was still living in North Carolina.

PLOT SUMMARY

The first-person narrator of "The Beginning of Something," Roseanne, explains that her mother's cousin Jessie died and that her whole family will be going to the funeral. Roseanne's mother is very upset because she was close to her cousin. Roseanne, however, was not very close to Cousin Jessie's daughter, Melissa, and resents that they are expected to be friends.

Melissa is upset by her mother's death. She hides under the covers for a while before getting out of bed in the morning, and she does not speak much to Roseanne. The girls sit on the front porch, and Roseanne thinks about how pretty Melissa is—"like a model"—even with her eyes swollen from crying.

Roseanne thinks about why Cousin Jessie died. She had severe diabetes. Roseanne does not seem to understand why her mother was so distraught when she got the news of Cousin Jessie's death, "like she was hearing something terrible and truly unexpected instead of word that Cousin Jessie was at rest."

Everyone is scheduled to go to the funeral home at one o'clock to "see if Cousin Jessie looks all right." Roseanne wants to eat lunch, but Melissa refuses. She only wants to sit on the swing and wait for her boyfriend, Jamie. Roseanne makes peanut butter and jelly sandwiches for both herself and Melissa, in spite of Melissa's refusal, and takes the dishes back into the kitchen when they are done eating. Mama is giving the house a thorough cleaning. Roseanne offers to help her, but she asks Roseanne to "keep an eye on Melissa."

When Jamie arrives, he brings his friend Travis. Roseanne and Melissa played with Travis when they were younger, and now Roseanne is attracted to him. While Jamie comforts Melissa, Roseanne talks with Travis. He invites her to go for a drive that evening after the visitation at the funeral home. Melissa tells her father, rather than asking permission, that she and Roseanne will be going out with the boys. Roseanne's mother agrees, but it is clear that she does not completely approve of the date.

Roseanne is nervous and excited. As she waits for the boys to pick her and Melissa up, she thinks about their visit to the funeral home earlier in the day. She was afraid to look at Cousin Jessie's body, but she noted how upset Melissa, Mama, and Cousin Roy were to see her

in the casket. When they returned home, the house was full of friends and neighbors bringing food. After everyone ate lunch, they returned to the funeral home for the visitation.

The four young people drive around for a while. Travis drives, and Roseanne sits beside him. Melissa and Jamie are in the backseat. They stop at McDonald's, and the boys go inside to get food while the girls wait in the car.

At the funeral the next morning, Roseanne is hot and uncomfortable, and she cannot seem to stop fidgeting. She notices that Melissa looks "like an angel" but also sees the way she is twisting and pulling at the tissue in her hands. Roseanne can think only of her date with Travis. They drove down by the river to eat their hamburgers. Leaving Melissa and Jamie in the car, Travis and Roseanne went to sit by the river. He surprised her with her first kiss.

When the girls got back to the house and went up to get ready for bed in Melissa's room, they caught each other's eye in the mirror. Roseanne felt that "it was like we were seeing each other for the first time." She seemed to suddenly understand what Melissa was experiencing and to genuinely feel for her. Later, when she heard Melissa tossing and turning in her bed, Roseanne joined her and rubbed her back to help her calm down and get to sleep.

Remembering everything that happened the night before, Roseanne resolves to stay at the cemetery as long as Melissa does, no matter how hot she feels in her hated dress. She promises herself that she will tell Melissa and Cousin Roy how sorry she is and that she will hug her mother.

CHARACTERS

Buddy

Buddy is Roseanne's little brother. He is nine years old. It is clear that Roseanne feels like an adult in comparison with him: although Roseanne herself might go to view Cousin Jessie's body, she says that Buddy "doesn't have any business at a funeral home" because he is so young. Perhaps because of the five-year difference in their ages, Buddy does not seem too important to Roseanne's day-to-day life.

Travis Cuthbert

Travis is Jamie's friend and Melissa's neighbor. Melissa and Roseanne used to play with Travis, running through the sprinkler with him on summer afternoons when Roseanne was visiting. Roseanne has not seen Travis in a few years because he has spent his summers at camp. As soon as Travis appears, Roseanne is attracted to him, noticing his "dynamite tan" and his muscles. Travis drives when he and Jamie take the girls out the night before Cousin Jessie's funeral. They stop at McDonald's for a snack and park by the river. Travis gives Roseanne her first kiss; Roseanne thinks "he was practicing as much as I was."

Daddy

Roseanne's father is a minor character in the story. Mama tells Roseanne, "Your daddy's a fine man," because he drove all night to get the family to Cousin Jessie's funeral quickly. Daddy also seems sensible, in the recent past pointing out to Mama that while she could not do much to help Cousin Jessie while she was in the hospital, she could do a lot to help Melissa and Cousin Roy after Cousin Jessie has died and therefore should delay her visit.

Esther

Esther is Cousin Roy's sister. Roseanne mentions that Esther is upset because she does not get to ride in the limousine with her brother.

Jamie Fletcher

Jamie is Melissa's boyfriend. He comes to visit with Melissa on the front porch on the morning after Cousin Jessie's death, and his presence does seem to give Melissa some comfort. Jamie and his friend Travis take Melissa and Roseanne out on a date, driving around town, stopping for hamburgers, and parking by the river.

Cousin Jessie

Cousin Jessie was Roseanne's mother's cousin. She suffered from "diabetes from the time she was first married." Roseanne's family travels to attend Cousin Jessie's funeral, driving all night to arrive as soon as possible so that they can be there to comfort Cousin Jessie's daughter, Melissa, and her husband, Cousin Roy. Cousin Jessie had been sick for a long time. Roseanne's mother puts all of her energy into cleaning the house, making it as nice as Cousin Jessie always kept it before she became so ill.

Mama

Roseanne's mother is very upset by the death of her cousin Jessie. The two women were close all their lives. Roseanne seems to find it embarrassing that Mama and Cousin Jessie would start whispering and giggling when they got together, remembering their teen years. Mama wants to hear every detail of Cousin Jessie's last days from Cousin Roy. She cannot seem to stop cleaning the house, and she takes on all of the arrangements for Cousin Jessie's funeral. Roseanne says that her mother often suffers from "what she calls remorse" and is "a bundle of nerves." At the end of the story, Roseanne seems to understand her mother better because she is starting to appreciate her own relationship with Melissa and has more sympathy for her mother's grief at losing Cousin Jessie.

Melissa

Melissa is Cousin Jessie and Cousin Roy's sixteen-year-old daughter. Roseanne says that she and Melissa have "never liked each other all that much, mostly I reckon because we're supposed to." Roseanne does not like feeling that she must be friends with Melissa simply because Mama and Cousin Jessie were always close. Roseanne also feels jealous of her cousin, who is beautiful, seemingly without any effort, whereas Roseanne only feels confident when she has makeup on. She also seems to envy Melissa's ease with boys. Melissa had "boys after her when she was twelve," while Roseanne feels like she is "making a fool of" herself when Travis appears.

Melissa does not seem to know how to handle Cousin Jessie's death. She withdraws into herself, not eating and hiding under her covers rather than getting out of bed in the morning. Whatever selfishness Melissa shows in this situation is understandable: her mother was ill for a long time, but a sixteen-year-old girl would likely have a very hard time preparing for her mother's death. However, Bridgers gives hints of Melissa's selfishness in other ways, such as through her choosing an expensive dress for a dance and refusing to ever wear it again, and her telling her father that she and Roseanne are going out with Jamie and Travis rather than asking for permission.

Roseanne

Roseanne is the fourteen-year-old narrator of the story. Her status as a somewhat awkward adolescent is established on the first page, where she explains her difficulty in finding something to wear because "my shape is changing. One day I'm pudgy-looking, and the next I've got this waist that nips in just perfect." Roseanne is caught halfway between being a girl and being a woman in terms of physical, mental, and emotional development.

Roseanne does not seem to feel much grief over Cousin Jessie's death. She justifies her lack of tears by thinking of "what you hear in church": Cousin Jessie "was real sick and now she's not sick anymore." Perhaps Roseanne truly does believe that Cousin Jessie is at peace now, but her lack of sympathy for those who are truly grieving seems selfish.

Throughout the story, Roseanne learns to cope with some major life events: the death of a loved one and her first experience with romance. Although she begins the story thinking only of herself and embarrassed by the grief and emotional needs of others, she learns to understand and sympathize with her mother more and to appreciate her relationship with Melissa and the value of someone who knows her family and her background.

Cousin Roy

Cousin Roy was Cousin Jessie's husband and is Melissa's father. He is very distraught by his wife's death and seems relieved to let Roseanne's mother take over the preparations for the funeral. When Roseanne's family arrives, Mama and Cousin Roy sit down so that he can tell her every detail of Cousin Jessie's last few days. Roseanne is surprised that he can remember so much, "like three days are marked in his brain, minute by minute."

Craig Watkins

Craig is a friend of Roseanne's. He sometimes comes to sit with Roseanne on the porch, but she does not consider her evenings with him to be dates because she believes "somebody has to spend some money to make it a date."

THEMES

Grief

It might seem obvious that a story set in motion because of a funeral will deal with the theme of grief, and indeed Bridgers does a good job, in relatively few pages, of portraying several

different ways of coping with grief. Roseanne's mother, for example, seems to have a need to be busy. Even before the action of the story, when she first heard that Cousin Jessie was in the hospital, she wanted to leave home right away, rushing to the hospital in spite of Cousin Roy's assurances that "Cousin Jessie wouldn't know she was there." After Jessie has died, Mama insists that the family leave as soon as possible and drive all night. Once they arrive, she spends her time cleaning everything in sight. She takes over organizing the funeral and the luncheon that will follow. Most likely staying busy helps her get rid of her "nervous energy" and keeps her mind off why she is there.

Melissa's reaction to grief seems to be a bit self-centered. Roseanne thinks that Melissa is "spoiled," and she does seem to think only of her own grief. She withdraws from everyone, hiding under her covers and spending hours painting her toenails. She seems to expect Roseanne to prepare food for her, and she informs her father that she and Roseanne are going out for a drive with the boys: "Didn't ask him. Told him in that sweet way of hers like her mama had somehow already given her permission." Melissa seems to think there is nothing wrong with expecting people to give her what she wants when she is unhappy. Readers can likely forgive Melissa for being a little selfish, however, because she is dealing with a huge loss.

Cousin Roy shows another reaction to grief; he seems to be numbed by his wife's death. He speaks very infrequently, lets his daughter manipulate him, and seems to have no desire to make funeral arrangements, happy to have Roseanne's mother take over.

Throughout the story, it is difficult to tell whether Roseanne feels any grief over Cousin Jessie's death. She admits, "I haven't cried a tear." She justifies her lack of response with what she has heard in church: that Cousin Jessie is no longer suffering now that she has passed on. Not only does Roseanne not seem to feel grief herself, she is unsympathetic to those who show their own grief. She is impatient with Melissa and her mother, saying, "This crying is getting to me." She does not understand her mother's compulsion to keep busy or Cousin Roy's need to relate the events of his wife's last few days. Bridgers cleverly sets up a comparison between Melissa and Roseanne. It is true that Melissa acts selfishly at times, but with good

TOPICS FOR FURTHER STUDY

- Just as Melissa must have struggled with her mother's illness from diabetes, Abby, the protagonist in Amy Ackley's *Sign Language* (2011), does not know how to cope with her father's cancer diagnosis. Read *Sign Language*, and then write a short story from Melissa's point of view in which she meets Abby. Think about what the two girls have in common. Do they both feel angry because their parents are sick? Does Melissa feel guilty after her mother dies? How do they balance the usual concerns of teenage girls—school, boys, friends—with the extra pressure of a sick family member?

- Find images that you feel represent the various scenes and characters from "The Beginning of Something." Be sure to choose stock images that are available for free use. Arrange the images in a PowerPoint presentation so that they tell the story. Then select a song that you think captures the story's mood, and play your presentation, set to the music, for your class.

- Bridgers believes that setting is very important to a story. In "The Beginning of Something," there are several instances of Roseanne's contrasting her mountain home with the eastern part of North Carolina, to which her family travels for Cousin Jessie's funeral. Read the story carefully for the details of setting that Bridgers provides. You may also do research online or at the library to find images of the area. Draw a picture of the setting of one of the scenes in the story, for example, Cousin Jessie's house with its front porch swing or the bank of the quiet river where Roseanne has her first kiss. Incorporate the details from the story as well as your own imaginative touches, and share the drawing with your class, explaining the different elements in your picture.

- The events are not described in chronological order in "The Beginning of Something." Instead, narrator Roseanne describes some scenes as flashbacks. Make a time line that puts each of the events of the story in order and charts how they have been rearranged. Share the time line with your class, and lead a discussion with your classmates about why Bridgers might have decided to present the events out of order. How does the nonchronological order affect the story, and what does it say about Roseanne and her memory?

reason. Roseanne has no such excuse, yet much of her behavior and thoughts are results of her own selfishness, until she begins to be more aware of the feelings of the people around her.

Family

When told that her entire family is traveling to Cousin Jessie's funeral, Roseanne's first words are "Not me." That initial reaction sums up Roseanne's attitude toward her relations at the beginning of the story. She seems to want to keep herself separate from them. She was embarrassed by her mother's behavior when she saw Cousin Jessie, when "the two of them would start

giggling and whispering behind their hands and hugging each other. Used to make Melissa and me sick."

Roseanne resents that she is expected to be friends with Melissa and calls the time the two girls spend together every summer "the longest month God ever made." Roseanne does not understand her mother's intense grief over losing her cousin and resents doing even the small things she can do to help Melissa feel better, like fixing her a peanut butter and jelly sandwich.

By the end of the story, however, Roseanne seems to have learned that family is indeed

Travis and Roseanne sit by the river. *(© Przemyslaw Wasilewski | Shutterstock.com)*

important. She declares her intention to tell both Melissa and Cousin Roy how sorry she is about Cousin Jessie's death, and the last sentence in the story is another promise: "As soon as I get a chance, I'm going to hug Mama."

STYLE

First-Person Narrator

Bridgers wrote "The Beginning of Something" with a first-person narrator. This means that the narrator refers to herself as "I." Bridgers uses Roseanne to give depth to the story by making her an unreliable narrator. Roseanne's perspective is limited, so readers cannot take what she says as the complete truth.

For example, Rose calls Melissa "spoiled." She recalls a time when Cousin Jessie "tried to sound like she was complaining" about Melissa's "expensive taste" in dresses, trying to prove her own declaration that Melissa is spoiled. However, only a few pages before, Roseanne was complaining about how much she hates the dress that she is going to wear to the funeral, not just because she does not like the style but because "Mama bought it on sale and anybody can tell."

If Roseanne were a completely reliable, impartial narrator, readers could accept as fact her statement that Melissa is spoiled, but because Roseanne is a character in the story and has her own feelings and prejudices about what is happening, readers must look at everything she says with a more critical eye. Though Melissa might indeed be spoiled, the events of the story must be judged through the filter of the unreliable narrator. Thus can Roseanne's jealousy, which affects how she describes Melissa, be detected.

Stream of Consciousness

Stream of consciousness is a style of narration that attempts to capture a character's thought processes. Roseanne's narration is an example of stream-of-consciousness narration. The words of the story sound almost as if Roseanne is talking to the reader, telling about what happened at her cousin's funeral. Because stream of consciousness is supposed to reflect how a person thinks, the style is usually not as formal as other styles of writing. Also, the progression of ideas might not be organized in a logical order, such as when Roseanne brings up something that happened a long time ago because she is reminded of it by what is happening now. The conversational style and rapid leaps in thought of stream-of-consciousness narrative are clear in the following quotation:

> I feel like I'm going on and on. Diarrhea of the mouth. That's what happens when a person gets feverish. You feel like you've got to get

COMPARE & CONTRAST

- **1980s:** Teens communicate with friends and set up dates face to face or by telephone.

  Today: Many teens today have cell phones, allowing them to communicate with friends at any time through texting, social media, and video chats.

- **1980s:** Family members dealing with a serious illness in the family, like Cousin Jessie's diabetes, might have problems taking time off work to care for their sick relative. If someone like Cousin Roy took time off work to care for a sick loved one, he might be fired from his job.

  Today: According to the Family and Medical Leave Act of 1993, employers are required to allow their workers as much as twelve weeks of leave in a year to care for a parent, child, or spouse with a serious health condition. Employers do not have to pay employees for the time off (although some employers do provide benefits), but employees must be able to resume their jobs with equivalent benefits and salary when they return from leave.

- **1980s:** Patients with diabetes use injections of human insulin to control their illness. Some patients begin to monitor their own blood glucose levels, but doctors are not in agreement over whether this is a safe development—there is concern about whether patients should have to do their own testing and whether they are responsible enough to maintain their own care without frequent doctor visits and office testing.

  Today: Patients with diabetes often use insulin analogs (artificial rather than human insulin). Self-monitoring of blood glucose levels is standard. Many diabetics have blood glucose meters, which are small computerized machines that easily and quickly test blood, reducing possible errors. Some patients have continuous subcutaneous insulin pumps that keep insulin and blood-sugar levels stabilized. Many websites offer online tools to help patients track their blood levels and treatment plans.

---

everything said before you pass out of heat exhaustion. My mind's been racing for hours. It's like I've got a top spinning in there, whizzing and making heat. Everywhere I've been it's been so hot and tomorrow I've got to wear that dress. I ought to take some aspirins or something.

Some stream-of-consciousness works are much more disjointed and confusing than "The Beginning of Something." Sometimes the style makes it difficult to follow what the narrator is thinking. The story might lack punctuation or have ideas or scenes linked together for no obvious reason. Bridgers's story is not quite so drastic in its use of the style, but it has the lack of linear organization and the feel of being a single person's thoughts as they occur in a natural flow.

HISTORICAL CONTEXT

The 1980s

A story like "The Beginning of Something," because it focuses so much on the thoughts of a single character and her interactions with a few other people, seems not to rely much on events outside her circle of family and friends. Any story, however, is a product of its time.

At the start of the 1980s, Ronald Reagan was elected. During his presidency, US politics were dominated by conservatives who called for a return to old-fashioned moral and social values. Internationally, perhaps the most significant issue for the United States was the Cold War. After the Soviets invaded Afghanistan in 1979, international relations between the Soviet Union

At Cousin Jessie's funeral, Roseanne can only think of Travis kissing her the night before.
(© Christian Knospe / Shutterstock.com)

The 1980s were also a time of contrast. AIDS was first diagnosed in 1981, although mainstream America was not really aware of the disease until the middle of the decade. While for some this increased the prejudice felt toward homosexuals, gay rights also started to become more widely accepted. The rise of the "yuppies" (young urban professionals), whose image glorified wealth, social climbing, and consumerism, contrasted with huge charity projects like Live Aid, rock concerts held to raise money to help victims of famine in Africa.

MTV was launched in the 1980s, and videos began to be as important as the music itself in the recording industry. New wave, hard rock, and pop music were all popular throughout the 1980s, and hip hop was emerging by the latter part of the decade. Video games, both in arcades and on home systems, became a favorite pastime for many kids. Personal computers became much more affordable in the 1980s, making it possible for many more workplaces, schools, and homes to have computers.

CRITICAL OVERVIEW

"The Beginning of Something," being a shorter work, has not received much critical attention. Bridgers's novels, however, have been extensively reviewed as examples of young-adult literature, and the reviews have varied widely. Ted Hipple, in his book *Presenting Sue Ellen Bridgers*, has nothing but praise, calling Bridgers "an outstanding writer.... She writes realistic novels in which adolescent characters are confronted with lifelike and significant problems." Hipple commends the "excellence of her writing and the wisdom and vision she brings to bear on that writing." In a review in *Library Journal*, Jeanne Buckley calls *Sara Will* "a quietly moving book," and Barbara Chatton, in a review of *Permanent Connections* in *School Library Journal*, asserts that Bridgers's "characterizations ... are excellent, providing vivid insights into their lives and troubles." Diane Haas, writing in *School Library Journal* about *Home before Dark*, agrees, describing Bridgers's characters as "almost painfully real."

However, these very positive reviews are balanced by an almost equal number of lukewarm or negative comments. In a review in *School Library Journal*, Sara Miller calls *All Together Now* a

and the United States and other countries in the West deteriorated. The threat of nuclear war seemed very real to many Americans. The situation did not improve until Mikhail Gorbachev became the general secretary of the Communist Party in 1985, bringing reforms that eventually led to the dissolution of the Soviet Union.

Within the United States, the "war on drugs" was fought to put an end to the illegal drug trade. First Lady Nancy Reagan helped support this cause by creating the "Just Say No" campaign, which encouraged kids to refuse drugs. The economy was also a problem in the early 1980s; a severe recession caused unemployment to rise to 10.8 percent at the end of 1982, the highest level since World War II. The auto industry in the United States was hit particularly hard by the recession, but by the end of the decade the increasing competition from foreign companies forced car manufacturers to improve in quality and efficiency.

"warm, well-written if overly sentimental narrative." Miller believes that Bridgers's technique of telling the story from different points of view causes readers to lose sight of the novel's heroine, "and more important—lose a sense of dramatic tension." A *Publishers Weekly* review describes a similar flaw in *All We Know of Heaven*, pointing out that "Bridgers breaks her tale into too many short chapters narrated by too many characters," which "leads to a diffusion of tension and drama." Even Bridgers's characterization, so highly praised by other reviewers, is not appreciated by the *Publishers Weekly* reviewer, who thinks that the novel "relies heavily on homespun truths spoken by country folk straight from central casting."

In addition to these criticisms about Bridgers's style, some reviewers criticize her message and content. A review of *Keeping Christina* in *Publishers Weekly* points out that Bridgers "fumbles a little" in the novel's resolution, "pinning almost all the blame" on one character rather than painting a more realistic, more complicated picture. Janet French's review of *Notes for Another Life* in *School Library Journal* is among the harshest. French quotes the publisher's blurb describing the book as "a family chronicle for all ages"; French believes, however, that

> it would have been more accurate to describe it as a propaganda vehicle for female domesticity. Good women subordinate their talents and yearnings to the home and their children; all other paths lead to havoc.

The one thing critics seem to agree on is Bridgers's ability to realistically portray North Carolina. Hazel Rochman, in the *New York Times Book Review*, praises the "immediacy and candor" with which Bridgers writes about her home state. Rochman believes that *Permanent Connections* "shows clearly not only the affection but also the meanness and defeat in a small Appalachian town." The *Publishers Weekly* review of *Keeping Christina* states that "Bridgers gets the bouncy milieu of Annie's North Carolina high school down pat," and Haas agrees, writing that *Home before Dark* "evokes life in the rural South."

CRITICISM

Kristen Sarlin Greenberg

Greenberg is a freelance writer and editor with a background in literature and philosophy. In the

THE 'SOMETHING' IN THE TITLE IS THE RELATIONSHIP BETWEEN ROSEANNE AND MELISSA— A MORE MEANINGFUL, ADULT RELATIONSHIP THAN THEY HAD BEFORE AND ONE THAT HAS THE POTENTIAL TO PARALLEL THE LIFELONG FRIENDSHIP THEIR MOTHERS SHARED."

following essay, she examines "The Beginning of Something" as a coming-of-age story.

Sue Ellen Bridgers's "The Beginning of Something" is a kind of coming-of-age story. The narrator, Roseanne, experiences two major rites of passage: her first brush with romance and the first time death has taken someone close to her. The two elements seem to be in harsh contrast. A young girl's first kiss should be a happy, life-affirming thing, full of hope and promise, whereas a funeral brings mourning and finality. Bridgers uses Roseanne's reactions to these two contrasting life events to show how she begins to change from a somewhat self-centered teen to a more caring and attentive young woman.

At the beginning of the story, Roseanne thinks only of herself. She does not want to go to Cousin Jessie's funeral although she knows that it is important to her mother. She complains about the dress she has to wear. She dismisses her mother's relationship with Cousin Jessie as "silliness" and says that the secrets and laughter Mama and Jessie shared "used to make me ... sick." Roseanne cannot understand why her mother is so upset by the loss of her cousin and dear friend, and she is impatient with the grief that Melissa shows.

The first interaction between the girls occurs the morning after Roseanne's family has driven all night to go to the funeral. Roseanne has slept only a couple of hours when Melissa wakes up and begins to cry. Roseanne does go to Melissa and offer some comfort, but it seems to be from a sense of obligation rather than from a true desire to bring comfort. Roseanne says that she "couldn't leave her like that." The word "couldn't" is significant, as if Roseanne does not have any choice about how to act.

WHAT DO I READ NEXT?

- Bridgers's first novel, *Home before Dark* (1976), established her as a voice in the then-emerging genre of young-adult literature. The book tells the tale of Stella, whose family is settling in one place after traveling throughout Florida as migrant workers for all of Stella's fourteen years. There is much for Stella to adjust to in this new settled lifestyle while she faces the usual trials of growing up.

- In "The Beginning of Something," Roseanne illustrates how teenagers' thoughts and emotions can flit from one extreme to another. Gary Soto's *Partly Cloudy: Poems of Love and Longing* (2009) also captures this changeability. The poems are told from the points of view of several different narrators who struggle with young love in its many forms.

- Themes of grief and healing are central to *The Girl Who Fell from the Sky* (2010), by Heidi W. Durrow. The heroine of this novel, Durrow's first, is Rachel Morse. Rachel's mother was white, and her father was African American, which was never a difficult issue for her while growing up in Chicago. After Rachel's parents are killed and she goes to live with her grandmother in a predominantly black neighborhood, Rachel is forced to examine her sense of her own identity in addition to learning to deal with the tragedy.

- *When Will I Stop Hurting? Teens, Loss, and Grief* (2004), by Edward Myers, explores the process of grief and bereavement, specifically as it relates to teens. The volume includes firsthand accounts of teens who have experienced loss and learned to cope.

- "The Beginning of Something" introduces some major life events in its plot: the death of a parent and the anxiety of first love. Jane Austen's *Sense and Sensibility* (1811) features these same events, showing that young adults, whether now or two hundred years ago, face similar milestones and difficulties.

- Erin Vincent, in her memoir *Grief Girl: My True Story* (2007), describes what happened after the death of her parents in a traffic accident. Vincent was fourteen years old at the time. With her eighteen-year-old sister, Vincent had to learn to deal with the loss of her mother and father at the same time that she took on adult responsibilities, looking after herself and a younger sister. Although she has written a portrait of a grieving family, Vincent also includes humor.

The next time Roseanne offers help is when she asks her mother, who has been cleaning non-stop, "Can I help you do anything?" However, she does not ask out of genuine concern for her mother or a willingness to be of material help in cleaning up for the visitors who will come later. Instead, Roseanne asks because her mother is "sniffling again" and the "crying is getting to me."

Roseanne surprises the reader and, it seems, herself when she tells Travis that she is going to accompany Melissa to the funeral home to view Cousin Jessie's body, "in case she breaks down over it." Although Roseanne is willingly offering to be of help in this case, she is still acting from selfish motives. She wants to impress Travis and is immensely gratified by his reaction; when he looks at her like she is "God's gift to the bereaved," she wishes she "had a picture." She wants to be seen as caring and strong by this boy she has a crush on, but she still ignores the needs of her grieving family. She does follow through on her promise to go with Melissa to the funeral home, but when they get there, Roseanne cannot make herself look at Cousin Jessie's body. She is not mature enough yet to face up to adult responsibility.

Perhaps because Roseanne does not know how to deal with the grief of her mother and Melissa, she fills her thoughts with her blooming romance with Travis. During the visitation at the funeral home, she is feverish with excitement as she looks forward to her date that evening. During the funeral itself, she recalls in detail everything she did with Travis: driving through the summer night, eating burgers, and awkwardly kissing by the river.

Clearly Roseanne's interest in Travis and the excitement she feels about her first kiss are important to her, but can it be said that the relationship helps move her forward to adulthood? In *Presenting Sue Ellen Bridgers*, Ted Hipple asserts, "Love is found in Bridgers's books, not so much as an act in itself but as a catalyst." With this in mind, the reader can look at Roseanne's actions and thoughts and see that when she focuses on Travis, she is still being selfish. First love is important on a person's path to adulthood, but it is not what sparks a real change in Roseanne.

The true transformation in Roseanne takes place the evening before the funeral, after the date with Travis, when Roseanne and Melissa are looking in the mirror while preparing for bed. Up to that point, it seems that both girls have always resisted being friends; Roseanne explains that they "never liked each other all that much, mostly I reckon because we're supposed to." However, while looking in the mirror, their relationship seems to shift. Roseanne describes the moment as "truly strange because it was like we were seeing each other for the first time." Melissa sees that Roseanne "was there with her." Roseanne finally seems to understand "that something terrible had happened to" Melissa, "had been happening most of her life. Her mama had been dying for a long time, and her being pretty and popular hadn't changed that."

In an article in the *ALAN Review*, Gail P. Gregg and P. Sissi Carroll write, "The issue of when one gives willingly, and when one gives out of a sense of obligation, to her own detriment, is central in much of Sue Ellen Bridgers' fiction." This issue is indeed central to "The Beginning of Something," as we see in this pivotal scene with the two girls. Roseanne has several reasons for making an effort to help others throughout, but because she does not offer that help completely willingly, she is not happy about it—she brings little comfort to others and feels uncomfortable

Mama deals with her anxiety and grief by cleaning the house. (© runzelkorn / Shutterstock.com)

herself. It is only when she begins to give of herself willingly that she proves she is truly maturing.

The moment of transformation, when Roseanne stops thinking of herself and truly feels for Melissa, is her first step toward being an adult. Soon after this, Roseanne gets into bed with Melissa and rubs her back to help her calm down and sleep. It is the first time Roseanne does something only out of a desire to help someone else rather than for selfish reasons, like to impress a boy, or out of a sense of obligation. Roseanne sees that Melissa is struggling and genuinely wants to help her. Because she is thinking of Melissa and not herself, she does it without feeling "one bit embarrassed."

This is not to say that Roseanne suddenly becomes a saint. During Cousin Jessie's funeral, she still spends most of her time thinking of her date with Travis. The romance is important to Roseanne, but it is also a distraction. She shows that she is maturing by pushing her excitement about Travis aside and turning her thoughts toward her family. There is still an echo of Roseanne's jealousy when she describes Melissa's dress, which is blue, "a soft color. Soft summery material, too ..., all glittery and shiny, while the rest of us are black and gray and midnight blue." However, rather than thinking only of her own feelings, she also notices the signs of Melissa's distress, "her hands working a Kleenex." Roseanne still hates her own dress and frets that she will "melt" outside in the "bright, sunny, July Sunday," but she resolves to stay at the cemetery "as long as Melissa does." Roseanne does not make the decision for any selfish reason or to impress anyone. Instead she simply wants to be there to support her cousin.

Roseanne's kiss with Travis becomes less important as a thing in itself and more significant because "just Melissa knows." This is how Roseanne's relationship with Travis becomes the "catalyst" Hipple describes—the secret the girls share signals the bond that has formed between them. The "Something" in the title is the relationship between Roseanne and Melissa—a more meaningful, adult relationship than they had before and one that has the potential to parallel the lifelong friendship their mothers shared. Roseanne's new connection with Melissa is representative of her growing appreciation of her family as the people who best know and love her. This appreciation is illustrated by the final line of the story, in which Roseanne promises, "As soon as I get a chance, I'm going to hug Mama."

There really is not as much of a contrast as it might at first appear between the major elements of the story, the funeral and the first kiss. Both are milestones Roseanne must pass on her way to adulthood. Bridgers uses these life events as outward signs of the change that is going on inside Roseanne as she learns the importance of her family connections and begins to be able to feel genuine empathy for others.

Source: Kristen Sarlin Greenberg, Critical Essay on "The Beginning of Something," in *Short Stories for Students*, Gale, Cengage Learning, 2014.

Sue Ellen Bridgers

In the following excerpt, Bridgers addresses being labeled a young-adult author and the importance of setting in her work.

. . . Being labeled a writer of young adult literature, when I don't always write in that category, is an issue I deal with when I'm speaking

> I ALWAYS THINK I AM WRITING ABOUT THE CLASS I CAME FROM. WE THOUGHT OF OURSELVES AS UPPER MIDDLE CLASS, BUT MIDDLE CLASS COVERS A LOT OF TERRITORY. WE WERE UPPER IN A SMALL TOWN WHERE UP WASN'T VERY HIGH."

to people who aren't knowledgeable in the young adult field. When I'm at state NCTE [National Council of Teachers of English] conferences around the country, or the ALAN branch of NCTE [Assembly for Literature for Adolescents], I'm with people who understand and celebrate young adult literature, so I feel renewed and inspired by their interest and enthusiasm. On the other hand, I'm occasionally in situations where I hear "Oh, I read your book and I liked it, even though it's for young people." The young adult category is relatively new, having been developed in the late '60s and '70s.

People who are denigrating toward young adult literature usually haven't read any and assume that because it is not written for adult readers, it's substandard in some way. A lot of young adult literature is better written than most adult literature. It's just that the subject matter is chosen for its appeal to the young reader. Older readers usually enjoy it too, when they get a chance at it. So being categorized as a young adult writer is both a blessing and a curse.

I'm *very* appreciative of my young adult audience and of the academic community who supports and teaches this genre, the high school teacher who is faced with the problem of finding something his or her students really want to read. I don't argue with the teaching of the classics. Students need to be exposed to those writing styles and those ideas. But they also need to read for pleasure and have the opportunity to explore the lives of people more like themselves, because that's what sets the stage for life-long reading. Writing for young people feels like a vocation. Now I'm being read by a second generation which is quite gratifying.

I wrote most of my first book, *Home Before Dark*, while I was a student at Western. I had written the first 50 pages in Chapel Hill while I was a stay-at-home mom and had put it away, thinking it was a failed short story. When I first had the idea of a migrant family putting down roots, I was concentrating on writing short stories and hadn't given much thought to the novel form. I wasn't interested in writing a novel, and I didn't realize that the story was formulating, whether I was conscious of it or not. One day it floated back into my mind, and I located the pages and continued working on it. When I went to Western to finish my bachelor's degree, I took some creative writing courses there, and I asked the teacher, Bill Paulk, if I could work on the novel instead of the assignments he was making. Most of the time I was able to do that and found it helpful to read sections aloud and get feedback from the other writers. When it was finished, I did not know what to do with it. A short novel about a migrant family, especially about a 14-year-old migrant child, didn't seem to have a market. I hadn't read more than a couple of young adult books. In the early '70s, one of my daughters had urged me to read a Judy Blume and a Paul Zindel, which I'd liked, but I thought of myself as a Southern writer of short fiction at the time and didn't see *Home Before Dark*'s potential in the young adult field.

So not knowing what to do with this manuscript, I sent it to *Redbook Magazine* because Anne Molligen Smith, the fiction editor there, had bought my story "Sitting Duck" and published it in 1972. In the '70s, *Redbook* published a condensation of a novel every month, and they offered to buy the manuscript for condensation. Anne also suggested I send it to Knopf. That wasn't the normal procedure. Usually the magazine bought a book from a publisher rather than the other way around. So in a way Anne Smith was acting as an agent for me.

She gave me Pat Ross's name at Knopf. Pat was a young adult editor, but I was not aware of that at the time. Pat called me a few days after receiving the manuscript and said she was very interested. Later she called again to say the manuscript had been read in both the adult trade and young adult trade departments because they were trying to decide how to categorize it. Finally the marketing decision was made to pitch it as a young adult book, although it was quite different from the books being published at the time.

Most young adult books of that period were written in the first person and had villainous adults because the writers were setting up situations in which there could be problem solving by the young protagonist. If the teenager has wonderful parents and a great support group, you don't have much of a story. The main thing is that these stories were told from the point of view of the young person, which didn't make great reading for adults. Most adults didn't want to go to that place again if they could help it. So the fact that *Home Before Dark* had well developed adult characters, parents who had a physical relationship, and a love story involving adults made it different from the typical young adult book. Of course I didn't know anything about the genre, but when Knopf asked if they could publish it as young adult fiction, I said "That's fine with me." I was excited to have the book published at all, and particularly by Knopf because I'd always loved Knopf's list and the look of their books. I knew I was in very good company there and didn't want to rock that little boat. I'm sure *Home Before Dark* was better reviewed than it would have been as an adult book because it was in a smaller field. That was one of the considerations with the marketing department.

The next book, *All Together Now*, was not only about a retarded man by the name of Dwayne Pickens but also about a community. I knew Dwayne needed a companion to make the story work, and my first idea was for that person to be a boy, which really didn't interest me very much. When I conceived this companion as a girl, she had to be younger than I'd planned if Dwayne were to believe she was a boy. So Casey became a 12-year-old girl and the book was marketed for young adults. Actually, there were several interconnected stories in that book, and only one was Casey's. In a review in the *Washington Post*, Katherine Paterson compared the story to a square dance. That is a nice image of couples together, taking their turns with the music.

And so I found my books popular in the young adult field. I was very happy with that then, and I have never been dissatisfied with it, only irritated with readers who dismiss young adult literature out of hand.

... One difference between the people in my novels set in Appalachia and those in eastern North Carolina is the way they talk. Their pronunciations and their expressions are different. I have to make sure I use expressions that people here would say rather than eastern Carolina expressions, which come more naturally to me. For example, I'd never heard "you'ns" or "pshaw" spoken until I moved here, although I'd seen both in writing. I'd never heard a grown woman call her mother "Mommy" or the word "stout" used to mean strong. I'd never heard the expression "as tight as white on rice," "land's so poor it would hardly raise a cussfight," or "as dead as four o'clock." I'd never heard a paper bag called a poke. Then there's the addition of the "r" sound to many words that changes the pronunciation here: "tarred" for tired, "warsh" for wash, "swaller" for swallow. There's a mountain anecdote about a tourist saying to a native, "People talk funny around here, don't they?" to which the native replies, "Yeah, but they don't hurt nothing and most of 'em leave after Labor Day."

For several years I've been playing around with a group of short stories about a girl who lives in western Carolina, but her mother comes from eastern Carolina, so I'm including some of the differences between the cultures. They seem to come to mind while I'm writing rather than as differences I'm conscious of every day.

Of course, rural people are rural people. I grew up in a rural area of eastern North Carolina. Daddy was a tobacco farmer, and so in many ways living here is not that different. The men I knew talked very much like Wendell Berry's men in Port William, Kentucky. I think my dad would recognize himself in Berry's world and be pleased. There is more difference between urban and rural lifestyle than there is in other regions of the country. I find that readers in Iowa and Kansas appreciate what my stories are about even though they are set in the South.

Mountain people seem to live in closer proximity to their families than people do now in Pitt County. They tend to make lives for themselves here. There are still small farms here and also a big Christmas tree industry, whereas the agricultural world I grew up in with big tobacco farms in eastern North Carolina no longer exists. Acres after acres of farm land have become suburban sprawl, and that's happening here too to some extent. Right down the road from us a lovely piece of pasture land is being bulldozed. It's truly a bloody gash on the landscape.

I always think I am writing about the class I came from. We thought of ourselves as upper middle class, but middle class covers a lot of territory. We were upper in a small town where up wasn't very high. I wrote about migrant workers in *Home Before Dark* because there were migrant children in our school when I was a child, and I always regretted not making more effort to befriend them. But Stella's father, James Earl, came from a good solid farm family, which I would call a middle-class family for that time. I don't write about people who are particularly well educated. There's not a lot of talk about their "professions." Most of the stories take place in the family setting, where the work is not crucial except in the sense that it earns them a living which, in turn, provides the environment they live in. In *Notes For Another Life*, the grandfather is a pharmacist with his own business. The family lives in a nice house and has all the advantages of small-town living.

All Together Now takes place in the '50s, and the Flanagans live in one of those big old rambling houses that young couples today are busy restoring. The family owns a hardware store and probably would have been upper class in a town of that size in the '50s.

In *All We Know of Heaven*, Charlotte and her husband have a higher standard of living than most of the other people in the book. The story takes place in the Depression, and since the South was already depressed, things didn't change all that much for my family. Our bank in Winterville was one of the few in the state that didn't close, which helped folks considerably. Charlotte is from a successful farm family, and her husband has a cotton mill, so they manage just like my grandparents did. Charlotte and Mac's lives are emotionally unsettled, though, because the niece they are rearing falls in love with a troubled young man, marries him over their protests, and has a brief, tragic life with him.

I first wrote that book in third person, but the sensibility of the voice was Charlotte's. She is so much like me it's scary. She knows everything. Well, actually it's not so much a matter of knowing everything as it is that she always has an opinion about what people should do. Though she's very often right, nobody pays much attention to her, so it would serve her well not to get so involved. But she does anyway. I think of her as a loving person with good intentions, even if she is bossy.

But some of my early readers didn't want to hear Charlotte's voice. They didn't trust her judgment. I changed to a multiple point of view to quiet her down a bit and found I enjoyed writing the other voices as much as hers. She remains the voice of reason, however. One of our sons-in-law was really adamant about not liking Charlotte and actually convinced me to make the change. "But that's my voice," I told him and he said, "I know." So much for our family dynamics.

Titles for my books are sometimes difficult to find, and sometimes they just fall in place. I named my first book *What Will The Robin Do Then?* from the old English nursery rhyme, but the editors of *Redbook* asked me to change it to *Home Before Dark*, which was on my alternate list, because they thought the original title was too obscure. *Notes For Another Life* got its name from the opening scene in which a woman and her granddaughter are on their way to see the girl's father in the hospital, and they start singing to give themselves courage. I knew then that the story was going to be about growth, and it was also going to be about music. I was thinking about notes both as instruction and as music. I saw that these kids needed a path toward another life. It seems to be a hard title for people to remember, but I still like it. *Permanent Connections* was the title of an earlier unpublished story, but as soon as Rob Dickson was clear in my mind, I knew it was the perfect title for a book about family's hold on us. *Keeping Christina* just sounded right for a story about a girl who invades a family structure and tries to destroy it.

Emily Dickinson's poem, "My life closed twice before its close," gave me the title for *All We Know of Heaven*. The book was originally called *Rachel Weeping* from a line in Jeremiah—Rachel is weeping for the children of Israel. I came to that title easily because of the tragedy in the story. Actually, there's a painting—I can't remember the artist—but it is an American painting from the colonial period of a woman and her dead infant called "Rachel Weeping." But it seemed too sad a title. Besides, there's no Rachel in the book. So Ellyn Bache, the publisher of Banks Channel Books in Wilmington, and I discussed several possible titles. I told her I had always thought the line from Dickinson was a good possibility, so we looked at the poem again, and there was a lovely logic to it because Bethany's life did close twice before its close....

Source: Nancy Carol Joyner, "An Interview with Sue Ellen Bridgers," in *Appalachian Journal*, Vol. 26, No. 4, Summer 1999, pp. 411–13, 415–18.

Gail P. Gregg and P. Sissi Carroll
In the following excerpt, Gregg and Carroll ask Bridgers about what is important to her in her writing and how writing books and screenplays differs.

...After chatting for an hour or so, we moved from specific questions to an open conversation regarding her art and craft—and her artistic processes. Sue Ellen is particularly concerned with clarity in her writing. When composing, she reads her words aloud or has her husband, Ben, read her words aloud in an effort to ensure clarity of thought and to hear the "voices." Reading aloud also helps her insure that there are no extra words. At times, Ben asks questions of what she has written in an effort to help her clarify points. She added that this was why she always chose to read her presentations to audiences—to hear her literary voice. In passing, she mentioned that she compared her presentations to giving a sermon—she has a message to give. It became readily apparent to us that Sue Ellen chooses her conversational words very carefully as well—she pauses before responding and while in the process of responding seems to weigh every word. She also, at times, changes her words after speaking when she doesn't think that they have accurately depicted her thoughts—if they didn't "sound" right. As Sara Will moved to her shoulder, Sue Ellen closed this part of the interview by stating that she spends many days editing but, she likes to gain distance from her words by waiting a period of time to revisit what she has written.

As we moved closer to our time of departure, we asked Sue Ellen about the projects currently on her agenda, especially her move into screenwriting with son, Sean, an actor who lives in Los Angeles. Sue Ellen became very animated when talking about the movie *Paradise Falls*, which has had great success and won awards at several different film festivals including Charleston and Houston, and in Atlanta, where it won "Best Drama Under One Million Dollars." Sue Ellen refers to it as a story about "the fallacy of redemptive violence"—a fallacy, since "There is no redemption in violence, because it pushes one further away." For Sean, the screenplay and movie is a necessary "story of loss" which grew from his own longing for the mountains of home after he moved away. The mother and son pair are now working together on a second screen play; filming will begin shortly and expected release in early 2000. She explained that working with her son is a pleasure and a challenge; she writes too many words and, by dramatizing for her, Sean shows her where she needs to tighten her language. Sean, she says, finds it impossible "to say 'No!'" to his mother.

When asked about writing movies versus writing books, Sue Ellen responded that she regards them as two separate entities. She does not accept producers' decisions about which books to make into movies as a legitimate indication of literary quality. She also stated that if she takes money for allowing one of her works to be turned into a movie, then she has to be willing to put up with changes that the movie producers will, inevitably, make....

Source: Gail P. Gregg and P. Sissi Carroll, "'What's It Like to Be You?': A Conversation with Sue Ellen Bridgers," in *ALAN Review*, Vol. 27, No. 1, Fall 1999, pp. 9–13.

Ted Hipple

In the following excerpt, Hipple describes Bridgers's formation as a writer.

... She published short stories in small literary magazines that gave authors complimentary copies as payment. The work on these stories provided a kind of training ground for her as a writer, an opportunity to learn that, for her, character development is the essential element in fiction, the one to which all other aspects of storytelling must be subordinated. In these stories she sharpened her skills as a painter of verbal portraits, skills that are evident in all of her novels. Yet there are other similarities between these early stories and the later novels. The stories were placed in small-town North Carolina. The themes that would later inform her longer works took root in these stories. Love and the importance of families, particularly vertical families, were common thematic explorations.

... Donald Gallo has assembled three volumes of original short stories by noted authors of young adult fiction; Bridgers's work has appeared in two of them. In *Visions* her story is "The Beginning of Something." The setting is typical Bridgers—rural North Carolina. Again, she mixes adolescents with their horizontal and vertical families. Teenager Roseanne is traveling across the state to the funeral of Cousin Jessie,

her mother's relative and best friend, just as Roseanne and Jessie's daughter Melissa are good friends. The funeral is described, with a number of adult reactions portrayed. But what really happens that weekend is that Roseanne gets her first kiss from a friend of Melissa's boyfriend. After the funeral Roseanne thinks, "I'm going to tell Melissa how sorry I am. I'm going to tell Cousin Roy [Melissa's father], too, because I haven't told him yet. But I'm not going to tell anybody about Travis Cuthbert kissing me. It's as private as grief but it doesn't need sharing."

Gallo's next collection, *Connections*, features another Bridgers story, this one a continuation of the previous one. In "Life's a Beach" Cousin Roy has remarried, only six months after Jessie's death, to the tearful chagrin of Roseanne's mother. Still, they must accept the generous offer of Roy's new bride that Roseanne come to spend the summer at the beach house with Melissa. There she and Melissa go after the same boy, Scott, Roseanne feeling sure that she will lose; after all, Melissa is prettier, quicker witted, more experienced. Yet it is she—Roseanne—whom Scott likes.

But Bridgers as a writer of short stories, then and now, is no match for Bridgers as a writer of novels, in her own estimation or that of her many readers. And, in 1976, Bridgers became a novelist. That year was for her one of those banner years when things happen in such a way that life can never again be the same. In that one twelve-month period Bridgers realized two major goals: she published a novel and she graduated from college....

Source: Ted Hipple, "A Writer's Life," in *Presenting Sue Ellen Bridgers*, Twayne Publishers, 1990, pp. 7, 9–10.

SOURCES

"Biography," Sue Ellen Bridgers website, http://www. sueellenbridgers.com/bio.htm (accessed September 2, 2013).

Bridgers, Sue Ellen, "The Beginning of Something," in *Visions: Nineteen Short Stories by Outstanding Writers for Young Adults*, edited by Donald R. Gallo, Laurel Leaf, 1987, pp. 213–28.

Buckley, Jeanne, Review of *Sara Will*, in *Library Journal*, Vol. 110, No. 1, January 1985, pp. 98–99.

Chatton, Barbara, Review of *Permanent Connections*, in *School Library Journal*, Vol. 33, No. 7, March 1987, pp. 168–69.

"Computer Revolution," in *American Decades*, edited by Judith S. Baughman, Victor Bondi, Richard Layman, Tandy McConnell, and Vincent Tompkins, Vol. 9, *1980–1989*, The Gale Group, 2001.

Deeb, Larry C., "Diabetes Technology during the Past 30 Years: A Lot of Changes and Mostly for the Better," in *Diabetes Spectrum*, Vol. 21, No. 2, April 2008, pp. 78–83.

French, Janet, Review of *Notes for Another Life*, in *School Library Journal*, Vol. 28, No. 1, September 1, 1981, p. 133.

Gregg, Gail P., and P. Sissi Carroll, "'What's It Like to Be You?': A Conversation with Sue Ellen Bridgers," in *ALAN Review*, Vol. 27, No. 1, Fall 1999, pp. 9–13.

Haas, Diane, Review of *Home before Dark*, in *School Library Journal*, Vol. 23, No. 5, January 1977, p. 99.

Hipple, Ted, *Presenting Sue Ellen Bridgers*, Twayne Publishers, 1990.

Joyner, Nancy Carol, "An Interview with Sue Ellen Bridgers," in *Appalachian Journal*, Vol. 26, No. 4, Summer 1999, pp. 410–23.

Linden, Carl A., "Glasnost," in *Encyclopedia of Russian History*, edited by James R. Millar, Vol. 2, Macmillan Reference USA, 2004, pp. 559–62.

Miller, Sara, Review of *All Together Now*, in *School Library Journal*, Vol. 25, No. 9, May 1, 1979, p. 70.

"The 1980s: The Arts," in *American Decades*, edited by Judith S. Baughman, Victor Bondi, Richard Layman, Tandy McConnell, and Vincent Tompkins, Vol. 9, *1980–1989*, The Gale Group, 2001.

"The 1980s: Lifestyles and Social Trends," in *American Decades*, edited by Judith S. Baughman, Victor Bondi, Richard Layman, Tandy McConnell, and Vincent Tompkins, Vol. 9, *1980–1989*, The Gale Group, 2001.

Review of *All We Know of Heaven*, in *Publishers Weekly*, Vol. 243, No. 37, September 9, 1996, p. 66.

Review of *Keeping Christina*, in *Publishers Weekly*, May 31, 1993, http://www.publishersweekly.com/978-0-06-02 1504-0 (accessed September 3, 2013).

Rochman, Hazel, Review of *Permanent Connections*, in *New York Times Book Review*, July 26, 1987.

Urquhart, Michael A., and Marillyn A. Hewson, "Unemployment Continued to Rise in 1982 as Recession Deepened," US Bureau of Labor Statistics website, 1983, http://www.bls.gov/opub/mlr/1983/02/art1full.pdf (accessed September 15, 2013).

FURTHER READING

Bridgers, Sue Ellen, *Notes for Another Life*, Knopf, 1981.
    Notes for Another Life, Bridgers's third novel, tells the story of siblings Kevin and Wren, who live with their grandparents. Their mother's career ambitions make them feel abandoned by her, especially since their father's mental illness prevents him from being with the family. While Wren works toward her goal of becoming a concert pianist and falls in love for the first time, Kevin struggles with the fear that he shares his father's illness.

Harris, Maxine, *The Loss That Is Forever: The Lifelong Impact of the Early Death of a Mother or Father*, Dutton Adult, 1995.
    Harris has collected over sixty stories from people who lost a parent when they were young, including some well-known names, such as Eleanor Roosevelt and Virginia Woolf. Although the stories describe the grief inevitable with such a tragic topic, they also reflect the growth and recovery that follow.

Helfrick, Robb, *North Carolina: Simply Beautiful*, Farcountry Press, 2003.
    Bridgers said in an interview with Nancy Carol Joyner, "The setting is extremely important to me. I want to give the reader a visual impression they can be grounded in." In her short story "The Beginning of Something," Bridgers draws distinctions between Roseanne's perceptions of the clear mountain air and flowing, rocky streams of western North Carolina's mountains and the river where she and Travis share their first kiss, which "hardly move[s] at all," and the warm, "sticky" air in the eastern part of the state. Helfrick's photography captures the beauty of Bridgers's home state, from the coast to the mountains.

Hoffman, Alice, *Green Heart*, Turtleback, 2012.
    Hoffman explores the themes of grief and recovery in this fairy tale–like novella. The heroine, Green, loses her family, retreats into her garden, and only slowly learns to feel hope again.

SUGGESTED SEARCH TERMS

Sue Ellen Bridgers AND The Beginning of Something

Sue Ellen Bridgers AND North Carolina

Sue Ellen Bridgers AND writing process

Sue Ellen Bridgers AND young-adult literature

North Carolina AND geography

North Carolina AND mountains

North Carolina Piedmont

teens AND grief

Christmas Day in the Morning

PEARL S. BUCK

1955

"Christmas Day in the Morning" is a holiday short story by Pearl S. Buck, the first American woman ever awarded the Nobel Prize for Literature. The story concerns a man in his sixties who wakes up at four o'clock on Christmas morning because he always woke at four during his childhood on his family's farm. He remembers back to when he was fifteen and found out, just a few days before Christmas, how much his father really loved him. He decided then to do something special for his father, to give him a break from his labors that Christmas morning. Fifty years later, the son reflects on the meaning of his gesture.

Since its original publication, on page 10 of the *Collier's* magazine issue of December 23, 1955, this simple, moving story has become a perennial holiday classic. It can be found in *A 2nd Helping of Chicken Soup for the Soul: 101 More Stories to Open the Heart and Rekindle the Spirit* (1995), edited by Jack Canfield and Mark Victor Hansen; *Christmas in My Heart: A Fourth Treasury; Further Tales of Holiday Joy* (1998), edited by Joe Wheeler; and *Believe: A Christmas Treasury* (1998), edited by Mary Engelbreit. In 2002 it was adapted as a picture book for children, with illustrations by Mark Buehner. Like the various published versions, the picture book edits the story, in this case leaving out the final paragraphs, about the character deciding to write a card to his wife. Beyond the *Collier's* original, the version included in the collection

Pearl S. Buck *(© Hulton-Deutsch Collection / Corbis Images)*

Believe offers perhaps the most complete text available. The version of "Christmas Day in the Morning" referenced in this entry is the one in *A Family Christmas*, compiled by Caroline Kennedy and published in 2007.

AUTHOR BIOGRAPHY

Pearl Comfort Sydenstricker was born in Hillsboro, West Virginia, on June 26, 1892. Her parents, Absalom Sydenstricker and Caroline Stulting, were Presbyterian missionaries who were stationed in China before she was born. At the time of her birth, they were back in the United States recovering from the loss of several of their children to tropical diseases. A few months after her birth, her parents returned to China to resume their missionary work.

In her early years, the young Pearl lived in Zhenjiang (Chen-chiang), though the Boxer Rebellion forced the family to move briefly to Shanghai when she was nine. Later, she moved to Shanghai by herself to attend Miss

Jewell's boarding school. After finishing her schooling, she moved in 1910 to Virginia to attend Randolph-Macon Woman's College, in Lynchburg. She graduated with honors in 1914 and briefly taught psychology there, but returned to China to care for her ailing mother and serve as a missionary. In 1917 she married John Lossing Buck, who was also involved in missionary work. They lived in Nanjing (Nanking), and she cared for their daughter, Carol, who was born in 1920 with special needs, and meanwhile taught English at several universities. She returned to America with her husband in 1925 to earn a master's in English from Cornell University, returning to China afterward.

Buck's first novel, *East Wind: West Wind*, was published to acclaim in 1930. Her second book, *The Good Earth*, about the lives of Chinese peasants, was published in 1931 and won the Pulitzer Prize the following year. It remains one of the best-known books in the English language from the twentieth century. She went on to publish frequently, putting out a novel every few years, including *A House Divided* (1935), *Dragon Seed* (1941), and *Pavilion of Women* (1946). She also published many short stories and books of nonfiction, frequently centered on international relations. She divorced John Buck in 1935 after starting a relationship with her editor, Richard Walsh, whom she married and lived with in the United States until his death in 1960.

In 1938, Buck was awarded the Nobel Prize in Literature, becoming the first American woman and only the fourth woman ever to earn the honor. In addition to publishing frequently, she was very active in international humanitarian causes to promote understanding between Eastern and Western cultures. In 1941 she founded the East and West Association, and in 1949 she started an adoption agency, Welcome House, to help place children from the poorest parts of China in Western homes. Buck died in Danby, Vermont, on March 6, 1973, of lung cancer.

PLOT SUMMARY

The opening paragraphs of "Christmas Day in the Morning" take place in the present day. It is Christmas morning. Rob, the protagonist, is about sixty-five years old. He wakes up at four o'clock, as he does every morning, a habit that became ingrained in him in the course of his childhood. Normally he just goes back to sleep, but this time he stays awake, thinking about that one special Christmas fifty years ago, when he was fifteen.

A few days before the Christmas Day he remembers, he overhears his parents talking. His father, Adam, tells his mother, Mary, that he feels bad about waking young Rob so early in the morning to milk the cows. Mary makes the case that Rob is no child and that Adam must do what he has to do to keep the farm running. Still, Adam feels bad about always having to wake Rob at four o'clock when a growing boy needs his sleep.

Hearing this, Rob has a revelation. He realizes that his father loves him. It is an idea that had never occurred to him in the difficult life his overworked family of farmers is forced to lead.

Lying in bed that Christmas Eve, fifty years ago, Rob thinks about what kind of gift he could give his father. He has already bought him a necktie from the store, but he feels that is not enough. Looking out at the stars, he remembers the day when he was young when he asked his father what a stable is, and found out that it is just a barn, no different from the barn they have on the farm. The connection between the humble origins of Jesus, who was born in a stable according to Bible stories, and his own situation leads Rob to think up what he determines will be the perfect Christmas gift for his father: he decides that he will rise early on Christmas morning and go out to the barn, to get the milking and the chores that go with it done before his father gets there.

Throughout that night he wakes often, impatient for the time when he can go. Finally, it is fifteen minutes before three o'clock. He puts his clothes on and quietly slips out of the house, into the night air, and goes to the barn. There, things go just as he has planned: he milks the cows, stores the large cans of milk, cleans up any signs of his work, and locks the barn behind him before going back into the house.

He makes it to his bed just in time, before his father comes to wake him at four o'clock. Pretending to hardly hear his wake-up call, Rob gives his father the impression that he will be following him out to the barn in just a few minutes. Then he curls back under his covers and waits. The wait is nerve-wracking as he anticipates his father's return.

After what seems like a long time, his father comes back into the house and goes to Rob's room. He knows exactly what Rob has done, and he is delighted. He moves close to Rob and gives him a massive hug. In response, Rob tells his father that he really does want to be good. His statement is a burst of emotion motivated, as the story explains, by the feeling of love for his father overflowing him.

Now that they are both awake, Rob dresses, and he and his father go downstairs. When his mother and sister come down, his father tells them about the nice thing that Rob did for him, and Rob, though a little embarrassed, is overcome with pride. His father explains that this is the best Christmas gift he has ever gotten, and that he will remember it every Christmas for the rest of his life. As the story's first paragraph explained, his father would go on to live for twenty years more. That gesture, more than any tangible gift he ever received, stayed in his memory for the rest of his life, and the delight he took from it stayed on Rob's mind every Christmas as he grew to be an old man.

The story returns to the present day, fifty years after that Christmas. Thinking about the good feeling that came to him from being generous and showing his love, Rob decides that he wants to express his love to his wife. It is something he has not done in a long time. He wants to write her a card, telling her that his love for her now is even greater than it had been when they were young. As he thinks about it, he realizes that his love for her is directly related to the moment he overheard his father talking to his mother, which was the moment that he first fully understood that his father loved him. That overheard conversation started a chain reaction: Rob's father's love stirred up his own love for his father and ultimately the love that he would feel for his wife. Showing his love for his father with that simple gift of milking the cows improved his life, and he is certain that showing his love for his wife will affect him as well. He takes a card and starts writing his message to her, on that happy Christmas.

CHARACTERS

Adam

Adam is the father of Rob, the story's protagonist. He is one of the main characters in the story.

Adam is not a very outwardly loving man. Readers can tell this by the surprise that registers with his son as soon as Rob hears that his father is concerned about his well-being. This concern must be something far out of the ordinary, because it affects Rob deeply. The best Christmas present that Rob can think of giving his father is a brief break from the drudgery of the farmwork, which shows how hard Adam is always working and how few interests he has beyond his family's basic survival.

Although the story builds suspense around how Adam will react when he finds out that Rob has taken care of his work, the father's response is nothing but unequivocal appreciation. He is moved to tears. It is, he says, the best Christmas gift he has ever gotten, a claim that is supported in the way that he remembers this gift for the next twenty years of his life. When his wife and his daughter come downstairs that Christmas morning, Adam rushes to tell them about the wonderful gift Rob has given him—he is not only grateful but proud.

Mary

Mary is Rob's mother. She does not have much to do with this episode, but her appearance in one brief scene is crucial to the reader's understanding of the story.

A few days before the Christmas of his fifteenth year, Rob overhears his parents talking about the work that their boy is required to do on the family farm. Rob's father is burdened with guilt because he is making the boy rise before dawn to milk the cows. He tries to convey to Mary how soundly Rob is always sleeping when he goes to wake him up.

The picture that Adam paints is a touching one, but Mary is not moved. She points out that there is just no other way, that Rob must take his turn doing the farmwork. Her explanation seems cold and unemotional, but it is also logical. She does not seem to harbor any negative feelings toward her son, but she is willing to admit that his labor is needed to make the farm run effectively. If only for a moment, Adam may indulge in the fantasy that he could possibly free Rob from his responsibilities, but Mary is mindful of the family's needs and is not inclined to even think about such an impossible scenario.

Implied by her explanation is concern for her husband. She says that Rob is responsible for doing chores because it is "his turn," indicating that the person who has been responsible for the predawn milkings up to this point—Rob's father, Adam—has earned a break.

Rob

Rob—whose wife calls him by the full name of Robert in some versions—is the protagonist of the story. Most of it takes place when he is fifteen years old and living on his parents' farm. That main portion of the story is bracketed with scenes of Rob at sixty-five years of age, waking at four in the morning because it is a habit developed in his youth and thinking about that one particular Christmas, and what it has meant to his life.

The story explicitly says little about what Rob was like before the events depicted here. His "loitering in the mornings" is mentioned, at least, and readers can assume that as a young man Rob was generally hesitant about doing his chores: that he complained, moved slowly, or in other ways conveyed that he objected to participating in the farmwork he was required to do. When his father is thanking him for the Christmas gift later on, Rob tells him that he did it to show that he wants to do good, which further indicates that his behavior up to then left doubts about his intents.

His previous attitude changes a few days before Christmas when he overhears his parents, Adam and Mary, talking. Again, it is not stated, but readers may reasonably infer that before hearing that conversation, Rob may have thought that his father gave him chores to do because he did not really love the boy. When he hears his father tell his mother, in a moment of candor, that he wishes he did not have to make Rob awaken at four every morning, Rob realizes how much his father loves him.

That starts a series of events. The short-term result is that Rob decides to respond to the knowledge of his father's affection by doing something special for his father. He knows that the tie he bought in town does not qualify as special. So he wakes up before his father on Christmas morning and milks the cows.

His father recognizes the gesture for what it is: a heartfelt sign of Rob's love. Although it was something that cost the boy nothing, an action that took no more than an hour or so to complete, Adam is moved to tears. He promises that he will remember it for the rest of his life.

Remembering Adam's gratitude for this simple gesture, some fifty years later, moves Rob to write a note to his wife. Like his father, he has not been a very expressive man, and he has not told his wife that he loves her lately. But he has been thinking for fifty years about how a simple expression of love affected his father, and he wants to have a similar effect on his wife, in case she feels unloved.

Rob's Sister

Rob's sister is mentioned a few times in the story—in the longest versions he has more than one sister—but she is not described explicitly. When Rob overhears his parents talking and decides that his father loves him, he mentions how his parents are just too busy to show their affection for any of their children. At that point in the story, it is not clear how many children there may be. But in thinking about what the family members usually give each other for presents, Rob recalls one sister. And on Christmas morning the narrative clearly states that Rob's father tells the story of Rob's gift to his wife and daughter. No details are given, however, about whether Rob's sister is older than Rob or younger, or anything else about her.

Rob's Wife

Some versions of the story, most notably the 2002 book illustrated by Mark Buehner, omit the role that Rob's wife plays. In the longer versions, though, she has the important role of highlighting the significance of what Rob learned in his youth.

Readers do not meet Rob's wife in certain versions of the story, and though in the longest versions her name is revealed to be Alice, in others she remains anonymous. Rob's relationship with her is implied by the way he feels about their relationship. He regrets that he has not told his wife that he loves her, and he feels that it is important for her to know that his love for her is even greater, at age sixty-five, than it was when they were young. They have obviously had a long relationship if they knew each other when they were young, but their relationship has perhaps gone stale, or has at least become routine, with Rob taking his wife for granted and becoming quiet toward her, just as his parents were toward Rob and his sister.

THEMES

Love

As the narrator points out at the end of this story, love is something that, once awakened, grows. Rob traces the entire sequence of events of his life back to the moment when he heard his father express concern for him, which was the first moment in his life when he realized his father loved him. After that idea sank into his head, Rob became focused on finding a way to show his father that he loved him, too. His expression of love—milking the cows without being told to—was received much more enthusiastically than Rob could have imagined. His father's emotional reaction to it made an impression on him about the power of love. Fifty years later, thinking back about that experience, Rob decides that it is time to express his love for his wife, whom he feels he may have taken for granted lately.

While the message that Rob receives from the recollected events is a message about love, the main focus of the story readers see unfolding before them is the *expression* of love. Adam, the father, loved his son even before Rob knew it; but it is only when Rob becomes aware of his love that the boy's own feelings toward his father come out. After Rob milks the cows, the love his father expresses for him is different from the concern that Rob recognized earlier in the story. Adam's concern for his son's health and well-being is a fatherly concern, but seeing the trouble that Rob goes to in coming up with a gift for him makes Adam melt with a love that is more akin to gratitude. Similarly, readers are told that Rob loves his wife and always has, but his decision at the end of the story to express his love for her in writing shows that he has realized, after reflecting on the long-ago incident with his father, that love is not all that powerful unless it is shown.

Memory

"Christmas Day in the Morning" is a story about two different kinds of memory. The first is the kind ingrained in the mind through rote repetition. Rob is sixty-five at the time of the story. The narrator does not say how long he was responsible for milking the cows on his father's farm, but it is explained that fifty years later he still wakes at four each morning, even though he has no cows to tend to. He

TOPICS FOR FURTHER STUDY

- Search the Internet for a Christmas tradition from some other culture around the world that interests you. Write a brief summary of the tradition and its history, and then write a short story, in the same style as Buck's, putting a father and his teenaged son from that culture into a situation similar to the one Rob and his father are in.

- In "Christmas Day in the Morning," Rob and Adam are not in the habit of expressing their emotions verbally, which is what makes Rob's gift so moving. As an old man, though, Rob feels that his wife will not understand his love for her well enough unless he does tell her of it in words. Verbal and nonverbal expressions of love are both important, but which is more important? Write a philosophical essay in which you explain the relative benefits of each way of expressing one's emotions and their relative significance, using hypothetical or real examples as appropriate.

- The story says that Rob's sister sewed presents for everyone. Research rural American stitchery, find some examples of such stitch work, and present photos to the class with a PowerPoint presentation, explaining the history and significance of the materials and patterns used.

- Watch the 1983 film *Bush Christmas*, an Australian story directed by Henri Safran and starring John Ewart, John Howard, and a teenage Nicole Kidman in her first film role. The film is a story for young adults about a family living in the outback and their hopes to race their prize horse to win enough to save their farm. After watching the film, write an essay comparing the aspects of farm life in Australia at Christmastime to farm life in 1950s America at Christmastime.

- In Buck's story, Rob does something nice for his father because he cannot afford to buy him a fancy gift: he states explicitly that they are a poor family. Research the social programs that were made available to poor rural families from the Great Depression onward, and write a paper explaining what help this family could have gotten from the government to keep their farm going.

- Contemporary medicine emphasizes the need to get enough sleep, identifying lack of sleep as a real danger for a modern generation that has too much stimuli to pay attention to. Research theories about sleep and its restorative powers as well as the chores that would be done on a small family farm early in the twentieth century. Then, write out a schedule for Rob and his parents on the farm, starting at four in the morning with milking the cows. Make sure that all the farm chores are covered and Rob's well-being is accounted for.

---

became so accustomed to waking in those years that the habit became a part of his internal clock, absorbed into his cells. His mind knows what time it is even without his looking at a clock, even when he is in the middle of sleeping, and, even these decades later, his mind feels that it is important for Rob to awake. This kind of memory has little to do with active thought and everything to do with the power of recurring habit.

The other kind of memory constitutes the main part of the story. Rob is reminded of something significant that happened, and he thinks about it, filling in the associated components as he remembers them. The details of what he remembers—the books that his parents bought him each Christmas, for instance, and the many matches he lit to check the clock while waiting for the right time to wake and milk the cows—make the past event real to him, and they help

Buck's story takes place on a dairy farm. *(© Lishansky Photography | Shutterstock.com)*

him recall the emotions he had at that time, fifty years ago. That, in turn, affects his behavior in the present, as he knows that the gift for his wife will evoke the same loving emotions that the gift for his father once did.

Christian Symbolism

This story takes place on the Christian holiday of Christmas, the celebration of the birth of Jesus Christ. For Christians, Christmas is one of the most important days on the religious calendar. It is the celebration of the most important person in Christian theology. Over the centuries, this day has been recognized through prayer and reflection, but also with acts of kindness toward others, including the exchange of gifts. Because they are struggling financially, the gifts exchanged in Rob's family are generally focused on fun as well as usefulness; the narrator makes a point of showing that his parents tried to give him "something more too" in addition to something needed. This recollection leaves Rob with the feeling that the Christmas gift he bought for his father, a necktie, is too impersonal—it is a

gift in name alone, as it does not reflect the feelings that he has for his father.

Exchanging gifts for Christmas is a Christian tradition. The only place where the Bible is specifically referred to in the story comes when Rob recalls asking his father what a stable is: he is thinking of the biblical story of Jesus's birth, which explains how the parents of Jesus were forced to go to the city of Bethlehem to fulfill a tax decree, but they could not find housing and so ended up staying in a stable, where Jesus was born. The most common version of the Bible available to Rob's family would have been the King James Version, translated into English in 1611. Neither it nor other standard editions, however, use the word *stable*: the Gospel of Luke says that Jesus was born in a *manger*, while none of the other gospels discuss his birthplace at all. This indicates that Rob knows his biblical stories from word of mouth, as they have been passed down to him from the tellings of his parents or other persons, or from sources that he has read other than the Bible.

STYLE

Framing

This story begins when Rob is in his sixties, and it ends at that same time. The main part of the story, however, occurs at a different time and place. A story within which another story is placed is called a *framing* device: the future story is like a frame around the story of Rob when he was fifteen.

Using a framing device like this gives the author the opportunity to show the long-term effects of the events on the character. Rob may not have entirely realized how significant his gift to his father was at the time: he saw that his father, mother, and sister were pleased, but that would not necessarily make his one simple act a life-changing event. From the perspective of many years later, however, he can say with assurance that his father was profoundly moved by his gift. Rob himself is still thinking about it half a century later, so the gift of milking the cows was clearly more significant than anybody could have realized at the time.

Buck's starting in the future and jumping to the past tells readers in advance that there will be significant consequences for the relatively simple story they are about to read. Returning to the future a few pages later fulfills the promise made at the beginning of the story.

Point of View

Most of this story is told from Rob's point of view, although that point of view is split between two different versions of the same man. It starts with his perspective as a man in his sixties but shortly goes back in time to his perspective as a fifteen-year-old boy. The narration stays with Rob's perspective, for the most part giving readers information that only Rob could know and only giving information Rob could know.

Buck nearly breaches the structure of the story's point of view when her narrator says that Rob's father remembered his gift year after year for the rest of his life. From Rob's point of view, there would be no way of knowing what was in his father's mind—unless he expressed it. Readers need to interpret the use of "remember" to mean that the father talked about the gift every year, remembering it out loud. If he just thought about it, there would be no way that that could be reported from Rob's point of view, which is the style this story establishes for itself and successfully commits to.

HISTORICAL CONTEXT

Christmas Gifts

The tradition of exchanging gifts at Christmastime has its roots in the Gospels, emulating the story of the magi, the three wise men (also referred to as the "three kings") who are said to have traveled to Bethlehem to bring gifts of gold, frankincense, and myrrh to the infant Jesus. In some cultures gift exchanges are still held on the sixth day of January, the twelfth day after Christmas, which is when tradition holds that the wise men arrived with their gifts.

The practice of exchanging gifts at the end of the year began with the Saturnalia of ancient Rome, a festival that many consider to have been the basis of the Christian celebration of Christmas. Originally a one-day feast on December 17, Saturnalia developed into a week-long celebration that was popular for centuries. In the fourth century, Christians used this festive time to convert pagans, telling them that they could still celebrate Saturnalia, but capping its end with the observation of the birth of Jesus on December 25. Gift exchanges were a part of the Saturnalia ritual.

The roots of the gift-exchange tradition also reach back to the presents that were distributed to the poor on Saint Nicholas's Eve by French nuns in the thirteenth century. Saint Nicholas was a bishop of the fourth century who was known for his generosity, and is considered to be the model for the mythical Santa Claus. Traditionally, the celebration of his feast day, December 6, includes giving candy to poor children. The nuns who emulated his work were said to have given out so many gifts anonymously while children slept that rumors began that Saint Nicholas himself was distributing presents, leading to the legend of Santa Claus.

In the 1800s the practice of gift giving at Christmas became standard. Stores advertised goods specifically to be given as presents by the 1820s. In the 1840s, advertising began using images of Santa Claus to remind people of the spirit of giving. By the 1860s stores rearranged their patterns in acknowledgment of people's inclination to buy gifts for friends and family: Macy's, for instance, took the bold move of keeping their New York City store open until midnight on Christmas Eve in 1867 so that

COMPARE
&
CONTRAST

- **1955:** Roughly 16 percent of the US labor force works on farms.

  Today: About 2 percent of the US labor force works on farms.

- **1955:** American magazines and public spaces are given over to observances of Christmas, with the assumption that the majority of people are Christian.

  Today: American society has become more conscious of the diverse backgrounds of its citizens and recognizes more varied religions that do not include Christmas in their traditions.

- **1955:** People living on farms can only buy whatever Christmas gifts can be found at the store in the nearest town, or perhaps in the Sears catalog.

  Today: A person living on a farm can order a Christmas gift online from across the globe and have it delivered to one's doorstep.

- **1955:** Buying Christmas presents is common, but many people, like Rob in this story, struggle to find a personal gift that is not commercial, one that will really mean something to the recipient.

  Today: As the Christmas shopping season is pushed back before Halloween by some

stores, the struggle against commercialism becomes more and more difficult.

- **1955:** Milking machines have been available for small farms since the beginning of the century, but they still have to be manually operated by farmers.

  Today: Automatic milking systems on corporate farms are robotic, milking cows when they step into position.

- **1955:** Students in rural schools have their schedules arranged around farm life: days start and end early, and school years are planned to accommodate the growing and harvesting seasons.

  Today: Since most farming is done by corporations, school years can be extended later into June and earlier into August.

- **1955:** Christmas cards are popular. A man like Rob thinking of writing a note of love to his wife at Christmas automatically thinks of writing it in a Christmas card.

  Today: According to Hallmark Corporation, more than a billion and a half Christmas cards are sent out each year. For interpersonal communication, the modern world also offers a wide variety of electronic media, such as texting and e-mails, to choose from.

---

customers who had not yet bought gifts would have an opportunity to do so.

In the present day, every year brings more and more charges of gift exchanges ruining the spirit of Christmas. But it is clear from "Christmas Day in the Morning" that, even in a rural area in the mid-twentieth century, the pressure was felt to find just the right present for a loved one.

Popular Magazine Fiction

Buck first published "Christmas Day in the Morning" in *Collier's*, a popular magazine. In

the middle of the twentieth century popular magazines were still publishing short fiction, but that practice soon began to end.

There are different opinions about the possible origins of the short story. Many literary critics like to trace it back to Nathaniel Hawthorne's volume *Twice-Told Tales*, published in 1837. Reviewing that book, Edgar Allan Poe gave a definition of the short story that has served to this day, as a narrative that can be read at one sitting.

In the later nineteenth century, cultural magazines began including short stories within their

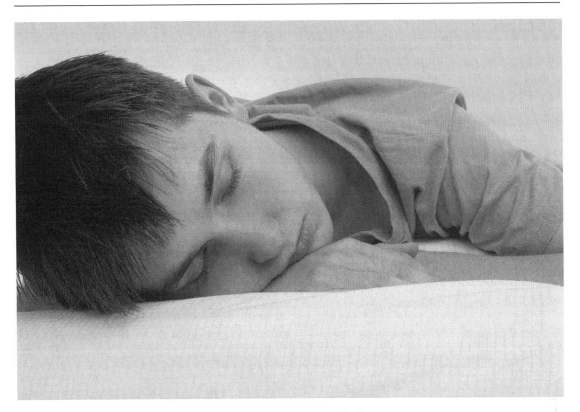

Rob pretended to still be asleep when his father came in to wake him up. (© Leah-Anne Thompson / Shutterstock.com)

pages, including *Harper's* and the *Atlantic* (both begun in the 1850s and still published today), *Scribner's Magazine* (published from 1887 to 1939), and *Collier's* (which ran from 1888 to 1957 and was relaunched in 2012). It was in the first decade of the twentieth century, though, that popular writer O. Henry (William Sydney Porter) made publishers see that the short story could be included in general-circulation magazines as a form of entertainment. Short fiction in magazines flourished in the first half of the century.

In the early twentieth century, various "little magazines" sprung up, publishing works of the post–World War I explosion of literary artists. Some of the more famous among these publications include the *Egoist*, *Blast*, the *Little Review*, the *Fugitive*, and *Contact*. With these magazines that focused specifically on artistic writing, the split between the short story and popular publications had begun. To this day, many small literary magazines that publish short fiction have small circulations (often less than a thousand subscribers, as opposed to the twenty-two million copies of *Time* shipped every week) and are generally associated with educational institutions.

The advent of other media eventually squeezed short literary fiction out of magazines. Whereas people once turned to magazine fiction for entertainment, the development of movies, radio, and finally television offered diverse entertainment for people with low reading skills. As television broadcasts became more widespread and popular in the years after the end of World War II in 1945, fewer and fewer people regarded fiction as a form of popular entertainment. Magazines focused on niche audiences, including those interested in literature, homemaking, crafts, politics, and television. *TV Guide*, for instance, was consistently among the magazines with the highest circulation figures from the 1950s through the late twentieth century.

In the 1950s, some of the magazines with the widest circulation, like *Collier's*, could afford to feature a short story from a top-name author like Pearl S. Buck. *Collier's* went out of business a few years after this story was published, however, and throughout the 1960s many magazines that had started publishing in the previous century either closed their doors or shifted their focus to general-interest subjects.

CRITICAL OVERVIEW

Buck is most known for her novels, her Nobel Prize for Literature, and her humanitarian work. Though she wrote short fiction throughout her life, most of it was the kind of populist writing that does not usually elicit the kind of attention or analysis that literary fiction garners. As Buck's biographer Paul A. Doyle puts it in his entry on the author for the survey *American Writers*, "While the shorter narratives are eminently readable, the majority are generally forgettable. They are mostly glossy magazine fiction with a persistent emphasis on romance."

One reason "Christmas Day in the Morning," in particular among Buck's short stories, has had enduring attention and continued readership is the fact that it was adapted as a picture book in 2002, with illustrations by Mark Buehner. In this medium, the story has gained universal acclaim from critics. Susan Patron, writing in *School Library Journal*, declares of *Christmas Day in the Morning*, "Moving and tender, this is a fine choice for reading aloud or family sharing." The *Publishers Weekly* review calls the book a "modest holiday tale" and notes that "Buck's understated yet moving piece ... will resonate with readers." Perhaps the most glowing praise came from Julie Yates Walton in the *New York Times*. "Nowadays," Walton wrote, "such a schmaltzy story line would typically evoke more smirks than tears. But between Buck's taut prose and Buehner's heartfelt paintings, only the most stoical among us could finish this splendid story aloud unmoved."

CRITICISM

David Kelly

Kelly is an instructor of creative writing and literature. In the following essay, he examines why "Christmas Day in the Morning" can be considered a successful story even though it does not follow the traditional structure for literary fiction.

"Christmas Day in the Morning" is a popular story that was published in *Collier's*, a popular, mass-market magazine. Readers look to popular fiction for a pleasant experience, but not necessarily for an enlightening one. Pearl S. Buck's story offers readers an experience that is more satisfying than they really ought to expect, given its structure.

> IN GENERAL, THE QUESTION OF ARTISTIC GREATNESS IS ONE THAT IS HARD TO PINPOINT: IF GREATNESS COULD BE IDENTIFIED IT COULD BE ISOLATED AND REPRODUCED, AND EVERYONE WOULD BE AN ARTISTIC GENIUS."

In literary fiction, the standard of whether a story works or not has traditionally been whether or not the author offers some valuable insight into one specific character, the protagonist. This is done within the limited space of the short story by building toward a clear, distinct moment when the character might experience some new way of looking at the world. The character might have some insight that puts a core belief into a new perspective. That peak can be called the moment of the character's change, or epiphany, or revelation—it is known by many different names. It could also, though, be the opposite of these: the moment when all signs have led to the protagonist realizing something and changing, but she or he resists these signs and does not change at all. Either version of the key moment tells readers something about the character and about humanity. The falling action is then just the amount of space it takes to clean up loose ends before the story comes to a close.

That is the design of almost all stories. Often, when people do not follow this standard pattern it is because they do not know what they are doing, in the same way that a painter who presents figures out of perspective to each other usually does so because he does not understand the basic principles of linear perspective. Every once in a while, though, a writer is able to break the rules and get away with it. That, apparently, is what Buck does, making "Christmas Day in the Morning" a successful story.

This story is upside down: instead of building toward a revelation, it lets its big revelation out immediately. By ordinary expectations, the rest of the story ought to be increasingly uninteresting, draining readers' interest instead of holding or building it. But Buck as a virtuoso artist keeps readers involved, sentence by

WHAT DO I READ NEXT?

- Buck is best known for her 1931 book *The Good Earth*, one of the great novels of the twentieth century and an early example of an American author engaging in a multicultural perspective. The story concerns life in rural China, which is where Buck spent her childhood.

- In 1909 Swedish author Selma Lagerlöf became the first woman ever to win the Nobel Prize for Literature. Like "Christmas Day in the Morning," Lagerlöf's holiday short story "Holy Night," about a shepherd visited by angels at the birth of Jesus, has been adapted as a picture book. Illustrated by Ilon Wikland, *The Holy Night* was published in 2004.

- Perhaps the most moving and best-known short story about Christmas gift giving is "The Gift of the Magi," by O. Henry. Loved by generations since its first publication in 1905, it tells of a young married couple and the sacrifices they make to show their love for each other through gifts they can hardly afford. It is often reproduced in anthologies and is included in *The Best Short Stories of O. Henry*, first published in 1945.

- Lemony Snicket, the pen name used by author Daniel Handler, is known for A Series of Unfortunate Events, his set of books for younger audiences. His take on a holiday tale is *The Latke Who Couldn't Stop Screaming: A Christmas Story*, which combines Christian, Jewish, and other traditions in his signature irreverent way. This book, illustrated by humorist Lisa Brown, was published in 2007.

- William B. Waits's 1993 book *The Modern Christmas in America: A Cultural History of Gift Giving* uses illustrations and historical examples to show what the modern view of gift giving is, and how it has come to be what

it is. Readers who feel, like Rob in the story, that actual physical gifts are too impersonal, will be glad to see that that attitude has been prevalent throughout most of the nation's history.

- Author Truman Capote usually wrote for adult audiences, but his short story "A Christmas Memory," originally published in *Mademoiselle* magazine in 1956 (one year after Buck's story), has become a sentimental favorite of holiday fiction. The story concerns a young boy and his aged cousin, who is his best friend, as they prepare for Christmas in the small, quixotic country town where they live. Published as a standalone book by Random House in 1966, it is also included in *The Complete Stories of Truman Capote*, from 2004.

- *A Foxfire Christmas: Appalachian Memories and Traditions* gathers interviews with people from one of the country's poorest rural areas, the highlands of northeast Georgia, who remember customs and oral traditions of Christmastime. As they discuss ornaments and toys that they were able to acquire despite their poverty, the picture of a way of life quite similar to the life in Buck's story comes through. The book was edited by Eliot Wigginton and his students at Rabun County High School and published in 1990.

- Poet Dylan Thomas sets a nostalgic tone to match Buck's in his story *A Child's Christmas in Wales*. The piece is a prose poem, not really telling a story but conveying a series of sensory impressions about what it was like at Christmastime in the country. Originally written to be broadcast on BBC Radio in 1952, it was so popular that it was printed in book form in 1954 and is available in a 1995 edition.

sentence and word by word, even while nothing of consequence is going on.

The story concerns a man in two phases of his life. In the present, Rob is an old man in his sixties who wakes up each morning at four o'clock because when he was a boy on his family's farm, his father woke him at that time each morning in order to milk the cows. It is Christmas morning, and knowing that takes Rob back in his memory fifty years, to the time when he decided to wake up even earlier, to milk the cows before his father could get out to the barn, his Christmas present. It was a decision spurred by a conversation he heard his father having with his mother when they did not know he was in earshot. The father was sad about having to wake his son so early each morning, and, hearing the regret in his voice, Rob suddenly realized the love his father had for him.

In life, it is a wonderful thing for a son to accept and understand his father's love. In a story, though, having this realization occur so near to the beginning, within the first couple dozen sentences in some versions, leaves the story little room to expand. Indeed, once the narrator reveals that "something in him spoke: His father loved him!" there is not really anywhere for the story to expand, emotionally.

The story does not build to Rob's revelation about his father's love in part because it does not show the time when he harbored doubts about his father's feelings. Readers can reasonably assume that Rob did have doubts, from the excitement that his revelation stirs in him—that there must be something there, something deeper than his father waking him early every morning. Buck does a clever, economical job of reflecting a coldness in Rob's mother's response to the father. She brushes off his concerns with an unemotional statement that nothing can be done, that a farm needs its young man working. This probably is close to the attitude that Rob expected his father to have.

There are in fact two big problems with the way Buck gives Rob his realization about how his father feels. The first, as noted, is that it comes so early in the story. Once Rob is moved by his father's love, nothing changes emotionally. Rob concocts a plan for a heartfelt Christmas gift, he anticipates how to make his plan happen, and he carries it out, and through all of this his father still loves him, and Rob still loves his father. From the first page on, there is action

but no emotional change. The story never takes an unexpected turn.

The second problem is that this revelation is nothing that Rob caused to happen. Buck makes a point of telling readers that nothing compelled Rob's father to tell his son of his love: Rob just happened to be walking by and heard his parents talking. Stories that rely on coincidence do not have much to tell readers, other than that it is always a good idea to be in the right place at the right time.

In a normal story structure the emotional peak would be near the end. The story of Rob and his father takes up most of the space of "Christmas Day in the Morning," but in the end there is a shift to the mature Rob's relationship with his wife. If the story of Rob and his father is static, it might be better seen as a buildup to establish his future emotional state.

Rob's relationship with his wife does indeed seem like his relationship with his father. His emotions are just as static. He plans to show his love for her, the way he once planned to show his love for his father, but, once again, nothing is at risk: Buck's narrator explains that Rob is certain of his growing love for his wife, and he is confident that she loves him. Writing a card to tell her that he loves her will make a nice gift. She will have a happy Christmas.

It seems that there is no subtext, no psychological situation smoldering under the surface of this story. Once Rob feels confident about how his father feels, he shows his father that he feels the same way, and they are both fine with how things are. His card to his wife will not have anything beyond the desired effect. The only psychological change is the one early on, when Rob (correctly) reads his father's concern as reflecting deeper emotion. Stories that are all surface, with no emotional complexity, can be popular with a reading public that does not want to be bothered with reading in depth, but seldom are they art.

So how does Buck make this story successful? In general, the question of artistic greatness is one that is hard to pinpoint: if greatness could be identified it could be isolated and reproduced, and everyone would be an artistic genius. There are, though, a few elements in "Christmas Day in the Morning" that indicate what makes it more than just a story about happy people making each other happy.

The family exchanges simple presents because they cannot afford luxuries. *(© Anna-Mari West | Shutterstock.com)*

The hardest element to examine is Buck's sense of just how specific readers need this story to be. It is hard to identify because she appears to know what to do simply by being gifted. She gives details that another writer would not give in some places, and then she omits details in others, and her choices all seem to be the right ones for this story to come alive. There is, for instance, no description at all about the bedroom that old Rob wakes up in each morning at four, but the physical surroundings of the boy Rob waking and sneaking to the barn, careful to avoid notice, are very clear, from the creaking floorboards to the frothing milk in the pail. The story gives the parents identities with names and dialogue, but Rob's wife has little to no physical presence or identity. The story does not tell readers why Rob at a younger age did not associate a stable with a barn, or what making the connection between the story of the Nativity and himself really meant to him. Why were these the right choices for Buck to make? It would be almost impossible to say.

What really makes this story succeed, however, is the way that Buck fills it with so much unfulfilled possibility. Readers reaching the end

may feel that not much has changed—love grew stronger, Christmases became happier—but there is no way readers can anticipate these outcomes at any step along the way. Readers become engaged with the story, are curious about whether Rob's plan to sneak away to the barn in the dead of night will succeed, but that episode would have little impact if they were not interested in the characters. Hanging over everything like a cloud is the question of why the boy is so desperate—whether one day's relief from milking the cows will really have the effect on the father that young Rob hopes it will. Rob's reading of his father seems obvious after the fact, but Buck's prose style is just flat and distant enough to let readers wonder whether things are going to turn out badly.

"Christmas Day in the Morning" does not build to a revelation about Rob's adult life. His wife seems added almost as an afterthought, to reaffirm the basic point that it is good to tell people you love them. The story is not about how Rob came to be the man he is, which is something that is settled on the first page. It is a story about feeling good about being loved and sharing love. Ordinarily a feeling, or a mood, is not enough to keep readers engaged throughout a narrative work, but Pearl S. Buck is no ordinary writer: she does not need the typical elements to keep readers engaged when she writes with such a mesmerizing voice.

Source: David Kelly, Critical Essay on "Christmas Day in the Morning," in *Short Stories for Students*, Gale, Cengage Learning, 2014.

Booklist

In the following review, a contributor to Booklist *calls the story "inspiring" and "beautiful."*

This inspiring story by a Nobel and Pulitzer Prize-winning author is reissued for the first time since 1955 with the oil paintings by the artist of *Fanny's Dream* (1996). Buck invests a simple story with poetic dignity and teaches a bone-deep lesson about love. On Christmas, a middle-aged man remembers a holiday morning when he was 15 and his farm family was just scraping by. Having overheard a conversation in which his father proclaimed his love, the teenager decides to do something special for Dad. The boy gets up very early on Christmas morning and does all the milking before his father arises, discovering that that love makes labor light. Buehner's paintings enhance the story, capturing the deep blue-white of a snowy farmland, punctuated by golden light spilling from windows, a pool of light from the boy's lantern as he goes to the barn, and the simplicity of a turn-of-the-century farmhouse interior. A beautiful Christmas message, powerfully delivered.

Source: Booklist, Review of *Christmas Day in the Morning*, in *Booklist*, Vol. 99, No. 4, October 15, 2002, p. 404.

Kirkus Reviews

In the following review, a contributor to Kirkus Reviews *comments on the illustrated version of* Christmas Day in the Morning, *considering the story "sentimental but touching."*

This longer story by Nobel Laureate Buck, originally published in 1955, is presented for the first time as an illustrated work for children. Early one Christmas, an older man thinks back to his best Christmas morning in the year that he was 15 and living on his family dairy farm. That year, the narrator of the story, Rob, surprised his father with a special, heart-felt gift by getting up in the middle of the night to do all the milking by himself so his father could have Christmas morning off. The boy's joy in planning the surprise for his father and the touching appreciation, pride,

THUS, *THE GOOD EARTH* SET THE STANDARD

FOR ITS AUTHOR."

and love in the father's gratitude are effectively conveyed in both the moving text and in Buehner's (*Snowmen at Night*, p. 1385, etc.) realistic paintings. His deep-toned, striking illustrations are mainly set at night, with snowy farm scenes lit only by glowing lantern and shining star. One spread shows the Nativity scene with puffy clouds in a turquoise evening sky shaped like angel heralds, and the following memorable spread of the barn at night repeats this element with subtle clouds in the shapes of the participants in the manger setting. Buck's sentimental but touching story memorably illustrates the value of a gift created with love, a gift like Buehner's.

Source: Kirkus Reviews, Review of *Christmas Day in the Morning*, in *Kirkus Reviews*, Vol. 70, No. 21, November 1, 2002, p. 1616.

Kang Liao

In the following excerpt, Liao explains how The Good Earth *overshadowed the rest of Buck's work.*

Before I begin my discussions, it is helpful to summarize what the representative critics and reviewers have said about Pearl Buck's works and to see where she stands in American literature, so that I can argue about different judgments, refer to the existing criticism, and avoid unnecessary repetition of opinions and evaluations. I shall also offer some reasons for her phenomenal success and, more important, for her present low status in American literature.

Although Pearl Buck had been publishing on average a book a year in her lengthy writing career from 1930 to 1973, the responses of most critics and reviewers to her works made her career appear like a meteor, burning brightest in 1938. No sooner had she received the Nobel Prize for literature that year than her brilliance began to dim in the eyes of the critical beholders. While it is arguable as to whether or not all her post-Nobel Prize books are inferior to her pre-Nobel Prize books, it is understandable that the phenomenal success of her early works, especially her second novel *The Good Earth*, set the high standard against which all her later works were measured. When they fell short of the expectation, no matter how little, she was naturally thought to be on the decline. Thus, the critics who had been encouraging before the prize became harsh after it.

Pearl Buck's first published book *East Wind: West Wind*, in Isidore Schneider's words, is an "ordinary, quite mechanical novel, full of plot and sentiment, but empty of any lifelikeness in its characters or significance in its thesis—the clash between modern and traditional China" (1930, 24). However, the emerging writer received much encouragement for her maiden work. In his review, Nathaniel Peffer evaluated the cognitive value of her book saying that "she tells more of contemporary China than a year of newspaper headlines or a shelf of volumes by political minded experts, and tells it entertainingly" (1930, 6). Approving her attitude toward China and a different culture, the reviewer for the *New York Times* commented, "Only one, who like the author, has lived all her life in China, yet being American still holds to Western concepts of romantic love, marriage and the scope of filial duty—only a lover of China, but no convert to her code of family and clan supremacy over the individual, could have written this beautiful novel" (8). As for the style of her book, Edwin Seaver said these encouraging words: "Mrs. Buck has written with a fine simplicity and delicacy and charm. One would say *East Wind: West Wind* was an exquisite book, did not the word, in this connection, so often connote preciosity" (10m).

Such compliments, we must bear in mind, were given to a new writer, whose book they compared, at most, with the best of Lafcadio Hearn. After Pearl Buck became a Nobel laureate, the critics would compare her not only with the best of her own work, but also with the masterpieces of other laureates. Commenting on the first novel that she published after the award, Hassoldt Davis said, "In *The Patriot* she has returned to the Orient to present a fictional biography which not only is compelling by its timeliness but is probably the best of her books since *The Good Earth*. It is none the less not comparable; though her craft is surer now. *The Patriot* lacks the wide cultural dimensions of the earlier book" (269). Thus the later novel, good as

it is, was eclipsed, as George Dangerfield judged the writer of *The Patriot* in the *Saturday Review of Literature*: "Certainly a story of this kind should tell us whether or not that rich vein, first revealed in *The Good Earth*, is really running thin. The answer is not a reassuring one" (5). In discussing the style of *Dragon Seed*, Paul Doyle compared it favorably with Hemingway's style. Then he decided, "In the sustained excellence of its style *Dragon Seed* comes close to *The Good Earth*; its prose does not, however, possess as much poetry and color as Buck's most famous novel" (P. Doyle 1980, 109).

This kind of comparison haunted Pearl Buck for the rest of her life. Her novel *Pavilion of Women*, in Mary McGrory's words, "is a searching, adult study of women written with high seriousness and sympathy, which should find a multitude of women readers" (6). J. J. Espey also predicted in *Weekly Book Review* that the novel would "be hailed as a moving and profound love story by the many thousand readers it is certain to have" (1946, 6). Indeed, the novel proved to be successful and was on the *Book-of-the-Month* Club list, but in comparison with *The Good Earth*, it lost its brilliance. As Margaret Williamson put it: "One puts down *Pavilion of Women* with a small sigh that it is hardly Mrs. Buck at her supreme best" (1946, 14). Commenting on the characterizations of this novel, the reviewer for *Kirkus* also compared it with Pearl Buck's highest achievement: "The figures never take on the emotional values that made her *Good Earth* so poignantly moving" (553).

Thus, *The Good Earth* set the standard for its author. Even in praising Pearl Buck's novel of 1949, Feike Feikema would mention its inferiority to what she had already accomplished: "While *Kinfolk* is not as juicy or as colorful in detail, not so poetic in style as *The Good Earth*, it has something else—the full play of a mature and warm mind that has brooded long and thoroughly on Good and Evil" (8X). *Imperial Woman*, in Pearl Buck's own opinion, is her best novel set in China. Rodney Gilbert, in discussing its artistic quality, also gave it "a very high rating" (1). Inevitably, the novel was compared with Pearl Buck's zenith. After confirming the function of making the past intelligible, Jane Voiles maintained, "But her imagination supplies no connecting link with the present so that the sense of communication experienced abundantly in *The Good Earth* doesn't come through in this novel" (1956, 18). Preston Schoyer, too, made the comparison in discussing the style of *Imperial Woman*: "Eminently suitable in its simple, rolling solemnity to the peasant life she describes so well in her masterpiece, *The Good Earth*, that style seems less felicitous in application to the exotic worldliness, the complex subtleties, the urbane sophistication, and the exquisitely mannered nonsense of imperial Peking" (12). *Letter from Peking*, in the words of the *Kirkus* reviewer, is a "minor production in the distinguished list of Mrs. Buck's writings" (336), but it could not escape the comparison, either. Fanny Butcher said, "That this novel is not another *Good Earth* is undeniable, but it makes no pretense of being so. It is written in depth—probing one woman's emotion—not in cosmic scope" (1957, 1). Similarly, *The Three Daughters of Madame Liang* was in the shadow. Having said some nice words about its useful insights into the temperament of modern-day Chinese, the reviewer for *Christian Science Monitor* concluded, "How they [the daughters] decide and how their decisions affect them make a mildly entertaining story that would please a casual reader whose expectations had not been pitched too high by memories of *The Good Earth*" (11).

Only when Pearl Buck was publishing novels under a pseudonym John Sedges was she free temporarily from her trademark of Chinese themes and the shadow of *The Good Earth*. Of the five John Sedges novels *The Townsman* is the most successful, and she rightfully regarded it as her best American novel (Cevasco 1981, 19). Commending this Kansan pioneer story, the reviewer for *Commonwealth* said, "Only rarely does a novel on immigration have the quality or the sensitiveness of *Giants in the Earth*. Yet despite its well-worn theme *The Townsman* manages to compel and hold attention. John Sedges tells the simple story of an English family well and there are several elements which set off this volume from most of its contemporaries" (193). One of the elements is the background description. The reviewers then were comparing it with the way of other writers rather than with Pearl Buck's way as W. S. Lynch put it: "Mr. Sedges writes with restrained fullness that fits the mood of his theme admirably. He handles his detail of background excellently, never letting the sodhouse, the calicoes, the furniture become obtrusive, in the Sears-Roebuck-catalogue way that many writers seem to think is necessary to

> AGAIN AND AGAIN IN PEARL BUCK'S POST-NOBEL PRIZE WORK, ONE CAN RECOGNIZE THAT IF MORE TIME HAD BEEN TAKEN FOR WRITING AND REWRITING AND FOR PROBING FOR DEPTH IN CHARACTER DEVELOPMENT, THE FINISHED PRODUCTS WOULD BE MORE TRULY ARTISTIC."

provide a convincing setting" (30). No one imagined the novel could be written by a non-Kansan, let alone by someone who lived most of her life in China. . . .

Source: Kang Liao, "A Neglected Laureate," in *Pearl S. Buck: A Cultural Bridge across the Pacific*, Greenwood Press, 1997, pp. 17–20.

Paul A. Doyle

In the following excerpt, Doyle examines how Buck's work is influenced by the Chinese novel.

. . . The earliest expression of Pearl Buck's literary theories is found in two informative addresses, concerned mainly with the Chinese novel, which were delivered in Peiping in February, 1932. In her analysis of the traditional Chinese story, she notes that the author is omniscient, although the author's presence is not advertised. She finds that the Chinese novel contains relatively little description and what description there is, is largely external. Characters are revealed by action and by dialogue, and seldom does one find exposition of internal states of mind. In the course of her remarks, Miss Buck does attack the Western behavioristic novel because it imposes a rigidity of viewpoint which condemns mankind to a narrow, mechanical, and one-sided type of existence.

She records that intellectuals and Confucian scholars deplored the indigenous Chinese novel. Nevertheless, she emphasizes the popularity of these tales. She notes that professional storytellers wandered throughout the country and set up booths where the people could gather to listen. The narrator of the tale took up a collection to pay for his time and effort. The ordinary Chinese particularly enjoyed these yarns, just as they delighted in plays given in the open air by roving groups of actors. This love of story, of the working out of a plot, engrossed Chinese audiences; and it is evident that Miss Buck regards this element with the utmost significance.

Miss Buck's most complete discussion of literary theory occurs in her Alumnae Address "On the Writing of Novels" delivered at Randolph-Macon Woman's College in June, 1933. At the outset of the speech she declares her enjoyment in writing fiction, but she does not like rules for writing. She has often been asked if the characters in her novels are real people, and she finds such a question difficult to answer. Characters in her work are, on the one hand, more simple than actual human beings and, on the other hand, more complex than real humans. She simplifies actual individuals when turning them into fictional figures so that they will fit the atmosphere, theme, and total picture. Anything which does not agree with the overall features of the scene and the story must be suppressed. At the same time, the novelist adds his own touches and flourishes to the characters, making them more imaginative and more complex than they are in real life.

Miss Buck states that she is more obsessed by characters than she is by a plot. Characters continually appear in her mind and call out to her to put them into a book. Such characters must be controlled and used to unify a book, although these individuals frequently want to dominate the author. The major characters direct the plot and shape it as it develops. Miss Buck claims that she knows the whole story, even the ending, before she begins to write.

Discussing various forms of telling a story, Miss Buck does not believe that one method is intrinsically better than another. The artist should choose the form which is most appropriate for his material. This is the only criterion which matters, and literary criticism which decrees otherwise, Miss Buck finds faulty. She insists that the modern techniques of novel writing are not superior to the older methods. The novelist who is interested more in form than in people, she argues, is not creative, only inventive. If the writer is obsessed with the story and the characters, then the story and characters develop the most suitable form for their revelation.

In regard to style, Miss Buck chooses some words from Virginia Woolf as the best definition of this quality. Good style consists of the use of "the far side of language." Style should bring meaning and emotion which goes beyond the words themselves. She feels that the simplest words are often the most powerful in bringing about such evocative effects.

Miss Buck admits that the didactic novel is now frowned upon by literary critics, and she herself acknowledges that the genuine artist should not be a preacher. She is, however, not satisfied with this condition. She asserts that a worth-while novelist like Thornton Wilder teaches through his writings, and she is personally attracted to the moral value in didacticism. Art may be didactic, she declares, if it describes life completely and firmly; but only the greatest genius could so handle art, and such a writer would avoid didacticism because it would disturb artistic proportion. The moralizer can never be a genuine artist because the picture of life portrayed would be distorted in order to fit the preachment. Life should be the teacher, not the novelist. She recognizes that the true artist should observe and portray life as it is and not twist it to fit a particular theory.

Five years later when Miss Buck traveled to Stockholm to receive the Nobel Prize, she gave her Nobel lecture on the Chinese novel. In this pivotal address, she explained the main influence on her work, as well as her philosophy of composition. She traces her origins as a writer to the traditional Chinese novel. According to Miss Buck, the Chinese reader was interested in action and in the effectiveness of character portrayal which arose from dialogue and the character's behavior, rather than from the author's analysis. The ordinary Chinese writer of novels, she declares, was not interested in technique; to the extent that he was concerned about technique, "he ceased to be a good novelist and became a literary technician."

Special attention to style was not a primary consideration because such concern could distract from the narrative. Speaking of the style of the native Chinese saga, Pearl Buck remarks: "[the style] was one which flowed easily along, clearly and simply, in the short words which they themselves used every day, with no other technique than occasional bits of description, only enough to give vividness to a place or a person, and never enough to delay the story. Nothing must delay the story. Story was what they wanted."

After much discussion of the indigenous Chinese novel, Miss Buck came to the central part of her own literary credo. Since this pronouncement is so important for an understanding of her writing, it is quoted in full:

And like the Chinese novelist, I have been taught to want to write for these people [the ordinary man and woman]. If they are reading their magazines by the million, then I want my stories there rather than in magazines read only by a few. For story belongs to the people. They are sounder judges of it than anyone else, for their senses are unspoiled and their emotions are free. No a novelist must not think of pure literature as his goal. He must not even know this field too well, because people, who are his material, are not there. He is a story teller in a village tent and by his stories he entices people into his tent. He need not raise his voice when a scholar passes. But he must beat all his drums when a band of poor pilgrims pass on their way up the mountain in search of gods. To them he must cry, "I, too, tell of gods!" And to farmers he must talk of their land, and to old men he must speak of peace, and to old women he must tell of their children and to young men and women he must speak of each other. He must be satisfied if the common people hear him gladly. At least, so I have been taught in China.

This crucial declaration with all its implications sums up many of the strengths and weaknesses of Pearl Buck's writing and indicates her basic philosophy in regard to literary production. From her statements on the Chinese novel, one can understand the development of Miss Buck's literary ideas and her allegiance to the doctrine of the storyteller. Yet one can also see the limitations of such a creed. As Lewis Gannett pointed out in a review of this speech when it was published in book form, such a doctrine would suggest that Zane Grey, Harold Bell Wright, Edgar Rice Burroughs, and Gene Stratton Porter are the really significant American novelists. Certainly, Miss Buck does not mean to suggest this; and, barring a few potboilers, her own work is on a far higher plane.

In the light of her statements made in the Nobel Prize acceptance speech, Pearl Buck seems to have become convinced of the value of reaching the least common denominator. More and more she wrote articles for magazines and began to dilute her creative efforts in the novel form with non-fiction studies, children's books, and humanitarian interests. She was criticized because of her desires to reach a mass audience. In answer, she asserted before the National Education Association: "One cannot dismiss lightly a magazine bought and read by three million people.... It is important. It is a serious thing for literature if three million people read—not literature, but something which gives them greater satisfaction."

Such an attitude would obviously preclude future attempts at reaching a more esthetic approach to the novel. Losing oneself in the lesser forms of writing, and turning to more ephemeral themes necessarily reduced time for contemplation, for revising and rewriting novels, and for careful reworking of creative materials in order to produce the most artistic effects. Again and again in Pearl Buck's post-Nobel Prize work, one can recognize that if more time had been taken for writing and rewriting and for probing for depth in character development, the finished products would be more truly artistic. Miss Buck comes to a point of subordinating her natural talent and ability to a narrow and limited creed of composition and to what is often communication for mass propaganda purposes.

In her biography of Pearl Buck, Cornelia Spencer has noted Miss Buck's growing desire to reach a mass audience and the importance she attached to this purpose. Cornelia Spencer approves of this development in no uncertain terms:

Underlying her interests and her writing and her other active life there was and there is one unchanging unity.... All she does must work toward mutual understanding between the common peoples of the earth and toward justice for all. Through her first books she interpreted China to the West. Now the base of her interpretation was enlarging and deepening to include common people everywhere. As the subject matter of her writing broadened so also must her audience. More and more, then, in keeping with her purpose she wrote where she would be read, not only by the student and lover of books but by the workman and the clerk and the stenographer. With deliberate intent she wrote that every one might read because she wants to write for people.

In addition to her adherence to the technique of the traditional Chinese novel, and her desire to reach the widest possible audience with her humanitarian interests, a third factor was apparently involved in Miss Buck's decision not to devote herself as fully as possible to the novel as an artistic form. This third element concerned a constitutional or temperamental excess of energy, which had too much drive and too many interests to confine itself to the strict, exhausting discipline of the novel as an art form. On one occasion Pearl Buck told her sister: "My great fault is that I can never give myself entirely to any one thing. I always seem to be concerned in several interests and I just have to be that way. I could not possibly choose one. The trouble is that I always have too many things I am interested in and live too many lives."

With all of these factors there exists perhaps, in part, a real-life counterpart of the Susan Gaylord dilemma witnessed in *This Proud Heart*, for Susan's genius was hampered by a wide variety of interests and her emotional and womanly needs. Finally, Susan isolates herself from distractions and gives herself to the total devotion of art. Unlike the fictional Susan Gaylord, Miss Buck, unhappily, did not make an ultimate dedicated choice of art....

Source: Paul A. Doyle, "The Nobel Prize: Glow and Afterglow," in *Pearl S. Buck*, Twayne Publishers, 1965, pp. 94–99.

SOURCES

Boyd, William, "A Short History of the Short Story," in *Prospect*, July 10, 2006, http://www.prospectmagazine.co.uk/magazine/william-boyd-short-history-of-the-short-story/#.Ui3vx9KsiSo (accessed September 8, 2013).

Buck, Pearl S., "Christmas Day in the Morning," in *A Family Christmas*, edited by Caroline Kennedy, Hyperion, 2007, pp. 160–64.

"Christmas Card-Sending in the U.S.," Hallmark Corporate Information, 2013, http://corporate.hallmark.com/Viewpoints/Christmas-Card-Sending-in-the-US (accessed September 10, 2013).

Dimitri, Carolyn, Anne Effland, and Neilson Conklin, "The 20th Century Transformation of U.S. Agriculture and Farm Policy," US Department of Agriculture, June 2005, http://www.ers.usda.gov/media/259572/eib3_1_.pdf (accessed September 10, 2013).

Doyle, Paul A., "Pearl Buck," in *American Writers: A Collection of Literary Biographies*, edited by A. Walton Litz, suppl. 2, pt. 1, *W. H. Auden to O. Henry*, Charles Scribner's Sons, 1981, p. 126.

"Little Magazines," in *Encyclopedia of American Literature*, rev. ed., edited by Carl Rollyson, Vol. 3, *Into the Modern, 1896–1945*, Facts on File, 2008, p. 141.

Patron, Susan, Review of *Christmas Day in the Morning*, in *School Library Journal*, Vol. 48, No. 10, October 2002, p. 57.

"Pearl S. Buck Biography," Biography.com, 2013, http://www.biography.com/people/pearl-s-buck-9230389 (accessed September 8, 2013).

Review of *Christmas Day in the Morning*, in *Publishers Weekly*, Vol. 249, No. 38, September 23, 2002, p. 30.

"Short Story," in *Encyclopedia of American Literature*, rev. ed., edited by Carl Rollyson, Vol. 3, *Into the Modern: 1896–1945*, Facts on File, 2008, pp. 226–29.

Walton, Julie Yates, "Children's Books," in *New York Times Book Review*, December 22, 2002, p. 19.

FURTHER READING

Buck, Pearl, *My Several Worlds: A Personal Record*, John Day, 1954.

This memoir does not tell the complete picture of Buck's life: it was published before "Christmas Day in the Morning" and therefore leaves out several decades of humanitarian work, and Buck is very reticent about the details about her failed marriage and subsequent relationship with her editor. Still, it is told in her captivating writing style and relates her sense of crossing between Eastern and Western cultures.

Conn, Peter, *Pearl S. Buck: A Cultural Biography*, Cambridge University Press, 1996.

This somewhat recent biography is considered to be the authoritative text about Buck's life, combining information from all existing sources.

Doyle, Paul A., "Pearl S. Buck's Short Stories: A Survey," in *English Journal*, Vol. 55, No. 1, January 1966, pp. 62–68.

Doyle wrote frequently about Buck and published a book about her life and work the year before this article was published, giving a solid scholarly view of the literary significance of her often-ignored short fiction.

Mauss, Marcel, *The Gift: The Form and Reason for Exchange in Archaic Societies*, W. W. Norton, 2000.

This book was first published in English in 1954, the year before Buck's story was published. French sociologist Mauss examines the ways gift giving has been viewed by different populations around the world, centering on case studies of Melanesia, Polynesia, and northwestern North America and on what their attitudes toward gifts say about each.

Middleton, David, *Quite a Sightly Place: A Family Dairy Farm in Vermont*, Commonwealth Editions, 2010.

Middleton, a renowned nature photographer, spent four years working on a family-run dairy farm that is still operated by the same family that ran it back in the 1860s. Some technology has changed, but Middleton is able to capture, in words and photographs, much of the feeling that Buck conveys in her story.

Spencer, Cornelia, *Pearl S. Buck: Revealing the Human Heart*, Encyclopìdia Britannica Press, 1964.

More sentimental than the standard scholarly work, Spencer's study of the author matches the tone of Buck's writing in this story, appreciating her for the humane values that make "Christmas Day in the Morning" come alive.

SUGGESTED SEARCH TERMS

Pearl S. Buck

Pearl S. Buck AND Christmas

Pearl S. Buck AND Christmas Day in the Morning

Pearl S. Buck AND gift

Pearl S. Buck AND farm life

short fiction AND Christmas stories

Pearl S. Buck AND popular

Christmas fiction AND 1950s

Christmas AND rural America

Pearl S. Buck AND Collier's magazine

A Cup of Tea

KATHERINE MANSFIELD

1922

Katherine Mansfield is highly regarded as an author of short fiction. Her work is realistic in its focus on women, sexuality, social and gender roles, and personal relationships but has also been considered modernist or experimental in its exploration of the interior world of its characters. Mansfield's fiction has been described as both avant-garde and impressionistic because of this tendency.

Her short story "A Cup of Tea" was originally published in 1922 and focuses on a young rich woman, Rosemary, who is interested in purchasing a very expensive gift for herself. For the moment, she opts not to spend this excessive amount of money on a frivolous item. When she is soon approached by a young woman begging for money for a cup of tea, Rosemary feels compelled to take her home and feed her, thinking the act of charity might amount to something momentous. Through this story, Mansfield examines the disparities between the rich and the poor in her society but also focuses on Rosemary's view of herself as a woman.

"A Cup of Tea" was originally published in May 1922 in a literary magazine, *Story-Teller*, and later appeared in Mansfield's collection *The Dove's Nest and Other Stories*, which was published in 1923, just after Mansfield's death. The story is available in modern collections of Mansfield's fiction, including *The Collected Stories of Katherine Mansfield*, published in 2006.

Katherine Mansfield, 1913.

Katherine Mansfield (© *Pantheon / SuperStock*)

AUTHOR BIOGRAPHY

Kathleen Mansfield Beauchamp was born on October 14, 1888, in Wellington, New Zealand. She was the third daughter of Harold and Annie Burnell Dyer Beauchamp. A fourth daughter was born soon after but died as an infant. Later, a fifth daughter, and then a son, entered the Beauchamp family. In 1903, Mansfield and her family traveled to England, where she and her sisters attended school for several years. The whole family returned to New Zealand in 1906.

Mansfield published four short stories in 1907 in the periodical *Native Companion*. In 1908, she returned to London to live there. She married George Bowden in 1909, a man she had known for only a few weeks, but was in love with another man, Garnet Trownell. Trownell's parents thought Trownell and Mansfield were too young to marry. Biographers are unclear as to whether Mansfield became pregnant before or

after her marriage to Bowden. Sources are also uncertain regarding the identity of the baby's father.

Mansfield ran off with Trownell to Glasgow, Scotland, not long after her wedding to Bowden. Mansfield's mother returned to England and then took Mansfield, who was also rumored to be romantically involved with several women, to Bavaria. There, Mansfield suffered a miscarriage. She returned to London in 1910 and lived with Bowden for a time. The same year, Mansfield received an operation to remove an infected fallopian tube.

In 1912, Mansfield became the assistant editor of the literary magazine *Rhythm*. The same year, she became romantically involved with writer and literary critic John Middleton Murry. After spending some months traveling abroad, Mansfield and Murry returned to London and attempted, ultimately unsuccessfully, to keep *Rhythm* financially viable. Mansfield was then befriended by D. H. Lawrence and Frieda von Richthofen; she and Murry traveled with the couple. Murry and Mansfield returned to London in 1914, the year that World War I began.

Mansfield at this time became interested in the work of Russian writer Anton Chekhov. Over the years, she studied his writing and translated his published letters. She felt an affinity with the Russian writer because of their similar interest in the disparities between external reality and one's inner world. In 1915, Mansfield's brother arrived in London to join the war effort. He was killed in a training accident in France not long after. Murry and Mansfield traveled to the south of France, where Mansfield hoped to recuperate from the serious cough she had developed. As time went on, Mansfield's condition, ultimately diagnosed as tuberculosis, would only worsen.

In 1916, Mansfield and Murry returned to England, settling in Cornwall. Mansfield was embraced by a regional literary circle that included Virginia Woolf and T. S. Eliot, among others. After traveling alone to France, having separated from Murry in 1917, Mansfield suffered a pulmonary hemorrhage in 1918. Mansfield was joined by her close friend Ida Baker, called Lesley Moore by Mansfield. The two were trapped in war-torn France for some time. Once she was able to safely return to England, Mansfield reconciled with Murry, and the two were married. Although she sought the care of a physician, Mansfield's condition continued to worsen, and in 1919, she traveled to the Italian Riviera to convalesce. Mansfield continued to write and publish short fiction, despite the severity of her pulmonary tuberculosis. She and Moore, who stayed with her in Italy, returned to London in 1920. The following year, Mansfield and Moore traveled to Switzerland and were soon joined by Murry.

Mansfield wrote a number of short stories during this time period and published *The Garden Party and Other Stories* in 1922. The same year, her short story "A Cup of Tea" appeared in the May issue of the literary magazine *Story-Teller*. Mansfield traveled between Switzerland, Paris, and London during this year and sought various treatments for her illness, eventually settling in Fontainebleau, France. In 1923, she wrote to Murry and asked him to join her. On January 9, 1923, Murry arrived, and Mansfield died later that evening after suffering a pulmonary hemorrhage.

MEDIA ADAPTATIONS

- Ruth Sergel adapted Mansfield's short story into a one-act play. The play, *A Cup of Tea*, was published by Dramatic Publishing in 1954.

- An audio recording of "A Cup of Tea" is available through LibriVox in *Short Story Collection*, Vol. 27. The collection as a whole or the individual story is available as a free download at http://librivox.org/short-story-collection-vol-027/. The running time is twenty-two minutes and nine seconds.

PLOT SUMMARY

"A Cup of Tea" opens with a description of the young, wealthy, married Rosemary Fell, who is out shopping one afternoon in winter. She finds herself at her favorite antique shop. The shop is her favorite because of the way the shopkeeper dotes on her. When Rosemary arrives, the shopkeeper informs her of a very special box he wishes to show her. It is an enamel box with a delicate image of an embracing couple on the lid. Rosemary is enchanted and wishes very much to have it. The price, however, is extremely high. Rosemary thinks it quite costly even for someone as rich as herself. She hesitates and then asks the man to hold it for her.

When Rosemary exits the building, she finds that it is raining. To Rosemary everything seems cold and grey. At that moment, she hears a voice asking to speak with her. Turning, Rosemary sees a young woman near her own age shivering and looking bedraggled. The woman asks Rosemary for money for a cup of tea. Rosemary asks if she has any money at all, and when the girl replies that she does not, Rosemary exclaims, "How extraordinary!" She decides that it would be exciting to take the girl home.

Thrilled by the novelty of the act, Rosemary insists the girl come home with her. The girl hesitates and expresses her suspicion that

Rosemary is being insincere or will take her to the police station. When Rosemary convinces the girl that she means no harm, she escorts her to her car, and they proceed to Rosemary's house. Rosemary is delighted to have the girl experience the charm and warmth of the house. She takes her to her own room. Not wanting to have the girl "stared at by the servants," Rosemary attempts to help the girl out of her wet outer clothes on her own. The girl stands before the fire, dazed, and finally confesses to Rosemary, who had assumed the girl was being dull-witted or deliberately difficult, that she is about to faint from hunger. Rosemary then rings for a servant to bring the tea service.

While they wait for tea, the girl begins to cry and tells Rosemary that she feels she cannot go on with her life. Rosemary attempts to reassure her. Tea is brought in, along with sandwiches and bread and butter. The girl eats heartily. Rosemary asks her when her last meal was, but at that moment, Rosemary's husband, Philip, enters the room. Rosemary attempts to introduce the girl but does not yet know her name. The girl informs them that her last name is Smith, and she is thus introduced to Philip as Miss Smith. After studying Miss Smith for a moment, Philip asks Rosemary to come with him to the library. There, he asks her to explain the presence of the girl in their home.

Rosemary recounts the story to Philip, who then asks her what she intends to do with the girl. Rosemary fumbles. She stresses that she wants to be nice to Miss Smith, to help her, but really does not know practically what this entails. Philip tells her, "It simply can't be done." Rosemary is flustered and demands to know why she cannot attempt to try and help her. Philip points out how "astonishingly pretty" the girl is. Rosemary expresses surprise, and Philip assures her of Miss Smith's loveliness. He tells Rosemary she is making an enormous mistake but seems content to allow her to continue with her experiment. He simply wishes to be informed if the girl will be dining with them. Flustered, Rosemary exits the room.

Before returning to Miss Smith, Rosemary gathers some money. After half an hour, she reappears in the library and tells Philip that Miss Smith will not be dining with them. Philip expresses mild surprise, asking sarcastically if Miss Smith had another engagement. Rosemary tells Philip that the girl insisted on leaving, so all Rosemary could do was give her some money and let her be on her way. Sitting on her husband's knee, with her hair freshly done, she then attempts to reassure herself of Philip's affection for her. Rosemary tells Philip about the expensive box and asks if she can have it. He gives her permission to buy it. She then pulls Philip close and asks him if she is pretty.

CHARACTERS

Philip Fell

Philip is Rosemary's husband. His role in the story is not a large one, but he exerts much influence over his wife and her actions. Rosemary defers buying the box that she covets until Philip gives her permission to do so at the end of the story. His reaction to Miss Smith's presence in his home is not a positive one. He questions his wife's decisions, but rather than scold her or tell her to turn the girl away, Philip seems to manipulate Rosemary by preying on her vanity and insecurity. He tells Rosemary how beautiful he finds Miss Smith to be. Soon, Rosemary has shown the girl the door but has given her some money to ease her conscience. She then flirts with Philip, asks for permission to buy the box, and begs to know if he finds her attractive.

Rosemary Fell

Rosemary is the protagonist of "A Cup of Tea." As the story begins, the reader is introduced to Rosemary, who is young, wealthy, and pretty. She has been married for two years. Her husband, Philip, appears later in the story. The text reads, "She had a duck of a boy. No, not Peter—Michael." This suggests that Rosemary and her husband have a son, and that Rosemary is not particularly attached to the child, as it seems irrelevant what he is called. An alternative reading is that Rosemary and Philip have two sons, but that Rosemary only regards one of them as "a duck of a boy," indicating that she is more fond of one than the other.

Rosemary covets an antique enamel box but, despite her wealth, decides it is too expensive to buy at that moment. She asks the shopkeeper to hold on to it for her. Standing in the rain, Rosemary feels keenly the regret of not having purchased the box. When a girl asks her for money to buy a cup of tea, Rosemary decides she will take her home and help her. She fashions a romantic notion of herself, thinking she is about to have an adventure because she is rescuing a poor stranger. Rosemary considers that her actions are similar to those of characters in books she has read, and she eagerly plucks the girl from the street and takes her home. Rosemary, however, seems a little unsure of what to do with her once she gets her there. Rosemary is frustrated by the girl's unresponsiveness, as the girl seems eager neither to thank Rosemary nor to tell Rosemary the story of her poverty. Rosemary removes the girl's wet coat and hat while the girl stands silently. When the girl speaks up to tell Rosemary that she is about to faint, Rosemary rings for tea.

When her husband asks to speak with her, Rosemary is at first eager to tell of her good deed but then dismayed that her husband thinks her rescue is pointless. Finally, she is driven to jealousy when her husband points out how pretty the girl is. Throughout the story, Rosemary demonstrates her shallowness. Helping Miss Smith is an act that is more rooted in her own desire for adventure and a need to shape her view of herself than it is about providing assistance to someone in need.

Shopkeeper

A shopkeeper owns the antique store Rosemary is fond of frequenting. She observes how pleased the shopkeeper always seems to be to serve her. Although Rosemary is aware the shopkeeper is flattering her so that she will spend money in his store, she also believes that there is something else motivating his actions. She recalls the way he has told her that he prefers to sell things to people who appreciate them. This recollection underscores Rosemary's belief in the shopkeeper's admiration of her good taste. Knowing his customer, the shopkeeper tells Rosemary he has shown no one else the beautiful box she comes to desire, and he promises to keep it for her.

Miss Smith

The girl whom Rosemary rescues from the rainy street later supplies her last name to Rosemary and is then referred to as Miss Smith. For most of the story, however, she is referred to as "the girl." Rosemary assumes she is a young woman approximately the same age as herself. The girl asks Rosemary for the price of a cup of tea. She is described as possessing large eyes and chapped hands. She shivers in the rain. Rosemary is surprised that the girl's voice does not seem to be that of "a beggar." When Rosemary invites the girl to come home with her, the girl is naturally suspicious and imagines Rosemary means to turn her in to the police. Her starvation wins out over her suspicions, however, and she follows Rosemary to her car.

At Rosemary's home, Miss Smith is shown to Rosemary's room. She stands, dazed and mute, while Rosemary questions her and tells her to sit down. The girl allows her coat and hat to be removed but continues to stand silently, until she finally informs Rosemary that she is about to faint. As they wait for tea to be brought, the girl sobs and confesses that she cannot bear to go on the way she has, suggesting that she might kill herself. Rosemary begs her to stop crying and insists she will help her.

After the girl has eaten, she seems content. She supplies her last name when Rosemary is attempting to introduce her to Philip. Miss Smith then remains by the fire as Philip and Rosemary leave the room to discuss her fate. Not long after, Rosemary returns to Miss Smith, supplies her with some money, and escorts her out. Rosemary tells Philip that Miss Smith insisted on leaving. Yet this scene is not narrated directly.

THEMES

Social Class

Mansfield depicts two distinct social classes in "A Cup of Tea." Rosemary is a member of the upper class. She is extremely wealthy: "They were rich, really rich, not just comfortably well off." Miss Smith is the poorest of the poor. With no money of her own at all, she begs in the streets. Rosemary's wealth entitles her to spend large amounts of money on items such as vast quantities of fresh flowers and pricey antique enamel boxes. When Rosemary is approached by the girl begging for money for tea, Rosemary is astonished by the quality of the girl's voice. She marvels that "it wasn't in the least the voice of a beggar."

It is clear from the way that Rosemary regards the girl with such curiosity that she has been wealthy all of her life. She finds it "extraordinary" that someone would be unable to afford a cup of tea. Although she observes that the girl is shivering and that her hands are raw and chapped from the cold, Rosemary does not contemplate the discomfort the starving, freezing girl must be experiencing. From her privileged perspective, she is able to view the girl as an interesting object to take home. She finds that the girl is easily prompted to come with her. "Hungry people," Rosemary observes, "are easily led." Rosemary continues to be fascinated by the girl and watches the way she experiences Rosemary's lavish home.

However, when Rosemary tries to assist the girl in removing her wet coat and hat, Rosemary becomes irritated. She is unable to understand why the girl is not more helpful or grateful. She thinks, "if people wanted helping they must respond a little." Here, Mansfield underscores once again how Rosemary's wealth distances her from the girl. Rosemary is unable to respond with empathy or compassion, and it is not until the girl informs her that she is about to faint does Rosemary begin to comprehend the effects of cold and hunger. Rosemary's desire to help someone less fortunate than herself soon comes to an end, however. When her husband, Philip, meets the girl and privately tells Rosemary how pretty the girl is, Rosemary sends the girl away with some cash. Mansfield critiques the wealthy class and its inability to comprehend the needs of the poor. Even though Rosemary intends to prove to the girl that "rich people had hearts,"

TOPICS FOR FURTHER STUDY

- "A Cup of Tea" focuses on Rosemary Fell's experience and perspective as she attempts to rescue a poor young woman. The girl, who identifies herself only by the last name Smith, says little, and the reader is not allowed access to her thoughts. Write a version of the story from Miss Smith's perspective. Consider the circumstances that might have led to her poverty, and contemplate what compels her to approach Rosemary. How does Miss Smith perceive Rosemary and Philip? What does she think of Rosemary's motivations and intentions? Is she fearful? Hopeful? Include the scene that Rosemary does not directly recount but rather summarizes for Philip, in which she gives Miss Smith money just prior to Miss Smith's departure. Do you think Rosemary asked her to leave? Or did Miss Smith insist upon leaving, as Rosemary tells Philip? Just as Mansfield offers the reader insight into Rosemary's thinking, take the reader into Miss Smith's thoughts.

- Indian-born Kashmira Sheth's 2010 young-adult novel *Boys without Names* focuses on an eleven-year-old's experience with poverty. Seeking opportunities in the city after leaving a rural village in India, Gopal and his family are poor and homeless, looking for work. With a small group, read Sheth's novel, and consider the ways in which the protagonist and his family are affected by poverty. How does it change them? How do they cope as the events of the novel unfold? Consider the sense of loneliness, isolation, and despair experienced by Gopal. How does he survive? Discuss these issues with your group, and continue to analyze the story's themes and characters in an online blog you create.

- Mansfield depicts an enormous gap between the rich and the poor in "A Cup of Tea." Research wealth, poverty, and social class in England during the 1920s. What were the causes of poverty during this time period? What was the impact of World War I on the working class? How did the wealthiest of the British classes come by their money? Did education or social welfare programs help improve the situation over time? Write a research paper in which you discuss your findings. Be sure to include a list of all your sources.

- In a number of her works, Mansfield examines the notion of feminine identity as a social construct. In addition to "A Cup of Tea," read other short pieces by Mansfield such as "The Tiredness of Rosabel," "Miss Brill," "The Garden Party," "At the Bay," or "The Woman at the Store." In what ways does Mansfield treat femininity and female and male views about gender in the stories you have selected? Are there common themes among the stories? Do any of the female characters resemble one another? In what ways are they different? Write an essay in which you compare Mansfield's treatment of female gender identity in these stories.

she only succeeds in proving that rich people have money.

Identity

In "A Cup of Tea," Rosemary attempts to cultivate her own identity. She is motivated both by her need to view herself in a particular way and by her concern over the way others perceive her.

She convinces herself, for example, that the shopkeeper's fawning over her is more than just flattery, that he, in fact, respects her excellent taste and regards it as a quality that not many people possess. When the girl outside the shop asks her for money for tea, Rosemary hatches an idea: "And suddenly it seemed to Rosemary such an adventure. It was like something out of a

Rosemary meets Miss Smith in an antique shop.
(© *Lee Torrens | Shutterstock.com*)

novel by Dostoevsky, this meeting in the dusk." She sees herself as a character in a novel and delights in the feeling of adventure that taking the girl home will bring her.

It is important to Rosemary to be perceived by the girl as generous and kindhearted. Attempting to reassure the girl, Rosemary smiles, and "she felt how simple and kind her smile was." Once Rosemary has gotten the girl into her car with her, she thinks, "She was going to prove to this girl that—wonderful things did happen in life, that—fairy godmothers were real, that— rich people had hearts, and that women *were* sisters." The girl's view of Rosemary is important to Rosemary for a time, but Rosemary becomes easily irritated with the girl for not being more responsive to Rosemary's assistance.

Rosemary is equally flustered with Philip's inability to regard her actions in a positive light. She tells Philip that she wants to be nice to the girl and take care of her, but Philip tells

Rosemary that she is "quite mad" and that assisting the girl in any long-term fashion "simply can't be done." Rosemary's response indicates the difference between her true motives and what she wants others to believe. Although she attempts to tell Philip that she wanted to be nice to Miss Smith and to help her, Philip's refusal to admire her actions results in Rosemary's revelation that in fact her "good deed," her attempt to help, is really an act of impulse. "Why not?" she asks Philip; "I want to. Isn't that a reason?" She mentions reading about such things. Philip cuts her off, but it is clear that her romantic view of herself, inspired by the characters she has read about in novels, informs her decisions where Miss Smith is concerned.

Rosemary's sense of identity flounders, however, after Philip comments on Miss Smith's beauty. Before long, Rosemary has sent Miss Smith on her way—though she tells Philip that the girl insisted on leaving. Rosemary then proceeds to question Philip about her *own* beauty, clearly threatened in her position as the object of Philip's desire by his comment about Miss Smith.

STYLE

Literary Impressionism and Realism

Mansfield's work has been associated with a variety of literary trends and movements. Aspects of her writing have led some critics to identify her as an avant-garde or experimental author and position her within a movement known as the modernist movement. Literary modernism as it evolved in the 1920s rejected past literary trends as insufficient in their ability to portray the post– World War I world, with all its destruction, chaos, and instability. Modernist writers experimented with a variety of narrative modes and techniques. Julia van Gunsteren, in *Katherine Mansfield and Literary Impressionism*, notes that scholars of the modernist movement "grouped [Mansfield] rather loosely and vaguely under Modernism."

Gunsteren more specifically places Mansfield within the literary impressionist movement, which, she maintains, "derives its coherence from the assumption that human life consists of the involvement of an individual character in a reality which is apprehensible only in terms of sensations." The critic goes on to note that Mansfield's writing does incorporate some realistic modes, stating, "Mansfield portrays ordinary people, who speak ordinary language sometimes tinged with dialect and describes situations drawn from within a common range." However, Gunsteren ultimately rejects the identification of Mansfield as a realist because of the author's emphasis on the sensory perception of reality.

In "A Cup of Tea," Mansfield employs both realist and impressionist techniques. Rosemary is a young, wealthy wife who is out shopping. Her exchange with the shopkeeper about the antique box is realistically portrayed and includes a detailed description of the coveted item, as well as natural dialogue between Rosemary and the shopkeeper. When Rosemary exits the shop, however, filled with regret at having not purchased the item, her perception of reality is altered and is conveyed through the filter of her emotions. Her ability to "read" her environment through her senses has been colored by her experience. It is dark and raining out: "There was a cold bitter taste in the air, and the new-lighted lamps looked sad. Sad were the lights in the houses opposite. Dimly they burned as if regretting something." Mansfield's impressionism comes through in these lines. She emphasizes her protagonist's sensory perceptions and the way her reality is altered.

By incorporating elements of both realism and impressionism in "A Cup of Tea," Mansfield presents a story that is told in a straightforward manner in terms of plot. At the same time, she presents her character's interior world in an impressionistic way, evoking the character's thoughts and feelings through her sensory interpretation of reality.

Limited Omniscient Third-Person Narration

Mansfield makes use of what is known as a limited omniscient third-person narrator in "A Cup of Tea." The story is written from the perspective of Rosemary Fell, but it is composed in the third person. Rosemary is referred to by her name or by personal pronouns such as "she." This is in contrast to a story told in the first person, in which the narrating character refers to himself or herself as "I." When a writer employs an omniscient third-person narrator, he or she allows the reader access to the private thoughts of any and all characters in the story.

Omniscient narrators are all-knowing and present the reader with facts about the characters, their thoughts, the setting, and sometimes the characters' futures. They already know what will happen in the story, and they are often associated with the author of the story. A narrator with limited omniscience restricts the reader's access to the perspective of one or a few characters at most. In "A Cup of Tea," the reader is allowed to know Rosemary's world from her perspective. The reader's understanding of other characters is accessed through the filter of Rosemary's viewpoint and thoughts. In a story as brief as "A Cup of Tea," this method of narration allows the reader to quickly develop an understanding of Rosemary, her motivations, her opinions of other people, and her view of the world. It also allows the reader to assess the differences between Rosemary's thoughts and actions. This is a vital component of the reader's experience.

In "A Cup of Tea," Rosemary acts in a manner that appears to be charitable and kind, but her inner monologue reveals that she acts not out of genuine concern for Miss Smith, but out of a desire for adventure and a need to be perceived—both by herself and by others—as extraordinarily generous. The discrepancy between thoughts and words that the limited omniscient third-person narration reveals also highlights Rosemary's insecurities where her husband is concerned. After Rosemary asks her husband for permission to buy the antique box, and he acquiesces, the text reads, "But that was not really what Rosemary wanted to say." She then goes on to ask her husband if she is pretty, revealing how deeply hurt and anxious she feels after her husband has commented on Miss Smith's beauty.

HISTORICAL CONTEXT

Literary Trends in 1920s England

In England in the 1920s, writers whose careers began before World War I (1914–1918) found themselves confronted with a new understanding of their world. The violence and brutality of the war in Europe altered the way writers understood reality, language, and their place within the new, postwar world. Modernism was a literary trend that began roughly at the turn of the century; it involved the rejection or evolution of Victorian literary modes. During the early years of the twentieth century, realism was a popular narrative mode that emphasized the accurate depiction of both individuals and society. Some

COMPARE & CONTRAST

- **1922:** In the aftermath of World War I, so recently ended in 1918, Great Britain experiences high unemployment levels after a very brief period of postwar economic improvement. Poverty rates decline over the course of the decade as wages rise, but many people still live in poverty and are unable to find work.

  Today: At the close of the first decade of the twenty-first century, the poverty rate in Great Britain is 22 percent, according to studies by the Joseph Rowntree Foundation. Unemployment and underemployment are major factors contributing to the current poverty levels. Recent figures indicate that in terms of physical health, the gap between rich and poor people is greater in 2010 than it was during the 1920s.

- **1922:** With the onset of World War I in 1914, British suffragists—those activists fighting for women's right to vote—put their goals on hold in order to not detract from the war effort. After the war, suffragists take up the fight once again, winning partial enfranchisement in 1918 and full enfranchisement in 1928. Women's rights advocates also fight for revisions to divorce laws—attempting to make it easier for women to file for divorce—and for the development of and access to birth control.

  Today: Divorce rates are declining in Great Britain, down 1.7 percent in 2011 from the rate the previous year. In 2011, there were approximately 10.8 divorcing individuals per thousand married people. Recent figures indicate that about 76 percent of women in Great Britain aged sixteen to forty-nine use birth control. In some parts of the United Kingdom, access to birth control and to abortion remain limited.

- **1922:** In British fiction, modernist experimentation with narrative styles and techniques evolves in the postwar years. The limits of language and the power of image and symbol become the focus of some modernist writers. The exploration of the interior world of fictional characters and the juxtaposition of this interior reality with the world as perceived through the senses continue through the use of literary impressionism.

  Today: Twenty-first-century British authors explore a wide range of narrative techniques and also write in more traditional, realist narrative modes. Due to the multicultural nature of modern Great Britain, many native British writers, such as acclaimed authors Zadie Smith, Nadeem Aslam, and Hari Kunzru, are born of immigrant parents from around the globe and consequently have infused contemporary British literature with global culture and issues. Notable female short-fiction writers include Alison Moore, Jackie Kay, and Anneliese Mackintosh.

---

writers, influenced by European trends in both art and literature, began to experiment with narrative styles and techniques. These writers were loosely identified as modernists.

A number of avant-garde or experimental movements are often regarded as subsumed by modernism. These movements arose or evolved in the aftermath of World War I and reflect writers' attempts to come to terms with the dissolution of the world as they once knew it. Some authors—symbolists and imagists—incorporated heavy use of symbols or images in their fiction or poetry, while others—surrealists—attempted to convey the inner workings of the subconscious mind and often experimented with nonlinear narration. Literary impressionism is also

Miss Smith insists she only wants a cup of tea, though Rosemary wants to do a lot more for her.
(© M. Unal Ozmen / Shutterstock.com)

typically regarded as a part of the literary modernism of the years surrounding World War I. *Literary impressionism* is a way of describing works of literature in which the characters' understanding of their realty is acquired through their sensory impressions. English modernist writers of this period, those who explored these various techniques and approaches to literature, included T. S. Eliot, Virginia Woolf, D. H. Lawrence, Henry James (an expatriate American), and Katherine Mansfield.

Social and Gender Issues in 1920s British Culture

In much of her work, including "A Cup of Tea," Mansfield touches on topics of social issues, such as social class, wealth, and poverty, along with gender issues, specifically women's place in society and in marital relationships. During the aftermath of World War I, unemployment rates in Great Britain were high. While many still remained in poverty, numbers were decreasing during the 1920s. As Marguerite Dupree explains in an essay for *The Cambridge Urban*

History of Britain, "Rising real wages during the war and during the interwar years for those in work meant that the market reduced the problem of low pay, the principal cause of poverty before the First World War."

Some critics have noted that there is disagreement among historians regarding the extent of poverty in Great Britain during the interwar years, that is, the years between the end of World War I and the beginning of World War II. Keith Laybourn observes in *Modern Britain since 1906: A Reader* that although "the scale of poverty might be open to question," the primary causes of poverty are more discernible. Laybourn asserts that surveys of this time period point to the "unemployment of the chief wage-earner" as "the most important cause of poverty." Laybourn goes on to discuss the health effects of unemployment and poverty on the British population.

In the aftermath of the war, there were other notable developments in the domestic sphere, particularly in issues pertaining to women's rights. Christine Bolt, in *The Women's Movements in the United States and Britain from the 1790s to the 1920s*, explains that the divorce rate increased after the war, although women still continued to choose marriage and motherhood. Some advancements were made in the area of reproductive rights during this time frame. Birth control became a topic of discussion, and the fight for development of and access to birth control was waged by activists. However, Bolt observes that in many ways, birth control became a family planning issue; it was separated from the feminist movement and from the notion of female sexual freedom.

CRITICAL OVERVIEW

"A Cup of Tea" has not received a great deal of individual attention because it is one among many short stories penned by Mansfield. One approach to Mansfield's work popular among critics is to find themes that span the breadth of her body of writing. Vincent O'Sullivan, in an essay on Mansfield for *The Critical Response to Katherine Mansfield*, examines the predatory nature of human beings and asserts that in stories such as "A Cup of Tea," Mansfield is concerned with the way women prey upon each other. O'Sullivan identifies other stories in which women prey on men and men prey on women. The critic further notes that in much of Mansfield's fiction dealing with women and men, there "is the sense of one partner inevitably exploiting the other."

James Gindin, in an essay for the *Dictionary of Literary Biography*, studies the way Mansfield treats social issues in her later fiction. Gindin finds that Rosemary in "A Cup of Tea" is primarily motivated by a sense of "social guilt." Similarly, in *Katherine Mansfield's Fiction*, Patrick D. Morrow maintains that Rosemary attempts to be a "Good Samaritan" but finds it "isn't always the smart thing to be." Morrow characterizes "A Cup of Tea" as "a sarcastic, and above all ironic story." In *Katherine Mansfield and Literary Modernism*, Ana Belen Lopez Perez analyzes the role of the city in Mansfield's fiction. In discussing "A Cup of Tea," Perez states, "For Rosemary, the city becomes the space where she satisfies her whims and fancies, including those of a consumer who identifies consumption with a form of liberation."

CRITICISM

Catherine Dominic

Dominic is a novelist and freelance writer and editor. In the following essay, she examines Mansfield's exploration of female identity in "A Cup of Tea" and argues that Rosemary Fell struggles to confidently construct a notion of her own identity.

In the short story "A Cup of Tea," Katherine Mansfield explores female gender identity and marriage, among other topics. Throughout the brief tale, Rosemary Fell tests out different views of herself as a woman. She does so with some enthusiasm, except where the issue of her role within her marriage is concerned. In her relationship with her husband, Philip, Rosemary falters. She is unsure of herself, uncertain as to how to get what she wants, unclear about her husband's attachment to her.

The story is told in the third person, from Rosemary's perspective. Using this limited omniscient narration, Mansfield exposes Rosemary's interior monologue to the reader. Rosemary is first presented to the reader as modern, pretty—but not beautiful—well dressed, and well read. Married, and a mother, Rosemary is adored by her husband. Rosemary's wealth is also central to her character. It provides her with a sense of herself as a sophisticated woman with excellent taste. Out shopping one day, Rosemary enters an antique shop. The reader is informed that "the man who kept it was ridiculously fond of serving her. He beamed whenever she came in. He clasped his hands; he was so gratified he could scarcely speak."

Rosemary is aware that this is flattery, but she thinks that still, "there was something." She does not specify what that something is, but she thinks about how the shopkeeper has expressed to her his reluctance to sell his things "to someone who does not appreciate them." Rosemary knowingly assumes that he considers her to be a person with "that fine feeling which is so rare," the feeling of genuine appreciation of his antiques, which he so admires. On the day when the story takes place, the shopkeeper presents Rosemary with an enamel box featuring an image of a couple embracing on the lid. She covets it, yet the price is very high, "even if one is rich." Rosemary asks the shopkeeper to hold it for her, and she leaves the building, immediately feeling pangs of regret.

In the opening scene, Rosemary embraces the notion of herself as a sophisticated woman with good taste and enormous wealth. Her hesitation at the antique store, however, is significant—she *wants* the enamel box, but she does not buy it. The reader has already been told that Rosemary and her husband are "really rich." Mansfield has described a typical scene in a flower shop, in which Rosemary purchases a vast quantity of flowers. Four bunches of this, and some of those and "all the roses in the jar," but not the lilac. She hates lilac. This demonstrates Rosemary's impulsive nature as well as the willingness with which she parts with her money, yet she does not buy the box. The expense is great, even for the very rich, so Rosemary delays her gratification and exits the store. The box, however, will become an issue again in the story.

In the meantime, Rosemary keenly feels a sense of regret over the box. When she decides to rescue the beggar girl from the street, Rosemary is positively delighted with herself. She smiles in such a way that the girl cannot help but sense her kindness, or so Rosemary thinks. In the car, Rosemary contemplates her desire to prove her good-natured intentions to the girl. She intends to show her that "fairy godmothers were real, that—rich people had hearts, and that women *were* sisters." This last point she also attempts to make verbally to the girl, stating, "We're both women. If I'm the more fortunate, you ought to expect . . ." But Rosemary never finishes the sentence. Her statement that they are both women is intended to convey the sense of sisterhood she imagines. It is important to Rosemary, the way she is viewed by another woman. She seeks common ground, a sense of belonging that

she perhaps does not feel elsewhere in her world, in her marriage.

Not long after this moment, however, as the girl stands mute and unmoving in Rosemary's bedroom, Rosemary thinks that the girl "looked rather stupid." She is annoyed that the girl is being difficult, as if she is being deliberately mulish as Rosemary tries to help her. Rosemary thinks to herself, "if people wanted helping they must respond a little, just a little, otherwise it became very difficult indeed." The warm sense of sisterhood has vanished. The girl finally confesses that she will faint if she does not eat something. Rosemary immediately calls for tea, as well as brandy, and this request sends the girl into tears. She insists that she never drinks brandy and wants only tea.

Rosemary considers the moment to be "terrible and fascinating." She encourages the girl to stop crying, gives her a handkerchief, and experiences what is possibly the only genuine feeling toward the girl she has yet demonstrated. She is "touched beyond words." Compelled by this sense of sympathy, Rosemary feels a gush of sisterhood and believes the girl feels the same way, because the girl confides in her that she cannot continue to live the way she has been. According to Rosemary, the girl is able to confide in her because she "forgot everything except they were both women." Rosemary pleads with her to stop crying, promises to help her, and when tea and sandwiches and bread and butter are brought, encourages the girl to have her fill.

Rosemary's feelings about the girl and about herself fluctuate in this brief encounter. Once she has gotten the girl home, she seems irritated that the girl is behaving stupidly, that she does not seem helpful or grateful. When the girl begins to weep, Rosemary becomes aware of her desire for connection and reflects on sisterhood once more.

Rosemary does not bask in the glow of sisterhood for long. Before she can really speak with the girl, Philip arrives. He examines the girl, now introduced as Miss Smith. He takes in the scene and asks to speak privately with his wife. Alone with Rosemary, he insists, "Explain. Who is she? What does it all mean?" Rosemary laughs and tells Philip how she brought the poor girl home. Philip presses her, wondering what she plans to do with the girl. Rosemary answers briskly enough at first but

WHAT DO I READ NEXT?

- *The Garden Party and Other Stories* was published in 1922, the same year Mansfield published "A Cup of Tea." The title story is one of Mansfield's best-known works of short fiction.

- D. H. Lawrence, a personal friend of Mansfield's, is also considered a modernist writer. Famous for novels such as *Women in Love* (1920) and *Lady Chatterly's Lover* (1928), he also published numerous short stories. The collection *England, My England and Other Stories* was published in 1922, the same year that Mansfield's "A Cup of Tea" first appeared in print. The collection is available in a 1996 edition.

- Mansfield was a great admirer of the work of Anton Chekhov. His short fiction, published in the late nineteenth and early twentieth centuries in Russian literary magazines, is available in modern collections such as *Anton Chekhov's Short Stories*, published in 1979.

- Sheila Heti's 2012 title *How Should a Person Be?* is experimental in its blending of genres and literary styles. Heti's work has been described as a novel-from-life, or part novel, part self-help guide. In *How Should a Person Be?*, she explores the notion of identity and specifically the construction of female identity.

- Mexican-born author Francisco Jimenez examines such issues as race, poverty, and identity in the young-adult short-story collection *The Circuit: Stories from the Life of a Migrant Child* (1997).

- Alison Moore is a British novelist and short-story writer. Her collection *The Pre-War House and Other Stories*, published in 2013, explores themes of motherhood and despair and uncertainty.

- R. W. Stevenson's *Modernist Fiction: An Introduction* (1997) surveys the themes, styles, and techniques of literary modernism in works by British and American modernist writers.

- Amy Ephron's 1999 novel *A Cup of Tea: A Novel of 1917* was inspired by Mansfield's short story. It tells the story of Rosemary and Philip before they were married.

---

soon stumbles, moving from an assertion that she will "be frightfully nice to her" to saying she will "look after her. I don't know how. We haven't talked yet. But show her—treat her—make her feel—." Rosemary's inability to complete her thoughts here is key. She has not thought through a plan and does not know what actually *helping* someone—aside from giving them a meal—looks like.

This point did not seem to matter much to Rosemary before Philip's arrival. Forced to outline what she wants to do, how she intends to help, Rosemary questions her own intentions. Philip expresses his doubts about both her sanity in the matter and her ability to do much to help the girl. This frustrates Rosemary. She states, "I want to. Isn't that a reason?" The reader is reminded of the description of the impulsive Rosemary in the flower shop, snapping up what she wants to take home—then a bunch of roses, now a beggar. Yet she is uncertain of herself in her husband's presence and begins to doubt her ability to formulate or execute a plan where the girl is concerned. She falls back on an idea of herself and her own agency in the world that is usually effective, stressing that she can simply do what she wants—she wants all the roses, but not the lilac. She wants to bring home the girl but not bother with details. Her *wanting* is usually reason enough for the action she takes. Now, she is thrown by Philip's wondering what comes next.

Rosemary's cigarette smoking seems to be a habit that hides her nervousness and insecurity.
(© Zoommer / Shutterstock.com)

Philip, pressing Rosemary further and knowing she has not thought the whole thing through, takes his time, saying slowly that the girl is "so astonishingly pretty." His statement has the effect of surprising his wife and making her blush. He asks if the girl will be staying for dinner, and once again he emphasizes her loveliness. Here Philip demonstrates his ability to manipulate his wife. It is unlikely that as a man of means, and one most likely being used to having some say regarding who gets invited into his home, he would be pleased with the presence of a bedraggled beggar in his wife's room. Rather than assert his dominance as the man of the house in an aggressive fashion, he slyly strikes at his wife where he knows her to be weak. He appeals to her vanity, knowing she will be jealous of Miss Smith if she believes that he is attracted to her. After leaving Philip in the library, Rosemary goes to her desk and retrieves some money, all the while fuming at her husband's words. She returns to her husband half an hour later telling him that Miss Smith had to leave.

Rosemary then sits on Philip's knee. The reader is informed that she "had just done her hair, darkened her eyes a little, and put on her pearls." Threatened by Miss Smith's looks, feeling jealous, and wanting to reclaim her husband's affection and attention, Rosemary has dressed up for him and applied more makeup. Her view of herself as a woman has been altered by her husband's gazing at another woman, and she must once again attempt to assert her agency, limited as it is in the domestic sphere she occupies. She asks Philip if he likes her. He holds her close, tells her that he likes her, and orders her to kiss him. Rosemary pauses. Now, she asks him if she may buy the enameled box.

Some critics and readers have regarded this request as evidence of Rosemary's own attempt to manipulate Philip. She uses her sexual attractiveness to get what she wants. However, Rosemary has shown that she often just buys or takes what she wants. Here, she specifically and pointedly defers to Philip. The submissiveness may either indicate that because of the box's great cost, she felt it genuinely necessary to ask Philip if she could purchase it. This would emphasize the imbalance of economic power in the relationship. Alternatively, Rosemary may be using her submissiveness as a weapon, as a deliberate way to manipulate Philip, not about the box specifically, but as a way to maintain a position in the relationship whereby she remains the primary object of his affection. By behaving in a submissive way, she ensures that Philip feels secure as the dominant figure in the household. She gives him the opportunity to give his permission to her. In this manner, Rosemary buys future permission to do as she pleases. If she "behaves" and asks permission for large purchases, Philip is more likely to be tolerant of her other expenditures.

Mansfield takes pains to inform the reader that asking permission to buy the box is not *really* what Rosemary wants to ask Philip. Rosemary goes on to press "his head against her bosom" and ask, "am I *pretty*?" Rosemary can only see herself—at least in this moment—through Philip's gaze. His validation of her beauty is more important to her than the box and more important to her than Miss Smith's sisterhood ever was. Given the sensual nature of the embrace, it is plain that Rosemary seeks both the emotional validation his words can give and the reassurance that his physical embrace will bring her.

Notably, the pose of Rosemary and Philip at the end of the novel mirrors that of the couple whose image appears on the enamel box Rosemary so covets: "On the lid a minute creature stood under a flowery tree, and a more minute creature had her arms around his neck." As Rosemary presses Philip's head to her bosom, her arms would be around his neck. The repetition of this imagery emphasizes what Rosemary truly desires—a sense of connection with her husband. She seeks the loving embrace of the couple on the box, longs for the idyllic nature of the relationship she sees there, where a "pink cloud like a watchful cherub" hangs above their heads.

Repeatedly, Rosemary sees herself from the outside. She considers the way the shopkeeper regards her. She longs for Miss Smith to see regard her with a sense of solidarity—to be seen not just as a rescuer, but as another woman, as a sister. She wants to know that Philip sees her as beautiful; she wants him to love her. Throughout the story, though, she is filled with doubt. Perhaps the shopkeeper is just flattering her. Perhaps Miss Smith, once she stops crying and stops eating, will not see her as a sister. Perhaps Philip does not find her beautiful or worthy of his love and attention. Although Rosemary is depicted as shallow and vain, she also displays a sense of vulnerability in her inability to craft a version of herself that she can believe in for any length of time.

Source: Catherine Dominic, Critical Essay on "A Cup of Tea," in *Short Stories for Students*, Gale, Cengage Learning, 2014.

Edward Wagenknecht

In the following excerpt, Wagenknecht praises Mansfield's use of descriptive language.

...Perhaps the first of Katherine Mansfield's qualifications for writing was her great faculty of observation. Examples might be chosen almost at random. Of the naked children braving the water "At the Bay" she observes that "The *firm compact* little girls were not half so brave as the *tender, delicate-looking* little boys." To the Burnell children the mirror in Aunt Beryl's dressing table is "very strange; it was as though a little piece of forked lightning was imprisoned in it." Sometimes, as in the case of Geraldine's cat in "Widowed," the detail is so vividly presented that it is unforgettable.

With this faculty for observation she had extraordinarily keen sense impressions. When Beryl goes bathing it is not enough that she puts on her bathing suit: rather, "she drew on the *limp, sandy-feeling* bathing-dress *that was not quite dry* and fastened the *twisted buttons*." So, when Kezia goes with Pat to see the duck beheaded: "She put her hand in his *hard, dry* one." Inevitably the apparently slight addition makes the thing live. When "Sun and Moon" come down to be slobbered over by their parents' eccentric guests, they observe "a skinny old lady *with teeth that clicked*." But the passage I like best of all is the description of Fenella in "The Voyage," trying to prepare for bed in the cabin of a ship: "The hard square of brown soap would not lather, and the water in the bottle was a kind of blue jelly. How hard it was, too, to turn down those stiff sheets; you simply had to tear your way in."

Very characteristic of Katherine Mansfield's psychological interest is her penchant for transferring sense impressions or even for attributing

"

physical properties to the immaterial. She speaks of the music which "breaks into bright pieces, and joins together again, and again breaks, and is dissolved. . . . ." Of a cruel laugh she records, "It had a long sharp beak and claws and two bead eyes," while a "weak worn old voice" suggests "a piece of faintly smelling dark lace." In "Six Years After" the *thoughts* of a selfish lazy husband, having come to a point where further reflection would be inconvenient, *feel the need of a cigar!*

It must be obvious that with such gifts Katherine Mansfield is a wonderful descriptive writer. How could a whole chapter enable us to see more clearly than this sentence the terrible "Woman at the Store." "Looking at her, you felt there was nothing but sticks and wire under that pinafore—her front teeth were knocked out, she had red pulpy hands, and she wore on her feet a pair of dirty Bluchers." Her child is equally vivid in one sharp, unlovely attitude: "A mean, undersized brat, with whitish hair and weak eyes. She stood, legs wide apart and her stomach protruding."

Of Katherine Mansfield's longer descriptive passages I like best the picture of early morning at the beginning of "At the Bay" and the psychological portrait of the horrible Mrs. Harry Kember in the same story. It is worth noting how she begins in the first instance—"Very early morning"—with a perfect study of still life. On page 2, when the sheep enter, the picture begins to stir, but it is not fully awake until Florrie the cat appears on page 4. As for Mrs. Kember she surely is one of the most convincingly horrible women in literature!

Yet much more striking than Katherine Mansfield's ability to see and to chronicle detail is her power to use it suggestively, to give us the

implications of a whole character in a single reaction or a single gesture. When the temperamental Stanley Burnell leaves the house of a morning in a bad mood, he rushes out to catch the coach, shouting meanwhile to his wife, "No time to say good-bye." Katherine Mansfield comments cruelly, "And he meant that as a punishment to her." Is not the character of Stanley fixed in our minds for good and all? In "Marriage à la Mode," when we hear that "It was over a year since Isabel had scrapped the old donkeys and engines and so on because they were so 'dreadfully sentimental' and 'so appallingly bad for the babies' sense of form,'" we understand at once just what it is that has been happening to Isabel, and we are prepared for the domestic tragedy which follows.

Katherine Mansfield is sometimes accused of trite themes and of artificial development. She realized the danger of artificiality and struggled hard against it. Her loyalty to truth was absolute: she would always rather abandon a story than force what seemed to her a not wholly inevitable development upon it. Yet it seems to me that even so famous a story as "Bliss," interesting as it is, quite fails to be convincing. The wife's deception is too thoroughgoing, there is not sufficient preparation for the outcome, it startles like a trick ending in an O. Henry story. The revelation of the husband's perfidy, coming after the wife's day of bliss, is indeed strongly ironical, but it is almost as definitely a piece of coincidence as the return of Paula's old love in *The Second Mrs. Tanqueray*.

As to the triviality, that is another matter. It is undeniable in many of the early stories, but I do not find that the mature Katherine Mansfield was ever trivial. Chances are that those who bring this charge against her do not understand what she is doing. Her avoidance of plot was intentional; she did not see life arranging itself into plots; so why should she arrange her stories in that way? Often when she seems at first glance most trivial, she is really most profound. She has learned from the psychologists that there are no little things. The human soul is what she is after and whatever reveals that soul is to her important, be it a handclasp or an avalanche. Take for example "The Fly," that marvelous story of her last days. Actually nothing happens in "The Fly" save that a man kills an insect by dropping ink on it. But the implications of the story go to the very roots of life. Humanity is symbolized twice in that story: in the fly—its pitiful struggles, its helpless heroism in the face of a power that has doomed it from the start; and again in the man—its thoughtless cruelty, its strange combination of sentimentality and callousness.

An interesting technical device in the writing of Katherine Mansfield is her tendency to shift, frequently and without warning, from the conscious to the subconscious. The women at the Bay are sure that some day Harry Kember will murder his wife: "Yes, even while they talked to Mrs. Kember and took in the awful concoction she was wearing, they saw her, stretched as she lay on the beach; but cold, bloody, and still with a cigarette stuck in the corner of her mouth." Similarly, disregarding time-order, Katherine Mansfield shifts from the present to the past and back again. As she remarks in connection with "The Weak Heart," "What I feel it needs so peculiarly is a very subtle variation of tense. . . ." Certainly she well understood how to manage such shifting. She writes as the mind works: so why should it not be clear? Excellent illustrations occur in "The Man Without a Temperament" and "Life of Ma Parker"; perhaps the best of all are in "The Daughters of the Late Colonel" and the two long stories about the Burnells—"Prelude" and "At the Bay." Here Linda thinks of her father, of her childhood days in Tasmania, and at once we are off with her mind as it lives over again those experiences she had with him. A careless reader must surely wonder where Linda's father came from and how he happened so suddenly to enter the story.

The development of Katherine Mansfield's skill in story-telling is a subject worthy of careful study. Indeed it seems to me that only those who know the early stories—*In a German Pension* and *The Little Girl*—can fully appreciate the wonder of the later collections—*Bliss, The Garden Party,* and *The Doves' Nest*—or can fully understand what Katherine Mansfield achieved and how unusual was her development. It is not primarily a question of mere writing in the earlier stories, not only a matter of technical immaturity, in, for instance, the all-important matter of exposition. It is rather a journalistic touch, a cynical exaggeration, a delight in smart cleverness for its own sake, all of which was later very definitely outgrown. Many of the *Pension* stories are told in the first person. "I" is a somewhat aloof, superior, cynical young person who, for example, considers child-bearing "the most ignominious of all professions." Later Katherine Mansfield's ideal was purely objective. As she says in her journal, "I can't tell the truth about Aunt Anne unless I am free to enter into her life without self-consciousness." . . .

Source: Edward Wagenknecht, "Katherine Mansfield," in *The Critical Response to Katherine Mansfield*, edited by Jan Pilditch, Greenwood Press, 1996, pp. 22–24.

Rhoda B. Nathan

In the following excerpt, Nathan discusses Mansfield's short stories as a whole.

Assessing an artist's contribution to his field is tricky at best. The subject must be scrutinized in his time, in the universal terms of his craft, for his original work, and in his derivative techniques. He must be measured against other practitioners of the genre, those past and contemporaneous. His good work must be separated from his mediocre efforts, his early work from his last. Periods of productivity must be weighed against arid patches in his creative landscape. Katherine Mansfield is not exempt from such treatment. Even the negative critical judgment of colleagues and critics in her day must be counterbalanced against favorable reviews. For example, her friend and fellow writer Virginia Woolf wrote this about her less than half a year after her death: "While she possessed the most amazing *senses* of her generation . . . she was as weak as water when she had to use her mind." The truth or falsity of Woolf's harsh criticism must be balanced against the indisputable fact that Mansfield's short stories continue to be anthologized frequently in our own day while those of her more distinguished rival do not.

In one area, at least, the task of critical evaluation is simplified by the author's scope. Mansfield, unlike most of her colleagues, wrote only short stories. Although she began one full-length novel, *Juliet*, she abandoned it. Notes in her *Journal* hint at another novel extending the New Zealand theme and tentatively called *Karori*, but nothing came of it. Her contribution was to the short story only. She is probably unique in this distinction. There is scarcely a writer of her time, and few since, who did not go on to write at least one novel. Whether she lacked the broader powers and vision to construct novels, as some of her detractors have hinted, is moot. The stories she left are sufficient. Berating her for failing to write at least one distinguished novel is analogous to faulting the composer Hugo Wolf,

> HER NARRATION IS ECONOMICAL AND
> COLORFUL, RARELY DISCURSIVE. HER MOST
> SUCCESSFUL STORIES ARE THOSE THAT ORIGINATE
> IN HER OWN CHILDHOOD, HER LOVE AFFAIRS AND
> MARRIAGES, AND THE CHARACTERS SHE
> ENCOUNTERED IN HER TRAVELS."

master of the German art song, or lied, for not writing at least one celebrated opera.

The conventionality of Mansfield's fiction—the term is not used in a pejorative senses—is another useful factor in limiting and directing critical evaluation. All the standard elements of the short story are present in most of her fiction in harmonious balance, much as the well-crafted stories of specialists such as J. F. Powers, J. D. Salinger, and John Updike during their *New Yorker* period. When Mansfield was experimental, it was primarily in her composition of a handful of spoken monologues, often constructed as flashbacks that reveal character, plot, theme, and tone. Her best short stories, "Miss Brill," "The Garden Party," "Bliss," and "The Dill Pickle," among others, are narrated conventionally from a subjective point of view. They comprise integrated elements of the short story as it has been defined by theorists such as Poe in the nineteenth century and Frank O'Connor in the twentieth.

The single most palpable quality permeating Mansfield's stories is her perfectionism. The exemplary New Zealand cycle, episode by episode, through character and conflict, develops with single-minded intensity a unified theme of complex family life recollected through a veil of nostalgia for an unrecoverable past. The action varies but the setting is remarkably unified, supporting the controlled tone of longing. In its finished state, "Prelude" offers the clearest evidence of its author's relentless polishing. Compared to "The Aloe," the original version of the story written just a year earlier, the final story shows clear evidence of "much reshaping and rewriting," according to Murry's introductory essay. In short order the reader discovers the

truth of Murry's description of the first version as "less perfect," and agrees with him that the belated publication of "The Aloe" many years after Mansfield's death does indeed offer the "more critically minded a unique opportunity for studying Katherine Mansfield's method of work."

. . . As well plotted and carefully constructed as Mansfield's stories are, they cannot be confined to any single tradition. The two recognized historical "schools" are the psychological tradition laid down by Poe and the socially observant tradition associated with Maupassant. There are other categories as well: the plotted and the plotless story, the stories of initiation, symbolist stories, and so on. The categories are both endless and overlapping, but Mansfield, like other writers, cannot be confined to any single formula, whether it be the rules set down in Poe's "The Philosophy of Composition," Chekhov's social realism, James's psychological realism, Maurice Maeterlinck's symbolism, or Joyce's stream-of-consciousness technique. Her short stories do not fit into any single framework, any more than does the entire body of Cheever's or Updike's short fiction. As she wrote, she continued to experiment. "Her First Ball" and "The Garden Party" are stories of initiation. They are also fully plotted psychological studies. They have some traces of social realism. "Je ne parle pas français" is a rare attempt at plotlessness. The story "Psychology" is not psychological but a fragment designed to produce a "single effect" with "deliberate care" in obedience to the Poe formula.

Mansfield's youthful devotion to Wilde's brittle comedy surely is responsible for the languid witty dialogue in "Marriage à la Mode" and "Bliss." "A Cup of Tea" is the perfect magazine story. It has all the elements required for a popular journal, including a surprise ending. Its slick commercial "feel" does not negate the perfection of its construction. "Poison" and "Taking the Veil" are effective demonstrations of the symbolist credo that states of mind are most effectively conveyed through concrete images. "The Child Who Was Tired," Mansfield's most feeling and conscious tribute to Chekhov's social realism, is actually far removed from Chekhov's profound but abstract social concern. Chekhov's "Sleepy" expresses his outrage against societal abuse; it is a protest against oppression and close to political socialism. Mansfield's version is more personal and limited. Her sad story focuses on the child herself as a helpless object of personal cruelty, not social injustice. Her symbolical ending of the child's dream gives the story a twist towards the allegorical. Chekhov's has none of that fanciful quality. His story is close to being a documentary of social inequity, its central character serving as an instructive example of victimization.

The following stories reveal still other debts to traditional sources even as they bear the stamp of her originality. "The Canary," a first-person oral monologue to an unseen audience, is reminiscent of Poe's unidentified monologists whose narrations explain their current emotional state in terms of their past history. The speaker in "The Canary" begins: "You see that big nail to the right of the front door? I can scarcely look at it now and yet I could not bear to take it out." The story is secondary to the tone and symbolism. The speaker is highly agitated. Her loneliness is implicit in her attachment to the dead bird, itself a symbol of her yearning for beauty in a pinched sterile life. The nail that held the suspended cage remains on the wall as a symbol of her loss and pain. It is a nail driven through her heart.

In "The Garden Party" also, literal objects have a wider symbolic reverberation than their limited objective selves. When Laura Sheridan leaves the party on her mission to the bereaved family of the dead man, "the kisses, voices, tinkling spoons, laughter, the smell of crushed grass [are] somehow inside her." As the great lawn recedes in the distance behind her, a newer unfamiliar reality is symbolized by the narrow dark lane leading to the cramped hovel in her line of vision. "Women in shawls and men's tweed caps" supplant the trailing skirts and frock coats of the afternoon's festivities. Shadows replace sunlight, silence follows the murmur of tea-party chatter. Only the large garden-party hat, still propped on Laura's bowed head, remains constant, worn in the dusk as a badge of penance as it has been worn in daylight as a symbol of her corruption.

Socially observant narrative that makes its point through irony in the Maupassant tradition may be discerned in plotted stories like "Sixpence." Mrs. Bendall, a timid woman, is bullied by Mrs. Spears, an overbearing visitor, into goading her husband to whip their beloved small son. The child's infraction is minor, and the family is loving and forgiving. Under subtle criticism of her "superior" neighbor, Mrs. Bendall is made to feel incompetent and lax in the performance of her "moral" duty, introducing a new and ugly atmosphere into her peaceful home. Her tired husband, angry at being assaulted by his overwrought wife to do *his* duty as a man, whips the child, and is crushed by the child's forbearance in his pain and humiliation. The worm has been found in the apple. The child forgives his parents but their happiness has vanished.

The irony of the serpent's evil in this Eden is implicit in the throwaway remark about Mrs. Spears's own "exemplary" sons. They have indeed attained perfection in deportment, but it is noted that they prefer to play outside their home, in the toolshed, behind the kennel, even in the trash bin. Her callers marvel that "you would never know there was a child in the house." Mrs. Bendall then recalls that "in the front hall of her neighbor's well-run home, under a picture of fat, cherry old monks fishing by the riverside, there was a thick dark horsewhip."

The contrast between Mrs. Spears's "soft sugary voice" and the repeated brutal whippings that have shaped her children's decorum is an irony lost on Mrs. Bendall but not on the reader. Her visitor's hypocrisy in the execution of her maternal obligation is yet another unnoted irony. Does Mrs. Spears administer the whippings? Of course not. It would be unseemly for a mother, the symbol of nurture. Who does it then? Why, their father, of course—the respected symbol of authority. Ironically, just as Mrs. Bendell, under the influence of her persuasive friend, is working herself up to persuading her husband to inflict corporal punishment on his beloved child, he "staggers up the hot concrete steps.... hot, dusty, tired out," and spoiling for a fight. He needs no convincing. "He felt like a man in a dark net. And now he wanted to beat Dicky. Yes, damn it, he wanted to beat something." The story ends on yet another ironic note. The beaten child, holding up his face in forgiveness, wipes out the father's rage and accepts the sixpence offered him in penance by his father, who is now beating himself for his unprecedented act of brutality.

This is a story crammed with irony. Whereas little Dicky Bendall makes his small mischief in the open, Mrs. Spears's model sons do theirs secretly, away from the bullwhip. In the arena of conflict the tables are turned and turned again. The timid mother is ironically stripped of authority in her own home and is forced into violating her principles. The "superior" guest is exposed as inferior in human terms. All the plotting of the two women to force the man to an act abhorrent to his nature proves to be unnecessary. He has come home in a brutalized condition and was ready to assault someone. "Sixpence" is withal a touching story in its understanding of frailty and the ironies of interpersonal maneuvering for power. The symbols of the omnipresent whip, the sugary voice, and the sixpence coin are effective emblems of control and subordination. It is worth noting that Mansfield must have taken Chekhov's observation about "props" in the theater seriously and adapted them to her own use of symbols. His remark that the audience may be sure that the gun hanging on the wall in the first act is bound to go off in the third is applicable to Mansfield's use of emblems, from the first mention of the tight headband on Mr. Bendall's head to the angry pucker left by his hat when he beats his child at the end.

Mansfield culled her characters from all levels of society, from the privileged station of the Sheridans to the shabby rooms of Ma Parker, from New Zealand to the Continent, from the beefy Germans of the Bavarian Alps to the fleshless spinsters of post-Victorian England. Her themes are manifold. Like all serious writers she tried to tell the truth about her own life, the life about her, and the imagined life. In short, her contribution to the genre of the short story cannot be neatly categorized. She ranged far and she roamed freely, but certain conclusions may be drawn as a guide to the basic constants in her fiction.

Her technique is invariably efflorescent—from the bud to the flower, so to speak. She begins with a single incident or clue, such as the landlady's intrusion into Miss Ada Moss's room in "Pictures" or the unblemished weather on the day of the Sheridans' garden party. We take it on faith that the tension in the story will derive from that single bit of information. She rarely disappoints us. She builds on the fragment layer by layer, establishing the mood—almost always an atmosphere of psychological tension—until the small incident, which Henry James used to call the "germ," unfolds into crisis, climax, and resolution.

A prevailing mood of tension is a constant in Mansfield's work. Unlike her literary model Chekhov, who did little by way of manipulation after he laid down the bare facts of his

characters' troubles, she adds, alters, and controls. Miss Brill's illusory self-image is shattered when she is forced to confront herself in a glass held up by her detractors. Laura Sheridan's innocence is destroyed step by step in a calculated series of ugly events that oblige her to confront the truth about her insulated life and the tragedy of others. The unsuspecting lover in "Poison" is forced by an insignificant incident—his mistress's casual inquiry about the mail—to face her inconstancy. Unrelieved tension is the governing mood of the allegorical "A Suburban Fairy Tale," generated by irremediably obtuse parents and their imaginative child.

In stories such as "Prelude," "Her First Ball," "The Doll's House," and "Bliss," tension is created through a contrived alternation between fulfillment and deprivation, satisfaction and yearning, self-indulgence and guilt. Their total sustained effect is one of delicate balance between opposing forces that prevail to the end. Witness the unanswerable question Bertha asks at the end of "Bliss" and Laura's unfinished question at the end of "The Garden Party." They keep their climate of mystery to the very end because their underlying tension is unresolved.

Finally, Mansfield's stories are usually "good reads." Their meaning is accessible even to the general reader who does not wish to trouble his head about the hidden significance in her fables. Their point of view is almost uniformly subjective, and their dialogue is witty, often sparkling. Her narration is economical and colorful, rarely discursive. Her most successful stories are those that originate in her own childhood, her love affairs and marriages, and the characters she encountered in her travels. Her least successful stories are static monologues such as "A Married Man's Story" and "The Lady's Maid." Taking Brander Matthews's definition of the true short story as "complete and self-contained" and marked by a "single effect," we may conclude that Mansfield's finest stories have the requisite "totality" of the prescription. If she failed to rise to James's mandarin detachment, or Chekhov's selfless compassion, or Joyce's psychological intensity, she left at least two dozen works of brilliance and polish and a smaller number of perfect stories.

Source: Rhoda B. Nathan, "'With Deliberate Care': The Mansfield Short Story," in *Critical Essays on Katherine Mansfield*, edited by Rhoda B. Nathan, G. K. Hall, 1993, pp. 93–94, 96–99.

SOURCES

Bolt, Christine, "The War, the Vote, and After: Doldrums and New Departures," in *The Women's Movements in the United States and Britain from the 1790s to the 1920s*, University of Massachusetts Press, 1993, pp. 236–76.

Borland, Sophie, "Health Gap between Rich and Poor 'Bigger Than Any Time since 1920s,'" in *Daily Mail* (London, England) online, July 23, 2010, http://www.dailymail.co.uk/news/article-1296992/Health-gap-rich-poor-bigger-time-1920s.html (accessed September 12, 2013).

"A Brief History of Divorce," in *Guardian* (London, England), September 18, 2009, http://www.theguardian.com/lifeandstyle/2009/sep/19/divorce-law-history/ (accessed September 12, 2013).

"Contraception: Patterns of Use Factsheet," Family Planning Association website, November 2007, http://www.fpa.org.uk/factsheets/contraception-patterns-use (accessed September 12, 2013).

Dupree, Marguerite, "The Provision of Social Services," in *The Cambridge Urban History of Britain*, Vol. 3, *1840–1950*, edited by Martin Daunton, Cambridge University Press, 2000, pp. 351–94.

Gindin, James, "Katherine Mansfield," in *Dictionary of Literary Biography*, Vol. 162, *British Short Fiction Writers, 1915–1945*, edited by John H. Rogers, Gale Research, 1996, pp. 209–26.

Gunsteren, Julia van, Introduction to *Katherine Mansfield and Literary Impressionism*, Rodopi, 1990, pp. 9–28.

Laybourn, Keith, ed., "Britain on the Breadline: Slump, Poverty and the Politics of Realignment during the Inter-War Years, 1918–39," in *Modern Britain since 1906: A Reader*, I. B. Tauris, 1999, pp. 105–35.

MacInnes, Tom, "UK Poverty: The Facts Considered," in *Guardian* (London, England) online, December 2, 2011, http://www.theguardian.com/news/datablog/2011/dec/02/poverty-working-fmailies-with-children-uk (accessed September 12, 2013).

Mansfield, Katherine, "A Cup of Tea," in *The Collected Stories of Katherine Mansfield*, Wordsworth Classics, 2006, pp. 332–38.

"Modernism," in *Dictionary of Literary Terms*, edited by Kathleen Morner and Ralph Rausch, National Text-book, 1994, p. 138.

"Modernism," Literature Network, http://www.online-literature.com/periods/modernism.php (accessed September 12, 2013).

Morrow, Patrick D., "Stories from the Posthumous Collection, *The Dove's Nest and Other Stories*," in *Katherine Mansfield's Fiction*, Bowling Green State University Press, 1993, pp. 94–113.

O'Sullivan, Vincent, "The Magnet Chain: Notes and Approaches to K.M.," in *The Critical Response to Katherine Mansfield*, edited by Jan Pilditch, Greenwood Press, 1996, pp. 129–54.

Perez, Ana Belen Lopez, "'A City of One's Own': Women, Social Class and London in Katherine Mansfield's Short Stories," in *Katherine Mansfield and Literary Modernism*, edited by Janet Wilson, Gerri Kimber, and Susan Reid, Continuum International Publishing Group, 2011, pp. 128–38.

Sedghi, Ami, and Simon Rogers, "Divorce Rates Data, 1858 to Now: How Has It Changed?," in *Guardian* (London, England) online, December 20, 2012, http://www.theguardian.com/news/datablog/2010/jan/28/divorce-rates-marriage-ons (accessed September 12, 2013).

Smith, Angela, ed., "A Chronology of Katherine Mansfield," in *Katherine Mansfield: Selected Stories*, Oxford University Press, 2002, pp. xxxviii–xli.

FURTHER READING

Baldick, Chris, *Literature of the 1920s: Writers among the Ruins*, Edinburgh University Press, 2012.

Baldick offers a survey of literary trends throughout the 1920s, discussing modernism, literary fiction, and genre fiction and the influence of social issues and historical events on the development of fiction during this time.

Bonikowski, Wyatt, *Shell Shock and the Modernist Imagination: The Death Drive in Post–World War I British Fiction*, Ashgate Publishing, 2012.

Bonikowski analyzes post–World War I fiction, demonstrating the ways in which the traumas of the war influenced the fiction of modernist writers such as Ford Madox Ford and Virginia Woolf, among others.

Drury, Elizabeth, and Philippa Lewis, *Forgotten London: A Picture of Life in the 1920s*, Batsford, 2011.

Drury and Lewis's work incorporates over 250 photographs taken throughout the 1920s in London. They offer a visual account of daily life in the city and provide representations of a variety of lifestyles and social classes.

Moran, Patricia, *Word of Mouth: Body Language in Katherine Mansfield and Virginia Woolf*, University of Virginia Press, 1996.

Moran studies the language and imagery surrounding the human body as well as eating, breathing, and physical longing in the works of Woolf and Mansfield. Moran demonstrates the ways in which these elements of the authors' works reveal anxieties rooted in notions of female gender identity.

Smith, Angela, *Katherine Mansfield: A Literary Life*, Palgrave, 2000.

Smith's biography of Mansfield examines the author's journey as an artist, tracing her literary influences and discussing the impact of her personal life on her fiction.

SUGGESTED SEARCH TERMS

Katherine Mansfield AND A Cup of Tea

Katherine Mansfield AND literary impressionism

Katherine Mansfield AND modernism

Katherine Mansfield AND feminism

modernism AND World War I

Great Britain AND 1920s AND poverty

British social class AND interwar years

Katherine Mansfield AND Virginia Woolf

Katherine Mansfield AND D. H. Lawrence

British modernist fiction AND short story

The Infant Prodigy

THOMAS MANN

1903

"The Infant Prodigy" is one of Thomas Mann's best-known short stories. It describes the performance of an eight-year-old Greek musical prodigy with the improbable name of Bibi Saccellaphylaccas. Much of its charm derives from it humorous satire of social types of the bourgeois culture of pre–World War I Europe (with a hint of the sinister fascism that would arise from the wreckage of that culture after the war). But it is also a serious meditation on the nature of art. Its main themes are the necessary artificiality and manipulative character of performance and the consequent inability of the performer to express art genuinely to his audience. The story, originally published in German as "Das Wunderkind" in 1903, can be found in English in the Mann collection *Stories of Three Decades* (1936), translated by H. T. Lowe-Porter.

AUTHOR BIOGRAPHY

Mann was born on June 6, 1875, in the German city of Lübeck. Mann's father was a successful merchant and, after his early death in 1891, left his family well provided for. Mann received a gymnasium (prep-school) education and studied at several universities in Munich without taking a degree. He chose to pursue a career as a journalist and began publishing occasional pieces in the 1890s, with his first short story, "Little Herr

Thomas Mann (© MARKA / Alamy)

Friedemann," appearing in 1898. The successful publication of his first novel, *Buddenbrooks*, in 1901 established his career as a writer.

"The Infant Prodigy" came at a turning point in Mann's career, marking the beginning of a new relationship between artist and art. The story was the product of the moment when he changed from a struggling to a sought-after writer, as he commented in a letter to a friend (cited in Bürgin and Mayer) just three weeks before the story was published:

> I am no longer sitting in my little room alone, free and without obligations, creating art for art's sake. I feel as though I have fallen within range of an immense spotlight which has made me visible to the public eye and that I am now burdened with the responsibility of using my talents, which I have been foolish enough to reveal to others. The *Neue Freie Presse* has sent a telegram requesting a short story from my precious pen for their precious Christmas issue. Seriously, they have done just that, and after the second telegram I have promised them some sort of literary trifle.

That short story, published in Vienna's *Neue Freie Presse* on December 25, 1903, was "Das Wunderkind." Mann nevertheless considered the finished story successful. It immediately became a

popular favorite and a regular feature of his public readings.

Mann married in 1905 and went on to an artistically and professionally successful career, producing novels such as *The Magic Mountain* (*Der Zauberberg*, 1924) and *Doktor Faustus* (1947). His works deal with abstruse philosophical issues that are at the same time at the center of human life, such as the interplay of intellectual and emotional growth and the drive for artistic creativity. He was awarded the Nobel Prize for Literature in 1929.

Originally highly conservative in outlook, Mann's consciousness was raised by the experience of living though the cultural disaster of the First World War and realizing how the structure of prewar European society had led to its own downfall. Thereafter, Mann became increasingly progressive and was a supporter of the Weimar Republic that replaced the German monarchy in 1919. In 1930 Mann turned his celebrity against the growing power of the Nazi Party in German politics in a series of public speeches. Happening to be on vacation in Switzerland when Hitler came to power in 1933, he considered it would be safer not to return to his native country. By a similar coincidence, he was delivering a lecture at Princeton University in 1936 when Nazi Germany annexed Austria and, considering it would be better to leave Europe altogether, he took an appointment teaching at the school. During the Second World War he recorded a number of propaganda addresses broadcast by radio into Germany. After the war he moved to Kilchberg, Switzerland (a suburb of Zürich), where he died of atherosclerosis on August 12, 1955.

PLOT SUMMARY

"The Infant Prodigy" opens with the main character, Bibi Saccellaphylaccas, entering a concert hall. The audience immediately becomes still, much anticipating the young piano virtuoso's performance. The concert hall itself is richly decorated, as is young Bibi. Although he is quite young, only eight years old, he is dressed in silk, and it is noted that at a break in the white silk on his legs, the dark brown color of his skin can be seen, for the child is Greek. It is implied that the concert audience is impressed simply because those in attendance were told that they would be impressed by this young prodigy.

Despite Bibi's rather adult dress, he exudes the innocence of childhood, but also with a tired expression and facial lines that come with aging. His exact age is unknown; his countenance makes him appear older than he is, but the audience believes him to be seven, so the narrator of the story gives his age as eight and remarks that the audience is willing to believe whatever they are told about him because he is a prodigy and also because an average audience will believe anything it is told.

When the child sits down to play, the reader learns that the entire music program consists of his own compositions. While Bibi is not yet capable of scoring the compositions, the impresario of the show suggests in the program that the music has artistic merit nonetheless. The narrator suggests that this interpretation of the child's compositions presents itself as an objective critical view of the music's worth but is really designed to, again, shape the audience's opinion in favor of the music.

Bibi sits down to play at his well-traveled piano. It is his own piano, specially adapted so that his feet can reach the pedals. When the child lifts his hand to play, it is noted that while the hand itself looks like the hand of a child, the wrist is strong, muscled and well developed, rather like an adult's wrist.

As he prepares to begin, it becomes clear that as young as he is, Bibi knows he has a role to play. He knows that he must charm the audience and persuade them to be amazed by his playing. However, inside his young heart, Bibi truly loves to play the piano. He feels an emotion that he knows he cannot express to the audience, so he does not try to do that. The audience breathlessly awaits the music as Bibi deliberately hesitates. He begins to play, and the audience relaxes to listen.

At this point the narrative shifts to describe the theater more fully—its size, its grandeur, its excessive decor. Despite the hall's immense size, not a seat in the auditorium is empty; in fact, people are standing in the aisles and at the back of the concert hall as well. The cost for those seated at the front of the auditorium was quite high, and indeed the people in attendance are of the best classes of society. It is suggested that those from the higher classes are motivated to appreciate the music more than are those of lower social classes; even children of the upper class are there, as if their parents believe that is important for them to have the chance to appreciate the performance of a prodigy.

Contrasted with these people is Bibi's mother—a severely overweight, heavily powdered woman who wears a feather in her hair. Bibi's impresario—that is, his manager—sits next to his mother, and he has a rather exotic appearance and large gold buttons on his cuffs. The royalty of the area is also in attendance, an older, wrinkled princess who sits in a chair that is something like a throne, with a Persian rug at her feet. She sits deep in her comfortable chair, whereas her attendant lady, being only an attendant, sits at strict attention. The princess has the luxury of comfort, but the lady-in-waiting does not have that luxury.

Bibi plays powerfully and well, with a bit of theater added to the performance in order to keep command of his audience. When he finishes playing a piece, he gets off the stool and awaits the applause, which the audience delivers enthusiastically. Bibi takes three curtain calls before he sits down again to play. When, after his *Rêverie*, the next piece, *Le Hibou et les moineux* (The owl and the sparrows), is finished, he receives an ovation and is called out four times; a worker at the theater presents him with three laurel wreaths, which Bibi graciously accepts. Even the princess is impressed with his performance.

Bibi pretends to admire the wreaths, though he has seen their likes many times before. He sits down to play more. Internally, he is thinking about a better piece he will soon play; yet he knows the audience will not appreciate it as much as *Le Hibou*, which, being the first thing he ever composed, he now finds silly. Still, he knows that he must give the audience what it wants.

As he plays, a sharp distinction is drawn between Bibi, who may indeed be a prodigy and a genius, and the audience members, who, despite their class or lack of it, are all equivalently ignorant. They are different from him, and while he has moments of separateness from them while he plays, he looks at them, and the sight of them reminds him that he has a responsibility to them. He knows that they are unable to fully appreciate what he is doing for them; that they cannot understand the subtleties of variation and style; only he alone in the whole hall can understand that.

The audience members, meanwhile, are making judgments of their own. One gentleman thinks that Bibi's gift is a miracle, a great blessing from God, and that no amount of work or genius will counteract what God gives or withholds. This is the man's comfort to himself for not having any special gifts or talents. A businessman thinks to himself that Bibi plays pretty well and, despite the cost of the whole affair, has probably made a good profit, so it is good business. A piano teacher in the audience acknowledges that while Bibi has talent, his technique is off, and if he were her student, she would punish him. A girl in the audience filters the music through her emotions, wondering how something so passionate could be unconnected to romantic love. A military officer equates Bibi's artistic talent with a good day's work, much like his own, and since each has attended to his duty, the officer deems Bibi worthy of his respect. The music critic, somewhat cynically, seems to have some insight into Bibi's genius as well as his showmanship but also acknowledges that he cannot of course publish the harsher critical truths he knows to be true.

The concert program is finally over. Bibi is presented with more tributes, more wreaths and bouquets of flowers, so many that he cannot possibly hold them all. He has to come out from behind the curtain many times before the audience is satisfied. The audience approves with even louder applause when Bibi's manager kisses him, and the music critic notes to himself that the action was probably more perfunctory than given out of true affection. The kiss was given because the audience wanted to see it.

Bibi plays one more time; it is a piece which turns into the Greek national anthem. The music critic thinks to himself that it is rather gimmicky and feels he should criticize it as inartistic in his write-up of the performance, but knows that he too is at the mercy of an audience, and so he will not criticize it.

After the concert, Bibi makes his way to his mother and his manager. A large group forms around him, while another forms around the princess. Bibi is taken to meet the princess, who questions him about his talent; he answers her politely but thinks she is as ignorant as everyone else around him. As the people start to leave, the music teacher, despite Bibi's success with the audience, still criticizes his playing. No one acknowledges her.

At this point, the narrative shifts away from Bibi to members of the audience: a beautiful young woman and her two vain brothers; a girl with messy hair who believes herself to be a

genius; and the old man who believes Bibi's talent is God's gift, given to the child but not to him. The girl with the messy hair observes the beautiful woman and her two brothers and feels she hates them, but she watches them until they turn the corner and are out of sight.

CHARACTERS

Lieutenant Adolf

Adolf is one of the brothers of the elegant young lady, whom he thinks pompous because she adopts an air of superiority over him—perhaps because she is his older sister, as she seems to be, and does not appreciate his identity as an officer. Like his sister, he makes no comment on Bibi, but he does inspire the only allusion to popular music (specifically, via diasporic African dance) in the story.

Applauder

The person who leads the audience in applauding Bibi when he takes the stage is referred to as a natural mob leader. This suggests the presence of a *claque*, a group of professionals skilled at influencing the applause and responsiveness of an audience at a public performance. Although such groups have existed since antiquity, they became especially prevalent in the nineteenth century as performances in front of large bourgeois audiences became increasingly important. Claques existed in every large city in Europe and the United States. At Bibi's concert, the impresario has perhaps hired a claque, led by the person who initiates the opening round of applause. This person has a greater importance than the line and a half devoted to him or her portends, since this is the first sign that the story will concern itself with the constructed and manipulative nature of performance.

Audience

The audience as a whole functions as a single character in "The Infant Prodigy," serving as an antagonist to Bibi, at least in his and their internal monologues. Much of the text of the story consists of the narrator's revelations of the private thoughts and reactions of individual audience members (mostly unnamed), but these can be conceived of as specific instances of the more general case. Indeed, after Bibi's first piece, the narrator presents thoughts collectively ascribed to the foremost people in the audience: "Look what slim little hips he has! Clap, clap! Hurrah, bravo, little chap, Saccophylax or whatever your name is! Wait, let me take off my gloves—what a little devil of a chap he is!" The audience's inability to properly articulate the performer's name (ironically from a contemporary perspective, they render it closer to ancient Greek, which many of them would have studied in school) reveals the failure of the audience to even grasp his artistic nature, and exposes the inanity of their evaluation of the artist. Calling Bibi a "devil" probably alludes to the Mephisophelean facet of the stage persona of Franz Liszt, the first solo performer in the modern sense, who exploited romantic ideas about the devil and possession.

Businessman

The businessman evaluates Bibi's performance entirely in economic terms, calculating that from the seated concertgoers alone, the income must have cleared six hundred marks (for comparison, Mann noted in his diary how well pleased he was to have received an advance of four hundred marks for his 1901 novel *Buddenbrooks*—both figures are within the range of a year's middle-class income).

Critic

One of the audience members is the critic of a local newspaper or magazine. He is often thought to represent Mann's most authentic voice in the story. The critic is "an elderly man in a shiny black coat and turned-up trousers splashed with mud." The absence of mud on anyone else's clothes (at least, no other mud is mentioned) would indicate that he may have worn the pants a number of times without washing them, or perhaps indifferently traipsed over muddy ground on the way there; either way, he is unconcerned with externals. He alone seems to understand the true character of Bibi's performance: that while it is true artistry, that alone is irrelevant to the mass audience that must still be persuaded of its greatness through deception and manipulation, because that is the only way the masses can understand it. He is just as conscious as Bibi that it is impossible to communicate these insights to his own audience. He muses, "Of course I can't write all that, it is too good. Of course, I should have been an artist myself if I had not seen through the whole business so clearly." This seems at first like an excuse for his own failure as an artist—the stereotype of

the critic as a failed artist—but it is also a deeper recognition of the fact that the performer must have the qualities of the deceiver and the artist in equal measure.

Girl with Untidy Hair

The girl with untidy hair forms a couple with the gloomy-faced youth. As she leaves the concert hall she observes, "We are all infant prodigies, we artists." In the context, this perhaps means that she realizes that the persona of the artist is quite different from his real identity, which cannot be communicated through art.

Impresario

Unnamed like most of the characters in "The Infant Prodigy," the impresario is Bibi's manager, who is responsible for the business aspects of Bibi's concert tour. The story especially highlights his careful orchestration of every aspect of the performance, except its musical quality, in order to impress and satisfy the audience. From his viewpoint, the audience must be controlled and made to understand that it is seeing an exhibition of real artistry, which it would not recognize in and of itself. He is Bibi's teacher in this art as well as, figuratively speaking, his creator.

Bibi is not responsible for showing the audience that his performance possesses "real artistic significance," but rather the impresario is responsible for telling them so in the program, so that they will believe it whether they are capable of understanding it or not. The statement that "the programme sounded as though the impresario had wrested these concessions from his critical nature after a hard struggle" suggests a reluctance to deal in art at all rather than pure showmanship.

Officer

A military officer in the audience is obsessed with his own rank in the social order, and thus accords Bibi respect according to his implicit rank as an artist.

Old Gentleman

The old man, one of the audience members, like the others evaluates Bibi entirely though comparison with his own experience—the seeming ease with which Bibi is making his career being compared to the old man's failure to seriously study the piano as a child and the presumed struggle (likely in business, since he is successful enough to attend the concert) that he has had in life. He thinks of Bibi as a kind of Christ child, and indeed he is, as a performer, a mediator between art (the divine) and audience. Although it is not fully represented in the translation, his gaudy taste, his inexperience with music, and above all the common form of German he speaks—or rather thinks—mark him as an outsider among the aristocratic class that makes up the audience.

Piano-Teacher

One of the audience members is an elderly female piano teacher. She evaluates Bibi's performance in terms of her own pedagogical technique, oblivious to the fact that Bibi's skill as a pianist far exceeds that of her own child students. She is so presumptuously reflective, and perhaps so ignorant of her own profession, that she mistakenly believes that one of Bibi's pieces is by Chopin.

Princess

One of the attendees is an aged princess, the leader of the fashionable set in the unnamed city where the concert takes place. Her influence is vital for promoting Bibi's success, but it is just as important for her to have an opportunity to hold court and be seen as a patron of the arts, helping to solidify her own identity.

Princess's Lady-in-Waiting

The princess is attended by a lady who is perhaps more a social secretary than a lady-in-waiting.

Bibi Saccellaphylaccas

Bibi is the title character of "The Infant Prodigy." He is an eight-year-old musical prodigy who can both perform and compose on a level of equality with adult musicians. Bibi reconciles within his name the prosaic common man, in the perfectly ordinary name (or nickname) Bibi, and the artist, in the imposing exoticism of his Greek surname. Saccellaphylaccas (a name evidently invented by Mann) is improbably composed of the Greek roots for *shield* and *protection*, suggesting that the sacredness of the art has to be defended from the common herd; yet in the name as a whole, art is indiscriminately mixed with the common man, since art can hardly be said to exist without its audience. Bibi reconciles other paradoxes within himself. He has the soft face of a child, but it is lined and tired like that of an old world-weary man. Because he is just a boy, a romantically piqued teenage girl in the audience rejects the idea of Bibi as a romantic subject, since a kiss from him would be like a kiss from her little brother; but after the climax of the performance,

the impresario kisses him on the lips, sending a galvanizing charge through the audience.

Bibi is quite conscious that he is constructing a performance to control and manipulate the response of the audience, even while he is confident in the artistic worth of his performance. Yet, contemptuous of the audience's ability to appreciate the true worth of his performance, he demonstrates a cynicism far beyond his years. For him the audience is composed of "idiots" who must be controlled and led, not equals capable of appreciating his art. Indeed, Bibi's insight must be closer to Mann's own than to an eight-year-old's, prodigy or not.

Bibi Saccellaphylaccas's Mother

Bibi's mother accompanies her young son as his guardian; about his father the narrator says nothing. She naturally sits in the front row at the performance but seems a little out of place. Most likely she comes from a lower class than the other audience members.

Young Girl

A girl in the audience, called young but seeming adolescent or teenaged, rejects Bibi as a romantic subject because he is too young. Although she has the ignorance of youth, she also has the quick, open imagination of youth, speculating that Bibi might represent "passion all by itself, without any earthly object," a typically Neoplatonic idea that builds up the portrayal of Bibi as an inspired artist.

Young Lady

An aristocratic young woman in the audience picks up her cloak and fur shoes from the coat check after the performance. She seems to have been so unimpressed that she makes no comment at all about Bibi or his music.

THEMES

Music

In the present day musical performance has a standard character. An audience comes to a concert hall, focuses attention on the performance, especially on a soloist or a soloist leading a larger group of musicians, and engages in a dialogue with the performer through a well-understood language of adulation and gratitude denoted by applause, bows, curtain calls, standing ovations,

TOPICS FOR FURTHER STUDY

- Virginia Euwer Wolff's *The Mozart Season* (1991) is a young-adult novel about a child prodigy. Write a paper comparing the insight into the psychology of an infant prodigy presented in that novel with Mann's ideas in "The Infant Prodigy."

- Find words or phrases in the English translation of Mann's "The Infant Prodigy" that seem unusual or out of place to you, and perform n-gram searches (http://books.google.com/ngrams) to find how the uses of these terms have changed over time. Using screen captures of your results (or repeating the searches live) give a report on your findings and their significance to your class.

- The ethos of self-sacrifice that characterized the Japanese armed forces in World War II, exemplified above all in the kamikaze pilots, is often, but wrongly, attributed to the traditional Japanese chivalric code of Bushido or some form of Buddhist philosophy, but actually derived from German romanticism, which was the dominant cultural influence among Japanese intellectuals of the day. This is reflected in *Kamikaze Diaries: Reflections of Japanese Student Soldiers*, translated by Emiko Ohnuki-Tierney in 2006 from the diaries of several kamikaze pilots, and in the 2002 monograph by the same author,

Kamikaze, Cherry Blossoms, and Nationalisms: The Militarization of Aesthetics in Japanese History. The writings of Mann, despite his staunch opposition to fascism, were a chief conduit of the German literary and philosophical tradition to these young Japanese men. Write a paper comparing their views of Mann with the views Mann himself expressed during the war, in his lecture series published as *The Coming Victory of Democracy* (1938) and his propaganda addresses in *Listen, Germany! Twenty-Five Radio Messages to the German People over BBC* (1943).

- Hikari Oe was a Japanese child prodigy in musical composition and is considered one of the leading chamber-music composers in contemporary Japan. He suffers from severe autism and several physical handicaps and can hardly communicate through language. His father is the Nobel Prize–winning novelist Kenzaburo Oe. Themes based on the latter's relationship with his son are frequent in his work, as well as forming the subject of a series of memoirs, beginning with *A Personal Matter* (1964, translated by John Nathan in 1969). Give a report to your class on the course of Hikari Oe's difficult and inspiring life struggle.

and the gift of flowers. This is played out archetypically in "The Infant Prodigy," and modern readers still recognize it on the basis of their own concertgoing experiences. As in any modern concert performance, Bibi's appearance onstage is met with long and thunderous applause, and then when he sits at the piano and raises his hands to the keys, "a breathless stillness reigned in the room—the tense moment before the first note came." His performance is highly theatrical: "With every note Bibi flung himself back from the waist as though he were marching in a triumphal procession." More applause follows the

performance of each piece and rises to a crescendo at the end with repeated curtain calls for Bibi.

To modern audience members this kind of performance probably seems inevitable and universal, but in the past this was far from the case. No matter how gifted, the young Wolfgang Amadeus Mozart (1756–1791) was seen by his patrons as a servant, and so even his performances could not be allowed to unduly dominate the attention of the noble patrons in his audience. As Mozart's biographer Peter Gay notes, "There is a much reproduced painting of 1766 by Michel

Bibi is a prodigy on the piano. *(© GSPhotography | Shutterstock.com)*

Barthélemy Ollivier which shows the ten-year-old Mozart bravely at the keyboard while a select, elegantly garbed assembly help themselves at a lavish buffet table." But Franz Liszt (1811–1886) transformed the nature of performance. Because of its sacred character, religious music has always received more respect than its secular counterpart and had something of the ecstasy of religious experience attached to it. Liszt managed to refashion performance of his secular music into a romantic exaltation that called for rapt silence, the concentration of the audience, and the veneration of the performer as a nearly divine figure. Liszt was able to fundamentally change performance because the audiences had also changed. No longer strictly aristocratic, his audiences were largely bourgeois and were willing to view the concert experience as the purchase of an essentially sacred experience in the form of a secular commodity, rather than mere entertainment they ordered from servants.

Neoplatonism

Performance fascinated Mann. He was highly conscious of the isolation of the artist from the audience by virtue of the act of creativity, which the audience can understand not in the same way as the artist, but only in a comparatively incomplete and superficial way. This is displayed abundantly in the parade of self-centered thoughts of audience members that Mann reveals to the reader in "The Infant Prodigy." But performance is at the same time a point of connection between artist and audience, since it is essentially an act of communication. This more difficult idea Mann expresses in metaphors drawn from Neoplatonism, the school of philosophy that arose in the late Roman Empire and remained dominant in Western civilization down to the Enlightenment. Neoplatonism showed an increased concern with the role of divine and even demonic interactions in the human mind, and used ideas drawn from magic to explain human interactions. As the concert progresses, Bibi takes possession of the audience, like an ancient Greek god possessing a seer or poet:

> He sat and played, so little, so white and shining, against the great black grand piano, elect and alone, above that confused sea of faces, above the heavy, insensitive mass soul, upon which he was labouring to work with his individual, differentiated soul.

Bibi acts on the audience to transform them, like a god remaking the world, and brings the fruition of his artistic endeavor to work in their souls. His soul is described as differentiated, meaning that it looks at what comes prior to the process of creation, namely god, while the mass or undifferentiated soul of the audience looks toward the limit of creation at matter; it is a difference of control and obeisance, or sending and receiving. This process is essentially magic through which thought or language takes on a physical existence, but Mann means it to suggest rather than describe the process that is taking place during the performance. The audience responds to Bibi's performance always with more applause, which finally becomes so thunderous that "a perfect storm arose in the hall." This recalls lightning striking as a metaphor for inspiration, which goes back to Neoplatonic discourse, since lightning is the language in which god is said to communicate to humanity. But in this case the artist is communicating to the audience, making performance a microcosm or repetition of inspiration and creation. The audience responds not only with applause, but with heaps of floral wreaths and bouquets, recalling the flowers that decorated ancient Greek temples during ritual sacrifice. Foremost among these are laurel wreaths, sacred to Apollo, the god of music and inspiration. In particular, the impresario hangs a laurel wreath around Bibi's neck, representing the crowning of the laureate poet (in the most general sense, as creator).

STYLE

Translation

The original German title of Mann's story, "Das Wunderkind," uses familiar enough a loan word in English that it might well have stood without translation. In any case, the original translator, H. T. Lowe-Porter, chose to render it as "The Infant Prodigy." *Wunder* (equivalent to the English *wonder*) suggests something of the miraculous, which is indeed a part of Bibi's character that the translated title does not express. The word *infant* also seems out of place in describing Bibi as an eight-year-old boy. The reason for that lies in the change of language over time. The Google Ngram Viewer allows a researcher to search for a word or phrase in a vast corpus of published books, magazines, and newspapers and sort the results by years. An n-gram search reveals that the phrase *infant prodigy* was about twenty times more common than *child prodigy* in the early 1900s. By the year 2008, however, the balance had changed so that *child prodigy* was about five times as common as *infant prodigy*. Similarly, an ordinary Google search for "infant prodigy" returns about fifty thousand hits, while "child prodigy" returns over eight million hits. So Lowe-Porter was simply following an idiom that now seems dated; the idiom has changed because the word *infant* has become more specialized in its meaning over time.

Realism

Mann is often classed as the last realist, the last great writer of the twentieth century, or at least the last great German writer, to write in the documentary style of the nineteenth-century novelist. On the one hand, this means that he devotes detailed description to the sights and impressions that one would experience as a spectator of a given scene. One might imagine that a well-written newspaper review of Bibi's concert in "The Infant Prodigy" would not be unrecognizably dissimilar from Mann's fiction. But more importantly, the insight that Mann provides into his characters' thoughts and interior lives is equally a report of the probable, not the improbable. The emphasis is on realistic events of everyday life, even if it is the everyday life of people whose lives might be more interesting than the reader's. Realism emerged in the middle of the nineteenth century as a reaction against romanticism and other heightened and stylized transformations of reality in literature. But in Mann's case the more instructive parallel is with the transformation of literature that came after him in the form of modernism. From this perspective, the significance of the realism of "The Infant Prodigy" consists in its sequential narrative of events and Mann's interest in the psychology of his characters.

COMPARE
&
CONTRAST

- **1900s:** Musical performance exists only in the form of public concerts.

  Today: While public performance is still an important aspect of a musical career, most music is experienced through recordings.

- **1900s:** Europe has an ordered, essentially aristocratic social structure.

  Today: While a hierarchy of wealth and power still belies the facade of egalitarianism that exists in the Western democracies, matters of taste and manners are tailored by and to mass audiences, as mediated by business concerns through marketing, rather than dictated by social hierarchy.

- **1900s:** European culture is thoroughly international; movement and travel through western Europe is essentially unrestricted.

  Today: Although Europe is politically united through the European Union and various pacts, to a degree it has not been since the days of the Roman Empire, strong economic and migratory boundaries have been erected in the wake of the world wars and the Cold War.

Modernism

Mann's fiction, however, does show prototypical elements of modernism. Although there is nothing on the surface of "The Infant Prodigy" that seems to break with traditional narrative, Mann nevertheless constructs his narrative out of randomly assembled fragments that strictly speaking occur simultaneously rather than sequentially. The effect can be seen in the narrative's sudden shifts between the fragments of thought of the minor characters, which can be compared to T. S. Eliot's reuse of bits of conversation overheard at random in bars in *The Waste Land* (1922). More particularly, these diverse perspectives do nothing to advance the plot, the single goal of realism, but rather comment upon it, detaching the reader from the narrative. More fundamentally, the overall effect of the story approaches magic realism, inasmuch as its main point is Bibi taking possession of or casting a spell over the audience. This is presented in the traditional language of Neoplatonism, with its discussion of the differentiated and undifferentiated soul, hearkening back to the theme of the occult in romantic literature. But the effect is quite new and different. The reader is not supposed to imagine the reality of the supernatural through the willing suspension of disbelief, but to perceive that the story's metaphors describe a reality that cannot be directly described in language; this reality is worth grappling with because it is a vital part of the human experience that is mysterious precisely because it cannot be commented upon in any ordinary way, but can only be suggested through art.

HISTORICAL CONTEXT

Loris Margaritis

While the familiar career of Mozart as a child prodigy, with its universal appeal, is undeniably one basis for Bibi's character, it has another and more proximate source in Loris Margaritis (1895–1953), a Greek musical prodigy whom Mann had seen on his tour of Germany in 1903 at age nine playing his own compositions for the piano. Margaritis went on to a successful adult career as a pianist and conservatory professor and held various posts in the culture ministries of Greek governments both before and after World War II. His stage appearance in 1903 as recorded in photographs was just as Mann describes Bibi's, wearing a white silk costume that was a cross between contemporary children's clothes and the dress of Mozart's period. Years later,

Bibi is to play to a packed crowd in a concert hall. *(© Oleksii Sagitov / Shutterstock.com)*

Margaritis's wife sent Mann a polite note containing a picture of her husband in the costume of his wunderkind days and the assurance that he had recently discovered and enjoyed reading "The Infant Prodigy."

Antifascism

Perhaps with insufficient perception because he was not yet especially interested in politics per se, Mann was a political and social conservative in 1903 when he wrote "The Infant Prodigy." But he progressively moved to the left throughout his life and became a mortal enemy of the Nazi regime that took over Germany in 1933 and plunged Europe into general war in 1939. As it happens, the seeds of Mann's distrust of fascism are present in his 1903 story. The story begins with the actions of one who may be a claqueur, a professional hired by the impresario to manage the audience's applause and other responses to Bibi's performance. He is described as "a leader of mobs, a born organizer." Surprisingly, this situation allegorizes with great exactness German business interests' efforts to seize control of the government through the use of Hitler

as a demagogue thirty years later. Mann surely means to make a political statement here, showing that he was aware of and concerned about the power of elite classes to perpetuate their control of society through manipulation of the masses, whose broader interests are intrinsically opposite those of the business elite.

Internationalism

The period from the nineteenth century through the beginning of World War I in 1914 is rightly thought of as the period of the birth of nationalism. People had long thought of themselves as citizens of Frankfurt or Buda, or subjects of the Prince of Württemberg or the Venetian Doge, but not as Germans, or Hungarians, or Italians. Following the French Revolution, however, and the appeal to national pride in Germany to raise armies to fight against Napoleon, the early nineteenth century saw the rise of national consciousness. The period between 1870 and 1914, in turn, was an age of international freedom in Europe of a kind that never existed before or since. Bibi, as a Greek, would have been free to travel to the Austro-Hungarian and German empires and anywhere else in Europe without a passport. The Greeks in Bibi's audience in whatever German city it takes place in are free to live and work there without a work visa or other papers. Even today in the European Union, there is no similar freedom to travel and work.

CRITICAL OVERVIEW

Although "The Infant Prodigy" is today one of Mann's most frequently reprinted works, it has been studied comparatively little because of scholarly concentration on Mann's novels and those shorter works, such as "Tonio Kröger" and "Death in Venice," that are more directly related thematically to the longer works. Among brief notices on the story, Lewis A. Lawson, in *A Gorgon's Mask*, characterizes "The Infant Prodigy" as a "study of the cleavage that exists between the unreflective majority and the artist."

The isolation and aloofness of the artist is a common theme in Mann's work. G. Peter McMullin, in *Childhood and Children in Thomas Mann's Fiction*, notes that the insight granted the reader into Bibi's thoughts is just as fragmentary as in the case of the audience, and he seems equally contemptuous of them as they are of him. This would seem to exclude Bibi from the healthy innocence that McMullin finds Mann endows most of his child characters with. Edward S. Brinkley, in his article "Fear of Form," treats "The Infant Prodigy" in light of the revelation about Mann's homoerotic (and highly Hellenic) attraction to young men revealed in his recently published journals. Although the teenaged girl in the story finds Bibi to be too young for a romantic fixation, Brinkley reads such a fetishistic attraction into the music critic's opinion of the wunderkind. Eric Wilson, in "The Private Games of Thomas Mann," notes that the revelation of Bibi's inner life expresses one of Mann's common themes, the subtlety in a work of art which is beyond the comprehension of the mass audience and only the artist can appreciate.

The most extended study of "The Infant Prodigy" comes in Esther H. Lesér's *Thomas Mann's Short Fiction: An Intellectual Biography*. She sees the story as woven from a conversation of three leitmotifs or themes: those of Bibi, the audience (suggestively referred to as simply "the people" in the original German), and the publicity organization represented by the agency of the claqueur and the impresario. This is represented above all in Bibi's self-conscious manipulation of the audience. Juxtaposing the three elements, "Mann simultaneously shows Bibi's real personality, the [people's] viewpoint, and the spiritual relations between the artist and his audience." Of the people themselves, Lesér notes, "each is hopelessly self-centered, deliberately cultivating personal weaknesses that bar him from the *Wunderkind*'s world."

As an aside, Mark M. Anderson, in his article "Mann's Early Novellas," notes that Mann's use of music in his short stories—music named and described in the text, of course, rather than heard—derives from the melodramas popular on the stage a hundred years ago rather than from the leitmotifs of Wagnerian opera. Although the critic does not mention "The Infant Prodigy" directly in this regard, this interpretation of sourcing certainly seems to prevail in Bibi's cheap manipulation of the audience's emotions.

CRITICISM

Bradley A. Skeen

Skeen is a classicist. In the following essay, he explores the historical basis of Mann's "The Infant Prodigy" in the lives of Mozart and Liszt.

Thomas Mann's fictional infant prodigy is deeply indebted to the historical personage of Wolfgang Amadeus (he actually preferred the French form Amadé) Mozart. His father, Leopold, had been a composer of the second rank and the *Kapellmeister* (assistant conductor) in the orchestra of the Prince-Archbishop of Salzburg (in the eighteenth century an independent state nestled between Bavaria and Austria). Born in 1756, Mozart grew up in a house filled with music and musical instruments and began to play the harpsichord at age three and the violin at age five. He was also composing simple pieces by then (no doubt fleshed out into formal structured pieces by his father). His sister Maria Anna was nearly as precocious, and Leopold was not slow to put his children on the stage where he made his own career. With Mozart as violinist accompanied by his sister at the harpsichord, three weekends of concerts in the imperial capital of Vienna brought in as much income as Leopold earned in two years. This experiment left no question about the course to be pursued by the family, which went on its first concert tour when Mozart was seven years old.

WHAT DO I READ NEXT?

- John Green's Printz Award–winning book for young adults *An Abundance of Katherines* (2006) treats the problems a child prodigy in mathematics encounters as he transitions to adulthood.

- *Buddenbrooks* (1901) is Mann's first novel. It tells the story of four generations of a family in the nineteenth century. In many respects, the novel was inspired by the history of Mann's own family.

- Richard Winston's *Thomas Mann: The Making of an Artist, 1875–1911* (1981) is an important biographical study of Mann, although it does not take into account his diaries, only recently discovered at the time of its publication.

- Nobel Prize winner Kenzaburo Oe's *Rouse Up O Young Men of the New Age!*, published in Japanese in 1983 and in English translation in 2002, is a novel based on his relationship with his son Hikari Oe, a prominent autistic-savant composer in Japan who began his career as a child prodigy.

- Ervin Nyiregyházi was a Hungarian piano prodigy born in 1903, the year Mann's "The Infant Prodigy" was published. His father, an opera singer, reported that he began playing classical pieces on his harmonica by age two as well as making his own compositions. He was reluctant to perform as a child prodigy, preferring to study to perfect his technique. However, his mother forced him to perform (and may have controlled him through systematic abuse). He became the focus of a famous psychological study by the psychoanalyst Géza Révész, *The Psychology of a Musical Prodigy*, published originally in German in 1916 (with the pianist's name as the title) and in an English translation in 1970. After becoming an alcoholic, Nyiregyházi fell into obscurity after 1925.

- Nyiregyházi moved to California in 1928 and lived in poverty, mainly working in films, supplying the hand close-ups in a large number of Hollywood films in scenes where the characters play piano on-screen. But in the 1970s he had a second concert career, including a tour of Japan, and wrote a number of compositions (none of which were recorded). Nyiregyházi's life is the focus of the biography *Lost Genius: The Curious and Tragic Story of an Extraordinary Musical Prodigy* (2007), by Kevin Bazzana. Several of his 1970s recordings of pieces by Franz Liszt are available on CD and MP3.

- Zhanna Arshansky, born in the Ukraine in about 1927, had a career as a child prodigy on the piano, performing in a radio concert as early as age six. Of Jewish descent, she was captured by the Nazis in 1941 and was marched with her family and thousands of other Jews to a mass grave outside of Kharkov to be executed, but she escaped at the last minute when her father bribed a guard with a gold watch. She survived by taking a Russian name and, ironically, working to entertain German troops. Coming to the United States after the war, she eventually became a professor of piano at Indiana University. Her story is told by her son Greg Dawson in *Hiding in the Spotlight: A Musical Prodigy's Story of Survival, 1941–1946* (2009).

Many *Wunderkinder* or child prodigies, as they were called, toured Europe in the eighteenth century, and Mozart, accompanied always by Leopold and sometimes by his whole family, spent his seventh, eighth, and ninth years continuously on the road. While other child performers could give simple if impressive performances, Mozart showed a real musical understanding that dumbfounded his audiences and even the professional composers who sought him out, improvising with great facility and playing complicated compositions at sight. Mozart not only

"

MOZART WAS PROBABLY THE ONLY BOY TO

HAVE BEEN DANDLED ON THE LAPS OF BOTH MARIE-

ANTOINETTE, QUEEN OF FRANCE, AND MARIA

THERESA, EMPRESS OF AUSTRIA."

fulfilled his childhood promise but surpassed all of his contemporaries and became probably the greatest of all composers, the leader in a very narrow field of equals that might include Claudio Monteverdi (the inventor of opera), Johann Sebastian Bach, Ludwig van Beethoven (who made his own European tour as a wunderkind in his early teens), Richard Wagner, and Dmitri Shostakovich.

Johann Wolfgang von Goethe, as great a poet as Mozart was a composer, saw Mozart perform at age seven and wrote in his old age an appreciation of his fellow genius, long after Mozart's untimely death at age thirty-five in 1791. Perhaps this is why the wunderkind in "The Infant Prodigy," by Mann, a deep admirer of Goethe, "looked as though he were nine years old but was really eight and given out for seven." The artificiality, the purposeful constructedness, of Bibi Saccellaphylaccas's public persona is one of the many things he shares with Mozart. Just as Mozart was carefully managed by Leopold, Bibi's unnamed impresario takes care of every detail of his public image and determines the shape of his career. Bibi, too, is not only a performer but even at his tender age a composer.

Leopold in his letters (cited in Gay) speaks of the care he took in his own person and his son in their "producing themselves." They made a point of both snobbishly and subserviently appealing to the highest nobility. Leopold took care to dress himself and his son in the richest finery of the local fashion in each city where the young Mozart performed, positively dressing the boy as an adult, complete with a tiny sword and an elaborately styled wig, as was then the fashion. Mann parallels this too in his Bibi, but there is a difference. Bibi does not garb himself in a more fashionable and more dandyish version of the clothes worn by his audience but in a carefully designed stage costume: "He was dressed entirely in white silk, which the audience found enchanting. The little white jacket was fancifully cut, with a sash underneath it, and even his shoes were made of white silk." Pointedly, he wears short pants, in 1903 something done only by children. This outfit seems to be a sort of fancy-dress version of eighteenth-century clothes and is purposefully designed to invoke the image of Mozart. It is not the way the seven-year-old Mozart dressed, but the way that an ordinary concertgoer used to seeing operas and plays set in the eighteenth century, knowing little more than that Mozart had been a famous child prodigy, might imagine he had dressed. The idea of a stage performer wearing period dress of a past era, an entirely modern idea, was already established at the turn of the last century.

Leopold Mozart made sure to appeal to the highest nobility, dedicating the young Mozart's published compositions to royalty and great nobles. This was amply rewarded with gifts of expensive jewelry and cash given to the boy, but never with the appointment as court composer or to a court orchestra that Leopold had hoped to obtain for his son. Bibi's impresario follows the same strategy, but again, in a more modern form. At Bibi's concerts,

> the front seats cost twelve marks; for the impresario believed that anything worth having was worth paying for. And they were occupied by the best society, for it was in the upper classes, of course, that the greatest enthusiasm was felt.

Although the impresario's production now depends more on bourgeois commerce than on *ancien régime* patronage, the patron still has a role, represented by an aged princess (meaning a great noble, rather than a member of a royal family) who leads the high society where the concert in the story takes place. Her acceptance of Bibi as a respectable performer is worth more than any money she might give. She is given a prominent seat in the front row and is as much on display as the wunderkind. Because the impresario has attracted her, the rest of the moneyed class in the city must attend Bibi's concert, too. The galleries are filled with those even from the masses of the city grasping to have the same experience as her. After the concert, the princess's lady-in-waiting went

> over to Bibi; she smoothed down his silk jacket a bit to make it look suitable for a court function, led him by the arm to the princess, and solemnly indicated to him that he was to kiss the royal hand.

This too is an updating of Mozart's experience. Mozart was probably the only boy to have been dandled on the laps of both Marie-Antoinette, queen of France, and Maria Theresa, empress of Austria. But Bibi's encounter is reduced in the direction of a modern royal receiving line.

Other features of Bibi's concert are more modern and recall Franz Liszt more than Mozart. In the mid-nineteenth century Liszt created the modern persona of the performer, appealing for the first time to bourgeois rather than aristocratic taste. Liszt too cultivated a striking appearance, with his long hair flowing down to his shoulders (the rock star Roger Daltrey did not have to change his hairstyle when he played the Hungarian pianist in Ken Russell's 1975 film *Lisztomania*). This is aped by Bibi, who "had smooth black hair reaching to his shoulders; it was parted on the side and fastened back from the narrow domed forehead by a little silk bow." Even today, classical music is sometimes called *longhair* music because of Liszt. Liszt made the solo performer the center of rapt attention on the stage, as Bibi very much is, rather than a pleasant diversion in the background, as Mozart often was at his concerts. Liszt also incorporated a political or nationalist sentiment into his persona. He exploited the nationalism of his era with his Hungarian Rhapsodies and other patriotic pieces, as Bibi does with his own *Rhapsodie grecque*.

The ultimate measure of Mozart is his fulfillment of his youthful promise in exceeding the skills of the composers of his day and indeed in surpassing every other composer who came after him. As a performer, Bibi exceeds Mozart in his captivating hold over his audience, but that has more to do with the changing nature of performance and audience expectations than with the qualities Bibi has infused into his music. Yet since there is no way for the reader to hear the music, it cannot be evaluated. The most that can be said is that the music teacher and other audience members at the concert seem to think very little of his music, as unreliable as the report of their random thoughts must be judged. Certainly Mann believed that the common man was impressed by showmanship above and beyond art.

But then, the music that Mozart had written by his ninth year, though competent, is not itself particularly impressive. What Bibi's audience is mesmerized by is the experience of the performance per se, not the music. What prospects, then, does Bibi have? Is he doomed to fade away after a season of fame like a modern pop star? By the time Mozart was in his early teens, he was in possession of letters of recommendation by fellow composers like Franz Josef Haydn (then the most lauded composer in Europe) and Johann Christian Bach (Johann Sebastian's most talented and successful son) and many others, attesting the brilliance of his compositional skill to patrons who might not trust their own judgment in such matters. In contrast, Mann seems wholly unconcerned with Bibi's future as a composer. If contemporaries like Gustav Mahler (conductor of the Vienna Court Opera and the most important composer in Austria in 1903) or Richard Strauss (then the leading composer in Germany, known today for his *Also sprach Zarathustra*) are even aware of Bibi, let alone ready to praise him as a composer to the world, the reader learns nothing of it.

Source: Bradley A. Skeen, Critical Essay on "The Infant Prodigy," in *Short Stories for Students*, Gale, Cengage Learning, 2014.

Esther H. Lesér

In the following excerpt, Lesér examines "The Infant Prodigy" in depth and includes a discussion of Mann's own background in music.

... Mann rapidly wrote "The Infant Prodigy" for the Christmas issue of the *Neue Freie Presse*, 25 December 1903, and it has become one of his most popular short stories. The English "infant prodigy" and the German "*Wunderkind*" both describe a young child with an unusually early-developing artistic talent, but "*Wunderkind*" also offers a heightened resonance of "miracle child," here indicating both the titular hero and the protagonist.

In the introduction, Mann uses "*Leute*" ("people") repeatedly, a collective noun which in German has no singular form. *Leute* is a Hydra. Each hydra-head of the *Leute* functions separately but is restricted by the common body in its individual development. *Leute* is one of Mann's leitmotifs throughout "Das Wunderkind"; finally the *Leute* becomes a collective character with a composite mind, even another protagonist. The third active power presented in the introductory paragraph, the "publicity machine" (*Reklameapparat*), provides unity throughout the story.

When the infant prodigy appears, his behavior mirrors the setting, which seethes with decadent *fin*

> **ALTHOUGH HE EMPHASIZED HIS LACK OF INTEREST IN POLITICAL AND PRAGMATIC REALITY IN A NAÏVE ESTRANGEMENT FROM THE WORLD, HE WOULD SUBSEQUENTLY SHAPE AND FICTIONALIZE THE PATTERNS OF HIS REALITY ACCORDING TO THE WAY HE CONCEIVED OF IT."**

de siècle colors and ornamentation. The child's affected gestures are studied and effeminate, and his immaturity is exaggerated to attract the public, making him appear his mother's toy rather than a little boy with individual rights. Mann points out his clothing, his hair, his behavior, and especially his name: "He was called Bibi Saccellaphylaccas,", another name, like Tonio Kröger's, whose first element clashes significantly with the last. Mann himself indicates this conflict, the gap between the ordinary citizen and the artist, when he discusses the impresario's reaction to the name. Any young lad in Munich might be called "Bibi," but "Saccellaphylaccas" immediately evokes distant Greece, a conflict between the innocence of the heart and the intricate burden carried by a child with a premature insight. The *Wunderkind* is a little boy with a soft unformed but lined face, the characteristics of his trade. Later Thomas Mann describes his strong well-trained hands, the dark complexion he inherited from his Greek ancestors, " . . . already a little tired," and the extravagant clothing and hair style his impresario requires.

Thomas Mann ironically picks up the notion of the deception inherent in the "artist"'s presentation of his art, earlier introduced by Tonio Kröger in his conversation with Lisabeta: "A little lie, they think, belongs to beauty. Where, do they [the people] think, would edification and elevation from the everyday living come from, if one did not contribute a little effort and accept things as they are presented? And they are quite right in their 'Leutehirnen'" (EHL). The "publicity machine" builds its success on the predictable uniformity of its audience, so the impressive French titles of the *Wunderkind*'s modest creations, like "*Le hibou et les moineaux*" ("The Owl and the Sparrows") are bound to make an effect.

Mann then deliberately reveals the *Wunderkind*'s mind and emotions. "Bibi made his face for the audience, because he was aware that he had to entertain them a little." The performing artist's feeling of superiority toward his audience is perfectly clear; little Bibi knows all the tricks to ensure an audience's response, but he genuinely feels music deeply, because it is a beloved world where each performance promises him an intimate *geistig* experience.

Mann himself knew the musical world well. He had taken violin lessons since he was seven years old, and he played quite well by ear, first with his mother, and later with Ilse Martens and Carl Ehrenberg. As a youngster, he loved to act out the role of the virtuoso, just as he had enjoyed his puppet theater. Later in his life, he described a band he had seen during his boyhood on a happy vacation at Travemünde, and its "little, long-haired gypsy-looking" conductor named Hess. He had also heard a nine-year-old Greek pianist named Loris Margaritis at the Munich conservatory where the Greek boy had studied. Much later, Margaritis's wife sent Mann a photograph of Margaritis at nine years old, with a letter stating that the pianist had enjoyed "The Infant Prodigy" very much.

The *Leute* observe the performance, the bows, and the entrances and exits of the *Wunderkind* and record humorous caricatures of the mother, the impresario, and other characters. Each episode has clear contours and a well-enunciated message, highlighted from at least two opposing angles. As Bibi plays, mentally commenting on his selections, and the *Leute* focus on him, the story's rich multiple angles become clearer. Mann simultaneously shows Bibi's real personality, the *Leute*'s viewpoint, and the spiritual relations between the artist and his audience.

The *Wunderkind*, as artist and as ally of the impresario, and the *Reklameapparat* are followed by the third protagonist, the *Leute*, represented by ten different characters from the gray, chewy, plump mass of the *Leute*, ten "*Leutehirne*" or "people-brains," willingly subordinate to the impresario. Each is hopelessly self-centered, deliberately cultivating personal weaknesses that bar him from the *Wunderkind*'s world: "All those people sat there in their regular rows, looking at the prodigy and thinking all sorts of things in their regular brains [*Leutehirnen.*]" First Thomas Mann describes the "grey old man," using an interior monologue which supports his physical characteristics. The seal ring on the old man's index finger, omitted in the translation, shows that the old man has had a less refined upbringing than might be expected from an aristocrat, a finely crafted bit of irony confirmed by his sketchy experience with music and his use of a common form of German. His reactions are good-natured but naïve; for the price of a ticket, he receives romantic thoughts and "elevation."

The next "*Leute*" are a businessman concerned with nothing but economics, a selfish small-town piano teacher, and a young girl, whose fantasies are extinguished by the mere thought of cod liver oil. Her awakening womanhood, joined with an ardent imagination, suggests abstract disembodied love, which for her is a sensitive intellectual topic. The witless officer recalls the hapless versifying lieutenant in "Tonio Kröger."

"Then there was a critic, an elderly man in shiny black coat and turned-up trousers splashed with mud. He sat in his free seat and thought: '... He has in himself all the artist's exaltation and his utter worthlessness, his charlatanry and his sacred fire, his burning contempt and his secret raptures. Of course I can't write all that, it is too good ....'" The critic's sharp insight has isolated him; his intelligence prevents him from escaping into illusion, as other "people-brains" do. But not being an artist himself, he cannot share Bibi's world; he serves the *Leute* as the *Reklameapparat* requires him to do. The critic's definition of Bibi also shows the essence of Mann's concept of the artist. The *Wunderkind* becomes the central figure between the *Leute* and the *Reklameapparat*, while the critic is sometimes thought to represent Mann.

As soon as he has left his piano, Bibi becomes only a sweaty little boy. The crowd's attention is divided between two curiosities, Bibi and the old princess who is seated in the first row. When the two confront each other, the old princess acts candidly and routinely and the professional artist, a little boy, now that he has left the stage, shrinks in importance. He does not care enough about disclosing his personal experiences to answer the princess's dispirited questions coherently. After the musical experience which had united them, the princess and the infant prodigy part without having built any bridge

of comprehension between them. Finally, "Outside in the cloakroom there was a crowd," 179; *GW*, 8: 347), and some highlights of various characters, both previously noted and newly appearing, break through the stuffiness. Mann again highlights the piano teacher with her envious display of professionalism and then a sparkle of beauty: a young blond blue-eyed aristocratic girl with her two lighthearted officer brothers, followed by an uncouth, ungroomed, puberty-stricken, pseudo-intellectual girl, an old gentleman, and a depressed young lad. As the crowd dissipates, the individuals lose appeal, and the *Wunderkind* fades totally; the *Wunder* is over. The German text abandons the word *Leute*.

Mann's unity of composition and the essence of his message appear in the basic elements of the story—the *Wunderkind*, the *Reklameapparat*, and the *Leute*; the presentation of Bibi Saccellaphylaccas as Bibi plus Saccellaphylaccas, "Child" plus "Artist"; Bibi's relation to the *Leute*; Bibi as seen by "others," the *Leute*; and the interaction of the *Wunderkind* and the *Leute* as governed by the *Reklameapparat*. The interaction, relation and definition of these elements express Mann's conception of the artist, the commoner, and the reigning business apparatus at this point in his life. Mann himself was pleased with his "Infant Prodigy." On 14 December 1903 he wrote to Fischer: "At the moment I am writing a sketch for the Christmas issue of the *Neue Freie Presse*, 'The Infant Prodigy.' It will be better than 'A Gleam'" (EHL).

"The Infant Prodigy" was an immediate success. On 11 December 1903, Thomas Mann presented it in a lecture at the newly founded *Neuer Verein* in Munich, and soon after, the *Neue Freie Presse* asked for a similar story for the considerable sum of 300 marks. He often read "The Infant Prodigy" in public, its immense popularity deriving from its omnipresent delectable humor and subtly ironic portraits, which never descend to cynicism.

Some of Mann's impressions and moods were troubling during early 1904, and he discussed them candidly in a long letter to Heinrich (27 February 1904), reacting to "Jagt nach Liebe," a novella Heinrich had sent him, clearly though unconsciously revealing the essential cause of his later estrangement from Heinrich and also the motivation for his *Betrachtungen eines Unpolitischen* (1918), where he logically expressed long-held ideas that he, while writing, was beginning to overcome. The letter also illustrates his frame of mind in early 1904:

> Much more peculiar, strangely interesting, still rather inconceivable for me is the development of your *Weltanschauung* toward liberalism, which is also formulated in this work. Strange, as [I] said, and interesting! ... First, I understand little about "Freedom." For me it is a purely *geistig*-moralistic concept, synonymous with "honesty." (Some critics call this in me "coldness of the heart.") But for political freedom I have no interest at all. Has not the powerful Russian literature emerged from beneath overwhelming pressure? This would at least prove that the struggle for freedom is better than freedom itself. What actually is "freedom"? Because so much blood has already flowed for this concept, it has for me something eerie, weird, unfree, something outright medieval.... (EHL)

This passage exquisitely characterizes young Mann's abstract thought, and his eagerness to clarify his own feverishly evolving metaphysical system of representation. Although he emphasized his lack of interest in political and pragmatic reality in a naïve estrangement from the world, he would subsequently shape and fictionalize the patterns of his reality according to the way he conceived of it. At this moment, when his budding love for Katia Pringsheim had aroused his will and emotions and lured him toward the world of light, money, wit, and elegance, such expression was difficult for him, since he hoped to court her properly and then establish with her a sound family unit in a world he really neither knew nor cared about. Heinrich's new-found self-identification, his expression of exploding sensuality and heated sociopolitical ideas, are secondary to the impact that Heinrich's style, ideas, imagery, and *Weltanschauung* made upon his brother Thomas by triggering his intellectual defense mechanisms. Heinrich's position forced Thomas to reevaluate his own concepts and define them coherently to harmonize with his intellectual and his personal world, a considerable strain in early 1904. *Buddenbrooks* had provided him with fame and money, but his work on *Fiorenza* was slow. He wrote to Ida Boy-Ed, 22 February 1904: "... I am nervous and tired. Lately I have come to realize my fame in the form of social events and intrusion by people and I find myself now in the near feverish state of *geistig* digestion" (EHL).

Mann's vital decisions did not come to a head for a long time. Katia, the daughter of a wealthy university professor who loved Wagner, collected rare art, and opened his house to colorful Munich society, did not even think about marrying at the moment. As she put it, "I was twenty and I felt well and happy under my skin, and also, I was very content with studies, [my] brothers, the tennis club and everything, and I really did not know why I now should leave it so soon" (EHL). Thomas Mann remained in anxiety and hope....

Source: Esther H. Lesér, "*Bürger* and *Künstler*: The Contour of a New Beginning," in *Thomas Mann's Short Fiction: An Intellectual Biography*, edited by Mitzi Brunsdale, Fairleigh Dickinson University Press, 1989, pp. 135–39.

SOURCES

Anderson, Mark M., "Mann's Early Novellas," in *The Cambridge Companion to Thomas Mann*, edited by Ritchie Robertson, Cambridge University Press, 2002, pp. 84–94.

Brinkley, Edward S., "Fear of Form: Thomas Mann's *Der Tod in Venedig*," in *Monatshefte*, Vol. 91, No. 1, Spring 1999, pp. 2–27.

Bürgin, Hans, and Hans-Otto Mayer, *Thomas Mann: A Chronicle of His Life*, translated by Eugene Dobson, University of Alabama Press, 1969, p. 20.

Gay, Peter, *Mozart*, Penguin, 1999, pp. 1–24.

Kurzke, Hermann, *Thomas Mann: Life as a Work of Art; A Biography*, translated by Leslie Wilson, Princeton University Press, 2002, pp. 116–59.

Lawson, Lewis A., *A Gorgon's Mask: The Mother in Thomas Mann's Fiction*, Rodopi, 2005, p. 97.

Lesér, Esther H., *Thomas Mann's Short Fiction: An Intellectual Biography*, edited by Mitzi Brunsdale, Fairleigh Dickinson University Press, 1989, pp. 135–39.

Mann, Thomas, "The Infant Prodigy," in *Stories of Three Decades*, translated by H. T. Lowe-Porter, Alfred A. Knopf, 1951, pp. 173–80.

McMullin, G. Peter, *Childhood and Children in Thomas Mann's Fiction*, Edwin Mellen Press, 2002, pp. 50–52, 98–101.

Wilson, Eric, "The Private Games of Thomas Mann," in *German Quarterly*, Vol. 47, No. 1, January 1974, pp. 1–12.

FURTHER READING

Heilbut, Anthony, *Thomas Mann: Eros and Literature*, A. A. Knopf, 1995.

> Heilbut's authoritative study is a biography of Mann interwoven with insightful criticism of his novels and novellas. This was the first major work of Mann scholarship to take into account

his diaries, which were published only in 1975 and yet to be translated into English. This allowed Heilbut to explore Mann's work from a new and highly personal perspective, particularly in light of his struggles over his sexual identity.

Kenneson, Claude, *Musical Prodigies: Perilous Journeys, Remarkable Lives*, Amadeus Press, 1998.

This survey gives brief biographies of over forty child prodigies, beginning with Mozart and continuing through well-known modern performers who began as child prodigies, including Glenn Gould and Jacqueline du Pré.

Mann, Thomas, *The Magic Mountain*, translated by H. T. Lowe-Porter, Alfred A. Knopf, 1927.

Published in German in 1924, *The Magic Mountain* is generally considered Mann's most important work and one of the most important pieces of modern German and world literature. It consists of philosophical and literary discussions between inmates of a series of tuberculosis sanatorium.

———, *On Myself and Other Princeton Lectures*, edited by James N. Bade, Peter Lang, 1996.

This annotated volume, derived from Mann's lecture typescripts, contains two different versions of Mann's autobiographical piece "On Myself" as well as two lectures on German culture: criticism of Wagner and Goethe. They were delivered at Princeton University between 1938 and 1940 in order to raise the consciousness of American intellectuals regarding the threat posed by the Nazis.

SUGGESTED SEARCH TERMS

Thomas Mann

The Infant Prodigy AND Mann

realism

modernism

Neoplatonism

claque

Mozart

Loris Margaritis

The Lagoon

JOSEPH CONRAD

1897

"The Lagoon" is a short story written by British author Joseph Conrad in the summer of 1896. It was first published in *Cornhill Magazine* in January 1897, then in book form in the author's 1898 collection *Tales of Unrest*, which also contains his better-known novella *An Outpost of Progress*. In an author's note to that collection, Conrad claims that "The Lagoon" was the first short story he ever wrote and that its publication in *Cornhill Magazine* was his first appearance in a periodical publication. Conrad's biographers note, however, that he may have written earlier short stories.

In "The Lagoon," an unnamed white man traveling through a rain forest has to stop for the night to stay with a Malay friend, Arsat, who lives in a hut on a lagoon and whose lover is dying of fever. In an act of confession, Arsat tells the white man a tragic story of love and betrayal in his past.

"The Lagoon" is very much of a piece with Conrad's life and career. He spent much of his adulthood at sea, traveling throughout the regions he depicted in many of his short stories and novels, including the Malay Archipelago, the setting of "The Lagoon." Further, the short story is the first of his works featuring the listener/storyteller format that he would use successfully in such novels as *Heart of Darkness* and *Lord Jim*. It is noteworthy that Conrad, regarded as one of English literature's consummate stylists, wrote and spoke English as a third language, after his

Joseph Conrad (© Everett Collection Inc. / Alamy)

native Polish, then French. His spoken English was heavily accented, and to his annoyance, many people who encountered him concluded that he could not speak English.

"The Lagoon" is available in *The Nigger of the "Narcissus" and Other Stories*, published in 2007. The story is available on the Internet at the East of the Web website at http://www.eastoftheweb.com/short-stories/UBooks/Lago.shtml and at the Project Gutenberg website (http://www.gutenberg.org/files/1202/1202-h/1202-h.htm) as part of the collection *Tales of Unrest*.

AUTHOR BIOGRAPHY

Conrad was born Józef Teodor Konrad Korzeniowski on December 3, 1857, in Berdichev, Ukraine, which at the time was part of the Russian Empire. Ethnically, however, Conrad was Polish, for the region in which he was born had historically been part of Poland. He was the only son of a Polish poet, aristocrat, and patriot, Apollo Korzeniowski, and his wife, Ewelina Bobrowska. In 1861, Apollo was arrested for political resistance to the Russian Empire, and

the following year he was sent into exile in Vologda, three hundred miles northwest of Moscow. Young Joseph (called Konrad as a child) and his mother, who was also accused of unlawful revolutionary activity, followed, but Ewelina died of consumption in 1865. In 1868, after Apollo was granted permission to leave Russia, he settled in Kraków, Poland, where he died in 1869. Conrad was then placed under the care of his maternal grandmother and uncle. In the years that followed he suffered from poor health, and he was at best a mediocre student. His ambition was to go to sea, so in 1874 he departed for Marseille, France, where he joined the French merchant marine and made an initial voyage to the West Indies. During this period he was implicated as a gun runner in a conspiracy to place the Duke of Madrid on the throne of Spain during the Third Carlist War of 1872–76. ("Carlist" refers to Carlos, one of the claimants to the disputed Spanish throne.)

In 1878, after having amassed debt and gambling losses and making a feeble attempt at suicide, Conrad launched a sixteen-year career with the British merchant navy, beginning as an ordinary seaman but eventually rising to the rank of captain. During these years he would make voyages to the Mediterranean, Canada, and such exotic locations as Australia, Singapore, India, Borneo, Thailand, Java, Mauritius, and Celebes (in Indonesia). In 1881 he sailed to Asia for the first time. He first set foot on land in that part of the world on an island off Sumatra after spending some thirteen hours in an open boat because the ship he was on caught fire and had to be abandoned—an experience he recorded in his 1898 short story "Youth." A voyage to India provided him with material for *The Nigger of the "Narcissus,"* an 1897 novel. (*Narcissus* is the name of a ship; the derogatory word for the black sailor at the center of the novel is unfortunate, but the word reflects common usage at the time.) Conrad became a British citizen in 1886, the same year he earned his certificate as a master mariner (after having failed the examination on his first try). An 1887 voyage to Java provided him with background for his 1902 novel *Typhoon*.

After years at sea, Conrad returned to London in 1889, but in 1890 a Belgian company placed him in command of a steamboat in Africa. His four-month voyage up the Congo River formed the basis of one of his most famous and widely read works, *Heart of Darkness* (first published serially in 1899, in book form in 1902), a grim psychological tale of madness in the African jungle that would form the basis of the 1979 Vietnam War classic film *Apocalypse Now*. After his return from Africa, he needed months to regain his health. In the early 1890s he made voyages to Australia and Canada, but his life at sea ended in 1894, primarily because of poor health. In the years that followed he wrote steadily, although for several years he continued to try to find a berth at sea. In 1895 he completed his first novel, *Almayer's Folly*, followed in 1896 by *An Outcast of the Islands*; that year, too, he married Jessie George and wrote "The Lagoon," first published in 1897. In the late 1890s he became part of Britain's literary set, meeting and forming friendships with such luminaries as John Galsworthy, Henry James, Stephen Crane, Ford Madox Ford, and H. G. Wells, as well as with philosopher Bertrand Russell and French poet Paul Valéry. He achieved financial success through his writing, but until his death he seemed always to be in debt and complained to anyone who would listen of having no money.

Most critics regard Conrad's novels of the early twentieth century, including *Lord Jim* (1900), *Nostromo* (1904), *The Secret Agent* (1907), and *Under Western Eyes* (1911), as among his finest works. Despite a physical and emotional breakdown in 1910, he continued to write and publish later in life, producing *Chance* in 1912 and *Victory* in 1915; the latter novel was adapted for the stage and had a successful run in 1919. By this time he was employing a typist, for he found writing by hand awkward and painful; he was often able to produce by hand only some three hundred or so words a day.

In his later years, Conrad traveled widely, including a triumphant publicity tour through New York, Connecticut, and Massachusetts. In 1924 he refused an offer of knighthood, for as an artist he was uncomfortable with what he regarded as an honor typically given for political reasons. During the later years of his life he was plagued by rheumatism. He died on August 3, 1924, at his home in Canterbury, England, of heart failure.

PLOT SUMMARY

As "The Lagoon" opens, a man identified only as "the white man" is in a sampan, a kind of canoe, in the jungles of Indonesia, a mile or two from the sea. With him are a steersman and four rowers. Darkness is starting to fall, so he decides to pass the night in a clearing inhabited by an old friend, a Malay named Arsat. He directs his Malay steersman to guide the canoe up a creek that opens into a lagoon. The river and surrounding jungle are quiet and still; the jungle casts the surroundings into darkness. It becomes clear that the Malay rowers are native Muslims, and they are uncomfortable at the thought of spending the night in the lagoon, which they believe is haunted by evil spirits; Arsat, a stranger among them, has chosen to live in a place that others have abandoned. The white man disembarks at Arsat's rude hut, which sits on a platform over the water.

Arsat appears and addresses the white man as Tuan, meaning "sir," "master," or "lord." Arsat asks the white man whether he has brought medicine, which he has not. He leads the white man inside to his lover, a woman named Diamelen, who is gravely ill, as if with malaria.

Arsat, who has known the white man for some years, feels the need to unburden himself to his friend. He reverts to a time in the past when he and his brother (who is never named) were warriors for their ruler. During a time of peace, he confesses to his brother his love for Diamelen, a slave girl who waits on Inchi Midah, the wife of the island's rajah, or ruler. ("Inchi" is a title of respect.) The brother, wanting to help Arsat, offers a plan: When the ruler and his court go on a nighttime fishing expedition, he and Arsat will abduct the girl and carry her away. After this plan is successfully executed, Arsat and Diamelen, along with the brother, are in effect exiles from the country of their birth. The brothers relentlessly row Diamelen away from pursuit in a canoe.

After rowing through the night, the three beach the canoe along the coast to rest. As the two men sleep, Diamelen keeps watch. She quickly rouses them in alarm as a prau (a type of boat) appears, carrying the ruler's guards in pursuit. Arsat and Diamelen flee on foot while the brother fires a gun to hold off the pursuers. Arsat and Diamelen find another canoe; Arsat disables the canoe's owner, and he and his beloved board it as the brother appears, fleeing from the guards. The brother repeatedly calls out to Arsat, but rather than waiting or going back to help, Arsat, desperately wanting to

MEDIA ADAPTATIONS

- An audio version of "The Lagoon" was released by Books on Tape (Random House) in 1999. The text is read by Wolfram Kandinsky.

- Another audio version of the story is contained in the Conrad collection *Tales of Unrest* (2012), read by Walter Zimmerman for the Classic Connection (2012). The audiobook is available as an MP3 download.

- A third audio version of the story, read by Richard Mitchley for Audible, was released in 2012. It is part of a collection titled *Joseph Conrad: The Short Stories*.

ensure the safety of Diamelen, pushes off, allowing his brother, who fell once and lost ground, to be killed by the guards.

After completing his narrative, Arsat goes into the hut, where he discovers that Diamelen has died. Arsat is in despair as the sun rises, but he suggests that he is resolved to return to his home and exact revenge for his brother's death. As the white man and his boatmen depart, Arsat remains standing and staring at the sun.

CHARACTERS

Arsat

Arsat is a Malay (an ethnic group found today primarily in Malaysia, Indonesia, Singapore, Brunei, Burma, and Thailand) who narrates the story of his abduction of the servant girl Diamelen and his betrayal of his brother as the two men and Diamelen fled from the guards of the island's ruler. His listener is the unnamed white man, a European, who appears at his hut on the lagoon to spend the night. Arsat is deeply troubled because Diamelen is gravely ill with a high fever. He and the white man have a history of friendship and loyalty to each other during times of trouble and danger. Perhaps because he knows that Diamelen is dying, Arsat feels compelled to tell his friend the story of how he and his brother spirited her away from the grounds of their ruler, her master. He was so desperate to get her away to safety and find peace with her that he betrayed his brother by ignoring the brother's cries for help as he was being pursued by the ruler's guards. In the end, Arsat suggests that he will leave his place of exile on the lagoon and return to his homeland and seek revenge for his brother's death, although the story leaves Arsat's precise intentions ambiguous.

Arsat's Brother

Arsat's brother is never named, but his role in Arsat's narrative is pivotal. Arsat depicts his brother as bold, decisive, and supremely self-confident in his resistance to authority and willingness to take action. It is the brother who forms the plan for abducting Diamelen and who urges Arsat to action. At one point, Arsat says this about his brother: "My brother wanted to shout the cry of challenge . . . to let the people know we were freeborn robbers who trusted our arms and the great sea." Later Arsat says, "There was no braver or stronger man in our country than my brother." As he, Arsat, and Diamelen flee the ruler's guards, he stays behind and tries to hold them at bay with a gun. After a few shots, however, he has no more ammunition, so he runs after his brother and Diamelen, who have fled from pursuit. He calls for his brother to wait for him to catch up or help him, but the lovers continue on their way in a canoe they have commandeered. Ultimately, he is killed by the pursuing guards.

Diamelen

In Arsat's narration, Diamelen was a servant girl of Inchi Midah, the wife of the ruler of their island. After she and Arsat revealed their love for each other, she was abducted and carried away by Arsat and his brother. She joined Arsat in his exile on the lagoon, but in the narrative present she is ill and dies, apparently of malaria. The reader never hears directly from Diamelen.

Inchi Midah

Inchi Midah is briefly mentioned as the wife of the ruler of Arsat's island, and she is very briefly described as cunning and temperamental. Diamelen is her servant girl.

Steersman

The white man's steersman and first mate (or *juragan*) is, like the other oarsmen in the white man's canoe, a Muslim. He and his peers are depicted as superstitious, loath to spend the night on a lagoon they believe is haunted by ghosts and unwilling to associate with Arsat, who is still regarded as a stranger to the area.

Tuan (the White Man)

The unnamed white man is a European, perhaps Dutch or British, who travels through the jungle on the river and puts up for the night at Arsat's hut. Arsat addresses him as Tuan, a title of respect that can mean "lord," "master," or simply "sir." The white man has very little to say, but the narration makes clear that he has had former associations with Arsat during times of conflict. He listens to Arsat's tale of love and betrayal. In the end he responds to Arsat's narration by saying, "There is nothing," suggesting that he has been shaken by what he has learned of his friend and that his friend's story has shattered his illusions about loyalty and brotherhood. The white man can be seen as representative of a settled, ordered European culture in contact with the uncertainty and disarray found in strange and what were at the time regarded as primitive lands.

THEMES

Betrayal

The central theme of "The Lagoon" is betrayal. The story's betrayal takes place on two levels. The first is Arsat's betrayal of his ruler by running off with the servant girl of the ruler's wife, who, the reader soon learns, is Diamelen, the ill woman in Arsat's hut. Any sense that this is an act of betrayal is muted, however, for Arsat and Diamelen love each other, and the actions of Arsat and his brother are depicted as a form of heroic, decisive action designed to set her free. At one point Arsat says, "There is a time when a man should forget loyalty and respect. Might and authority are given to rulers, but to all men is given love and strength and courage."

The betrayal that lies at the heart of the story, of course, is Arsat's betrayal of his brother. It is the brother who says to Arsat, "We are two who are like one," and it is the brother who forms the plan for abducting Diamelen and fleeing with her. The narration makes clear that the brothers are close

and that the brother wants to come to Arsat's aid. The plan he forms works until the fugitives stop for rest, allowing the ruler's guards to catch up with them. As the brother holds the pursuers off with a gun, Arsat and Diamelen flee. They commandeer a canoe, but as the brother pleads for Arsat to wait for him to catch up, Arsat flees, abandoning his brother to death at the hands of the guards. This type of theme, involving a character who has to make a quick decision under extreme duress, then has to live with the consequences of a moment of weakness, is common in Conrad's fiction. This theme would be central to the author's novel *Lord Jim*, leading many critics to regard "The Lagoon" as an apprentice work that foreshadows the author's later motifs and themes.

Nature

Another common theme in Conrad's fiction is the indifference of the natural order to human aspirations and human suffering. This perspective was likely the result of the author's long career at sea. During these years, Conrad took numerous extended voyages. These voyages would have been marked by danger, principally from the weather and the power of the sea—and indeed, Conrad is regarded as a master in the depiction of storms at sea. Jungles, too, represent nature at its rawest and most threatening. He places his characters, such as Arsat and the white man, within this natural order, then explores how they behave when the veneer and the comforts and codes of civilization are absent and all that exists is an indifferent universe. The indifference of the lagoon—the expanse that figuratively separates the Malay Arsat from his European listener—is suggested by its extreme stillness. The surroundings are "motionless" and "unstirring." The walls of vegetation are "thick and somber." The darkness is "mysterious and invincible." The night in the wilderness is "hopeless and abysmal." The stillness is "profound and dumb." The earth is "an unquiet and mysterious country of inextinguishable desires and fears." In the hands of a different author, the death of Diamelen could be seen as a punishment for Arsat's betrayal of his brother, yet nothing in the story suggests that the reader is to interpret it in this way—that is, as the workings of a moral universe. The jungle has afflicted her with what seems to be malaria. Arsat has simply failed in his effort to find a place "where death is forgotten—where death is unknown." In the end, the white man concludes that "there is

TOPICS FOR FURTHER STUDY

- Locate images of the types of watercraft that would have been used in the region at that time, including the sampan the white man travels in and the prau used by Arsat's pursuers. Post these images on a website, along with descriptions, and along with images of other types of boats used in the South Pacific and the East Indies in the nineteenth century.

- Research the history of the East Indies, particularly as the Indies were affected by European colonization and imperialism. Write a report in which you comment on the lasting effects, if any, of this colonization and imperialism.

- During the nineteenth century, travel narratives became an increasingly popular form of literature, as the people of Europe and North America were learning for the first time about exotic and faraway lands and as anthropological research was growing in popularity. Conduct research on nineteenth-century British travel literature (including adventure fiction) and prepare a bibliography, with brief descriptions, of books you believe might interest your classmates. Distribute your bibliography to your classmates.

- Charles Johnson's young-adult novel *Middle Passage* (1990) is in its own way a form of travel literature, for it examines, in sometimes comic fashion, the Atlantic slave trade in the nineteenth century. Read the novel, then summarize it for your classmates in an oral report. Be prepared to comment on how Johnson (through his narrator, Rutherford Calhoun) and Conrad (through Arsat) achieve highly contrasting tones in their narrations.

- Locate a copy of one of the Allan Quatermain novels of H. Rider Haggard; two that continue to be read are *King Solomon's Mines* (1885) and *Allan Quatermain* (1887). These and other novels by Haggard are adventure tales set in Africa during the time when the European powers maintained colonies on the continent. Write a report in which you comment on Haggard's implicit attitude toward colonialism in his fiction. Suggest how that attitude differs from Conrad's.

- *The Coral Island*, an 1858 novel by Scottish author R. M. Ballantyne, has been enjoyed by generations of young adults and has remained in print since it was first published. It tells the story of three boys marooned on a South Seas Island. Read the novel, then write a one-act play that depicts a favorite or particularly dramatic scene from it. With classmates, perform your play for the rest of the class.

---

nothing," and Arsat looks "into the darkness of a world of illusions." The universe remains indifferent to his guilt, suffering, and loss.

Remorse

Yet another common theme that runs through Conrad's fiction and that can be found in "The Lagoon" is the relentlessness of remorse and guilt. This was a preoccupation with Conrad, who often depicts characters who have become exiled from their homeland, as Arsat is (and Conrad was, having been forced to leave his homeland as a child); who are forced to make a choice between allegiances (such as Arsat's allegiance to his brother and his love for Diamelen); who violate some sort of bond (particularly a fraternal bond); and who feel lasting remorse, requiring them to try to expiate their guilt. Arsat, having made a choice that led to the death of his brother, has exiled himself to the lagoon, and his senses of guilt and remorse are clear. In the spare dialogue toward the end of his narration, he asserts his love for his brother, but he acknowledges, "What did I care who died? I wanted

Sunrise and sunset highlight the contrasts in "The Lagoon." *(© Iakov Kalinin / Shutterstock.com)*

peace in my own heart." His words suggest that he remains tormented by his actions. His words are ironic, for the very thing he sought, peace, is the very thing that has eluded him because of the nature of the choice he was forced to make.

STYLE

Point of View

Broadly speaking, the point of view Conrad adopted for "The Lagoon" is third-person omniscient. This means that the story is narrated by an authorial voice that refers to the characters as "he," "she," and "they." As an omniscient, or "all-knowing," narrator, the narrative voice has access to the thoughts and emotions of the characters and has license to comment on the action. In "The Lagoon," however, the third-person narrative voice constitutes what is often called a framing story. Little happens in the third-person narrative present, other than the arrival of the white man and the death of Diamelen, but the narrative present provides a frame that

surrounds Arsat's narrative, which itself is told from a first-person point of view. The use of a framing story enhances Arsat's narrative by providing it with a context that implicitly comments on the story he tells. It also provides an atmosphere that contributes to the story's sense of foreboding and imminent revelation.

Imagery

Conrad was strongly influenced by the impressionist movement in the visual arts. That movement was centered in France, and French was Conrad's second language, which he picked up after he first went to sea out of Marseille. The goal of the impressionists was an art based not on sharp clarity and precision but rather on the struggle of the perceiver to seek truth that is often obscured by mists, fogs, uncertain light, shadows, and shifting perspectives. Accordingly, much of Conrad's work, including "The Lagoon," makes use of highly visual imagery that seems designed to confront the reader with an obscurity and density that suggest the elusiveness of truth and understanding. Thus, the story contains passages such as this one, which is highly characteristic of Conrad's use of visual imagery:

> The narrow creek was like a ditch: tortuous; fabulously deep; filled with gloom under the thin strip of pure and shining blue of the heaven. Immense trees soared up, invisible behind the festooned draperies of creepers. Here and there, near the glistening blackness of the water, a twisted root of some tall tree showed amongst the tracery of small ferns.

This sense of obscurity, invisibility, and shadowiness—of "impalpable vapour"—pervades the story and hints at the elusiveness of the truth that Arsat seeks.

Symbolism

Conrad uses symbolic action to good effect. Perhaps the best example is the detail in Arsat's narration where he notes that his brother called out for him three times. Readers of the New Testament will hear the echo of Peter's denial of Christ three times before the cock crows.

The principal symbol, however, is the lagoon itself. While the river that the white man navigates is a thoroughfare that leads to the sea and thus to the world beyond, the lagoon is a place of "weird aspect and ghostly reputation." It is a place of isolation, a kind of prison, where Arsat can dwell on his betrayal of his brother. He remains, however, an outsider, a stranger, and the Muslim rowers do not want to spend the night in the lagoon where Arsat lives "amongst the spirits that haunt the places abandoned by mankind." "Familiar ghosts are not easy to propitiate," as Arsat knows to his sorrow. Arsat's lagoon, then, is symbolic of his guilt and isolation.

HISTORICAL CONTEXT

Although "The Lagoon" does not refer explicitly to historical events, it does so obliquely in the reference to Arsat and the white man's having been loyal comrades during an earlier time of trouble. The reader is not told what that trouble was but is left to infer that it was likely a by-product of European colonialism. Overall, the story draws on a common motif in Conrad's fiction: the encounter between East and West, between "civilization" and "savagery," or progress and backwardness, and the effect that strange, faraway, primitive cultures and settings can have on Westerners and their value systems.

"The Lagoon" takes place during an era in history when the East Indies, as the region was called by Europeans, were still dominated by the Dutch. In the modern era, this region encompasses the Indian Subcontinent, Southeast Asia, and the islands of Oceania. In the late nineteenth century, the modern designation "Indonesia" was starting to be used to refer to the Dutch East Indies. For centuries, this region had experienced waves of immigration by Hindus, Buddhists, and finally Arab traders, such that by the end of the 1500s Islam was the dominant religion, as suggested by the white man's oarsmen. The first Europeans to explore the region were the Spanish and Portuguese. The Dutch arrived in 1596, replacing the Portuguese as the region's dominant European power; the English arrived in 1610, although the British East India Company had already been formed in 1600 to conduct trade in India.

Throughout the seventeenth and eighteenth centuries, the region was exploited by the Dutch East India Company, a private joint-stock company chartered in 1602 and given a monopoly over colonial activities in the East Indies. This company helped transform the Netherlands into a formidable maritime and trading power. Centered on the island of Java, the Dutch, with their fleet of not only trading vessels but also warships, subjugated an ever-widening circle of nearby islands, often through force. They subdued Sumatra in a war that extended from 1821 to 1838, Java in a war running from 1825 to 1830, and Kalimantan (a portion of the island of Borneo) in a conflict extending from 1859 to 1863. Throughout the remainder of the century, conflict continued to break out in such places as Java, Lombok, and Sumatra. The preindustrial peoples of the region were no match for the heavily industrialized Dutch, who argued that it was their moral obligation to impose colonial rule as a way of freeing the Indonesian people from their backward, oppressive island overlords.

The company ceded control of the region to the Dutch government in 1799. After the Napoleonic Wars of the early nineteenth century, the British and the Dutch, by treaty, defined separate spheres of influence (a development that led to British control of Singapore). The ongoing commercial rivalry of the British and the Dutch drove many of the islands' earlier inhabitants inland. Many became pirates, outlaws, and freebooters. (Recall what Arsat says

COMPARE & CONTRAST

- **1890s:** The British Empire spans the world, controlling millions of square miles and a quarter of the world's population. A popular expression is that the sun never sets on the British Empire.

  Today: Great Britain does not maintain an empire, but many of its former colonies, such as Canada and Australia, are part of the Commonwealth of Nations, a consortium of fifty-four nations, most of them former British colonies and dependencies, that cooperate on such matters as trade.

- **1890s:** The British merchant fleet comprises ten million tons, a figure that will rise to twenty million by 1914, nearly half of the world's ocean-going steam shipping.

  Today: Most goods, other than bulky commodities such as oil and grain, are shipped by air freight, although air cargo has lost market share because escalating air rates and falling ocean rates have widened the price gap between the two modes of transport.

- **1890s:** Britons learn of exotic and unfamiliar locations throughout the world through an extensive body of travel literature and often from explorers who give public lectures about their travels through such organizations as the Royal Geographical Society.

  Today: The world has shrunk, but people continue to pursue exotic experiences through "adventure vacations" in less well-traveled regions, including the South Pacific and Asia.

about his brother: "My brother wanted to shout the cry of challenge . . . to let the people know we were freeborn robbers who trusted our arms and the great sea.") The British and the Dutch exploited local conflicts between chieftains to expand their influence, and Conrad may have wanted the reader to imagine these conflicts when the narration mentions that the white man admires Arsat for his ability to "fight without fear." Some of the more far-flung islands in the archipelago—perhaps like the island on which "The Lagoon" takes place—remained relatively free of European influence, but that influence was nonetheless pervasive and ever present. Trading interests extended throughout the region, and it was this colonial exploitation of the remote regions of the world that Conrad often addressed, and condemned, in his fiction.

CRITICAL OVERVIEW

Many critics pay scant attention to "The Lagoon," regarding it as an apprentice work, although they also note that it foreshadows themes and motifs that would dominate Conrad's later work. In general, they do not think highly of the story. In the *Oxford Reader's Companion to Conrad*, Owen Knowles and Gene M. Moore write: "Generally regarded by critics as one of Conrad's more conventional and derivative tales, 'The Lagoon' has often been used . . . to anatomize . . . the overwrought landscape descriptions that the developing writer was soon to outgrow." Interestingly, Conrad himself appears not to have thought very highly of the story. In a letter (quoted by Knowles and Moore) he wrote that it was "a tricky thing with the usual forests[,] river—stars—wind[,] sunrise, and so on—and lots of secondhand Conradese in it.".

One critic who had virtually nothing good to say about "The Lagoon" is Daphna Erdinast-Vulcan. In *The Strange Short Fiction of Joseph Conrad* she calls the story a "crude specimen of Conrad's exoticism at its worst" and remarks that the narrative is "cliché-ridden and stilted." She finds the local people to be "universalized stereotypes of primitive 'natives.' Their discourse is made up of aphorisms and ready-made formulas

Arriving at Arsat's hut and finding the sick woman results in a long story. *(© Ammit Jack | Shutterstock.com)*

of superstition." Further, with regard to Arsat, she writes,

> Though supposedly different from the local people by virtue of his strangeness, their hostility, and his friendship with the white man, Arsat is, in fact, as faceless as the other natives, unindividuated, entirely true to type.

For Ian Watt the story also falls short. Writing about Conrad's early work in *Conrad in the Nineteenth Century*, he comments: "At times the seaman's style is a little too obvious.... In this mood Conrad's writing is as forced and hollow as when, in the opposite mood, its gloomy magniloquence genuflects to the melancholy romantic shade" of his father, the poet. Watt then quotes T. E. Lawrence, who wrote that Conrad's style is "not built on the rhythm of ordinary prose, but on something existing only in his head, and he can never say what it is he wants to say." In a similar vein, Joseph Shand, in "Some Notes on Joseph Conrad," writes that

> Conrad's style is very characteristic. It is slow, heavy, and rather involved, especially in descriptive passages. For Conrad ...seems so anxious

to make his readers see all the details of a setting that he often obscures the picture instead of revealing it.

Other critics, rather than focusing on Conrad's style, emphasize theme. Mark A. Wollaeger, for example, in *Joseph Conrad and the Fictions of Skepticism*, quotes from R. A. Gekoski's *Conrad: The Moral World of the Novelist*, who wrote that all the stories of *Tales of Unrest*, including "The Lagoon," center "on a character who, safe in a clearly defined understanding of life's regularities and values, is confronted with an experience so traumatic that it destroys belief, and opens up a vista of a universe implacable and terrifying." Wollaeger himself, however, in examining the narrative arc of the story, finds it not fully agreeable:

> Unsatisfactory in many ways, "The Lagoon" offers no resolution of the question of belief focused in Diamelen's death: is it retribution for the death of Arsat's brother or only a consequence of tropical disease? The narrative simply stops with a perfunctory reference to a "world of illusions," but neither the narrator nor Conrad decides which world is illusory—Arsat's or the white man's.

In "The Past and the Present: Conrad's Shorter Fiction," Edward W. Said remarks, in a comment distinctly applicable to "The Lagoon":

> It is no accident then that the *present* of almost all the stories ... is inevitably one of calm, of critical delay, of time circumstantially at a standstill. The reader looks in upon an atmosphere that exudes the feeling of something wrong, which has to be examined or recollected or relived or worked out.

CRITICISM

Michael J. O'Neal

O'Neal holds a PhD in English. In the following essay, he examines Conrad's use of setting in "The Lagoon."

Conrad's fiction is imbued with a strong sense of place. His attention to setting and its minute details is perhaps a function of his temperament, but it is just as likely an outgrowth of his extensive travels during the first decades of his life. Even during the years of his youth (1857–1873), he lived variously in the Ukraine, Russia, Austro-Hungary, Switzerland, and Warsaw and Kraków, Poland. Readers can imagine the frequently ailing boy escaping from loneliness and isolation through the romantic travel literature he read voraciously as a child, sparking his desire for a life at sea. Indeed, as the perfection of steamship technology opened up far corners of the world and as the burgeoning discipline of geography sparked interest in those corners, wanderlust was no uncommon impulse in boys of that era.

Conrad achieved that life at sea in the years 1874–1894, and a list of the places he saw reads like the index to a world atlas: France, the Mediterranean (Italy, Greece), Haiti and the West Indies, Constantinople, Australia, Singapore, India (Bombay, Calcutta), the Malay Archipelago, Thailand (Bangkok), Africa (especially the Congo River). These travels appear to have sharpened the young ship officer's focus on the kaleidoscopic details of his surroundings, which he used to great effect in his fiction. Particularly in the early years of his career as an author, the 1890s, he rode a continuing wave of interest in travel narratives, putting his powers of geographical and natural description to good use. Some readers and critics have argued that he

> SETTING PLAYS AN INTEGRAL PART IN DEFINING THE VISION OF HUMAN EXPERIENCE THAT READERS THINK OF AS PECULIARLY CONRADIAN, A VISION THAT EXPLORES NOT ONLY THE DARK CORNERS OF THE WORLD BUT ALSO THOSE OF THE HUMAN HEART, THE REAL OBJECT OF THE AUTHOR'S EXPLORATIONS."

put them to *too* much use and that his narratives can get bogged down in the details of setting, whether the author is describing a jungle scene or life aboard a ship. For some readers the settings are too minutely rendered, impeding the narrative flow and leaving the author exposed to parody. For other readers, these details of setting define their encounter with Conrad and are an irreducible part of his appeal. Each reader draws his or her own conclusion on this issue.

Setting in most of Conrad's fiction, however, is more than just window dressing, a way to appeal to the fiction-buying public's desire for the faraway and exotic. The author's goal was never to transport the reader just to a place on a map. Setting plays an integral part in defining the vision of human experience that readers think of as peculiarly Conradian, a vision that explores not only the dark corners of the world but also those of the human heart, the real object of the author's explorations. This use of setting for thematic purposes is apparent in "The Lagoon." Certainly it would have been possible for Arsat to tell his story in another locale—on the deck of a ship, in a tavern or marketplace—but the lagoon, the jungle, and the river that define the terms of the white man's journey create an atmosphere of foreboding, expectancy, and revelation that make the story in large part what it is, a story about truth peeking out from beneath obscurity.

One set of details about the setting emphasizes the river as it slices through the jungle. Here is one such passage: "At the end of the straight avenue of forests cut by the intense glitter of the river, the sun appeared unclouded and dazzling, poised low over the water that shone smoothly like a band of metal." These and similar details

WHAT DO I READ NEXT?

- Conrad's signature novel is *Lord Jim* (1900), which makes use of the storyteller/listener format the author employed in "The Lagoon." The novel tells the story of "Tuan," or "Lord" Jim, who attempts to find on a remote island settlement refuge from a moment of weakness and dishonor as a first mate on a ship. He redeems himself by protecting the settlement from a predatory bandit.

- One of Conrad's most widely read short stories is "The Secret Sharer" (1910). At the center of the story is a young, untested sea captain who hides aboard his ship a mysterious swimmer who fled from his own ship after having, as chief mate, committed an ignominious deed.

- Readers interested in the history of European colonization and the relationship between the European powers and the nations of East Asia and the South Pacific might start with H. L. Wesseling's 2004 volume *The European Colonial Empires: 1815–1919*.

- Patrick Brantlinger's *Rule of Darkness: British Literature and Imperialism, 1830–1914* (1988) traces the intersections between literature and European imperialism during the nineteenth and early twentieth centuries.

- *Hail, Britannia: Novels of European Colonialism* (2010) is an omnibus edition of five short novels about European colonialism by Conrad, A. E. W. Mason, Rudyard Kipling, G. A. Henty, and Winston Churchill.

- Coretta Scott King Genesis Award winner Sharon M. Draper is the author of *Out of My Mind* (2012), a young-adult novel that deals with the theme of betrayal.

- Another modern young-adult novel that deals with the theme of betrayal in the context of the relationship between brothers is Edward Bloor's *Tangerine* (1997).

- *The Netherlands East Indies at the Tropenmuseum* (2011), edited by Janneke van Dijk and Susan Legêne, reproduces artwork from the Dutch East Indies that is preserved in the Tropenmuseum in Amsterdam, Netherlands. The objects depicted provide insight into the culture of colonialism and colonial society in the region of the world where "The Lagoon" is set.

---

emphasize the separation of the jungle from the world beyond. The river, under a clear sky, is an illuminated thoroughfare that cuts through the obscurity of the jungle and leads to the open sea and beyond—or into the jungle, a place of mystery, of shadows and darkness. Truth is easy to find under a blue sky and brilliant sun. Truth is harder to find in darkness. And it is worthwhile in this regard to note that even though he was raised as a Catholic, Conrad was not a religious man, and in fact was an atheist. He expressed disdain for Christianity and its rituals and doctrines, and although he acknowledged that Christianity could on occasion be a force for compassion, in general, according to his view, it was distorted by colonists as a justification for exploiting native peoples. In his view, Christianity was emblematic of European arrogance and hypocrisy, and it was inadequate to play any sort of redemptive role in men's lives. This attitude toward religion is relevant, for throughout "The Lagoon" and other of Conrad's narratives, truth and understanding are to be achieved not through religious apotheosis and revelation but rather through observation of the human subject within a setting that strips away all of the supports of civilization that characters such as the white man enjoy. Another author, writing within a religious tradition, might use setting in a much different way.

Primarily, the jungle is a place of silence and stillness, of muteness, a place "bewitched" and inhabited by ghosts—as the Muslim oarsmen believe. The white man's boat "seemed to enter the portals of a land from which the very memory of motion had for ever departed." It is as though the boat and its occupants are being swallowed into a world utterly severed from the familiar, rational world of the white man's Europe. The image is distinctly classical, suggesting the often imagined westward voyage off the edge of the world, or a plunge into Hades, the Underworld.

After the white man disembarks at Arsat's hut, the sun sets in a "conflagration" that is extinguished by shadows, leaving behind the "intense blackness of the earth," the "night of the wilderness." Notice that the shadows quench the fire of the sun; the sun does not illuminate the shadows. This setting, with its stark contrast of light and dark, shadow and sunlight, its stillness and forbidding atmosphere, defines in large part the encounter between Arsat and the white man. It sharpens the reader's sense of something out of kilter, about to be revealed. The setting becomes a reflection of the white man's frame of mind, of his fascination with the "wonder of death," the "unrest of his race," "the suspicion of evil, the gnawing suspicion that lurks in our hearts." The earth, for the white man, becomes a "shadowy country of inhuman strife, a battlefield of phantoms." In this environment, the human heart is "helpless." It is this notion of a physical voyage as a symbolic voyage into the darkness and impenetrability of the heart that Conrad developed so effectively in his novella *Heart of Darkness*. "The Lagoon" in this sense clearly anticipates that later work.

Conrad in "The Lagoon" wants to escort the reader into a world of shadows, darkness, phantoms, and illusions—like a haunted dwelling or cavern whose mysteries erode the foundations of one's belief in rationality, regularity, predictability, and order. Here, in this setting, the white man learns for the first time the story behind Arsat's exile in the lagoon. It is a story of betrayal and guilt, one that undermines everything the white man had believed about his friend: "He liked the man who knew how to keep faith in council and how to fight without fear by the side of his white friend." The two men were brothers in arms—why and under what circumstances the reader is not told—but now the white man, who will pass onward to the sea and home to his familiar world, sees a very different side of Arsat. Interestingly, the narrative

The unnamed white man sits in the canoe and has the Malay men pole the boat through the water for him. (© trevor kittelty / Shutterstock.com)

never tells the reader anything directly about the white man's reaction to Arsat's confession; the reader is left to infer that reaction, contained in his response to Arsat's statement that he can see nothing: "There is nothing." The white man reenters the world of light and sunshine as the day breaks, leaving Arsat to gaze fixedly into a world of illusions, a world in which the exiled human heart can find no escape from despair and death. That world is defined by its setting, and in particular by Conrad's imaginative re-creation of that setting.

Source: Michael J. O'Neal, Critical Essay on "The Lagoon," in *Short Stories for Students*, Gale, Cengage Learning, 2014.

Ted Billy

In the following essay, Billy provides an analysis of "The Lagoon," specifically discussing Conrad's negative portrayal of European culture in his work.

In his Malayan tales, Conrad frequently contrasts Eastern and Western attitudes and usually disparages European culture. He derides Western hypocrisy and rapacity, by-products of modern civilization, and casts a favorable light on the traditional values and instinctive qualities of his fictional South Seas natives. In "The Lagoon," however, Conrad does not draw such a sharp contrast between the white trader and the Malayan warrior. The nameless white man suffers from delusions of self-aggrandizement, but he is not the only character blinded by egoism, for Arsat's confession of how he won Diamelen and ran off with her instead of avenging his brother's death, the pivotal tale within the tale, implies that he, too, is motivated by desire. The lagoon in Conrad's title comes to represent a psychological morass in which the dream of possession leads to a petrification of selfhood. In his struggle to overcome his psychic immobility, Arsat seems to cultivate yet another myopic obsession. He intends to recover his former identity, a pursuit that can only lead to death, either metaphorically or literally. Conrad demonstrates that serenity always lies beyond the reach of those who pursue self-interest or are haunted by the consequences of their previous actions.

The conclusion of the tale is problematical because Conrad presents the perspectives of both the white man and the Malayan without endorsing either viewpoint. To the white man, Arsat's commitment to vengeance seems to be a needless sacrifice. When the Malayan expresses love for his dead brother, the white man answers with a hollow echo of that sentiment: "We all love our brothers" (*TU*, 202). And when Arsat, facing moral solitude, remarks quietly, "I can see nothing," the white man's response is unfeeling: "There is nothing" (*TU*, 203). There is nothing to do, the white man believes, but to go on with the business of living. But Arsat views his situation as a personal crisis; for Diamelen's death marks the end of his enslavement to his obsession and his renewed commitment to his slain brother and his Malayan culture. Still immersed in the darkness of his sensual desire, Arsat can see nothing, but he hopes to find a way back to his former self. This solemn "friend of ghosts," who has been living as an outsider to be with the woman who is sole object of his desire, proclaims his new desire to regain his cultural identity through an act of self-destructive revenge. He vows to negate one betrayal by adding to his original treachery.

> THE WHITE MAN, NEVER NAMED AND NOT REALLY DRAMATICALLY PRESENT, LEAVES THE SCENE OF CONRAD'S DRAMA AS POWERLESS A SPECTATOR AS DIAMELEN ON HER DEATHBED."

After making this vow, Arsat stands "still with unmoved face and stony eyes, staring at the sun" (*TU*, 204). This pose suggests Conrad's general assessment of humanity, civilized or primitive, as capable of progressing only from one form of blindness to another. Furthermore, Conrad accentuates the motif of spiritual myopia in the grim tableau that closes the story: "Arsat had not moved. He stood lonely in the searching sunshine; and he looked beyond the great light of a cloudless day into the darkness of a world of illusions" (*TU*, 204). The white man seems to view Arsat's self-destructive decision as uncivilized, while Arsat himself believes his vow is based on brotherly love. But Conrad complicates this apparent resolution by undermining the perceptions of both Arsat and the white man. They have been blinded by self-interest, and only the Malayan seems to recognize the extent of his own blindness.

Conrad's refusal to name "the white man" throughout the tale suggests that the character represents a cultural stereotype. Arsat has lost his former identity, but the white man has no formal identity at all. The white man functions mainly to give commands, which are wordlessly executed by grunting Malayans who work for him. His canoe brings confusion to a previously undisturbed landscape that is "bewitched into an immobility." Conrad adds another sinister touch by focusing on the carved dragon-head on the prow of the white man's boat, comparing the progress of the vessel to "some slim and amphibious creature leaving the water for its lair in the forest" (*TU*, 188). The white man, spiritually akin to the amphibious dragon, makes an unwarranted intrusion on the silence of the forest. His first command is the only line of dialogue in the initial five hundred words of exposition. Not surprisingly, Conrad depicts the jungle as a postlapsarian, snake-infested paradise: "Here and there, near the glistening blackness of the water, a twisted root of some tall tree showed amongst the tracery of small ferns, black and dull, writhing and motionless, like an arrested snake.... Darkness oozed out from between the trees, through the tangled maze of the creepers, ...darkness scented and poisonous of impenetrable forests" (*TU* 188–89). The white man's destination, the "marshy bank" of a "stagnant lagoon," would be a perfect lair for a poisonous snake.

Despite years of friendship, the white man has a condescending attitude toward Arsat. Conrad wryly notes that the trader likes the Malayan a little less than he likes his pet dog. To the white man "in the midst of his own pursuits," Arsat is little more than a trained animal who can be useful on occasion. To the Western psyche, caught up in its own endeavors, everything alien to European culture is a curiosity to be either plundered or swept aside. The presence of the white man at Diamelen's deathbed provides the occasion for another of Conrad's ironic asides, a comment on the restlessness of Western culture: "The fear and fascination, the inspiration and the wonder of death—of death near, unavoidable, and unseen, soothed the unrest of his race and stirred the most indistinct, the most intimate of his thoughts" (*TU*, 193). For a Western individual in the nineteenth century, the dread of personal annihilation is the most absorbing thought of all. Nature, itself, also arouses a sense of dread. In contrast to the natives, who have an instinctive rapport with the organic world, the white man can only feel uneasy when confronting the dumb stillness of nature. Conrad juxtaposes the "gnawing suspicion" and the "powerful disturbance" at the root of the white man's being with the profound stillness of the environment. The white trader interprets the organic facade as "the placid and impenetrable mask of an unjustifiable violence" (*TU*, 193). His code of conduct has not prepared him to deal with the incomprehensible. Without his conventional frame of reference, he views the scene as a shadowy land of phantoms struggling to possess vulnerable human hearts.

The white man's subjective vision mirrors his "inextinguishable desires and fears," for the key word in Conrad's sermon on the vanity of human wishes is "possession," the passion for ownership shared by Arsat and the white man. Arsat even hints at this mutual defect when he acknowledges his inability to understand the forces that impel the white man: "[Y]ou went away from my country in the pursuit of your desires, which we, men of the islands, cannot understand . . ." (*TU*, 194). In narrating his story, Arsat makes a revealing comparison: "We are of a people who take what they want—like you whites" (*TU*, 196). The white man may appear to lack the blind rapacity of the uninhibited Kurtz, but Conrad groups him with Arsat and his brother as believers in the will to power: "We are men who take what we want and can hold it against many" (*TU*, 197). Thus, Conrad does not reduce the white man to the neutral role of observer, as some critics claim, but instead employs him as a representative of pernicious colonial influence, which promotes turmoil and unrest, even in peaceful times.

Conrad links the white man to Arsat in yet another revealing way. The lagoon's "weird aspect and ghostly reputation" frighten the polers, who distrust Arsat because he is a stranger and, more importantly, because he has no fear of ghosts (*TU*, 189). Arsat's disregard for superstition causes the polers to associate him with "unbelievers"—the white men in league with the "Father of Evil," who make "an offensive pretence of disbelief" (*TU*, 190). Although Arsat does not fear ghosts, he is haunted by remorse, by the bittersweet knowledge that he has attained the object of his desire at the cost of betraying his brother and his Ruler. Furthermore, despite the undeniable melodrama of his subject, Conrad makes sport of the sentimental connotations of the word *heart* throughout the tale. For him, the romantic heart is an excessively glorified incinerator burning with the fires of delusive passion. Here the author seems to have taken to heart the message of Buddha's Fire Sermon, for Arsat suffers from a "burnt-up heart" and announces Diamelen's death by saying, "She burns no more" (*TU*, 203). Conrad implies that for Arsat and Diamelen intense life means feverish desire. Appropriately, Arsat's passion fades from the scene with "the dying embers of the fire" (*TU*, 201).

In "The Lagoon," the briefest of his short stories, Conrad chronicles the eclipse of Arsat's passion but not his pride. Employing a technique he also uses in Kurtz's speeches in *Heart of Darkness*, written a few years later, Conrad couches much of Arsat's dialogue in self-referential language. Like Kurtz, Arsat has kicked himself free from the universe and now spouts solipsistic redundancies: "I hear, I see, I wait. I remember . . ." (*TU*, 193). Diamelen's death has simply become part of Arsat's "fate," since she functions only as a prized possession in his thinking. Arsat's betrayal of his Ruler and subsequent desertion of his brother are secondary to the ultimate fact in his self-absorbed consciousness: "I had her there! I had her! To get her I would have faced all mankind. But I had her—" (*TU*, 202). Even when he reports Diamelen's physical condition to the white man, his words reveal his self-preoccupation: "[S]he hears nothing—she hears not me. She sees nothing. She sees not me—me!" (*TU*, 191). Conrad undercuts the pathos of Arsat's situation at the end by depicting him as a "friend of ghosts," an outsider beyond the pale of human solidarity. Instead of embodying impersonal devotion to discipline, the hallmark of the most positive characters in Conrad's fiction, Arsat's single-minded fixation perverts life.

Conrad's ending, stressing silence and immobility, functions as a summary of the whole story. In fact, the pathetic closing tableau recalls a scene Conrad refers to periodically throughout the tale: Diamelen's deathbed. Diamelen is a pivotal nonparticipant in a story that revolves around her capture and possession. Her qualities imply nonexistence (she is silent, motionless, unseeing, unhearing), because she has been defined by Arsat more as an object than a subject. In her wordlessness and powerlessness, Diamelen shares traits with Kurtz's African mistress and Mrs. Schomberg, among others. She lies on her deathbed as helplessly as when she sat in the canoe during her abduction. In her fever, she hears nothing, except perhaps what the white man fails to hear, as the woods whisper "the wisdom of their immense and lofty indifference" (*TU*, 194).

Critics have attached significance to the flight of the white eagle following Diamelen's death (*TU*, 202). To view this as a token of Arsat's redemption would be to misconstrue Conrad's ironic perspective. For just as Arsat's possession of Diamelen is a nonpossession; so, too, his belated commitment to avenge his brother's death is a nonaction, a decision made in a vacuum. Conrad's ending defuses whatever tension has accumulated in the course of Arsat's narrative. The postures Arsat and the white man assume at the close of the story suggest the sentimental attitudes and delusive passions of conventional melodrama, since Conrad covertly sabotages the poignancy of the tableau. In a sense, Arsat exchanges one obsession for another, unmindful of the self-destruction implicit in his conversion to vengeance. The white man, never named and not really dramatically present, leaves the scene of Conrad's drama as powerless a spectator as Diamelen on her deathbed. Unveiling "the dark world of illusions" for an instant, Conrad places the reader in the role of the white man looking back at the wake of his stream of words, looking to find symbols of redemption, looking at a universe of mirrors, and looking for a new obsession to make life meaningful once again.

Source: Ted Billy, "Despair and Red Herrings: 'The Lagoon,'" in *A Wilderness of Words: Closure and Disclosure in Conrad's Short Fiction*, Texas Tech University Press, 1997, pp. 171–76.

SOURCES

Allingham, Philip V., "Joseph Conrad," Victorian Web, 2000, http://www.victorianweb.org/authors/conrad/pva 39.html (accessed August 14, 2013).

Barnard, Bruce, "Air Cargo Market Losing Share to Ocean Carriers," in *Journal of Commerce*, September 6, 2011, http://www.joc.com/air-cargo/cargo-airlines/air-cargo-market-losing-share-ocean-carriers_20110906.html (accessed August 14, 2013).

Belich, James, *Replenishing the Earth: The Settler Revolution and the Rise of the Angloworld*, Oxford University Press, 2009, p. 111.

"The British Empire," Victorian School, http://www.victorianschool.co.uk/empire.html (accessed August 14, 2013).

Conrad, Joseph, Author's Note to *Tales of Unrest* (1898), Project Gutenberg website, http://www.gutenberg.org/files/1202/1202-h/1202-h.htm (accessed August 8, 2013).

———, "The Lagoon," in *The Nigger of the "Narcissus" and Other Stories*, edited by J. H. Stape and Allan H. Simmons, Penguin, 2007, pp. 215–30.

"Conrad, Joseph," in *Merriam-Webster's Encyclopedia of Literature*, Merriam-Webster, 1995, p. 267.

Erdinast-Vulcan, Daphna, *The Strange Short Fiction of Joseph Conrad*, Oxford University Press, 1999, pp. 55, 57–58.

Friend, Theodore, *Indonesian Destinies*, Harvard University Press, 2003, p. 121.

"History of the Society," Royal Geographical Society website, http://www.rgs.org/nr/rdonlyres/53ac53b8-ef0a-4129-a97a-dbdd83eb59ec/0/historyofthesocietypdf.pdf (accessed August 18, 2013).

Knowles, Owen, and Gene M. Moore, "Lagoon, The," in *Oxford Reader's Companion to Conrad*, Oxford University Press, 2000, p. 196.

"Profile: The Commonwealth," BBC News website, February 1, 2012, http://news.bbc.co.uk/2/hi/europe/country_profiles/1554175.stm (accessed August 17, 2013).

Ricklefs, Merle Calvin, *A History of Modern Indonesia since c. 1300*, 2nd ed., Macmillan, 1993, pp. 138–42.

Said, Edward W., "The Past and the Present: Conrad's Shorter Fiction," in *Joseph Conrad*, edited by Harold Bloom, Chelsea House, 1986, p. 34; originally published in *Joseph Conrad and the Fiction of Autobiography*, Harvard University Press, 1966.

Shand, Joseph, "Some Notes on Joseph Conrad," in *The Art of Joseph Conrad: A Critical Symposium*, edited by R. W. Stallman, Michigan State University Press, 1960, p. 14; originally published in *Criterion*, Vol. 3, October 1924–July 1925, pp. 6–14.

Stape, J. H., and Allan H. Simmons, eds., "Chronology," in *The Nigger of the "Narcissus" and Other Stories*, Penguin, 2007, pp. vii–xi.

Vickers, Adrian, *A History of Modern Indonesia*, Cambridge University Press, 2005, p. 14.

Watt, Ian, *Conrad in the Nineteenth Century*, University of California Press, 1979, p. 31.

Wollaeger, Mark A., *Joseph Conrad and the Fictions of Skepticism*, Stanford University Press, 1990, pp. 39–40.

FURTHER READING

Hynes, Samuel, ed., *The Collected Stories of Joseph Conrad*, Ecco, 1996.

> Readers interested in Conrad's short fiction will find the author's twenty-two published short stories in this volume. The collection also includes a chronology of Conrad's life and Conrad's own notes on the stories.

Karl, Frederick R., and Laurence Davies, eds., *The Collected Letters of Joseph Conrad*, 9 vols, Cambridge University Press, 1983–2008.

> Conrad was a prolific correspondent who wrote to friends, professional associates, literary figures, and many others in English, Polish, and French. This collection of his letters was launched with an initial volume in 1983 and consisted of nine volumes as of 2008.

Knowles, Owen, and Gene M. Moore, eds., *Oxford Reader's Companion to Conrad*, Oxford University Press, 2002.

> This volume is an A-to-Z encyclopedia that distills a wide range of information about Conrad's life, works, and historical and cultural context.

Much of the information is recent, and the volume is the first to pull together otherwise scattered information about the author.

Meyers, Jeffrey, *Joseph Conrad: A Biography*, Cooper Square Press, 2001.

> Meyers is a distinguished biographer who has written biographies of several notable literary figures. In this biography of Conrad, he focuses on the author's troubled childhood, his difficult life at sea, his debt and mental instability, and his tumultuous affair with American journalist Jane Anderson.

Porter, Andrew, ed., *The Oxford History of the British Empire*, Vol. 3, *The Nineteenth Century*, Oxford University Press, 2001.

> This collection of essays provides a comprehensive account of the spread of the British Empire during the nineteenth century and up to the start of World War I. Readers interested in the settings of Conrad's fiction can focus on this volume's Part II, which examines British colonialism in Asia and the East Indies.

Stape, J. H., ed., *The Cambridge Companion to Joseph Conrad*, Cambridge University Press, 1996.

> In this volume, Conrad scholars examine the author's life, give detailed readings of his works and narrative techniques, discuss his relationship with his era's cultural developments, trace his influence on later writers, and summarize recent developments in Conrad scholarship. The volume also contains a chronology and guide to further reading.

SUGGESTED SEARCH TERMS

Joseph Conrad

Joseph Conrad AND The Lagoon

travel literature AND nineteenth century

British Empire

European imperialism

European colonialism

Dutch East India Company

East Indies

Malayan Archipelago

South Seas exploration

The New-Year Sacrifice

LU XUN

1924

Lu Xun, an author of immense fame in China, was a modern, educated man in a time of great political change, the opening decades of the twentieth century. Though primarily a writer of stirring polemic essays, Lu Xun took a brief interest in writing fiction and produced two collections of short stories. "The New-Year Sacrifice," a story condemning the ruthlessness of village superstition, was part of the second volume of short stories, *Pang huang* (*Wandering*), published in 1925. The story was originally published in *Dongfang Zazhi* (Eastern miscellany) in 1924. In the story, a weak-willed narrator who believes himself a worldly scholar encounters a woman known only as Xianglin's Wife, a beggar woman who was formerly a maid in his uncle's household. Their interaction during the spiritually significant days leading up to the New Year sends the narrator into a spiral of uncertainty and self-doubt, and he proceeds to remember her troubled life as a widow.

The story, which is alternately titled "New Year's Sacrifice" or "The New Year's Sacrifice," can be found in such Lu Xun volumes as *The New-Year Sacrifice and Other Stories* (2002) and *Capturing Chinese: Lŭ Xùn's "The New Year's Sacrifice"* (2011), both translated by Yang Xianyi and Gladys Yang, and *The Real Story of Ah-Q and Other Tales of China: The Complete Fiction of Lu Xun* (2009), translated by Julia Lovell. While the pinyin Chinese spelling of "Lu Xun" is now favored by scholars, the

Statue of Lu Xun (© *Dorling Kindersley* | *dk* | *Alamy*)

Wade-Giles spelling of "Lu Hsun" also appears generally in older volumes of his stories.

AUTHOR BIOGRAPHY

Lu Xun was born Zhou Zhangshou (later changing his name to Zhou Shuren) on September 25, 1881, in Shaoxing, China. He would create the pen name Lu Xun in 1918. While still a young boy, he watched his father succumb to alcohol-related health problems such as edema, unaided by the various traditional herbal remedies prescribed by country doctors, instilling in the son a distrust of his country's superstitions and rural medicines. He was educated at the Jiangnan Naval Academy, a decision which brought some shame to his family but offered free tuition. Later he transferred to the Jiangnan Military Academy, where he was exposed to Western lessons in science.

In 1902 Lu Xun traveled to Tokyo, Japan, to continue his studies, his interest in science growing at the same pace as his distrust in the rural practices of the Chinese countryside. During a brief return home in 1903 he was married to Zhu An, a wife chosen by his mother. Because of her bound feet and traditional upbringing, Lu Xun had little interest in his new wife, though he went through with the ceremony and never divorced her. After returning to Japan and engaging in medical studies for a couple of years, he abruptly dropped out of the program and enrolled as a student of literature at the German Institute in Tokyo. David E. Pollard writes in his introduction to *The New-Year Sacrifice and Other Stories*, "He was now resolved to take literature as his vocation, to 'cure minds' instead of bodies."

As a writer of literature and essays on current events, Lu Xun would become a household name in China within a very short time. Returning to Shaoxing in time for the Xinhai Revolution in 1911–1912, he rode out the political turmoil as a teacher. In 1912 he accepted a job with the new republic's government in the Ministry of Education and moved to Beijing. He joined the literary journal *Xin Qingnian* (New youth) in 1917. His interest in writing fiction lasted until 1926, with two major collections published, *Na han* (1923; *Call to Arms*) and *Pang huang* (1925; *Wandering*), in which "The New-Year Sacrifice" is the first story. He then focused entirely on his political essays.

During the turbulent years after the revolution, as politicians made good on their threats to imprison those who spoke against them, Lu Xun appeared in public with little worry, for he was too famous to be assassinated. However, he was forced for his safety to leave Beijing in 1926 due to an essay he wrote condemning the government after an attack on a student protest. He moved to Shanghai, where he stayed for the remainder of his life. Lu Xun continued to give extremely popular lectures across China and was courted by multiple factions of the Communist Party. He died of tuberculosis on October 19, 1936. Chairman of the Communist Party Mao Zedong would use the facts of Lu Xun's life and popularity for the purposes of propaganda. Pollard writes, "After the Chinese Communist Party assumed power in 1949 it was a crime even to hint that Lu Xun had any shortcomings." That is no longer the case today, but Lu Xun remains a highly respected writer and household name in China.

PLOT SUMMARY

"The New-Year Sacrifice" begins with the narrator ruminating on the year's end and the approach of the New Year. The days are dark, and the smell of gunpowder from celebratory fireworks fills the air. The narrator returns to his hometown of Luzhen after a long absence, staying at the house of Mr. Lu, an uncle. A grumbling Neo-Confucianist, his uncle is more interested in arguing about politics and government reform than making pleasant conversation with his nephew.

The narrator visits with his old friends, finding each family busy with chores in preparation for New Year's celebrations and the New Year's sacrifice. The sacrifice, given to the God of Fortune, consists of carefully prepared food set out at dawn for the god to enjoy. Every home in Luzhen takes part in this important tradition, which the narrator finds pleasing despite not being a superstitious man. Returning to his uncle's home as it begins to snow, the narrator examines the Taoist scrolls hanging on the wall. In the middle of the display is the Chinese character for *longevity*, one scroll has fallen to the floor, and the other reads, "Understanding of principles brings peace of mind." The only books in the room are Neo-Confucian or traditional philosophic texts of China. The narrator, a modern man, finds the room distasteful with its commitment to old ideas. He plans to leave town as soon as possible.

Also souring the narrator's mood was an earlier run-in he had with Xianglin's Wife, a woman whom he had known in his childhood in Luzhen but who has changed dramatically since then. That run-in is related.

Seeing that she is now a beggar, the narrator stops walking so that she may come to him to ask for change. Instead, Xianglin's Wife, recognizing the narrator as an educated man and a traveler, whispers a question which has been on her mind: "Do dead people turn into ghosts or not?"

The narrator, incredibly uncomfortable and even frightened by the question from such a poor soul, weighs his options. Though he does not believe in spirits, he knows the people of Luzhen are still very superstitious. He sees how badly she wants an answer and wonders if it would give some hope to her in her misery to hear him say yes. He decides to say that it is possible there are ghosts. She immediately asks another question:

"That means there must be a hell too?" Surprised, the narrator responds that if there are ghosts then logically there would be a hell. She asks a third question: "Then will all the members of a family meet again after death?"

Stumbling over his words, the narrator realizes he has failed to answer the questions correctly and is only making things worse with his hesitations. Frightened of the ramifications of what he has said to Xianglin's Wife, he tries to reverse himself: "In that case ... actually, I'm not sure.... In fact, I'm not sure whether there are ghosts or not either."

After saying this, he quickly leaves, afraid of answering any more of Xianglin's Wife's questions. He worries that she was not simply looking for comfort but had another reason for asking, even a sense of something bad about to happen. The narrator feels guilty for his answers. If something bad were to happen he would feel responsible. But he laughs off his discomfort and paranoia over such a simple conversation, especially because he said, "I'm not sure," thus ridding him of any direct responsibility for any disaster his words could lead to. He considers the phrase "I'm not sure" to be a way of giving advice while remaining safe from guilt. If someone inexperienced boldly gives advice without including this phrase, then they can be blamed for anything bad that happens as a result. But if they finish their piece of advice with "I'm not sure," then they cannot be blamed because they expressed uncertainty. The importance of saying "I'm not sure" is reinforced for the narrator by the strange meeting with Xianglin's Wife.

Despite having said "I'm not sure," the narrator, even after a night's sleep, dreads any repercussions of his talk with Xianglin's Wife. He decides he must leave Luzhen the next day and return to the city. That evening he overhears his uncle loudly exclaim, "What a moment to choose! Now of all times! Isn't that proof enough she was a bad lot?" The narrator asks the servant why Mr. Lu is so upset, only to learn that Xianglin's Wife has died. The narrator asks how she died, to which the servant curtly replies that she died of poverty.

Though his worst fears have been realized, the narrator is actually relieved of his great stress from the day before. He still feels momentary guilt but finds himself much happier knowing that no more harm can come from his conversation with Xianglin's Wife. He shares a dinner table with his uncle, who is moody at the inauspicious timing of Xianglin's Wife's death. Though the narrator wants to discuss it, he knows that to mention death or a dead person just before the New Year's sacrifice is incredibly bad luck to a person who, like his uncle, believes in spirits. The narrator gathers that his uncle dislikes his presence in the house, seeing him as just as bad as Xianglin's Wife. The narrator tells Mr. Lu that he will leave the next day, and his uncle does not try to stop him.

After dinner the narrator sits in reflection. Though the snowy landscape is quiet, the households of Luzhen are brightly lit and busy with preparation for the sacrifice. He considers that Xianglin's Wife was a mystery to those who knew her. He believes that her death was the end of a pointless life, and that both she and the town will benefit from her absence, as the town was tired of seeing her. This thought, that her death was the end of something painful for both her and the people of Luzhen, relaxes the narrator. But he cannot help but remember what he knows of her life.

Xianglin's Wife first appears in Luzhen when the narrator's uncle's household needs a maid, and Mrs. Wei brings her to the family. She is twenty-six years old and wears a white band in her hair, signifying mourning. The family learns that her husband recently died. The uncle disapproves, as he does not want a widow in the house, believing they are bad luck. The narrator's aunt,

however, intuits Xianglin's Wife's incredible work ethic and hires her. The family never asks her real name. She seldom speaks, but they do learn that her husband was a woodcutter. In addition to his wife, Xianglin left behind a mother, father, and younger brother. After months of working at Mr. and Mrs. Lu's house, Xianglin's Wife becomes healthy and happy. The town agrees that she is an excellent worker. She can prepare the New Year's sacrifice, usually a job for several maids, all by herself.

One day she sees her husband's cousin pacing the opposite riverbank where she is washing the family's rice. Upset, she tells the uncle and aunt, who conclude she must have run away from her husband's family after her husband's death. Time passes, and they forget about the cousin, until Mrs. Wei appears again at their door, with Xianglin's mother beside her. The mother-in-law calmly explains that she needs Xianglin's Wife to come back, as it is a busy time in their household; Xianglin's Wife is the property of her mother-in-law now that her husband is dead. The aunt reluctantly agrees. She gives Xianglin's mother the wages that Xianglin's Wife earned but never spent. After Mrs. Wei and the mother-in-law leave, the narrator's aunt cannot find the rice basket. They search the house, but it is not there. They find it at the riverbank, where witnesses describe having seen a boat pull up to the shore. Two men jumped out of the boat and forced Xianglin's Wife to come with them; she put up a fight but was eventually subdued by being gagged and tied up. Then the mother-in-law and Mrs. Wei arrived.

The uncle is beside himself over the disgraceful behavior at the riverbank, and Mrs. Wei's appearance at their house after lunch further infuriates him. Both he and the aunt berate Mrs. Wei for bringing Xianglin's Wife to the house only to help her be taken away again in such a violent manner. They are afraid of what the people of Luzhen will think of the family after such scandalous actions. Mrs. Wei apologizes profusely, saying that Xianglin's Wife did not tell her she was a runaway when she asked for help finding work. The family is mollified, and the incident is forgotten. Only the aunt regrets Xianglin's Wife's abduction, as she was such a good worker, especially compared to the other maids the family hires to replace her.

After several New Years, Mrs. Wei returns to the house with news of Xianglin's Wife. She was married off to the son of a mountain family by the mother-in-law: after she was brought back to Wei Village, the mother-in-law immediately forced her to marry the sixth son of the Ho family, in Ho Glen, so that Xianglin's mother would have enough money to afford a bride for her younger son. The aunt is scandalized, but Mrs. Wei considers this an excellent management decision. Xianglin's Wife had to be tied up on the way to her new husband's house. She shouted and cursed until she was hoarse, then sliced her head open while banging it on the altar. She put up such a fight because it is dishonorable in their culture to marry again after being widowed. But Xianglin's Wife finally grew used to her new life. She gave birth to a son and is living happily with her new husband, without a mother-in-law to push her around. After hearing this, the aunt no longer speaks of Xianglin's Wife, having given up hope of her return.

Two years later, Mrs. Wei brings Xianglin's Wife, once again wearing a white mourning band in her hair, back to the narrator's uncle and aunt. Mrs. Wei explains that the woman's second husband has died of typhoid fever, while her son was killed by a wolf. Xianglin's Wife tells the very moving story of the death of her son, Amao. She had given him beans to shell on the front porch and left him alone. Though she knew wolves might attack when starving in the winter, she never expected a wolf to roam into the village in the spring. She found Amao was missing from the porch and began desperately asking around the village after him. They searched all day until finally finding one of his shoes in a gully. A little farther on, they found his body partially eaten in the wolf's den. His hand was still clutching the basket his mother had given him for the beans.

The aunt is brought to tears by this story and agrees, much to Mrs. Wei and Xianglin's Wife's happiness, to take her on again as a maid. Despite all that has happened to the woman, the people of Luzhen still refer to her as Xianglin's Wife. To the aunt's disappointment, age and sorrow have slowed the woman's once-incredible work ethic. She is forgetful and never smiles. Additionally, the uncle gripes that she gives off negative, contaminated energy and could be a damaging influence to have in their house. They decide that she cannot have a part in the sacrifices: "They would have to prepare all the dishes themselves. Otherwise they would be unclean and the ancestors would not accept them." Without the sacrifices to prepare for, Xianglin's Wife has nothing to do for the New Year; the aunt would rather complete all the tasks herself than let a morally unclean person spiritually contaminate the silverware, dishes, or candlesticks.

In town, the people of Luzhen act coldly toward Xianglin's Wife, until they hear the sad tale of Amao's death. She repeats the heart-breaking story for all of the townspeople, including some who seek her out just to hear it. Unfortunately, soon all the people of Luzhen know the story by heart. Meanwhile, Xianglin's Wife continues to take any opportunity to repeat it. She scares small children with the story and is teased by those who can repeat it word for word before she gets a chance. Soon the townsfolk are disgusted by her obsession with the story and avoid her.

For the following New Year's sacrifice preparations, Xianglin's Wife is left out while other servants are hired to help. Amah Liu, in charge of washing the sacrificial vessels, interrupts Xianglin's Wife as she attempts to tell the story of Amao's death yet again. Instead, Amah Liu asks how Xianglin's Wife got the large scar on her forehead. Xianglin's Wife does not respond, for she got it banging her head on the altar during her second marriage. Amah Liu chastises her for allowing herself to be wed again, for it is a sin: "Just think: when you go down to the lower world, the ghosts of both men will start fighting over you." Amah Liu even tells her that the devil will divide her in two to satisfy them both.

Xianglin's Wife is scared of this possibility, having never considered it before. Amah Liu tells her to atone for her sins by purchasing a threshold at the Temple of the Tutelary God. Xianglin's Wife begins to save her money for this large purchase.

Meanwhile, the townspeople now begin to tease Xianglin's Wife about her scar, but she nonetheless focuses on working to buy a threshold so that her sin may be forgiven. Finally, she saves up enough money and returns from the temple triumphant. Believing herself to be morally clean, she hurries to help with preparations for the coming New Year's sacrifice—but the aunt still will not let her take part. She is devastated and permanently withdraws into herself. She becomes fearful and listless, until finally the family fires her. The narrator reflects that from there she must have become a beggar, though he does not know how soon this happened after she was fired.

A burst of fireworks nearby wakes the narrator up from his reverie. Dawn is near, and the whole town is alive with fireworks and noise in celebration of the New Year. The narrator can finally relax completely as he listens to the noise. He believes that the New Year's sacrifice has been accepted by the gods, and great fortune will shine down on the people of Luzhen.

CHARACTERS

Amah Liu

Amah Liu is asked to kill the animals for the New Year's sacrifice at the Lu household, but as a vegetarian, she refuses. Instead she washes the sacrificial vessels while Xianglin's Wife tends the fire. She cruelly teases Xianglin's Wife about her scar, saying it would have been better if she had succeeded in killing herself, as it is a grave sin to remarry. She points out that her two husbands will fight over her in the afterlife, and she will likely be split in two to appease them. She terrifies Xianglin's Wife into buying a threshold at the temple, so that she may atone for her sin. Xianglin's Wife is convinced that this expensive purchase will absolve her.

Amao

Amao is Xianglin's Wife's young son through her second marriage. When he is still very young his mother sets him on the front porch to shell beans into a basket. He is then seized by a wolf and carried to its den, where the townspeople find his corpse still holding the basket his mother gave him. Xianglin's Wife repeatedly recites the story of his death to the people of Luzhen, who, though at first interested, soon become tired of hearing about his fate.

Mr. Ho

The unnamed sixth son of the Ho family is Xianglin's Wife's second husband. He lives in a rural mountain community and is a strong worker. Despite being young and fit, he dies of typhoid fever shortly after marrying Xianglin's Wife.

Mr. Lu

Mr. Lu, an uncle of the narrator's (seemingly a distant one), adheres to Neo-Confucianism, a philosophy that favors rationality and ethics, although he is very superstitious. He dislikes the narrator. He also dislikes Xianglin's Wife, becoming enraged and blaming her when she dies on New Year's Eve. When Xianglin's Wife was first brought to his house by Mrs. Wei, he frowned at the idea of having a widow as a maid, but his wife took the woman in anyway; they have trouble finding good servants, so exceptions must be made despite his high standards. Mr. Lu is deeply concerned with honor and reputation. When Xianglin's Wife returns for the second time, he believes that she is morally degraded after remarrying and cannot be allowed to touch sacrificial objects.

Mrs. Lu

An aunt of the narrator's, Mrs. Lu first took in Xianglin's Wife over her husband's disapproval because she appeared, and proved, to be such a hard worker, eliminating the need to hire others. The aunt is upset to see Xianglin's Wife go and compares all maids who serve the family after her unfavorably to Xianglin's Wife. When she returns to the family, the aunt is moved to tears by Xianglin's Wife's story of her son's death. However, because she has been married twice, the aunt shares her husband's opinion that she is morally contaminated and so will not let her touch the sacrificial materials. After Xianglin's Wife buys a threshold at the temple and believes herself absolved, the aunt still will not let her help with the sacrifices, and thus destroys any hope she had of finding peace of mind while working for the Lu family again. As she deteriorates owing to her heartbreak and disappointment, the aunt is vocal about her displeasure, eventually firing Xianglin's Wife.

Luzhen Townspeople

The people of Luzhen are superstitious villagers, sharing a traditional Chinese belief in spirits and fortunes. The narrator, who has been educated and lives in the city, is uncomfortable with their antiquated ways. When Xianglin's Wife joins the Lu household for the second time, the townspeople like to hear the story of her son's death, until growing tired of it. They ridicule her for her scar and the sin she committed by marrying after her first husband's death. They call her Xianglin's Wife and do not bother finding out her real name. Once she has become a beggar, the people of Luzhen do not associate with her.

Narrator

The unnamed narrator is an educated, modernized man who travels to his hometown of Luzhen for the New Year celebrations. Though he generally scoffs at Luzhen's superstitious traditions, he finds the practice of the New Year's sacrifice to be beautiful. He is a nephew of Mr. Lu and his wife. Mr. Lu allows his nephew to stay with him during the holiday, though they do not get along well, especially after the death of Xianglin's Wife. The narrator's troubling conversation with Xianglin's Wife just before her death triggers his memories of the beggar woman from when she was a maid in his uncle's house. Though he tries to answer Xianglin's Wife's questions according to what the locals of Luzhen believe, he fails to comfort her, or to realize that she has sought his opinions specifically because he does not believe in the local superstition. Still, when the New Year comes in, the narrator looks across the city with peace in his heart. He is not troubled by the sad fate of the lonely woman.

Servant

The servant of Mr. Lu tells the narrator that his uncle is upset at Xianglin's Wife because she has died on the eve of the New Year. The servant does not see the terror on the narrator's face because he keeps his head bowed respectfully. When the narrator asks how she died, the servant scoffs as if the answer is obvious: she died of poverty.

Mrs. Wei

Mrs. Wei is a go-between for the upper and lower classes who finds suitable servants for the Lu household. Having brought Xianglin's Wife to them without knowing she ran away from home, Mrs. Wei then aids the mother-in-law in getting Xianglin's Wife back. The narrator's uncle and aunt are disgusted by Mrs. Wei's behavior, but she soothes them by promising that she did not know the woman was a runaway. Later, she comes to visit and has news of Xianglin's Wife, telling Mr. and Mrs. Lu of the sordid details of the woman's second marriage and how she has yet found happiness with her new husband and son. After their deaths, Mrs. Wei brings Xianglin's Wife back to the Lu household to work. She is greatly relieved that they accept her once again as a maid.

Xianglin

Xianglin was the first husband of Xianglin's Wife. He was ten years younger than his wife and came from a family of woodcutters. His mother-in-law retains control of his wife after his death. He is survived by a younger brother who is unmarried.

Xianglin's Mother

Xianglin's mother—who is considered Xianglin's Wife's mother-in-law even after Xianglin's death—grieves the elder son, who died, but still has an unmarried younger son and the daughter-in-law, who has run away from their home. She finds Xianglin's Wife through Mrs. Wei and comes to take her back to their village. After two men forcibly abduct her from the riverbank, Xianglin's Wife is married off by her mother-in-law into a mountain family, who pay a higher price for her because their location is so isolated. Thus the mother-in-law makes enough money to afford to find a bride for her youngest son, with some cash left over. This behavior appalls Mrs. Lu, but Mrs. Wei shrugs it off as normal for those from the country and good fiscal management.

Xianglin's Wife

Xianglin's Wife, whose real name is neither given nor asked for in the course of the story—though her surname is said to likely be Wei—is the young widow of a woodcutter named Xianglin who becomes the favorite maid of the Lu household. She works tirelessly and silently and smiles slightly, happy to be of use. Being a runaway, however, Xianglin's Wife is effectively kidnapped by her mother-in-law and two men, who take her back to their village; from there, she is married off to the sixth son of the Ho family, who live in the mountains. She resists, gashing her head open on the altar in what seems an attempt to commit suicide; this act results in a permanent scar on her forehead. Despite her struggle, she learns to enjoy her life in the mountains, until both her husband and son die untimely deaths.

Xianglin's Wife once again returns to the Lu household, with the help of Mrs. Wei, but cannot work as hard as she used to. The townspeople at first sympathize with the frightening story of her son's death, but they soon grow weary of her. She is not allowed to help with sacrifices because she is tainted by the sin of remarriage and is left with nothing to do but tend the fire. Terrified of being punished in the underworld for her sin, she purchases a threshold at a temple at great cost, but it has no effect on her daily life at the uncle and aunt's house; she is still considered a moral liability. She gives up hope and is soon fired by the family. She becomes a beggar on the streets of Luzhen, where she recognizes the narrator during his visit home. Noting that he is well educated and well traveled, she asks him if ghosts are real, if there is a hell, and if families are reunited in the afterlife. He answers yes to all three questions, though he also indicates that he is not sure. Shortly after, she passes away, just short of the New Year.

THEMES

Death

After the death of her first husband, Xianglin's Wife must wear the white mourning band that so disturbs Mr. Lu, who believes widows are bad luck. When she appears again at the Lu household years later with a new mourning band, it certainly seems to the family and the reader that death follows the woman. Xianglin's Wife loses two husbands and a son, all at a young age. In the superstitious town of Luzhen, these deaths, along with her sin of remarriage, make Xianglin's Wife a pariah, despite the fact that the deaths were not her fault. Her unceasing repetition of the story of Amao's death only seals her fate of ostracism from Luzhen and the Lu household. The sad tale is a constant reminder of her bad luck, as well as of the second marriage which the villagers find scandalous. In addition to the deaths of the men in her life, Xianglin's Wife tries to kill herself during her second wedding ceremony, resulting in a large scar on her forehead. After they tire of hearing the story of her son's death, the villagers mock her attempt on her own life by asking about the scar. Meanwhile, with each New Year an old year dies, time after time in the course of the story.

In the final days of the present year, Xianglin's Wife asks the narrator a series of questions about death. His bumbling answers seal her misery. She asks if there are ghosts, if there is a hell, and if families are reunited after death. When he answers yes to all three, she, taking his word because he is a scholar rather than a superstitious man, conceives that (as Amah Liu warned) her husbands will indeed fight over her in the underworld. She passes away as the old year dies, a sacrifice to the New Year and the god of luck.

Superstition

While the people of Luzhen are wary of Xianglin's Wife for both the bad luck she brings as a widow and her contamination as a sinner, evidence in the story contradicts their superstition. Xianglin's Wife's bad luck is strictly her own, never spreading to the Lu household, the narrator, or the village folk who tease and torment her in Luzhen. Lu Xun condemns superstition at every turn, from the modern, educated narrator's silly belief in the power of saying "I'm not sure" to avoid being blamed after giving unhelpful advice; to the Neo-Confucian uncle who, despite believing in progress and rationality, hotheadedly blames Xianglin's Wife for dying so close to the New Year, with no kind words for the poor beggar woman who has died from poverty; to the aunt who out of superstitious fear will not let Xianglin's Wife be useful in preparations for sacrifices; to Xianglin's Wife herself, who spends an enormous amount of money on a threshold to absolve her sin, only to find her treatment at the Lu household unchanged.

The superstitions of village life are deeply rooted in traditional Chinese religious beliefs, but Lu Xun, as a scholar of Western teachings and promoter of a modernized China, uses "A New-Year Sacrifice" to illustrate how such superstitions can create inhuman treatment of an innocent person. After all, with superstitions removed, Xianglin's Wife is only a hardworking woman who enjoys putting herself to the fullest use in the Lu household. This is a blessing for the family, not a worrisome addition to the household. The narrator and his uncle both aspire to be reasonable and modern, yet they are as bad—if not worse—than the villagers who cruelly tease Xianglin's Wife. The villagers simply act out what they know as right: superstitions passed down from earlier generations. But the educated narrator and his Neo-Confucian uncle succumb to superstition while posing as modern or scholarly. The narrator especially looks on his uncle's fear of mentioning death at dinner on New Year's Eve with condescension. Yet he is as superstitious as his uncle—witness his relief at Xianglin's Wife's sacrificial death—and both share the fault for Xianglin's Wife's mistreatment and death with the other citizens of Luzhen who knew her. The superstitions did nothing to keep the people of Luzhen safe from Xianglin's Wife's bad luck, because they were never in any danger. Xianglin's Wife suffered and died because of the superstitions of those who selfishly feared contamination by her bad luck rather than help her escape her fate.

TOPICS FOR FURTHER STUDY

- Read Stacey Zolt Hara's children's book *Bella's Chinese New Year* (2011), about an American girl in Singapore who learns about the customs of the holiday. How does Hara create an atmosphere of openness and acceptance of different cultures in the book? Read the book out loud to a class of younger students, and ask what they have learned about the Chinese New Year when you are finished reading. Organize a few activities based on the Chinese New Year to accomplish with the class, such as learning to write the Chinese character for "good luck" or making a paper lantern.

- Write an essay in which you examine the significance of New Year's celebrations to the life of Xianglin's Wife. How many New Years are described in the course of the story? What exactly does each New Year entail? How does her life change with each passing New Year? Why do you think Lu Xun chose the New Year as the festival around which to tell the story of Xianglin's Wife?

- The narrator describes his uncle as a Neo-Confucian. What does this term mean? Who was Confucius? Research in print and online to discover the meaning of *Neo-Confucianism* as well as the history behind the term. Then write an essay in which you explain what Confucius taught, what a Neo-Confucian believes, and how the narrator's uncle is portrayed as a Neo-Confucian in "The New-Year Sacrifice." Does the uncle live up to the descriptions you have found? Do you think Lu Xun has a positive or negative view of Neo-Confucianism? To what extent does the author's view, as gleaned from the sense of the story as a whole, seem to align with the narrator's? Use evidence from the text to support your argument, and cite your sources.

- Early in "The New-Year Sacrifice," the narrator's uncle makes reference to a reformist named Kang Youwei, who was closely associated with fellow reformists Liang Qichao and Emperor Guang Xu. Create a blog inspired by one or all three of these Chinese figures. Research the life and ideological stance of your chosen figure(s) and make at least five posts, including pictures and links to outside sources, some of which may concern later historical figures considered to be the reformists' ideological descendants. Add a brief post in which you discuss the reformists' relevance to Lu Xun's story.

- Choose a different short story by Lu Xun to read. How would you compare the story to "The New-Year Sacrifice"? Are there any similar characters, themes, or plot devices? How are the stories different? Some popular short stories by Lu Xun to choose from include "Diary of a Madman" (or "A Madman's Diary"), "The Real Story of Ah-Q" (or "The True Story of Ah Q"), "A Happy Family," and "The Divorce."

STYLE

Unreliable Narrator

An *unreliable narrator* is a narrator whom the reader cannot or should not trust completely. The narrator of "The New-Year Sacrifice" is not unreliable because he lies, exaggerates, or leaves out important details. Instead, he is unreliable in the advice he gives the reader and in his perspective on Xianglin's Wife. Speaking of the usefulness of adding the phrase "I'm not sure" to the end of any presumptuous advice a person gives to someone in need of help, he says, "by concluding their advice with this evasive expression they achieve blissful immunity from reproach." In a short story of superstitions, the

Fireworks mark the celebration of the New Year's sacrifice. (© *Botond Horvath | Shutterstock.com*)

narrator's belief in the power of "I'm not sure" to wipe away guilt in case of disaster is peculiar in that it comes from an educated outsider. As much as he tells the reader and himself that he is free of guilt if something bad happens to the beggar woman, the narrator is troubled by the conversation with his family's former servant, especially by the possibility that something bad is on the horizon for her. The narrator has revealed himself to be as superstitious as the people of Luzhen at whom he scoffs.

When he is done telling the story of Xianglin's Wife, the narrator is not disturbed or agitated by her treatment and fate, but instead feels serenely at one with the town, feels that good luck will rain down on the villagers in the New Year. Julia Lovell writes in her introduction to *The Real Story of Ah-Q and Other Tales of China*, "The story ends with an incongruous exhalation of relief by the narrator, ... a jibe at the moral cheapness of catharsis." The narrator feels that just by remembering her painful life he has done good, conveniently forgetting the damning conversation he had with Xianglin's Wife just before she died. He failed to give her comfort then, but now uses her sad memory to comfort himself. Like her life, Xianglin's Wife's story is controlled, compromised, and abused by people who do not care about or even consider her real feelings.

Motif
A *motif* is a repeating image, event, character, theme, or phrase in a story that has significance to the work. Lu Xun uses several motifs in "The New-Year Sacrifice" to illustrate the hopelessness of Xianglin's Wife's situation. When she first appears at the Lu household, she is wearing a blue jacket, green bodice, and black skirt and a white mourning band in her hair. Years later when she appears again, her outfit is unchanged: black skirt, green and blue top, and, most significantly, the mourning band is back in her hair.

Though her outfit is the same, she has aged with stress and sadness and no longer looks as young as she did. Similarly, the motif of New Years passing fills the story of Xianglin's Wife's life, from her initial success in the Lu household, when she works so hard to prepare the sacrifice that no additional help need be hired; to her return, when she is not permitted to touch the sacrificial objects; to her final, tragic New Year, when she dies alone and unloved. A third motif occurs in Xianglin's Wife's repetition of the story of her son. Not only does she repeat this story throughout town until every villager knows the tale by heart, but the story itself is repeated word for word in the text of "A New-Year Sacrifice." Lovell writes, "Lu Xun forces his readers to join Luzhen's callous listeners, allowing us first to 'chew deliciously' on her sorrow then to share the townspeople's sense of boredom." Thus the reader is implicated in the cruel treatment of the luckless woman.

In Lu Xun's story, the motifs stay the same—the image of the white hair band, the New Year celebrations, and the terrible story of the son's death—but the circumstances around the motifs always change for the worse. Xianglin's Wife may wear the same outfit but is weighed down by sorrow; her New Years progress slowly and painfully toward her death; and the villagers use her story against her after they cannot stand to hear it anymore.

HISTORICAL CONTEXT

Chinese New Year

The New Year in China is celebrated at the end of the lunar year rather than at the end of the Gregorian (or Western) calendar used in New Year's celebrations in the United States and elsewhere. Specifically, the Chinese New Year falls on a later date than the Gregorian New Year, in late January or early February, and is also known as the Spring Festival. The festival celebrating the New Year is the longest of the Chinese holidays and includes fireworks, giving gifts (especially red envelopes with money inside), feasts, visiting relatives, honoring ancestors, and making sacrifices of food to the gods, such as those seen in "The New-Year Sacrifice." The Chinese New Year has influenced the celebration of the New Year in many nearby countries, such as Japan and Singapore. The Chinese New Year is also celebrated in America in China-towns, such as in San Francisco, where a large Chinese New Year parade is held.

In the days leading up to the New Year, families gather together to pray, prepare sacrifices, and clean and purify their homes. After a large feast on New Year's Eve (seen in "The New-Year Sacrifice" in the uncomfortable dinner scene between the narrator and his uncle), New Year's Day and the days following are a celebratory time to rest and relax from school or work. Inauspicious events, such as Xianglin's Wife's death, are very carefully avoided by those superstitious of encountering bad luck or sour omens during this spiritually significant time. Many of these traditions are present in "The New-Year Sacrifice": the narrator returns to his village hometown from the city to visit old friends and relatives, the smell of gunpowder from fireworks lingers in the air, the New Year's sacrifice is made to the gods, and a feast is shared between the narrator and his uncle.

Modernization

During Lu Xun's lifetime, the long dynastic tradition in China was overthrown. In the revolution of 1911–1912, called the Chinese Revolution or Xinhai Revolution, the Qing dynasty—the last dynasty to rule over China—was replaced with the Republic of China. After a long history of successful isolation from the world, the Chinese population had realized, particularly after the 1895 defeat by Japan in the First Sino-Japanese War, that the country had fallen behind its neighbors in what had become a race to modernize in Asia. After replacing the dynasty with a republic, China set about the difficult process of modernizing (which typically meant Westernizing) its practices in education, medicine, and military programs while simultaneously attempting to protect its ancient culture and traditions.

As Lu Xun grew in fame after the revolution, he became a voice for the modernization of the country through his essays, lectures, and short stories. In "The New-Year Sacrifice," he rejects traditional village superstitions, illustrating the terrible harm they can cause. However, he also pulls the narrator down from his pedestal of modernity, demonstrating that just becoming educated is not enough to help the country move forward. The narrator has an education but uses it to condescend to Xianglin's Wife—telling her

COMPARE
&
CONTRAST

- **1920s:** Lu Xun completes his second volume of short stories in 1925, ending his career in fiction. Though he does not publish fiction again, he continues to write essays and give lectures on the state of China. He is a much-beloved critic of government and encourages the modernization of China.

  Today: After Lu Xun's death, Mao Zedong expropriated the writer's life as Communist propaganda, making it illegal to speak poorly of him. Though today that law is no longer in effect, Lu Xun remains an extremely popular figure in Chinese history. Students, scholars, and lovers of history and literature read his work, which is widely translated and published throughout the world.

- **1920s:** Traditionally an isolated and prosperous country, China emerges from the bloody revolution of the early 1910s, in which the last dynasty in China was brought down. No longer isolated in their own traditions and practices, Chinese citizens seek to modernize in order to compete globally. Lu Xun endorses this push towards modernization after learning Western science and teaching methods as a student in Japan.

  Today: China is a global superpower, modern and yet still loyal to its ancient traditions.

- **1920s:** The narrator views the village of Luzhen (based on Lu Xun's birthplace of Shaoxing) as backwards compared to the big city where he lives. However, he appreciates the beauty of the traditional New Year's sacrifice.

  Today: As one of the largest countries in the world, China is home to bustling cities such as Beijing as well as villages even smaller than the fictional Luzhen, where everyone knows each other. There is a great range of peoples, beliefs, technology, and education in China.

---

what he thinks she wants to hear, rather than his true feelings towards ghosts and the underworld. By condescending rather than being honest, the narrator causes great harm. Lu Xun suggests that for China to progress, those with access to modern education must help those in the villages who still believe in ancient superstitions.

CRITICAL OVERVIEW

"The New-Year Sacrifice" has been praised since its publication for its indictment of the prioritization of callous superstition over sympathy. The people of Luzhen indulge in their fear of Xianglin's Wife rather than extend compassion toward a woman in need. In his introduction to *Capturing Chinese: Lǔ Xùn's "The New Year's Sacrifice,"* Kevin Nadolny writes, "The tragic tale of Xianglin's Wife illustrates the lack of freedom that women had in feudal China. Even though she is a hard worker, she cannot escape her obligations to her mother-in-law." In addition she is a widow twice over, causing the town to view her as sinful.

David E. Pollard writes of Lu Xun's fiction in *The True Story of Lu Xun*, "We read in his stories of characters rendered inert by hopelessness." Xianglin's Wife's hopes of redemption are dashed when the threshold she buys at the shrine has no effect on the prejudice she faces at home. When, in the last day of her life, she seeks help from the narrator, his answers do nothing to ameliorate her grief. Of Lu Xun's portrayal of the dark side of society, Yiyun Li writes in her afterword to *The Real Story of Ah-Q and Other Tales of China*, "It is what remains unchanged [in the world] that will make literature live on, and it is perhaps for this reason that Lu Xun's stories will still be read fifty or a hundred years from now."

Pollard, in his introduction to *The New-Year Sacrifice and Other Stories*, writes, "It

Hsiang Lin's wife goes to wash the rice and is kidnapped. *(© wasanajai | Shutterstock.com)*

would be difficult to find a Chinese person who has not heard of Lu Xun and, given a secondary school education, read some of his works, too." His legacy remains prominent in Chinese literature. Lovell writes, "Lu Xun distinguished himself . . . through the controlled craftsmanship of his narratives, his critical intelligence, and the sardonic humour that overlays his recounting of even the blackest episodes."

CRITICISM

Amy Lynn Miller

Miller is a graduate of the University of Cincinnati and currently resides in New Orleans, Louisiana. In the following essay, she considers the guilty parties behind the misery of Xianglin's Wife and examines Lu Xun's subtle methods of showing the reader who is to blame in "The New-Year Sacrifice."

Xianglin's Wife loses not only two husbands and a son in "The New-Year Sacrifice" but also her name, her happiness, and finally her life. She is essentially sacrificed by Luzhen's superstitious inhabitants to the God of Fortune, leaving behind only memories in the minds of those who are glad to finally be rid of her. "The New-Year Sacrifice" is a tragic story but is told by Lu Xun's scholarly narrator as if it were an emotional triumph. The backwards beliefs of the villagers condemn Xianglin's Wife to poverty and death, yet at her death the people do not come to a realization of the wrongs they have committed, as they might in a fairy tale. Even the educated narrator and his Neo-Confucian uncle have no epiphany of guilt upon hearing the news of her death. Instead, the uncle curses the poor woman for her bad timing in dying so close to the New Year celebrations, and the narrator believes that the town is at peace without her troublesome presence: "In this world of ours the end of a futile existence, the removal of someone whom others are tired of seeing, was just as well both for them and for the individual concerned." Xianglin's Wife is stripped of her name, her life, and her story by the outdated superstitions of a rural backwater. Lu Xun's stunning condemnation of such superstitions demonstrates the need for China's modernization in the face of

> XIANGLIN'S WIFE IS AN INNOCENT VICTIM, SACRIFICED BY THOSE WHO NEVER CARED TO KNOW HER, WHO NEVER EVEN ASKED HER FOR HER REAL NAME, ON AN ALTAR OF BASELESS SUPERSTITION."

such inhumanity. Nadolny writes, "Lu Xun uses these characters and story to shock the reader into action ... to wake the Chinese up to bring change into their society."

When Xianglin's Wife first asks the narrator her three ominous questions, Lu Xun has not yet introduced her backstory. After we know more of the woman's tragic life, a return to those loaded questions is necessary. She asks if there are ghosts, if there is an underworld, and if families are reunited after death. Clearly Amah Liu's cruel taunts to her when she was still a maid in the Lu household have not left her mind. She is fearful—now so close to death—that the time will come soon when her husbands will meet her in the afterlife and demand she be ripped in half so they may both have her for eternity. The narrator, who we learn knows her backstory well, thinks not of the significance of these questions to her personal history but instead considers his answers from a condescending perspective. Of course, being an educated, well-traveled, and modern man, he does not believe in such things as ghosts and the underworld. But, considering that the village folk do, he assumes Xianglin's Wife is looking for reassurance in the existence of an afterlife. He lies to her, to alleviate what he believes are her simple rural worries.

What the narrator does not consider, as he looks down on her as a superstitious simpleton, is that Xianglin's Wife desperately wants him to say no—no, there are no ghosts, there is no underworld, and most importantly families do not reunite after death. This is precisely what the narrator believes. Imagine the relief the woman would have felt upon hearing him refute the superstitious beliefs of the Luzhen villagers that have tormented her so. Xianglin's Wife even subtly leads him toward the correct response, calling him well educated and well traveled, implying he is different, better than the villagers

of Luzhen. But the narrator fails catastrophically at picking up these small hints or even considering her life of struggle before giving the easy answers that he assumes a simple villager would prefer to hear. The superstition and bad luck that have plagued her through a lifetime strike a final blow with the narrator's lies. Considering her state as a beggar woman, she would have eventually succumbed to her poverty and died no matter what the narrator answered, but she is not given release from the guilt that the people of Luzhen have piled upon her shoulders. Instead, believing herself damned for an eternity of suffering, she passes away that night, before the New Year dawns.

Lu Xun highlights the disinterest of the community in Xianglin's Wife's troubles with her unusual name. Even after her second marriage the townspeople as well as the Lu household refer to her as Xianglin's Wife—never asking for her real name. The startling lack of curiosity around town about who she is in effect strips her of her personhood. Xianglin's Wife is always in the state of possession, that is, being someone else's possession, and is reminded of this every time someone says her name: she is the wife of Xianglin, owned even after his death by first her mother-in-law, who kidnaps her from the riverbank; then by her second husband in the mountains; then by the Lu household, until she is used up; and finally by the townspeople of Luzhen, where she lives off their spare change and meager charity, which is not even enough to keep her alive. Xianglin's Wife's life belongs to others and, tragically, so does her story. Lu Xun's choice of narrator emphasizes how little anyone in Luzhen cared for the out-of-luck woman. The narrator's strange emotional responses—relief on learning she is dead, relaxation after remembering her life of struggle—do not match the feelings of the thoughtful reader, who sees past the village's worries of contamination and bad luck to the core fact of the story: Xianglin's Wife is an innocent victim, sacrificed by those who never cared to know her, who never even asked her for her real name, on an altar of baseless superstition.

Lu Xun never rises above the narrative mire to scold or chastise the people of Luzhen for their behavior. Rather, he sinks the reader deeply into murk. Lovell writes, "He most unsettlingly implicates the intellectual narrator, the crowd and the reader in the violence of literary

WHAT DO I READ NEXT?

- Gene Luen Yang's young-adult graphic novel *American Born Chinese* (2006) narrates the stories of several characters who must navigate between their Chinese heritage and American culture, including a new student in a school in which he is the only Chinese American, and a popular boy who must accept his Chinese roots in order to succeed after his social standing is ruined by a visit from his eccentric cousin.

- *Palm-of-the-Hand Stories* (2006), by Japanese author Yasunari Kawabata, translated by Lane Dunlop and J. Martin Holman, collects Kawabata's very short, experimental fiction for the first time. The differences between Western and Eastern conceptions of a story, as well as nuances of Japanese culture as they struggle between tradition and modernization, are on display in these short, elusive stories.

- *Diary of a Madman and Other Stories* (1990), by Lu Xun and translated by William A. Lyell, collects much of Lu Xun's best fiction, including his ever-popular "Diary of a Madman."

- In Adeline Yen Mah's memoir of her childhood, *Chinese Cinderella: The True Story of an Unwanted Daughter* (1999), Mah is seen as bad luck in her family after her mother dies during childbirth. Though Mah survives, her remaining family's superstitions and her new, harsh stepmother make Mah quickly realize that she is not welcome as a daughter in her own home.

- *Chinese Theories of Fiction: A Non-Western Narrative System* (2006), by Ming Dong Gu, proposes a literary theory specific to Chinese literature, using critical and literary work from within China to examine the methodology of the writing of Chinese fiction. Gu compares Chinese theories of fiction to those of Europe and elsewhere, legitimizing the place of Chinese fiction in world literature.

- *Six Records of a Floating Life* (1983), by Shen Fu, originally published in 1809 and translated by Leonard Pratt, is the memoir of a man's life in China long before modernization would take hold. Balancing his career, family, and reputation, Shen illustrates the value system and traditions of the Qing dynasty—the last of China's dynasties.

- *Chinese Gods: An Introduction to Chinese Folk Religion* (2009), by Jonathan Chamberlain, explains the many intersections among established religions in the Chinese belief system, including Taoism, feng shui, Buddhism, ancestor worship, Confucianism, and many other ancient practices still honored today, as well as introducing the major gods worshipped in shrines and at celebrations such as the New Year.

- *Waiting* (1999), by Ha Jin, winner of the National Book Award and PEN/Faulkner Award, is the story of a Chinese doctor caught in a love triangle with two women: one representing traditional Chinese values, the other modernity and radical change. A masterful work written by a contemporary giant in Chinese and Chinese American literature, *Waiting* is notable for its insider's portrayal of Communist China.

- *Strange Tales from a Chinese Studio* (2006), written by Pu Songling and translated by John Minford, is a beloved eighteenth-century collection of short stories and folktales in which demons and spirits play an important part in the human characters' often humorous and bumbling moral adventures.

- In *The Vintage Book of Contemporary Chinese Fiction* (2001), edited by Carolyn Choa and David Su Li-qun, twenty-one short stories by contemporary Chinese authors focus on life, both rural and urban, in modern-day China, with particular emphasis on themes of childhood and adolescence.

voyeurism." The reader shown Xianglin's Wife through the subjective lens of the unreliable narrator is at a loss to find Xianglin's Wife's personal spark. She has no qualities that particularly humanize her. When she finally has something to say, repeating the tale of her son's death, the story quickly becomes tiresome, and the reader's eyes scan past the familiar, pathetic lines. Lovell writes, "Time and again, Lu Xun pulls this trick, drawing himself and his audience into his crowds of numb spectators." Even so, there is something not right about the narrator's responses—relief, happiness, even comfort—to the terrible fate of Xianglin's Wife. The reader does not know her because the characters never bothered to find out who she was. But the reader can recognize in the behavior of the more vocal characters the hypocrisies and fears that created such an empty vessel.

Lu Xun does not openly suggest another option for Luzhen. Instead he stirs up anger in the reader over the nonsensical treatment of Xianglin's Wife. His foolish narrator, a modern man like the author himself, does not understand what Lu Xun most emphasized in his life. Modernity in a single individual is not enough to create progress. The entire society must change. Pollard, introducing *The New-Year Sacrifice and Other Stories*, writes, "Modernity was in fact a key concept in all his thinking; not modernity as a fashion, but as a basis for China to first survive, then prosper." Lu Xun lived and wrote in a tempestuous time in China's long history. Traditions long unquestioned were uprooted in favor of a modern approach. "The New-Year Sacrifice" is Lu Xun's lesson in the danger of unquestioned traditions towards helpless individuals. Xianglin's Wife is distrusted as a widow, scorned as a woman who has remarried (even though it was against her will), prevented from helping prepare the religious sacrifices that once gave her joy, and condescended to by the narrator in a moment when she most needs the promise of an escape from her luckless life. Yet in reality Xianglin's Wife is a hardworking woman who is never given a chance to thrive, to enjoy her life as her own. The villagers fear her as a harbinger of bad luck, but it is the people of Luzhen who cast bad luck onto her. She never harms, never speaks in anger, never casts a mean glance, but the village will not support her, until finally her luck runs out.

Source: Amy Lynn Miller, Critical Essay on "The New-Year Sacrifice," in *Short Stories for Students*, Gale, Cengage Learning, 2014.

Jon Eugene von Kowallis

In the following excerpt, Kowallis describes Lu Xun's importance in Chinese culture and history.

The influence of Lu Xun (1881–1936) in China's cultural, literary, and artistic life over the last seventy years has been inestimable. Hailed at death as "The Soul of the Nation," he wore in life the laurels of "Father of Modern Chinese Literature," "Leader of the New Culture Movement," and "Founder of the Woodcut-Engraving School." But he was first and foremost a classical scholar—a poet from a backwater town, propelled by the times through mining, engineering, seamanship, medicine, philology, and pedagogy into the careers of educator, writer, publicist, and polemicist. His novella *The True Story of Ah Q [A Q zheng zhuan]*, replete with classical language and references, won enough recognition at home and abroad to culminate in consideration for the Nobel prize, despite a halting English translation with annotations nearly double the length of the text.

In 1981 Lu Xun became the subject of an international conference held at Asilomar, California, not so much to dissect his works as to dispute his legacy—a legacy still hotly contested in China today between the cultural organs of the state and the mimeographs of its dissidents: for, coming as he did squarely out of the old culture to actively forge the new, Lu Xun was an intellectual titan, a literary colossus, and an ideological iconoclast, the likes of whom China will, in all probability, not see again in the near future.

Though he became the symbol of leftist opposition to the Kuomintang or Nationalist government in the 1930s and lent his name to the Communist cause, he steadfastly maintained an independent position and questioning spirit to the end, never surrendering his intellectual freedom to doctrinaire Stalinism, as did Gorky in the Soviet Union. In the eyes of the Chinese intelligentsia, therefore, Lu Xun maintained his integrity from start to finish, and so the validity of his cultural direction has never been negated by the posthumous distortion to which it has been subjected. If a "loyal opposition" is ever to emerge in China, it will be pursuant to the independent intellectual and moral stance set down by the life and works of this great rebel. In short, Lu Xun is very much alive today, simply because he never allowed himself to make the compromises of a Gorky and would never mount a pedestal of his own free will. His literary

> THE SENSITIVITY TO AND ECONOMY OF LANGUAGE IN HIS SHORT STORIES AND ESSAYS HAS DRAWN UNTRAMMELED PRAISE FROM NATIVE CRITICS, REGARDLESS OF THEIR IDEOLOGICAL ALLEGIANCES."

accomplishments were staggering, and the profundity of his insights on Chinese society unrivaled, yet the crux of his artistic impulse remains the outburst of an irascible conscience at pointless inhumanity. His works offer a critique of the national psyche at times so penetrating, so unnerving that even those who set themselves up as apostates to tradition and harbingers of a new order fly at its onslaught back to the comfortable clichés of the days of foot binding, demure daughters, and obedient sons.

From his experiences reading and translating Eastern European literature against the backdrop of a crumbling imperial order and later in the days of the foundering Republic, Lu Xun came to ascribe purgative powers to literature as a vehicle for psychological inquiry into the spiritual ailments of a people. Early in youth he ruminated on the nature of the ideal citizen, juxtaposed against what he and his contemporaries termed "the Chinese national character." More than anything else, he found the people of his country lacking in compassion (*ai*, literally, "love") and earnestness (*cheng*, also "sincerity," "faith," "conviction"). Initially, he believed this character defect was attributable to lengthy periods of rule by alien invaders (the Mongols, Manchus, and others) that had bred slavish attitudes among their Chinese vassals. But by middle age he had concluded that China's ills were wholly of its own making and could not, in good conscience, be laid at the doorstep of any foreigner. He argued that the greatest danger inherent in aggression was the arrogant indifference of potential victims and the shameless opportunism that often surfaces among a vanquished people. The rulers of the Ming dynasty, as he wrote many times, epitomized the folly of China. Paying no heed to the ever-lengthening shadow of Manchu might building on their northern frontiers, "they busied themselves instead in China with the slaughter of innocent men, as though they had no regard for human life." Yet "the decadence and corruption of the Ming was actually deprived of reaching its peak, simply because Li Zicheng and Zhang Xianzhong rebelled." Then, as the armies of peasants and outlaws swarmed into Peking, "because the rich and powerful were beside themselves lest their former slave become an emperor, they casually invited the 'great Manchu army' in to defeat him." But seeing Chinese flee before their might, the Manchu horsemen were not disposed to stop at Peking, and so went on to finish the conquest of the entire land, destroying the Ming house in their wake.

Lu Xun found himself much troubled by the values of an elite who would choose to give up the whole *tianxia* ("empire") into the hands of foreigners rather than endure the sight of the loss of one city to their own slaves, for he saw in this a recurrent theme in Chinese history. The Manchu statesman Gang Yi (1834–1900) had suggested it again on the eve of the Qing dynasty's collapse with his cavalier remark "Better to hand something over to a friend than have it taken by a household menial." Lu Xun ascribed no better motives to China's later rulers, Yuan Shikai (1859–1916), the northern warlords, and then Chiang Kai-shek, all of whom he saw as too anxious to make concessions to Japan in order to buy time for their personal political agendas.

But what has any of this to do with present-day realities or with universal literary truth? In Lu Xun's oeuvre we find a vast gamut of the literary spectrum employed to analyze social reality, yet we also see social reality recast through the prism of allegory, imagery, and metaphor into lyrical and philosophical art forms valid for all time—relevant to China and the world still in that they address the predicament of modern life—our faults, failings, and innermost fears, in a way that many other Chinese authors have failed to do. As the late critic T. A. Hsia summarized it, Lu Xun's lyrical imagery is imbued with "a kind of terror and anxiety, an experience which we might call modern." His art verges on the fable, borders on the morality play—in a sense Ah Q is a modern Everyman who attains his first glimpse of enlightenment only at the edge of the grave; Aigu in *Divorce* [*Lihun*] faces a hearing as absurd as Kafka's *Trial* and awaits a fate nearly as arbitrary as that of Joseph K. Interpretation of Lu Xun's works can be done at various levels of meaning, and this is a worthwhile undertaking for all, not merely the domain of the specialist. Literature can serve as a stepping stone into a highly complex conceptual framework, but it can also lure a sophisticated Chinese thinker out from his own societal preoccupations to engage the Western reader in a serious dialogue about cultural priorities—if only the latter is willing to hear him out.

In the context of cultural synthesis, Lu Xun's genius at absorption from foreign literature was phenomenal. And in fiction, his stepping out of tradition into a blending of Chinese and Western forms is even more impressive. The sensitivity to and economy of language in his short stories and essays has drawn untrammeled praise from native critics, regardless of their ideological allegiances. These qualities along with his exceptionally sensitive powers of observation are traits that Jaroslav Průšek attributed directly to the influence of classical Chinese poetry, perhaps the most succinct yet stylized of literary forms, on his prose. But in his classical poetry, he was less of the formalistic innovator and more the conduit of an ancient idiom into the modern context. In technique he deviates from the precedents set by Huang Zunxian (1848–1905), who advocated the revitalization of classical poetry through the liberalization of its formalistic requirements and the addition of new vocabulary. For Lu Xun took, with few exceptions, to the highly stylized forms of *jueju* (quatrains) and *lüshi* (full-length regulated verse) poetry—forms with detailed, strict rules for rhyme and tonal prosody that evolved according to pronunciations and standards set up over a thousand years ago. Instead of "new vocabulary," he relied, like his Tang precursor Li He (791–817), on the mythological and shamanistic imagery of the *Chu ci* lyrics, but used it to reflect feelings of modern alienation as well as to comment on and respond emotionally to the excesses, injustices, and vicissitudes of his own day....

Source: Jon Eugene von Kowallis, Introduction to *The Lyrical Lu Xun: A Study of Classical-Style Verse*, University of Hawai'i Press, 1996, pp. 3–6.

SOURCES

"Chinese New Year," History.com, http://www.history.com/topics/chinese-new-year (accessed September 2, 2013).

Denton, Kirk A., "Lu Xun Biography," MCLC Resource Center website, 2002, http://mclc.osu.edu/rc/bios/lxbio.htm (accessed August 21, 2013).

Li, Yiyun, Afterword to *The Real Story of Ah-Q and Other Tales of China: The Complete Fiction of Lu Xun*, Penguin Books, 2009, pp. 412–16.

Lovell, Julia, Introduction to *The Real Story of Ah-Q and Other Tales of China: The Complete Fiction of Lu Xun*, Penguin Books, 2009, pp. xiii–xxxix.

Lu, Xun, "The New-Year Sacrifice," in *The New-Year Sacrifice and Other Stories*, translated by Yang Xianyi and Gladys Yang, Chinese University Press, 2002, pp. 163–205.

Nadolny, Kevin, ed., Introduction to *Capturing Chinese: Lǔ Xùn's "The New Year's Sacrifice,"* Capturing Chinese Publications, 2011, pp. xi–xv.

Pollard, David E., Introduction to *The New-Year Sacrifice and Other Stories*, Chinese University Press, 2002, pp. viii–xxxvi.

———, *The True Story of Lu Xun*, Chinese University Press, 2002, pp. xi–223.

FURTHER READING

Lu, Xun, *Selected Stories of Lu Hsun*, translated by Yang Hsien-yi and Gladys Yang, W. W. Norton, 2003.

This Lu Xun collection (using the Wade-Giles spelling of his name) gathers his most acclaimed short stories, such as "The True Story of Ah Q," "The New Year's Sacrifice," and "A Madman's Diary," with an introduction by the contemporary master of Chinese and Chinese American fiction Ha Jin.

Mann, Susan L., *Gender and Sexuality in Modern Chinese History*, Cambridge University Press, 2011.

Mann explores the changing world of gender and sexuality throughout China's history, including in government laws and regulations, traditions of marriage and childbirth, and how practices have been adjusted, abolished, or strengthened with China's modernization and emergence as a global power.

Schell, Orville, and John Delury, *Wealth and Power: China's Long March to the Twenty-First Century*, Random House, 2013.

Schell and Delury examine China's history of isolation and war for hints of the future superpower it would become. Experts in their field, the authors chose eleven of China's most important figures to study in depth, including Mao Zedong, Chiang Kai-shek, and Empress Dowager Cixi.

Tai, Jeanne, comp. and trans., *Spring Bamboo: A Collection of Contemporary Chinese Short Stories*, Random House, 1989.

Tai's collection of modern Chinese short stories features ten then-young Chinese writers who embrace the long-standing historical and mythical traditions in China while contextualizing those practices and beliefs in modern-day situations.

SUGGESTED SEARCH TERMS

Lu Xun

Lu Hsun

Lu Xun AND New Year Sacrifice

New Year Sacrifice AND short story

New Year Sacrifice AND 1924

Chinese fiction AND New Year Sacrifice

Xianglin's Wife AND New Year Sacrifice

Xianglin's Wife AND Lu Xun

One Throw

W. C. HEINZ

1950

"One Throw" is a brief yet rewarding baseball story written in the middle of the twentieth century by the highly regarded sportswriter and novelist W. C. Heinz. A longtime journalist, Heinz's first forays into reporting for the *New York Sun* through the late 1930s followed sundry subjects, until he became the paper's key correspondent in Europe in the closing years of World War II. Upon returning, he shifted from one realm of physical achievement under duress to another, less extreme one: that of sports.

While he would become best known for his writings on boxing, including his novel *The Professional* (1958)—which Ernest Hemingway once called the only good boxing novel he had ever read—Heinz also demonstrated keen insight into football, baseball, and other sports. He helped revolutionize sports journalism by focusing not merely on the athletes' competitions but on their personal lives as well, including how their wives and families were affected by their lifestyles, how they coped with public adversity, and how their integrity was tested by their circumstances. The focus of "One Throw" is a talented minor-league baseball player who is growing despondent about the small-time scene he is wallowing in. He meets a man who just might be able to help him improve his lot.

"One Throw" was first published in *Collier's Weekly* on July 15, 1950, packed onto a single page as a "short short." The story is available in

W.C. Heinz (© Eddie Adams / Corbis)

many anthologies—including *Fielder's Choice* (1979), edited by Jerome Holtzman; *Baseball's Best Short Stories* (1995), edited by Paul D. Staudohar; and *The Fireside Book of Baseball*, 4th ed. (1987), edited by Charles Einstein—as well as in, with various revisions, the mixed fiction/nonfiction collection *What a Time It Was: The Best of W. C. Heinz on Sports* (2001).

AUTHOR BIOGRAPHY

Wilfred Charles Heinz was born on January 11, 1915, in Mount Vernon, New York, the only child of his salesman father, Frederick, and mother, Elizabeth. Among his childhood activities was the pastime of flipping baseball cards with friends—pitching cards into the air or against walls under various rules to try and win

the others' cards. Slender as a youth, Heinz played hockey through high school, gaining a firsthand understanding of the value of athletic competition, but recognized that despite his dreams, an athletic career was not in the making.

Meanwhile, he became a devoted reader, being drawn to such authors as Mark Twain, Edgar Allan Poe, Alfred Tennyson, and Honoré de Balzac. On his seventeenth birthday, he received Grantland Rice's edited anthology *Omnibus of Sport*, and his interests in sport and literature were fused. Heinz attended Middlebury College, in Vermont, becoming a contributor and sports editor for the college's newspaper and yearbook and graduating in 1937 with a degree in political science.

That fall Heinz gained employment as a messenger boy with the *New York Sun*, running errands for fifteen dollars a week. He was soon promoted to copy boy and cub reporter, and when he wrote an insightful article on cleaning women traveling the elevated trains to Manhattan in the early mornings, he was promoted to city reporter. He would proceed to report on such topics as corrupt politicians, roller-coaster track walkers, pushcart fires, and street shootings. Heinz married Elizabeth Bailey in 1941, and they would have two daughters.

After America entered World War II, Heinz served as the *Sun*'s junior war correspondent, writing up duly admiring, patriotic pieces on secondary figures in the war, namely those, including cooks and clerks, manning aircraft carriers in the Atlantic. When the *Sun*'s primary war correspondent was captured by the Germans, Heinz stepped up to replace him, covering the advances of American forces from the D-day invasion of the beaches of Normandy, France, in 1944 to the conquest of Germany in 1945. In the face of the intense drama of the war, he honed a minimalist style, including few of his own comments and simply allowing the events and their participants to speak for themselves. Having emerged from this crucible in which men's valor and integrity were at the heart of the experience, Heinz returned to the United States and made one request: that he now be assigned to sports.

Already admired for his wartime journalism, Heinz saw his career as a sportswriter take off as he covered in his column "The Sport Scene" everything from hockey to bicycling to horse racing to boxing to baseball. When the *New York Sun* folded in 1950, he turned to freelance writing, contributing nonfiction and fiction to periodicals such as the *Saturday Evening Post*, *True*, and *Collier's Weekly*, which published "One Throw" in July 1950. Pieces such as Heinz's intimate profiles of Rocky Graziano in "The Day of the Fight" and of Graziano's wife, Norma, in "The Fighter's Wife" established Heinz as a forerunner of what would be known as New Journalism, adding extra literary dimensions to what until then had been a strictly objective profession.

Among Heinz's celebrated books were *Run to Daylight!* (1963), an intricate working profile that would help turn Vince Lombardi into a football coaching legend; *M.A.S.H.* (1968), written with H. Richard Hornberger under the joint pseudonym Richard Hooker, which inspired the hit movie and TV series about a field hospital during the Korean War; and *Once They Heard*

the *Cheers* (1979), a nostalgic look at the athletes who had so inspired Heinz in their heydays. Heinz died at the age of ninety-three on February 27, 2008, in Bennington, Vermont.

PLOT SUMMARY

"One Throw" opens with a first-person narrator noting his arrival at a hotel, the Olympia, in a town so small that that hotel is the only one. Loitering in the lobby, he chats with the man behind the desk to confirm that a baseball player named Maneri indeed plays in that town. (The terms *play ball* and *ballplayer* are classically used to refer to baseball.) The narrator indicates some familiarity with Maneri's situation, as he has read about the young man's great potential. Phil Rizzuto, with whom Maneri is compared, was in that era the star shortstop for the New York Yankees, the vaunted major-league organization Maneri is now playing for, though on a minor-league team. The man behind the desk imagines that the Yankees must know what they are doing, keeping such a talented young player so far from the majors, but he reveals that Pete Maneri himself is a bit downhearted about the situation. A question of the narrator's suggests that he was unaware that Maneri (along with a few other players) is currently living in the Olympia.

Pete happens to enter the lobby just then. He greets and chats affably with the man behind the desk, Nick, though Pete's tone hints at a less-than-sunny frame of mind. The narrator introduces himself as Harry Franklin, remarking that he recognizes the ballplayer from photos. Maneri speaks modestly of his abilities, even self-deprecatingly, though Nick objects. Franklin reveals himself to be a baseball fan who, since there is a doubleheader that evening, will attend the games. In fact he used to play ball as well, for the minor-league team in Columbus, Ohio.

Franklin and Maneri go down to the hotel bar, with Franklin having "a couple" (suggesting beers), while Maneri has cola. Franklin says he now sells hardware. The older man asks Pete what he is doing in this low league when word has it he ought to be playing higher up. Pete seems disappointed and puzzled: he has an outstanding batting average (.300, which means getting a hit 30 percent of the time, is a benchmark

MEDIA ADAPTATIONS

- A facsimile of the original *Collier's Weekly* version of Heinz's "One Throw" is available online at http://www.unz.org/Pub/Colliers-1950jul15-00038.

for excellence); he leads the league in stolen bases (racing to the next base while the pitcher winds up and pitches); and, on the defensive side, he declares himself an incomparable fielder. However, the manager, Al Dall, ignores him even when he comes up with key hits or fielding plays. Meanwhile, Maneri gets chewed out if he makes the slightest mistake, such as when he attempted to advance to second base when the ball was "loose" (as dropped by a fielder on the hit or a throw) and got caught in a rundown—when the fielders chase a runner back and forth, repeatedly throwing the ball ahead of him until they can tag him. (For a rundown to occur, the original throw to get the runner will be so far ahead of him that he has time to stop and turn around.)

Franklin begins to suggest that the manager is intentionally suppressing Maneri's advancement through the Yankees' minor-league system simply so that his own team will continue to perform well. The true goal of the organization is to channel all worthy talent to the major-league team as efficiently as possible, but a minor-league manager will nonetheless want the performance of his particular team to reflect well on his own managing abilities. Thus, it is indeed in Dall's personal interest to keep Maneri on his team. Maneri laments that a big-time Yankee scout like Eddie Brown, never being told of Maneri's talent, would probably never even pass through the town.

As Franklin sees it, Maneri's best option may be to act out in order to get the Yankees' attention. Franklin reports that once, having been in a similar situation, he began playing poorly enough to sabotage his minor-league

team's games, which led to the manager's griping to his superiors. When the major-league team sent scouts to assess the situation, Franklin evidently impressed them enough to be not demoted but promoted, to Columbus. Franklin goes so far as to suggest that the boy has nothing to lose by trying such a trick, and the boy agrees. He declares that he will attempt Franklin's approach. By now, Franklin as narrator is revealing a certain mischievousness: he acknowledges that he is steaming Pete up, which may strike the reader as mean, and that he does do some strange things. Franklin communicates to Maneri his excitement over the coming evening.

Franklin goes to the old wooden ballpark. The evening's first game is uneventful, with only about four hundred fans in attendance. Maneri's team, the home team, wins handily, 8–1. Franklin reports that Maneri was not challenged in the field, as none of his chances for plays were difficult, but he did hit a double, display patience at the plate by getting walked twice, and show his speed while running the bases.

The second game proves more exciting. By the ninth and last inning, Maneri's team is winning 3–2. However, the opposing team, down to their final out in the top of the ninth, rallies and loads the bases (getting men on all three bases in the field). Even a single could score two runs and give the opposing team the lead, and the home team would be left only one more chance at the plate, in the bottom of the ninth. On the other hand, if the opposing team fails to score, the home team need not bat again, and the game ends. (A tie would lead to extra innings.) Franklin hopes the ball is hit to shortstop— which is most common—and indeed it is, taking one big bounce off to Maneri's right. Making a backhand stab at the ball, he must leap and turn despite his momentum to make a long throw across the diamond to first base to get the out—a very challenging play to execute—and he succeeds. The batter is out, and the game ends.

Back at the hotel, Franklin hangs around until Maneri arrives. The elder man is interested in chatting, but Maneri appears despondent and simply wants to go to bed. Franklin sways him by assuring him that he "did the right thing," and they go back down to the taproom. Franklin now interrogates Maneri, twice asking him why he failed to throw the ball away and twice being told that Maneri does not know why. Franklin then declares that he will tell him why he failed to throw it away: because he is going to be a major leaguer, and he is going to be a major leaguer because he failed to throw the ball away. Franklin tried to get him to throw the ball away as a test, as he is, in fact, Eddie Brown.

CHARACTERS

Eddie Brown

Known to the reader and to the other characters throughout the story as hardware salesman Harry Franklin, the narrator reveals himself to be none other than "the great Yankee scout" Eddie Brown in the final line—indeed, the final words—of the story. All along he seems to be a sympathetic individual. He appears to be especially curious about Maneri because he has read about his situation, and he professes to wonder why the kid remains down there in the minors. When Pete expresses his displeasure with the circumstances, the narrator seems to respond by speaking in Pete's best interests. Though his suggestion to play poorly on purpose is ethically suspect, he figures that such a ruse might ultimately get Maneri promoted.

The reader likely takes the narrator's statements at face value, at least up until the point where he hints and then acknowledges that he is intently eliciting Pete's displeasure. Even so, while Franklin is evidently the sort of person to stir up trouble, there is little reason to suspect he is not who he says he is: a retired semiprofessional ballplayer who learned a dubious thing or two in the minors. After the game, it may seem as though Franklin is cruelly pleased with Pete's failure to botch what proved the game-ending play, obliging the poor kid to talk when he would rather call it a night. The reader soon learns, however, that Franklin is pleased because he is actually Eddie Brown and has been testing this promising young man, and Maneri has passed with flying colors.

Al Dall

While Pete's manager does not appear in the story, his presence hangs over it, because his treatment of Maneri is leaving the standout shortstop disheartened. The portrait of Dall provided by Pete is of a man who is inclined for no apparent reason to belittle one of his better players—if not his best player—for occasional

mistakes while overlooking decisive contributions, as if intending to quash his spirit. It is no surprise that Dall's treatment frustrates Maneri. Whether or not Maneri's frustration is affecting his play on the field, however, is an open question. In the two games that Eddie Brown watches, Pete makes no mistakes in the field, while on offense he shows some power by hitting a double. Also, though one might expect him to be eager to impress, he patiently earns two walks (by declining to swing at four pitches out of the strike zone each time). From this information, as well as his season statistics thus far, it would seem that Pete is playing just fine despite Dall's oppressive treatment.

In this light, it is conceivable that Dall's treatment is strategic, perhaps even commanded by the Yankees' head office. If a player's on-field abilities are already proven, what remains uncertain is how he will mentally adapt to the heightened competition of the majors. If he starts out poorly, he may get disheartened, and his playing may suffer further; if, on the other hand, he has already demonstrated that, even if disheartened, he is capable of maintaining his focus and performing well, then it is that much clearer that he is ready for the majors. Indeed, the fact that Eddie Brown is at the games that evening—and intent on not just witnessing but testing Maneri—is evidence that Dall has not, after all, kept the Yankees in the dark about the quality of Maneri's play.

Harry Franklin
See Eddie Brown

Pete Maneri

At the heart of the story is Pete Maneri, an excellent baseball player who finds himself mired on a minor-league team in a two-bit town that feels like the middle of nowhere. His all-gray clothing helps figure him as overcast in spirit and also as entering the story in an ethically questionable state of mind—not black or white but somewhere in the middle. Pete's conversational remarks suggests that he is trying to stay positive, but he cannot quite deny that he wishes he were closer to the majors, as there is at least one other minor-league team, Kansas City, and probably several, between him and the Yankees.

Although his fielding position is never directly stated, Pete presumably plays shortstop, which is the position played by Phil Rizzuto and which the description of the game-ending play supports. This infield position is found to the left of second base (if one is looking from home plate) and is a key position where the fielder must be sure-handed, because more ground balls tend to go here than anywhere else. Typically the best infielder plays shortstop, needing wider range than the third baseman and a stronger arm than the second baseman. Throws from shortstop to first base are especially challenging if the fielder must range deep to his right to make a backhand play, with his momentum carrying him even farther from first base.

Maneri prides himself on his fielding and his speed, and his batting average of .365 likely puts him among the league leaders. Yet there he remains, in a town and on a team whose namelessness heightens the sense that he is nowhere special. He is just resentful enough, it turns out, to give consideration to Harry Franklin's suggestion that perhaps the best way to get the Yankees' attention would be to start screwing up, rather than playing so consistently well—to make the bosses pay attention to him. How Maneri responds when he is presented with the perfect opportunity to literally throw the game away constitutes the crux of the story.

Nick

Nick is the worker at the front desk of the hotel. He is amiable with both the narrator, whom he has just met, and Pete Maneri, whom he has gotten to know over the season. His old-fashioned sense of hospitality—not just serving but befriending his clientele—helps bring Pete into contact with the man who turns out to be Eddie Brown.

THEMES

Injustice

The first half of "One Throw" is a tale of injustice—or so it seems. The reader is presented with the pitiable circumstances of Pete Maneri: despite being billed as a future superstar, he is languishing on a mid- to low-level minor-league team and, moreover, being treated dismissively by the coach. Given his abilities, Pete imagines that he ought to be playing in a higher league, and no player likes to have his accomplishments ignored and his mistakes magnified and broadcast.

Interestingly, Maneri himself seems mostly disinclined to speak ill of his manager or go so far as to declare that the situation is unjust. When asked by Franklin how he feels about this particular minor league, he does not at once begin griping about the quality of the league or the Yankees' failure to promote him but says, "I suppose it's all right. I guess I've got no kick coming." Instead of at once blaming his manager for failing to notice his talents, he more broadly laments, "There's nothing wrong with my playing ... but who cares?" When Al Dall is brought up, Pete does not truly bad-mouth him but more diplomatically says, "Maybe he is all right, but I don't get along with him." In other words, Pete is mostly resigned to his situation, for the time being, at least.

Franklin, rather, is the one who makes a point of identifying the injustice, especially through leading questions like "What are they trying to do to you? ... What's the trouble? ... Who manages this ball club?" Of course, ultimately, Maneri is being paid by the Yankees organization to play for their minor-league team, and they have the leeway to treat him as they see fit. They would be foolish to allow a young player to squander his talents in permanent irrelevancy, and Maneri is wise to accept their plans as being, in the end, in everyone's best interest: they, like him, want him to be the best ballplayer he can be. One might conclude, then, that what seems like injustice is simply the way things happen to be for the present. Only under Franklin's provocative influence is the situation fully framed in Maneri's mind as unjust.

Deception

Franklin's remedy for the injustice he has identified is a ruse, a bit of calculated deception. His tale of his own experience securing promotion through deception is a cunning one. Had he merely theoretically posited that such a scheme, botching plays so that the team starts losing, would work, Maneri might have shrugged it off as too far-fetched. Instead, Franklin himself offers the proof that such a scheme can work, as it did for him, gaining him promotion to Columbus. This is enough to lead Maneri to consider the merits of the plan; he would like nothing more than to find his way to a higher league, perhaps even if it involves deception.

Yet as the reader realizes in retrospect, Harry Franklin is not who he says he is, and so

TOPICS FOR FURTHER STUDY

- The success of Heinz's story depends to some extent on the reader's understanding of the game of baseball. Write a story set in a specialized milieu with which you are familiar—whether that of a different sport, a style of dance, a religious community, a gaming community, or any other social niche—featuring a protagonist who is confronted with a moral dilemma. Carefully consider how much esoteric situational language, or jargon, to use, trying to strike a balance between realistically reflecting the community and making the story accessible to all readers. Post your story online, and get feedback from your classmates as to how successful it is.

- With at least two classmates, produce a film version of "One Throw," which, being mostly dialogue, lends itself to performance. You can try to reproduce the baseball scene(s) on a field, using close-ups to obscure the absence of many players and a large crowd, or you can convey the baseball action by zooming in on Eddie Brown in an empty part of the bleachers listening to the game on the radio (as prerecorded by your production team). Present the film to your peers in class or online.

- Read the story "Jamesie," by J. F. Powers, which follows a boy as he hangs around an early twentieth-century baseball game in which his favorite local player, Lefty, is pitching—but not as well as he usually does. Write an essay in which you compare this story with Heinz's "One Throw," discussing the moral standing of Lefty and Pete Maneri, the relevance of their levels of ability to the plot, the lesson conveyed by each story, and any other topics you find interesting.

- Write a research paper on the integrity of the New York Yankees organization over the course of baseball history as reflected in individual players. Try to write objectively, as Heinz strove to do, concealing any favor or disfavor you harbor toward the polarizing club. Be sure to discuss the virtues and shortcomings of major figures from the past, such as Babe Ruth, Lou Gehrig, Joe Dimaggio, and Mickey Mantle, as well as from the contemporary era, such as Andy Pettite, Mariano Rivera, Alex Rodriguez, and Derek Jeter.

- Stage a debate with a friend or write a paper on whether or not Pete Rose, who holds the all-time record for hits but was found guilty of gambling on baseball, deserves to be permanently banned from baseball's Hall of Fame. If you write a paper, include discussion of the relevance of this issue to "One Throw."

---

there is no reason to believe that the story about his promotion to Columbus his true. Almost certainly, the tale of successful deception is itself a deception. The presence of multiple layers of deceit illuminates the overarching problem with it: once one commits to the realm of deception, one can never be sure of what is true and what is not. Indeed, where Franklin is the sort of person who would encourage another to be deceptive, who believes that deception is occasionally justified, it stands to reason that he cannot be trusted, as he might have some unspoken reason for being deceptive himself at any given time. Maneri might subconsciously realize that

Franklin cannot be trusted and also understand that the realm of deception is not one that a person can virtuously inhabit.

Integrity

The question that the story hangs on—what will Maneri do when he has the chance to execute Franklin's plan?—boils down to the question of Maneri's integrity. From a certain perspective, Franklin's plan may seem just: a player, based on his talent, deserves to be promoted, but unfair treatment by a selfish manager is keeping him where he is; thus to counter that unfairness with deception is legitimate, perhaps even the only solution. Of course, first of all, it is not certain that the manager is acting selfishly—this is only a conjecture, and one made by Franklin, at that. Then, to execute Franklin's plan, Maneri would not only be deceiving his manager, he would be deceiving his entire team, operating contrary to the team's goal of performing as well as possible in order to win as many games as possible.

Some might conceive that winning should not be the goal of sporting activity, and with children that may be a relevant point, but this is a professional organization, staffed by men who are being paid to dedicate their talents to the success of the team. Regardless of his rationale, if Maneri were to sabotage even a single game, he would, in effect, be a traitor, one who is secretly working against the community to which he has pledged his allegiance. Baseball is a team sport, and the individual cannot prioritize his own interests above the team's and simultaneously maintain respectability among his peers.

As it happens, Pete's integrity is precisely what Eddie Brown as Harry Franklin has set out to test. It is not difficult for Brown to cajole Pete into discussing his situation, and Pete appears grateful to have the chance to speak freely with someone on the matter; it would be unwise of him to share any frustrations with his teammates, since not only might they resent him, but word could get back to the manager, who might conclude that Pete is incapable of setting his ego aside to simply contribute to the team. If Pete had followed through with Franklin's plan, that is what it would have revealed, that his ego is more important than the success of the team—a toxic quality in a professional athlete.

Success

There may be many routes to success in a given endeavor, as well as many definitions of what constitutes success. A person might consider oneself successful for having a lucrative career, or a fulfilling career, or a trophy wife or husband, or a loving family, or all of these things. One might attain these things through perseverance, innate qualities, sheer luck, or even deception. With a baseball team, there is actually only one solid definition of success, which is winning.

There are different approaches to winning a game—good pitching, power at the plate, impeccable fielding, speed on the base paths, and so forth—but if one takes integrity into account,

The narrator and the kid first meet in the hotel lobby. (© Kzenon / Shutterstock.com)

what cannot lead to unqualified success is deception. There are written rules against, say, scuffing the ball, because it gives the pitcher an unfair advantage, and there are unwritten rules as to personal conduct on the field, such as with regard to stealing signs. There may not be an official rule against throwing the ball away on purpose to cause one's team to lose, but ethically, this would be a failure of integrity.

Pete Maneri wants to succeed as a baseball player, but part of his personal definition of success is to perform to his utmost ability, while he recognizes that as a ballplayer, he is first and foremost committed to the success of his team. As such, by definition, it is not possible for him to succeed at the expense of his team. It is a clever ruse that Eddie Brown has concocted to test this promising young man so, and in the end, Maneri succeeds in sustaining his integrity, deciding against traitorous deceit even in the face of seeming injustice, and proving his worth as a ballplayer and as a human being.

STYLE

Morality Play

"One Throw" has been succinctly characterized by Alvin Hall as a "morality play on the diamond," meaning a work (about baseball) that follows the dramatic style in which an explicit moral dilemma is presented, often as put forth by a subtly or perhaps brazenly sinister character who represents evil or a specific vice, and with other concepts similarly personified. Morality plays were common in the Middle Ages, especially among Christian playwrights, featuring religious thematic approaches.

Heinz's story indeed resembles a play in that it consists almost entirely of dialogue in stationary settings, namely, the hotel lobby and the taproom in the basement; at the baseball field, while dialogue is absent, the perspective does not move around within the games being played but remains at Brown's vantage point in the stands. Beyond his playing abilities, Pete Maneri, as he is depicted before Harry Franklin's corrupting influence overtakes him, can readily be seen to represent certain virtues, like humility, patience, and perseverance. Franklin, on the other hand, appearing in the seemingly harmless guise of a hardware salesman and former ballplayer, represents impatience, selfishness, and deception. Franklin quite deliberately tempts Maneri toward sin. By aggressively telling Maneri to "take over" and not let Dall "ruin" his career, he even elicits a commitment to the dark side: "'I'll try it,' the kid said."

The references throughout the story to Maneri as a "kid" emphasize his ethically vulnerable position: in learning the ropes of a new realm of society, he is liable to misunderstand what is and is not proper behavior. In the end, his moral compass proves sound, as he declines to follow Franklin's ill-advised suggestion. In speaking with Maneri afterward, Franklin figuratively throws off his sinister disguise, with theatrical dialogue that suits the occasion—Brown has, after all, been acting toward this premeditated moment all along—and reveals himself to be the savior figure who will reward Maneri for his virtuousness with ascent to the major leagues.

Surprise Ending

Many readers will be pleasantly surprised by the ending of "One Throw." The story itself has a distinct and steady trajectory toward a defining finale, but the finale the reader expects is the throw itself, the "one throw" that will likely either make or break the protagonist Maneri. The setup is successfully ambiguous in that, though the reader may instinctively recognize Harry Franklin's advice to be ethically unsound, the argument he presents is a rational one: he frames Maneri's present discontent as the fault of a particular person, Al Dall, who could stand in the way of Maneri's deserved promotion indefinitely. Franklin essentially characterizes Maneri as oppressed, and disregard for authority is one of the most basic ways of coping with oppression. Henry David Thoreau, author of "Civil Disobedience"—objecting to the Massachusetts government's use of funds, he was jailed for a night for refusing to pay the poll tax—might have bought Franklin's argument. Refusing to support a supposedly corrupt manager by refusing to contribute one's talents to the team is not so far removed from a labor strike, an ethically sanctioned approach to improving one's working circumstances. By virtue of Franklin's reasoning, the reader can easily imagine that Maneri might go through with the intended sabotage.

However, Heinz has sprinkled a few clues to keep the reader guessing with regard to where the story is headed. Through the first two-thirds of the story, Franklin seems to be genuinely advising Maneri in the player's best interest, yet when he concludes his story about sabotaging his team's games and gaining promotion to Columbus, the narrative text begins tilting the other way. The reader may raise an eyebrow when Franklin says that in counseling Maneri he is "egging him on." The reader may raise both eyebrows when the narrator states, "Maybe you think this is mean to steam a kid up like this, but I do some strange things." Instead of figuring his encouragement as a rational attempt to help another cope with oppression, Franklin as narrator figures it here as one man drawing out another's darker emotions in an unkind way, suggesting that he is actually goading him toward improper action. The vague reference to the narrator's occasional strangeness can only be taken at face value—whether he has benevolent or malicious designs remains up in the air.

After Maneri proves to make the game-winning throw, there occurs the only break in the text, lending a finality to that throw, as if Maneri has just closed the book on his opportunity for advancement. Franklin comes across as excited to chat and not so much disappointed as intrigued by Maneri's decision. Even when Franklin positively declares, "You're going to be a major-league ballplayer someday," the reader, like Maneri, may take this as empty pep talk that only heightens the ballplayer's awareness of his present minor-league despondency and his failure to fulfill the plan. Franklin's insistence, asking several times why Maneri made the throw he did, is frustrating to Maneri, but at last the disguise is dropped, and the great scout Eddie Brown is revealed holding the key to the future that Maneri has been looking for all along.

HISTORICAL CONTEXT

Mid-twentieth Century Baseball and the New York Yankees

"One Throw" presents itself as taking place at precisely the time of its publication, the summer of 1950. By this point in history, the New York Yankees were the acknowledged powerhouse of Major League Baseball. There were then sixteen teams in all, divided into the American and National Leagues, and since the World Series had been established in the century's first decade, crowning a champion among all teams, the Yankees had been the victors a hugely disproportionate twelve times, most recently in 1949—which would prove the first of five straight championships. In sum, as Harvey Frommer puts it in *New York City Baseball: The Last Golden Age, 1947–1957*, "Throughout baseball, the Yankees were viewed as aristocrats, winners."

Alongside such hallowed figures as Joe DiMaggio, Yogi Berra, and Mickey Mantle, shortstop Phil Rizzuto was among the most prominent Yankee stars during their period of overwhelming dominance through the middle of the century. He was the regular shortstop beginning in 1941, though, like many players, having been enlisted during World War II, he played for the US Navy team while hostilities continued; when he returned, he suffered from recurring bouts of malaria. In 1950, Rizzuto hit .324, led American League shortstops with a .982 fielding percentage, and won the league's Most Valuable Player award. By the mid-1950s, having played in nine World Series, Rizzuto "seemed to fans to have always been a Yankee," in Frommer's words. Yet he was aging, with his statistics trailing downward and talented players lined up to

replace him; and so in midsummer 1956, the Yankees released him, and his career ended. Referring to the fates of Rizzuto and other Yankees, Frommer notes, "Actions such as these—the unceremonious release of Yankee legends—earned for the organization its reputation as a callous, calculating, cold corporate entity," one with an "endless stream of spare parts and new parts from the highly productive farm system."

The "farm system" is a colloquial term for the set of minor-league clubs affiliated with a major-league team. While various leagues had been in existence since baseball evolved in the late nineteenth century, the farm system as such was formulated in the first half of the twentieth century. In 1901, minor-league teams created their own association and ranked the leagues from levels A down through D, with the higher minor-league teams able to draft players from any of the lower teams. In 1903, major-league teams were enabled to draft players from the minors in a similar manner. However, by 1919, the minor leagues regretted the continual loss of talent to the majors and withdrew from the existing drafting agreement. Thus, while some major-league team owners also owned minor-league teams—and so could arrange for promising players to advance their skills in the minors until they were ready to be "called up"—otherwise the minors functioned independently. Major-league teams would trade for or purchase players from minor-league teams much as they would from each other. Under a new drafting agreement forged in 1921, a given minor league—by then class AA, or double A, was the highest—could withdraw entirely from a year's draft, meaning it would neither lose nor gain talent to or from other leagues.

With this added uncertainty over prospects, the pioneering owner Branch Rickey, of the St. Louis Cardinals, moved to establish a minor-league empire of sorts, an extensive system of teams at all minor-league levels, all owned by the parent club, in which talent could be protected and nurtured. Because a successful farm system could only be built if the youngest talent could be found and identified early—rather than ripened talent being plucked once proven—scouts came into play, helping the parent club invest both broadly and wisely in potential stars. By the early 1930s, major-league owners widely acknowledged that having a farm system had become a necessity.

COMPARE
&
CONTRAST

- **1950:** With only sixteen teams in Major League Baseball and flourishing numbers of minor-league teams for each major-league team—often over a dozen—the ratio of minor leaguers to major leaguers is over 26 to 1, reflecting the low likelihood that any given minor leaguer will make it to the top.

  Today: The thirty teams in Major League Baseball are generally limited to five or six minor-league teams each, and so (judging from the standard twenty-five-man major-league roster) the ratio of minor to major leaguers is closer to 10 to 1. Still, only the most promising talent will be given a chance at the major-league level each year.

- **1950:** As television increases in popularity, newspapers are relied on less for daily reports. With the *New York Sun* ceasing operations in January 1950 and others following suit over the next two decades, the number of New York dailies will be reduced from ten to three. Sportswriters like Heinz

  become fewer and more limited in their publication options.

  Today: In the twenty-first century, printed newspapers are considered an endangered species, with many shifting to online-only content, accessible by computer, smartphone, or electronic pad, to remain financially solid. With the Internet, sportswriters have an array of options for "publishing" their writings, though self-driven media such as blogs do not bring payment for their efforts.

- **1950:** The average major-league baseball player makes $11,000 for the year, nearly equal to the salary of US senators, $12,500.

  Today: Constantly rising in the era of free agency and intense competition among teams for the biggest stars, the average annual salary of major-league baseball players reaches $3.2 million in 2012. By contrast, as of 2012, the majority of US senators and representatives earn a yearly salary of $174,000.

By midcentury, the Yankees' farm system had come to rival the Cardinals' as one of the best. With the highest minor leagues now labeled AAA, or triple A, the Yankees had three such teams, in Kansas City, Missouri; Newark, New Jersey; and Oakland, California. In addition, they had an array of lower minor-league teams, in such locations as Springfield, Massachusetts; Binghamton, New York; Butler, Pennsylvania; Akron, Ohio; Norfolk and Bassett, Virginia; Augusta, Georgia; Beaumont, Texas; Quincy, Illinois; Muskegon, Michigan; Grand Forks, North Dakota; and still other cities. One can easily imagine how, at a time in history when newspapers were distributed locally and options for long-distance communication were limited to letters, telegrams, and the telephone, a minor leaguer might come to feel abandoned in such an extensive farm system as the Yankees'. The depth of their system would be characterized by

manager Casey Stengel in 1955 (cited in Frommer) in revealing terms:

> We start out to get us a shortstop and now we got eight of them. We don't fool we don't. I ain't yet found a way to play more than one man in each position although we can shift them around. . . .

The Yankees' dominance on the baseball diamond grew tiresome for many opponents as well as fans of the game—offering evidence that victory alone is not necessarily satisfying for spectators. In the words of Yankee second baseman Jerry Coleman (cited by Frommer), "People watched the Yankees ... admired the pride of the Yankees, but unfortunately, the Yankees became so successful, people hated them for their success." In effect, as Frommer suggests, the Yankees' businesslike approach to victory minimized the humanity of the players and reduced the sympathetic connection established

The kid plays baseball in a small ballpark with old wooden bleachers. (© Paisarn Praha / Shutterstock.com)

by fans: "It wasn't just their success year after year that rankled Yankee haters. It was the way they achieved success. With machine-like efficiency, with methodical consistency, their pursuit and attainment of excellence became boring." The historian later reiterates, "The public image of the Yankees was one of corporate efficiency and expertise, where all the individual stars blended in the pursuit of victory." Whether or not a virtuous fictional player like Heinz's Pete Maneri would happily fit into such a culture of mechanical success is left to the reader's imagination.

CRITICAL OVERVIEW

While Heinz's novels, especially his widely praised boxing novel, *The Professional*, have been given due regard, his short stories are few in number, were published sporadically, and have elicited little commentary. In the *Dictionary of Literary Biography*, Edward J. Tassinari observes that Heinz's stories typically extol "the fortitude

of the code hero, who may suffer for his honesty but adheres to an abiding respect for the sport that prohibits him from profaning its essence." (Tassinari points out that Heinz frequently used the name Eddie Brown or just Eddie for the solid "professional working man" in his short fiction, including for a world-class boxing trainer, an infallibly honest fight referee, an artistically minded football coach, and the renowned baseball scout.) "One Throw" is said to focus on a test of "the inner fiber of a promising but troubled young minor league shortstop." Critically speaking, Tassinari only reports that "this simple story was considered by Heinz to be completely true as to dialogue and characterization."

In *Extra Innings: Writing on Baseball*, Richard Peterson finds this story (and many others) too melodramatic for his taste. He states, "The problem with the conventional baseball short story is that what passes for realism too easily slides into formulaic characters and plots and morally predictable and nostalgically sentimental outcomes." He offers only a single clause on Heinz's story in particular: "the green hero must . . . resist a Faustian temptation to compromise his great talent," referring to the fabled German magician—a common referent in literature—who makes a deal with the devil. More favorable in his assessment is Alvin L. Hall in *The Cooperstown Symposium on Baseball and American Culture, 1999*, where the story is deemed "a wonderful morality play on the diamond." Hall acknowledges that "the story seems predictable in a sense" but notes that the "surprise ending" inverts that supposed predictability. He concludes that "One Throw" is "an exceptionally fine character-building story for youngsters to read. The shortstop whose 'virtue is its own reward' gets an added bonus for his honest effort."

Most of the attention paid to Heinz has been with respect to his journalism. In his foreword to the Heinz collection *What a Time It Was*, David Halberstam, himself a respected sportswriter, notes how Heinz's writing drew him to the profession, as "here after all was journalism, simple and understated, which was both true and literary." Halberstam continues:

> He wrote simply and well—if anything he underwrote—but he gave his readers a feel and a sense of what was happening at a game or at the fights, and a rare glimpse into the personalities of the signature athletes of the age. He was immune from the great sin of that era's sportswriting—clichés.... [T]he people he wrote about were very real; they lived real lives, and on occasion they even felt real pain.

Halberstam elaborates on how natural Heinz's nonfiction felt, the author not artificially erasing himself but, by acknowledging his role in the story, allowing the reader to vicariously experience that role. In a phrase, Heinz's journalism "has the feel of fiction—because it contained so much truth."

In his introduction to the same Heinz collection, Jeff MacGregor affirms that "Heinz had an ear for dialogue, for the truth of what people said and how to write it." He goes on to state that "what characterizes the writing of Bill Heinz is its drive and its deceptive simplicity. Never strident or overwrought, never hagiographic or adulatory, Bill Heinz wrote sports with a gimlet eye."

Richard Orodenker has high praise for Heinz in *The Writers' Game: Baseball Writing in America*. With regard to his nonfiction, Orodenker emphasizes Heinz's skill in drawing subjects out through conversation, with results that reflect the strong authorial presence of New Journalism:

> He is sports literature's most tectonic writer, a consummate interviewer who built elegant narrative structures around moments of golden quotation. He did not just quote but actively engaged his subject in dialogue, revealing his own character in the bargain.

Tassinari declares, "Sportswriter W. C. Heinz is considered by many of his peers to be one of the best pure writers of his time."

CRITICISM

Michael Allen Holmes

Holmes is a writer with existential interests. In the following essay, he takes a magnified look at the changes Heinz made to his 1950 story "One Throw" upon its republication a half century later.

Reading a short story by an expert literary stylist is a pleasure. One of the pleasures of rereading a masterful story is the chance to pay attention to and gain an understanding of just how the writer constructed it, including what particular phrasings are used, how the mood is established, and where key lines are presented. A degree even more interesting is the chance to read two different versions of the same story, because now one is given insight into what the author, given the chance to revisit a story published years before, was inclined to change. One might imagine that such changes would most always be for the better, given that the writer has presumably honed his or her craft over the course of a career distinguished enough to allow the opportunity to republish earlier works.

W. C. Heinz's classic short story "One Throw," originally published in *Collier's Weekly* in 1950, has been republished a great number of times, in baseball anthologies as well as academic textbooks—evidence that the craft of the story is to be admired. What might be considered the definitive publication of the story came with the collection *What a Time It Was: The Best of W. C. Heinz on Sports*, issued in 2001, over fifty years after the original version. However, a close examination of this version as compared with the original suggests that the changes made may not have been for the better.

It is easy to see why Heinz first felt compelled to revisit the story, as subsequent versions feature a single change made as more of a technical

WHAT DO I READ NEXT?

- Heinz's most admired work of fiction is *The Professional* (1958). The novel follows a devoted boxer named Eddie Brown as he prepares for a crucial fight, as related by a sportswriter. The boxer is not a natural prodigy but one whose intense and persistent training keeps him just on the cusp of the set of the world's most talented boxers.

- Heinz's name is often mentioned alongside that of Red Smith, another renowned sportswriter from the mid-twentieth century. Some of his best columns, primarily for New York newspapers, are collected in *Red Smith on Baseball: The Game's Greatest Writer on the Game's Greatest Years* (2000), spanning the years 1941–1981.

- A generation before Heinz was the columnist and dramatist Damon Runyon, perhaps best known for his gangster-era story collection *Guys and Dolls* (1932), of which two stories were adapted as the musical of that name. Runyon was also known for his sportswriting, and anecdotes have the dying Runyon touting Heinz as the best young sportswriter in New York. A modern collection of Runyon's sportswriting is *Guys, Dolls, and Curveballs: Damon Runyon on Baseball* (2005).

- Notable in the sportswriting generation following Heinz is David Halberstam, who contributed the foreword to Heinz's collection *What a Time It Was*. The state of the New York Yankees around the time of the action of "One Throw," in particular their storied rivalry with the Boston Red Sox, is presented by Halberstam in *Summer of '49* (1989), with a cast of characters including Joe DiMaggio, Ted Williams, and Phil Rizzuto.

- Among the most admired baseball novels of all time is *The Natural* (1952), by Bernard Malamud, about baseball phenom Roy Hobbs, who tries to make a comeback after his career is interrupted by an unfortunate confrontation with a mysterious woman. Robert Redford starred in the 1984 film version of the novel.

- One of the most recent novels with a plot revolving around the game of baseball is *The Art of Fielding* (2011), by Chad Harbach, about Henry Skrimshander, the star shortstop for Westish College, whose presumed major-league future is threatened by a wayward throw. The story owes a great debt to Herman Melville's whaling classic *Moby-Dick* (1851).

- Included in the middle-grade collection *Baseball Crazy: Ten Short Stories That Cover All the Bases* (2008), edited by Nancy E. Mercado, are Jerry Spinelli's "The Great Gus Zernial and Me," Maria Testa's "Smile Like Jeter," Joseph Bruchac's "Ball Hawk," and others.

- Mexican American author Gary Soto's collection *Baseball in April and Other Stories* (1990) centers on the everyday exploits of Latino preteens and teens living in California's Central Valley. Because Soto often uses Spanish words, a glossary is included.

---

correction than a stylistic one: in the original version, the reader learns that in the second game of the doubleheader, "the home club picked up three runs ... and they were in the last of the ninth with a 3–2 lead and two outs"—but as any baseball aficionado will realize (though perhaps not on the first reading), where "last of the ninth" in this context can only mean "bottom of the ninth," this is incorrect, since if the home team is winning after the visiting team bats in the top of the ninth inning, the bottom of the inning is not played. Sure enough, when the story was published in, for example, the anthology *Fielder's Choice* in 1979, the corresponding text was revised to "and they were in the top of the ninth with a 3–2 lead and two outs." Other than this

WITH THOSE REMARKS INCLUDED, BROWN'S
OVERARCHING DECEPTION IS SUBTLY HINTED AT,
AND HIS KNOWING UNKNOWINGNESS BECOMES A
PART OF THE FEEL OF THE STORY."

change, Heinz, perhaps wisely, left the remainder of the story intact. An identical version was published in the fourth edition of *The Fireside Book of Baseball* in 1987.

In the version of the story published in *What a Time It Was*, however, there are well over a dozen minor changes, and they are worth tracing through the story. The first change is very minor: in a line of Eddie Brown's dialogue—"I mean if he's such a good ballplayer what's he doing in this league?"—a dash and comma are inserted, so that it now reads, "I mean—if he's such a good ballplayer, what's he doing in this league?" A number of the changes are of this sort, additions of punctuation to what might be considered run-on or ungrammatical text. These changes are interesting because many critics had by then praised Heinz's realistic dialogue, and as reported by Edward J. Tassinari in a 1996 *Dictionary of Literary Biography* essay, the story had been judged by Heinz himself to be "completely true as to dialogue and characterization." Indeed, for one who reads the original version and then approaches the 2001 version, the inserted punctuation may give pause (so to speak). It might look more proper on the page, but it sounds stilted compared to the smooth flow of the original, which perhaps better reflects how a person such as a New York baseball scout, as opposed to a city gentleman, would actually talk.

The most significant changes to the text occur next, as the following lines of dialogue are removed entirely:

"What kind of a kid is he?"

"He's a nice kid," the guy said. "He plays good ball, but I feel sorry for him. He thought he'd be playing for the Yankees soon, and here he is in this town. You can see it's got him down."

One can imagine why the lines were removed: this dialogue might be seen as preempting or rendering redundant what follows. The reader is about to learn directly from the story's dialogue

everything that is reported there by the desk employee, Nick, and so it is theoretically wiser to remove those remarks to eliminate the redundancy and purify the story. Yet such reflexive heavy-handed editing may not be so wise. In this instance, the repetition can be seen to serve a distinct purpose. The conversation that Eddie Brown proceeds to have with Pete Maneri is not one that he naturally ambles into and then naturally executes; rather, as the reader may deduce after reading the story, Brown was surely already aware that Maneri was living at the Olympia, perhaps even knew that he would be passing through the lobby at that time of day. He wanted, even planned to have just such a conversation with the kid. If the reader is exposed to the above-quoted lines spoken by Nick, they reinforce the notion that Brown is going into this conversation from a knowing perspective—and yet he interacts with Maneri as if he knows little to nothing about him. With those remarks included, Brown's overarching deception is subtly hinted at, and his knowing unknowingness becomes a part of the feel of the story.

As a side note, the removal of those lines spoken by Nick also drastically reduces his role in the story. With those lines, he is depicted as a sympathetic individual who pays attention to and seeks to understand his clientele, including Pete; without them, he is simply a desk employee who reports basic information while offering no opinions or perceptions. His only take on the situation becomes "I guess the Yankees know what they're doing"—hardly an insightful comment.

In addition, the extension of the dialogue between Nick and Brown with the above lines renders slightly more realistic Maneri's coincidental entrance during that dialogue—though if Brown is aware of Maneri's schedule, it is not coincidental after all. Either way, the longer Nick and Eddie chat at the desk, the more likely it is that Pete might happen to enter. Regarding that coincidental entrance, Heinz seems to have decided that it was too conspicuous. The next bit of revision is the removal of Nick's line "This is a funny thing," so that upon Pete's entrance he merely remarks, "Here he comes now." From one perspective, calling attention to any coincidence in the text is unwise, being likely to prod the reader to perceive the coincidence as artificial, and so should be cut. As noted above, however, this is a coincidence from the reader's perspective but likely a "chance" meeting that

Brown has anticipated. If Nick remarks, "This is a funny thing," this is actually more realistic because he, like the reader, would be unaware that Brown could have planned the chance meeting, and so it would have been striking to him. One would expect him to make such a comment about the seeming coincidence. Thus, arguably, it makes more sense for Heinz to signal an awareness of the coincidence (which is likely not coincidental) than to eliminate any reference to it.

Another curious deletion follows: Heinz removes the one and only detailed description of any person in the story, namely, Maneri: "He had on a light gray sport shirt and a pair of gray flannel slacks." One can only imagine that Heinz removed this line for the sake of consistency—since no other character is physically described, why should Maneri be? (Though the line about him looking "just like" Phil Rizzuto is left in.) Yet Maneri is clearly the focus of the story: the attention of the narrator as well as the reader is on this particular ballplayer, so it stands to reason that the narrator would both notice and relate Maneri's appearance. Also, it makes sense that Nick's dress—perhaps a basic hotel uniform—would not be described, nor would the narrator likely describe his own clothes. On top of all this, whether Heinz intended it or not, Pete's all-gray outfit contributes to his characterization, suggesting both cloudiness of spirit and the fuzzy grayness of moral ambiguity, neither black nor white.

There are no further omissions as extensive as the above; most of the remaining changes are slight alterations of wording and punctuation. The word *that* is added to form the narratorial comment "you could see that he was exaggerating." Later, instead of saying "That's," Brown remarks of his own ballplaying, "That was twenty years ago." Again, these changes may make for more proper speech, but they do not necessarily better reflect the way Brown would speak.

The removal of the ellipsis after the text "'Is that right?' the kid said. . . . " perhaps merits little comment, though again it seems to reflect a literary tweediness. Time is often inferred to pass between lines of text, making such an ellipsis technically unnecessary. A somewhat amusing change is the alteration of "taproom" to "grill-room," and instead of having "a couple"—suggesting a couple of mugs of beer—Brown now has "a cup of coffee." By the late 1980s, Heinz was writing essays for *TV Guide* with titles like "Why Can't TV Encourage Class Instead of Crass?," so perhaps he thought removing the references to alcohol consumption would make the story feel cleaner. Indeed it does—but the notion that Brown would be drinking beer adds to his depiction as a casual, even jocular character, which he is later revealed to be when he tells the reader, "I do some strange things." Furthermore, the notion that he is bringing this "kid" into a taproom—a barroom—adds to the sense that he is drawing Maneri into a morally questionable side of society. Altogether, then, Brown's drinking beer can be seen to give the story more depth than his drinking coffee does.

The next portion of removed text is another minor redundancy. When Brown asks Maneri what the trouble is, Maneri originally responds, "Well, I don't get along very well here. I mean there's nothing wrong with my playing. . . ." In addition to *well* being repeated, Maneri soon states of Dall, "I don't get along with him." Thus, in the 2001 version, the earlier line merely reads "Well, there's nothing wrong with my playing." The words *I mean* were also removed, perhaps considered an unnecessary verbal tic. Yet if speaking spontaneously, people often repeat themselves and use phrasings like "I mean" and "You know" and so forth. The text may look better to the shrewd editor with little to no repetition, but this does not mean it more accurately reflects people's speech—in fact it may mean the contrary.

To enumerate the remaining changes is largely to catalog changes of the same categorical types as the earlier ones. "Maybe he is all right" is revised to "Maybe he's all right"; the original wording may slow the reader down, but the emphasis on *is* yet makes for realistic speech. Brown's comment of Dall "He's not worried about you" is removed—descriptive, but presumably considered redundant. "He bawls me out" is revised to "He bawled me out"; this makes Maneri's speech more consistent, sticking to the past tense, but it also lessens the broader implications made by the use of the present tense. The original reads "What chance is there for a guy like Eddie Brown or somebody like that coming down to see me in this town?" The 2001 version more succinctly reads "What chance is there for a guy like Eddie Brown to see me in this town?" Where the original reads "I never even saw him, and I'll never see him in this place," for the 2001 version, "I never even saw him" was removed.

The narrator knows the kid has the makings of a major-league player because he cannot throw the ball away. (© David Lee | Shutterstock.com)

In both of these cases, the dialogue is less redundant but no more realistic, and perhaps less so considering that Maneri is becoming emotionally agitated and would likely sputter somewhat in his speech. Brown's remark "I was lousing up his ball club and his record" is removed—descriptive, but likely deemed redundant. The original reads "It's not much ball park in this town. . . . The first game wasn't much either." The later version reads "It's not much of a ball park in this town. . . . The first game wasn't much of a game either." Again, the speech is refined but arguably not improved. "One big bounce" becomes "one bounce." The break in the text after the throw is eliminated. The text "because I'm not a hardware salesman and my name's not Harry Franklin" becomes "because I'm not Harry Franklin."

Heinz is a writer who was widely admired by his sportswriting peers mostly for his nonfiction, as well as for his novels. Included in *What a Time It Was* are only five short stories, two of which are actually extracts from his novels. Perhaps the immediacy of journalism was ideal for Heinz, because he could churn out on instinct a masterful piece of writing that would ever remain a product of that point in time. The permanence of novel writing perhaps also suited him too, because once a novel is published, few authors undertake the grand and likely fruitless effort of rooting out inconsistencies for a later edition. Tassinari suggests that with his novels, as with his journalism, Heinz relied on instinct: "According to Heinz, writing a novel is analogous to painting an enormous mural; the writer-artist finds it impossible to take a figurative step back and assess the work in progress and must instead carry it all in his head." The republication of his short stories left Heinz plenty of time and room to take a figurative step back and reconsider them—but in doing so, he was perhaps guided more by formulaic literary strictures with regard to redundancy and consistency and less by the instinct that had served him so well throughout his career. With "One Throw," the unrevised original is the one that rings true.

Source: Michael Allen Holmes, Critical Essay on "One Throw," in *Short Stories for Students*, Gale, Cengage Learning, 2014.

Rick Baillergeon

In the following review, Baillergeon praises Heinz's ability to put his reader in the middle of the action.

W. C. Heinz is one of the most versatile and acclaimed writers of our time. Perhaps overlooked in his storied career is the superb combat reporting and feature writing he produced during World War II. *When We Were One: Stories of World War II* is a collection of smaller pieces Heinz wrote during the latter stages of World War II and some longer magazine articles he wrote after the war.

Each piece highlights Heinz's ability to put the reader into the middle of the action and captures the emotions exuded on the battlefield. Although the collection is filled with outstanding examples of Heinz's writing, two are particularly stirring. In "The Morning They Shot the Spies," Heinz discusses his emotions as he witnesses the execution of three German spies. In "Dawson Holds Line Above Aachen," he recalls a company commander emotionally breaking down while discussing his soldiers' heroism against the Germans.

Books such as *When We Were One* remind us that wars are fought by humans. We must never forget the most important dimension of warfare—the human dimension.

Source: Rick Baillergeon, Review of *When We Were One: Stories of World War II*, in *Military Review*, Vol. 84, No. 1, January–February 2004, p. 88.

Mark Ellis

In the following review, Ellis calls Heinz's writing "riveting."

Heinz is a longtime sportswriter and author of *The Professional* as well as a coauthor of *MASH*. During World War II, he was a young correspondent for the *New York Sun*, and this collection of his war pieces begins with his personal observations aboard the USS *Nevada*. The battleship had been restored after the attack at Pearl Harbor and was now supporting the Allied invasion on D-Day. From D-Day, Heinz continues his war coverage with stories from the Siegfried line and Aachen. Heinz was one of the few reporters who witnessed the execution of three German spies captured after the Battle of the Bulge, an experience he writes about with clarity and controlled emotion. In his of-the-moment dispatches, Heinz does a good job of telling the story of the war and profiling its

fighting men and scenes of horror. His narrative brings all the chaos of battle to the reader. In the newspaper dispatches, of course, there is little room for historical background. But the book also includes several longer magazine pieces, most memorably an account of returning years later to the Normandy beaches with a D-Day hero and his son. This book of wartime observations will be riveting for the interested reader. Recommended for all public libraries and academic libraries with historical collections.

Source: Mark Ellis, Review of *When We Were One: Stories of World War II*, in *Library Journal*, Vol. 127, No. 11, June 15, 2002, p. 78.

Morey Berger

In the following review of Heinz's 2001 collection, Berger praises his "enlightening narrative skill."

In more than 60 years of writing for newspapers and magazines, Heinz has covered baseball, boxing, football, horse racing, and even bike races. But he has also written respected novels (*The Professional*), coauthored Vince Lombardi's *Run to Daylight*, and collaborated with H. Richard Hornberger to write the comic classic *MASH* under the joint pseudonym Richard Hooker. Drawing on both fiction and nonfiction written throughout his long and influential career, this new collection showcases his wide-ranging sports knowledge and enlightening narrative skill, whether the subject be the talented but accident-prone outfielder Pistol Pete Reiser or the original pound-for-pound fighting genius Sugar Ray Robinson. Heinz's anthology should be attractive to most public libraries and all sports collections. [Heinz had more entries than any other writer in the recent *The Best American Sports Writing of the Century*.—Ed.]

Source: Morey Berger, Review of *What a Time It Was: The Best of W. C. Heinz on Sports*, in *Library Journal*, Vol. 126, No. 10, June 1, 2001, p. 172.

SOURCES

"Average Salary Hits Record $3.2M," ESPN website, December 7, 2012, http://espn.go.com/mlb/story/_/id/8724285/mlb-average-salary-38-percent-32-million (accessed September 10, 2013).

Brudnick, Ida A., "Congressional Salaries and Allowances," Congressional Research Service, January 15, 2013, http://www.senate.gov/CRSReports/crs-publish.cfm?pid =′0E%2C*PL%5B%3D%23P%20%20%0A (accessed September 10, 2013).

Carchidi, Sam, "Flipping over Baseball Cards," Philly. com, June 23, 1989, http://articles.philly.com/1989-06-23/ entertainment/26106528_1_baseball-cards-card-collectors-card-lands (accessed September 10, 2013).

Frommer, Harvey, *New York City Baseball: The Last Golden Age, 1947–1957*, Macmillan, 1980, pp. 126–48, 213.

Goldstein, Richard, "W. C. Heinz, 93, Writing Craftsman, Dies," in *New York Times*, February 28, 2008, p. B7.

Halberstam, David, Foreword to *What a Time It Was: The Best of W. C. Heinz on Sports*, Da Capo Press, 2001, pp. ix–x.

Hall, Alvin L., *The Cooperstown Symposium on Baseball and American Culture, 1999*, edited by Peter M. Rutkoff, McFarland, 2000, pp. 64–65.

Heinz, W. C., "One Throw," in *Collier's Weekly*, July 15, 1950, p. 38, http://www.unz.org/Pub/Colliers-1950jul15-00038 (accessed September 6, 2013).

———, "One Throw," in *Fielder's Choice*, edited by Jerome Holtzman, Harcourt Brace Jovanovich, 1979, pp. 47–52.

———, "One Throw," in *What a Time It Was: The Best of W. C. Heinz on Sports*, Da Capo Press, 2001, pp. 233–36.

MacGregor, Jeff, Introduction to *What a Time It Was: The Best of W. C. Heinz on Sports*, Da Capo Press, 2001, pp. xiii–xvi.

Marshall, William, *Baseball's Pivotal Era, 1945–1951*, University Press of Kentucky, 1999, pp. 300–301.

"Morality Play," in *Encyclopìdia Britannica* online, 2013, http://www.britannica.com/EBchecked/topic/391805/ morality-play (accessed September 8, 2013).

"1950 Minor League Affiliations," Baseball-Reference. com, http://www.baseball-reference.com/minors/affiliate. cgi?year=1950 (accessed September 10, 2013).

"1950 New York Yankees Minor League Affiliates," Baseball-Reference.com, http://www.baseball-reference. com/minors/affiliate.cgi?id=NYY&year=1950 (accessed September 9, 2013).

Orodenker, Richard, *The Writers' Game: Baseball Writing in America*, Twayne Publishers, Twayne's United States Authors Series No. 663, 1996, pp. 10, 13, 96–98, 106–107.

Peterson, Richard, "Only Fairy Tales: Baseball Fiction's Short Game," in *Extra Innings: Writing on Baseball*, University of Illinois Press, 2001, pp. 73–88.

Rader, Benjamin G., *Baseball: A History of America's Game*, 3rd ed., University of Illinois Press, 2008, pp. 90, 142–49.

Rembert, Ron, "Baseball Immortals: Character and Performance On and Off the Field," in *Baseball/Literature/ Culture: Essays, 2002–2003*, edited by Peter Carino, McFarland, 2004, pp. 136–45.

Tassinari, Edward J., "W. C. Heinz," in *Dictionary of Literary Biography*, Vol. 171, *Twentieth-Century American Sportswriters*, edited by Richard Orodenker, Gale Research, 1996, pp. 132–44.

"Teams by Name," MiLB.com, http://www.milb.com/ milb/info/teams.jsp (accessed September 10, 2013).

Ziglar, Toby, "Is Baseball an American Religion? A Sociological Analysis," in *Baseball/Literature/Culture: Essays, 2002–2003*, edited by Peter Carino, McFarland, 2004, pp. 106–15.

FURTHER READING

Asinof, Eliot, *Eight Men Out: The Black Sox and the 1919 World Series*, Macmillan, 2011.

> The biggest ethical scandal in baseball history occurred a good century ago, when eight members of the Chicago White Sox, who resented their team's miserly owner, plotted with underworld gamblers to throw the World Series and lose to the Cincinnati Reds. Asinof's definitive, novelistic account of the series, the scandal, and the aftermath was first published in 1963.

Bjarkman, Peter C., ed., *Baseball & the Game of Life: Stories for the Thinking Fan*, Birch Brook Press, 1990.

> The contributors to this collection, including Robert Coover and W. P. Kinsella, use baseball as a springboard for philosophical explorations of a variety of issues.

Klinkowitz, Jerry, *Short Season and Other Stories*, Johns Hopkins University Press, 1988.

> This collection of twenty-two baseball vignettes explores the ballplaying and personal lives of the players on one fictional class A minorleague team, the Mason City Royals, over the course of a promising season.

Leinweaver, Mark, and Ryan Bradley, eds., *Minor Moments, Major Memories: Baseball's Best Players Recall Life in the Minor Leagues*, Globe Pequot Press, 2005.

> Baseball stars including Cal Ripken Jr., Gary Carter, Keith Hernandez, and Gary Sheffield have contributed stories about how they enjoyed their days in the minors to this collection.

SUGGESTED SEARCH TERMS

W. C. Heinz AND One Throw

W. C. Heinz AND baseball

W. C. Heinz AND boxing

W. C. Heinz AND interview

sportswriting AND baseball

minor league baseball AND fiction

baseball AND short stories

baseball AND ethics OR morality

W. C. Heinz AND Damon Runyon

The Piece of String

GUY DE MAUPASSANT

1883

Guy de Maupassant's brief story "The Piece of String" focuses on the consequences of social bias and how an innocent man can be deemed guilty by the general populace even if he should be vindicated. Like many of Maupassant's short stories, "The Piece of String" depicts a rural village in Normandy and the lives that peasants lead there. As is also common in his stories, "The Piece of String" contains unexpected plot developments. The story is concise and does not waste words, and there is no sentimentality or romance associated with peasant life. The peasants are clearly poor, are bent from years pushing ploughs, and have endured a lifetime of hard work. But Maupassant did not admire peasants and sought to illustrate the animosity that he thought was common amongst them.

"The Piece of String" was written in 1883 for *Le Gaulois*, a weekly newsmagazine. It was included in Maupassant's short-story collection *Miss Harriet*, published in 1884, and in the multivolume compilation of short stories *The Works of Guy de Maupassant*, published in 1903. Recent English translations of Maupassant's short stories are not plentiful. However, there are several good translations from the first half of the twentieth century. "The Piece of String" is included in *Best Short Stories of Guy de Maupassant*, published in 1944, and a more recent translation was published in the journal *New Literary History* (Vol. 20, No. 3) in the spring of 1989. "The Piece of String" is also available on the Project Gutenberg website, at http://www.gutenberg.org/files/3084/3084-h/3084-h.htm.

Guy de Maupassant (© *MARKA* | *Alamy*)

AUTHOR BIOGRAPHY

Henri-René-Albert-Guy de Maupassant, known as Guy de Maupassant, was born on August 5, 1850, at the Château de Miromesnil in Normandy, France. He was the elder of two sons of Laure Le Poittevin and Gustave de Maupassant. When Maupassant was eleven years old, his parents, after years of arguments, separated. Maupassant lived with his mother and younger brother and was tutored at home until he was thirteen years old, when he was allowed to attend classes at a Catholic seminary. Eventually his mother permitted him to attend a secondary school in Rouen, from which he would graduate in 1869. Sometime in 1867, Maupassant was introduced to the French novelist Gustave Flaubert, who would later become his literary mentor.

After completing his secondary education, Maupassant enrolled in law school in Paris, but he soon dropped out to enlist in the French army during the Franco-Prussian War. The brutality of battle and the French defeat shocked Maupassant, whose mother had largely sheltered him from reality. After the war ended, he became a clerk in the Naval Ministry office. He continued to work in this position for eight years, until 1880. During this time, Maupassant began to write, under the guidance of Flaubert. His first short story, "Boule de suif" ("Ball of Fat"), was so well received that Maupassant was encouraged to quit his job at the ministry and begin writing as a full-time endeavor. During this time, Maupassant also worked for two newspapers, *Gil Blas* and *Le Gaulois*, where he published weekly human-interest stories. Maupassant's work for both newspapers led him to develop a concise style of writing, with no wasted words.

The ten years between 1880 and 1890 were filled with an outpouring of short stories and novels from Maupassant, including almost three hundred stories and six novels. Many of the short stories were reworked pieces that he had previously written as newspaper stories. These reworked stories were subsequently published in *Le Gaulois* as part of a featured title: "The Sundays of a Parisian bourgeois." "The Piece of String" was one of the stories written during this period. It was first published as "La ficelle" in *Le Gaulois* on November 21, 1883. Maupassant published his stories in several collections, including *La maison Tellier* (*Madame Tellier's Establishment, and Short Stories*) in 1881. Among Maupassant's novels, his first, *Une vie* (*A Life*), was published in 1883. This was followed by *Bel-Ami* in 1885 and *Mont-Oriol* in 1887. Until the end of the decade Maupassant published a new novel each year, with *Pierre et Jean* (*Pierre and Jean*) in 1888, *Forte comme la mort* (*Strong as Death*) in 1889, and *Notre cœur* (*Our Heart*) in 1890.

Maupassant never married, although he did father three children. He often frequented prostitutes, whereby he contracted syphilis, which was not diagnosed until 1877. As sometimes happens with syphilis, the disease progressed to his brain, which led to severe headaches and mental illness. He attempted suicide in January 1892 and was committed to a private asylum in Paris, where he died on July 6, 1893.

PLOT SUMMARY

The setting for "The Piece of String" is Goderville, a small village in Normandy. As the story opens, it is market day, and the local peasants are heading into town. The men are described as bent and crooked from too much time bent over a plough and too many years reaping corn. Some of the peasants are leading cows, while their

MEDIA ADAPTATIONS

- "The Piece of String" is available as a free MP3 audio download, presented by Listen to Genius at http://listentogenius.com/author.php/351. The story is narrated by Stefan Rudnicki, and the running time is seventeen minutes.

- *Normandy Stories* is an audiobook including eleven of Maupassant's short stories set in Normandy. Although "The Piece of String" is not included, this two-disc, 158-minute audiobook, published by Naxos in 2004 and read by Oliver Montgomery, includes other stories that depict rural peasant life.

wives follow behind. The women are not as bent, and they have greater energy. Both men and women are dressed for market day in freshly laundered clothing. A very few of the peasants are able to ride in a cart, pulled by an old nag, but for most of them, walking is their mode of transportation.

The marketplace is described as very crowded, with great throngs of people present, all jostling one another and making a din of noise. As might be expected of an old-time marketplace, there are animals and feed, and thus the market smells of animals and farm life. The description in the opening paragraphs creates a lively image of country village life.

The protagonist, Maître Hauchecorne, appears in the sixth paragraph. He is described as "economical." This is why, when he sees a piece of string on the ground, he bends down to pick it up. When he sees that Maître Malandain is watching him, however, Hauchecorne becomes ashamed at having been seen picking up such an inconsequential item as a piece of string. The two men have become enemies and bear animosity toward one another. Hauchecorne hides the string under his shirt and pretends to be searching for something else on the ground. Soon he heads for the market, where he is lost in a crowd of people.

At the market, people carefully examine the goods for sale. Whether their interest be in a cow or in chickens tied up to be sold, each item is cautiously assessed before a decision is made; the peasants worry about being cheated. There is much haggling over prices, but the impenetrable expressions on the sellers' faces give away nothing about what they are thinking. Eventually the market square empties, as those peasants who have journeyed from the countryside head to the inns for lunch, while the local villagers return to their homes.

Hauchecorne goes to Jourdain's for lunch. The inn is filled with other peasants who have likewise journeyed to the market. The great fireplace is filled with roasting meats. There is much conversation amongst the peasants who sit eating together and discussing the weather and the goods sold and bargains purchased during the morning marketplace.

In the midst of the lunch, the town crier beats his drum outside and shouts that a pocket-book containing five hundred francs was lost that morning on the road to Beuzeville. If it is found and returned, there is a twenty-franc reward. The peasants continue to eat and talk and wonder about the likelihood that the pocket-book will be found. As they finish their lunch, a corporal arrives asking for Hauchecorne, who identifies himself and is asked to go to the mayor's office.

The mayor wastes no time in telling Hauchecorne that he was seen picking up the lost pocket-book that morning. Hauchecorne is nearly speechless, as he is frightened at being accused and confused as to why he has been accused. He quickly denies having picked up the pocket-book, but the mayor tells Hauchecorne that he was seen by Malandain, the harness maker, who has testified that he witnessed Hauchecorne picking it up. Immediately Hauchecorne pulls the piece of string from his pocket and tells the mayor that the string was what the harness maker saw Hauchecorne pick up. The mayor insists that Malandain is a man of integrity who would not have mistaken a piece of string for a pocket-book. Hauchecorne swears by "the truth of the good God" that he picked up the string and not a pocket-book. The mayor, however, is insistent and informs Hauchecorne that he was even seen continuing to search the ground in case any money had fallen from the pocket-book. Hauchecorne is both angry and frightened about not being believed. He asks to be searched, and nothing is found.

The mayor warns that he will turn the matter over to the prosecutor, and Hauchecorne is dismissed. Meanwhile, word of the accusation has spread, and Hauchecorne is surrounded by people who ask if he found the pocket-book and kept it. He tells everyone the story of the string, but is only mocked. Everyone who stops him is told the story. Moreover, Hauchecorne himself stops many people and tells the story. No one seems to believe him, and many people laugh. By the time it is dark and he must walk home, Hauchecorne is filled with anger and despair since no one believes him.

Along his journey home, Hauchecorne tells people the story of the string and even shows them the place along the road where he stopped. When he arrives home, he tells everyone in his small village the story of the string, and still no one believes him. Hauchecorne becomes sick with worry and indignation at being accused and laughed at by everyone to whom he tells the story. The next day, a farmhand turns in the pocket-book, which he says he found on the road. Because he does not know how to read, he waited for his master to tell him who the pocket-book belonged to, so that he could return it.

Hauchecorne again tells everyone his story of the string, but now he adds that the pocket-book was found and thus he has been declared innocent, as he was all along. All that day he tells and retells his story to everyone he sees, even strangers. He includes the fact that he was much injured by being accused of lying. Although he seems to be feeling better now that the truth has been discovered, Hauchecorne is bothered that still no one appears to believe his story. He also thinks that they may be talking about him when he is not there.

The next week Hauchecorne again goes to the market, but only to tell his story. When he passes Malandain's door, the harness maker laughs at him. Others also laugh at him and call him a "great rogue" and an "old scamp." A horse trader suggests to Hauchecorne that the one who returned the pocket-book may not be the one who found it. Hauchecorne now understands that people believe that he took the pocket-book and then had an accomplice return it. In the eyes of everyone, Hauchecorne is still considered guilty. He is so upset that he cannot eat his dinner at Jourdain's and soon leaves for his home.

Hauchecorne recognizes that he cannot prove his innocence. Moreover, he acknowledges that he is indeed capable of having taken the pocket-book and deceived everyone, and thus, even though he did not take it, he feels shame and guilt. He continues to tell everyone the story, elaborating on it with each telling. How to add to the story is all that he thinks about whenever he has a moment alone. The more often he tells the story, the less he is believed. Hauchecorne's heart is heavy with pain at not being believed, and he wastes away from not eating. Now people ask him to tell the story so that they can laugh at him. Hauchecorne has become the village joke. Soon he is so unwell that he cannot leave his bed, and shortly after, Hauchecorne dies. His last words protest his innocence.

CHARACTERS

Corporal of Gendarmes
It is the corporal who goes to Jourdain's to ask Hauchecorne to accompany him to the mayor's office.

Maître Hauchecorne
Hauchecorne is the protagonist in "The Piece of String." He is a Norman peasant, and although his age is not given, he is referred to as an old man who is bent over from severe arthritis. Most of the male peasants are described as bent over from years of walking behind a plough, and thus, readers might reasonably assume that Hauchecorne is a farmer. He is pragmatic and "economical" and does not waste anything, so readers understand that he is not one to pass by something that might be useful later. He picks up the string because he thinks it might come in handy at some point.

When Hauchecorne is accused of having picked up the pocket-book and not returning it, he is unable to convince the mayor of his innocence. Deep down, Hauchecorne conceives that "he was, perhaps, capable of having done what they accused him of"; had he seen the pocket-book on the ground, he might indeed have picked it up, denied the act, and had an accomplice return it, a trick he could have boasted about afterward. One reason he finds it so difficult to convince anyone that he is innocent is because he knows that if the opportunity had presented itself, he might have been guilty of the crime.

Hauchecorne is an outsider in Goderville, where much of the story takes place. He is from Bréauté, which is presumably more rural, since he journeys to Goderville to attend the market. It may be that Hauchecorne is of a lower social class, since he is from the country, and that may account for his desire to be seen as innocent. Although Hauchecorne knows he is innocent, actually *being* innocent is not enough for him. He psychically requires that everyone in his own village and in Goderville accept and acknowledge his innocence. Even though someone else admits to having picked up the pocket-book, and even though it is returned, his air of guilt damages his reputation, which is partly his own doing. In defending himself so desperately, he acts guilty, and thus in the eyes of the villagers, he is guilty.

He originally hides the string because he feels ashamed for having picked it up. Having done so revealed something about his personality that he does not want to acknowledge and does not want others to know. As the narrator reports, being economical is a typical trait of the Norman peasants who live in this area. However, even to Hauchecorne himself, his actions appear more miserly than normal. As a result, Hauchecorne is convinced that others are gossiping about him. At the story's end, he dies from grief and the loss of a will to live. Being laughed at by others, the fear of which led Hauchecorne to hide the piece of string when he picked it up, is something that he cannot bear. He would rather die than be the subject of interminable jokes.

Maître Fortuné Houlbrèque

Houlbrèque never actually appears in "The Piece of String." However, it is his pocket-book that is lost, which sets in motion the downfall and subsequent death of Hauchecorne.

Monsieur le Maire

The *maire*, or mayor, of Goderville is described as pompous and serious. He takes his position as mayor quite earnestly, and he is also the notary, thus occupying a legal position. The mayor interrogates Hauchecorne about the missing pocket-book. He chooses to believe Malandain's story of how Hauchecorne picked up the lost pocket-book. Malandain lives in Goderville, while Hauchecorne lives in a different village. The mayor's familiarity with Malandain may in part make his version of what happened along the road appear more believable. It is also likely that the mayor sees Malandain as a closer social equal than the peasant, who is a countryman of little social standing. The mayor is not a peasant; he would not understand why Hauchecorne felt compelled to pick up a piece of string, which would be worth nothing to the mayor, who holds a position of some authority and thus is not as poor as Hauchecorne. Hauchecorne turns red with shame when he must tell the mayor about the string, which further suggests that there is unequal social standing between the two.

Maître Malandain

Malandain is a harness maker. He is a sworn enemy of Hauchecorne and sees him picking up something from the ground. It is never clearly established whether he sees that it is a piece of string or genuinely thinks that Hauchecorne has picked up a pocket-book and kept it. No matter what he might actually know, Malandain takes advantage of the situation by telling the mayor that he witnessed Hauchecorne picking up the pocket-book and that the old peasant furthermore searched the ground for any money that might have fallen out. The mayor describes Malandain as "a man worthy of credit," and thus his word is not disputed.

The first time that Malandain appears in the story, he is watching Hauchecorne walk down the road. Malandain's mere presence fills Hauchecorne with shame for having picked up the piece of string. The two men once had a quarrel, and given their estrangement and Hauchecorne's supposedly shameful act, Malandain now possesses power over Hauchecorne. Malandain lives in Goderville, while Hauchecorne lives in the country in a village that perhaps does not have a market, since the peasant journeys to Goderville to go to the market. This suggests a difference in social class. Malandain makes harnesses. He may also be poor, but he is not a farmer, or a rural peasant, as Hauchecorne is.

The second time Malandain appears is at the mayor's office, where he confronts Hauchecorne and tells his story of having seen the old peasant pick up the pocket-book. It is not explained how he "sustained his testimony," but it is apparent that he is quite convincing, since the mayor believes in Hauchecorne's guilt.

Marius Paumelle

Paumelle is the farmhand who finds the pocket-book. He cannot read and so is unable to return the lost pocket-book to its owner immediately. The delay allows for Hauchecorne to be accused. Later, Paumelle is thought to have been Hauchecorne's accomplice.

THEMES

Guilt

Guilt is one of the central themes of "The Piece of String." Hauchecorne is accused of picking up a pocket-book from the road and then not returning it. Although he is innocent, he is thought to be guilty because he acts guilty. When he first picks up the piece of string, he notices that Malandain is watching him. Rather than stand straight and look his enemy in the eye, Hauchecorne is ashamed at having been seen. He not only continues to search the ground, which further piques the interest of Malandain, but also hides the string under his shirt. These appear to be the acts of a guilty man, with something to hide. What Hauchecorne hides is his shame, but for the harness maker who watches, these acts appear to reflect guilt, which may account for what Malandain later tells the mayor he witnessed.

While it may be argued that an individual is innocent until proven guilty in a court of law, the court of public opinion is a very different matter. It is the people of Goderville and of Hauchecorne's smaller village of Bréauté who determine that he is guilty. In a sense, Hauchecorne also judges himself guilty. He admits to himself that had he found the pocket-book, he might not have immediately turned it in. Rather, he is capable of having stolen the pocket-book and "even of boasting of it as a good trick"; Hauchecorne labels the keeping of the pocket-book a "trick" of which he might boast to his friends. But stealing is not simply a trick, and thus Hauchecorne admits his liability. He may not have stolen the pocket-book this time, but it is a crime that he could have committed. It may even be a crime that he has committed in the past; Maupassant's readers are not told about Hauchecorne's past. All in all, he feels guilty, which motivates him even more to proclaim his innocence.

Hauchecorne cannot tolerate being thought guilty of theft. Because he is not actually guilty of carrying out the crime for which he is accused, but only of knowing that he is capable of committing such a crime, Hauchecorne is determined to be judged innocent by everyone. It is not enough that his friends and acquaintances know, or at least tacitly accept, that he is innocent. The narrator in "The Piece of String" tells readers that Hauchecorne even accosts strangers to tell them of his innocence. Eventually his extreme protestations of innocence, which appear as overacting to all who hear his story, begin to sound like guilt. Even when the pocket-book is found and returned, Hauchecorne continues to be judged guilty of having taken it. Hauchecorne knows that Malandain caused the problem, and yet he never seeks revenge. Instead, Hauchecorne obsesses over the accusation until he dies. His disinterest in how his enemy has treated him may well be a manifestation of Hauchecorne's own sense of guilt: he imagines that he deserves to be guilty and thus cannot seek revenge against the man who accused him.

Social Class

In "The Piece of String," Maupassant is careful to distinguish between the different social classes that appear in the story. In the opening paragraphs, the narrator describes the peasants as they journey toward the marketplace as "bony" and the women as wearing "scanty little shawls." These are the poorer peasants, who wear simpler clothing and are too poor to have any extra fat on their bodies. They walk, carrying their chickens and ducks or leading a cow or calf. The distance is not great, perhaps less than two miles, but these are men and women who work hard. The men are bent from working a plough to dig up the earth for planting. They are too poor to afford a carriage or buggy. Although they are poor, they are described as wearing freshly starched garments. The women cover their hair with a white cap, but the men are not described as wearing hats to protect their heads.

The peasants fear being cheated, even when buying from other peasants. They bargain and weigh every purchase with great care. At Jourdain's, where everyone gathers to eat after the marketplace empties, the peasants are described as "the aristocracy of the plough," a term that comes across as sarcastic, since it describes peasants who are bent from years of hard work on the land. In a sense those who have goods to sell and can afford to eat the hearty food at the inn are the "aristocracy" of farming, but Maupassant does not use the term to elevate their social

TOPICS FOR FURTHER STUDY

- In "The Piece of String," Hauchecorne is falsely accused of a crime. Although he is innocent, he finds it impossible to prove his innocence, such that simply the suggestion of guilt is enough to destroy his reputation. Use fellow classmates to stage a trial in which Hauchecorne is given the chance to prove his innocence. Read the story carefully for the evidence that you will use and then stage a defense. Ask one of your classmates to be the prosecutor, and another six to be the jury. Stage this as you would a real trial, with secret deliberations and paper ballots. After the decision is rendered, discuss the kinds of evidence and what parts of the story most clearly establish guilt or innocence. Try to answer this question: how does an innocent man prove he is not guilty?

- The scene that opens "The Piece of String" is similar to what is seen in Pieter Brueghel the Elder's painting *The Battle between Carnival and Lent*, with a marketplace crowded with people. Locate a copy of this painting, and in an oral presentation, provide a comparative analysis of the painting, drawing connections between specific themes and characters that appear in the painting and are suggested in "The Piece of String." Choose at least four close-ups of the tableau of the painting to present using PowerPoint.

- "The Piece of String" begins with one significant event: Hauchecorne picks up a piece of string. Eventually this small event leads to his death. Think of one simple event in your own life, and write a short story that develops from that single event. Present your story to the class in an oral report, and explain the choices you made in developing your short story and why you made those choices.

- During the 1780s, Queen Marie-Antoinette wanted to escape from the pressures of her life and had a fake peasant village constructed on the grounds of the Petit Trianon, a château at Versailles that was given to her as a wedding gift. The idyllic village was called Hameau (hamlet). The 2006 film *Marie Antoinette*, directed by Sofia Coppola, includes a scene of this rustic peasant village. Research peasant life in nineteenth-century France, and watch this film. Then write a paper in which you compare the results of your research with how peasant life is depicted in both the film and in "The Piece of String." Present an argument on the degree of authenticity in each of these depictions.

- Read Anton Chekhov's short story "A Problem," and write an essay in which you compare it to "The Piece of String." Both stories deal with a crime that is not what it appears. In your essay, be sure to discuss, among other topics, how each set of characters responds to the situational conflict created by the author.

- Hauchecorne's obsession with proving his innocence eventually leads to his death. *Stop Pretending: What Happened When My Big Sister Went Crazy* (1999), by Sonya Sones, is a young-adult novel in verse about what happens when a thirteen-year-old girl's older sister begins to suffer from mental illness. Both this novel and "The Piece of String" depict various symptoms of mental disruptions. Based on the perceived degree of success of the novel and the story, consider which format—verse or short story—may be best suited to this topic. Then prepare an oral presentation that explains your viewpoint and compares the messages that Sones and Maupassant relate to their respective audiences.

The people going to Goderville seem to be much like the animals they lead to market.
(© Margo Harrison / Shutterstock.com)

positions. In fact, this use of the term suggests just the opposite.

Hauchecorne is one of the peasants who lives outside Goderville. He lives in the smaller community of Bréauté and journeys to Goderville to the marketplace. The narrator describes Hauchecorne as "economical," which suggests that he is careful with money. This is also said to be a typical trait of the Norman peasants who live in this area. This nature of being economical is what motivates him to pick up the piece of string, even though he has no immediate need for it. Hauchecorne, who ultimately pays a heavy price for his place in society, is of a lower economic and social class.

Maupassant also describes the wealthier peasants who congregate in the marketplace. They are distinguished from the poorer peasants by elaborate hats. The men's hats are "high and long-napped," which distinguishes them from the poorer peasants who journey to the marketplace on foot and with bare heads. The wives of the wealthier peasants also wear more elaborate headdress than the wives of the poorer peasants, who wear only a simple white cap. Although they are also peasants, these peasants are of a higher social class than Hauchecorne.

Those who live in Goderville are also distinguished from the peasants. Malandain lives in Goderville. He has an occupation, that of harness maker, and is not described as a peasant. The mayor also claims that Malandain is a credible witness, even though he is either mistaken about Hauchecorne or deliberately lying. The mayor is perhaps the most important person in Goderville. He is also a notary and so holds a position of some legal authority. He judges Hauchecorne guilty because it is inconceivable to him that anyone would bend down to pick up a piece of string. The mayor has no knowledge of poverty or of how peasants live. In contrast, Hauchecorne is immediately frightened, first in being summoned by the mayor, who is both a social and a legal superior, and then in being accused of the crime.

What readers find in Maupassant's story is a convergence of social classes and economic values that eventually leads to Hauchecorne's death. Hauchecorne imagines that if he explains the string and swears by God that he is innocent, he will be believed. As a peasant, however, his story fails to ring true to the townspeople. Malandain, by virtue of his position as a tradesman, carries the great weight of credibility and is more valued in this society, and thus his version of the events is not questioned. The mayor, because he holds the highest position in the town, has the power to speak up and exonerate Hauchecorne, but this exoneration is not forthcoming. Hauchecorne has no value in the world that the mayor inhabits.

STYLE

Irony

Irony refers to a reality that is different from what is presented; irony uses words to convey a meaning different from the actual words and can be used to expose the difference between what is real and what only appears to be real. For instance, the peasant farmers in town for the market are called "the aristocracy of the plough." Farmers are not aristocracy, but Maupassant uses irony to make a point about social-class distinctions. Irony also exposes what is real versus what is expected or wished to be real. Irony can be considered a kind of grim humor. One kind of irony is situational irony, in which the situation is different from what it should be. In "The Piece of String," situational irony exposes the hypocrisy of small-village life and the injustice that a small village can exert through gossip. Although the pocket-book is found, and someone else admits to having taken it, Hauchecorne's extreme protestations of innocence only make him appear more guilty. He is even accused of having hired someone else to assume the blame. The great irony, of course, is that he is innocent.

Narrative Voice

In a short story or novel, the narrator is the voice that tells the story. When the narrator is a person within the story, speaking in the first person, the story is limited to only that person's point of view. That person tells the story and interprets it for the reader, including only the details experienced by or related to the narrator. In some cases, authors use multiple narrators, whereby several characters tell their stories. This gives the reader the opportunity to see the characters from multiple perspectives. In contrast, a third-person narrator can provide an omniscient view of the action. In "The Piece of String," the narration is third person. This allows readers to witness Hauchecorne's emotions and his growing frustration from inside his mind, and readers are also given the end of the story after he gets delirious and dies, which could not happen if he himself were providing first-person narration.

Psychological Realism

The term *psychological realism* refers to an effort by the writer to focus his or her work on the interior motives and circumstances that define a character. In psychological realism, the story does not simply present the actions of a character; instead, the writer attempts to create a depth of characterization that will help the reader understand why the character makes the choices he or she does. For example, in "The Piece of String," Maupassant provides glimpses into Hauchecorne's mind. It is not enough that he is innocent of the charges; readers know that from reading the story. What matters is why he is compelled to so ardently defend himself. The interior motives and the psychological effects of the circumstances on his mind add depth to the story. For Hauchecorne, having everyone know he is innocent becomes more important than whether he is actually innocent. However, it is important to recognize that Hauchecorne might have picked the pocket-book up if he had seen it on the ground. The reader knows this because he eventually admits to himself that he might have done so. But what is not known beyond a doubt is whether he would have actually returned the pocket-book with the money still inside. Although he says he might have boasted of finding the pocket-book and deceiving everyone, he never indicates whether or not he would have kept the money. Through psychological realism, Maupassant creates a complex character, and as a result, characterization becomes as significant as the events that occur.

Short Story

The telling of stories is a very old narrative form. The short story must, because of its brevity, define characters through momentous actions, since there is little time to develop characters through the establishment of cause and effect for arrays of intricate actions. The short-story author must unite plot, themes, characters, mood, and tone using only a few scenes in order to create a narrative that reveals the author's purpose in constructing the story. "The Piece of String" is quite brief, fewer than a dozen pages. There is no backstory. The story begins with market day and Hauchecorne picking up and concealing a piece of string. Although there is a brief reference made to Hauchecorne and Malandain being enemies, because of a quarrel, all that readers know about these characters and about the other villagers and peasants is provided in a few brief descriptions. The first words of the story, for example, reveal that the peasants are worn and bent from hard work, information that will be important in understanding the kind of people who populate the story that follows.

HISTORICAL CONTEXT

Peasant Life in Late Nineteenth-Century Normandy

The historical French province of Normandy is on the north coast of France and is sometimes called "old France." (After the French Revolution, the province was divided into the two administrative departments of Upper Normandy and Lower Normandy.) The area where "The Piece of String" is set is evidently not on the rail line and seems far from Paris. Both men and women labor in the fields, and although the women wear dresses to labor, they are not restricted by the corsets that have recently come into vogue in cities, where women are expected to restrain their bodies. The women in Normandy wear shorter skirts, a blouse, and an apron. A kerchief or white cap, called a *coiffe*, is used to hold hair out of the way and to keep it clean and free from the dirt of the fields. Normandy had a tradition of weaving and embroidery, as well as lace making, and thus such items might have also decorated a woman's clothing, since they were valued occupations for women when farming occupations were not available.

Traditional harvesting by hand was how farmers in Normandy brought in their crops in the late nineteenth century. In many places, fruit trees were planted around fields, rather than in an area set aside for an orchard. The integration of fruit trees and farmland within a small space made it easier to work both areas, since fruit was also harvested by hand. Dairy production, particularly of cheese, was also common in this area, as it is in the modern day. Most farmers used a scythe for mowing and not the newer machines, which were just beginning to be used in other rural areas of France. As Maupassant describes in his short story, it was labor in the fields that bent the bodies of the men who had to push a plough; many farmers were too poor to own a horse or mule to drag a plough. In turn, the need to spread their knees wide for a firm stance from which to reap the corn left the peasants' legs crooked. Farming by hand was hard on farmers' bodies, but it was typical of peasant life in late nineteenth-century Normandy.

Cooking and Food

Peasant women of Normandy cooked in fireplaces which, though smaller than the one described at Jourdain's in "The Piece of String," nevertheless served as a means to both cook food and provide heat for the small houses. The cauldron that hung in the fireplace of many peasant homes in Normandy continued to be a mode of cooking into the twentieth century. Most foods were cooked by boiling, with soups and stews being a common dish on the peasant table. Whatever could be found was thrown into the soup, with new ingredients added each day, as they became available. The chicken, pigeon, and mutton roasting in the fireplace at Jourdain's in Maupassant's story would not have been common in simpler peasant homes. People ate with pocket knives, which were used to cut off pieces of bread; spoons were the only other utensil in common use. Aside from stew, the other common dish was porridge, which was made by boiling water and adding flour or some kind of grain to the cauldron of water. Depending on the level of poverty, peasant diets might have also included boiled eggs, if chickens were available. Few chickens were eaten. They were, however, often sold at markets to raise needed cash. If a peasant family could afford to do so, they would buy a pig, since pork could be added to many dishes, and the fat from a pig could flavor many of the blander soups that were served. Bread was the primary staple of the Norman diet, but in the late nineteenth century, bread was very different from what is eaten today. Flour was far less pure

COMPARE
&
CONTRAST

- **1880s:** Following the end of the Franco-Prussian War in 1871, France, having lost, was forced to pay Germany a large sum of money. This caused an economic decline in France that would last for many years.

  Today: Economic problems in France create new tensions with Germany, where strict austerity measures have limited many of the economic inflationary problems that other members of the European Union are facing. Previously the balance of trade between Germany and France was relatively even, but that has changed, with France now at an $86 billion trade deficit with Germany and French government debt rising.

- **1880s:** The railroads have become the modern means of transportation, and by 1880, there are more than six thousand locomotives in operation in France. Each year more than fifty thousand passengers and twenty-one tons of freight are transported across France. In "The Piece of String," most of the peasants journey to the neighboring market on foot. The first railway line linking Normandy to Paris had just recently been built in 1858, but there are no lines to conveniently link the small villages. Foot and cart transportation continue to be the most common mode of transportation.

  Today: High-speed railways have linked Paris to many of France's most populated cities. Since the opening of the tunnel beneath the English Channel in 1994, high-speed trains now link even London and Paris in just over two hours.

- **1880s:** France pours so much money into building a centralized system of railroads that there is no money for infrastructure,

including roads, canals, and other mediums of transportation.

  Today: The French government is planning on further expanding high-speed rail lines to additional cities but is also making some economic cutbacks in order to improve infrastructure. Money has been allocated for additional improvements to roads and for a new canal project to link the Seine to the Rhine-Scheldt waterway in Germany.

- **1880s:** As the end of the nineteenth century approaches, the term *fin de siècle* (end of the century) is first applied to French art and French artists whose emphasis on symbolism and egotism is thought to represent the century's end. Maupassant is considered an important fin de siècle writer whose short stories depict masculinity in chaos in the period following the Franco-Prussian War.

  Today: At the beginning of the twenty-first century, popular art has assumed greater importance. There is also a greater emphasis on conceptual art and art by women artists, such as Monique Frydman.

- **1880s:** At the end of the nineteenth century, French artists produce a series of postcards in which they predict what life will be like in the year 2000. One postcard predicts that firefighters will be able to fly, using a sort of wing apparatus, as they fight fires in high-rise buildings. Another depicts tennis players able to fly, with games played in the air over the crowds of onlookers.

  Today: Firefighters remain restricted to ladders and ladder trucks, as well as climbing interior stairs, to fight fires in high-rise buildings; nor can tennis be played by winged players hovering over the crowds.

then, as it was often adulterated with additives that could not be identified. Oil and salt, two staples of bread making, were often unavailable as well. Nevertheless, in some areas a third to half of a peasant's budget might be spent on bread, no matter its quality.

Hauchecome was ashamed to be seen picking up a piece of string, but hiding it led to him being accused of something worse.

(© Madlen | Shutterstock.com)

CRITICAL OVERVIEW

Maupassant's career was a brief one—just ten years. There are no records of his novels or stories being reviewed, and there are few recently published editions of his work to attest to his influence. However, this is not to suggest that Maupassant's literary career lacked either importance or a legacy. In the obituary published in the *New York Times*, Maupassant is referred to as one of French literature's "most unquestioned glories." After noting that Maupassant was to be credited with the revival of the short story, the writer completed the obituary by remarking, "His name will remain as that of one of the finest prose writers that France has ever produced."

Three days after Maupassant's death, there appeared in the *New York Times* a lengthier tribute, in which a number of critics and authors celebrated Maupassant's life. Among the many writers who contributed to this tribute, a few stand out. French poet and essayist Sully Prudhomme comments on the "perfection of form" that Maupassant brought to literature. Another French author and playwright, Ludovic Halévy, notes Maupassant's "masterly assurance, precision, clearness, and concision" in his "marvelous

tales." French novelist, essayist, and short-story writer Émile Zola points out that Maupassant "brought to us the best qualities of the French genius, neatness of observation, and health of style." In his focus on the short stories, Zola attests that Maupassant "leaves, in his tales, masterpieces wherein are resplendent all the qualities of the race." In all in this tribute, eighteen authors wrote about the influence that Maupassant had on literature and French literary studies, especially the short-story genre.

It is worth considering the influence that Maupassant has had on American writers as well. In the United States, late nineteenth-century novelist and short-story writer Kate Chopin so admired Maupassant that she read and translated several of his stories into English. In "*The Awakening* as Literary Innovation: Chopin, Maupassant and the Evolution of Genre," Elizabeth Nolan credits Maupassant as a major influence in Chopin's development as a writer, particularly in her literary innovations. Chopin wrote about her admiration for Maupassant in 1896, mentioning that she marveled at his direction and clarity. Nolan suggests that Chopin regarded Maupassant, "who had died three years previously, in terms of posthumous mentorship." Like Maupassant, Chopin was interested in the inner consciousness of the protagonist, and thus she studied his techniques and what he brought to the short-story genre and adapted them to her own writing.

Maupassant continues to be of interest in the twenty-first century, having been the subject of several recent biographies. All three of these biographies, by Nadine Satiat (2003), Frédéric Martinez (2012), and Marlo Johnston (2012), were published in French and as of early 2014 had not been translated into English.

CRITICISM

Sheri Metzger Karmiol
Karmiol teaches literature and drama at the University of New Mexico, where she is an adjunct professor in the University Honors College. In the following essay, she discusses Maupassant's "The Piece of String" as exemplary of the power of the short-story genre to illuminate truth.

Writers of fiction have a responsibility to alert their readers to injustice, to danger, and to the need for social change. This is true even if the

WHAT DO I READ NEXT?

- *A Parisian Affair and Other Stories* (2004), by Maupassant and translated into English by Siân Miles, includes thirty-four of Maupassant's short stories, including several of the best-known stories, such as "Boule de Suif" and "The Necklace."

- *A Life* (1999) is an English translation by Roger Pearson of the first of Maupassant's novels, *Une vie*, which covers almost thirty years in one woman's life.

- *Maupassant and the American Short Story: The Influence of Form at the Turn of the Century* (1994), by Richard Fusco, is one of the few texts to provide a critical analysis of Maupassant's importance in the development of the short-story genre in the United States.

- An English-language biography of Maupassant, simply titled *Maupassant* (1975), by Michael G. Lerner, is the most recent biography in English.

- Although Maupassant wrote some poetry, he is not well known as a poet. In *Six French Poets of the Nineteenth Century: Lamartine, Hugo, Baudelaire, Verlaine, Rimbaud, Mallarmé* (2000), E. H. and A. M. Blackmore present the poetry of Alphonse de Lamartine, Victor Hugo, Charles Baudelaire, Paul Verlaine, Arthur Rimbaud, and Stephane Mallarmé. This collection provides an opportunity to study the poetry created by Maupassant's literary contemporaries.

- Gustave Flaubert was an important friend and mentor to Maupassant. *The Letters of Gustave Flaubert*, Vol. 2, *1857–1880* (1982), translated into English by Francis Steegmuller, provides a glimpse into Flaubert's opinions on life and literature.

- *The Orphans of Normandy: A True Story of World War II Told through Drawings by Children* (2003), by Nancy Amis, is the true story of one hundred orphaned girls who were forced to flee their orphanage in Normandy and walk to a town 150 miles away. Aimed at younger readers, the volume includes drawings that the girls created, their own stories, and many descriptions of the countryside.

- *Kira-Kira* (2004), by Cynthia Kadohata, is a novel about a Japanese American girl who is ostracized by the Georgia community and school in which she lives. Though not guilty of any crime, she must find a way to live in a community where she and her family feel like outsiders. This middle-grade novel includes many of the same themes found in Maupassant's "The Piece of String."

- *Beyond the Divide* (1983), by Kathryn Lasky, is a young-adult novel about a family that is shunned by their community after they break one of the community's rules for what constitutes moral and ethical behavior. This novel, too, addresses many of the themes found in "The Piece of String."

- *The Friends* (1973), by Rosa Guy, deals with class issues and poverty, as well as race and ethnicity, as a young girl tries to fit into a community that has rejected her. This novel, set in 1960s Harlem, is intended for young adults.

writer does not admire the subject of his or her fiction, as was evidently the case with many of the stories of Guy de Maupassant, who had no particular affection for peasants. Literature provides readers with a way to view ideas, history, and customs that might otherwise never be experienced. At its best, literature clarifies the injustices of poverty, of class bias, and of discrimination. In short—literature educates readers to the need for social change. In his short story "The Piece of String," Maupassant uses the economical nature of the protagonist,

Hauchecorne, a trait that the author pronounces normal for "all true Normans," and turns it into a negative attribute that ultimately leads to Hauchecorne's death. As a result, Maupassant's short story functions as a kind of moral compass that reveals the flaws in the village's legal system, the economic bias that affects perception and judgment, and the damaging effects of guilt.

In "The Piece of String," there is clear evidence of economic bias and social-class prejudice based on economic distinctions. Like many short stories, "The Piece of String" reveals the world as it really exists. This is the reality of peasant life in Normandy during the nineteenth century. Peasants' bodies are worn out from years of pushing a plough and performing hard labor in the fields. They cannot afford the modern machinery that eases farming; their bodies are the machines. They are poor, people whom Maupassant describes as "bony" and "withered." The protagonist, Hauchecorne, is a peasant and is so "economical" that he stoops to the ground, although it is painful to do so, to pick up a piece of string that is so small that it is described as a "bit of thin cord." The string is an inconsequential item that was dropped to the ground, but it is not an insignificant item to Hauchecorne. This is the peasant class of Normandy, a group of hardworking farmers who spend their lives doing hard labor in an area where the climate can be harsh. They live in penury at a subsistence level, leading lives that have little value to people like the mayor and the harness maker.

To really understand the power of Maupassant's story, it is important to first consider why the short-story genre is such an effective choice for a story that focuses on what is imagined, what is real, and what is true. Edgar Allan Poe thought the short story second only to poetry in a hierarchy of literature. In some cases, according to Poe, the short story is even superior to verse in its ability to reveal truth. The short story possesses the same kind of emotion and ability to illuminate life as poetry. Because the short-story prose narrative is similar to poetry in its ability to tell a story, the short story is just as capable of evoking emotion or of illuminating a social issue. In her essay "The Short Story: An Overview of the History and Evolution of the Genre," Viorica Patea argues that the short story is a narrative in which no word is wasted but in which the truth can be found in its brevity. The truth of

peasant life, with all its harshness, is what readers are exposed to in "The Piece of String." Achieving succinctness, the short story compresses events and heightens the reader's response. In this sense, the short story is not unlike poetry, which is also capable of revealing ideas and motives, with only a few carefully chosen words and images. However, the short story can also reveal surprises. Patea claims that "short fiction makes room for commonplace things and events, yet the ordinary or the uneventful are never allowed to remain so." This is true in "The Piece of String," where, though picking up a piece of string seems like an ordinary-enough act, by the end of the story Hauchecorne dies because he cannot bear to be thought guilty of a petty crime and ridiculed when he is really innocent. Patea also points out that the short story is often peopled with characters who exist on the margins of society, which is certainly the case with Maupassant's protagonist Hauchecorne, who is physically compromised, almost miserly in his outlook, and so much of an outcast amongst the villagers that he is automatically assumed to be lying.

Because of the transformation from the ordinary to the unexpected, the short story is ideally positioned to challenge what readers think they know about truth. Maupassant's reader is given only brief glimpses into Hauchecorne's life. Much of what readers know about this old peasant is presented through his physical description and his actions. However, we do not know many specifics about Hauchecorne's existence before the morning when he bends down to pick up a piece of string. Readers do know that he is careful with money, "economical," in Maupassant's wording. Hauchecorne also suffers from severe arthritis and thus is likely to be in some pain. Those who eat in Jourdain's are farmers, what Maupassant calls "the aristocracy of the plough." Hauchecorne is also less than honest. He admits to himself that he might have kept the pocket-book had he found it. The great irony is that he did not find it, and is in fact quite innocent of the crime of which he has been accused. All of those descriptions and actions make up for the limited knowledge that readers are provided in "The Piece of String." The strength of the short story derives from how readers use that limited knowledge and where it leads them.

Because Maupassant's short story covers only a brief moment in the life of Hauchecorne, it is up to the reader who seeks the truth to read carefully and dissect the parts of the story that are important to understanding the events that unfold. Patea suggests that "the short story has the potential to challenge notions of conventional truth." That is certainly what happens in "The Piece of String." The missing pocket-book is found and returned to its owner. The man who finds the pocket-book admits to having picked it up on the road, where it was lost. These facts are all true, and they should, in a traditional court of testimony, be enough to exonerate Hauchecorne. The question, then, is why Hauchecorne continues not to be believed. In a conventional case, the accepted truth would be proved through evidence, and Hauchecorne would be cleared of any guilt. That is not the case in "The Piece of String." One possible reason for people's doubting him is the issue of class bias that Maupassant raises in this story. Hauchecorne is a peasant, and he is uneasy at being summoned by an authority figure like the mayor; it can be deduced that his lower rank accounts for his need to repeat "Here I am, here I am" as he follows the corporal out the door. Hauchecorne knows that he is at a disadvantage when summoned and is nervous when faced with someone of authority. As it turns out, he is justified in being nervous. He is not believed. His accuser, Malandain, is thought to be a credible witness. The only difference between the two men is social rank—one a peasant and one a harness maker. The latter is engaged in a trade, for which he has presumably been trained, and he lives in the town. Malandain is clearly of a higher social rank than Hauchecorne. Living in town and having a trade make Malandain more believable. They make him, as the mayor claims, "a man worthy of credit." That credibility is determined by

economics and/or social class is, of course, an injustice, but it is an injustice with which Hauchecorne must live, or he must die. In the case of a peasant, the conventional truth may not be sufficient.

In writing about an injustice, whether a single act of oppression or a lifetime of cruelty, it is the writer's words that tell the reader of the trauma and pain of injustice suffered by others. Literature reinforces lessons about injustice and helps readers to understand the truth of their world. In fact, literature teaches readers how to confront perceptions of the truth and to deal with the world in which we live. Maupassant makes clear in "The Piece of String" that perception and reality are vastly different concepts. Patea points out that "the short story probes the nature of the real, which proves to be more complex than the reality of mere appearances." In "The Piece of String," what people think happened trumps what they know did not happen. An innocent man is found guilty, not because he is guilty but because he is thought to be guilty. Because the mayor and the harness maker denounce Hauchecorne as a liar, he is judged to be so.

Poe thought that an important strength of the short story is its ability to reveal the truth, and even went so far as to argue in a review of Nathaniel Hawthorne's *Twice-Told Tales* that revealing the truth is often the direct intention of the short-story writer. Maupassant uses the short-story genre to illuminate the destructiveness of economic and class bias and show how what people perceive and think matters far more than what is true. In "The Piece of String," Hauchecorne is wronged by nearly everyone to whom he tells his story. He is never vindicated; his innocence is never pronounced by the harness maker who accused him or by the mayor who judged him. Hauchecorne is vindicated only for the reader. This is a virtue of the short-story genre, which possesses the power to judge and vindicate the innocent. It provides truth for the reader. Hauchecorne dies accused, the subject of laughter and jokes. It is within the power of the short-story writer to free Hauchecorne from the yoke of guilt. This is what Maupassant accomplishes in "The Piece of String."

Source: Sheri Metzger Karmiol, Critical Essay on "The Piece of String," in *Short Stories for Students*, Gale, Cengage Learning, 2014.

Hauchecome becomes obsessed with the issue of the string, wasting away as he insists on his innocence. (© Voronin76 | Shutterstock.com)

Laurence A. Gregorio

In the following excerpt, Gregorio interprets "The Piece of String" through the Darwinian concept of "survival of the fittest."

I have chosen for more complete analysis under the Darwinian lens one short story from among many possibilities. "La Ficelle" is a text that offers several points of interest, both thematic and narratorial, for the sort of analysis I propose. It was first published in November, 1883 in *Le Gaulois* and figured in the published collection entitled *Miss Harriet* in the following year. It is a work that is typical of Maupassant for its setting in the Norman peasant society, for its narratorial perspective and for its thematics. It comes from around the midpoint in his publishing career, so it is more mature than some earlier efforts. This *nouvelle* is among Maupassant's better known short stories, often chosen as representative or simply as one of his best for inclusion in anthologies or for translation.

The text opens on market day in the Norman town of Goderville as the peasants from surrounding areas are making their way in for the morning. The protagonist, Maître Hauchecorne from Bréauté, while walking into town, happens to spot a piece of string lying on the ground and bends over to pick it up. He notices that his enemy from some past dealings, Maître Malandin, has been observing him, so he hides the string in his shirt, pretends to be looking for something else on the ground, and continues on his way. Later in the day, however, Hauchecorne is summoned before the mayor and he learns that he is accused by Malandin of having found a lost wallet and not returning it to its owner. Hauchecorne protests his innocence, and the matter would seem to be resolved when the lost wallet is handed in by another peasant. But no one believes Hauchecorne's story, and he is tacitly accused in public opinion of having found the wallet and given it to an accomplice to turn in when suspicions arose. Hauchecorne becomes the object of ridicule and ostracism, and soon dies of grief, claiming his innocence to the last.

Let us begin with the level of narration. The text is narrated in the third-person voice of an omniscient extradiegetic speaker. Almost completely absent is the free indirect narrative discourse that typifies much of Maupassant's fiction, hence there is already a measure of distantiation between narrator and the characters and events narrated. It is clear from the start that this narrator sets himself apart from those characters and events, and the reader is given to understand—if only by the narrator's choice of descriptive vocabulary—that the narrator looks down on this textual society from a position of something like moral superiority. For example, his use of the term "l'aristocratie de la charrue" (CN1, 1082) to denote the clientele of the local eatery betokens an attitude of disdain and sarcasm where this society is concerned. Such downward vision lends itself easily to a judgmental tone and to the implicit moralizing that accompanies the narration of this somber action; but there is sufficient narrative distance of vision set between speaker and characters virtually to qualify as a perspective on a species entirely apart. It is as though the narrator has—and wants to have—nothing in common with the creatures whose adventures he is recounting.

It cannot precisely be said that the narrator of "La Ficelle" is taking the tone of a scientist or

> THE READER CAN ONLY INFER THAT ONE OF HIS LIFE NEEDS IS MEMBERSHIP IN THE HERD SINCE HE SOON DIES AFTER BEING CUT OFF FROM SOCIAL ACCEPTANCE."

an empiricist in the "laboratory of life;" Maupassant does not tend to strike this pose in his writing. Nonetheless, this narrator leans a bit in that direction. Narrative distance here gives the impression of objectifying characters and events. Narrative voice becomes all the more objective, too, with the frequent use of passive voice and impersonal constructions.

...All of the descriptive vocabulary tends toward explicitly characterizing the peasant society as beasts of burden, rendered bestial by their work. Later in the text, of course, they are rendered bestial by their actions. There is nothing surprising here: this is a *topos* of Naturalist fiction; Zola, in *La Terre* and *Germinal*, for example, made a point of similar descriptions. In "La Ficelle" the process of identification between human and animal is unmistakable.

...Note that the struggle for survival in which Hauchecorne finds himself engaged is not economic in the financial sense. Material prosperity is indeed the principal means of identification and exchange in the textual rural society, but it does not figure in the central conflict here. Money is indeed at the source of Hauchecorne's conflict in two ways: first, his feud with Malandin dates back to a financial transaction involving a horse's halter, and second, it is a wallet full of money that he is accused of finding and retaining unrightfully. But these are only the pretexts for the real conflict for social inclusion or acceptance that is, for Hauchecorne, the cause of a life-threatening crisis. So, while the society is understandable in the light of the principles of Malthusian economics, the narrative's central conflict turns out to be Darwinian in the original sense of the term. Rather than having to do with finances, it has to do instead with the economy of nature.

The struggle in question here pits the protagonist against his milieu, the individual against

his species. It is not the usual Darwinian struggle of individual against peers for limited resources or for reproductive success; as was just noted, the matter leaves the resources (albeit, defined as limited in the world depicted in the narrative) aside for the remainder of the text after the wallet is returned to its owner. From that point forward, the struggle for Hauchecorne is for a commodity which, for him, is as important as physical sustenance, as it turns out. The rest of society makes it a point to deny him the credence he obviously desires, and it is obviously to fulfill a need of its own that it takes this course: as a group, they find it entertaining to induce Hauchecorne to tell his story only to greet it with ridicule and disbelief. "Les plaisants maintenant lui faisaient confer 'la Ficelle' pour s'amuser..." (CN1, 1086). No one in the social unit shows the slightest sign of awareness that this protocol is a cruel one for Hauchecorne, and it goes on unabated since society is strong enough to pursue its needs in the absence of any force—the Church, some coterie of friends, some neutral altruist, etc.—to sway the struggle in Hauchecorne's favor. As the text is written, any such force is nowhere in sight. Such a force would be motivated by a concern for justice, a feeling of pity for the weak, or simple charity—a motive or combination of motives based in morality. But the Darwinian environment of nature is utterly (even maddeningly, for us) amoral, blind to the priorities of notions like "right over wrong" or "good over evil." This is exactly the milieu that "La Ficelle" portrays, bereft of any moral support whatever for the protagonist, not even, as we shall see, from the narrator. No force, divine or natural, textual or not, will intervene to spare Hauchecorne, as he is left to survive only as best he can. The only relevant truth is not that Hauchecorne really did pick up a piece of string, but rather that only the tough are likely to survive in nature. Harsh, cruel and amoral, certainly, but it is the law of the Nature that Darwinism describes.

Tacitly, the herd detects a weakness in Hauchecorne and is willing to exploit it regardless of its effects on the survival of a lone, weak individual. Weakness is the salient characteristic of this individual: the narrative focuses on his advanced age and his rheumatism, as we have seen, but it is also made clear that the question of real innocence versus presumed guilt is one that taxes Hauchecorne greatly. His need for belief and vindication is as compelling as any other in his life as we read it. The effects of his loss in this struggle make it evident that it is a question of survival for him: he falls physically ill and soon dies as a direct result of his ostracism. The reader can only infer that one of his life needs is membership in the herd since he soon dies after being cut off from social acceptance. Meanwhile, society gets what it needs from Hauchecorne (i.e. entertainment or a target for its hostility), but the reverse is not the case.

It has already been indicated that financial economics are not the focus of our study at this juncture. The action of the text leads our attention away from money and property, and towards other concerns for the central character. The other economics, the economy of nature, is still to be addressed in a Darwinian model of interpretation for "La Ficelle."

Evolutionary biologists are often confronted with baffling phenomena which, if their theory of life is to be of use, must be understood for their evolutionary logic. Their task is to understand the economy of nature where survival strategies and struggles may not always be easily understood, and to do so they must seek to divine what advantage a species gains by being as it is. Why does a species evolve a particular trait or behavior that seems at first glance to be without sense or gratuitously unmotivated? Why, for example, would the seventeen-year locust evolve the eccentric practice of burying itself in the ground for a seventeen-year stretch, only to emerge for a short time, reproduce and dig in for another seventeen years? Why indeed? There must be something gained for the advantage of the species, or else the behavior would not be "selected for" in evolutionary history. Only by crafting answers to such questions, by arriving at the internal logic of the life system, can science come to an understanding of evolution and retain evolutionary theory as a viable model for interpreting nature.

In the present application of Darwinian thought as a model of interpretation of Maupassant's short story, we are at the point where we must ask what the species (i.e. the rural society of Goderville) has to gain in ostracizing and harassing the individual who is old, defenseless and weak, but who has nothing material from which the society would stand to profit. Simple jealousy can be ruled out as a motive since there is nowhere any indication that Hauchecorne is to be envied for his wealth or lands, for example.

One other plausible motive might be gratuitous nastiness, given the usual dim view that is cast upon human nature in Maupassant, but this may be set aside if we assume that species behavior is directed towards some gain that will aid in the struggle for survival; in this case, the entertainment value of leading an old man to retell his story, or bullying a defenseless Hauchecorne, does not profit the society much. So why does society seem to conspire for the suffering of this character?

If there were no answer to this question, the action would be gratuitous and the Darwinian model would come to a dead end. The absence of an answer would mean that the Darwinian reading would take us only so far and no further, after providing valuable insights up to this point into the thematics, characterization and narration of the text. The matter would remain at the point of Maupassant's customary pessimism about human nature, and the rural society of Goderville would be simply bent on persecuting Hauchecorne for the mere sake of it. Granted, that may not seem odd for a society of uncultured dolts whose transcendence and moral character are recurrently portrayed by Maupassant here and elsewhere as most lacking. On the other hand, however, the peasant society throughout Maupassant's fiction, and especially in "La Ficelle," is shown to be frugal to the point where one can reasonably assume that all conduct, all expenditure of effort, will have at its source some profit incentive—this is a plot which revolves, after all, around a character who, despite his rheumatism, bends over and picks up a string out of parsimonious obsession. So the question remains, what is to be gained by society's persecution of Hauchecorne? The answer, if there is one, must lie in the notion of the economy of nature and must shed light on the internal logic of the species in its milieu.

The solution is in the peasant society's perception and structuration of the struggle for survival in perennially hard times. Signs in the text show us graphically that success in society is measured by two standards, money and possessions, on the one hand, and standing in public opinion where finances are concerned, on the other. The tight-fistedness of the characters is proof enough of the first. Proof of the second, public opinion of one's shrewdness, is evident in the prevailing opinion of the innkeeper Jourdain, for example: the narrator's choice of descriptive term reflects social opinion of this "*malin* qui avait des écus" (CN1, 1082, italics added). Society affords him respect and envy because of his business sense....

Source: Laurence A. Gregorio, "A Darwinian Reading of 'La Ficelle,'" in *Maupassant's Fiction and the Darwinian View of Life*, Peter Lang, 2005, pp. 47–49, 54–57.

Trevor A. Le V. Harris

In the following excerpt, Harris examines Maupassant's narrative style in "The Piece of String."

...It is certainly true that the story strikes many readers as in some sense typical of Maupassant's work, with its evocation of the seamy avarice of the Norman peasantry, the cruel comedy of its ending and the familiar limpidity of the prose. In these opening paragraphs we are presented with a truly simple scene, a straightforward description of down-to-earth peasant folk on their way to the local market and one's first reaction is to enjoy the simplicity and to admire the seemingly effortless manner in which Maupassant sets the scene for the events which are to follow.

All but the most casual readers, however, will not fail to be struck by a certain neatness in the narration, a detachment—one is even tempted to say, a rather haughty disdain in the way Maupassant organises the elements of his description. There is something a little too picturesque about Maupassant's peasants for them to be totally convincing. In the same way, there is something in the celebrated *clarté* of the writing, in its selectivity, which arouses a certain suspicion and makes this reader feel that it is just too neat, too simple, to be totally devoid of complexity.

A fundamental aspect of the simplicity of the text is, clearly, the size of the narrative units which the reader is required to assimilate. The five paragraphs of the extract quoted here are all comparatively brief and, on two occasions, reduced to a single sentence, as though the narration lacked the necessary energy or enthusiasm to develop the idea which it introduced. This is reinforced by the absence of any complexity at the lexical level, if only by virtue of the size of the units used: there are very few words here of more than two syllables. More important, the terms Maupassant uses are familiar by any reader's standards, with very few words which might be deemed difficult or rare. Indeed, if one considers the nouns used here, the vocabulary seems

THE REDUCTIVE TREATMENT OF THE PEASANT MEN AND WOMEN IS FURTHER EMPHASISED BY THE WAY IN WHICH THE NARRATION ESTABLISHES AN ANALOGY BETWEEN THE PEASANTS AND THEIR ANIMALS."

almost banal in its simplicity, as though it had been selected from a lexicon of elementary French. The same could also be said of the verbs used. It is no doubt this combination of brevity and familiarity which induces Léon Daudet—never an enthusiastic reader of Maupassant—to see this prose as characterised by the 'phrase courte et frottée.'

Indeed, the syntax of the extract also demonstrates a number of features which reinforce the lexical simplicity. Given that this is a descriptive passage, it is scarcely surprising that Maupassant makes little use of those adverbials which normally signal the chronological development of the narrative. Slightly more unusual, perhaps, is the near-total absence of cohesive links between the paragraphs. The latter constitute a series of images which seem to bear little relation to each other. More unusual still is the fact that, when Maupassant does use a familiar adverb, it is used in a rather unfamiliar way. At the beginning of the third paragraph we read, 'Puis, un char à bancs passait.' The adverb *puis* is strange here, since in the vast majority of cases it is used to mark a succession in time. However, the preceding sentence could hardly be deemed an 'event.' It is rather a description of the peasant women, a static image drawing on adjectives and past participles. There is, therefore, no succession of events to signal to the reader.

This is one way in which the sentence subverts the normal criteria of usage. But the sentence which *puis* introduces here is also unusual in the sense that one would expect a past historic rather than the imperfect *passait* to follow. The action described in this clause sits awkwardly with the durative or repetitive notions evoked by the tense chosen. Instead of the chronological relationship of succession most readers might have expected at this point, the narration insists on the durative aspect, maintaining the distance and detachment of the preceding sentences and paragraphs. Indeed, the more one concentrates on this, the more unsettling it becomes. The narration invites the reader to consider the event as an habitual one. On market day at Goderville, as the local farmers and their wives made their way towards the town square, a cart 'would pass by.' The accent is placed on the frequentative aspect of the scene being described. The uniqueness of the description falters and beyond it we are offered a fleeting view of the peasants' routine existence. The result is a curious conflation of two normally discrete modes of perception. This market-day becomes a market-day like any other. That which is apparently specific is repetitive. The unique becomes banal. There is already a sense in which Maupassant's simplicity seems a little strange.

The syntactic simplicity of this extract is also located in the systematic avoidance of co-ordinating or subordinating expressions. For example, of the thirty-six common conjunctions listed by Grevisse, Maupassant uses only four: *puis, car, ou, et*. While there is only one occurrence of each of the first three, *et* is used eighteen times. The reader's intuitive knowledge will tell him that the frequency, in some ways, is hardly surprising. Notwithstanding this fact, it is the discrepancy between the frequency of *et* and that of the other three conjunctions used which seems rather odd. The syntactic feature of co-ordination has been reduced to its most basic aspect: addition. In a similar way, if one considers the use of relative pronouns here, they are conspicuous by their absence. There are only four occurrences: *dont, qui* (twice), *que*.

The cumulative effect of these features of the language is to produce a description in which the components are arranged almost invariably by a process of juxtaposition or accumulation, so that the overall tenor of the piece begins to resemble that of a list. The narrator snatches a detail here, a detail there, places them side by side, or adds a series of adjectives without attempting to establish any hierarchical relationship between them. In the first paragraph, for example, the description of the male peasants is achieved by means of three clauses each introduced by *par*. Indeed, the ternary pattern is used on four other occasions in this short extract and may therefore be taken to constitute one of the main structuring-principles of the text.

It would no doubt be unwise to read too much into such a technique at this stage. And yet, one has to recognise that Maupassant is taking advantage of one of the most prominent figures of classical rhetoric, while at the same time undermining the way in which the ternary rhythm aims to organise the material it presents to the reader or listener. Broadly speaking, the force of the device, as in Caesar's famous saying or in the terms in which Shakespeare has Mark Antony address the people of Rome, resides in its balance and plenitude. It forms an elegant, autonomous trinity. In much of this, however, Maupassant's usage seems to be at odds with the traditional characteristics of the trope. When he gives us his description of the peasants, there is no real sense in which the details he provides can be held to exhaust the descriptive possibilities. When he presents their *blouse* as 'bleue, empesée, brillante,' these three adjectives do not encompass all the potential qualifications of the peasants' mode of dress. The use of the ternary rhythm here fails to produce a finite, self-sufficient structure. Indeed, after the initial ternary progression, the details which are selected lead on to others, equally important or equally banal, suggesting further ways in which the clothes can be described: 'leur blouse bleue, empesée, brillante, comme vernie, ornée au col et aux poignets d'un petit dessin de fil blanc, gonflée autour de leur torse osseux.' There is a sense in which the reader feels that the series might have been extended indefinitely. One detail evokes another in no real order of preference or importance. The walls of the ternary structure are breached, the details spilling over these limits into a potentially endless list of additional information. The hermetic unity of the ternary rhythm has become an open-ended incremental technique.

The essence of that technique, repetition, is much in evidence elsewhere in the extract, a number of terms being used more than once. Ten of the nouns and three of the verbs are repeated. Leaving aside those repetitions which are context-conditioned, a number of the other terms which are repeated do not easily admit of a similar explanation. While the words *hommes* and *femmes* are, no doubt, logical variants for *paysans* and *paysannes*, the fact remains that the generic force of the first pair of terms is reinforced by the second pair and that, even before he describes the crowd on the square at Goderville, Maupassant is concentrating on the collective as opposed to the individual characteristics of the people he is describing, observing them from a distance, noting down details of their appearance and movement, much as an ornithologist might observe birds from a hide. Indeed, at one point in his description Maupassant refers not to 'les paysans,' nor even to 'les hommes,' but to 'les mâles.'

The whole thrust of the narration is towards a reductive treatment of human character, the emphasis being placed on an awkward rigidity of movement, and the repetition of the words *tête, bras, taille, poitrine* in the descriptions both of the farmers and of their wives establishes a parallelism which points up the fact that Maupassant is assessing the appearance and movement of the female of the species with the same distance and detachment. The men lead the animals, while the women are invariably to be seen 'derrière l'animal.' The males walk 'à pas tranquilles,' while the females have a step which is 'plus court et plus vif.' Where the women are concerned, the narrative distance is underlined by the deletion of those physical attributes Maupassant's contemporary reader would have recognised as signs of feminine beauty: colour and arrangement of the hair, fullness of the bust and narrowness of the waist. The Goderville peasant women have 'la tête enveloppée,' 'la taille sèche' and 'la poitrine plate.'

The reductive treatment of the peasant men and women is further emphasised by the way in which the narration establishes an analogy between the peasants and their animals. In this case the parallelism is more striking and points up very clearly the way in which the limitation of the terms used creates a set of equivalences and similarities between the various elements of the text. Having described the 'blouse bleue' which the peasant men wear as 'un ballon prêt à s'envoler,' Maupassant adds, 'd'où sortait une tête.' The peasant women are then shown as carrying 'de larges paniers d'où sortaient des têtes de poulets par-ci, des têtes de canards par-là.' In this way, not only is the semantic component of volume repeated in each case ('ballon'/'larges'), but so is the structure of the two descriptive phrases ('*d'où sortait une tête*'/'*d'où sortaient des têtes*'), establishing a relationship of identity between the peasants and their animals. Similarly, later in the extract another linguistic parallel reiterates this resemblance. Above the general din in the market square at Goderville, the only sounds which emerge are, 'un grand

éclat poussé par la robuste poitrine d'un campagnard en gaieté' and 'le long meuglement d'une vache attachée au mur d'une maison.'

Other details underline the extent to which the narration presents the peasants and their animals as equivalents. The voices of the Goderville crowd are described as 'criardes, aiguës, glapissantes,' the last adjective suggesting that the noise produced by the peasants is animalistic. Or, again, the square is shown as full of 'une cohue d'humains et de bêtes mélangés.' Finally, the smell generated by the large gathering is described as 'humaine et bestiale, particulière aux gens des champs.' It is as though their constant proximity to animals has caused the peasants to assimilate, by some strange process of osmosis, certain animal characteristics....

Source: Trevor A. Le V. Harris, "Narrative with No Loose Ends: 'La Ficelle,'" in *Maupassant in the Hall of Mirrors: Ironies of Repetition in the Work of Guy de Maupassant*, St. Martin's Press, 1990, pp. 2–6.

SOURCES

Bloom, Harold, ed., "Biography of Guy de Maupassant," in *Guy de Maupassant*, Chelsea House Publishers, 2004, pp. 15–17.

Bond, Anthony, "Anyone for Underwater Croquet? Bizarre 19th Century Postcards Reveal How French Artists Thought We'd Be Living in 2000," in *Daily Mail* online, September 10, 2012, http://www.dailymail.co.uk/news/article-2200930/Bizarre-19th-Century-postcards-reveal-French-artists-thought-wed-living-2000.html (accessed August 10, 2013).

Dobbin, Frank, *Forging Industrial Policy: The United States, Britain, and France in the Railway Age*, Cambridge University Press, 1997, pp. 95–105, 153–57.

"1893: Maupassant Dies; In Our Pages: 100, 75 and 50 Years Ago," in *New York Times*, July 7, 1993, http://www.nytimes.com/1993/07/07/opinion/07iht-edold_16.html (accessed August 12, 2013).

"Guy de Maupassant's Work: Quality of His Style and Secret of His Popularity," in *New York Times*, July 9, 1893, http://query.nytimes.com/mem/archive-free/pdf?res=FA0A17FD3B5F1A738DDDA00894DF405B8385F0D3 (accessed August 12, 2013).

Harmon, William, and C. Hugh Holman, *A Handbook to Literature*, 11th ed., Pearson Prentice Hall, 2009, pp. 298–99, 361, 445, 511–12.

Käsebier, Gertrude, "Peasant Life in Normandy," in *Monthly Illustrator*, Vol. 3, No. 11, March 1895, pp. 269–75.

Leick, Romain, "Rocky Relationship: Attraction and Repulsion Define French-German Relations," in *Der*

Spiegel online, August 16, 2012, http://www.spiegel.de/international/europe/french-intellectuals-put-the-franco-german-axis-on-the-couch-a-850197.html (accessed August 10, 2013).

Maupassant, Guy de, "The Piece of String," in *Best Short Stories of Guy de Maupassant*, World Publishing, 1944, pp. 67–76.

Miller, Jonathan D., "France," in *Infrastructure 2013: Global Priorities, Global Insights*, Urban Land Institute/Ernst & Young, 2013, p. 38, http://www.ey.com/Publication/vwLUAssets/Infrastructure_2013/$FILE/Infrastructure_2013.pdf (accessed August 10, 2013).

Nolan, Elizabeth, "*The Awakening* as Literary Innovation: Chopin, Maupassant and the Evolution of Genre," in *The Cambridge Companion to Kate Chopin*, edited by Janet Beer, Cambridge University Press, 2008, pp. 118–31.

Patea, Viorica, "The Short Story: An Overview of the History and Evolution of the Genre," in *DQR Studies in Literature*, No. 49, 2012, pp. 1–25.

Patrick, Jonathan, "Maupassant's Men: Masculinity and the Franco-Prussian War," in *Fin de Siècle*, edited by Anne Fremiot, University of Nottingham, 1998, pp. 17–26.

Poe, Edgar Allan, Review of *Twice-Told Tales*, by Nathaniel Hawthorne, in *Essays and Reviews*, edited by G. R. Thompson, Library of America, 1984, pp. 571–74.

"Upper Normandy Living," Complete France, December 11, 2012, http://www.completefrance.com/living-in-france/upper_normandy_living_1_1738185 (accessed August 12, 2013).

Weber, Eugen, *Peasants into Frenchmen: The Modernization of Rural France, 1870–1914*, Stanford University Press, 1976, pp. 201–10.

"What Is Fin de Siecle?," in *Art Critic*, Vol. 1, No. 1, November 1893, p. 9.

Zeldin, Theodore, "Eating and Drinking," in *A History of French Passions, 1848–1945*, Vol. 2, *Intellect, Taste and Anxiety*, Oxford University Press, 1993, pp. 725–30.

FURTHER READING

Devlin, Judith, *The Superstitious Mind: French Peasants and the Supernatural in the Nineteenth Century*, Yale University Press, 1987.

> This book examines common legends and folklore, clerical reports, and physicians' descriptions to explore religious belief, witchcraft, belief in ghosts, prophecy, magic, demonic possession, and medicine in rural nineteenth-century France. The text provides a fascinating opportunity to explore the culture and belief systems of the people who populate Maupassant's stories.

Herbert, Robert L., *Monet on the Normandy Coast: Tourism and Painting, 1867–1886*, Yale University Press, 1994.

> Herbert discusses more than fifty of Monet's drawings and paintings and provides analysis of the artist's efforts to show the transformation of Normandy's coast from fishing villages to tourism destinations. The works highlighted illustrate how much the coast of Normandy changed even though the interior small-village life of peasants remained unchanged during those years.

McNamara, Carole, Sylvie Aubenas, Stephen Bann, and Dominique de Font-Reaulx, *The Lens of Impressionism: Photography and Painting along the Normandy Coast, 1850–1874*, University of Michigan Museum of Art, 2009.

> This book includes more than one hundred reproductions of paintings, photographs, and drawings that reveal life along the coast of Normandy during the nineteenth century.

Patton, Susannah, *A Journey into Flaubert's Normandy*, Roaring Forties Press, 2006.

> This text is a literary guidebook to Normandy. It includes maps, photographs from the nineteenth and twentieth centuries, and artwork, with a focus on the small towns where Gustave Flaubert, Maupassant's mentor, once lived and journeyed.

Perrot, Phillippe, *Fashioning the Bourgeoisie: A History of Clothing in the Nineteenth Century*, translated by Richard Bienvenu, Princeton University Press, 1994.

> This text is a study of how France's first department stores, opened in Paris in the mid-nineteenth century, changed fashion by making available ready-to-wear clothing that gave rise to a new bourgeoisie lifestyle and blurred class distinctions.

Wawro, Geoffrey, *The Franco-Prussian War: The German Conquest of France in 1870–1871*, Cambridge University Press, 2003.

> Wawro offers a history of the Franco-Prussian War, which had a profound influence on Maupassant's life. The French defeat in this war heavily plunged the nation into debt and caused economic hardship, as the French were forced to pay huge sums of money to Germany.

Webster, Jane, *At My French Table: Food, Family and Joie de Vivre in a Corner of Normandy*, Viking, 2008.

> This is a combination memoir and guide to the food and restaurants of Normandy. The book includes many photographs of the region and information about antique fairs and street markets, as well as profiling local people.

SUGGESTED SEARCH TERMS

Maupassant AND The Piece of String

Maupassant AND short story

Maupassant AND biography

Maupassant AND criticism

Maupassant AND Normandy

Maupassant AND novel

Maupassant AND Franco-Prussian War

peasant life AND Normandy

farming AND Normandy

A Prayer from the Living

BEN OKRI

1993

Ben Okri is a Nigerian novelist and short-story writer. A year after his birth, Nigeria, until 1960 a British colony, gained its independence. Okri's writings are consequently rooted in his experience as a citizen of a country in transition and turmoil. In his fiction he explores themes of race, war, identity, and death. In the short story "A Prayer from the Living," Okri writes vividly of the experience of famine, starvation, and dying. The work, which was inspired by the famine in Somalia in the early 1990s, centers on an unnamed narrator who is searching among the dead for his loved ones. Just as they have starved to death, he, too, is starving and quickly approaching death. The narrator regards those already dead as lucky, and happy. When he looks at the dead, he has two experiences of them—he regards them as corpses, and as smiling, singing figures. If he can find his loved ones and know they are at peace, he too can stop struggling to remain alive.

"A Prayer from the Living" was originally published in 1993 in the *New York Times*. It is available in the anthology *Under African Skies: Modern African Stories*, edited by Charles R. Larson and published in 1997.

AUTHOR BIOGRAPHY

Okri was born on March 15, 1959, in Minna, Nigeria, to Grace and Silver Oghekeneshineke

Ben Okri (© Jeremy Sutton-Hibbert / Alamy)

Loloje Okri. The year after he was born, British colonial rule officially ended in Nigeria. Okri's parents were well-off. His father worked in a managerial capacity for Nigerian Post and Telecommunications. He and his family traveled to England in 1962. There, his father earned a law degree. Okri was subsequently educated in both Nigeria and Britain.

Okri and his mother returned to Nigeria in 1966 and were followed later by his father, who set up a legal practice in a slum region, Ajegunle, a district of Lagos. In 1968, Okri entered Urhobo College for his secondary education, which he completed in 1972. Although he did not earn a place in a Nigerian university, he found a job at a paint store and pursued his writing. Okri published short fiction in magazines and newspapers. In 1978, he was admitted to Essex University in England. He finished his first novel there; *Flowers and Shadows* was published in 1980. The same year, he earned his bachelor of arts degree in comparative literature.

Okri worked as the poetry editor of *West Africa*, a literary journal, from 1981 through 1987. For about a year, from 1984 through 1985, he was employed as a BBC World Service broadcaster for the program *Network Africa*. Over the years, Okri has also reviewed literature for the *Guardian*, the *Observer*, and the *New Statesman*. He has won various literary prizes, including the *Paris Review*/Aga Khan fiction prize for the 1986 short-story collection *Incidents at the Shrine*. He published the acclaimed novel *The Famished Road* in 1991. The work earned Okri the prestigious Man Booker Prize.

Okri continued to publish short-fiction collections and novels. In 1993, he published the novel *Songs of Enchantment*, along with the short story, "A Prayer from the Living," which first appeared in the *New York Times*. In the early 2010s, Okri published the essay collection *A Time for New Dreams* (2011) and the poetry collection *Wild* (2012). As of 2013, Okri resided in London.

PLOT SUMMARY

"A Prayer from the Living" opens with the narrator, referring to himself only as "I," entering a village, accompanied by other unnamed individuals. They move among the houses, searching. The narrator comments that certain unsympathetic people, "the little godfathers who controlled everything," have taken all the food meant for the villagers. Yet the narrator goes on to say that he has little need for food at this point; he has not eaten for three weeks. He speaks of how those who have already died look at the living with "pity and compassion."

The narrator observes the way the white people who have come to film them and bring assistance cannot understand the sense of calm they see in the starving villagers. The white people expect to see fear in the villagers' eyes, the narrator supposes.

Repeatedly the narrator declares that the dead are not dead. They sing, and they celebrate. He mentions the soldiers, and how they fight for the right to control a land that once was beautiful but now is little more than a cemetery. The narrator describes the way he searches for his family and his lover. He does not know if they are dead or alive. He mourns the loss of a past in

MEDIA ADAPTATIONS

- "A Prayer from the Living" was adapted into a short film in 2002. The film was directed and produced by Alex Reuben. It was shown at the 2003 VideoDance Festival in Athens and Thessaloniki, Greece.

which the future seemed full of possibility. Now, he muses, there is only death.

He and his companions turn over bodies, searching for faces that are familiar to them. He notes that all of the dead are familiar in a way; they are all related in death. The narrator also observes that death contorts the faces so that they are yet unfamiliar. He finds his brother first and scatters dust on his body, symbolizing burial. Not long after, he finds the rest of his family. He describes the way his mother clutches a bone.

At sunset, the narrator hears singing coming from the unfinished building that once served as a school. He describes the sound as magical. Making his way toward the school, he wonders at how long that journey seems to take. A cow wanders into the building in front of him, and he follows the creature in. The school is filled with the dead. He insists, however, that the dead in the school are alive, although he realizes that this is a paradoxical statement to make. The narrator believes that at the end of their lives, these individuals thought of other people who were suffering, and that in their last moments of living, they prayed for the living. He makes himself comfortable among the dead and begins to pray as he believed they prayed, marrying his prayer with the song of the dead.

He finally looks down at the body next to him and sees the face of his lover. He keeps up his singing, not moving his mouth but singing silently, as he begins to process the fact that he has found the answers he sought. His loved ones have all gone on. He sees a white man enter the room holding a television camera, and he witnesses the man weeping.

The narrator observes that the dead linger around him and smile, waiting patiently but joyfully for him. He knows that human life has nothing left to offer him, and he considers how he feels betrayed by life, knowing as he does now all of its evils. The narrator sees the cameras filming the room and notes that the cow still wanders through the schoolroom. As he looks at the living, he considers them dead, because they are chained to the cruel world. He breathes his last breath and lets himself die. The final thought he shares with the reader is that he smiled at the reporters, and that this must have confused them. He believes that if they had been able to understand him they would have known that he was saying good-bye.

CHARACTERS

Little Godfathers
The narrator refers to the "little godfathers who controlled everything." He informs the reader that these individuals stole the food which aid workers had brought for the starving villagers, and that they redistributed it, feeding themselves "and members of their clan." Although the narrator does not elaborate on this situation, the comment about the godfathers presumably refers to armed leaders of other clans from the surrounding area, who raided supplies and capitalized on the humanitarian aid that was brought to the village.

Narrator
"A Prayer from the Living" focuses primarily on the experiences of one character, the narrator himself. He enters the village using the collective term "we," but in the story he has no direct contact with anyone else. He has come to the village to confirm what he suspects—that his loved ones have all died. The story consists of his search through the village. As he turns over the bodies, looking at faces, he comments on the presence of soldiers and television reporters. The narrator periodically wonders about their perceptions of the village, of those who have starved to death in it. Yet he is largely occupied with his quest. He finds that his loved ones have died, and he subsequently relinquishes his own grasp on life and slips away as well. Before he dies, the

narrator encounters the spirits of those who have died. In those spirits, the narrator sees life and joy. The spirits sing, and they pray. While the reader may interpret these spirits as the delusional effects of starvation on the body or as insane visions brought about by the horrors the narrator has witnessed, the spirits are real to the narrator. They give him comfort as he transitions from this world into the world of the dead.

Narrator's Companions

The narrator uses the term "we" at the beginning of the story. It seems as though he enters the village with others, who, like him, are seeking their loved ones amongst the corpses. Once he begins to find members of his family, the narrator no longer mentions these companions with whom he entered the village. He does not speak with them or appear to have any contact with them. They exist near one another but do not interact. At the same time, they share the bond of suffering and loss.

Soldiers

The narrator observes that the soldiers "fought amongst themselves eternally" and that they did not care about those who died. He states that they battled for control over the land, which had once been beautiful but was now little more than a "fabulous graveyard." Although Okri does not specifically identify the country in the story, critics have noted that the story was published at a time when there was civil war and famine in Somalia, a situation in which the United States and the United Nations intervened. The soldiers, according to the narrator, have not improved the situation in the country.

White Ones

Referring at several places in the story to white people, the narrator mentions in passing the fact that they are reporters and aid workers. He speculates that they expect the villagers who have not yet starved to death to be weeping. Yet it is the white ones who weep, or at least one of them: at the conclusion of the story, a "good-hearted white man" enters the school, filming the scene, and the narrator sees him crying. The narrator hopes that the camera has somehow captured his silent singing. He additionally smiles at the reporters as he dies. The narrator suspects that his smiling "must have puzzled the reporters." Yet through the singing only he can hear, and through his smile, he attempts to convey that he

is moving on toward a more peaceful state, and that he is relieved to be leaving suffering and pain behind him. Just as with the unnamed companions and the soldiers, though, the narrator does not interact with the white ones. The only exception is the "good-hearted white man," who, upon seeing him in the room with the dead, weeps.

THEMES

Death

Death is one of the overriding themes of "A Prayer from the Living." From the first sentence to the last, death pervades the story. The narrator and his unidentified companions enter the "town of the dying" at sunset, as the day itself is dying. The narrator regards death in terms of both endings and beginnings. He notes the way the villagers died—through starvation—and the way they exist now, as joyful and "luminous" beings. He also comments that he is not afraid to die through starvation—as they did. As he wanders through the village he emphasizes the positive nature of those who have died. "The only people who weren't dead," he states, "were the dead." They sing "golden songs"; they are "jubilant." The narrator further observes, though, that the dead villagers do not matter to the soldiers. The soldiers do not care about how many villagers have died, or that the land they seek to rule has become a "graveyard."

The narrator, upon finding his dead loved ones, enacts a burial ritual, covering their bodies with dust. Once he enters the school, the narrator's eagerness for death increases, particularly after he finds the corpse of his lover. He notes, "The dead in the school were—forgive the paradox—*alive*." Death for the narrator has come to mean a new life, a release from the suffering of the world. Just before he dies, he contemplates the nature of human life, describing it as "full of greed and bitterness, dim, low-oxygenated, judgmental and callous, gentle, too, and wonderful as well, but ... human life had betrayed me." Throughout the story, Okri infuses the notion of death with a sense of spirituality. The actual process of dying of starvation is not depicted. The three weeks in which he has had nothing to eat occur prior to the beginning of the story. This suffering is not portrayed. By the end, the narrator has ceased thinking of food. Death, now, is

TOPICS FOR FURTHER STUDY

- Okri's work employs elements of magical realism while treating grave themes such as suffering, death, and despair. Likewise, Jose Cruz Gonzales makes use of magical realism in his young-adult plays, which treat the serious issues young people face. Edited by Coleman A. Jennings, *Nine Plays by Jose Cruz Gonzales* was published in 2008. Gonzales, the son of Mexican migrant workers, helped his family by working in the fields with them. Select one or two of Gonzales's plays and read them with a small group. How does Gonzales's background inform his work? What themes does he explore? Consider the ways race and ethnicity are treated in the plays. In what ways is magical realism incorporated into the plays? How does Gonzales's use of magical realism compare with that of Okri? Discuss these issues with your group. Continue your discussion in an online blog you create.

- When "A Prayer from the Living" was published in 1993, there was an ongoing famine in Somalia. Research this time period in Somalian history. What events contributed to the famine? How many people were affected? How was the involvement by the United States and the United Nations received by Somalis? Did the assistance help or hurt those most affected? When did foreign troops withdraw? When and how did Somalia begin to recover from the famine? How did political instability affect the ability of aid workers to distribute famine relief supplies? Create a time line—either in print or online—and pinpoint the key events

during this crisis. Present your time line to the class.

- In "A Prayer from the Living," Okri depicts the narrator's belief in an afterlife. The narrator sees the dead as living, as going about their normal activities, as singing joyfully. Somalia is a predominantly Muslim nation. Research Muslim beliefs regarding the afterlife, and explore other cultural beliefs on this topic that may exist among other segments of the population, such as the Bantu people, an ethnic minority in Somalia. Write a research paper in which you outline the various beliefs about death and the afterlife among Muslims and Bantus in Somalia. Discuss as well customs related to burial. Although it does not need to be incorporated into your paper, consider the ways the beliefs of the narrator in Okri's story compare to what you have learned.

- Okri is a Nigerian writer who, in "A Prayer from the Living," addresses the crisis of famine and civil war in Somalia. Both Somalia and Nigeria are nations with a colonial history. Select either Nigeria or Somalia and research the history of colonization and subsequent independence. When was the nation first colonized and by whom? What resources drew the colonizing nations there? How was independence gained? Was the transition of power violent or peaceful? What struggles has the nation endured politically since gaining independence? Present your findings as a PowerPoint presentation.

peaceful, as his smile at the end of the story indicates.

Otherness

In "A Prayer from the Living," the narrator regards the aid workers and the reporters (who

are in the village due to the widespread famine) as the "white ones," underscoring the fact that there are racial and cultural differences at play. He also draws attention to the presence of soldiers, who have done nothing to improve the situation in the village and who have

The gunrunners and the "godfathers" steal relief supplies, leaving many people without food.

(© Peter Kim | Shutterstock.com)

demonstrated a callousness regarding the dead and dying. In the introduction to Okri's story in the anthology *Under African Skies*, Larson explains that the work was written in response to the Somalian famine, and to what has since been characterized by critics as a misguided intervention by the US military. Larson's explanation and the text of the story both emphasize the notion of the "otherness" with which the outsiders to the region—the soldiers, reporters, and aid workers—regard the villagers.

The narrator regards himself, his companions, and the villagers as a community, and he sees those who have intervened in an effort to ameliorate the conditions resulting from war and famine as outsiders. Further, the narrator senses that the "white ones" (he describes the journalists and aid workers in this manner) and the soldiers regard the villagers as foreign and incomprehensible. To the soldiers, reporters, and aid workers, the villagers are "the others."

The narrator comments in several portions of the story about the way the aid workers, reporters, or soldiers misunderstand the villagers, or the way they have demonstrated a disregard for them. The narrator states, "I suppose this is what the white ones cannot understand when they come with their TV cameras and their aid. They expect to see us weeping. Instead, they see us staring at them, without begging." He goes on to wonder, "Maybe they were secretly horrified that we are not afraid of dying this way." He further emphasizes that the soldiers are unaffected by the deaths of the villagers, as they are only interested in establishing leadership in the devastated country.

In the end, the narrator finds that at least one of the outsiders sheds his notion of the "otherness" of the villagers. Rather than seeing differences, one "good-hearted white man" is able to weep for those who have died. In the last line of the story, though, the narrator once again draws attention to the misunderstanding the outsiders have about the villagers. He smiles as he dies, and thinks, "If they had understood my language, they would have known that it was my way of saying goodbye." He attempts to communicate, but even until the moment of his death, he fully believes that those outsiders—who have come to the village to bear witness to the villagers' suffering and death—ultimately fail to understand what they are seeing and whom they are failing to help.

STYLE

Postmodernism

In literature, *postmodernism* is a general term that refers to a rejection of the notion that reality can be effectively conveyed, explained, or understood through scientific or objective methods. According to postmodernist theory, reality is essentially constructed by the human mind as it attempts to comprehend its own subjective experience. A hallmark of postmodernism is skepticism regarding explanations of reality that assert objective certainty, or validity for all groups of people. Its focus is on relative, individual truth. Much of Okri's work has been described as postmodern in that therein, Okri experiments with narrative techniques and conveys the subjective nature of his characters' perception of reality.

In "A Prayer from the Living," Okri employs an unnamed first-person narrator (referring to himself as "I"). The use of a first-person narrator underscores the notion of subjectivity and individuality. The story conveyed is a depiction of the reality known to the narrator. At the same time, unnamed narrators, by virtue of their anonymity, are sometimes understood as a representation of humanity as a whole, as an "everyman." Okri is depicting the narrator's personal reality but at the same time exposing to the world—through the eyes of the narrator—the horrors of war and famine, of isolation, suffering, and death. Okri also incorporates the spirits of the dead as an integral part of the story, in this way mingling elements of spiritualism with the historical realism of famine and civil war in this portion of the world. The melding of these perspectives is another postmodern element in the work. Similarly, the construction of the story as a tale told by a dead man, in its inversion of traditional narrative technique, is suggestive of the work's postmodernist qualities.

Magical Realism

The term *magical realism* originated in 1925 when it was used by a German art critic, as Stephen Hart explains in an essay for *A Companion to Magical Realism*. Later, it was applied to fiction. Its first use in this capacity, notes Dana Gioia in an article for the journal *Sniper Logic*, came in 1949 when it was used by Cuban novelist Alejo Carpentier. Beginning with works such as the 1967 novel *One Hundred Years of Solitude*, by Gabriel García Márquez, the term was used to describe what became a trend in Latin American fiction. Works of magical realism are those in which a realistic story is infused with elements of the fantastic, supernatural, or absurd. Such elements are accepted as part of the framework of the story, part of that tale's reality. Okri's works, particularly the novel *The Famished Road*, have been analyzed in terms of their magical realism.

In "A Prayer from the Living," Okri incorporates elements of the supernatural. The spirits that the narrator perceives are regarded as part of the narrator's reality. The closer the narrator moves toward his own death, as he reports, the more of this other world is perceivable: "Every day, as I grow leaner, I see more things around us. I see the dead—all who had died of starvation. They are more joyful now; they are happier than we are." He hears them singing and insists that they carry on with "their familiar lives." Later, approaching the school building, the narrator describes the singing of the dead as "the most magical sound I had ever heard." For a full paragraph he describes the joyful singing and the way it recalls the "beginning of all creation." Making himself comfortable among the bodies, he prays. Not long after, the narrator describes the moment of his own passing. His ultimate demise emphasizes that in the reality of the story, he has written the tale after his death.

HISTORICAL CONTEXT

Famine and Civil War in Somalia in the 1990s

In 1991, Somalia's dictator, Mohamed Siad Barre, who had been in power since 1969, fled Somalia's capital city of Mogadishu when the militias of rival clans captured the city. Warring clan leaders and their followers then fought for power. During this period of civil war, Somalian citizens numbering in the thousands were injured or killed. One of the clan leaders, Ali Mahdi Mohamed, declared himself president of the Republic of Somalia. The following year, in addition to the ongoing battles between rival clans, a drought-induced famine struck the country. Hundreds of thousands of Somalis died as a result of warfare, disease, or starvation. US president George H. W. Bush ordered emergency supplies and rations to be airlifted into Somalia beginning in late 1992. Furthermore, the United Nations Security Council approved a military mission designed to guarantee that food and supplies would reach the people in need instead of being raided by warlords. The UN mission in Somalia was led by the United States and was referred to as UNOSOM. In addition to its humanitarian aims, UNOSOM also sought to stabilize the collapsed Somalian government.

In October 1993 Somali militiamen shot down two US helicopters. A battle then erupted in Mogadishu, in which eighteen US service members and hundreds of Somali militiamen and civilians were killed. In 1994, the United States ended its role in the mission to Somalia. In total, the mission cost the United States $1.7 billion, as Anabel Lee Hogg explains in a chronology of the Somalian famine and warfare for the *Atlantic*. The United Nations and the

COMPARE
&
CONTRAST

- **1993:** In Somalia, there is a drought, extensive famine, and a civil war. A US-led UN coalition enters the country in 1992 in an effort to provide food and supplies, but this humanitarian mission leads to military operations intended to stabilize the government. Somali militiamen shoot down two US helicopters, resulting in further escalation of the violence in the region.

  Today: Somalia continues to face humanitarian crises caused by violence, drought, and food insecurity. As of October 2012, according to Refugees International, there are over 1.3 million Somalis displaced within the country and over a million refugees living in neighboring countries. Overall, 3.7 million Somalis are in dire need of humanitarian assistance.

- **1993:** In Nigeria, a colony of Great Britain until 1960, the first presidential election since 1983 presents an opportunity to end the existing military dictatorship. However, Nigeria has a history, since gaining independence, of democratic elections being derailed by military coups, and the results of the 1993 election are canceled by the military ruler of Nigeria, General Ibrahim Babangida. The presumed winner of the election, M. K. O. Abiola, is imprisoned for declaring himself president. He later dies in jail. The postcolonial transition to independence thus continues to be marked by political turmoil.

  Today: Nigeria has a civilian government. The president of Nigeria is President Goodluck Jonathan, who assumed the presidency after the death of President Yar'adua in 2010 and won the 2011 presidential election. Nigeria's legislative branch consists of elected members of a bicameral National Assembly (comprising two houses—a Senate and a House of Representatives).

- **1993:** The literature of many African countries is shaped by political events. Countries that were once colonies of nations such as Britain and France face the challenge of establishing a collective cultural and national identity. The contemporary literature of these countries is often studied through the filter of a postcolonial analytical framework. African writers during this time are also influenced by global literary movements and trends such as postmodernism and magical realism.

  Today: Many African writers who wrote during the turbulent postcolonial eras in their nations continue to publish fiction today. Their works are marked by an evolution in style and by a continued focus on the political themes pertinent to their homelands, as many nations continue to struggle with racial and ethnic tensions and political violence.

United States were viewed by some as having done more harm than good in their effort to intervene militarily in the civil war. As Sally Healy and Mark Bradbury explain in a summary of the civil war published in the journal *Accord*, "the mission failed to mediate an end to hostilities or disarm factions." The authors further explain that the mission was "criticized for fueling the war economy, causing a proliferation of factions and shoring up warlord power structures."

African Literature in the 1990s

In the 1990s, African literature was shaped by global developments in fiction characterized as postmodernism, postcolonialism, and magical realism. The term *postcolonial* emerged as a

Even the horses and cows are starving. (© Trazos sobre Papel | Shutterstock.com)

theoretical construct, a framework for understanding the history, literature, and culture of nations once held as colonies by European nations. The term *neocolonialism*, prevalent in the 1980s, implied possibility and progress, but when political and economic trouble persisted in former colonies, new nomenclature was necessary. As Simon Gikandi explains in an essay on postcolonialism for the *Encyclopedia of African Literature*, "as the term 'neocolonial' appeared inadequate, a new term—'postcolonialism'—emerged as a possible alternative." Gikandi explains that some African intellectuals rejected the notion of postcolonialism, as "the issues privileged by postcolonial theory (difference, hybridity, and performativity) were not necessarily liberating in societies in which the invocation of these terms had been the basis of warfare, violence, and genocide." Nevertheless, the term became widely used as a means of understanding the postcolonial experience.

Postmodernism is also a theoretical construct applied to the work of African writers during this time period. It is rooted in the philosophical notion that reality is something individually and subjectively perceived, rather than something that can be conveyed as objective or as true for all groups. Okri's *The Famished Road* and several of his other works are frequently examined as examples of African postmodern literature. As Robert Bennett explains in an overview of Okri and his work in *Postcolonial African Writers: A Bio-Bibliographical Critical Sourcebook*, Okri's writings are regarded as postmodern in that they "mix genres, cross cultural boundaries, and intertextually parody both African and European traditions." Other African authors whose work has been considered in this light include Nuruddin Farah and Femi Euba.

Related to the dominance of postmodernism and postcolonialism in African fiction of this time period is the emergence of magical realism in the works of African writers. Brenda Cooper, in an essay for the *Encyclopedia of African Literature*, maintains that

> the heart of the emergence of magical realism in Africa lies with postcolonialism and postmodernism. While postcolonial writing comes in many shapes, sizes, and modes, it is probably

true to say that magical realism is a form of postcolonial writing that most aggressively harnesses some of the tools of postmodernism—parody, irony, pastiche, and syncreticism."

Magical realism incorporates elements of the supernatural, fantastic, or the absurd into works that are otherwise narrated in a realistic fashion. In an essay in *A Companion to Magical Realism*, Stephen Hart explains the relationship between magical realism and postcolonial African politics in Okri's *The Famished Road*. Hart states that Okri "is able to combine in an arresting manner a vision of the supernatural with a sense of the real political problems faced by Africa today." Hart goes on to offer a general sense of the way magical realism effectively migrated across the globe. He explains,

> Particularly for writers in countries which had recently escaped from the clutches of colonialism, magical realism appeared to offer a literary idiom which could reflect the raw political tensions which accompanied the movement towards nationhood.

Other African authors writing in this mode included Syl Cheney-Coker and Kojo Laing.

CRITICAL OVERVIEW

Critical analysis of Okri's work is often focused on his use of magical realism or is rooted in the assessment of his fiction as postmodern or post-colonial. In general, critics have largely focused on *The Famished Road* as the most significant of Okri's works. The work is typically regarded as exemplifying the magical realist mode in its blending of realism and myth. In his overview of Okri's work in *Postcolonial African Writers*, Bennett states, "Critics have praised Okri for his ability to creatively experiment with new literary forms." Bennett discusses the way Okri has become gradually more experimental over time. He mentions that Okri's short fiction has received less critical scrutiny than his novels.

In his introduction to "A Prayer from the Living" in *Under African Skies*, Larson describes the story as a "powerful response to the famine in Somalia." Larson further underscores that in the story, "Okri defines a central moral issue of our time: the justification of intervention in cultures other than our own, which too often for the West has meant misunderstanding and ignorance of other people's ways." Similarly, in

Seeing Witness: Visuality and the Ethics of Testimony, Jane Blocker regards "A Prayer from the Living" as an effort "to give voice to Africa's contemporary experiences of the Western media."

CRITICISM

Catherine Dominic

Dominic is a novelist and freelance writer and editor. In the following essay, she asserts that Okri's language and imagery underscore the contrasts and paradoxes inherent in "A Prayer from the Living" and that ultimately, the tale is marked by a sense of hopelessness and despair.

"A Prayer from the Living" is a bleak tale of suffering and death. In it, Ben Okri juxtaposes the lives of the living and the peace attained in death. Throughout the story, the language and imagery employed by Okri underscore this interplay between the grim reality of living and the joyful nature of death in this forsaken place. The narrator's belief in an afterlife suggests that even in a world of pain and suffering, there is the possibility of release. For many readers, though, the narrator's belief in an afterlife may be regarded as superstition or as the result of hunger-induced hallucination. For these readers, the story takes on an even more devastating tone. Okri offers little hope for the living, for those the narrator leaves behind as he perishes at the end of the story. Okri infuses "A Prayer from the Living" with contrast and paradox. Living and dying are conflated. Prayer is both hopeless and necessary. The world is depicted as devoid of love, yet it is love that motivates the narrator to search for his family and his lover. By the end of the story, the notions of futility and despair, and the images of suffering, are overwhelming. Okri thus effectively conveys the relief with which the narrator departs the world of the living.

As the story opens, the narrator describes the village he enters, searching for his loved ones. Death is everywhere. As the narrator, through his own starvation, gets closer to his own death, he describes the way his clarity of vision intensifies. He begins to see the dead, both as they died—starved corpses on the ground—and also as happy, "living their luminous lives as if nothing has happened." Although he does not portray the suffering endured by those who have died before him, he captures in brief images the

> THE LANGUAGE AND IMAGES THAT OKRI USES TO DESCRIBE THE NARRATOR'S THOUGHTS AND EMOTIONS ARE FILLED WITH DARKNESS AND HOPELESSNESS. THE ABSENCE OF LOVE IS BLAMED FOR THE SUFFERING INDUCED BY THE DROUGHT AND FAMINE."

horror of their deaths. He sees his "old friends" who have passed on before him, "clutching onto flies." The narrator insists, "Now they feed on the light of the air." The imagery is poetic in its compression. The weeks and weeks of slow starvation ending in death are only hinted at, yet those small phrases tell their own story to readers who take the time to consider the corpse "clutching onto flies" and what brought that individual to that point at the end of his or her life.

The narrator describes "the white ones" who are in the village, "with their TV cameras and their aid." Emphasizing the way the villagers are objectified by the white ones, the narrator describes what he believes the white ones see— the narrator starving to death, staring back. He wonders if the white ones are "secretly horrified" that anyone left in the village is unafraid to die. Here, the narrator regards the efforts of those who believe they have come to help as futile. The reporters are bringing the plight of the villagers to the world, yet the villagers are still starving to death. The aid workers have attempted to bring food and supplies, but these have been raided, as the narrator notes earlier. All the white ones can do now is watch the others die, it seems.

The narrator once again portrays the dead he has encountered in the village as not dead. They sing; "they carried on their familiar lives." The only other people in the village who are not dead are the soldiers. The narrator describes the way the soldiers care nothing for the dead but fight over the land. Just as he contrasts the differences between the joyful dead and the gruesome reality of starvation, the narrator depicts the land in terms of contrasts. Once it was "beautiful and civilized." Now it is a "fabulous graveyard."

Continuing his search for his family and his lover, the narrator is spurred on by his need to know if they have died or not. As he journeys through the village, he contemplates what he describes as the "source of the drought and famine—the mighty mountain of lovelessness." In his despair, he thinks of the "grim spirits of negation" descending from the peaks of that mountain, chanting "their awesome soul-shrinking songs." The effect of the songs is to "steal hope" and "make us yield to the air our energies." The songs "make us submit to the clarity of dying." The language and images that Okri uses to describe the narrator's thoughts and emotions are filled with darkness and hopelessness. The absence of love is blamed for the suffering induced by the drought and famine. While drought is outside the realm of human control, the ability of humans to care for those who are starving is not. Yet there has been a failure, the narrator observes, a failure in the human capacity to love and to nurture. From that void, war and death have emerged.

The narrator continues his search and begins to find his family members. First, he finds his brother. Enacting a ritual resembling burial is important to the narrator, who scatters dust on his brother's body. Next he finds his mother. Here he includes another compressed poetic image that conveys volumes about her suffering before she died—she "holds on tightly to a bone so dry it wouldn't even nourish the flies." He again enacts the burial ritual, scattering dust across her corpse. Next, he hears singing coming from the building that was once the school.

As he listens to the singing, the narrator likens the voices raised in song to "the joyous beginning of all creation, the holy yes to the breath and light infusing all things." Okri's language emphasizes the vitality inherent in this singing. His imagery infuses this passage with notions of creation, of birth and growth, of the colorful vibrancy of living. The narrator states, "It was the true end of my quest, the music to crown this treacherous life of mine, the end I couldn't have hoped for, or imagined." Paradoxically, this singing represents both beginnings—new life—and endings, the end of the narrator's quest and his own death. In this paragraph, Okri again posits death—"the end" that the narrator speaks of—as something wondrous. As the dying narrator believes, suffering is for

WHAT DO I READ NEXT?

- Okri's *The Famished Road* is widely considered his masterpiece. Originally published in 1991, the work exhibits elements of postmodernism and magical realism and has been compared to Chinua Achebe's novel *Things Fall Apart*. It is available in a 1993 reprint.

- *A Time for New Dreams* is Okri's 2011 collection of essays. The collection features linked essays in which Okri deals with themes of childhood, beauty, education, economics, and self-censorship, along with the relationship between poetry and life.

- Chinua Achebe is one of the best-known Nigerian writers and has been counted among the most prominent modern African writers. His highly acclaimed novel *Things Fall Apart* was published in 1958, just two years before Nigeria's independence from Great Britain. The work explores the changes British colonialism brought to traditional tribal life. Achebe's incorporation of mythic elements in the novel is sometimes regarded as a precursor to the magical realism that would later characterize works of postcolonial African fiction, such as Okri's *The Famished Road*. The work is available in a 1994 edition.

- Colombian author Gabriel García Márquez published his novel *One Hundred Years of Solitude* in 1967. It is regarded as a seminal work of magical realism. The novel is available in a 2003 edition.

- Caroline Pignat's young-adult novel *Greener Grass*, published in 2009, deals with the issue of famine. Set in Ireland in the nineteenth century, it offers a child's perspective on widespread famine and starvation. The work is notable for its lyrical, poetic language.

- Robert D. Kaplan's *Surrender or Starve: Travels in Ethiopia, Sudan, Somalia, and Eritrea*, published in 1988, is an exploration of the causes of and responses to twentieth-century famine throughout Africa. Kaplan discusses the role of international aid and the impact of civil war on famine-affected areas.

---

the living, but in death, there is the hope of joy and life.

Having come to regard the singing as representing a "joyous beginning," the narrator begins to make his way toward the sound. Yet his weakness slows him. He imagines it takes an eternity to cover the distance:

> After maybe a century, when history had repeated itself and brought about exactly the same circumstances, because none of us ever learned our lesson, or loved enough to learn from our pain, I finally made it to the schoolroom door.

As in the extensive poetic passage about lovelessness and the mountain, Okri again describes the great sin of humanity as a failure to love. No one has loved *enough*. No one has learned the lessons taught by pain. Okri indicts society for its failure to love and care for and heal its members. The notion of futility resurfaces here as well. History repeats itself. The "same circumstances" are repeated over and over. The famine, the suffering, the death—all are viewed as inevitable.

Once inside the school, the narrator describes a room full of the dead. The entire paragraph that follows is one of contrast and paradox. Previously, the narrator had described the dead outside in the village as "singing golden songs in chorus, jubilant everywhere." Now, however, the narrator notes, "all the dead here were differently dead from the corpses outside.

The dead in the school were—forgive the paradox—*alive*." He characterizes the atmosphere as serene. Somehow, the dead in the school achieved a vitality so intense that what the narrator witnessed outside, the jubilant dead, seem like corpses once again by comparison. The narrator attempts to convey why these dead seem so different. He states that "here the air didn't have death in it. The air had prayer in it." This initially seems to be a positive statement. Prayer is associated with holiness, or the striving toward sanctity, a seeking of blessing. Yet in the next sentence the narrator claims, "The prayers stank more than the deaths." The assertion is startling, and seems to imply both futility and decay. The narrator goes on to wonder if somehow the dead had "made the room holy because they had, in their last moments, thought not of themselves but of all people who suffer." He is now doing the same thing, "praying for the whole human race." By the end of this paragraph, the narrator has connected prayer to both hopelessness and holiness. Prayer is associated with the smell of rotting corpses and also with "serenity." The narrator describes as a "paradox" the notion that the dead are alive. This paradox is underscored by the paradoxical portrayal of prayer. Yet pray he does, even though, as he goes on to explicitly state, he imagines that "prayers are possibly an utter waste of time." Still, he prays for every living thing. He begins to sing, joining "the great anguished cry of all mankind." As he sings, he sees that the body next to him is that of his lover. At this moment, a "good-hearted white man" enters the school and records him with his camera. The white man weeps, the narrator observes. It is the only moment of connection with another living human that the narrator experiences in the story.

In his last moments, the narrator senses the dead all around him. They wait. They are peaceful, and they do not hurry him. He considers the way life is filled with "greed and bitterness," though it could be "gentle, too, and wonderful." In the end, however, he realizes, "Human life had betrayed me. And besides, there was nothing left to save in me. Even my soul was dying of starvation." As he dies, he sees the living—the reporters filming the scene—"as the dead, marooned in a world without pity or love." He smiles as he goes, thinking that if the reporters had "understood my language, they would have known that it was my way of saying goodbye." Again, in the last sentence of the story, Okri

emphasizes the paradoxes surrounding human life and death. The narrator wants to say goodbye, seeks to have one last moment of connection with his fellow humans, but they are unable to understand him. He reaches out with love as he slips into death, but the living cannot feel it. Once more, the loveless nature of the world, of human life, is emphasized. Throughout the story, Okri employs language and imagery that contrast the hope of life after death with the suffering endured by the living. Paradoxically, the prayer *from* the living that the narrator, in his last moments of life, conducts *for* the living, is regarded as futile.

Source: Catherine Dominic, Critical Essay on "A Prayer from the Living," in *Short Stories for Students*, Gale, Cengage Learning, 2014.

David C. L. Lim

In the following excerpt, Lim explains Okri's idea of "universal civilization."

ALL THINGS ARE LINKED: OKRI, SENGHOR AND THE UNIVERSAL CIVILIZATION

Okri's African Way is but one of the many Ways flowing in and out of each other like the river of creation which became a road which then branched out to the whole world. In Okri's philosophy, all Ways flow into the great sea of humanity to constitute what he calls the "universal civilization." This notion of "universal civilization" has not received as much scholarly attention as the *abiku* and famished-road motifs, but it is pivotal to, if not the culmination of, Okri's vision in which "All things are linked" (483). It is mentioned perhaps for the first time in his essay "Redreaming the World," where, by way of clearing the ground for the introduction of the term, he reminds contemporary victors not to forget the mathematics of destiny, that "to swallow the history of others into your own history is to expect to be constipated with the history of others." To "strangled nations" and "wounded peoples," he asks them not to "hold themselves down with rage about their historical past or their intolerable present" but instead to find the humility and strength to distil their experience into the highest creativity. It is only when people recognize the logic of the rise and fall of things, Okri writes, that there may be hope "for us all to create the beginnings of the first true universal civilization in the history of recorded and unrecorded time." The idea surfaces next in Okri's essay "Time to Dream the Best

Dream of All," where he urges the United Nations to commit itself steadfastly to its "universal goal": "the realisation of the human potential, the eradication of poverty, the enhancement of liberty, and the triumph of justice." Despite the UN's shortcomings, Okri says, it is today "the only organisation still vaguely capable of articulating the notion of one world, a sort of symphony of humanity." It is not until *Astonishing the Gods* (*ATG*), though, that the notion receives its fullest treatment. From the allegorical novel, we learn that the dream of the Invisibles is to "initiate on earth the first universal civilisation where love and wisdom would be as food and air" (*ATG* 131), a place where

> the most ordinary goal was living the fullest life, in which creativity in all spheres of endeavour was the basic alphabet, and in which the most sublime lessons possible were always learned and relearned from the unforgettable suffering which was the bedrock of their great new civilisation. (*ATG* 28)

After *ATG*, 'universal civilization' is invoked in several other works. In his essay "The Joys of Story-Telling I," for instance, Okri reflects on the postmodern collapse of the great systems (in whose name nations and individuals have wreaked violence upon others), and how it is *celebrated* rather than mourned by strong poets, "albeit with some sadness in their hearts," because they know that the last remaining towers of certainty must collapse before "a true world history and genius" can begin. Only then, he writes, "might the world hope as one and struggle as one, towards the first universal golden age." In *IR* [*Infinite Riches*], the third book of the *abiku* trilogy, the notion surfaces as the "grand picture of humanity" (112–13), a composite of "the great jigsaw that the creator spread all over the diverse peoples of the earth, hinting that no one race or people can have the complete picture or monopoly of the ultimate possibilities of the human genius alone" (112).

Even from these few examples it is clear that the 'universal civilization' is a central constant in Okri's writings. What is perhaps not so evident is how much it recalls, if not has its roots in, Senghor's lesser-known Negritudist conception of the "Civilization of the Universal." For Senghor, the universal civilization is the reconciled totality of the inherently *equal* parts of a divided but interdependent world. It is a pan-human order, to be achieved through a world-historical "dynamic symbiosis" wherein only the fecund

elements of each part are retained and the harmful discarded. Senghor also believes, rightly or wrongly, that Africa stands to benefit from "an infusion of the inquisitive spirit and a higher development of analytical reason," while "Western Europe, now locked in a dehumanizing worship of machines and material wealth, will benefit from the African contribution of its greater emotional and spiritual development, vitality, and understanding of the interconnectedness of all life in the universe." Although there are essentialist moments in Senghor's conception here that would furrow the brows of postcolonial critics, it would serve us well not to throw out the baby (Senghor's attempt to validate Africa's place in the world) with the bathwater (his essentialist view of the inherent differences between the West and Africa). In any case, Okri, despite being influenced by Senghor, does not draw wholesale from him but radicalizes his ideas. For instance, where Senghor envisages the realization of the universal civilization as a distant but actual possibility, Okri sees it more as an impossible ideal to be pursued but never to be fully attained, as attainment would only lead to the cessation of the infinite overcoming of self-limitations. Like the road-builders' Heaven in *ATG*, Okri's universal civilization is a transgressive utopia which, instead of insisting on arrival, celebrates process over product. . . .

Source: David C. L. Lim, "Songs of Enchantment," in *The Infinite Longing for Home: Desire and the Nation in Selected Writings of Ben Okri and K. S. Maniam*, Rodopi, 2005, pp. 97–99.

SOURCES

"Ben Okri," British Literature Council website, http://literature.britishcouncil.org/ben-okri (accessed September 16, 2013).

Bennett, Robert, "Ben Okri," in *Postcolonial African Writers: A Bio-Bibliographical Critical Sourcebook*, edited by Pushpa Naidu Parekh and Siga Fatima Jagne, Routledge, 1998, pp. 364–73.

Blocker, Jane, "A Cemetery of Images: Photography and Witness in the Work of Gilles Peress and Alfredo Jaar," in *Seeing Witness: Visuality and the Ethics of Testimony*, University of Minnesota, 2009, pp. 51–60.

Cooper, Brenda, "Realism and Magical Realism," in *Encyclopedia of African Literature*, edited by Simon Gikandi, Routledge, 2003, pp. 640–43.

Gikandi, Simon, ed., "Postcolonialism," in *Encyclopedia of African Literature*, Routledge, 2003, pp. 175–76.

Gioia, Dana, "Gabriel Garcia Marquez and Magic Realism," in *Sniper Logic*, No. 6, 1998, http://www.danagioia.net/essays/emarquez.htm (accessed September 16, 2013).

Graff, Ann-Barbara, "Ben Okri," in *Dictionary of Literary Biography*, Vol. 231, *British Novelists since 1960, Fourth Series*, edited by Merritt Moseley, The Gale Group, 2000, pp. 200–206.

Hart, Stephen M., "Magical Realism: Style and Substance," in *A Companion to Magical Realism*, edited by Stephen M. Hart and Wen-Chin Ouyang, Tamesis, 2005, pp. 1–12.

Healy, Sally, and Mark Bradbury, "Endless War: A Brief History of the Somali Conflict," in *Accord*, No. 21, 2010, http://www.c-r.org/accord-article/endless-war-brief-history-somali-conflict (accessed September 16, 2013).

Hogg, Annabel Lee, "Timeline: Somalia, 1991–2008," in *Atlantic*, December 2008, http://www.theatlantic.com/magazine/print/2008/12/timeline-somalia-1991-2008/307190/ (accessed September 16, 2013).

Larson, Charles R., ed., "Ben Okri," in *Under African Skies: Modern African Stories*, Noonday Press, 1997, pp. 238–39.

"Nigeria," *CIA: World Factbook*, https://www.cia.gov/library/publications/the-world-factbook/geos/ni.html (accessed September 16, 2013).

"Nigeria: Eight Years On, Memories of '93 Election Still Burn Bright," in *AllAfrica*, June 13, 2001, http://allafrica.com/stories/200106130001.html (accessed September 16, 2013).

Okri, Ben, "A Prayer from the Living," in *Under African Skies: Modern African Stories*, edited by Charles R. Larson, Noonday Press, 1997, pp. 240–43.

"Postmodernism," PBS website, http://www.pbs.org/faithandreason/gengloss/postm-body.html (accessed September 16, 2013).

"Somalia: Overview," Refugees International website, http://refugeesinternational.org/where-we-work/africa/somalia (accessed October 26, 2013).

FURTHER READING

Gaylard, Gerald, *After Colonialism: Africa Postmodernism and Magical Realism*, Witwatersrand University Press, 2006.

Gaylard explores the rise of experimentalism in African fiction in the postcolonial era and the way postmodernist and magical realist works gradually grew out of a social realist tradition.

Harper, Mary Jane, *Getting Somalia Wrong? Faith, War and Hope in a Shattered State*, Zed Books, 2012.

Harper examines the recent history of Somalia and criticizes current perceptions of the failed state as a breeding ground for Islamist extremists. Harper demonstrates that in parts of the country, solid foundations for government and economy are being built, albeit on a small scale.

Okoro, Dike, ed., *Speaking for the Generations: An Anthology of Contemporary African Short Stories*, Africa World Press, 2010.

Okoro has gathered short fiction written by African writers from around the continent. The work offers an overview of various styles, themes, and cultures and presents stories dealing with politics and exile along with childhood, family, love, and death.

Warnes, Christopher, *Magical Realism and the Postcolonial Novel: Between Faith and Irreverence*, Palgrave Macmillan, 2009.

Warnes offers an overview of magical realism and explores it specifically as a postcolonial concept. Warnes analyzes the use of magical realism by authors such as Okri, Salman Rushdie, and Gabriel García Márquez, among others.

SUGGESTED SEARCH TERMS

Okri AND A Prayer from the Living

Okri AND postmodernism

Okri AND postcolonialism

Okri AND magical realism

Somalia famine AND 1990s

postcolonial Nigeria

African fiction AND postmodernism

African fiction AND postcolonialism

African fiction AND magical realism

history of magical realism

African fiction AND spiritualism

African fiction AND myth

Teenage Wasteland

ANNE TYLER

1983

Anne Tyler's "Teenage Wasteland" is a classic work of young-adult literature that deals with the theme of alienation of youth from the society of their parents. The story's central character, Donny, is cut off from his disjointed family and failing in school. He seems to be in danger of failing in life. Tyler subtly introduces the thematic notion that the fault that is apparently Donny's lies rather with his parents and with society as represented by his school and other authority figures. While seeming to take up the call against youth culture so often seen in middle-class society, Tyler rather explores the middle-class anxieties of parents who want to shift blame anywhere but on themselves.

"Teenage Wasteland" was first published in *Seventeen* magazine in November 1983. It can be found in the anthology *Tales of Psychology: Stories to Make You Wise* (2002), edited by Alma Bond.

AUTHOR BIOGRAPHY

Tyler was born in Minneapolis, Minnesota, on October 25, 1941. Her father was a chemist, her mother a social worker. While Tyler was young, the family lived in a series of Quaker communities in the mountains of North Carolina. As a result, Tyler did not attend a public school until she was eleven years old. She was homeschooled

Anne Tyler (© Geraint Lewis / Alamy)

by socially conscious intellectuals who had chosen to abandon mainstream American culture. Her parents were actively involved in political protests against racism and the militarism represented by American participation in the Vietnam War.

In college, Tyler married Iranian-born Taghi Modarressi. While he finished medical school to become a psychiatrist, Tyler worked as a librarian to help support the family. Once he took a job at a hospital in Baltimore, Maryland, Tyler devoted herself to raising their two daughters and to writing. She has produced over a dozen novels, of which *Dinner at the Homesick Restaurant* (1982) and *The Accidental Tourist* (1985) were nominated for the Pulitzer Prize, while *Breathing Lessons* won the Pulitzer in 1989. Her novels, generally set in Baltimore and sharing some minor characters, concern the pressures of family life. Modarressi also became a successful novelist, first in Farsi and then in English. His works deal with the destructive impact of the Iranian Revolution on Iranian

society. Modarressi died in 1997. Tyler's most recently published novel is *The Beginner's Goodbye* (2012), but she has announced the working title of a new novel, *A Spool of Blue Thread*, which she intends to be her last work.

Unlike most contemporary novelists of her prominence, Tyler does not go on book tours or give public readings. She rarely grants interviews, and when she does it is only through correspondence. However, it is evident that the subject matter of her works roughly parallels the life stages of her family at the time of writing, and her short story "Teenage Wasteland" (originally published in *Seventeen* in 1983) was written during her daughters' teenage years. Her writing habits at that time were highly regimented, limited to the hours between her children leaving for school in the morning and their returning home again in the afternoon. Joseph C. Voekler quotes Tyler on her writing process in his *Art and the Accidental in Anne Tyler*:

> I work until the children come home—3:30 or 4 in the afternoon. If things are going well, I feel a little drugged by the events in my story; I'm desperate to know what happens next. When the children ring the doorbell I have trouble sorting my lives out.... I save my afternoons for them, and feel lucky to have such indisputable, ultra real ties to the everyday world; but still in those first few minutes I'm torn in two directions, and I often wonder what it would be like to live all alone in a shack by the sea and work 23 hours a day.

At that time in her life, during the early stages of writing, she left ideas written down on note cards lying all over her house wherever she happened to think of them. She also avoided the distraction of reading until the composition was well developed and then worked methodically until the novel or story was finished.

PLOT SUMMARY

"Teenage Wasteland" opens with an image from the central character's childhood. This teenager, now grown, had as a baby a rather angelic appearance, with white-blond hair and a little cowlick. This image is juxtaposed with the current appearance of the teenager. As he grew up, his hair became darker, and the cute cowlick disappeared as his hair grew longer. In addition, the teenager's hair suggests he is lax in his hygiene, for his hair is somewhat dirty as well as being too long. His face is still endearing to his mother despite the fact that he has also outgrown his round cheeks and has a distinct Adam's apple, a physical indication of puberty in a male.

The teenager begins to do poorly in his private school. The school calls his mother and requests a conference with her. The mother, Daisy, goes alone to the conference because her husband is working. She learns that Donny is not only a poor student but also a disruptive one. Daisy is ashamed because she herself was once a teacher before she had a family of her own. She feels that she has somehow failed because she, the former teacher, is now at a school conference for her own troubled child. She explains to the principal that she is aware her son has problems, so he is not allowed any privileges like television on school days.

Daisy also tells the principal that when she asks her son about homework, Donny claims he finished it all in study hall or does not have any homework to do. At the principal's suggestion, she checks her son's homework assignments daily, sitting by him while he completes his work. Inwardly, she notes how poor his work is; how he seems to take no interest or pride in learning or doing a good job with his assignments.

Because of her motherly efforts to get her son back on track, Daisy is often behind in her own housework and does not give as much attention to her daughter. The sacrifices wear on her, darkening her mood. She often takes her frustration out on her husband, who is surprised and confused by her attitude, so she attempts to check it, realizing that he could not possibly understand how difficult the situation is for her.

A couple of months later, the school calls again, requesting a meeting with both parents. While Donny's grades have improved slightly, his attitude and behavior have not. They have become worse, with Donny skipping classes, smoking in the furnace room, and assisting another classmate with breaking into a locker. He also left campus during a physical education class being held outdoors, and when he returned, it seemed he had been drinking alcohol. Again, Daisy is dismayed, thinking to herself how she and Matt, her husband, must appear to the principal. They must look to him like failures themselves. The principal wants to arrange a meeting

with a psychologist, confident that the psychologist will be able to end the boy's problems.

Donny at first resists the psychologist. After a short time, however, he begins to improve his hygiene and takes a little better care of himself. At a meeting between Donny, his parents, and the psychologist, the psychologist assures Daisy and Matt that Donny has no serious mental problems but is simply going through a difficult period in his life. Donny needs help academically and also with improving his self-esteem. Therefore, the psychologist suggests Donny would benefit from some academic tutoring and counseling with a therapist and tutor named Calvin Beadle. Donny, of course, does not want to go.

Daisy questions her own parenting in terms of Donny's sense of self-worth. She knows she praised him as a child, maybe even went too far, and also knows that when Donny's sister was born, it was a difficult transition for Donny. Daisy is bewildered and doubts her own parenting skills. She cannot see that she did anything so wrong that Donny would now be in this position, but she feels she must have done something terribly wrong because he is failing in school and acting inappropriately. She submits to the psychologist and sends her son to see Calvin Beadle.

Cal bears a strong resemblance to Donny. He is very casual and presents a sympathetic persona. When he questions Donny about school and his actions, Donny replies truthfully that he does not apply himself academically and that he breaks school rules of conduct. Cal sympathizes with him and suggests they meet three times a week, with the caveat that Donny can quit anytime he likes if he feels the sessions are not helpful. This pleases Donny because instead of having to follow the rules, he gets to make them.

As they leave Cal's office, which is also his home, Daisy notes that the place seems more like a teenage hangout than an office, a place to play ping-pong and listen to rock music. Clearly, Cal is trying to build rapport with the troubled teenagers in his care. Daisy is not sure how she feels about this, so she submits to her son's apparent positive response to Cal.

Donny begins his tutoring sessions with Cal three nights a week, upsetting the family dinner routine. It turns out that Cal's services are also very expensive, but Daisy decides it is worth it to see the changes she is seeing in her son. While the principal of Donny's school reports that Donny's grades have not yet improved, his attitude certainly has, and the principal confirms to Daisy that this is the right course for her son. At home, however, Donny is still sullen and rebellious and resists whenever his parents try to enforce rules. When Cal intervenes on Donny's behalf in this matter, suggesting that his parents be more lenient with him, Daisy halfheartedly resists but ultimately cedes all parental authority and lets her son make his own rules. She is convinced that he will not then have to suffer through an unhappy adolescence like she had. Cal has also given Daisy and Matt rules: not to intervene and to direct all questions from the school and from Donny's teachers to him.

However, one teacher, Miss Evans, disobeys this rule and calls Daisy directly. She informs Daisy that she had seen improvement in Donny's academic performance when Daisy supervised his work, but now Donny's grades have slipped again; he is failing the class. The teacher suggests that Daisy reassert her parental decision-making power over her child instead of handing it over to a tutor. Daisy examines the sacrifices she has made for her son's well-being and becomes angry. She calls Cal and tells him she wants to work with her son again as far as his studies go. Cal assures her that her son's success is not bound up in academics alone, and again, Daisy defers to him and decides that Miss Evans must be narrow-minded.

Cal continues to see Donny and forms a relationship with him that is more like a friendship; Cal lends Donny an album by The Who, and they go to a concert together. Cal allows Donny's new girlfriend to come to Donny's tutoring sessions as well, and Daisy tells herself it is because Cal cares so much about her son. However, Daisy is hurt that Donny refuses to let his girlfriend, Miriam, come over to his house and have dinner with his parents.

It is through Miriam that Daisy learns Cal was once married but got a divorce because his ex-wife was too controlling. As Daisy and Matt drive up to Cal's to pick up their son, they can see Donny outside playing basketball. Daisy can hear music coming out of the house, and she names the song: "Teenage Wasteland," by The Who. Her husband confirms the identification; the scene before them is indeed a teenage

wasteland. Daisy realizes her husband thinks she is commenting on the scene at Cal's rather than identifying the song title. Daisy mourns that her son, despite all the sessions at Cal's, still seems so lost and directionless. She knows that many of Cal's students have not had positive outcomes—one was physically attacked and stabbed in a bar, and one was sent to boarding school. Other students have been withdrawn from Cal's services. Still, others have been with him for years, so Daisy does not argue the point with her son.

A call from school announces Donny's expulsion for having alcohol and tobacco in his locker. The school informs Daisy that Donny has packed his belongings and is walking home on foot. When he does not show up at home, Daisy becomes worried and finally calls Cal, and Donny is indeed at Cal's house. When Daisy arrives to pick Donny up, Cal encourages Daisy to listen to her son's version of what happened at school; Donny claims he was set up, and Cal indignantly suggests that Donny's civil rights were violated when his locker was searched without a warrant. Daisy knows from the expression on her son's face—the same one he wore when he lied as a small child—that he is lying about what happened at school.

Daisy's biggest concern is to get her son back into school, so she enrolls him in a public school and stops his tutoring sessions with Cal. Donny fights this bitterly, but Cal does not. Cal agrees with Daisy that he did not make much progress with her son and suggests that Donny is emotionally disturbed.

Donny goes to school, but he seems defeated and forlorn. He makes no friends at his new school and joins no clubs. One day, he runs away. The police are called, and they search for Donny but cannot locate him. The police tell his parents that if Donny does not want to be found, he will not be.

Three months later, Donny is still missing. His parents wait in vain for a phone call, as no phone call comes. Their daughter now stays away from home as much as possible. Daisy cannot sleep at night. She lies awake going over her son's life in her mind, trying to determine who is at fault: she and her husband, Cal, or both. In the end, she cannot answer the question of what went wrong but knows on some deep level that her son is lost to her.

CHARACTERS

Calvin Beadle

Cal is in many ways the antagonist, or villain, of "Teenage Wasteland." When Donny starts to fail at school, he is sent for a psychological evaluation and then referred to Cal, who supposedly specializes in helping troubled youth. Cal evokes middle-class anxieties over the 1960s youth counterculture. The environment he creates for his students is entirely unstructured, allowing them to do whatever they please without a word of criticism or advice; he prevails upon Donny's parents to treat him in the same way. This has the predictable result of causing Donny to do even more poorly at school.

Despite his distaste for authority and structure, from Daisy's perspective all Cal does is set rules for her to follow. She is not supposed to question Donny about his schoolwork and cannot even talk with his teachers: she must let Cal act as mediator. Miss Evans, one of Donny's teachers, informs Daisy that, besides her son's continuing academic decline, he uses Cal's name as a talisman, as if it has some magical power to make him succeed without effort, a fantasy. When Donny is finally expelled from his private school, Cal's suggestion to Daisy and Matt is to send Donny to another private school that is presumably just as unstructured as the environment he himself has created for his young clients.

Cal enables Donny in denying all responsibility for his own actions. When Donny is expelled for hiding beer in his locker, Cal insists that the school is at fault since they had no right to search Donny's locker. Daisy, as a former teacher, knows very well that the school has every right to conduct such a search. Donny's excuse is that he was framed by another boy. He is unable to offer any evidence or argument that could support this plea, however, such as the name of the boy who supposedly held a grudge against him and put the beer in his locker or how he could have gotten Donny's combination. When Daisy tries to question her son on these points, Cal insists that Donny must be trusted absolutely, even when he is obviously lying, and enlarges the conspiracy theory, suggesting that the school itself framed Donny.

Amanda Coble

Amanda is Donny's younger sister. Her character as well as her role within the family is very little developed. The only information Tyler gives is that Daisy would rather spend time with Amanda than help Donny with his schoolwork and indeed seems to have favored Amanda since the time she was born, a fact that is not lost on Donny. Amanda's name, Latin for *she who must be loved*, no doubt relates to this.

Daisy Coble

Daisy is Donny's mother. Her relation to her son is largely based on fantasy. She first saw him as the fair-haired boy, the angelic answer to her family's problems, but this idea, as well as her interest in her son, was abandoned with the birth of her daughter. By the time she again turns her attention to Donny, he is a stranger to her. She responds with a new fantasy, this one fraught with her own anxieties and insecurities.

Trying to piece together her broken relationship with her son, Daisy frets over pop-culture advice on child rearing and concentrates her mental effort on chastising herself for having praised him too much or not enough, for being too strict a disciplinarian, or for being too lax. Her new fantasy revolves around a second chance. If she only had her life to live over again, she would do everything perfectly. Even in her imagination, however, she cannot articulate what she would change. She indulges in these pointless musings to distract herself from the possibility of doing something now that might help her son, instead contenting herself with doing what she is told to do by those she considers authorities: Donny's principal, his psychologist, his tutor, and his teacher. Daisy is mystified by her son's failure but never makes any effective effort to find out what is actually going on.

Though Daisy was once a teacher herself, her own character seems adolescent. Aside from her failure to master the situation with Donny, when she is confronted with authority, even the very minor authority of a private-school principal whom she is paying for a service, she reacts like a teenager, ashamed of her own appearance and bracing herself for disapproval. She actually becomes jealous of Calvin Beadle when Donny seems to prefer his company to hers. Her chief concerns over Donny seem to be how his failure will reflect on and impact her; she worries that others will think that she is a bad mother. The work that she must do to help Donny is a burden to her that fills her with fatigue and hostility. Her question about Donny's running away is what *she* could have done to prevent it. The final image of the story, Donny lost in a yard of dry bones, suggests that the real wasteland is inside her.

Donny Coble

Donny's character is an enigma since it is presented to the reader almost entirely through the eyes of his mother, Daisy, who has no real insight into her son. To the reader, he remains as much a phantom as he is to his mother. When Donny was born, his mother seemingly entertained a fantasy of him as a fair-haired boy, someone from whom great things could be expected in the future, but she let him drift away, probably paying as little attention to him as necessary for his basic care as he matured from an infant to a child; now that he is a young man, she does not know him at all.

Unable to find any direction at home, Donny transfers the disrespect his parents have earned to his teachers; his obscene insult against the psychiatrist who evaluates him reveals the attitude that he must have learned to hold toward his parents and which he projects to other authority figures. He thus falls in with other directionless young men, neglecting the effort that is required from him at school but whose purpose he cannot understand and indulging in the slight carnal pleasures of drinking and smoking. Donny responds to the freedom given him by his tutor, Calvin Beadle, but seems to ultimately see that that is just as pointless as the discipline others wish (but are unable) to impose on him. He leaves because there is nothing real offered to him from any quarter.

Matt Coble

Matt is Donny's father. He is a rather rumpled insurance salesman. He seems to be alienated from his family and especially from his son. He has little connection to either his son or wife and, because they are the main characters of the story, plays only a marginal role. Matt seems too exhausted at the end of each day to take much notice of his family. He does observe, however, from the thuggish appearance of the students who populate Calvin Beadle's home office, that it seems to be a teenage wasteland, characteristically misunderstanding his wife's reference to a song title.

Miss Evans

Miss Evans is one of Donny's teachers. During the period of Donny's tutoring with Calvin Beadle, when teachers are supposed to communicate with him instead of Donny's parents, she nevertheless calls Daisy to tell her that Donny is now failing her class. Miss Evans suggests that Daisy take over supervising Donny's homework herself again, since when she did that before the boy was at least passing.

Principal Lanham

Lanham is the principal of the private school that Donny attends. His solution to Donny's problems is to send him to the psychologist and then support the specialist tutor, which does no more to help Donny than the ineffectual efforts of his parents. As a person of authority, Principal Lanham intimidates Daisy, a measure of her own ineffectualness.

Miriam

Miriam becomes Donny's girlfriend. The story reveals little about her, except that Daisy has a low opinion of her. To Daisy, Miriam is "an unappealing girl with blurry lipstick and masses of rough red hair. She wore a short bulky jacket that would not have been out of place on a motorcycle." The name *Miriam* itself is the Hebrew version of Mary, the mother of Jesus, which suggests that Donny may be looking to her as a mother figure.

The Psychologist

The psychologist to whom Donny is referred by the school is never named. He seems to be incompetent. He does not make any attempt to gain a personal understanding of Donny but approaches him through a series of standardized tests. This procedure is unable to identify Donny's very real problems. The psychologist also refers Donny to Calvin Beadle for tutoring and is evidently unable to see Cal's own profound incompetence.

THEMES

Family

The Cobles are meant to be a typical American suburban family. That there is something deeply wrong with the family is suggested by their unusual family name: the family is something

TOPICS FOR FURTHER STUDY

- The character of Donny represents the white and the male as the typical case, privileging white and male status in society. In contrast, *Colonize This! Young Women of Color on Today's Feminism* (2002) presents a collection of essays by young women belonging to a broad spectrum of races, ethnicities, and nationalities about their difficulties in modern society, making an appeal to a reform of feminism as a possible solution. Write your own story that deals with the same issues of alienation as "Teenage Wasteland" but without privileging maleness and whiteness.

- Originally written in Farsi, Tyler's late husband Taghi Modarressi's *The Virgin of Solitude* (translated in 2008) deals with the alienation of an Iranian teenager, Nuri, from his culture, which is being torn down around him by the Iranian Revolution in 1979. Read Modarressi's novel, and write a paper comparing Nuri with Donny from "Teenage Wasteland."

- Tyler grew up in isolated Quaker communities in North Carolina. Write a paper comparing the social world of teenagers in such communities with the suburban world inhabited by Donny in "Teenage Wasteland."

- The phrase "teenage wasteland" has become widespread in popular culture, thanks to the popularity of the song by The Who. Search the Internet for uses of the phrase in book and article titles, on blogs, and in videos. Report back to your class with a summary of your findings and their significance using a PowerPoint presentation.

---

cobbled together, an assemblage hurriedly thrown together that barely serves its purpose. The mother, Daisy, worked as a fourth-grade teacher but quit her job to raise their children, Donny and his sister, Amanda. The father, Matt, is an insurance salesman. Their character

as a family is established in the story through the parents' encounters with Mr. Lanham, the principal of Donny's school. When Daisy, first alone and then with her husband, goes to the school for conferences, she does not think of herself as equal to Lanham; instead Daisy imagines that they seem like naughty school children themselves, being called in before the school authorities. She admits to herself that they have failed as parents.

Matt is too tired and befuddled when he comes home from work to deal with any family problems. Daisy finds it burdensome, if not exhausting, to merely supervise her son's homework, let alone deal with the whole burden of going to school, with its social and academic pressures, that her son must endure. She is jealous of time spent helping her son that she would prefer to spend with her daughter. She is unable to bring any imaginative effort to helping her son; the father is far too withdrawn to even contemplate such a thing. They are summoned to observe as bystanders each step in Donny's academic failure. Daisy is reduced to doubting everything she has done in the past. It does not occur to her to try and find solutions to their present difficulties or envision a future. Her emotional paralysis is relieved by hostility directed toward her husband.

In short, they are a family only in name. They function as individuals (and that not well) with little real connection to each other. How Donny evaluates and reacts to this situation can only be guessed at, because the story, essentially told from Daisy's perspective, is never able to offer any insight into Donny's character. The most that can be said is that he eventually realizes that it is in his interest to leave, which reflects his recognition that he has no family at all in any meaningful sense.

Youth

As early as the 1930s, one can see alarmist popular fears about youth expressed in films like the Dead End Kids series or *Reefer Madness*: the youth are seen as failing to move on with the upward mobility of the middle class pioneered by their parents and are being destroyed by their alienation from society and dissipated through petty crime, drug use, gangs, and a general lack of respect for authority. The stereotype was as much alive in the 1950s or 1970s and is actually presented in a quite mild form in Tyler's

Fifteen-year-old Donny is starting to rebel against his parents. (© *PHOTOCREO Michal Bednarek | Shutterstock.com*)

"Teenage Wasteland." The purpose of Tyler's story is to explore the possibility that the causes of such alienation lie outside of the young people themselves.

The 1960s were a watershed period in US history. The youth counterculture, popularly known as the hippie movement, was presented in mass media as a pack of young degenerates that virtually heralded the end of civilization. Dropping out of society was presented as a generational betrayal, but to the youth themselves, it was an impulse to change society, which they viewed as having failed them. By the 1980s, it was possible to present Calvin Beadle as a representative of the youth counterculture. He gives his students license to indulge in undisciplined rejection of society. He offers no alternative, and his program is really nothing more than time wasting: a waste of youth's potential. This is a parallel of what society imagined the hippie movement had been, since it offers no serious challenge to the status quo.

One may doubt, however, that Tyler herself subscribes to this oversimplified distortion. The message of "Teenage Wasteland" may be that by the 1980s the counterculture was as bankrupt as the society it rebelled against and that some new way had to be found, but her true motives in writing remain as enigmatic as Donny's own unexplored motivations.

STYLE

Characterization

In "Teenage Wasteland," Tyler is exceptionally successful at conveying character through subtle, seemingly incidental physical descriptions. For instance, the story beings with a description of Donny:

> He used to have very blond hair—almost white—cut shorter than other children's so that on his crown a little cowlick always stood up to catch the light. But this was when he was small. As he grew older, his hair grew darker.

Without ever using the hackneyed phrase "fair-haired boy," which denotes a favored child, full of promise, Tyler evokes it and with it the natural tendency of a new family to impose impossibly high hopes on their firstborn. Moreover, this image also suggests both the crown of a prince and the halo of an angel. The darkening of Donny's hair, irrelevant in and of itself, signals to the reader Donny's fall from grace within the family romance, in other words his alienation and marginalization. Tyler sets up the entire conflict of the story entirely through suggestive description.

When Donny's mother, Daisy, is introduced, she imagines how she and her husband seem to other people: like "the kind of people who are always hurrying to catch up, missing the point of things that everyone else grasps at once." In this instance, the self-perception is immediately followed by a physical description: "She wished she'd worn nylons instead of knee socks." The physical description serves to concretize the more abstract character description, providing an outward sign that can be read to determine character.

Literary and Cultural Allusion

Written for a young-adult audience and seemingly straightforward in its portrayal of modern American teenagers, "Teenage Wasteland" does not at first glance seem to provide much in the way of references to great works of literature. This is deceptive, however: Tyler shows great subtlety in her interaction with literature and history. The word *wasteland* itself is a richly evocative literary term whose associations add depth to the story, but another striking example is the name of the story's antagonist, Calvin Beadle. The name may at first just seem a little strange, but this strangeness is a signal to pay careful attention to it.

A *beadle* is an official in the Church of England usually responsible for the business aspects of a parish. If a casual American reader has any familiarity with the term at all, it may very well be because of the beadle in Dickens's novel *Oliver Twist*, who is in charge of the workhouse orphanage where Oliver grows up. As a representative of institutional oppression, this beadle is extraordinarily cruel, famously keeping his charges on a starvation diet and abusing them in other ways. It is precisely because the state has no place for Oliver except one in which he is harshly downtrodden that he runs away from the authorities that have charge over him and seeks freedom, or a better life, or at least immediate relief, in the criminal underground.

Calvin is the name of an important Protestant theologian of the Reformation in the sixteenth century. He became dictator of the city of Geneva and established an authoritarian regime with harsh punishments for natural and inevitable human inclinations—for example, any outward display of secular celebration such as dancing or singing, or for working on the Sabbath, even if remaining idle one day out of every seven put a poor citizen of Geneva at risk of hunger.

Calvin Beadle's name, then, seems to recall the oppressive structures of society that he, as a representative of the 1960s counterculture, is meant to be rebelling against. On further reflection, however, the terms that make up Calvin Beadle's name symbolize the character's own oppressive role. His rebellion has been co-opted into the social structure (he is after all recommended by Donny's school) and amounts to nothing more than a destructive lethargy that is just as poisonous to Donny's development as a free and educated person as is the regimentation of the school itself. The crisis of the story is Donny's realizing that Cal does not represent another option and that he really has no options except to flee the situation that he is in.

HISTORICAL CONTEXT

Education

Education ought to be an overwhelming experience of personal discovery and learning about the world that leaves the student bewildered but also filled with the joy of grasping new ideas and finding new insights. Ideally, the feelings will be so intense that the student can hardly imagine that he is not the first to feel them, leaving him at a loss to express the excitement and confusion inside him and wondering, as the Noble Prize–winning German novelist Thomas Mann asks in his Princeton lectures, "How can you others understand?" Although many American students have this experience, it is generally not because of the education that they are given, but in spite of it.

Historical circumstances created quite a different education for Donny in "Teenage Wasteland." The infamous report of the Trilateral Commission (founded to enable cooperation

COMPARE & CONTRAST

- **1980s:** Secondary education is generally geared toward preparing students for life in regimented workplaces and for lives as consumers.

  Today: The principle goals of education have not changed much for over a century but are now subordinated to performance on high-stakes standardized tests under federal programs like No Child Left Behind.

- **1980s:** Although the concept of young-adult literature is about a century old (going back to Victorian works such as adaptations of Homer and other classical literature and purposefully written young-adult novels, such as those of G. A. Henty and Robert Louis Stevenson), Tyler is unusual among established literary authors for publishing a young-adult work like "Teenage Wasteland" in *Seventeen* magazine.

  Today: Young-adult literature is a large section of the publishing industry, and many writers cross over between young-adult works and standard literature.

- **1980s:** Donny sees smoking as a rite of passage: because only adults are allowed to smoke, if he smokes, it may magically transform him into the adult he longs to be.

  Today: With the extreme health risks associated with smoking becoming more and more exposed, smoking is vanishing from adult culture and is no longer viewed favorably by teenagers either.

---

between North America, Europe, and Japan), titled *The Crisis of Democracy*, suggested that the rebellious youth culture of the 1960s was a threat to government—that was the crisis—and that it had come about because the schools and other institutions had failed in their "role in the indoctrination of the young," leaving them free to rebel against authority. Noam Chomsky, writing on what he terms in a book title *MisEducation*, explains how the commission's idea has been the basis of American education, starting in the nineteenth century as public education became shaped to the needs of the industrial economy:

> The indoctrination is necessary because schools are, by and large, designed to support the interests of the dominant segments of society, those people who have wealth and power. Early on in your education you are socialized to understand the need to support the power structure, primarily corporations—the business class.

Education for the creation of industrial workers was the fundamental basis of the late nineteenth-century educational reforms that created large urban school districts and established the model of education that is still followed in most American schools. Jesse Hagopian, writing in the *International Socialist Review*, notes that the new schools had as

> their main goals ... to control children during the day while both parents worked, provide basic education to the next generation of workers, and acculturate them to the rigid schedules of factory life governed by the ubiquitous whistles and bells.

This is not far above creating what Adam Smith in *The Wealth of Nations* suggested was the kind of worker favored by industrialists, a worker "as stupid and ignorant as it is possible for a human creature to become." Donny's school experience in "Teenage Wasteland" sounds much the same; he says, "It's like a prison there, you know?"

If the goal of education were to make students capable of independent and critical thought, it would not proceed through rote memorization of facts to be regurgitated on standardized tests but would allow students to

Daisy, a former teacher, is especially worried about her son's performance at school.

(© Terence Mendoza | Shutterstock.com)

discover the truth through their own searches. The teacher can do no more than create an environment for that kind of discovery. This is the kind of experiential education that the philosopher John Dewey advocated (and is probably more similar to the education that Anne Tyler herself received from her homeschooling parents) but which is rarely implemented fully in modern American schools. For Dewey, writing in "The Economic Basis of the New Society," the goal of education is "the production of free human beings associating with one another on terms of equality." Instead American education serves to create a mass of people easy to be controlled. People are directed away from social and political realities and the issues that actually matter to them and toward a consumer society.

Donny does not appear to have found the joy of learning. He too would ask, "How can you others understand?" By this, he would mean that no one can understand the emptiness and desolation he feels inside because his growing consciousness is being starved. While Calvin Beadle

thinks that he is leading his charges in rebellion, he is perfectly serving the most authoritarian interests of the state and the economic forces that control it. His students become an apathetic herd with little ambition beyond consuming the commercial products that are passed off to them as their own youth culture, symbolized by Tyler in the popular music that seems to be the only form of instruction that Cal gives Donny and his other students. That emptiness is the teenage wasteland. Donny leaves because he realizes that his school, his parents, and the so-called alternative offered by Cal will do nothing to turn the wasteland into a productive paradise.

CRITICAL OVERVIEW

Tyler's critical reputation depends mostly on her novels at the expense of her short stories. Tyler encourages this by refusing to have a collection of her short stories published. As a consequence, even the text of a story like

"Teenage Wasteland," originally published in a popular magazine, is hard to access. Although the story is frequently reprinted in literature anthologies intended for classroom use in high schools, such collections are sources unlikely to be referenced by literature professors.

Tyler is principally known as a novelist. Although the uniqueness of her background leaves her largely estranged from the mainstream of American culture, her time spent as a child in North Carolina and her education at Duke University in the same state lead critics like Joseph Allen Byrant, in his *Twentieth Century Southern Literature*, to consider Tyler a southern writer. Susan S. Kissel, in her *Moving On*, finds a prominent southern theme in Tyler's work, namely, the virtual removal of the father figure in her novels, whether through their withdrawn remoteness from the family or their ineffectiveness. In Kissel's view, this is Tyler's comment on the collapse of the white patriarchal culture in the South in the late twentieth century. This analysis certainly has bearing on "Teenage Wasteland," where the father is both withdrawn from his family and completely ineffective in remedying its difficulties.

Tyler, who is famously reclusive and only rarely grants interviews, considers her short stories in some sense inferior to her novels and so discourages their recirculation. In the Twayne volume on Tyler, Elizabeth Evans reports that "a notation by Tyler in her papers in the Perkins Library of Duke University declares that most [of her short stories] are not to be republished or anthologized. . . . Tyler clearly prefers the novel form and has said that when she gets a good idea she reserves it for a novel." This attitude naturally has the effect of discouraging criticism on "Teenage Wasteland."

Consequently there is only a single extended treatment of the story in print, in Robert W. Croft's encyclopedic overview *An Anne Tyler Companion*. Croft suggests that the story is really about Donny's parents:

> "Teenage Wasteland" tackles the thorny problem of raising teenagers. With great sensitivity to the parents, Tyler describes Matt and Daisy Coble's efforts to help their son Donny through this difficult stage of his life. Hindered by a lack of communication with their son, Matt and Daisy ultimately have to face failure when Donny runs away.

Croft observes that a child running away is a common theme in Tyler's work. Her focus is on the effect of this action on the parents:

> Donny leaves his parents, especially his mother, broken and racked with guilt, wondering how they could have broken through the barriers he put up and helped him. Donny's exact motivation for leaving is left unclear, and the reader, like Daisy, never figures out exactly what his problem is. In the final analysis, that is appropriate because Tyler's focus remains on the effect of Donny's running away on his parents.

CRITICISM

Rita M. Brown

Brown is an English professor. In the following essay, she traces Tyler's "Teenage Wasteland" through T. S. Eliot's The Waste Land *back to Chrétien de Troyes's* Perceval, *the ultimate source of the wasteland of the story's title.*

The source of the title of Anne Tyler's short story "Teenage Wasteland" seems at first quite straightforward. When Donny's parents, Daisy and Matt, go to consult with his tutor, Calvin Beadle, they find their son not studying but in the tutor's driveway playing basketball with other boys of questionable appearance. The boys are listening to a stereo, which is playing a song that sparks Daisy's memory: "Daisy recognized [it] from the time that Donny had borrowed the album. '*Teenage Wasteland*,' she said." Her husband however, misunderstands her and thinks she is making a general comment on the scene before their eyes:

> The players looked like hoodlums, even her son. Why, one of Cal's students had recently been knifed in a tavern. One had been shipped off to boarding school in midterm; two had been withdrawn by their parents.

At first impression, the term *teenage wasteland* seems to refer here to the general pointlessness of the lives being led by Donny and his friends, an idea that can be linked to the general criticism of American youth culture that has been current since the 1960s. Young people, unlike the generation that struggled against the Depression and overcame fascism in World War II, are said to be wasting their potential on television, or drugs, or video games, or whatever concerns a particular social critic at the moment.

DONNY HAS LIVED HIS WHOLE LIFE WITHOUT HAVING HEARD A BACH CELLO SUITE OR HAVING SEEN A PAINTING BY JACQUES-LOUIS DAVID, OR IF HE HAS, THEY WERE EXPERIENCES THAT HAD NO MEANING FOR HIM—JUST BROKEN IMAGES THAT HE COULD NOT CONNECT WITH."

The song reinforces this impression. Written by Peter Townsend and performed with his band, The Who, in the early 1970s, the song is not properly called by its frequent refrain "teenage wasteland." Although the song is frequently mistakenly referred to by this phrase, the true title is "Baba O'Riley." This alludes to Meher Baba, The Who's guru. Baba came from the Parsi community in India and created his own New Age–style religion in which he conceived of reality as an illusory product of the imagination; he also claimed to be an incarnation of God on earth. The song is meant as a tribute to him; it contains an instrumental passage based on Indian classical music. The song is also a tribute to the minimalist composer Terry Riley, who was influenced by Indian classical music. The lyrics of the song refer to Townsend's experience at the Woodstock concert in 1969. He was appalled that the entire audience was intoxicated, or "wasted" in the slang of the day, on LSD or other drugs and thought the phrase "teenage wasteland" apt to describe them.

The word *wasteland* has literary associations of which Townsend may have been unaware but which the reader may credit Tyler with taking into account. One of the most seminal and important works of twentieth-century literature is T. S. Eliot's *The Waste Land*. Eliot wrote this lengthy poem in 1922, in the immediate aftermath of World War I. Therein he describes the wreckage of Western civilization left behind by the war. The damage was not only physical. Unlike in the American Civil War or later World War II, the massive loss of life in World War I was concentrated in small areas of what had been countryside: the trench lines running from Switzerland to the English Channel. Cities and their civilian populations had been spared the direct effects of the fighting. What had been destroyed was an entire generation of young men, with millions of soldiers from France, Great Britain, Italy, the United States (to a lesser degree), and Germany killed, millions more maimed, and even more psychologically scarred by the experience of the fighting. The war laid waste to Western civilization itself, which had in effect caused the war.

By the war's end, the faith that people had had in institutions like the church and the state, even in art and literature, and especially in the idea of progress and faith in the future, had been destroyed. If physical objects of culture such as the statues and architecture of the Roman Empire were to be seen lying in broken heaps in the modern city of Rome, World War I had left culture itself lying in broken bits. Everything that had seemed to go together to make civilization whole had lost its meaning because it seemed to belong to a world that was dead, that had killed itself. It is not that people could no longer listen to the Bach cello suites or look at a painting by Jacques-Louis David, but they could not do so with the same meaning, the same sense that all the little pieces connected to a whole that was ultimately good and purposeful. The devastation of the war seemed to be the tragic and meaningless end that civilization had been building towards. The future of civilization seemed to be the world continuing to tear itself apart with political ideologies like fascism and Stalinism, philosophical ideas like deconstruction (the idea that communication between artist and audience is impossible), and so-called modern art, which privileged what the old civilization would have considered ugly and bizarre. If one could still look at a painting by Jacques-Louis David, one could not do so with the same sense of connection people had felt in 1913.

This is much the same wasteland that Daisy and Matt see Donny and his friends inhabiting, the institution of education having failed like every other part of civilization. It is not that Donny is not receiving an education, but he inevitably rejects it because he can tell it has no meaning. It is not doing anything to integrate him into Western civilization. The youth counterculture of the 1960s realized that what they were told was civilization was no longer culture, but a consumer culture that at best imitated traditional culture, and so rebelled against it.

WHAT DO I READ NEXT?

- *The Accidental Tourist* (1985) is Tyler's best-known novel and has been adapted into a film (1988) by Lawrence Kasdan. The book was nominated for the Pulitzer Prize. Like most of Tyler's work, it is set in her adopted home city of Baltimore. The plot concerns a marriage that disintegrates after the murder of the couple's adult son.

- *Santa Claus in Baghdad* (2008), edited by Elsa Marston, is a collection of short stories about the difficulties of the teenage years in a broad spectrum of Arab cultures.

- *The Outsiders* (1967), by S. E. Hinton, is a classic young-adult exploration of teenage alienation.

- Taghi Modarressi was Tyler's Iranian-born husband who died in 1997. A psychiatrist, he also wrote several novels in Farsi and later in English. His *The Book of Absent People* (1986) is a surrealist account of an aristocratic Iranian family's survival during the Iranian Revolution.

- Donna Gaines's *Teenage Wasteland: Suburbia's Dead End Kids* (1991) presents a nearly anthropological study of a group of alienated teens in suburban New Jersey, focusing on their obsession with death and their own perception of the meaninglessness of their existence. She suggests that news coverage of such youth is often misleading and sensationalist and that many school-based programs meant to help simply fail to address the true nature of the problem.

- *Breathing Lessons* (1998) is Tyler's Pulitzer Prize–winning novel. It examines the struggles of a middle-class American family, particularly as the mother tries to reconcile her son and daughter-in-law, whose marriage is teetering on the edge of divorce. It has been adapted as a television movie.

Television, which is essentially a collection of commercial products (television shows plus ads), replaced education as the main force of acculturation. The message of shows like *Leave It to Beaver* privileged conformity over creativity and integration with a meaningful culture. Even the music that plays on the radio is a set of commercial products that are pushed aside every few weeks or months as new products are marketed.

The idea of patriotism that reemerged in America in the 1950s supposedly to strengthen the West against the threat posed by Communism merely covered over the injustices of class and race inequality and the growing transformation of the nation into a national security state that even President Eisenhower warned of. Everything seemed to be tending toward a third and finally destructive world war. The hippies rejected this but no longer had an authentic culture to turn to. Donny has lived his whole life without having heard a Bach cello suite or having seen a painting by Jacques-Louis David, or if he has, they were experiences that had no meaning for him—just broken images that he could not connect with. Donny and his parents are left as bewildered individuals who cannot connect to each other even as a family.

Eliot drew the very idea of the wasteland as a metaphor for the collapse of Western civilization from another broken image of the past. The word comes from the medieval poet Chrétien de Troyes's epic *Perceval*. Perceval is one of King Arthur's knights. During his travels, he is going through a green and beautiful land of farmers' fields and suddenly comes across a tract where the green shoots of corn have been cut down, as have the trees in the forest and along the embankments between the plots of land, where all the peasants have fled. The land has been laid waste by an army besieging a nearby castle. Later, Perceval meets the Fisher King, who has suffered a wound that is magically prevented from healing. He sees a vision of religious icons, including a grail or cup—the Holy Grail—which, he learns, has the power to heal the king. Perceval sets out on a quest to find the Grail.

According to the scholar Jessie Weston, in her *From Ritual to Romance*, the meaning of the Grail quest is that if the king were healed, the wasteland too would be made whole again. While no modern critic would read the poem in this way, Eliot seized on this idea, making the central theme of his poem the unrealizable hope that some way of healing the wasteland of all of Western civilization could be found. Eliot explained these intentions in notes that his publisher had him add to the poem to pad its length sufficiently to issue the work as a short monograph (to turn it into a viable commercial product). He later dismissed the whole idea of his work being based on Weston's as a joke.

Tyler, however, is free to read Eliot in light of Weston, joke or not. In any case, this perspective permits a reading of "Teenage Wasteland" that frees the reader from its evident nihilism. Perceval was the son of a knight, but when he was a very small child, his mother took him far away from knightly civilization and made sure he did not even know what armor and swords were, because his father and older brothers had all been killed in the course of their knightly service in warfare, and she did not wish to see her only remaining son die the same way. One day, two knights ride by their distant manor, and as soon as he sees them, Perceval knows he will settle for no other way of life and runs to tell his mother that he plans to leave immediately to fulfill his destiny to become a knight. As poor as his chances are, Donny, too, leaves because he realizes that he has to go somewhere else to find meaning.

Source: Rita M. Brown, Critical Essay on "Teenage Wasteland," in *Short Stories for Students*, Gale, Cengage Learning, 2014.

Elizabeth Evans

In the following excerpt, Evans discusses some of the main themes in Tyler's short stories.

Anne Tyler's stories—some 50 of which are in print—have never been collected; indeed, a notation by Tyler in her papers in the Perkins Library of Duke University declares that most are not to be republished or anthologized. Although Tyler clearly prefers the novel form and has said that when she gets a good idea she reserves it for a novel, she is a fine short-story writer, and her work has been included in annual *Best American Short Stories* and has won O. Henry awards.

Elements of Tyler's stories have found their way into her novels: "I Never Saw Morning" (1961) and "Nobody Answers the Door" (1964), for example, are part of *If Morning Ever Comes*; "ReRun" (1988) appears as chapter 2, part 1, of *Breathing Lessons*; and "The Country Cook: A Story" (1982) is chapter 5 of *Dinner at*

TYLER'S STORIES NEED CRITICAL ATTENTION; HER PLACE AMONG CONTEMPORARY SHORT-STORY WRITERS HAS YET TO BE SERIOUSLY CONSIDERED."

the Homesick Restaurant. "People Who Don't Know the Answers," chapter 5 of *Saint Maybe*, appeared in the 26 August 1991 *New Yorker*. As such reviewers as John Updike have noted, each of the 10 chapters of *Dinner at the Homesick Restaurant* is rounded like a short story. Indeed, as Doris Betts (quoting Tyler's mother) reports, "each had been designed so it could be published as a separate story."

Some of Tyler's stories focus on situations and character types the author has not chosen to treat extensively in her novels. "A Misstep of the Mind" (1972) relates the violent rape of a teenager who by chance surprises a burglar in her home, a black man who comes to represent the crumbling safety that heretofore had surrounded this young woman's life. Although blacks appear in a number of Tyler's novels—for instance, the tobacco-typing-shed workers in *The Tin Can Tree* (1965) and, of course, Daniel Otis in *Breathing Lessons*—none has been so central to the narrative as Maroon in "The Geologist's Maid" (1975) and Ida in "The Common Courtesies" (1968). The perpetually angry Maroon (she and all of her sisters are named for colors) rules her professor-employer's sick room and house, and Ida, another maid, is effective, if more stereotyped: "Ida was colored, but her heart was in the right place." Powerfully sinister women—the mother in "A Knack for Languages" (1975) and the totally selfish Mrs. Brauw in "As the Earth Gets Older" (1966)—are character types treated in Tyler's stories. Her novels are filled with strong women, but—except for the disturbing episodes of child abuse Pearl Tull commits in the early years of *Dinner at the Homesick Restaurant*—she never returns to this unsettling character type.

Tyler's major novels are all closely involved with their geographic setting, Baltimore—a setting she used in the 1963 story "The Baltimore Birth Certificate," published four years before

After Donny runs away, Daisy thinks she sees a basketball out of the corner of her eye.
(© digitalvox | Shutterstock.com)

she made Baltimore her home. Tyler had used various places for story settings before claiming Baltimore as her particular place: "I Play Kings" (1963) begins in Raleigh, North Carolina, but the major action takes place in New York City; "Dry Water" (1965) takes place in Sandhill, North Carolina, the setting Tyler used for *If Morning Ever Comes*; "The Feather behind the Rock" (1967) follows a grandson and his grandparents through their cross-country drive from their home in Wilmington, North Carolina, to San Francisco; "The Genuine Fur Eyelashes" (1967) takes place in the tenant tobacco land of North Carolina, where the family attend a daughter's graduation from ninth grade at reform school (they bring the present she had requested—a pair of "genuine fur eye lashes").

Even though geographic place rings true in Tyler's short stories, she clearly prefers the detail and presence of Baltimore, which has figured so prominently in her work since 1972, when she published *The Clock Winder* and has her protagonist, Elizabeth Abbott, settle in Baltimore. Her narrative techniques are evident in the Baltimore stories: humor, strong characterizations, convincing portrayal of everyday life. In these stories she occasionally shows her skillful use of photographs and letters, two major devices in her novels. And in several stories, including "With All Flags Flying" (1971), she writes about very old characters and with the same gentle grace she uses to portray Daniel Peck (*Searching for Caleb*) and Daniel Otis (*Breathing Lessons*). . . .

Anne Tyler's short stories appear in two forms: those that are later woven seamlessly into a novel and those that remain discreet stories. As I have shown in this chapter, Tyler uses themes in short stories that do not appear in her novels, particularly the important issue of cross-cultural relations, which she explores in stories like "Your Place Is Empty," "Uncle Ahmad," "A Knack for Languages," and "Linguistics."

In several stories Tyler presents the plight of women trapped in domestic routine and limited by society's expectations. These woman are often unable and indeed unwilling to abandon their domestic life. At the same time the tension between fulfilling responsibilities and gaining a sense of self weighs heavy on these women, a dilemma that figures prominently in most of Tyler's novels. In "Under the Bosom Tree" (1977) a recently widowed 67-year-old woman faces her first birthday after her husband's death. Her preoccupied family fails to share her grief or to appreciate her struggle to survive. As she describes the first mornings after her husband's death, she takes her place among Tyler's enduring characters: "I woke up feeling just—oh, elated. I thought, 'Look at me, I made it through the night on my own.' I was proud of that."

In "Laps" the mother of a 14-year-old sees her life as an endless repetition of swimming pool visits for the daughter and the domestic routine of meal preparation and family care. As she gathers her belongings from the poolside to start home, her reflections on past and present show how completely she is paralyzed by her routine: "It occurs to me that I left the breakfast dishes undone. I have spent the day uselessly, wasted it, and see nothing ahead of me but more days to waste the same way."

Tyler's stories need critical attention; her place among contemporary short-story writers has yet to be seriously considered. Intriguing characters and quick humor, as well as societal and family issues, are among obvious aspects that invite critical response. Most of all, the stories need to be read for the good writing and moving experiences. An especially good example is the final paragraph of "Some Sign That I Ever Made You Happy" (1975), a story in which a man discovers the letters his father wrote to his wife after she died. The last letters (written six weeks before the father's death) reveal that the couple missed happiness altogether. Daily the husband had thought of the past, searching "out some sign that I ever made you happy."

Moved by these letters, the son tries to rekindle love in his marriage to avoid the regret he found in his father's letters. His gesture fails because his wife is busy with kitchen chores. As he walks into the living room he experiences an epiphany of cold recognition that reminds one of Gabriel's chilling moment in James Joyce's "The Dead": "So he went. In fact he found that he was even relieved to go. He was looking forward to a quiet half hour with the paper. But just as he was reaching toward the mantel he froze, struck suddenly by an unexpected sorrow, and for several minutes he stood motion-less, hoping against hope that the sorrow was the kind that would lessen as time went on" ("Sign," 130).

Tyler's reviews of the stories of Elizabeth Bowen, Eudora Welty, Caroline Gordon, John Cheever, and Hortense Calisher document delight in these novelists' *stories*—the sheer pleasure of having the Calisher volume in hand is "greedy satisfaction" ("Teacup," E1), even though the stories had been available in separate volumes.

Thus far there is no single volume of Tyler's stories, and one would be a welcomed addition to her canon. Readers can hope that eventually *The Collected Stories of Anne Tyler* will appear on library shelves.

Source: Elizabeth Evans, "The Short Stories," in *Anne Tyler*, Twayne Publishers, 1993, pp. 21–22, 41–43.

Alice Hall Petry

In the following excerpt, Petry looks at various literary influences on Tyler's work.

… Not surprisingly, most of the little critical attention that has been directed towards Tyler has consisted of efforts to fit her work into traditional literary classifications. She has been variously termed a realist, a romantic, a Victorian, a postmodernist, a minimalist, a sentimentalist, a feminist, a non-feminist, and a naturalist—terms which generally are mutually exclusive, or at least stridently incompatible. This confusion is hardly assuaged by concomitant efforts to identify Tyler's literary forebears and contemporary cousins. Her eccentric characters and tragicomic world view have led several commentators to place her within the school of Charles Dickens—a reasonable connection to make, though Tyler herself maintains that she is hardly a devotee: "Dickens isn't someone I've read much of—*Great Expectations* while a daughter was reading it in high school is the only title that comes to mind. I write about those off-beat characters and that blend of laughter and tears because in my experience, that's what real life consists of." Other commentators place her in the intensely modern, angst-ridden school of such contemporary writers as John Irving, John Cheever, and John Updike, though she herself is inclined to disagree: "I think John Irving is a skillful writer, but I disliked *Garp* and would never model a character after T. S. Garp. (Or after anyone in any book, for that matter.) And since I don't see any similarity between my writing and John Irving's, I don't think either one of us has influenced the other." It would appear, indeed, that Tyler's true literary forebears, the figures within whose tradition she seems most clearly to be working, are the writers of the Concord circle, the great Russian playwrights and novelists of the nineteenth century, and the writers of the modern South.

One would do well to keep copies of Emerson, Thoreau, and Hawthorne on hand when reading Tyler's novels. She is deeply interested, after all, in the nurturance of the self (and especially a mature sense of self-reliance) and in the often contrary connections between self and family, and self and community. Her novel *The Clock Winder*, for example, explores how a young woman's interactions with the Emerson family reveal her—and their—often-unsuccessful efforts to determine the needs of the self and the precise nature of self-reliance in the contemporary world. Likewise, in books like *A Slipping-Down Life*, *Celestial Navigation*, *Searching for Caleb*, *Earthly Possessions*, *Morgan's Passing*, and *The Accidental Tourist*, Tyler returns to the Thoreauvian question of what the individual truly needs to survive. As her characters accumulate and discard furniture, clothes, baby supplies, relatives, and even modes of thought, Tyler reveals the tensions inherent in modern man's contrary urges to amass and to minimalize. Thoreau's call for simplicity resonates throughout Tyler's novels, as characters repeatedly seek to strip down their existences by abandoning belongings, running away, or, more maturely, by living deliberately, often in tiny apartments or trailers.

Nathaniel Hawthorne seems also to be an important Tyler precursor. Robert McPhillips made a tentative suggestion in this direction in his 1988 review of *Breathing Lessons*, arguing that Tyler's fiction "belongs to the tradition of the American romance pioneered by Hawthorne far more than to that of the realistic or naturalistic novel." To be sure, the stylistic qualities that have come to be associated with Hawthorne—

THE WORLD AS TYLER PERCEIVES IT IS A DECIDEDLY MESSY AFFAIR."

including the slightly fey quality of *The Marble Faun* or the use of outsiders like Miles Coverdale to observe and comment upon others in *The Blithedale Romance*—are strong elements in Tyler's work. But so too are other Hawthornesque elements. For example, many of her novels—most dramatically *Earthly Possessions*, *Dinner at the Homesick Restaurant*, *Searching for Caleb*, *The Accidental Tourist*, and *Breathing Lessons*—read very much like Hawthornesque allegories, with characters transparently representing particular moral stances or possible modes of action. As another instance, Tyler is concerned with the burden of the past, be it personal, familial, or (less commonly) historical. Macon Leary can barely function a full year after his son's death (*The Accidental Tourist*); the legacy of Justin Montague Peck hangs like a pall over generations of his descendants (*Searching for Caleb*); Charlotte Emory seeks to run away from the oppressive weight of her childhood home, as much as from her uncomprehending, guilt-ridden husband (*Earthly Possessions*); and Ezra, Jenny, and Cody Tull continue to suffer from their unsettling childhoods long after they have reached maturity (*Dinner at the Homesick Restaurant*). Not surprisingly, the burden of the past often leads Tyler's characters to abandon the physical homes of their youth, to yearn, like Jeremy Pauling, to move to a spare cubicle in the desert or at the very least to put a sturdy lock on the door (*Celestial Navigation*). As is evident from Tyler's frequent habit of equating a house with the family that lives within it, she could appreciate fully what Hepzibah and Clifford Pyncheon suffer in *The House of the Seven Gables*. Tyler herself disavows any kind of indebtedness to writers like Hawthorne, Thoreau, and Emerson—"I'm not conscious of 19th-century influences, nor am I fond of 19th-century writers." It seems possible, however, that these influences may be traced to Tyler's having been raised according to her father's "Emersonian ideal." Literary influence can be most powerful when it is least conscious.

Tyler's apparent indebtedness to Russian writers is perhaps less surprising. On the most obvious level, many of her characters speak of Russian authors: the senior Merediths chastise Leon for reading "Communist" authors like Tolstoy (*Morgan's Passing*); Duncan Peck of *Searching for Caleb* immerses himself in Dostoyevsky, "because I think he's a writer that impassioned adolescents ... feel particularly drawn to"; Maggie Moran of *Breathing Lessons* attempts to read Dostoyevsky, a writer Tyler chose because of his "long, hard book[s]." But more important than these references are Tyler's use of themes, techniques, and character types drawn from the Russian masters, though she herself maintains that there are limits to this indebtedness. Benjamin DeMott in a fine review of *Dinner at the Homesick Restaurant*, for example, observed that "there's a touch of Dostoyevsky's 'Idiot' in Ezra, a hint of the unposturing selflessness whose effect on people denied faith in the possibility of human purity is invariably to intensify cynicism"—but Tyler remarks that "I can say for sure that I've never created a Dostoevskian character." Similarly, Paul Binding argues that, like Tyler, both Chekhov and Turgenev "present, in shapely works of fiction, a large gallery of related persons who define themselves in part through these diverse relationships," while Martin Levin in 1972 pointed out that Tyler "fills her pages with ... richly-idiosyncratic characters who amble about in Chekhovian fashion." The eccentric characters who populate Tyler's world would certainly seem to owe far more to the example of Chekhov than Dickens, while Tyler's much-discussed use (or misuse) of language—skewed dialogue, non sequiturs, illogical trains of thought—would be instantly familiar to anyone who had just read *The Cherry Orchard*. Tyler herself admits that "I did so much admire Chekhov during my college days that I may very well unconsciously echo him." Though Tyler confesses that she no longer aspires to be "another Tolstoy," she nonetheless puts to excellent use her extensive knowledge of Russian literature, and especially Chekhov.

The body of writing that has been most frequently associated with Tyler is, however, Southern literature. As the "Note About the Author" in the Berkley paperback editions of her novels attests, Tyler "considers herself a Southerner"; and though she harbors serious doubts about that statement, she nonetheless has been frank about her indebtedness to some Southern writers, especially Eudora Welty. As she recalls in her essay "Still Just Writing," Tyler had discovered in her high school library a book of Welty's short stories:

> She was writing about Edna Earle [of "The Wide Net"], who was so slow-witted she could sit all day just pondering how the tail of the C got through the loop of the L on the Coca-Cola sign. Why, I knew Edna Earle. You mean you could *write* about such people? I have always meant to send Eudora Welty a thank-you note, but I imagine she would find it a little strange.

To Welty, then, may be attributed Tyler's sense of authorization, her feeling that she could pursue a career devoted to recording in writing what she saw about her in the South. To Welty Tyler may also owe her keen eye for detail, her overriding interest in characterization, and "the ordering poles of her fiction: a sense of distance on the one hand and a gift of sympathy on the other."

Then again, these qualities are likewise evident in two other Southern women writers with whom Tyler has been associated repeatedly: Flannery O'Connor and Carson McCullers. It is easy to overstate the O'Connor connection. Tyler's own impatience with organized religion and her usually scathing portraits of ministers remove her dramatically from the insistently Roman Catholic world of O'Connor, as does her careful avoidance of violence. There are no drownings or bull gorings in Tyler's world, in which the very few acts of violence—Janie Rose's tractor accident (*The Tin Can Tree*), Timothy Emerson's suicide (*The Clock Winder*), Ethan Leary's murder in a Burger Bonanza (*The Accidental Tourist*)—either occur offstage before the opening of the novel or are passed over quickly. Further, Tyler is most comfortable with the world of the urban South, not the remote farms of most of O'Connor's characters, for whom the city is a kind of Hell. On the other hand, Tyler does share with O'Connor a tendency to use unlikely characters, like Jake Simms (*Earthly Possessions*) or Muriel Pritchett (*The Accidental Tourist*), as agents of revelation, though the epiphanies they engineer have nothing to do with God's grace and much to do with more accurate perceptions of the self.

Tyler's indebtedness to McCullers is more pronounced. They both write of characters who seem not quite to fit in their family circles, who yearn to run away, and who, more often than not, forge painfully a kind of compromise perspective that enables them to endure in a not-always-pleasant world. Perhaps more importantly, Tyler seems receptive to McCullers's dictum that we must learn to "connect" with one another, that love is one of the few defenses we have against a world that seems antagonistic towards a strong sense of both selfhood and freedom—existential ideas that become increasingly evident after *A Slipping-Down Life.*

The Southern writer who is mentioned most often in relation to Tyler is William Faulkner, although too much has been made of the few parallels that exist between them. To be sure, *Dinner at the Homesick Restaurant* is, like *As I Lay Dying*, a deathbed novel using multiple points of view; but Tyler has never read *As I Lay Dying*, and in fact she does not seem to have a high opinion of what little Faulkner she has read. Certainly the vast differences between Tyler and Faulkner would tend to offset what little they seem to have in common. For one thing, Tyler evinces slight interest in race: she rarely uses black characters as anything but domestics (the exception is Mr. Otis, in the digressive second part of *Breathing Lessons*), largely because she feels ill-equipped to address the black experience in America: "I would feel presumptuous writing about black life as if I really knew what it was like." Further, Tyler does not share Faulkner's interest in the myriad Southern speech patterns. Though early in her career she stressed her interest in the richness of Southern dialects, her characters sound suspiciously like Northerners. Tyler also lacks the Faulknerian interest in the ante-bellum South (only *Searching for Caleb* ranges back to the nineteenth century), while she "doesn't share Faulkner's obsession with the South's perceived fall from an Edenic state of grace, after the Civil War, perhaps simply because she was born in Minneapolis." And though she experiments with point of view in books like *Celestial Navigation* and *Dinner at the Homesick Restaurant*, there is nothing even remotely comparable to the experimentation of Faulkner's *Absalom, Absalom!* or *The Sound and the Fury*. Indeed, her disinclination to experiment may be seen as a conscious reaction against Faulkner: "his whole approach to writing—obviously he was knitting off in all directions—was completely wrong for me. If it were possible to write like him, I wouldn't. I disagree with him. I want everyone to understand what I'm getting at." And she certainly parts company with Faulkner in her

apparent lack of interest in the matter of sexual activity—a lack for which she has been roundly criticized. Tyler is quite defensive, however, on this score: "While I'm writing a novel I feel personally acquainted with my characters—almost in love with them, in fact—and responsible for the way they're presented. So I have never felt comfortable about exposing their sex lives. I believe I've been wrong about that in only one instance: *Celestial Navigation*. As I look back upon that book I see that it must be hard for readers to credit Jeremy with any sexual capability, and that I really owed it to them to show how he managed it. But Jeremy is the character I've felt most protective of, and so I let the book down on that account." But where Faulkner and Tyler seem very close is in their mutual insistence on one of the most important elements in human existence: the need to endure.

The world as Tyler perceives it is a decidedly messy affair. In addition to the burden of personal and familial pasts, her characters suffer from peer pressure (*A Slipping-Down Life*), child abuse (*Dinner at the Homesick Restaurant*), genetically-based predispositions (*Searching for Caleb*), and poor self-image (*Morgan's Passing*). Most live in terror of the outside world, like Macon Leary compiling guidebooks to minimize contact with it (*The Accidental Tourist*) or Jeremy Pauling holing up in his studio in agoraphobic panic. Others try to escape but cannot, like Charlotte Emory, whose only successful departure is as the hostage of a befuddled bank robber (*Earthly Possessions*). Much of the apparent chaos in Tyler's fictional worlds is due to the fact that everything seems to happen as an incongruous blend of utter chance and utter doom: Jake Simms just happens to take Charlotte hostage, while Ethan Leary just happens to be in a fast-food restaurant when a teen-aged thug decides to murder all the customers; the Pecks seem destined from birth to buy only Fords and to despise plaids (*Searching for Caleb*), while Emily Meredith is destined to embark on a career in puppetry that seems genetically encoded (*Morgan's Passing*). The Tyler characters who do try to remain functional in this chaotic world rely on various strategies. One such strategy is the cultivation of ritualistic behavior, like the purchase of a new red toothbrush every winter (*If Morning Ever Comes*). Others try to create the illusion of control by assuming identities (Morgan Gower in *Morgan's Passing*) or acting more integrated than they really are (Elizabeth Abbott of *The Clock Winder*). Others immerse themselves in the world of games (especially Monopoly and solitaire), where the rules are clear and winning a real possibility. Others frantically demand to know "the point," be it the point of pursuing an unsuccessful music career (Drumstrings Casey in *A Slipping-Down Life*), of getting to class on time (Justine Mayhew Peck in *Searching for Caleb*), or of holding a funeral for a cremated husband (Serena Gill in *Breathing Lessons*). Others just as frantically try to blame someone, anyone, anything for all that happens, since blame implies an understood order and a feeling of control. Still others use a medium that is quite appealing to Tyler: the fine arts. Most notably in Janie Rose's "tin can tree" and Jeremy Pauling's "pieces" (*Celestial Navigation*), Tyler's characters try to integrate the seemingly antithetical fragments of the world, rendering incongruous images, ideas, and events into meaningful wholes over which they, as artists, exert control. Photography likewise is a frequent pursuit in Tyler's novels, as characters attempt to "freeze" particular moments, to save them from the exigencies of change, of passing time, and of seeming chaos.

In the course of writing her eleven novels, however, Tyler seems to have evolved a means of dealing with these exigencies that has little in common with rituals, role playing, or games. In their stead, her characters have come to rely on a strategy that exerts a measure of genuine, rather than illusory, control over their lives and the world. It is seen as early as *Searching for Caleb*, in which the fortune teller Madame Olita explains to Justine Peck that one of the most painful elements of man's existence, the weight of the past, need not be overwhelming: "you can always choose to *some* extent. You can change your future a great deal. Also your past. . . . Not what's happened, no . . . but what hold it has on you" (135, 129), In a similar vein, Macon Leary of *The Accidental Tourist*, buffeted by the shocking death of his son and the dissolution of his twenty-year marriage, eventually comes to the realization that one may "choose what to lose" (301, 310).

It is an upbeat stance, and one quite unusual for the contemporary American literary scene. No wonder she defies classification. Humanists like Anne Tyler are, after all, very rare indeed.

Source: Alice Hall Petry, "Understanding Anne Tyler," in *Understanding Anne Tyler*, University of South Carolina Press, 1990, pp. 5–17.

SOURCES

Bail, Paul, *Anne Tyler: A Critical Companion*, Greenwood, 1998, pp. 1–11.

Bryant, Joseph Allen, *Twentieth Century Southern Literature*, University of Kentucky Press, 1997, p. 197.

Chomsky, Noam, *Chomsky on MisEducation*, Rowman & Littlefield, 2004, pp. 15–35.

Choquette, Diane, *New Religious Movements in the United States and Canada: A Critical Assessment and Annotated Bibliography*, Greenwood, 1985, pp. 122–36.

Croft, Robert, *An Anne Tyler Companion*, Greenwood, 1998, pp. 231–32.

Crozier, Michel, Samuel P. Huntington, and Joji Watanukie, *The Crisis of Democracy: Report on the Governability of Democracies to the Trilateral Commission*, New York University Press, 1975, p. 162.

Dewey, John, "The Economic Basis of the New Society," in *The Later Works, 1925–1953*, Vol. 13, *1938–1939, Experience and Education, Freedom and Culture, Theory of Valuation, and Essays*, edited by Jo Ann Boydston, Southern Illinois University Press, 1988, pp. 309–22.

Eliot, T. S., *The Frontiers of Criticism: A Lecture Delivered at the University of Minnesota Williams Arena on April 30, 1956*, University of Minnesota Press, 1956, p. 11.

——, *The Waste Land and Other Poems*, Harcourt Brace Jovanovich, 1962, pp. 47–54.

Evans, Elizabeth, *Anne Tyler*, Twayne's United States Author Series No. 620, Twayne, 1993, pp. 1–20.

Hagopian, Jesse, "A People's History of the Chicago Teachers Unions," in *International Socialist Review*, No. 86, November 2012, http://isreview.org/issue/86/peoples-history-chicago-teachers-union (accessed September 6, 2013).

Kissel, Susan S., *Moving On: The Heroines of Shirley Ann Gau, Anne Tyler, and Gail Godwin*, Bowling Green State University Popular Press, 1996, pp. 69–98.

Mann, Thomas, "Richard Wagner and the Ring of the Nibelung," in *On Myself and Other Princeton Lectures: An Annotated Edition based on Mann's Lecture Typescripts*, edited by James N. Bade, Peter Lang, 1996, pp. 81–110.

Smith, Adam, *An Inquiry into the Nature and Causes of the Wealth of Nations*, Vol. 3, Stirling, 1819, p. 194.

Troyes, Chrétien de, *Perceval; or, The Story of the Grail*, translated by Ruth Harwood Cline, University of Georgia Press, 1985, pp. 50–94.

Tyler, Anne, "Teenage Wasteland," in *Tales of Psychology: Stories to Make You Wise*, edited by Alma Bond, Paragon, 2002, pp. 254–65.

Voelker, Joseph C., *Art and the Accidental in Anne Tyler*, University of Missouri Press, 1989, pp. 67–88.

Weston, Jessie L., *From Ritual to Romance*, Dover, 2001, pp. 11–22.

FURTHER READING

Dickens, Charles, *Oliver Twist; or, The Parish Boy's Progress*, Richard Bentley, 1838.

    In *Oliver Twist*, Dicken's second novel, the protagonist begins life as an orphan in a workhouse. He eventually rebels against the institutional cruelty to which he is subjected and runs away to become one of the crowd of child pickpockets who plagued London and other major European cities of the time.

Modarressi, Taghi, *The Pilgrim's Rules of Etiquette*, Doubleday, 1989.

    This novel by Tyler's late husband narrates the personal crisis of an Iranian professor when one of his students is killed in the Iran-Iraq War. The professor flees his alienation from the oppressive fundamentalist regime that rules Iran into reintegration with the nation's past.

Salwak, Dale, ed., *Anne Tyler as Novelist*, University of Iowa Press, 1994.

    Salwak has collected a series of new and reprinted critical articles and reviews of Tyler's novels.

Tyler, Anne, *Dinner at the Homesick Restaurant*, Knopf, 1982.

    This Pulitzer Prize–nominated novel is Tyler's favorite among her works. It explores the different constructions put on their childhoods by three adult siblings reunited for their mother's funeral.

SUGGESTED SEARCH TERMS

Anne Tyler

Teenage Wasteland AND Tyler

social realism

suburbia

alienation

wasteland AND Eliot

wasteland

The Who

education

The Third Bank of the River

JOÃO GUIMARÃES ROSA

1962

"The Third Bank of the River" is a story by Brazilian author João Guimarães Rosa that revolves around a man's curious decision to devote himself to a river. While bodies of water in particular may not be hallmarks of Rosa's work, nature more broadly is, with the majority of his tales taking place somewhere in the *sertão*, the rural central highlands set off from both the coastal cities and lowland jungles of Brazil, a region that compares both physically and thematically with America's Wild West. In the great distances between isolated communities, a person's sense of self is given the chance to expand to fill the wide open spaces, with nature as the ever-present intermediary. The relationship between one solitary-minded man and a wide, silent river is at the heart of "The Third Bank of the River."

Rosa was writing in an era when the intellectual, introspective trends of the modernist movement were being reshaped by the playfulness of postmodernism and the fantastic interludes of magic realism. Rosa's own style lay somewhere in between these two trends, as he played with the features of narrative, but not so much as to disrupt the telling of the story at hand, and he manipulated the boundaries of realism, but not so much as to move into the realm of fantasy. "The Third Bank of the River" shows the strengths of such a middle way. The story was first published in Portuguese in 1962 as "A terceira margem do rio" in the

The boy brings his father's food to the boat. (© ffoto29 | Shutterstock.com)

volume *Primeiras estórias*, meaning "First stories" (though this was published some sixteen years after Rosa's debut collection). The story was translated into English by Barbara Shelby for the collection as renamed *The Third Bank of the River and Other Stories* (1968). The title story has been included in several anthologies; for example, a translation by William L. Grossman can be found in *Modern Brazilian Short Stories* (1967) and *The Oxford Book of Latin American Short Stories* (1997).

AUTHOR BIOGRAPHY

Rosa—who is alternately referred to as either Rosa or Guimarães Rosa by both American and Brazilian critics—was born on June 27, 1908, the first of six children to Florduardo Pinto Rosa and Francisca Guimarães Rosa. His hometown of Cordisburgo is in the state of Minas Gerais, lying just on the edge of the *sertão*, a region covering about a third of Brazil's territory. Rosa's German ancestry has been noted in the name of his hometown as well as

in both his appearance and his temperament. His forefathers were cattlemen who migrated inland from the coast, enabling his own father to be successful in the same business. Rosa's childhood on a farm was filled with the rumbling of ox hooves by day and by night.

Rosa traded the farm life for studies at boarding school in the larger town of Belo Horizonte around the age of ten. By then he was already dabbling in foreign languages such as French. Around age seventeen, he went to medical school at the University of Minas Gerais. In between studying, he began contributing stories to a magazine in Rio de Janeiro, *O Cruzeiro*, and won four literary prizes. He married Lygia Cabral Pena, with whom he would have two daughters, in June 1930 and graduated in December 1930, delivering a speech for the ceremony. He became a physician the following year, based in Itaguara.

Rosa's early professional life was filled with intrigue. Even before his graduation, a revolutionary force was coming together in the nation, with political heads of Minas Gerais among the leaders, and Rosa enrolled as an army doctor. His experience was such that he could later state (as quoted by Eduardo F. Coutinho), "As a physician I came to know the mystical greatness of suffering; as a rebel, the value of consciousness; and as a soldier, the importance of the proximity of death." Between periods of military conflict, his medical practice often involved journeys on horseback to towns near and far, sometimes lasting several days. The revolution succeeded; but by the time the dictatorial government resulting from the revolution was overturned in 1933, Rosa had shrewdly switched sides, and he attained the rank of captain with the Brazilian Força Publica. Longing to expand his range of experience further, he joined Brazil's diplomatic service in 1934, traveling by way of Rio de Janeiro (then the capital) to Hamburg, Germany, in 1938. That year he remarried, to Aracy Moebius de Carvalho.

While he was relocating to Germany, Rosa won a national poetry contest with the manuscript "Magma" (which was never published) and earned a highly commended second prize in a short-fiction contest for his thousand-page collection *Contos*—a result he was disappointed with. He remained in Hamburg into the early years of World War II, to endure four months of imprisonment at Baden-Baden in 1942. Afterward, while alternating periods in Colombia and France, he worked on and revised his stories, and in 1946, he published them as *Sagarana*, a collection blending traditional genres with nuanced narration, original language, and ethical incisiveness.

Thereafter, Rosa's life was marked by both his ongoing diplomatic activities and his literary production. He was back in Rio de Janeiro by 1951 but did not publish again until 1956. In that year, he published two substantial volumes: *Corp de baile: Sete novelas* (Corps of ballet: Seven novellas), a collection of lyrical short fiction, novellas, and novels, and *Grande sertão: Veredas* (Great backlands: Paths), a stream-of-consciousness novel with no chapter breaks that has been compared to James Joyce's *Ulysses* for its epic force. Rosa accumulated a number of literary awards in his later years, including a lifetime achievement prize from the Brazilian Academy of Letters. Among other works, *Primeiras estórias*, which contains "A terceira margem do rio" ("The Third Bank of the River"), was published in 1962. Though Rosa once claimed that he was so full of stories that he could never finish writing them down, he would

not get the chance to prove himself: having endured a heart attack and near-death experience in 1958, he suffered another heart attack on November 19, 1967, while at work in his study in the Copacabana *bairro* of Rio de Janeiro, Brazil, and died at age fifty-nine.

PLOT SUMMARY

The narrator of "The Third Bank of the River" begins by clarifying that his father had always seemed quite normal, even conventional, as people who knew him confirmed. The narrator adds that he found his father no less rational than other people. His father spoke little, and his mother was the one who ran the household. One day, the father makes plans to acquire a canoe.

The canoe would be of particular dimensions, allowing just enough room for one person, and would be sturdy enough to last for decades in the water. The mother objects, finding it ludicrous that a man of the father's age should suddenly take up a hobby like fishing or hunting. The father keeps quiet. The house is rather near the river. When the canoe is ready, the father bids the family good-bye and heads out, despite the mother's insistence that if he leaves, he should never return. He has packed almost nothing. Taken aside by the father, the narrator asks to accompany him, but the youth is told to turn back. Instead, the narrator heads to a grove of trees to watch: the father launches his canoe into the river, and there he stays.

The father neither heads for the opposite bank of the river nor returns to where he came from, but settles himself in the middle. He would never leave the canoe again. Baffled, the family and friends gather, and with the mother remaining levelheaded—as if she, knowing the father best, might have anticipated such a course of action—the others come to the conclusion that the father is mad. It is idly supposed by a few that he may be holding a vow, made for whatever reason, or may have some repulsive disease. Rumor spreads up and down the river, and the people declare that he never lands. When the father's relatives imagine that the food he has stashed away must be getting low, they suspect he will come ashore.

But the narrator has been bringing his father food ever since the second day, after the family

MEDIA ADAPTATIONS

- *A terceira margem do rio* is the title of a film adaptation of the story from 1994. Directed by Nelson Pereira dos Santos for Centre National du Cinéma and Regina Filmes, with a running time of ninety-eight minutes, the film was nominated for the Golden Berlin Bear at the Berlin International Film Festival and won a Silver Daisy in Brazil. The movie poster, showing a close-up of a young girl with a glow around her, suggests that the story line has been altered somewhat; the cast credits cite a character called Nhinhinha, the name of a phenomenal child in Rosa's story "The Girl from Beyond," from the same collection as "The Third Bank of the River."

spent the night calling to the father from the firelit shore. The narrator places the food—simple things like corn bread or bananas—in a niche in the bluff along the riverbank. In time, the mother, without saying anything directly, begins to aid the son's support of the father, leaving leftovers in conspicuous places.

The mother seeks outside help. She gets an uncle to help manage their farm and affairs, a tutor for the children, and a priest to exorcize whatever spirit is possessing the father—to no avail. A pair of soldiers also fail to compel the father to return to the bank. When anyone tries to reach him by boat—such as the reporters seeking his picture—the father eludes them by winding his way through nearby swamplands.

The family tries to adapt to the father's persistence in always holding to the middle of the river, whether in sweltering heat or midnight cold. They think of him when enjoying pleasures unavailable to him, like good cooked food or a warm bed on a rainy night. Weeks, months, and years pass.

The narrator actively wonders how the father does it—how he might get sleep by tying the canoe to an islet—how he could survive without fire, on what little cold food he had—how his strength could never fail him, even amidst floodwaters. The family stops talking about the father but can never forget him.

The narrator's sister gets married, but the mother cannot bear to celebrate. As the narrator matures, he is said to resemble his father, but he knows that the father's appearance must be savage by now. The narrator wonders whether the father even loves his family anymore. When his sister gives birth to a son, she wants to show the father and wears her wedding dress to the riverbank, holding the baby and calling to the father. He never shows up, and the family mourns together.

The sister and her husband move far away, and the narrator's brother goes to the city. Eventually the mother, growing old, joins the sister, leaving the narrator as the father's only remaining kin there. Marriage is unthinkable to the narrator; he feels burdened, and he knows, despite having never been told, that his father needs him. The son grows determined to understand why the father is out there. Some say the canoe maker might have known, but he is dead. Others reconsider the early rumor that, like Noah, the father is responding to a divine call. The narrator's age begins to show in his few white hairs.

The narrator is full of sorrow as well as guilt, a guilt that he cannot quite understand—he wonders if he should blame his father or the river. He imagines that one day the father will lose all his strength and will be carried miles downstream to plunge down a cataract to his death. Weighed down by his sorrow and guilt, the narrator resolves to relieve them. The son wonders aloud if he is crazy, then affirms that he is not. In fact, the family no longer speaks that word; if anyone is crazy, they believe, then everyone is.

The narrator heads to the riverside and, holding a sheet to signal with, awaits his father. He eventually appears, and the narrator's words practically shout themselves: he declares that the father has done his part and can come back now; his son will take his place. For the first time since he took to the river, the father responds, waving and then directing his canoe to the shore. The narrator panics, feeling as if the father has returned from the spirit world, and flees. Now, he wants only forgiveness. The father was never heard from again. The narrator believes he has failed utterly, but he is too fearful to end his own life. He only asks that when his death comes, he be cast adrift in a canoe, abandoned to the river.

CHARACTERS

Brother

The narrator's brother is said to move to the city—one imagines a regional city some distance away—after the family's disappointment when the father fails to meet his grandson.

Father

The father is the curious focal center of Rosa's story. Because his earlier life, before his decision to take to the river, is not shown at all, he remains an enigma. Rather than having a genuine personality, a manner of perceiving and responding to the world, he has only his designs, his intention to spend the rest of his life on the river. When his family members make comments that bear no relevance to his intention, he simply ignores them. He thus seems less a person than the embodiment of a course of action. This is the case for the reader as well as for the rest of his family, for whom this is frustrating because they did formerly know him as an ordinary person. From their perspective, his apparent total indifference even to his family—to the most momentous event of his daughter's creating a new person in the world—is not just inexplicable but intolerable.

The mystery of the father appears to be the very point of the story. There are conjectures sprinkled throughout as to why he might be doing what he is doing, but these are virtually all dismissed by the narrator. By the end, the narrator seems to have at least figured out that the father is doing what he is doing because he feels compelled to, but why he should feel so compelled remains unstated.

Mother

The reader's impression of the mother is founded on the very few characteristics revealed by the narrator. She is portrayed as a somewhat cool disciplinarian in being the one "who gave the orders and scolded us every day"; the narrator says nothing about the degree to which she *cared* for her children. This hints at her possible resentment of the fact that she had to fill the disciplinary role left vacant by the taciturn father. Later the narrator states, "Mother almost never showed what she was thinking," suggesting that in light of the father's quietness, she grew into the habit of keeping her own feelings to herself, rather than exposing them to a "practical" husband who perhaps managed to demonstrate little sympathy.

Yet the mother demonstrates a keen devotion to her husband in several ways. Her threats over the father's leaving with the canoe may seem harsh, but while his behavior at that point may strike the reader as singular but not unreasonable, the mother could perhaps already sense that he meant never to return. Thus, she challenges him, as if in hopes that, being confronted with the stark reality of what he is doing, he might at last change his mind. Even once he is out in the river, she helps the narrator supply him with food, she does everything she can think of to bring him back, and she insists on a certain solemnity—declining to celebrate her daughter's marriage—in recognition of the father's ongoing, tragic absence from the family. The mother is said to at last leave their home near the river only "because she was growing old"; after so much devotion, she at last concedes defeat.

Narrator

Through the beginning of the story the narrator approaches his father's mysterious behavior objectively: he does not judge him and offers little personal opinion with regard to his potential motivations, instead simply describing what he does. The son's reverence toward the father is evoked in his question, "Father, will you take me with you in that canoe?" He does not know quite what is going on, but he wants to be alongside his father nevertheless. The narrator, too, is the one who thinks of supplying the father with food, and he seems to accept the fact that his father declines to personally receive the food; it is as if the son acknowledges that his duty as a son is not to judge but to follow as best he can. (The narrator's age at the story's opening is unspecified, but his manner suggests that he is fairly young, perhaps preadolescent.)

The narrator's position in relation to his father gradually shifts over the course of the story. More and more he questions his father's motivations and thinks about the effect his course of action has had on his family. In the end the uncertainty is unbearable, and the son resolves to figure things out by making one last appeal to the father—a bold appeal, going so far as to not just support him in his peculiar mission but to offer to take his place. Whether he is motivated by love or by curiosity, he at once regrets it. The response is perhaps what was desired but was not truly expected. The son cannot truly imagine facing the enormity of the task of taking his father's place, and so the entire episode in their lives comes to a dramatic end.

Sister

After the father has taken to the river, the sister marries and bears a child, a son. The narrator hints at the fruitlessness of her desire to introduce her father to his grandson when he says that "she got it into her head" to do so, as if she had not considered whether it was a wise idea. Indeed, she is very disappointed when the father never shows, and after that, she and her husband move somewhere far away. In finally abandoning the father in favor of living her own life, the sister serves as a foil (a contrast or counterpoint) to the narrator.

THEMES

Solitude

The father in "The Third Bank of the River" turns out to be the sort of person who is content with, even desires, an extraordinary degree of solitude. He succeeds in avoiding person-to-person contact with absolutely everyone, evading people who seek him out by losing them in the swamps, never even drifting ashore to greet his family. In going without conversation, he gives up a great deal: sympathy demonstrated through shared interest, forums for his thoughts, expressions of love. Yet he has always been a quiet person, and perhaps he views conversation as more of a burden and feels no need for validation from other people about what he does with his life. This might be regarded negatively as self-centered, or positively as self-reliant.

The individual who seeks to withdraw from society is not an uncommon type, especially in literature, where as a rule interesting personae are explored. Notably, if the father in this story really wanted perfect solitude, he could have gone to any number of places—the heart of the jungle, a mountaintop, the other side of the world—where no one would have ever found him. It is conceivable that the father is self-reliant in ways the narrator does not describe—perhaps he learns to fish so expertly that he does not even need his family's material support—but it seems that despite his desire for extreme solitude, the father either wants or needs to remain close to his family.

Family

The man's wife, daughter, and sons are profoundly affected by his actions. Because they are his family, they love him, and they would like nothing more than for him to return home. If given the chance, they probably would have told him that he could be as solitary as he liked, saying nothing at all if he so chose, even ignoring them completely, if only he would come back and be with them, be present as the father. A family functions interdependently, each person tangibly or just subconsciously relying on the others' presence for peace of mind and well-being. Parents are role models for their children, and having an absent parent can mean not having so clear a sense of how one should behave in the world. The way a son can instinctively take after his father is reflected in Rosa's story in the way the narrator both first wants to accompany the father in the canoe and later cannot leave him; he compulsively remains at the father's beck and call, even if the father never actually beckons or calls him. Even the father's complete lack of communication with the son does not break the bond between them.

This is not the case with the rest of the family. The father's decision to remain adrift in the river is understandably difficult for them to bear. Because of their sympathetic connection with him, they cannot quite enjoy all that they used to enjoy—food, comfort, society—knowing that these enjoyments are out of their father's reach. They cannot help but imagine him stuck out in the rain when they would otherwise be able to bask in the warmth and security of their own shelter. Finally, after his refusal to acknowledge the existence of his grandson—effectively declining to be a part of the family's future—they can bear to be burdened by his lingering distance from them no longer. Thus do the narrator's sister and brother recognize that the healthiest option for them is to move on, to leave their father in the past and turn to their own futures. The narrator, to the contrary, remains; but at length his own powerfully

TOPICS FOR FURTHER STUDY

- Write a story in which a first-person narrator relates the separation of another person from his or her family and discloses the consequences of that separation. You might reconstruct Rosa's circumstances, with the person strangely seeking solitude somewhere, or use any other situation that creates the separation, such as someone running away from home, someone going to jail, or someone going off to war.

- In an index at the close of Rosa's *Primeiras estórias*, sets of pictographs, drawn by illustrator Luís Jardim, are provided for each story—and every one (except for the eighth one, perhaps an oversight) includes an infinity sign. Choose any of the stories from the English translation, *The Third Bank of the River and Other Stories*, and write an essay exploring the themes of that story—including the notion of infinity—and remarking on the extent to which they intersect with those of the title story. A good choice is "The Aldacious Navigator," in which a girl tells an inventive story about a man who drifts away from his family out to the ocean.

- Read "The Bass, the River, and Sheila Mant," a coming-of-age story by W. D. Wetherell, available in his collection *The Man Who Loved Levittown* (1985). Set primarily along a New Hampshire river, the story deals with how a fourteen-year-old boy's affection for fishing clashes with his interest in a young lady. Write an essay in which you compare this story with "The Third Bank of the River," focusing on the characters of the fourteen-year-old boy of Wetherell's story and the father of Rosa's story. Discuss what value they find in the river, how this affects their relationships, how they ultimately seek happiness, and other topics that you deem significant.

- Research the Amazon River online. Find geographical and ecological information, describing the physical characteristics, wildlife, and route of the river itself, as well as cultural information, such as the roles it has played in shaping the cultures of the region and how it is thought of today. Assemble your findings into a multimedia presentation with photos, video, commentary, and any other elements that you find helpful (perhaps audio, a time line, or interactive elements such as quizzes). Also produce a written bibliography showing the sources for your presentation.

---

sympathetic connection with his father elicits not simple loyalty but moreover sorrow and guilt.

Guilt

The source of the narrator's guilt over the father's self-assigned fate is uncertain at first. One might suggest that the son should feel no guilt at all: his father has opted to take to the river through no fault of the son's, even declining the son's company, and has shown no gratitude for the son's persistent efforts to serve him. The reader may even want the narrator to counter the father's abandonment of the family by abandoning the father, just as his siblings have. But something keeps the son there, and the son is so absorbed in or preoccupied with that something that he is unable even to consider, say, a romantic relationship for himself. To draw a comparison with Christianity, he is devoted to the father much as a monk or nun is devoted to God or specifically Jesus Christ, who is understood to have died for humanity's sins.

The narrator of "The Third Bank of the River" does not appear to have committed any grave sins, or any sins at all, and yet he feels guilt over his father's ongoing self-sacrifice

The boat traps the father and keeps him safe. (© *Nanisimova | Shutterstock.com*)

nonetheless. One might conjecture that this is because he feels the sense of filial duty so strongly—perhaps especially because his siblings have renounced this duty—that he must not only accompany and serve the father always but also endure whatever he endures, suffer what he suffers. The father has set a dazzling example for the son: to give up everything and lose himself in the river. The son may not see any merit in this, but he certainly recognizes his father's sacrifice, and he rues it. As the father grows older and surely weaker, the son imagines that the father cannot persist much longer. And yet, for whatever reason—be it compulsion, fanaticism, or madness—the father cannot give up the task he has set himself. The crux of the matter is not so much that he must do it, one surmises, but that it must be done. The son ultimately recognizes this truth at the heart of his father's devotion to the river. The source of his guilt, then, is that he realizes that he and he alone can actually invert the circumstances and be his father's savior—he can assume the role of the sacrificed and let his father return to land and live, and soon die, in peace. Still, when the son, in at last successfully

hailing the father, gains the opportunity to viscerally consider abandoning himself to the river, it strikes him as madness.

Madness

Rosa lets the idea of madness linger around the edges of this story. It is brought up in the very first paragraph, as the narrator seeks to establish that his father was not crazy—at least not before he took to the river. But once the father is out there and refuses to come back, with the mother showing a stoical resignation, the family and acquaintances cannot escape the conclusion that the father must indeed be mad. No rational explanation presents itself as to why he should remain suspended in the river as he does. Still, the family goes to great lengths to avoid settling on the verdict of madness. As the narrator reports, they decline to ever again speak the word *crazy*, with regard to their father or anyone else. Their formulation of the logic of madness— "Either no one is crazy, or everyone is"—is significant: rejecting relative judgment, they commit to an absolute definition of the term whereby all individuals are seen to have their own unique worldviews and wills, such that no one person's uniqueness can be called madness—unless everyone's is.

This is philosophically sound, to an extent. But it leaves the narrator himself lingering in a mental state that approaches true madness. Were he to recognize his father as crazy, he could perhaps finally gain peace of mind, because he would be recognizing that there is no logic to his father's fate, so he would not have to feel guilt and responsibility about it. In effect, the narrator, like his siblings, could fully abandon the father to his bizarre behavior and move on. Instead, he feels compelled to resolve that behavior, to unwind it, to find a rational solution to it. In fact, he appears to find a solution—but it is not a good one. He manages to lure the father back to the shore, but only by offering his own life, indeed his own sanity, in exchange for the father's. To voluntarily commit oneself to a course of action that one believes would lead to a state of insanity may be, for any truly sane person, impossible. The son rhetorically asks and responds, "Was I crazy? No." But his elusive definition of madness renders his declaration meaningless. He has given up a normal life for a father who has abandoned him.

The reader may conclude that not everyone is crazy, but the father appears to be, and the son, sadly, drawn along by the father, in the end does too. On the other hand, his ultimate refusal to take the father's place may be the evidence that, unable to commit to insanity, he must be sane. However, his guilt over his failure only increases the strain on his emotional stability and his sanity. In light of his despair over his failure to save his father, the son in the end, in death, wants only exactly what in life he could not bear to face—to lose himself in the river, just like his father did.

STYLE

Brazilian Sertão *Literature*

One of the hallmarks of Rosa's fiction, as well as that of many other Brazilian writers, is the setting of the *sertão*, sometimes translated as the "backlands," meaning the backcountry or areas removed from the more heavily populated regions. Critic Luiz Fernando Valente, in a *Modern Language Studies* essay, refers to this setting as "the quintessentially Brazilian motif of the

'*sertão*.'" These are Brazil's central highlands, set away from coastal population centers such as São Paulo, Rio de Janeiro, and Recife and elevated above the dense Amazonian jungles. These highlands encompass a variety of landscapes, as Luis Harss and Barbara Dohmann relate in an essay on Rosa's works: "The *sertão* is many things: mountain range and valley, moor and marsh, glade and gorge, windy peak and chasm.... The *sertão* is changeable: an oceanic spread with shifting contours that tease the mind and deceive the eye." A description more immediately accessible to the American reader is offered by Mary L. Daniel, who in an essay on Rosa refers to *Primeiras estórias* as a "collection of 'Wild West' stories," evoking the familiar rural expanses, untamed individuals, and existential open-endedness of the storied American West.

In "The Third Bank of the River," the *sertão* is the background for the extreme isolation achieved by the narrator's father. His actions would hardly be practical near a city. Out in the *sertão*, the communities are thin, the fog lies thick, and the labyrinthine swamps are near enough at hand for the father to elude anyone who follows him. The open river there can accommodate the father's solitary designs. One senses a certain finality in the narrator's reference to how his brother "decided to go live in the city," as if the brother is thus transported to an entirely different world, nullifying his relevance to life in the *sertão*. The father and narrator, meanwhile, are left to resolve their standoff of wills, as it might be called, against the stark natural background of the unending flux of the river.

Fabulation

Rosa's stories function on the verge of a style that has been employed frequently and effectively by Latin American writers: magic realism. In such works, the setting is primarily realistic, but there are intrusions by supernatural or magical elements that are treated much like ordinary occurrences. Rosa's stories tend not to feature such sensational, typically impossible events, but they do stretch the boundaries of realism in a way that similarly shifts the consciousness of the reader. In "The Third Bank of the River," what the father undertakes is a quite astounding effort, to remain afloat on a simple canoe for years on end, permanently exposed to the elements, surviving on what little food is supplied by his family (or perhaps caught from the river), never partaking in society. If the father is not mad before he undertakes this effort, one can easily imagine that the effort itself might drive him mad. Yet this effort is not magical or super-natural. The narrator has difficulty explaining how the father can do it, but it remains just within the bounds of human possibility, enough so that the story does not demand the willing suspension of disbelief on the part of the reader (as magic realism does). On the other hand, to call Rosa's story a work of realism would be inaccurate; this may be a version of reality, but it is indeed an extraordinary, quite improbable one. Moreover, the cryptic title of the work, "The Third Bank of the River," suggests a location somewhere beyond ordinary reality.

A term that applies to such refashioning of reality, especially to moral or philosophical ends, is *fabulation*, with the root word *fable* meaning a story that presents a character in a moral dilemma or creates a moral confrontation to teach the reader a lesson. Aesop's fables, which use animals to emphasize characters' embodiments of certain vices and virtues, are a well-known example. Robert Scholes (as quoted by Valente) updates the notion of the fable in a definition he gives in *Fabulation and Metafiction*, one that speaks to the characteristic refashioning of reality: "Modern fabulation, like the ancient fabling of Aesop, tends away from direct repre-sentation of the surface of reality but returns toward actual human life by way of ethically controlled fantasy." That is to say, what the reader is presented with may be not straightfor-ward reality but a sort of fantasy world that operates within distinct boundaries. As Valente states, Rosa demonstrates "the fabulators' belief in the possibility for fiction to create an imagined reality that opens up and enlarges ordinary reality."

"The Third Bank of the River," then, can be seen to enlarge reality in that it presents a person whose actions—living in a canoe for years on end—surely stretch beyond those of anyone any reader has known. The father's actions may be difficult for the reader to realistically conceive; the story presents an imagined, fabu-lated reality. And it is precisely through this fabulated reality that Rosa opens up the possi-bility of exploring rational limits of solitude, independence, family love, and sanity. As for the story's moral lesson (something any fable

ought to have), Rosa leaves that less clear, as neither the father nor the son proves a faultless role model. Whatever the father's motivations for taking to the river in the first place, he is evidently relieved at the news that his son will take his place, suggesting repentance. The son tries to follow in his father's footsteps but can-not, and in the end he is consumed by guilt over his failure. Indeed one might say that, lacking a clear moral, this story is not so much a fable as a fabulation, and the reader seeking meaning may be advised to settle into a more intuitive appre-ciation for the characters and the tale.

HISTORICAL CONTEXT

Brazilian Literature into the Twentieth Century

Interestingly, while Rosa began his professional life in the course of a minor revolution (which was soon reversed) and was a Brazilian diplomat throughout his literary career—as which he wit-nessed World War II, the peace accords, and the onset of the Cold War—his fiction bears little if any relevance to the politics and history of his era. Instead, his stories are set in a fairly timeless *sertão* in which small-scale human experiences operate independently of contemporary events. "The Third Bank of the River," for example, has only one factor that even places the story in the modern era: the reporters' attempt to take the father's picture, with the technological innova-tion of the camera only implied, not specified, by the language.

Rosa's intents, rather, were inherently artis-tic, literary, and philosophical, and he proceeded to skillfully etch his name into the lasting record of Brazilian literature. This subset of Latin American literature has received proportion-ately less attention than others in part because of the isolation fostered by the Portuguese lan-guage, which is spoken in Brazil, Portugal, and only a few other places. Spanish, on the other hand, is spoken throughout the remainder of Latin America. In their 1960s investigation of ten essential Latin American writers, Harss and Dohmann chose only one Brazilian, Rosa.

The earliest written Latin American litera-ture was poetry, with the form of the novel being adapted through the nineteenth century. One early Brazilian epic in the vein of the celebration of the "noble savage" (the idea that Native

COMPARE
&
CONTRAST

- **1960s:** Deforestation in Brazil has been a concern since the 1500s, and the first nation-wide evaluation of vegetation in 1962 confirms losses of overwhelming proportions of forests—losses that increase after the economy booms and major highways are constructed during the late 1960s and early 1970s. Brazil's first three national parks were created in the late 1930s, and their number increases to fourteen by the end of the 1960s.

  Today: Brazil has become a model nation in the developing world with regard to wildlife protection, with sixty-four national parks and more than three hundred conservation areas altogether. Among these is Parque Nacional Grande Sertão Veredas, which is located on the border of the states of Minas Gerais and Bahia and is named after Rosa's great novel, *Grande sertão: Veredas* (Great backlands: Paths).

- **1960s:** Brazil enjoys a surge of attention on the world stage. Brasília, the new inland capital, is founded in 1960, bridging the coastal cities with the *sertão*. In soccer, Brazil wins the 1962 World Cup. The same year, there is a landmark bossa nova concert performed in Carnegie Hall in New York City by more than twenty Brazilians. Translations of Rosa's major works into English appear in 1963, 1966, and 1968 .

- **Today:** Brazil is considered one of the most promising economies in the world, contributing to the initialism BRICS (for Brazil, Russia, India, China, and South Africa) as one of five rapidly developing nations. Brazil's soccer team is among the foremost in the world, with a global high of five World Cup titles, and is hosting the event to much fanfare in 2014.

- **1960s:** An era of significant experimentation in Brazilian literature is marked by story collections such as Rosa's *Primeiras estórias* (1962) and *Tutaméia: Terceiras estórias* (1967), Nélson Coelho's *O inventor de Deus* (The inventor of God, 1962), and Samuel Rawet's *Os sete sonhos* (The seven dreams, 1967). Aside from Rosa, such writers are not well known to English-speaking audiences.

  Today: Catering to ever-increasing traffic on the Internet, the literary group Word Awareness has created a site featuring English translations of Brazilian stories, which have further been compiled into the first volume of *Contemporary Brazilian Short Stories* (2011). Brazilian writers are also granted exposure through the literary magazine *Granta*'s 2012 issue highlighting twenty of the best young Brazilian novelists, including Miguel Del Castillo, Luisa Geisler, and Chico Mattoso.

Americans, because they lived simple lives close to nature, were unspoiled and morally pure) was José de Alençar's *O Guarani* (1857). One of the most respected names in Brazilian letters is Joaquim Maria Machado de Assis, whose fiction is distinguished by a psychological realism that was well ahead of his time. Among his works is the 1884 story collection *Historias sem data* (Stories without date). Worthy successors to Machado de Assis were long in coming, though other novels of note appeared sporadically. José

Pereira da Graça Aranha's socially conscious 1902 novel *Canaã* (*Canaan*) ponders multiculturalism in Brazil by exploring the concerns of two German immigrants.

Modernism—a literary and artistic movement of the early twentieth century that emphasized breaks from tradition—came to the forefront of Brazilian fiction with Mário de Andrade's 1928 novel *Macunaíma*. This work, considered an important exploration of American identity, is about a young man from the

The river seems to represent life, or existence.
(© gary yim / Shutterstock.com)

does not deal with specific regions or communities but with elemental landscapes and their relevance to individuals. For this reason, Rosa is seen by many as having stepped beyond simple regionalism to produce works of universal regionalism. Rosa also made notable innovations in the language of fiction, such as by inventing new words to suit new ideas and rearranging syntax in ways that call attention to each and every idea in a text. Afrânio Coutinho, in *An Introduction to Literature in Brazil*, refers to Rosa as a "revelation." Daniel echoes this recognition of Rosa's historical relevance in remarking that his debut collection "shocked the critics, puzzled the public, and opened an exciting new era in Portuguese-language fiction." By 1967, Harss and Dohmann could hold up Rosa's works as being typical of the era in Latin American literature: "Our fiction as a whole, over the past years, has tried to find the point of confluence of the mythical and the personal, the social and the subjective, the historical and the metaphysical. Guimarães Rosa ... shows that the task has not been in vain."

CRITICAL OVERVIEW

Critics speak of Guimarães Rosa's works very favorably. In an essay in *Studies in Short Fiction*, Daniel identifies him as "Brazil's most original short story writer of the twentieth century, ... an erudite master of language and a bold stylistic-linguistic innovator." Luiz Fernando Valente, in a *Modern Language Studies* essay, comments that "Guimarães Rosa is unquestionably the most international of twentieth-century Brazilian writers." And Harss and Dohmann, in *Into the Mainstream: Conversations with Latin-American Writers*, call Rosa "the most notable writer of the century in the Portuguese language." Russell G. Hamilton Jr., in his 1969 essay "The Contemporary Brazilian Short Story," observes that Rosa "has become something of a legend. Critics and the enlightened reading public have built up what amounts to a cult around Rosa and his works." Hamilton acknowledges that Rosa's unique language can be difficult to grasp, but he affirms that the absorbed reader regardless finds "aesthetic serendipity"—that is, an unexpected artistic pleasure—in that language.

jungle who wields magical abilities in the civilized world of São Paulo. Later writers with modernist sensibilities showed an awareness of how scientific and technological innovations— the camera, the telephone, the airplane—were revolutionizing people's perceptions of themselves and of the roles and functions of society. Gilberto Freyre's novel *Casa-grande e senzala* (1933), whose title refers to the dwelling places of slaveholders and slaves, respectively, is a modernist masterpiece on Brazilian history that gave new direction to sociological study in the nation.

It was around the close of the modernist period that Rosa's first volume, *Sagarana* (1946), was published. By this time, accompanying a trend of social protest novels, modernism had started to focus on how particular landscapes played into the lives of local peoples, as seen in works by Graciliano Ramos and Jorge Amado. The land plays important roles in the fiction of Rosa, but in nonspecific ways—he

Critics celebrated *Primeiras estórias* and observed the ways in which it represented a departure from Rosa's earlier works—hence his reference to them as "first stories." Responding to the English translation in the *Saturday Review*, Donald A. Yates wrote, "While the stories of *First Stories* are on the surface modest, unplotted sketches, they are infused with a tone of mysticism which suggests insights and meanings that project far beyond their immediate scope." Alexander Coleman, in his review of *The Third Bank of the River and Other Stories* for the *New York Times*, declares, "Like Borges, once we are in Rosa's world, one sentence in, it is almost impossible not to go on. There is a magnet inside each story." After noting that "The Third Bank of the River" is "one of Rosa's best," Coleman goes on to conclude, "The book is full of ... stunning moments; it is a magnificent collection of stories that is already a landmark in modern Latin American letters."

Eduardo F. Coutinho, in a *Dictionary of Literary Biography* volume on Brazilian writers, notes of *Primeiras estórias*, "The new stories are much more condensed, characterized by a sharper philosophical tone, more lyrical, and freer from traditional plot." The volume is seen to surpass the unity of his debut collection, while "rationalism and common sense are called into question more vehemently here than ever before in Rosa's works." Coutinho refers to "A terceira margem do rio" as the "most intriguing" of several stories in the volume that pull together madness and mere absurdity. Coutinho relates that "this story, a jewel of narrative technique, is one of Rosa's sharpest criticisms of the supremacy of rational thought."

In their volume on Latin American writers, Harss and Dohmann offer a glowing assessment of Rosa's literary greatness:

> He is the original mesmeiro, to use one of his own terms: the man who is always himself. . . . What distinguishes him from other writers on the continent is not a literary tendency, which he transcends, but a frame of reference. He is a philosophic novelist in command of both vital forces and the powers of introspection. His work has stature because it gives the full measure of the man behind it.

Harss and Dohmann roundly declare of Rosa, "He not only fulfills a vision but culminates a whole literature." Eduardo Coutinho concludes that "Rosa's work is, par excellence, an art of its century."

CRITICISM

Michael Allen Holmes

Holmes is a writer with existential interests. In the following essay, he considers the title concept of "The Third Bank of the River" as a metaphor for nirvana.

There is no shortage of commentary on the metaphysical and mystical aspects of João Guimarães Rosa's fiction. Jon P. Vincent observes that his first volume, the story collection *Sagarana*, reveals "a mystic vision," while more broadly Rosa's dedication to "spiritual inquiry" has earned him the label of a "transcendent" regionalist. Barbara Shelby, who translated *Primeiras estórias* into English, in her introduction to that work draws attention to Rosa's connections to the American writer Ralph Waldo Emerson, who was among the founders of transcendentalism; Rosa's stories often feature protagonists "to whom nature and the intuition are the keys to knowledge." Mary L. Daniel finds in Rosa's writings "a pervasive telluric mystique"—suggesting he taps into an electrical current coursing over the earth's surface—and sees *Primeiras estórias* as presenting "the intangible conflicts and ecstasies of the human spirit in its ascensional pathway of *becoming*." Luis Harss and Barbara Dohmann declare of Rosa, "He is a mystic, part Catholic, part Taoist and Buddhist, with a religious sense of life, a fervent respect for all living things, and an unquenchable thirst for ultimate knowledge and enlightenment." The reader of the Brazilian edition of *Primeiras estórias* is at once cued to the expansive sense of the stories by the illustrations on the cover, which were drawn by Luís Jardim at Rosa's behest. Among the sets of drawings representing each separate story can be found an abundance of infinity symbols: two on the front cover and four on the back, with another twenty-one appearing in the volume's unique pictorial index. One spiritual concept that comes to the fore in considering the insinuations of infinity is that of nirvana.

The grasping for infinity is quite prominent in "The Third Bank of the River." One might naturally begin by considering the title, which may first come across as simply a clever play on words: any river has just the two banks, one on either side, and so the idea of a river's third bank is somewhat like the idea of, say, the side of the wind, or the top of the sun, or the surface of the

NIRVANA, IT TURNS OUT, IS AN
OVERWHELMINGLY INFINITE PLACE TO BE."

universe; it cannot really be said to exist; the phrase itself is a paradox (that is, a profound contradiction, a supposition of two things that cannot simultaneously be true), suggesting a sort of infinite placelessness—in being nowhere, it could be, and is, anywhere. Many spiritual traditions try to avoid paradoxes, but one tradition makes pointed use of paradoxes in focusing the mind, namely, Zen Buddhism. The idea behind a *koan*, a paradoxical statement used as a basis for meditation, is that the mind of the practitioner will at first struggle to rationally resolve the paradox but may eventually stumble upon a truth behind the statement that cannot be formulated through logic. The practitioner is thus conditioned to let go of the workings of the rational mind in order to access the intuitive, irrational functioning of the mind.

The classic example of a koan is "What is the sound of one hand clapping?" As Russell G. Hamilton Jr. notes in "The Contemporary Brazilian Short Story," Rosa invokes a koan in his later collection *Tutaméia: Terceiras estórias*: "A girl crosses the street. Is she the oldest or the youngest sister?" With each of these formulations, the question cannot be rationally resolved; instead, one must drift beyond the words to find some deeper intuitive meaning, which can only be hinted at by an instructor or peer. The latter question, for example, might be approached by considering the notion that all of humanity is related, in a sense, and one might alternately consider this girl from the perspective of the past or of the future. "The Third Bank of the River" implies a koan in the form of a question, "Where is the third bank of the river?" Reading the title, the reader may imagine that the story will reveal this—but the phrase never appears within the story itself.

Rosa begins his story with an eye-opening discourse by the narrator on whether or not his father might have been crazy. If the narrator's thoughts are taken at face value, one might conclude that a judgment of insanity is undeserved,

but since the narrator is the man's son, he can hardly be considered objective; the underlying suggestion is that the father *was* crazy in some sense. Here again the story can be seen as suggestive of spiritual traditions, in that individuals with striking, at times inexplicable dispositions have been at the heart of many religious movements. One way to describe Jesus of Nazareth is as misunderstood. Eugen Herrigel, in *The Method of Zen*, points out that Zen masters, who have essentially divorced themselves from habitual Western mentalities of all kinds, are "a people of a quite different mold from the ordinary. They seem to be ruled by a special star." This is an apt description of the father in Rosa's story.

The foundation for the mind-set of the Zen master is that provided by Buddhism, which uses ideas like *impermanence* and *nonself* to portray everything as always changing and, being interconnected with all other aspects of reality, without an individual self. Each and every person is instead seen as an aspect of the one universe. Parting with one's individual self is a complicated process whereby preferences, desires, discriminations, materialism, and egotism are all abandoned. One source of suffering, the Buddhist believes, is the thwarting of desires, which will go fulfilled or unfulfilled according to the fate of the universe, over which a person ultimately has no control. Moreover, whether one particular desire goes fulfilled or unfulfilled, it inevitably gives rise to further desires, trapping a person in an endless cycle of want. Full peace of mind can only be attained if one exits this cycle by giving up desire entirely. Now, many people would argue that desire is at the heart of the human experience. Without desire, what becomes of romance, and thus of love, and thus even of family? Can one create a family without the desire that bonds one to one's spouse and to the children produced? This question is in one sense beside the point, because the intent of the Buddhist tradition is not to prescribe a way of functioning as a cog in society, but to lead one to spiritual fulfillment. Some people may follow Buddhist teachings while enjoying a wide variety of life's pleasures, while others may feel moved to commit further, becoming monks or nuns and indeed giving up the possibility of having a family. In many religious traditions, there is a division between the ordinary believers and those who seek a higher spiritual calling and

WHAT DO I READ NEXT?

- Where *Primeiras estórias* contains brief stories averaging only a dozen pages, the stories in Rosa's debut collection, *Sagarana* (1946), are closer to forty pages each, demonstrating a wide range of narrative techniques and literary inventiveness. The title is taken from the Old Norse word *saga* and a Tupí Indian suffix, *-rana*, meaning "rough" or "crude." A translation by Harriet de Onis was published in 1966

- One of the earliest works of *sertão* literature was *Os Sertões* (1902), a piece of ethnographic nonfiction by Euclides da Cunha about an 1890s civil war in which a backlands community pitted itself against the republican forces. Da Cunha opens with a treatment of the terrain of the *sertão*, then scientifically considers the racial character of Brazil's peoples, and lastly narrates the war. An English translation was offered by Samuel Putnam in 1944 under the title *Rebellion in the Backlands*.

- A notable collection from the same era as Rosa's latter collections is Osman Lins's *Nove, novena* (1966), translated by Adria Frizzi as *Nine, Novena* (1995). Lins's postmodern approach is evident in the surreal "Baroque Story or Tripartite Unity," which features several different realities narrated by the same gunman.

- To get to the roots of Brazilian literature one should turn to the nineteenth-century writer Joaquim Maria Machado de Assis, from the Brazilian state of Minas Gerais, whose psychological insight was unmatched in his era. A recently assembled collection of his short fiction is *Chapter of Hats: Selected Stories* (2008), translated by John Gledson.

- Rosa's "The Third Bank of the River" has strong similarities to the Italian author Italo Calvino's novel *Il barone rampante* (1957), which tells of a twelve-year-old who defiantly climbs to the treetops in his family's garden and keeps his promise to never come down. Archibald Colquhoun's translation *The Baron in the Trees* appeared in 1959.

- Ineke Holtwijk, a Dutch newspaper correspondent, provides a startlingly realistic portrait of urban life in Rio de Janeiro in her book *Asphalt Angels* (2003), which follows thirteen-year-old Alex as he adapts to life on the streets with a gang of young people. The story is aimed at high-school students but, with drug use, prostitution, and violence present, is best suited to mature readers.

- A different portion of rural Brazil is treated in the young-adult novel *Keeper* (2003), by Mal Peet, in which a soccer hero called El Gato narrates his youth in the rain forest and how he makes his way to stardom.

---

distinguish themselves by their solitude and self-deprivation.

These issues are relevant to "The Third Bank of the River" because the crux of the story is the effect that the father's actions—abandoning his family to spend every moment of his life on a river—have on his son who remains nearby, the narrator. As befits a short story, the father is characterized briefly, with a few traits that suggest an outline while leaving the reader to fill in the blanks. One can only imagine why the father decided to forsake his family for the river—and one possible line of reasoning is precisely that which would be suggested for a Zen Buddhist. He was always a quiet person and was disinclined to discipline his children, a task he left to his wife. This suggests that the father had a calm personality and did not get worked up over what his children were doing. Perhaps the father had already reached a point where he did not quite desire anything anymore—not to indulge his pride by accomplishing things, inflate his ego through conversation serving to validate his ideas, or govern the direction of other people's lives. What he wanted, rather, one must presume, was a greater peace of mind, a freedom from all the interpersonal obligations that tangle one up in the material world of desires, including his wife's and his children's desires. He must have wanted to simply sink into—or rather float through—existence.

Even in this light, the father's actions remain curious. He might possibly have found peace of mind in a number of simpler ways, such as committing himself to a monastery somewhere, whether near or far from his family. Even then, of course, he would have experienced some degree of interaction with other people, even if just through nearness. In taking to the river as he does, he goes to an extreme, neither speaking with nor acknowledging the existence of any other people, including the members of his family. The demand of the river, in stark opposition to the demands of society, is that he maintain a perfect physical consciousness at virtually all times, a consciousness that has nothing to do with other people, or his sense of self, or any possible desires he or they might have. With no confirmation of his ego to be found in this extreme existence, his self completely dissipates.

The family cannot understand why the father should choose to abandon them so completely, having devised for himself an existence that seems, to use a phrase that Herrigel applies to the outward appearance of Zen, "utterly soulless." In fact, the father's existence on the river might be described as not just soulless or familyless but everything-less—and this is precisely what constitutes the experience of nirvana. In casual usage, *nirvana* is typically intended to mean a state of bliss, but its meaning in Buddhism is more elaborate. As Thich Nhat Hanh states in *The Heart of the Buddha's Teaching*, "Nirvana means extinction, above all the extinction of ideas—the ideas of birth and death, existence and nonexistence, coming and going, self and other, one and many. All these ideas cause us to suffer." Since most of a person's daily activities are founded in one's idea of oneself, specifically in creating happiness for oneself, to eliminate the idea of the self is to release oneself

from all personal motivations and be set adrift on the currents of the universe. Such is nirvana—theoretically.

Nhat Hanh attaches several analogies involving water to the idea of nirvana. To illustrate the notion that nirvana is not a separate dimension of experience but "is the ground of being, the substance of all that is," he invokes the difference between a wave and the water. Attached to concepts, the wave might conceive of itself as only a wave and be sad that it is not water, or that it must die when it crashes upon the shore, losing its waveness and becoming water. But as Nhat Hanh notes, "A wave does not have to die in order to become water. Water is the substance of the wave. The wave is already water. We are also like that. We carry in us the ground of interbeing, nirvana." Thus, if a person can erase the preconceived notions that define the self, in the absence of those notions, nirvana can be realized.

Nhat Hanh also describes the transformation of a cloud into rain, in an analogy that reconstructs the ideas of birth and death:

> When a cloud is about to become rain, she is not afraid. She may even be excited. Being a cloud floating in the blue sky is wonderful, but being rain falling on the fields, the ocean, or the mountains is also wonderful. As she falls down as rain, the cloud will sing. Looking deeply, we see that birth is just a notion and death is a notion.

Harss and Dohmann present some relevant words of the Buddha that Rosa is said to have quoted in his fiction: "Learn, from the rolling of the rivers." Nhat Hanh also offers a river-centered analogy attributed to the Buddha: "'My dear friends,' the Buddha said. 'The Dharma I offer you is only a raft to help you to cross over to the other shore.'" Here the water represents the trials of existence more than the spiritual fluidity of it. *Dharma* refers to the Buddha's body of teachings, and he is suggesting that these teachings will keep a person afloat, but the goal is to reach the other side.

These last analogies help the reader understand the truth behind "The Third Bank of the River." The father, of course, is not trying to get to "the other shore" but is trying to steer clear of the shore, all the while learning from the rolling of the river. Or perhaps, he *is* trying to get to another shore, but only a metaphorical one—to follow along neither the first bank nor the second bank but rather a spiritual third bank. What or where is this third bank? No one, perhaps not even Rosa, could answer this question for certain, as such a koan is not to be resolved. Still, one might conjecture that the third bank is precisely where the father happens to be: suspended in the middle of the river, devoted to it, endlessly following its contours with no motive, no design, no desires, and no purpose. Yet is the father content there? Has he attained a state of bliss? It would hardly seem that he has, because his search for peace of mind has led him to an endless struggle. Just so, some might consider the goal of complete detachment from oneself, including all of one's desires and dreams, to be an inevitable struggle without end. Such a goal may have been attainable for the likes of the Buddha and his most enlightened followers, but the average person may never be able to separate completely from his or her humanity. That the father cannot fully devote himself to nirvana may be signaled by the fact that he does not leave his family completely; though physically he stays clear of the shore, he remains tethered by the idea of the family, and this link to the world is eventually his downfall, as it seems.

The focus of the story gradually shifts away from the actions of the father in isolation to show how his actions affect the family, and finally how the son is compelled to respond. What appears at first to be the story of the father turns out to just as much be the story of the son. The reader may be inclined to imagine that the father, drifting along the third bank of the river, has attained nirvana. He certainly seems to have extinguished all concepts and cut his ties to the world. And yet he never completely loses sight of the ordinary existence that he left behind—it waits for him on the shore, embodied by his son. Thus, when the son offers him the chance to abandon his endless quest, luring him back to the world of desires, he cannot help but jump at the chance. Nirvana, it turns out, is an overwhelmingly infinite place to be. The mere idea of it is too much for the son—even to save his father, he cannot bear to face it. Thus does the father, drawn back toward the shore only to be denied, perish in the version of nirvana he found—along with all his concepts, at last he himself is extinguished. Of course, the narrator only relates that the father was never heard from again, and so the reader may imagine that he does finally find perfect solitude and nirvana somewhere. Still, the son can never escape the guilt over his failure to save his father from his

solitary fate, nor can he ever escape the allure that the idea of nirvana, the bliss of freedom from all thought, represents. As the story closes, the son's lingering mental distress is made clear. As if teased by a vision of heaven, or perhaps a glimpse of infinity, he cannot get the image out of his mind. Torn between his everyday reality and that glimpse of infinity, only upon death, when he can finally be propelled, paradoxically, "down the river, away from the river, into the river—the river"—only then will the son, too, attain something like nirvana.

Source: Michael Allen Holmes, Critical Essay on "The Third Bank of the River," in *Short Stories for Students*, Gale, Cengage Learning, 2014.

Jon S. Vincent

In the following excerpt, Vincent discusses the stories in the collection The Third Bank of the River and Other Stories.

Primeiras Estórias (*First Stories*), a book containing twenty-one short narratives, was published in 1962. It appeared in English in 1968 under the title *The Third Bank of the River and Other Stories*, in a fine translation by Barbara Shelby. It is claimed that Guimarães Rosa chose both the format and the title of his new book after a turning point in his own life, a near-fatal heart attack which he suffered in 1958. These are the "first stories" following whatever revelations might have accrued from the crisis, and they bespeak an author radically changed in outlook. Had his critics and faithful readers attempted to predict a fourth book, logic would probably have led them to anticipate something vaster and more ambitious than *Grande Sertão*, though prudence and an awareness of Guimarães Rosa's genteel intransigence might have produced more outlandish predictions, or, in the cautious, no predictions at all. Perhaps Guimarães Rosa considered the possibility of ever-progressive inclusion and thought it a bad idea. Perhaps the illness itself changed his mind. But these *estórias* (a term for "story" the author rescued from disuse to avoid the ambiguity of the homophone *história*, which means both "story" and "history") are certainly his first.

Some of the characteristics of the early Guimarães Rosa are still present in the book: there persists a fascination with the word and its potential, a view of the world sharpened by a sense of irony, and an engrossment with the duplicity of occurrences. But the focus here is

> THE DENSITY OF LINGUISTIC NOVELTY IS SO GREAT IN THIS BOOK THAT SOME CLAIM TO SEE IN IT A SELF-GENERATING AFFECTATION, ALMOST AS IF THE AUTHOR WERE IMITATING OR EVEN 'PLAGIARIZING' HIS OWN MATERIAL."

microscopic rather than cosmic, and the narrative process relies less on carefully paced climax than on epiphany. The controlled turbulence of the earlier diction has also been replaced by an incisive, condensed vocabulary and syntax which is something beyond mere economy of expression.

An element common to all the first stories is a modification of a substratum found in the previous three books. In *Sagarana*, the plots were all more or less conventionally constructed around the movement of protagonists toward some desired end, which is one reason that resonance in that work carries such a heavy charge of patterned familiarity, since the patterns were largely derived from traditional narrative forms. In *Corpo de Baile*, most plots were constructed around tensions, which implies tension relief as a principal goal of the characters and a principal source of reader experience. And in *Grande Sertão*, both the action and the mystical stratum were connected to yet another traditional narrative device, the quest motif. The stories in *PE* are also constructed around the hermeneutics of becoming, but here the anxiety and tension are relatively reduced in importance—not merely because each tale must come to a climax in a short time due to the brevity of the narrative, but because discovery and fruition are here as much part of effect as the search itself, previously so important. The point in a tale identifiable as a climax in the first three works has been seen as a point at which separate narrative planes finally coincided or crossed, where dramatic situations were unraveled, where mysteries or secrets were revealed, or where obscure motivations were clarified. Even in cases of highly ambiguous characters, such as Dona Rosalina, in "Lélio e Lina," the denouement provided the reader with a satisfactory number

of speculative possibilities about motivations and a plot closure which indicated completion and unrepeatableness. But in *PE* the discoveries made are of such an unorthodox nature, and the characters making the discoveries of such unfamiliar configuration, that released tension is at best oblique and understated; often it is subliminal. Another feature which works on behalf of attenuated response is the highly elliptical diction. As in all of Guimarães Rosa's works, language in *PE* is itself both attractive for its originality and somewhat unsettling because of its unconventionality. Like the structures of the tales themselves, however, language in these stories reverses the visible trend toward gigantism and shrinks to a laconic, eloquent shorthand. Where before Guimarães Rosa could pause and indulge in a leisurely display of linguistic symphonics, the stories in *PE* are delivered in minor keys, in eighth notes, and the loss of a single phrase is disproportionate to its length.

Plot summaries, which have deservedly fallen into general disrepute, have been shown to be of even less than the usual utility in the case of Guimarães Rosa's works. In this book, plot itself is both less revealing and less subject to summary than in the earlier volumes. But the stories in *PE* all share certain characteristics which facilitate useful generalizations. Most critics have commented on the frequent presence in these narratives of deranged or socially marginal characters, for example. One writer has advanced the idea that eccentric acts and "magic helpers" are of key importance, along with children, as determiners of narrative form in *PE*. The feature itself is not precisely a new one for Guimarães Rosa, but only in *Corpo de Baile* were madmen and children of pivotal importance, and then in only half the stories. Here, there is a being of special sensibility and vaguely alien nature as a principal in every tale. Most readers will probably leave the book with an awareness that some pretty peculiar characters are at the center of the transformations operated in *PE*, but it may be less apparent that they share certain traits. At least two of the types included here, children and bullies, may not strike all readers as at all eccentric, but it is fair to say that an appreciation for the implied oddness of these personages is in itself an important first step in grasping the processes at work in the book. It may seem artificial to attempt to establish a relationship between a story whose principal character is a wonder-struck little boy on his first plane ride and another featuring a slovenly Italian immigrant who lives in a haunted house and eats lettuce by the bucketful, but both these stories derive effects from reader appreciation of the roles of characters disengaged from certain aspects of social machinery. The perceptions of and about such beings comprise the meat of the stories.

The feature which all these beings share is their status, temporary or permanent, as outsiders or marginals. Since they are in but not of the locality of the tale, they enjoy both the relative safety of distance and the burden of increased perceptions, something in the manner of a de Tocqueville, whose Frenchness allowed him to observe another society as both grander and more outlandish than any insider could have found it. The example is overly simple, because the vantage points in *PE* are neither political nor quite so systematic, since in at least one case ("The Mirror") the alien being is the subject of his own observation, but the outsider's position is nevertheless metaphorically comparable. In addition to the quality of strangeness or not-belonging, every tale in the book involves a transformation or a becoming—a realization that something important has happened or is about to happen. Since these same marginals are always either responsible for the transformation or the only ones to perceive it, a useful term, applicable to the entire range of eccentrics, might be derived from the anthropological concept of "liminality," or the quality of being "at the threshold." As in "O Recado do Morro" (*Carpo de Baile*), children operate on the threshold along with the mad and the inspired, and as in "Conversation Among Oxen" (*Sagarana*), animals have the same capability as nonparticipant, prescient creatures. In four of the tales of *PE* a child or a group of children functions as the prismatic expanding device of the perception; in one, the liminal being is a cow. The latter example (from "Cause and Effect") is the only isolated liminal animal in the book and the only creature that functions as a "magic helper" in the traditional, folkloric sense. In another three stories, liminality is provided by hoodlums, either in fact or because of a sort of reciprocal perception, in which their very status as tough guys separates them from the other characters. In the twelve remaining tales, liminal beings are of much more obviously alien nature. In these stories, the liminal characters are either inexplicably eccentric, mentally deficient, or outright mad.

These liminal beings either precipitate or perceive the basic transformation, but each transformation in turn depends on an agent or vehicle. As each threshold is approached, an object in the tale assumes particular importance. The process here is similar to the traditional short story use of "active detail," in which one item in the tale becomes a key element in the climax and denouement, usually by repetition. The vehicles in the stories of *PE* range from the very traditional, such as the message-bearer in "Honeymoons," to the scarcely believable, such as the piece of cow dung in "The Aldacious Navigator."

The final common element is the transformation itself, which may be simply a revelation of an unknown truth, in the mold of the traditional short story, or a transcendence, in which the events and characters of the story culminate in an unexpectedly complete resolution. This final becoming, the transformation, is frequently of such an abstract or mysterious nature that any attempt to reduce it to a word or phrase is bound to be thwarted. Transformation is, in fact, the single most important source of effect in the stories of *PE*, but in no story is the change simply one of category or status. The changes which operate in *PE* may depend on an awareness of the duplicity of things; on an appreciation for the capacity things have for appearing to assume new attributes, without actually changing; they may be dependent on the hypersensitivity of the narrator or a liminal being; they may imply second sight.

. . . In "Notorious," events hinge on a theme at least secondarily present in all of Guimarães Rosa's works—the meaning of a word. The story works somewhat less well in English than in the original, because the Portuguese word *famigerado* probably has a somewhat more sinister ring than "notorious." In this story, a bandit chief informs the doctor that a young government man has been going about referring to him as *famigerado*, and he wants to know what the word means. Assured that the word has no pejorative connotations, the bandits ride off. In "The Dagobé Brothers" a similarly threatening situation is unexpectedly defused. Here the liminals are the three formidable brothers of a man murdered by one Liojorge. The expectation of revenge increases when the three uncharacteristically arrange for a funeral for their deceased sibling. Even more surprising is the appearance of Liojorge, whom the brothers immediately conscript as a pallbearer. Virtually all the other characters (and the reader) expect Liojorge to be dispatched at graveside, but instead the brothers admit that their brother was a scoundrel and reveal their intention to move away to the city. One of the dynamic features of this story is that Liojorge appears to the reader to be the threshold being throughout—on the verge of death—and the reversal showing the transformation to be in characters not established as likely candidates for change is a pleasant surprise not just as a plot turn but because it is an artistically appropriate solution. In "My Friend the Fatalist" another rustic is being terrorized by a bully, who has taken a shine to the man's wife and has even followed them when they moved from one town to another. The friend, also a bit on the daffy side, insists that the Greeks, who understood Fate, were right all along. He shows the terrified man his array of weapons and encourages him to take one. He loads a gun himself and follows the man into the street, where the bully is met and liquidated—with two bullets, one of them no doubt redundant.

Read simply as plots, these three stories appear to follow fairly conventional short-story models, and they come the closest of any in the book to having the "surprise ending" of the traditional form. In addition, the thresholds in these narratives are largely dramatic rather than metaphysical, and the transformations which take place, while definitive, are of something less than transcendent importance.

In sharp contrast to this very low threshold construct, three of the stories in *PE* involve marginals who are permanently alienated from their communities. "Sorco, His Mother, His Daughter," one of the most affecting tales in the book, concerns a man, Sorco, who has finally decided to send his mad mother and daughter off to an insane asylum. The whole town turns out to wait for the special railroad car the government has sent. Sorco appears with his two harmless but hopelessly demented relatives, and suddenly the daughter begins to sing a garbled chant. The mother joins in. The train arrives and they are taken away. As he turns to leave, Sorco himself begins to sing the same meaningless song, "... and then, with no agreement beforehand, without anyone's realizing what he was doing, all, with one voice, in their pity for Sorco, began to accompany that nonsense song" (218). The

liminality in this story is not only a permanent condition for the two central threshold characters but is transferred, temporarily, to all the others. Another permanent alien is found in "A Woman of Good Works." This curious tale, narrated in direct address to a plural "you," is about one of the town eccentrics, a crazy woman called Marmalade Mule. The narrator informs his listeners that, although the woman acted as the guide for the repugnant and arrogant blind man Clubfoot, she was really a benefit to the community. He goes on to explain that Clubfoot may have been her son, and that Marmalade Mule had murdered his father and blinded the boy, both deeds worthy of praise, since either of them left to prey on the community would have been worse than any crime. There is also reason to believe that she may have helped Clubfoot along a little when he died. Now, the narrator says, she's dead herself, but just before she died she found a dead dog in the street and carried it off. Why? To prevent illness? Out of pity? For solace? The answer is not, of course, provided, but it would appear that the woman, for all the sordidness of her life, has achieved a kind of grotesque grace foreign to those on this side of the threshold. Perhaps the least "real" of the liminals in *PE* is the character in "A Young Man, Gleaming, White," who appears to have descended to earth aboard a meteorite. Readers of Spanish American fiction will no doubt be reminded of the mysterious types in García Márquez' "The Handsomest Drowned Man in the World" and "A Very Old Man With Enormous Wings," who share the otherworldly appearance and uncanny winsomeness of this personage. The young man appears shortly after an unknown object comes out of the sky causing an earthquake and flood. Taken in by one of the residents, he is almost forced into marriage by an irate father who learns that the young man has placed his hand on his daughter's breast. But the young man appears to be able to get even the most irascible of people to like him. He discovers a treasure for the girl's father and then goes out one night and disappears. After his departure the girl he touched remains in a permanent state of bliss, and all the others experience *saudade* and something like death whenever they think of him. His gleam, it is said, remains.

Two other stories in the book are based on the reader's acceptance of the magical properties of things, but in them the tale hangs not on the surprise manifestation of an enchanter but on a process of internalization. In "Substance," a man named Seo Nésio has inherited a manioc plantation. At the behest of an old woman named Nhatiaga he takes under his care a mysterious girl called Maria Exita, who has been abandoned by the other members of a bizarre family—her mother deranged, her father a leper, her brothers murderers. Put to work at the most difficult job, splitting sheets of dried manioc on stone slabs in the sun, she becomes the focus of Seo Nésio's progressively obsessive attentions. He worries about possible rivals and starts appearing at the laborers' parties just to watch her. He finally goes to see her, and the gleaming substance seems to fuse with the perfect vision of the girl in his mind, driving away all doubts. The story ends with their shared epiphany of perfect love, white and complete. The liminality here operates on several levels, since the substance itself is the ostensible vehicle of revelation, but the girl herself has many of the characteristics of marginality and the old woman might be viewed as a magic helper. Also internalized is the crossing of the threshold in "The Mirror," in which the narrator directs a long metaphysical thesis about existence to an unheard listener. The monologue begins with a dense exposition on the function and place of mirrors, reminiscent in tone and content of the stories of such writers as Jorge Luis Borges. The narrator explains that one day he happened to glance at two mirrors at once and saw himself as a horrible, ugly creature. At that point in his life he began a long inquiry into his image, in which furtive glances and changed lighting were employed to attempt to change the image. Finally realizing that his "double" was the jaguar, the man settled on not seeing feline features in the mirror as a first step to curing his image problem. After avoiding mirrors for some months, he finally looked in one—and saw nothing. After some years, he looked again and saw a light, the beginning of an image, an intersection of planes and angles which indicated a soul in the process of becoming. The question posed by mirrors, he says, is whether or not one has managed to begin existence, and the answer is an unemphatic "Yes?". Here, though the object itself functions as the vehicle of liminality, the recognition of the threshold and the attempted crossing are carried out within the main character, who, though lacking the marginality usually implied in liminals, has by his own cognitive process placed himself at the edge of a transformation.

The tales in this book are not easily broken into categories to facilitate discussion of groups of stories, because the processes of fiction and the variety of effect make such analysis unmanageable. But it does appear that the axis of effect in all the stories is change, and in every case that change implies the crossing of a threshold. An approach to these twenty-one narratives through analysis of the changes is somewhat entangled due to the various ways in which transformations can legitimately be viewed. Three differing approaches, each having some features in its favor, might center on different aspects of the same problem: the degree of liminality (from testiness to outright madness), the agents of change (from objects to animals to time-space), or the character of the changed state itself (from a fleeting rediscovery of youthful vigor to a transcendence of self). In a number of tales, liminality is most apparent in the distinctive properties of a central character. This is the case of seven stories featuring animals or children or both as instruments of focus, and of five stories featuring either permanent alienation or internalization of threshold perception. Four tales hinge on liminal acts, and the remaining five feature principals characterized by a range of estrangement from simple malevolence to pure lunacy. In every case the importance of the transformation is weighed in terms of an abnormal perception of reality: either that of the threshold being or that of the community itself in regard to that being. And each story hinges on an agent of the change, which may be the same liminal being, but may also be some secondary liminal being, such as an animal. Stories in which animate threshold agents are not present have a physical object as a touchstone or key element in the process. In two cases the object is an abstraction: in "Notorious" it is a word, and in "Sorco" it is a song. "Hocus Psychocus" might be included in the same category, since the vehicle in this story is a play which technically does not exist. Only one story ("No Man, No Woman") features an agent of a nature so abstract as to be almost impossible to identify. Though the story takes place in a house, the object-transmitter here appears to be something like time-space, since the story revolves around a thing not even as concrete as memory, but on the *effort* to remember. The third element in each tale is the state achieved or recognized at the end, which in almost all cases is an unspecified condition of simply being beyond. In most stories it defies precise naming, though progress toward and recognition of this state is the principal source of effect in every tale.

At least two other features of these stories deserve consideration. One is time, which, though it occurs only once as the thematic core of a tale, is of extreme importance in at least half the tales and of implied consequence in all. Rather than a technical device, subject to authorial manipulation for heightened effect, time is of such importance in the book as to be considered one of the general themes of the work. The framing tales of *PE* are in part studies of the fluidity of time. "The Thin Edge of Happiness" concludes with the words, "It was—here now and gone again—happiness." And the final tale, "Treetops," begins with the sentence "It was once upon another time." This story also concludes with a section subtitled "The Moment Out of Time," which ends the story with, "And life was coming toward him." The framing of the volume with two tales in which temporality, though oblique, is of such importance, is a clue to another of the basic processes at work throughout the book. The stories in *PE* are all studies of the transitory, of attempts to seize the moment, or of unexpected visitations of chance. As in Guimarães Rosa's other works, there is here a clear sense of the becoming, the crossing (*travessia*) being as important as the stasis presumed to exist on either end of the movement, though here the tales all take place in the final stage of the crossing so that the becoming itself is emphasized. Stories such as "My Friend the Fatalist," "Cause and Effect," and "Nothingness and the Human Condition" are those in which closing or reaching a destiny is most approximated. But even in these tales the concept of time marching inexorably toward some preordained goal is vitiated by a persistent usage of ambiguous time referents which dislocate the presumed linearity of orderly occurrence. This is a feature of diction almost impossible to translate, and it is probably the most notable weakness of an otherwise excellent English version. In "Nothingness and the Human Condition," for example, the first sentence in Portuguese is a convoluted extrapolation of the ordinary story exposition, in which the narrator appears to deny rather than affirm the historicity of his tale. The English version includes the narrator's subsequent observation that "Each of us lives only his future past," but Aunt Liduína's death comes out occurring "with no warning" instead

of "almost suddenly." Another example, of the dozens possible in this extremely time-oriented story, is the English version's phrase "in sin against their common grief," which in the original is "to sin against *saudade*." *Saudade* is also the principal legacy of another character in *PE*, the gleaming young man. In addition, the song in "Sorco," the ascension of "The Girl From Beyond," the unendable play in "Hocus Psychocus," the question about beginning existence in "The Mirror," are all symptoms of passage in process. And each manifestation is a temporal marker of threshold.

The other feature worthy of note is the same one which first attracts or repels readers in all of Guimarães Rosa's works: language. Reading any of his books is an activity that takes a little getting used to, and critics note that *PE* is no exception to the general observation that the author writes in a difficult, hyperexpressive style. But use of language in this book is not what might be expected to be the next step in a trajectory of style which could be traced through succeeding stages in the first three works, though critics still suggest that many readers are likely to be driven away from this book because of the eccentric language use. The density of linguistic novelty is so great in this book that some claim to see in it a self-generating affectation, almost as if the author were imitating or even "plagiarizing" his own material. Mary Lou Daniel notes that the stories in *PE* are the densest of all the author's in the frequency of portmanteau words, the use of verbs formed from adjectives, and ("baroque") syntactic inversions, and she views some of the narratives (notably the "Aldacious Navigator") as so affected as to constitute self-parody. There is no question that any discussion of *PE* which ignores style is bound to suffer greatly by that omission, as there is no question that a great deal of what goes on can be analyzed by discussions of style alone. Even structural analysts admit that the reduction of the tales to the formulas favored by that system is greatly complicated by both the fantastic dimension and by the fact that the *fabula* cannot be adequately rendered without reference to the manner in which it is expressed, implying that, as in the case of *Grande Sertão*, *fabula* and *sujet* are in many ways inseparable. A full discussion of the kinds of effect produced by language itself could illuminate the book considerably, but in general the manipulation of language seems to have the same ends—among them novelty, surprise, and rhythm—envisioned in earlier works.

The particular linguistic feature of this book which sets it apart from the others is the variety of style and mannerisms which comprise tone. Point of view and implied listener are very important considerations in determining the tone of stories, and each tale in *PE* avails itself of a slightly different set of relationships in determining narrative form, with the result that the narrative voices in the stories have an extraordinary range of types and styles. Some are basically humorous (of the hebephrenic variety in "Much Ado"), some of a mysterious, almost nondirective sort, emanating from an unknown source ("No Man, No Woman"), others of a more or less conventional first person ("The Horse That Drank Beer") or third person ("Aldacious Navigator"). In almost all of them there is a dislocation of point of view or a fluctuating between two or more narrative perspectives, and there is almost always a changed point of view at the threshold. Whatever the stylistic variety, every tale in the book is different from every other one, and the tones range from an almost biblical diction ("A Young Man, Gleaming, White") to a serious, didactic tone ("A Woman of Good Works").

Guimarães Rosa has also provided some clues about the nature and style of each story, by including, in the index, a sort of pictographic resumé of each tale following the title. Included are a number of representational figures such as men on horseback, cattle, birds, and a train. But none is quite what one would imagine to be a visual representation of exactly what goes on in the story, because no resumé is without signs from its own cabala. Benedito Nunes has noted that among the symbols used are the standard signs now used for male (animus) and female (anima)—but he cautions that those characters also symbolize copper and iron. The Brazilian edition also features some very suggestive designs on the book jacket, which readers not familiar with Portuguese might find illustrative after having read the stories in English. Among the objects pictured: a flight of toucans, a man astride a horse which is standing next to a huge question mark, a turkey enclosed in what appears to be a halo, a sphinx, a Star of David. There are also several infinity symbols. In the pictographic index, all the stories in the book save one either begin or end with that symbol.

Source: Jon S. Vincent, "*Primeiras Estórias*: At the Threshold," in *João Guimarães Rosa*, Twayne Publishers, 1978, pp. 88–93, 99–107.

Charles E. May

In the following essay, May looks at "The Third Bank of the River" as a work of fabulism.

João Guimarães Rosa is generally agreed to be the most important writer in the development of modern Brazilian fiction. He signals a transition from the realistic regionalist tradition of the early part of the twentieth century to the modern magical realism that has characterized the work of better-known Latin American writers such as Jorge Luis Borges and Gabriel García Márquez. Guimarães Rosa has been called a "universal regionalist," a "transrealist," and a "surregionalist." These terms suggest that, although his content focuses on the people and places of the Brazilian backlands, his style effects a transcendental transformation of the settings and characters into universal spiritual emblems.

Having appeared in several short story anthologies, "The Third Bank of the River" ("A Terceira Margem do rio") is one of Guimarães Rosa's best-known tales. Although the story is grounded in a real place and features realistic characters, the central event of the story makes it highly fabulistic. The tale centers on a son's efforts to understand a father who, without explanation, goes into the river near his home in a small boat and lives his life there by eddying about in one place. The father is not so much a specific person as he is an embodiment of the role he plays, which is typical of the conventions of magical realism. Because all we know of him is that he is a father, his journey on the river, combined with the fact that the central focus of the story is the son's reaction to the event, can be explained only by his paternal status. The question the story poses is, What does the father communicate to the son by wandering aimlessly on the river?

The only other significant action in the story—as the other members of the family get married, have children, and move away—is that the narrator son remains, maintaining his affection and respect for his father. Whenever someone praises him for doing something good, he says, "My father taught me to act that way." The puzzle the son cannot reconcile himself to is why, if the father does not care about his family, he does not go up or down the river but stays so close to home. The central conflict the son faces is the sense of guilt he feels, for his father is always away and his "absence" always with him. At the end of the story, when the son himself has grown old, he calls the father to come in and let him take his place. The old man, however, seems to come from another world, and the son runs away in fear. The son's final hope is that when he dies they will put his body in a small boat in the "perpetual water between the long shores" and that he will be "lost" in the river.

There is no realistic motivation for the father's behavior, nor can it be explained as a parable of a father's abandonment of his social responsibility to his family. Instead, it must be approached as an embodiment of a universal spiritual act. The critic Allan Englekirk has described the father as a "liminal" character whose apparently irrational action to define truth and reality other than the way it is usually defined sets him apart as a heroic figure. James V. Romano has said that the most basic antithesis in the story is between the transcendence of spiritual life, as represented by the father, and the nontranscendence of spiritual death that is suggested by the son.

The river is a traditional metaphor for time that continuously moves yet simultaneously remains timeless and for change that is also permanence. The father's action thus symbolizes the human need to transcend time by remaining in one place as the river flows by. Human beings at their most heroic—some would say at their most insane—are never willing to accept the fact that life is contained, as is water within the two banks of a flowing river. They insist on transcending such limitations and, instead of allowing the river to sweep them on until they die, in seeking a timeless third bank. Although this is the basic responsibility that every father passes on to every son, such an effort means casting oneself off alone, and only a few are willing to attempt it.

In a fable such as this, characters do not act because of realistic or psychological motivation but because the underlying theme and structure demand that they do so. Unless readers recognize the fabulistic nature of the story and the spiritual nature of its theme, they may be tempted to dismiss the father's act as madness. As the son says, however, in his house the word "crazy" is never spoken, "for nobody is crazy. Or maybe everybody."

Source: Charles E. May, "The Third Bank of the River (A Terceira Margem do Rio) by João Guimarães Rosa,

1962," in *Reference Guide to Short Fiction*, 2nd ed., edited by Thomas Riggs, St. James Press, 1999, p. 1056.

SOURCES

"The Best of Young Brazilian Novelists," in *Granta*, No. 121, July 5, 2012, http://www.granta.com/New-Writing/Best-of-Young-Brazilian-Novelists (accessed September 20, 2013).

Coleman, Alexander, Review of *The Third Bank of the River and Other Stories*, in *Modern Latin American Literature*, Vol. 2, *M–Z*, edited by David William Foster and Virginia Ramos Foster, Frederick Ungar Publishing, 1975, pp. 290–91; originally published in *New York Times*, September 9, 1968, p. 4.

Coutinho, Afrânio, *An Introduction to Literature in Brazil*, translated by Gregory Rabassa, Columbia University Press, 1969, p. 231.

Coutinho, Eduardo F., "João Guimarães Rosa," in *Dictionary of Literary Biography*, Vol. 307, *Brazilian Writers*, edited by Monica Rector, Gale, 2005, pp. 328–39.

Daniel, Mary L., "Joao Guimaraes Rosa," in *Studies in Short Fiction*, Vol. 8, No. 1, Winter 1971, pp. 209–16.

"Guimaraes Rosa, Novelist, 59, Dies," in *New York Times*, November 21, 1967, p. 47.

Hamilton, Russell G., Jr., "The Contemporary Brazilian Short Story," in *To Find Something New: Studies in Contemporary Literature*, edited by Henry Grosshans, Washington State University Press, 1969, pp. 118–35.

Harss, Luis, and Barbara Dohmann, *Into the Mainstream: Conversations with Latin-American Writers*, Harper & Row, 1967, pp. 1–36, 137–72.

Herrigel, Eugen, *The Method of Zen*, edited by Hermann Tausend, translated by R. F. C. Hull, Vintage Books, 1974, pp. 23, 29.

Janér, Ariane, *The National Parks of Brazil*, Instituto EcoBrasil, 2010, http://www.ecobrasil.org.br/publique/media/Brazil%20National%20Parks%20-mar%202010.pdf (accessed September 20, 2013).

Martins, Wilson, *The Modernist Idea: A Critical Survey of Brazilian Writing in the Twentieth Century*, translated by Jack E. Tomlins, New York University Press, 1970, pp. 3–14.

Mittermeier, Russell A., Gustavo A. B. da Fonseca, Anthony B. Rylands, and Katrina Brandon, "A Brief History of Biodiversity Conservation in Brazil," in *Conservation Biology*, Vol. 19, No. 3, June 2005, pp. 601–607.

Nhat Hanh, Thich, *The Heart of the Buddha's Teaching: Transforming Suffering into Peace, Joy, and Liberation; The Four Noble Truths, the Noble Eightfold Path, and Other Basic Buddhist Teachings*, Broadway Books, 1999, pp. 136–40.

Rosa, João Guimarães, *Primeiras estórias*, drawings by Luís Jardim, Livraria José Olympio Editra, 1962.

———, "The Third Bank of the River," in *The Third Bank of the River and Other Stories*, translated by Barbara Shelby, Alfred A. Knopf, 1968, pp. 189–96.

Shelby, Barbara, Introduction to *The Third Bank of the River and Other Stories*, Alfred A. Knopf, 1968, pp. v–xi.

Skidmore, Thomas E., *Brazil: Five Centuries of Change*, 2nd ed., Oxford University Press, 2010, pp. 126–79.

Valente, Luiz Fernando, "Against Silence: Fabulation and Mediation in João Guimarães Rosa and Italo Calvino," in *Modern Language Studies*, Vol. 19, No. 4, Fall 1989, pp. 82–92.

Vincent, Jon S., "João Guimarães Rosa," in *Dictionary of Literary Biography*, Vol. 113, *Modern Latin-American Fiction Writers, First Series*, edited by William Luis, Gale Research, 1992, pp. 256–69.

Yates, Donald A., Review of *The Third Bank of the River and Other Stories*, in *Modern Latin American Literature*, Vol. 2, *M–Z*, edited by David William Foster and Virginia Ramos Foster, Frederick Ungar Publishing, 1975, pp. 291–92; originally published in *Saturday Review*, October 19, 1968, p. 32.

Poppino, Rollie E., *Brazil: The Land and People*, 2nd ed., Oxford University Press, 1973.

> With a focus on the activities of ordinary people rather than political events, Poppino's book includes a section devoted to the colonial exploration and settlement of the *sertão*: "Trail Blazer, Cowboy, and Prospector."

Twain, Mark, *Life on the Mississippi*, Penguin Books, 1984.

> First published in 1883, Twain's memoir of his days traveling up and down the Mississippi River as a steamboat pilot and in other capacities demonstrates a more grounded appreciation, so to speak, for the beauty and power of a river.

Vincent, Jon S., *João Guimarães Rosa*, Twayne's World Authors Series No. 506, Twayne Publishers, 1978.

> The most focused critical assessment of Rosa's works appearing in English, Vincent's text includes the notable chapter "*Primeiras estórias*: At the Threshhold," highlighting the many gateways between worlds found in that collection's stories.

FURTHER READING

Bartholomew, Aleck, *The Spiritual Life of Water: Its Power and Purpose*, Inner Traditions/Bear, 2011.

> Published by a small press in Vermont, this text seeks to connect with one aspect of nature—water—in all its capacities as profoundly as possible. Chapter titles include "Springs and Rivers," "Spirals, the Vortex, and the Etheric," and "Water's Cosmic Role."

Jackson, K. David, *Oxford Anthology of the Brazilian Short Story*, Oxford University Press, 2006.

> This is among the most recent collections providing critical commentary, biographical capsules, and stories from dozens of highly esteemed Brazilian authors. "The Third Bank of the River" and six other stories by Rosa are included.

SUGGESTED SEARCH TERMS

Joao Guimaraes Rosa AND The Third Bank of the River

Joao Guimaraes Rosa AND Primeiras estorias

Joao Guimaraes Rosa AND modernism

history of Brazilian literature

Brazil AND short story OR novel

Brazilian author AND Minas Gerais

Brazilian literature AND sertao

sertao AND geography

Buddhism AND river OR water

The War of the Wall

TONI CADE BAMBARA

1996

The story of "The War of the Wall," by Toni Cade Bambara, was first published in *Image* magazine in the early 1980s. Set somewhere in the South during the 1970s, the story is about the painting of what is known as a "wall of respect," a mural on the outside of a building in an African American community. The young narrator and his friend Lou are annoyed that a woman painter from the North is painting something on their favorite wall, and her demeanor irks them. From the beginning, they try to figure out how to drive her away. The story draws on the wall of respect movement that began among African Americans in Chicago in the 1960s, which showed how such walls can engender a deep pride in community, extending from the local to the national and international realms. In examining the nature of African American community, the story is exemplary of Bambara's work.

"The War of the Wall" was reprinted in *Deep Sightings and Rescue Missions: Fiction, Essays, and Conversations* (1996), a posthumous collection of Bambara's writings. A longer version of the story appeared in Carol Booth Olson's *The Reading/Writing Connection: Strategies for Teaching and Learning in the Secondary Classroom* (Pearson, 2007). This version, which is the one often used by educators, is available at http://iweb.tntech.edu/jcbaker/War%20of%20 the%20Wall%20Short%20Story.pdf and on a number of other Internet sites, including

The *"painter lady"* seems to appear out of nowhere with her cans of paint and begins to decorate the wall. *(© Maxx-Studio | Shutterstock.com)*

http://chute.district65.net/teachers/rochem/00CB 82C6-011F5307.8/WAR:WALL001.pdf. These versions of the story differ slightly at various points, in addition to the ending, from the version in *Deep Sightings and Rescue Missions*. This entry follows the text of the story that appears in *Deep Sightings and Rescue Missions* but also makes use of the ending as it appears in the longer version of the story.

AUTHOR BIOGRAPHY

Toni Cade Bambara was born Miltona Mirkin Cade on March 25, 1939, in New York City. She became known as Toni as a young child. Cade lived the first ten years of her life in Harlem. Later, she attended John Adams High School in Queens, New York. She attended Queens College and graduated in 1959 with a bachelor

of arts degree in theater arts and English. That same year her first short story, "Sweet Town," was published in *Vendome* magazine.

In the early 1960s, Cade worked as a family and youth caseworker, then as director of recreation in the psychiatric division of Metropolitan Hospital in New York City. She also continued to study, and in 1965 she was awarded a master of arts degree in American literature from City College of New York. From that year until 1969 she was an English instructor in the SEEK program at City College, after which she was an assistant professor at Livingston College at Rutgers University, in New Jersey, until 1974.

In 1970, Cade adopted the last name Bambara and edited and contributed to the volume of African American women's writing *The Black Woman: An Anthology* (1970), which includes some early work of writers who would later become very well known, such as Nikki

Giovanni and Alice Walker. One year later, Bambara edited *Tales and Stories for Black Folks* (1971), a collection of short stories that includes work by some of her students. In 1972, Bambara's first collection of stories, *Gorilla, My Love*, was published.

Two years later, Bambara moved to Atlanta, Georgia, with her four-year-old daughter, Karma Bene, whose father was Gene Lewis. In 1975, Bambara traveled to Vietnam as part of a women's delegation, spending ten days in Hanoi, the capital city, in July. From 1975 to 1979, she was a writer in residence at the Neighborhood Arts Center in Atlanta, and in 1976 she was visiting faculty at Stephens College, in Columbia, Missouri. A second volume of short fiction, *The Sea Birds Are Still Alive: Collected Stories*, was published in 1977, and Bambara's first novel, *The Salt Eaters*, appeared in 1980. It won the American Book Award in 1981.

In 1985, Bambara moved to Philadelphia and developed her longtime interest in filmmaking. She was the writer and narrator for *The Bombing of Osage Avenue* (1986), a documentary by Louis Massiah, which won the Best Documentary Award from the Pennsylvania Association of Broadcasters and the Documentary Award from the National Black Programming Consortium, both in 1986. Bambara wrote, edited, and narrated several more documentary films.

Bambara died of colon cancer on December 9, 1995, in Germantown, Pennsylvania, at the age of fifty-six. *Deep Sightings and Rescue Missions: Fiction, Essays, and Conversations*, a posthumous collection of Bambara's writings edited by Toni Morrison, was published in 1996. It includes the story "The War of the Wall." Bambara's novel *Those Bones Are Not My Child* was also published posthumously, in 1999, edited by Morrison. Bambara had worked for over twelve years on this novel, which is set in Atlanta during the time of the city's infamous child murders, whereby forty black children were murdered between 1979 and 1981.

PLOT SUMMARY

As "The War of the Wall" begins, on their way to school, two young boys, the unnamed narrator and his cousin Lou, see a woman preparing to paint on their favorite wall. It is the wall of a barbershop, and the neighborhood boys are used to playing all sorts of games against it. They tell the woman, who is from out of town, to stop, but she says she has permission from the owner to paint. The narrator recalls how he and Lou had chiseled the name of Jimmy Lyons on the wall when they heard he had been killed in the Vietnam War. The narrator expresses to the painter his anger that she is interfering with a wall that he says belongs to the kids of Talbro Street (in some versions, Taliaferro Street).

By the time they return from school and pass the wall again, the woman has painted it white and is making further preparations, taping string to the wall and chalking it. Mrs. Morris and her son are watching from their window, while the Morris girl twins have come outside. Side Pocket also comes to watch. The Morris twins bring the painter supper, and Side Pocket tries to talk to her, but she is too focused on her work to take any notice. She eventually tells Frieda Morris to thank Mrs. Morris for the food but claims that she has brought her dinner with her. After refusing the food, she returns to work.

Lou and the narrator go to the family restaurant to talk to the narrator's father and do some chores. At dinnertime the painter comes in the restaurant. It now becomes clear that she did not bring any dinner with her, because she proclaims herself very hungry. In fact, the reason the painter lady rejected the food the Morris twins brought was because it had meat in it, and she is a vegetarian; she does not want any dish that includes meat. But the narrator's mother gets impatient with her many questions about the menu. To the amusement of Lou and the narrator, the painter continues to ask what they think of as stupid questions about ingredients in the dishes on the menu, and Mama gets more impatient. The painter lady finally makes her order—with one additional request for cucumbers and beets in the salad. Mama tells her she will get whatever Lou has put in the salad and then tells her to sit down and be quiet.

Later, on a trip to the country, Lou and the narrator try to get Mama to criticize the painter, but Mama is restrained in her comments. She says the woman is an artist who is painting in public, and there is nothing wrong with that. Despite further attempts by Lou and the narrator to get her to condemn the painter, she declines.

Over the weekend, Lou and the narrator try to think up how they can reclaim their wall. On television they see a movie set in New York that shows a wall in a train station covered with graffiti done with spray paint. This gives them an idea. When they are back home, they buy a can of spray paint.

When they get to the wall, however, the entire neighborhood is there. As published in Bambara's posthumous collection, the story ends abruptly with the line, "And then we saw it—the wall."

Other versions of the story continue: The wall is extremely colorful. By showing one man with a horn and another seated at a piano, it alludes to African American achievements ifn music. The wall also depicts some faces. The narrator recognizes that of Martin Luther King Jr., and his father points out the face of Malcolm X, another African American leader in the 1960s. Harriet Tubman, famous for helping slaves escape, is depicted, as is Fannie Lou Hamer, the civil rights leader. As the narrator continues to look at the painting, he sees more familiar faces: the Morris twins, Frieda and Hattie. Then Side Pocket points out a number of red, black, and green flags and says they are flags of liberation from different countries in Africa. In addition to the various national African flags, those three colors constitute what is sometimes called the Pan-African flag, in which the red stands for the blood that connects all people of African ancestry, as well as blood that has been shed in the cause of liberation; black stands for black people; and green stands for the natural wealth of Africa.

Mama points high up on the wall, where Daddy, the narrator, and Lou are depicted, along with other kids from the neighborhood. Lou spots a rainbow painted on the wall, in the exact place where the kids had chiseled the name *Jimmy Lyons*; the name now appears in a rainbow. Mrs. Morris tells Frieda to read the inscription, which she does aloud. The painter has dedicated to the people of this street this "wall of respect," which she painted in memory of her cousin Jimmy Lyons.

CHARACTERS

Daddy
The narrator's father is called Daddy. His wife runs the local restaurant, while he works at the telephone company (or the firehouse, depending on the version). He takes the family and Lou out to the country to visit the narrator's grandparents for the weekend.

Mr. Eubanks
Mr. Eubanks is a local barber. He once intervened when Mrs. Morris's son was up against the wall, being questioned by the police, and the police let the boy go after Mr. Eubanks said he was not a troublemaker. When the painting on the wall is finished, Mr. Eubanks comes out of his barbershop to admire it, even though he is in the middle of shaving a customer.

Granddaddy
The narrator's family visits his grandparents' farm in the countryside. His grandfather thinks that graffiti artists should be punished by having to clean off all the paint.

Grandma
The narrator's grandmother speaks disparagingly of children who deface things like subway trains with graffiti.

Pop Jacobs
Pop Jacobs is a customer at the restaurant. He is happy because Mama piles more food on his plate to show her exasperation at the painter and keep her waiting.

Lou
Lou is a cousin and friend of the narrator's, and they seem to be almost inseparable. Lou works at the restaurant that is run by the narrator's family, where he makes the salads. Like the narrator, Lou is strongly against the painter, but he is more ambivalent about it than his friend. He admires the technical skill she shows as she prepares the wall and also her ability to concentrate on what she is doing. But this does not stop him from joining with the narrator in the plan to destroy the painter's work with spray paint. Lou is depicted on the wall as spinning a globe on his fingertip.

Jimmy Lyons
Jimmy Lyons is a man from the neighborhood who was killed in the Vietnam War. Mourning him, the young boys chiseled his name in the wall. He was going to teach them how to fish. It turns out that the painter is Jimmy's cousin, and she paints the wall in memory of him.

Mama

The narrator's mother is called Mama. She runs a restaurant in the neighborhood. Mama likes to observe good manners, and she gets irritated when she thinks the painter is being rude. However, later, she refuses to go along with her son and Lou's desire that she say bad things about the painter.

Frieda Morris

Frieda, wearing yellow ribbons, is one of the Morris twins. She brings a dinner plate for the painter and speaks softly. At the end of the story, with the encouragement of her mother, she reads the inscription on the painted wall.

Hattie Morris

Hattie, wearing red ribbons, is one of the Morris twins. Accompanying her sister, she brings the painter a jug of lemonade.

Mrs. Morris

Mrs. Morris is a woman who lives in the neighborhood. She is known as a good cook, and she gets her twin daughters to take food to the painter. She also has a son.

Mrs. Morris's Son

Mrs. Morris's son was once questioned by the police because he was out late.

Narrator

The narrator is a young boy in the neighborhood. His mother runs a restaurant, and his cousin Lou is his close friend. He is indignant when he finds the painter lady interfering with what he refers to as "our wall." He thinks the wall belongs to the kids in the neighborhood. He chides the painter lady quite aggressively. As he observes her both before and after school he is full of contempt, thinking her not only a fool but crazy, too. In the restaurant, he laughs at what he thinks of as her stupid questions about the menu, and he is disappointed when Mama refuses to say nasty things about her. The narrator, with the help of Lou, decides to do whatever it takes to sabotage the painter lady's work, and he tries to enlist his father's support for ideas that would accomplish this, but Daddy, like Mama, offers no encouragement. To accomplish his goal, he buys a can of spray paint. Like everyone else, though, when he sees the wall, he is enthralled by it. He is even depicted on the wall, looking at a row of books.

Painter Lady

The painter lady, as the boys refer to her, is from somewhere in the North. She gets permission from the owner of the barbershop to paint the wall outside. She focuses intensely on her work and shows great skill and efficiency. She takes little notice of the narrator or Lou or Side Pocket as they try to interact with her. The painter lady is a vegetarian who is very careful about her diet, and her questions about the menu in the restaurant exasperate Mama. It is later revealed, when the painting is finished, that the painter lady is the cousin of Jimmy Lyons, and she has painted the wall in memory of him.

Side Pocket

Side Pocket gets his name from his love of playing pool. He likes to hang out at the pool hall and to charm the girls. When the painting is finished and the people in the neighborhood gather around to admire it, Side Pocket points out the flags of liberation and explains what they are in an authoritative voice.

THEMES

Community

Bambara's story depicts a close-knit African American community in the South. It is the kind of neighborhood where everyone knows everyone else. The pool hall and restaurant seem to form the backbone of social life. The young boys form a community within a community when they gather at the wall to play their favorite games, such as handball and pop fly. They regard that wall as their own. Fairly recent events, it seems, have forced the boys to become more insular in their recreational activities. The narrator explains that the "crazies" from across town (meaning whites who felt threatened by racial integration) closed down the park and poured cement in the swimming pool rather than let African Americans use it. In the absence of those recreational options, the boys improvise games against the wall.

Lou and the narrator at first have a very narrow sense of community. They resent the painter lady not only because she is interfering with their wall but also because she is an outsider. She has out-of-state license plates on her car. Mama suggests that she is probably from the North, and it is obvious that the painter lady's

TOPICS FOR FURTHER STUDY

- If you were to create a wall of respect in your community, who would you depict on the wall, and why? Chart out such a wall, including some historical figures and writing notes explaining who they are. Create a Power-Point presentation about your wall and show it to your classmates. If you are artistically inclined, you could also draw or paint a representation of the wall you have in mind.

- Write a short story with a young protagonist who is suspicious of a newcomer to the neighborhood. What does the protagonist discover about the newcomer that makes the protagonist change his or her mind? Write the story bearing in mind Bambara's statement that she preferred not to portray the ugliest aspects of life; she liked to be upbeat and optimistic, while still presenting the truth.

- In a short story, much depends on the point of view—the viewpoint through which the story is told. In "The War of the Wall," the viewpoint is that of the young narrator. Rewrite the story from the point of view of the painter lady. How would each scene in the story unfold from her perspective? What would she be thinking? What would she be feeling? Draw on the characterization of her that the story already provides, but feel free to add more.

- Read *Fannie Lou Hamer: Fighting for the Right to Vote* (2002), by Laura Baskes Litwin, a biography of Hamer for young people. What were the main issues that Hamer tackled during the civil rights movement? Write a blog post in two parts. In the first part, describe Hamer's work in the struggle for voting rights. In the second part, discuss whether the ruling of the Supreme Court in June 2013, in which portions of the Voting Rights Act of 1965 were struck down, is a threat to the rights that Hamer campaigned for. Consult the *New York Times* article "Supreme Court Invalidates Key Part of Voting Rights Act," available at http://www.nytimes.com/2013/06/26/us/supreme-court-ruling.html?pagewanted=all&_r=0, or any other news source about the case.

lifestyle is different from that of the people in the neighborhood. This is shown by the difficulty she has in obtaining what she wants in the restaurant, and by the not-very-friendly response of Mama, who runs the restaurant. Mama later relents and tells her son that the painter is a "decent person." In fact, the older people in the community are more welcoming to the stranger from the North than are the younger people—perhaps because they have some idea of her intentions. It seems that the young are the ones who have the most to learn.

By the end of the story, the narrator and Lou have been exposed to a much wider sense of community than they had formerly been aware of. They learn that the painter they regarded as an outsider is in fact the cousin of Jimmy Lyons, a man who was admired by all the local boys and was killed in the Vietnam War. Moreover, when they see themselves depicted on the wall along with some of the great figures in African American history, they find themselves linked to a wider racial, cultural, and historical identity that is their fundamental heritage. The wall no longer belongs only to the neighborhood kids. It belongs, in a sense, to the entire African American community, with its long struggle for civil rights and freedom, as well as to the wider African liberation movement, as shown by the flags. As the whole neighborhood contemplates the colorful splendor of the wall, people gain an instant, visual appreciation for who they are, where they have come from, and where they are

The painter lady alienates the neighborhood by coming into the restaurant asking for vegetarian dishes.
(© Peter Kim / Shutterstock.com)

going as a wider racial and cultural community. For Lou and the narrator, this amounts to a coming-of-age experience: their mental and cultural horizons suddenly expand as they come into this new, more mature knowledge, and it is likely that, if they have not done so already, they will soon completely reevaluate their former hostility to the painter lady.

Creativity

Although the narrator is too young and inexperienced to appreciate it, the painter lady is an illustration of creativity in action. She presents the figure of the inspired artist. The narrator describes her "scribbling all over the wall like a definite crazy person" as she deftly moves between milk crate, stool, and ladder creating her artwork. "It was like those old music movies where the dancer taps all over the furniture, kicking chairs over but not skipping a beat, leaping over radios and all," the narrator says. Even Lou, who is almost as hostile to the lady as the narrator is, appreciates the skill she is displaying and looks like he wants to applaud. The painter lady maintains an unshakable focus on her work. She is oblivious to everything else. As she finally acknowledges the presence of the Morris twins, who have brought her dinner, she walks over to them looking like she is "in a daze, a trance, another place." The narrator does not understand this, but the painter is simply wrapped up in her artistic vision, inspired by what she is bringing to birth.

STYLE

First-Person Narration

The story is told from the point of view of the young, unnamed boy who narrates in the first-person voice. Everything is seen through his eyes, although he often identifies his views with those of Lou, so the occurrence of the plural "we" is almost as frequent as the singular "I." In this form of storytelling, the thoughts and feelings of the other characters are known only through what the first-person narrator says about them or through their actions as he describes them. The boy's age is never given, but perhaps he is around twelve or thirteen. The story thus features the kind of slang expressions that a boy of that age might use, such as "She was really running off at the mouth" (of the painter lady at the restaurant) and "her beat-up ole piece of car," as well as colloquial, nonstandard forms of speech that may be common in the neighborhood, such as when he says, "my mama don't take no stuff off nobody in her place."

Symbolism

The ordinary wall that the neighborhood boys play games against is transformed into a highly symbolic piece of art. By depicting local people, both children and adults, as well as notable figures in African American history and African flags of liberation, the wall symbolizes community in its widest sense. It is an all-inclusive entity that extends from local to national and international realms and stretches back into earlier twentieth- and nineteenth-century history. Community as depicted on the wall of respect is a source of pride and represents a people's deepest sense of identity. The painted vine that the narrator spots on the wall is a symbol within a symbol. On the vine are flowers that look like faces. The flags look like leaves on the vine. The vine thus symbolizes the organic nature of community. Everyone is connected to everyone else in a perpetually growing, changing tapestry of life.

Elsewhere in the mural, the kids shown looking at books, spinning a globe, or using microscopes and compasses symbolize the value of education, suggesting that education is a liberating force. The rainbow in which Jimmy Lyons's name is embedded is a universal symbol of hope as well as aspiration, as the description of Lou pointing out the rainbow suggests: "He had to tiptoe and stretch to do it, it was so high." As a final touch, the dedication "*To the People of Taliaferro Street*" gives dignity and significance to the ordinary folk of this neighborhood.

HISTORICAL CONTEXT

Wall of Respect Movement

The origin of the wall of respect movement lies in the formation of the Organization of Black American Culture (OBAC) in Chicago in May 1967, during the civil rights movement. A group of fifteen male and female artists within the OBAC came up with the idea to create an outdoor mural on a building on the South Side of Chicago. According to Jeff Donaldson, in his article "The Rise, Fall and Legacy of the Wall of Respect Movement," "the artists chose to depict 'Black Heroes' as positive role models for identity, community formation, and revolutionary action." Donaldson was one of the artists. Others included Sylvia Abernathy, Eliot Hunter, Wadsworth Jarrell, Barbara Jones-Hogu, Carolyn Lawrence, Norman Parish, and William Walker. By agreement, none of the artists' names appeared on the mural, titled *The Wall of Respect*. While the mural was being created, "the Wall became a site for impromptu musical or dance performances, poetry readings, and spoken word events," writes Donaldson. After it was finished, the wall received a lot of publicity and was at the center of community life in the South Side. In August 1967 it was the site of a large rally organized by the Student Non-violent Coordinating Committee, and in October 1967 a festival of African American creativity was organized there by the Forty-Third Street Community Organization. The building on which the mural was displayed was damaged by fire in 1971, and the City of Chicago decided in 1973 to raze the building.

The Wall of Respect inspired similar African American murals in Detroit, Boston, St. Louis, and Philadelphia. There were also murals produced to celebrate Hispanic, Native American, and Asian American culture. According to Edmund Barry Gaither, director of the Museum of the National Center of Afro-American Artists in Boston, as quoted by Norman Parish III in the *Chicago Tribune*, "'The Wall of Respect' was one of the most important artistic events of the 1960s." Gaither also said, "American art wouldn't have regained a sense of social consciousness if it wasn't for the 'Wall of Respect.'" Parish also quotes Margaret Burroughs, founder of Chicago's DuSable Museum of African American History, who said of the city's mural, "It was that piece of work that sparked the whole public art movement in America. Even corporations started painting murals."

African American Heroes

The wall of respect in Bambara's story commemorates four African Americans in particular, all of whom played an important role in the struggle

COMPARE
&
CONTRAST

- **1970s:** On the heels of the 1969 publication of Maya Angelou's memoir *I Know Why the Caged Bird Sings*, the work of African American writers becomes more accepted in mainstream American publishing, and Bambara is one of a number of black female writers who begin publishing their work during this decade. Alice Walker publishes her first novel, *The Third Life of Grange Copeland*, in 1970, and Toni Morrison's first novel, *The Bluest Eye*, is also published that year. Ntozake Shange's play *For Colored Girls Who Have Considered Suicide When the Rainbow is Enuf* is produced on Broadway in 1976 and is published in 1977. It wins a 1977 Obie Award and the Outer Critics Circle Award.

  1990s: Gloria Naylor publishes the bestselling *Baylor's Cafe?* (1992), set in a cafe? in New York in the post–World War II era. She also publishes *The Men of Brewster Place* (1999). Morrison continues to publish acclaimed novels, including *Jazz* (1992) and *Paradise* (1997). Octavia Butler, who has been publishing science fiction since the 1970s, achieves great success with the novels *Parable of the Sower* (1993) and *Parable of the Talents* (1998), as well as the collection *Bloodchild and Other Stories* (1995).

  Today: While Morrison continues to publish novels, such as *Home* (2012), a new generation of African American women writers begins to make its mark. These include Tayari Jones, author of *Leaving Atlanta* (2002) and *Silver Sparrow* (2011), and ZZ Packer, author of the short-story collection *Drinking Coffee Elsewhere* (2003).

- **1970s:** The Vietnam War, in which more than fifty-eight thousand US servicemen die, reaches an end point, as the United States, South Vietnam, and North Vietnam sign a cease-fire agreement in Paris in 1973, and all US forces are withdrawn. In 1974, however, war between North and South Vietnam resumes, and Saigon, the capital of South Vietnam, falls to the Communists in April 1975. South Vietnam surrenders, and Vietnam is unified under the Communist government in the north.

  1990s: The United States resumes diplomatic relations with Vietnam in 1994. Meanwhile, millions of people visit the Vietnam Veterans Memorial in Washington, DC, each year. Inscribed on the wall are the names of all the US servicemen and servicewomen who died in the war.

  Today: Millions of people continue to visit the Vietnam Veterans Memorial each year. The Dignity Memorial Vietnam Wall, a three-quarter-scale replica of the Vietnam Veterans Memorial, travels around the country so that people who are unable to go to Washington, DC, can still see the wall and honor those who served and died. In May 2013, the replica travels to Sacramento, California, one of more than two hundred cities in the United States that have hosted the traveling wall over the years.

- **1970s:** Continuing from the 1960s, when they were first established, affirmative action programs try to ensure that African Americans and other minorities are given the same opportunities in jobs and education that are available to whites. Affirmative action is seen as a temporary measure to reverse centuries of discrimination in favor of whites.

  1990s: Some black conservatives, as well as many whites, oppose affirmative action. They say it is no longer needed and has the effect of undermining genuine achievements by African Americans. Stephen L. Carter, a law professor at Yale University, writes *Reflections of an Affirmative Action Baby* (1992), in which he argues that equality of opportunity can be achieved without affirmative action.

  Today: The Supreme Court has ruled that race may be used as a factor in college admissions, but schools must show that there is no other alternative for creating diversity in the student body.

Seeing a train with graffiti on the news inspires Lou and the narrator to buy spray paint with the intention of defacing the mural. (© ChameleonsEye | Shutterstock.com)

for freedom and civil rights: Harriet Tubman, Martin Luther King Jr., Malcolm X, and Fannie Lou Hamer.

Harriet Tubman was born Araminta Ross around 1820 in Maryland. She was the daughter of slaves. In 1844, she married John Tubman, a free black man, and around that time she changed her name to Harriet. Five years later, Tubman left her husband and escaped via Delaware to Philadelphia. The following year, Tubman returned to Maryland to help the family of her niece escape. Over a period of eleven years Tubman made nineteen trips to Maryland, rescuing approximately three hundred slaves, including her parents and several siblings. She became known as Moses, and was also known for carrying a rifle, which she used not only for defense against enemies but as well to ensure that slaves about to escape did not back out. (She is depicted with a rifle on the wall of respect in "The War of the Wall.") During the Civil War, Tubman enrolled in the Union army as a cook and nurse, also becoming an armed scout and a

spy. After the Civil War, she lived in Auburn, New York. She died in 1913.

Martin Luther King Jr. was a Baptist minister from Georgia. He was educated at Morehouse College and Boston University, receiving a PhD from the latter in 1955. King, who was at the time pastor of the Dexter Avenue Baptist Church in Montgomery, Alabama, led the Montgomery bus boycott in 1955, which marked the beginning of the civil rights movement. King was one of the leaders of the Southern Christian Leadership Conference, which he cofounded in 1957. His organizational skills, inspiring oratory, and commitment to nonviolence made a huge contribution to ending racial segregation in the South. In the march on Washington that he helped to organize in August 1963, two hundred thousand people gathered at the Lincoln Memorial to protest racial injustice. It was on this occasion that King gave his famous "I Have a Dream" speech, in which he shared his vision of freedom and justice. He was awarded the Nobel Peace Prize in 1964. King was assassinated in Memphis, Tennessee, in April 1968.

Malcolm X was born Malcolm Little in Omaha, Nebraska, in 1925. He left school at fifteen and became involved in drugs and crime. He was sentenced to ten years in prison in 1946. In prison he read widely and was converted to the Nation of Islam, a sect of black Muslims who advocated the creation of a separate state for black people. Malcolm X was released from prison in 1952 and worked to promote the goals of the Nation of Islam. The sect grew rapidly as a result of his efforts, and he became a leading figure in the cause of black liberation in the 1950s and 1960s. He said that blacks could resist racism with violence if necessary. In 1964, however, Malcolm X broke with the Nation of Islam and its leader, Elijah Muhammad. He made a pilgrimage to Mecca and became an orthodox Muslim. Subsequently he believed that civil rights for African Americans might be achieved peacefully. This alienated some of his followers, and he was assassinated in Harlem in February 1965.

Fannie Lou Hamer was born in Mississippi in 1917 to a family of sharecroppers. In 1962, she attended a meeting in which civil rights activists were trying to persuade African Americans to register to vote. She became actively involved and was a member of the Student Nonviolent Coordinating Committee (SNCC). She spent the rest of her life working for civil rights, and she showed great determination in spite of being threatened and beaten. In 1964, she founded the Mississippi Freedom Democratic Party as a counter to the all-white Democratic Party delegation that attended Mississippi's Democratic convention that year. In 1965, she ran unsuccessfully for Congress. She died of cancer in 1977.

CRITICAL OVERVIEW

Bambara's short stories have long been admired for the accurate way they depict African American life in setting and dialogue. Alice A. Deck in the *Dictionary of Literary Biography*, in comments that might well apply to "The War of the Wall," writes,

> Much of Bambara's fiction is set outside of the home, on a sidewalk, in a movie theater, in a park or on an athletic field, in a local bar, or in a community center. Bambara's characters are rarely at odds with their geographical environment.... They move through their immediate neighborhood comfortably familiar with the

people and each building, street lamp, and fire hydrant they pass.

Bambara's commitment to a political message has also been noted by reviewers. The reviewer of *Deep Sightings and Rescue Missions* for *Publishers Weekly* comments that Bambara "viewed writing as a political act. The writings collected here show that, unlike many others, she rarely let her activist motives cripple her aesthetic sense or her intellectual honesty." Toni Morrison, in her preface to that posthumous volume, makes a similar point. Morrison writes of Bambara, whom she knew personally, "Any hint that art was over there and politics was over here would break her up into tears of laughter." Morrison remarks of "The War of the Wall," "Gently but pointedly she encourages us to rethink art and public space."

F. Gregory Stewart, in his entry "Toni Cade Bambara" in *Writing African American Women*, discusses "The War of the Wall." He comments that the people in the neighborhood are skeptical about the work the painter is doing

> until the ending where the mural is revealed and no further details are offered. Read either as a boon to the locals or a disappointment, the mural's very ambiguity echoes the apparent growing uncertainty of where African Americans fit within a multiethnic America.

Stewart's commentary refers to the briefer version of the story appearing in *Deep Sightings and Rescue Missions*. In the longer version of the story, the mural is not at all ambiguous. On the contrary, its message is clear and inspiring.

CRITICISM

Bryan Aubrey

Aubrey holds a PhD in English. In the following essay, he examines "The War of the Wall" in light of Bambara's own comments in published interviews about the purpose and nature of her work.

Bambara wrote mostly in the 1970s and 1980s, a time when the civil rights movement had recorded many successes in ending past discrimination against African Americans. Much had been achieved, but there was still a long way to go, and Bambara's work is strongly marked by its concern with the welfare of African American communities and with the injustices and discrimination that continued to exist. Bambara believed, as she told Kay Bonetti in an

WHAT DO I READ NEXT?

- *Gorilla, My Love* (1972) is Bambara's first collection of short stories. It contains fifteen stories set in the rural South and in the North. Eight of the stories focus on young children and adolescents as they live their day-to-day lives in their neighborhood and meet the challenges of growing up.

- *The Black Woman: An Anthology* (1970) is a collection of poetry, short stories, and essays edited by Bambara and including three of her own essays. Contributors include Nikki Giovanni, Audre Lorde, Alice Walker, and Paule Marshall.

- Brenda Wilkinson's *African American Women Writers* (1999) is written for young-adult readers. Wilkinson surveys the work of African American women writers from the earliest times to the modern period. In addition to Bambara, writers discussed include Margaret Walker Alexander, Maya Angelou, Gwendolyn Brooks, Octavia Butler, Nikki Giovanni, Lorraine Hansberry, Frances E. W. Harper, Zora Neale Hurston, Harriet Jacobs, Audre Lorde, Paule Marshall, Terry McMillan, Toni Morrison, Ann Petry, Ntozake Shange, Sojourner Truth, Alice Walker, Ida B. Wells-Barnett, Dorothy West, and Phillis Wheatley. The book is also illustrated.

- Sandra Cisneros is a leading Hispanic American writer who has won numerous literary awards. *Woman Hollering Creek andOther Stories* (1991) is a collection of stories set near the border between Texas and Mexico. Cisneros writes with knowledge, insight, and affection about the lives of her mostly female characters.

- *In Love & Trouble: Stories of Black Women*, by Alice Walker, was first published in 1973. Walker's first collection of short stories, it tells of many black women from a variety of backgrounds, exploring the dilemmas and conflicts they face in their lives.

- ZZ Packer is one of the younger generation of African American women writers. Her 2003 collection of eight short stories, *Drinking Coffee Elsewhere*, has been widely praised by reviewers.

---

interview in 1982, that a writer naturally serves the interests of the community to which he or she belongs, and Bambara identified strongly with belonging to an "oppressed people." She considered her task as a writer to be "to make revolution irresistible." One way she accomplished this, she told Bonetti, was by "celebrating ... victories within the black community." She believed that literature has a certain potency in contributing to positive social change. In 1983, she told interviewer Claudia Tate,

> I work to tell the truth about people's lives; I work to celebrate struggle, to applaud the tradition of struggle in our community, to bring to center stage all those characters, just ordinary folks on the block, who've been waiting in the wings.

The term *celebrate*, used by Bambara in both interviews, is key. Although she spoke in admiration of struggle, Bambara did not allow herself to get mired in the ugliness of life or its darkest corners; she wanted to uplift and nourish her readers with positive resolutions. In her essay "What It Is I Think I'm Doing Anyhow," she tells of how people would often come up to her and tell her nightmarish stories about their own lives, thinking that she could make use of the material, but Bambara was not interested. She did not believe that relaying the ugly aspects of life could lead anyone to the truth about "our deep-down nature," which was what she wanted to convey. Using a musical metaphor to describe the many different types of literature being written, she continued,

---

THE CONFLICTS THAT MAKE THE STORY
WORK ARE NEATLY EMBEDDED AT SEVERAL LEVELS
BUT DO NOT VIOLATE BAMBARA'S PRINCIPLE THAT
SHE DOES NOT DO 'UGLY.'"

I prefer the upbeat. It pleases me to blow three or four choruses of just sheer energetic fun and optimism, even in the teeth of rats, racists, repressive cops, bomb lovers, irresponsibles, murderers. I am convinced, I guess, that everything will be all right.

"The War of the Wall" is an illustration of all these tenets of Bambara's. It is a delightful, uplifting story with a young protagonist; it creates a picture of ordinary folks in their neighborhood and has several deft touches of humor; its extended conclusion is an optimistic, inspiring celebration of community as well as a proud affirmation of over a century of African American history. This does not mean that the author ignores gritty issues of race and politics as they affect the day-to-day lives of her characters, but she handles them with a light touch; the issues are there in the background but do not dominate the story.

Problems of race are made plain early on, when the narrator alludes to the fact that the local park has been closed and the swimming pool cemented over so that African Americans cannot use them. This is a reference to the desegregation of public facilities that took place during the civil rights era. In many towns in the South, the swimming pools were traditionally for use by whites only, and so strong was the desire in some communities to preserve this state of affairs that some swimming pools were indeed cemented over so that whites would not have to swim with blacks. This occurred, for example, in the town of Sanford, Florida, among others. The fact that some white communities were prepared to destroy their own pools rather than submit to legally mandated racial integration gives the reader some idea of the strength of feeling that prevailed in such matters during the 1960s and 1970s (and also an awareness of how far the country has traveled in matters of race since those long-ago days).

Another problematic issue that is touched on in the version of the story published in *Deep Sightings and Rescue Missions*—it does not appear in the extended version—is relations between the people in the neighborhood and the police. One night, the narrator recalls, the police stopped Mrs. Morris's son for no reason other than because he was out late at night. Then they got rough with him, shoving him up against the wall, simply because he was slow in answering their questions. The narrator adds that the police might have gotten even rougher had Mr. Eubanks not shown up and told the police that the boy was not the type to do anything wrong. The race of the police is unstated, but in many African American communities relations between the residents and the often white-dominated police force were tense—a problem that has not gone away even in the 2010s. The story says no more about the issue, but it is established as a fact in the neighborhood that everyone would have been aware of.

Nevertheless, the darker issues in the background do not contribute substantially to the overall mood and tone of the piece. The narrator of course expresses anger toward the painter lady, but that is not because of any larger feelings of injustice (his apparent anger about the incident involving the Morris boy notwithstanding) but because he thinks that the wall belongs to him and the other kids in the neighborhood. His concerns are local and practical. He and his cousin Lou just do not want other people, especially outsiders like the painter lady, messing with "their" wall.

The conflicts that make the story work are neatly embedded at several levels but do not violate Bambara's principle that she does not do "ugly." As she wrote in "What It Is I Think I'm Doing Anyhow," she was "not convinced that ugly is *the* truth that can save us, redeem us." So everything is handled very lightly, with good humor, until the power of the wall is conveyed right at the end. The main conflict is between the narrator and the painter lady, although in the little scene that takes place in the restaurant, Mama becomes part of the conflict, also against the painter lady. The community is not as much against the painter as puzzled by her; while Mrs. Morris sends the twins to her with food, the girls and Side Pocket, as well as Lou and the narrator, are bemused by what seems to be her unfriendly attitude. There are also the seeds of a slight conflict between Lou and the narrator. Lou, in spite of himself, seems to admire the skill of the painter, but the narrator will have none of it. The difference of opinion between the two cousins is handled in a typically amusing manner by the author. When Lou says something about how "hip" the painter lady's technique is, the narrator says, "I dropped my book satchel on his toes to remind him we were at war." The notion of war, then, far from being a reflection of the reality of life in an inner-city zone somewhere, is thus playfully reduced to a child's anger at someone (the painter lady) who is encroaching on his play space.

When the mural is finished and the people in the neighborhood gather to view it, "The War of the Wall" becomes a perfect illustration of Bambara's words quoted earlier, about celebrating victories—that is to say, achievements—in the black community. The comments the narrator makes reveal that while the community marvels at the work the painter lady has produced, it is perhaps not surprising that they appreciate it so much. This is a community that is already, it would appear, proud of its ethnicity and of the African American standard-bearers of the past and present. A signed portrait of Fannie Lou Hamer hangs in the restaurant, the narrator says, and he also recognizes Harriet Tubman because his grandmother has pictures of Tubman all over her house. Bambara said in her interview with Bonetti that part of her job was to "maintain some kind of continuity from the past" for the sake of the children in the community. The family she portrays in the story seems to be doing exactly that. Bambara also emphasized in the same interview that she maintained in her worldview an international dimension. She said, "The African family is worldwide. And to that extent I tend to have an international perspective because I'm concerned about everything that happens to the family." Thus in the story, the Pan-African flag is shown in the mural, with reference to several African countries.

Source: Bryan Aubrey, Critical Essay on "The War of the Wall," in *Short Stories for Students*, Gale, Cengage Learning, 2014.

Gay Wilentz

In the following excerpt, Wilentz discusses how Bambara's work reflects the theme of healing in the literature of the African diaspora.

In the creation of the African Diaspora, the cultural survivalisms and imperatives carried from the African coast were tempered by the specific cultures from which the enslaved Africans came, as recent studies have shown. Equally important, they were mitigated (and often violently) by the societies in which they entered. In the first part on African-based texts, I focus on healing in the Caribbean, specifically Jamaica; here, my discussion centers on African-based healing strategies of an African American community in the United States, a major site of the development of "Western" medicine, along with more hidden sites of healing, often ignored by the American medical establishment. Chapter 1 examined a discourse of healing through Afro-Caribbean oral medicines presented to the protagonist, Nellie—Toni Cade Bambara's *The Salt Eaters* explores a broader base of healing strategies in relationship to other systems, both conventional and alternative, including Native American. However, as is the case with the other works examined in this book, this novel is solidly grounded in the reclaiming of the healing practices and worldview of a violently transplanted and formerly despised culture group. In *The Salt Eaters*, Bambara presents her own take on Mervyn Alleyne's notion of the magical power of the word in Afro-Jamaican culture to identify an African American wellness narrative. Bambara, a politicospiritual healer, tells us of her impetus for writing: "That's what I work to do: to produce stories to save our lives" ("Salvation" 41). Through her evocation of the language and stories of healing, Bambara, in a literary laying on of hands, begins to develop a discourse to help cure the culturally ill. Significantly, the novel also moves us toward a comprehension of medical performance as envisioned by Makinde, in which biomedical practice joins hands with the traditional healers.

In her use of the magical power of the word, Bambara's aim to heal her community reflects a "prevalent strategy in contemporary Black women's writing," according to Athena Vrettos. Although Vrettos unfortunately does not mention Bambara in her article "Curative Domains: Women, Healing and History in Black Women's Narratives," her focus on Alice Walker, Gloria Naylor, and Paule Marshall, who envision "the fragmentation and alienation of Afro-American culture from traditions of its past as a disease that can be healed, and healed specifically by Black women" (471), can easily be expanded to

BAMBARA'S WELLNESS NARRATIVE IS A RITUAL OF RADICAL CHANGE, AND IT (RE)CREATES AN AUDIENCE WITH THE ANCESTORS AS PART OF A CONTINUUM OF BEING."

include Bambara. Vrettos further states: "Through representations of healing, Black women writers seek the inspiration and authority to heal, locating in language a new curative domain" (456). Furthermore, Joanne Gabbin, in "A Laying On of Hands," comments: "[Black women writers] have begun to explore the roots of their cultural traditions and, as symbolic agents in a kind of ritualistic, laying-on of hands experience, are cleansing, healing, and empowering their communities" (246). Along with Marshall's *Praisesong*, Gabbin discusses female empowering texts like Zora Neale Hurston's *Their Eyes Were Watching God*, Margaret Walker's *Jubilee*, and Toni Morrison's *Sula*; however, in her article she does not mention *The Salt Eaters*, a novel that, with the exception of *Praisesong*, deals with healing more explicitly than do the other texts mentioned. Despite the fact that this profound healing text is not discussed in either of these articles, Bambara actualizes these two women's theoretical positions. *The Salt Eaters*, as a healing text, most explicitly relates personal dysfunction to both cultural and global dis-ease. And Bambara, as authorial healer, takes on conventional medicine while creating a strategy for healing in her language and narrative structure. In her woman-centered and African-based discourse, Bambara performs a linguistic "laying on of hands" on her readers and community.

The Salt Eaters, in which two hours of a traditional healing at a community hospital extend out into concentric circles of the lifeblood of an African American community, is a complex novel, considered difficult by many critics and readers. Much of its complexity comes from Bambara's design: "To work at the point of interface between the political/artistic/metaphysical, that meeting place where all contradictions and polarities melt" ("Salvation" 43). But

the complexity also derives from Bambara's extensive use of allusions: New Age terminology, such as tarot, chakras, past lives, astrology, from the cultures that New Agers appropriate; Marxist political discourse and underground American resistance; and most important, African-based mythology, cultural traditions, and healing practices. For Bambara, as for her character Velma Henry and the healers themselves, being well is integrally connected to the acknowledgment of one's African heritage. To glean from the Rastafarian vocabulary, Bambara's "overstanding" is that one can "want to be well," cure the "affliction of disconnectedness," and save lives through residual African cultural practices, which often lie dormant in African American communities. The governing force of the novel is a challenge: How, as a culture, in this case, African American culture, do we begin to get well despite "the psychic and spiritual damage that is being done to us?" (Chandler 348).

For Bambara, whose aim is to produce "stories to save our lives," the link between language and healing is paramount. In her creation of this wellness narrative, she begins to work with Makinde's oral medicine in trying to find a language in which to perform the healing. In an interview with Kalamu ya Salaam, right after the publication of *The Salt Eaters*, Bambara details her design for healing her community, as well as the limitations of English as a language in which to conduct the healing. She comments that English (as well as other corresponding colonial languages) "has been stripped of the kinds of structures and the kinds of vocabularies that allow people to plug into other kinds of intelligences, [at a time when] certain types of language 'mysteries'—for lack of a better word—were suppressed" (48). Like her Caribbean sisters, Brodber and poet Marlene Nourbese Philip, Bambara is trying to disrupt the language to overthrow the dominant linguistic stranglehold that makes English a "foreign anguish" through her own metaphoric activity. Bambara tells us how she tries to invent a new kind of discourse that relates back to that other language in metaphors that include both the idiom of science and the ancestors: "I'm trying to break words open and get at the bones, deal with symbols as though they were atoms. I'm trying to find out not only how a word gains its meaning, but how a word gains its power" (48). In searching to find how words gain the power to heal, Bambara, who prematurely died of cancer as I was writing this book, takes on the role of ancestral spirit guide, and leads us linguistically through a healing, decentering both our language and the sense of linear narrative, making the connections to heal the whole person. In her holistic vision, "everything becomes a kind of metaphor for the whole" (Salaam 50). In what Bambara herself calls a "thrown-open" book, she traces the whole through a personal healing, the reconstruction of the community through the medicine people, the warriors, and the artists. Furthermore, she links this growth to combating the "national suicide" that Metzger identifies through our society's environmental disasters and nuclear wastes, especially the environmental racism committed on so-called minority communities.

... Bambara, as diviner-healer, guides her readers through breakdown and healing. Through the oral medicine of this wellness narrative, Bambara tells us that the "natural response to stress and crisis is not breakdown and capitulation, but transformation and renewal" ("Salvation" 47). In this novel, Bambara presents to us, as readers, a way to begin our own process of transformation as her authorial narrator comments during the storm: "One would tap the brain for any knowledge of initiation rites lying dormant there, recognizing that life depended on it, that initiation was the beginning of transformation and that the ecology of the self, the tribe, the species, the earth depended on just that" (247). The movement toward health is linked to a turning inward and outward, to recovering lost parts of ourselves, to the ritual of transformation, not only for individuals, but for the earth itself. When Bambara calls for an "ecology of the self," she is both returning to the source of health as part of a balance among self, community, and the earth, and expanding notions of political activism and spiritual growth as part of a healing act. *The Salt Eaters*, as part of this transformational process, explores the necessary relationship between personal health, cultural affiliation, political activism, and spiritual growth; moreover, it opens a door for the scientists to commune with the healers to fight for a healthy planet. Bambara's wellness narrative is a ritual of radical change, and it (re)creates an audience with the ancestors as part of a continuum of being.

Source: Gay Wilentz, "A Laying On of Hands: African American Healing Strategies in Toni Cade Bambara's *The Salt Eaters*," in *Healing Narratives: Women Writers*

Curing Cultural Dis-ease, Rutgers University Press, 2000, pp. 53–56, 78.

Elliott Butler-Evans

In the following excerpt, Butler-Evans discusses the particular kind of feminism in Bambara's short stories.

The several ways in which Toni Cade Bambara's short stories were produced assured them a wide audience. Collected and presented as single texts, they were widely anthologized in feminist anthologies, particularly those produced by "women of color"; and Bambara often read them aloud as "performance pieces" before audiences. Yet they have rarely been the object of in-depth critical attention.

Bambara's role as storyteller resembles Walter Benjamin's description of such a person. Benjamin's storyteller, a person "always rooted in the people," creates a narrative largely grounded in the oral tradition of his or her culture and containing something useful in the way of a moral, proverb, or maxim that audiences can integrate into their experiences and share with others. Hence, the story becomes the medium through which groups of people are unified, values sustained, and a shared world view sedimented.

Benjamin's reflections on the story in general are relevant to the cultural practices that informed the production of the Afro-American short story, which is largely rooted in the Black oral tradition. Many Afro-American writers, among them Hurston, Chesnutt, Ellison, and Wright, not only produced short stories but incorporated into their novels folklore drawn from the oral culture.

Working within this framework, Bambara attaches political significance to the short story. Introducing an early collection of her short stories for Black children, she discusses the historical link between Afro-American folktales and short stories. She creates for her readers an imagined setting in which Black families gathered in kitchens to share stories that challenged and corrected representations of Blacks in the dominant historical discourse, fiction, and film. She urges young readers to "be proud of our oral tradition, our elders who tell their tales in the kitchen. For they are truth." In an interview with Claudia Tate, Bambara elaborated on her commitment to the short story, stating that she viewed it as highly effective for establishing political dialogue:

> I prefer the short story genre because it's quick, it makes a modest appeal for attention, it can creep up on you on your blind side. The reader comes to the short story with a mindset different than that which he approaches the big book, and a different set of controls operating, which is why I think the short story is far more effective in terms of teaching us lessons.

Like her works in other genres, Bambara's short stories primarily aim at truth speaking, particularly as *truth* is related to the semiotic mediation of Black existential modalities. Of primary importance are the construction and representation of an organic Black community and the articulation of Black nationalist ideology. Nevertheless, her two short story collections, *Gorilla, My Love* and *The Seabirds Are Still Alive*, are marked by dissonance and ruptures; in both volumes, Bambara's insertion of themes related to the desires of Black women and girls disrupts and often preempts the stories' primary focus on classic realism and nationalism.

In *Gorilla*, Bambara's use of the young girl Hazel as the primary narrator results in a decentering of the stories. In each narrative, a subtext focused on issues with which girls and women are confronted threatens to displace the racial discourse that is in the dominant text. The stories in *Seabirds*, which are generally more explicitly political than those in *Gorilla*, directly inscribe the tensions between racial and gender politics. The stories in *Seabirds*, then, signal a pre-emergent feminist consciousness. In this collection, more complex development and representations of Black women of "the community," increased marginalization and deconstruction of mythologies centered on Black males, and the general highlighting of feminine and feminist issues indicate a heightening of tensions between gender and racial politics. . . .

Source: Elliott Butler-Evans, "Desire, Ambivalence, and Nationalist-Feminist Discourse in Bambara's Short Stories," in *Race, Gender, and Desire: Narrative Strategies in the Fiction of Toni Cade Bambara, Toni Morrison, and Alice Walker*, Temple University Press, 1989, pp. 91–93.

SOURCES

Bambara, Toni, "The War of the Wall," in *Deep Sightings and Rescue Missions: Fiction, Essays, and Conversations*, edited by Toni Morrison, Pantheon Books, 1996, pp. 57–66.

———, "What It Is I Think I'm Doing Anyhow," in *The Writer on Her Work*, rev. ed., edited by Janet Sternburg, W. W. Norton, 2000, pp. 157–58.

Bonetti, Kay, "An Interview with Toni Cade Bambara," in *Conversations with Toni Cade Bambara*, edited by Thabiti Lewis, University Press of Mississippi, 2012, p. 35.

Deck, Alice A., Review of *Deep Sightings and Rescue Missions*, in *African American Review*, Vol. 33, Spring 1999, pp. 170–72.

———, "Toni Cade Bambara," in *Dictionary of Literary Biography*, Vol. 38, *Afro-American Writers after 1955: Dramatists and Prose Writers*, edited by Thadious M. Davis and Trudier Harris, Gale Research, 1985, pp. 12–22.

Doerksen, Teri Ann, "Toni Cade Bambara," in *Dictionary of Literary Biography*, Vol. 218, *American Short-Story Writers since World War II, Second Series*, edited by Patrick Meanor and Gwen Crane, The Gale Group, 1999, pp. 3–10.

Donaldson, Jeff, "The Rise, Fall and Legacy of the Wall of Respect Movement," in *International Review of African American Art*, Vol. 15, No. 1, 1991, pp. 22–26, https://coral.uchicago.edu:8443/display/chicago68/The + Rise, + Fall + and + Legacy + of + the + Wall + of + Respect + Movement (accessed August 27, 2013).

"Fannie Lou Hamer Biography," Biography.com, http://www.biography.com/people/fannie-lou-hamer-205625 (accessed August 28, 2013).

"Harriet Tubman Biography," Biography.com, http://www.biography.com/people/harriet-tubman-9511430 (accessed August 28, 2013).

"History Red, Black & Green," Universal Negro Improvement Association and African Communities League website, http://www.theunia-acl.com/index.php/history-red-black-green (accessed August 27, 2013).

Lee, Trymaine, "In Black Sanford, a Place to Gather and Wait for a Verdict," MSNBC website, July 12, 2013, http://tv.msnbc.com/2013/07/12/in-black-sanford-a-place-to-gather-and-wait-for-a-verdict-2/ (accessed September 2, 2013).

"Malcolm X Biography," Biography.com, http://www.biography.com/people/malcolm-x-9396195 (accessed August 28, 2013).

"Martin Luther King Jr. Biography," Biography.com, http://www.biography.com/people/martin-luther-king-jr-9365086 (accessed August 28, 2013).

Morrison, Toni, ed., Preface to *Deep Sightings and Rescue Missions*, Pantheon Books, 1996, p. ix.

Olson, Carol Booth, *The Reading/Writing Connection: Strategies for Teaching and Learning in the Secondary Classroom*, Pearson, 2007, pp. 34–38.

Parish, Norman, III, "'Wall of Respect': How Chicago Artists Gave Birth to the Ethnic Mural," in *Chicago*

Tribune, August 23, 1992, http://articles.chicagotribune
.com/1992-08-23/entertainment/9203170088_1_mural-site-
controversial-mural-mexican-artists (accessed August
27, 2013).

Review of *Deep Sightings and Rescue Missions*, in *Publishers Weekly*, November 4, 1996, http://www.publish
ersweekly.com/978-0-679-44250-9 (accessed August 27,
2013).

Stewart, F. Gregory, "Toni Cade Bambara," in *Writing African American Women: An Encyclopedia of Literature by and about Women of Color*, edited by Elizabeth Ann Beaulieu, Greenwood Press, 2006, p. 45.

Tate, Claudia, "Toni Cade Bambara," in *Conversations with Toni Cade Bambara*, edited by Thabiti Lewis, University Press of Mississippi, 2012, p. 53; originally published in *Black Women Writers at Work*, edited by Claudia Tate, Continuum, 1983.

"Traveling Vietnam Wall Coming to Sacramento," in *Daily Democrat* (Woodland, CA) online, May 19, 2013, http://www.dailydemocrat.com/ci_23277595/traveling-
vietnam-wall-coming-sacramento (accessed August 29,
2013).

"Wall of Respect," Social Design Notes, June 7, 2005, http://backspace.com/notes/2005/06/wall-of-respect.php
(accessed August 27, 2013).

Williams, Pete, and Erin McClam, "Supreme Court Raises Bar for Affirmative Action in College Admissions," U.S. News, NBCNews.com, June 24, 2013, http://usnews.nbc
news.com/_news/2013/06/24/19115041-supreme-court-
raises-bar-for-affirmative-action-in-college-admissions?lite
(accessed August 29, 2013).

FURTHER READING

Franko, Carol, "Toni Cade Bambara," in *A Reader's Companion to the Short Story in English*, edited by Erin Fallon, R. C. Feddersen, James Kurtzleben, Maurice A. Lee, and Susan Rochette-Crawley, Greenwood Press, 2001, pp. 38–47.

> Franko provides a biography of Bambara and a critical analysis of Bambara's short stories. The book as a whole covers about fifty short-story writers, many of them African American and Asian American.

Gates, Henry Louis, *Life upon These Shores: Looking at African American History, 1513–2008*, Alfred A. Knopf, 2011.

> This is a well-illustrated book that surveys five centuries of African American history. There are over seven hundred images, including maps, fine art, photographs, cartoons, and posters.

Holmes, Linda Janet, and Cheryl A. Wall, eds., *Savoring the Salt: The Legacy of Toni Cade Bambara*, Temple University Press, 2007.

> This volume is an appreciation of Bambara's work and an assessment of her significance as a writer, filmmaker, and social activist. Contributors include Toni Morrison, Amiri Baraka, Abena Busia, Pearl Cleage, Sonia Sanchez, Nikki Giovanni, Eleanor W. Traylor, Audre Lorde, Rudolph Byrd, and Ruby Dee. The book includes some photographs of Bambara.

Valerio, Anthony, *Toni Cade Bambara's One Sicilian Night: A Memoir*, Bordighera Press, 2007.

> Valerio is an Italian American writer, and this is a memoir of his close relationship with Bambara.

SUGGESTED SEARCH TERMS

Toni Cade Bambara

The War of the Wall AND Bambara

wall of respect

ethnic mural

civil rights movement

Harriet Tubman

Fannie Lou Hamer

Malcolm X

Martin Luther King Jr.

Vietnam War

The Winner

BARBARA KIMENYE

1965

"The Winner" is a short story by the Ugandan author Barbara Kimenye. The story was included in Kimenye's collection of short stories *Kalasanda*, published in 1965, which depicts life in a traditional village in Buganda, a kingdom within Uganda. Written in the voice of a village gossip, Kimenye uses humor to create engaging characters and entertain her readers.

Written shortly after Uganda gained independence from Great Britain, the story is about the long-suffering Pius, whose life is turned upside down after he wins a small fortune in a soccer pool. He finds himself surrounded by greedy family and friends, but he is more concerned about the intentions of the assertive Cousin Sarah. "The Winner" has been included in *African Short Stories: A Collection of Contemporary African Writing* (1970), edited by Charles R. Lawson, and *Unwinding Threads: Writing by Women in Africa* (1983), edited by Charlotte H. Bruner.

AUTHOR BIOGRAPHY

Barbara Kimenye was born Barbara Clarke Holdsworth on December 19, 1929, in Halifax, a town in West Yorkshire, England. She was the daughter of a West Indian doctor and a Jewish mother who converted to Catholicism. As a

Pius is happy to win the football pool, but he does not become upset when he learns he must share the winnings with others.

(© Warren Goldswain | Shutterstock.com)

child, she attended a convent school. As a young woman, she studied in London, where she trained to become a nurse. She met Bill Kimenye in London, where the two married. Bill Kimenye was the son of a Bukoba chief in Tanganyika, which is now Tanzania. The couple moved to East Africa in the 1950s.

Kimenye divorced her husband and moved to Uganda in the 1960s with her two sons to be near friends. She took a job as secretary to Edward Mutesa II, who was the *kabaka*, or king, of Buganda, an independent realm in a federation with Uganda. She also worked as a journalist. In fact, Kimenye was one of the first female journalists in Uganda.

In 1965, she moved to Kenya, where she worked as a journalist for the *Daily Nation*. That same year she published her collection of short stories *Kalasanda*, which includes "The

Winner." She released the sequel, *Kalasanda Revisited*, shortly after the success of her first book. Kimenye followed her short-story collections by creating her most beloved fictional character, Moses. The Moses stories were written for children and focus on the adventures of a mischievous young boy and his classmates. The first of these books, *Moses*, was published in 1967. The Moses books have been translated into multiple languages and reprinted over the years.

Kimenye moved back to London in 1975, where she worked as a race relations adviser and continued to write stories for children. She returned to Uganda in 1986 and later to Kenya. Finally, she moved back to London in 1998, where she lived until her death on August 12, 2012.

PLOT SUMMARY

"The Winner" is told from the perspective of a village gossip. The story begins when Pius Ndawula, an older coffee farmer in the Bugandan village of Kalasanda wins a football pool worth seventeen thousand pounds. (The term *football* is used in the British sense and refers to soccer.) After the report of his winnings spreads, family, friends, and reporters descend on Pius's home. Most of his relatives want him to invest in their businesses.

Salongo, an old friend of Pius's, was the first person Pius informed about the winnings. He is the custodian of a landmark, Ssabalangira's tomb. The tomb is in need of repair, and Salongo hopes that Pius will give him money to improve the tomb as well as his home. Although he is described as "almost blind and very lame," Salongo makes his first journey out in years to visit Pius at his home. He believes that the journey will be worth his effort.

The crowd in Pius's house becomes overwhelming for him. A woman named Nantondo is able to slip into a picture reporters are taking without Pius's knowledge. She is reported as his wife by the newspaper, which angers Pius. He is particularly annoyed with a woman who introduces herself as Cousin Sarah. She takes charge of his home and comments that he needs a woman in the house. Salongo does not approve of Cousin

Sarah and warns Pius to stay away from her, saying, "She's a sticker!"

In the midst of the chaos, Pius has very simple plans for his winnings. He hopes to extend his *shamba*, or personal farm, where he grows coffee beans, and repair or replace his home. He also plans on investing in hens so that he can sell eggs. This part of the plan shows the changes then occurring in postcolonial Africa. He and Salongo believe that eating chicken and eggs causes infertility in women, but the female welfare officer is encouraging women to eat more eggs and chicken.

Although Pius is happy to be surrounded by family, his house becomes too crowded as the day progresses. The text describes a sea of *kanzus* and *busutis*. *Kanzus* are male garments, and *busutis* are female garments. The telegram that Musisi brought with the news that Pius has won begins to fall apart because so many people handle it. A reporter from the BBC attempts to interview Pius, but Salongo orders his friend not to answer any questions. Pius remains silent, frustrating the reporter's efforts.

Cousin Sarah offers to answer the reporter's questions on Pius's behalf. During the interview, she tells the reporter that Pius lives alone, but she will remain to take care of him for as long as he needs her. She also claims to be his closest relative through marriage. The household is shocked by her behavior. Pius is horrified by her answers, and Salongo reminds Pius that Cousin Sarah is "a sticker." By teatime, Pius is exhausted. Cousin Sarah serves *matoke*, a dish made of plantains, with the tea, but Pius is too tired to eat. Cousin Sarah chases people away from Pius so that he can rest.

Yosefu Mukasa and Kibuka visit Pius in the evening, and they are concerned by how tired Pius looks. They also meet Cousin Sarah, who tells Yosefu that he knew her late husband. Pius overhears their conversation and realizes that Sarah is not a close relation. Her husband was the stepson of one of his cousins, making her familial bond "virtually nonexistent." Kibuka tells Pius that he looks tired, and Salongo remarks that it is because the relatives are "scavengers." Pius insists that it is normal for family to come and share his joy, but Salongo is not convinced. Salongo adds that he is sure Cousin Sarah is out to get Pius because he knows her type.

Salongo's remarks amuse Yosefu, who asks Pius to come stay at his house and escape the crowd. The relatives are making fires and dancing, which Yosefu points out will make resting difficult for Pius. Cousin Sarah tells Pius that he should go, and she promises that she will look after the house while he is gone. Pius hesitates, but Salongo tells him to go so that he can get away from Cousin Sarah. Cousin Sarah overhears Salongo, and she gives him a contemptuous look.

Pius and Salongo both leave with Yosefu because Yosefu has promised to drive Salongo back to the tomb. Salongo is happy because Pius promised to give a portion of the winnings to help build a new house at the tomb. Pius relaxes with Yosefu and his wife Miriamu, and he remembers that the BBC interview is going to play on the radio. They listen to Cousin Sarah answer the reporter's questions, and Pius is reminded of Salongo's warnings about her intentions.

The next morning, Miriamu insists that Pius remain one more night and rest. After lunch, Musisi and Cousin Sarah arrive. Miriamu goes out to meet Cousin Sarah, and the two women become instant friends. Musisi has another telegram with him. He informs Pius that there was an omission in the first telegram, and Pius actually has to share the prize with three hundred people. This will leave Pius with roughly one thousand shillings. Pius is not displeased with the news and calls it a great deal of money, which confuses Musisi.

Cousin Sarah agrees that Pius does not need such a large sum of money as the original prize. She also adds that the family would not have given Pius any peace if he had won the full amount. Musisi informs Pius that his relatives have caused considerable damage to his home. They ate all of his plantains and trampled part of his garden. Cousin Sarah did stop them from digging up the sweet potatoes. Pius is upset, but Cousin Sarah tells him that she will have her sons help replant the garden after the relatives leave. Pius admires her ability to handle the situation. Musisi takes Cousin Sarah back to clear the relatives out of Pius's house, and he promises to bring Pius home the next day.

Pius is not happy about the state of his home when he returns. Cousin Sarah, however, explains how she thinks the house can be repaired and improved. Pius tells her his plans for the prize money, which still includes giving a potion to Salongo. Cousin Sarah gives him her ideas for the future of the household and tells him that she will send for her six hens so that they can sell eggs. Pius remarks that she sounds like she plans on staying.

Cousin Sarah admits that she is not happy living in the same household as her son and his new wife. She remembered that Pius was a kind man from a previous meeting, and she believed that he would need her to look after him once news spread that he had won the football pool. She explains that she is used to having her own way and did not quite consider that Pius might prefer to be alone.

The next week, Pius visits Salongo at the tomb of Ssabalangira. He gives Salongo one hundred shillings, which Salongo begrudgingly takes. Salongo bitterly comments that Pius will find life expensive with a woman living in the house and that Sarah will want to get married soon. Pius informs him that the wedding is scheduled for the next month. Salongo warns Pius not to marry Sarah. Pius is only concerned for a moment. He is certain that marriage is the right choice when he considers what she has already done. Pius stands up to Salongo and tells him that he will expect his friend at the wedding. Surprised, Salongo agrees to try to be there. He also offers Pius bananas and cabbage to take home to Sarah. He ends by declaring her "the real winner."

CHARACTERS

Kibuka

Kibuka comes to visit Pius with Yosefu. He comments that Pius does not look well.

Cousin Sarah Kivumbi

Cousin Sarah presents herself as a relative by marriage, but in reality, there is no familial bond between her and Pius. She remembers Pius from a previous meeting and comes because she is certain that he will need her. She takes charge of the household and announces her intention to stick around, which annoys Salongo and Pius. She chooses to remain with Pius even after she learns that he will not receive all of the prize money. Cousin Sarah believes the loss is good for Pius because it means that

his family will leave him alone. Pius is impressed with her plan to improve his home and farm. When he asks if she intends to stay, she admits that she is used to having her own way and never thought that he might prefer to be alone. By the end of the story, she and Pius plan to marry.

Miriamu Mukasa

Miriamu is married to Yosefu. She takes care of Pius when Yosefu brings him to their home. Miriamu meets Cousin Sarah, and the two women instantly decide to become friends.

Yosefu Mukasa

Yosefu is a friend of Pius's and the husband of Miriamu. He is concerned about Pius's health when he comes to visit. He asks Pius to come stay with him and Miriamu so that his friend can rest.

Musisi

Musisi delivers the telegram to Pius with the news that he won the pool, and he delivers the news to Salongo at Pius's request. He brings Cousin Sarah with him when he delivers the second telegram with the news that Pius must share the winnings with three hundred people. He also brings Pius home from his stay with Yosefu and Miriamu.

Nantondo

Nantondo is a woman who slips into a picture that is being taken by the press. Pius is angry that she is reported to be his wife. Pius also suspects that Nantondo is the person who told Salongo that Cousin Sarah is still at his home.

Pius Ndawula

Pius Ndawula is an older coffee farmer who lives in Kalasanda, a village in Buganda. News spreads that he has won a football pool worth seventeen thousand pounds, and his extended family comes to wish him well and ask for money. He generously welcomes them into his home, which results in overcrowding and damage. He also notifies Salongo of the news and promises to give him a share of the winnings.

Pius is annoyed when Cousin Sarah arrives and takes over his household. The crowd and attention from the reporters also exhaust him. His friends are concerned for his health, and he goes to rest at the home of Yosefu and Miriamu. While he is there, Musisi brings the news that a mistake was made, and Pius will have to share the pool winnings with three hundred other people, leaving him with one thousand shillings. Pius is pleased with the news. Impressed by Cousin Sarah's ability to manage his household, Pius decides to marry her.

Salongo

Salongo is the custodian of Ssabalangira's tomb. He is old, lame, and almost blind. He visits Pius hoping to secure funds for the tomb and his home. Salongo does not like Cousin Sarah, and he warns Pius to stay away from her. He is disappointed when Pius is only able to give him one hundred shillings of the winnings. Salongo finally accepts that Pius is going to marry Sarah and declares her the "real winner."

Welfare Officer

The welfare officer encourages women to eat eggs and chicken, which Pius believes causes infertility.

THEMES

Greed

The theme of greed is apparent throughout "The Winner." The friends and family of Pius visit under the pretense of congratulating him on his good fortune, but they inevitably ask him for money. Their greed is not limited to his money. They also take advantage of Pius's hospitality, showing a complete disregard for his property and his comfort. They eat his food, stay up late dancing, and damage both his house and his garden. The greedy guests do not offer to repair the damage or contribute to the food supply. Instead, they leave without saying goodbye once they learn that Pius is not entitled to the fortune they came to enjoy.

The greedy behavior is not confined to distant relatives. Pius's old friend Salongo also hopes to profit from the winnings. Salongo visits with the purpose of obtaining money for the tomb, and he leaves in a happy mood because Pius promised him a large sum. His expectancy is clear when Pius brings him one hundred shillings out of the meager sum he won. He "looked at it as if it were crawling with lice." He is obviously disappointed that the amount is not larger and blames Cousin Sarah for using up Pius's money.

Female-Male Relations

"The Winner" shows the complexity of relations between men and women in East Africa. Salongo has a distrust of women, which he conveys to Pius. He views the female characters as controlling and manipulative, and certain actions appear to support his view. For example, Nantondo sneaks into a picture with Pius and is reported to be his wife. Cousin Sarah takes over the household without consulting Pius, which both the men find to be both annoying and frightening. Cousin Sarah does not fit into societal expectations for women because she does not act subserviently.

Neither Salongo nor any other man intimidates Cousin Sarah. She represents the changing role of women in postcolonial Buganda. This change in society is also reflected in food customs. Pius considers how he and Salongo hold the traditional belief that eggs and chicken cause infertility when women eat them. This conflicts with the advice of the welfare officer who encourages women to eat protein to improve their health and the health of their children.

Cousin Sarah's behavior may not be typical, but other characters, including Yosefu and Miriamu, consider her "a fine woman." Cousin Sarah is honest about her shortcomings, admitting that she is used to having her own way and that she never considered Pius would not want her to stay. She distinguishes herself, however, by being useful and choosing to remain with Pius after he finds out that he has won much less money than he thought he had. Her industriousness and reliability impress Pius, who changes his opinion of her and decides they should marry. Pius's high estimation of Cousin Sarah causes Salongo to respect her, declaring her "the real winner."

Reversal of Fortune

A reversal of fortune occurs twice in "The Winner." The first reversal occurs when Pius learns that he has won a pool worth seventeen thousand pounds. The common coffee farmer instantly becomes wealthy. The news of the wealth, however, does not change his life for the better. Pius remains unaltered in character after receiving news of the winnings, but the news does change the people around him. Extended family and an old friend gather around

TOPICS FOR FURTHER STUDY

- Read *The False Princess* (2012), by Ellis O'Neal. Set in a fictional realm, this young-adult novel tells the story of Sinda, a teenage girl who was raised as the princess Nalia only to discover she was a decoy. Removed from the only life she has known, Sinda discovers a talent for magic from this reversal of fortune. Write your own short story about a reversal of fortune. Include at least one character from "The Winner" and one from *The False Princess* who meet because of magic.

- Research the oral stories of the Bugandan people and how they are interpreted in art. Consider the impact that these stories have had on modern literature. Design a website that provides an overview of important Bugandan legends and folktales. Be sure to include links to artistic and literary representations of these stories.

- Research the events that followed Ugandan independence, focusing on the politics of the 1960s and 1970s between Buganda and the rest of Uganda. Write a paper that explains the important events and people of the time. Create a multimedia presentation to accompany your paper and present it before the class.

- Read the young-adult novel *Climbing the Stairs* (2008), by Padma Venkatraman. This is the story of Vidya, a teenage girl in colonial India who dreams of going to college. Like Cousin Sarah, she is not subservient, but she has little hope of making her dreams come true after her father is injured and her life changes forever. Write a short play in which Vidya and Cousin Sarah meet. What advice would Cousin Sarah give to Vidya? Perform the play with a friend and record the performance. Present the recording in class.

- Choose a short story from *Kalasanda Revisited*, the sequel to *Kalasanda* and "The Winner." Consider ways that the characters interact and help each other. Create a blog for one character from each story. Have the characters discuss what they would do with the winnings from the next football pool. Make sure that your answers accurately reflect the characters Kimenye created.

Pius to take advantage of his good fortune. All of the attention leaves Pius exhausted and overwhelmed. Yosefu reacts to Pius's exhaustion by offering his own home as a refuge.

The second reversal of fortune occurs when Pius learns that there was a communication mistake and he will not receive the full amount. His share of the winnings will amount to one thousand shillings. Pius is pleased with the change because the original amount was more than he needed. This reversal of fortune is in Pius's favor because he is able to return to his old life with some improvements. His family leaves his home without causing any further damage when they learn the news. In the end, Pius gains enough

money to make repairs to his home, and he gains Sarah as a wife and companion.

STYLE

Foil

A foil is "any person who through contrast underscores the distinctive characteristics of another," according to William Harmon and Hugh Holman's *A Handbook to Literature*. The greedy characters in this story act as foils for Pius. His only desire is to fix his home and expand his farm. He does not want a fortune,

Pius has modest plans for his winnings, like investing in raising hens. (© Matt Howard / Shutterstock.com)

and he is relieved when he learns that he will only receive one thousand shillings. Pius further shows his generosity by giving Salongo one hundred shillings of his winnings. This behavior is in stark contrast to that of many of the people around him. His generosity is accentuated when he is compared to Salongo and his extended family, who take advantage of his generosity and try to collect money from him.

Point of View

"The Winner" is told from a limited third-person point of view. In *A Glossary of Literary Terms*, M. H. Abrams defines this point of view as that of a narrator who "tells the story in the third person, but stays inside the confines of what is perceived, thought, remembered and felt by a single character (or at most by very few characters)." The narrator only shares the thoughts and feelings of specific characters. A few thoughts of Salongo, Pius, Yosefu, Musisi, and Miriamu are revealed to the readers. Cousin Sarah, however, remains a mystery. Outside of the moment when Miriamu and Cousin Sarah mutually size each other up and become friends, everything that the

reader learns about her comes through her words and actions.

Tone

Kimenye makes use of an informal, humorous tone in "The Winner." The author establishes an informal tone by using simple language and descriptions to tell the story because, as Hebe Welbourn notes in her review of *Kalasanda*, the story is told by a stereotypical gossip. The language and descriptions engage the reader and make the story more believable. The humor can be seen in the descriptions of Cousin Sarah's unwanted interventions and Salongo's reactions to her behavior. The encounter between Pius and the reporter is another humorous episode that helps set the tone of the story.

HISTORICAL CONTEXT

The 1960s in Uganda

The 1960s was a time of upheaval in East Africa, particularly Uganda and Buganda, where "The

COMPARE
&
CONTRAST

- **1960s:** Buganda is part of Uganda but retains a certain level of autonomy. It has a *kabaka*, or king. Ugandan prime minister Milton Obote orders an attack on the Bugandan palace in 1966. King Freddie escapes, but in the 1967 constitution, the kingdom of Buganda is dissolved.

  Today: Buganda is again a subnational kingdom of Uganda with limited autonomy. It was reestablished in 1995 with the ratification of the current Ugandan constitution. The *kabaka* is Ronald Muwenda Mutebi II.

- **1960s:** Women in Uganda are expected to be subservient to men. However, women do have religious and political influence. Groups such as the Uganda Council of Women work for recognition of issues affecting women.

  Today: Uganda has laws protecting the rights of women. The protection of women's rights, however, varies in areas where leaders are more likely to adhere to traditional views of women.

- **1960s:** Uganda gains its independence from Great Britain in 1962. The nation experiences political divisions once independent. Obote rules in an increasingly authoritarian manner after he becomes president in 1966. A new constitution is drafted in 1967, and the nation faces years of dictatorial rule under Obote and later Idi Amin.

  Today: President Lieutenant General Yoweri Kaguta Museveni, who took control in 1986 but is now elected by popular vote, leads Uganda. Economic recovery has occurred after many years of mismanagement, but there is racial tension in Uganda, and the nation still faces conflict with militant groups such as the Lord's Resistance Army.

Winner" is set. Formerly a British colony, Uganda gained its independence on October 9, 1962. The new nation included the kingdoms of Ankole, Buganda, Bunyoro, and Toro. Buganda was the dominant kingdom in the region. In fact, the name Uganda comes from Buganda.

The British originally planned to integrate Buganda within Uganda. The *kabaka* or king, Frederick Walugembe Mutesa II, known as Freddie, however, "demanded that Buganda be separated from the rest of the protectorate," according to *Uganda: A Country Study*, edited by Rita M. Byrnes. Before independence, Buganda accepted an agreement whereby it "would enjoy a measure of internal autonomy if it participated fully in the national government."

After independence, Milton Obote was established as the prime minister, and the *kabaka* of Buganda became president and head of state. Regional divisions, however, remained strong. In 1964, the Uganda military mutinied, demanding more power, which Obote granted. On February 4, 1966, a vote of no confidence designed to remove Obote from power was passed in the Ugandan parliament. Obote responded by suspending the constitution and creating a new constitution in which the prime minister held the most power. Under the new constitution, Buganda's autonomy was revoked. When Bugandan leaders protested, Obote ordered the Ugandan army to march on the Bugandan palace on May 24, 1966. According to "The 1966 Crisis," the army was unable to catch King Freddie, and he fled to exile in England. Obote subsequently "imposed a new 'Republican' constitution on the nation and declared himself President without first calling an election."

Women in Uganda

Traditionally, women were considered subservient to men in Uganda. According to *Uganda:*

Pius's house is taken over by newfound relatives. *(© Oleg Znamenskiy | Shutterstock.com)*

A Country Study, "Women were taught to accede to the wishes of their fathers, brothers, husbands, and sometimes to other men as well, and to demonstrate their subordination to men in most areas of public life." Despite their subordinate status, women were very influential in society. They were religious leaders, and they had influence in politics. Women's groups were extremely influential during the independence process. "Early in 1962, the Uganda Council of Women, formed in 1946, spearheaded the women's cause," as Victoria Miriam Mwaka states in an article for *Women's Studies Quarterly*. The issues addressed included education, property rights, health care, and the right to work. During this time, women managed to make small progress. In the entry "Feminism and Literature" in *The Companion to African Literatures*, it is pointed out that women became accepted in literary circles: "Beginning in the 1960s ... women writers became more numerous and more widely read."

The 1970s and 1980s were difficult decades for women in Uganda because of the political unrest that followed the first few years of independence. Years of division and violence devastated the economy, and more women entered the workforce. Still, they were expected to act subserviently. The late 1980s and 1990s saw a rise in government support for protecting women's rights and interests. For example, the 1995 constitution made discrimination based on gender illegal. Additionally, Uganda became the first African nation to have a woman, Dr. Specioza Wandira Kazibwe, as vice president. Kazibwe served in that capacity from 1994 to 2003. The extent to which women's rights have been protected vary according to region and custom. Violence in northern Uganda, for example, has limited advances for many women. Additionally, local leaders have not always upheld the rights of women.

CRITICAL OVERVIEW

Kimenye's work has delighted several generations of readers. Critics, however, have not always been kind to her. Her unwillingness to discuss the political upheaval of Uganda in her works, even though her stories take place in a contemporary setting, was often condemned by her peers and critics. As Nancy J. Schmidt points out in an article for *African Studies Review*, one critic has called Kimenye "an uncommitted writer who does not deal with the issues affecting Africa today."

As is pointed out in the entry "Literary Criticism: East Africa" in *The Companion to African Literatures*, critics have also taken issue with the fact that Kimenye wrote her fiction in English. Some critics place higher value on Afro-centric literature written in African languages. Welbourn notes in "Village Gossip," her review of *Kalasanda*, that the book "has been conceived in English and would not really translate into Luganda." She does offer some praise for the work: "*Kalasanda* provides an entertaining diversion for anyone who enjoys village gossip." The entry on Kimenye in *The Companion to African Literatures* confirms the popularity of Kimenye's short stories by noting that *Kalasanda* and its sequel were reprinted regularly.

Despite the criticism that Kimenye's work has not been relevant to Ugandans, her Moses series was studied in East African schools, and the books became instant classics. They were translated into multiple languages and found receptive audiences. In fact, the series was relaunched shortly before Kimenye's death in 2012 to delight another generation of schoolchildren.

CRITICISM

April Paris

Paris is a freelance writer with an extensive background writing literary and educational materials. In the following essay, she argues that Cousin Sarah is an East African feminist character whose actions are interpreted through the bias of the other characters in "The Winner."

In her short story "The Winner," Barbara Kimenye explores societal expectations and the roles of women. Playing with female expectations and stereotypes in East Africa, the author creates a feminist overtone through the character of Cousin Sarah. She is both the controlling female whom Salongo fears and the industrious woman whom society prizes. Her character, however, is not contradictory. The characters

> IN THE END, THE READER LEARNS TO SEE HER AS A FEMINIST IDEAL FOR EAST AFRICA, A STRONG WOMAN WHO IS ABLE TO CONTRIBUTE TO THE LIVES OF OTHERS."

around her create their own interpretations of Cousin Sarah's motives based on their personal observations and worldview. In the end, the reader learns to see her as a feminist ideal for East Africa, a strong woman who is able to contribute to the lives of others.

Cousin Sarah is not a traditional female character because she deviates from the societal norms of a compliant woman by taking control of her own life, along with Pius's life. As Jean de Grandsaigne and Gary Spackey point out in "The African Short Story Written in English: A Survey," "The formidable cousin Sarah (who is no cousin at all!) does not hesitate to invent a fictitious family relationship with Pius Ndawula in order to further her marriage plans." At first glance, Cousin Sarah appears to embody the traits that men should avoid in women. She is a liar who is also manipulative and controlling.

Pius initially sees the worst in Sarah. He is annoyed and fearful when she does not conceal her intentions to remain in his home. He dislikes the way that she takes over the household and "kept loudly remarking that he needed a woman about the place." Pius's view of Cousin Sarah, however, is partially influenced by Salongo, who continually calls her "a sticker." Salongo says that he knows her type, and he seems convinced that marrying Cousin Sarah would be the worst thing that Pius could do. Salongo is not quiet with his opinion that she would bring Pius unhappiness. Early in the story, it is easy for the reader to agree with Salongo and assume that she is simply out to snare a wealthy husband. The view of her, however, changes as new characters are introduced and the story progresses.

Cousin Sarah's aggressiveness and stubborn determination are not the only ways in which she deviates from societal norms. She also breaks away from convention by taking the lead with

WHAT DO I READ NEXT?

- Doreen Baingana's *Tropical Fish: Tales from Entebbe* (2006) is a collection of linked stories about schoolgirls set in 1970s Uganda. It exposes readers to the work of a modern female author from Uganda.

- Published in 2000, *African Literature in English: East and West*, by Gareth Griffiths, introduces students to the works of authors from different regions in Africa. Complete with criticism and historical commentary, the volume helps students understand the circumstances under which authors worked.

- *East African Literature: Essays on Written and Oral Traditions* (2011) is a collection of essays that examines the literature of East Africa, including aspects of gender, style, and history. Edited by J. K. Egara Kabaji and Dominica Dipio, the text is an example of modern criticism from Africa.

- *Moses and the Movie*, by Kimenye, is part of the author's beloved series that features the character Moses. Published in 1996, this children's book shares the adventures of Moses as he tries to take part in a movie.

- In *The Oral Tradition of the Baganda of Uganda: A Study and Anthology of Legends, Myths, Epigrams and Folktales* (2010), Immaculate N. Kizza examines the oral legends and stories of the Bagandan people. Readers will enjoy learning about the myths and legends, which provide a greater understanding of Ugandan culture.

- *People and Cultures of East Africa*, by Peter Mitchell, is written for a young-adult audience, making it a useful introductory text on the subject of East Africa. Published in 2006, the book provides valuable information about the geography and cultures of East Africa.

- *Uganda: A Nation in Transition; Post-colonial Analysis*, by Godfrey Mwakikagile, provides valuable insight into the history, politics, and culture in postcolonial Uganda. Published in 2012, the book is ideal for anyone interested in studying the country and its people.

- *Uganda since Independence: A Story of Unfulfilled Hopes* (1992), by Phares Mutibwa, closely examines the cultural and political upheaval that occurred after Uganda gained independence in 1962.

- Set in Pakistan, *Beneath My Mother's Feet* (2008) is a novel that tells the story of Nazia, a teenage girl who faces a reversal of fortune and must work as a maid. Amjed Qamar's story examines how losing something can lead to greater gains in life.

- Published in 2012, *Curveball: The Year I Lost My Grip* is a young-adult novel by Jordan Sonneblick that tells the story of an American teenager who suffers a reversal of fortune, somewhat like Pius in "The Winner." When an injury ends Peter's athletic ambitions, he finds new interests and a new love.

Pius. According to the book *Uganda: A Country Study*, "Women's roles were clearly subordinate to those of men, despite the substantial economic and social responsibilities of women." Sarah serves Pius food, but she is not subservient. When she takes over his interview with the BBC, Cousin Sarah causes a stir among the spectators. Not only does she speak on his

behalf, she also makes public her intention to remain with Pius indefinitely. Again, Cousin Sarah seems to reinforce the idea that she is a troublesome woman, but other characters do not see her in the same light as her detractors. Yosefu, for example, does not judge Cousin Sarah as harshly as Salongo does. Although he is "taken aback" by Cousin Sarah's behavior, he does not condemn it. He was a friend of her late husband, which indicates he probably understands her character better than Salongo does. Yosefu finds the idea that Salongo knows Cousin Sarah's type amusing because Salongo has come into contact with so few women over the course of his life. Rather than warning Pius to steer clear of Cousin Sarah, Yosefu simply says that she is a "fine woman," a sentiment that is echoed by his wife, Miriamu, after she meets and sizes up Cousin Sarah.

Miriamu behaves like a traditional wife. She welcomes Pius as a guest in her home even though her husband gave her no notice to prepare. Miriamu cooks and cares for both Yosefu and Pius without complaint. In fact, she demands that Pius remain another night with them so that he can rest. She is a respectable woman in every way, which makes her encounter with Cousin Sarah very revealing. When the two women meet, they "decided to be friends." Like her husband, Miriamu comments to Pius that Cousin Sarah is a "fine woman." This statement indicates that she believes Cousin Sarah would be a very good wife for Pius and a useful addition to their community.

When seen through the eyes of Yosefu, Miriamu, and soon Pius, Cousin Sarah becomes the epitome of a positive feminist character in East African terms. As the entry "Women in Literature: East Africa" in *The Companion to African Literatures* states, a feminist character "asserts above all the indomitable will of women to participate fully in the life of their societies." Cousin Sarah epitomizes this definition. She helps control the damage that the relatives do to Pius's home, and she prevents them from eating all of the poor man's food. Additionally, she reveals plans to improve the home after she clears out the scheming crowd. Her main concern is for Pius and, by extension, his community. She looks after Pius because she believes that he needs her; she does not care about his fortune. In fact, she agrees with Pius that the original amount of the winnings was far too much, and she adds that his family would have given him no peace with such a large sum.

The news of Pius's winnings changes the people in his life. Even his old friend, Salongo, visits with the hope of gaining money from Pius. Tellingly, he calls the relatives who have the same expectations "scavengers." No doubt, he projects his own expectations of securing financial security from Pius onto Cousin Sarah. While he is concerned about his friend, Salongo views the other guests as rivals for the money that he needs for the tomb and his home. His attitude and comments suggest that he believes Cousin Sarah will be a financial drain on Pius. Disappointed that Pius does not share more of his meager winnings, Salongo blames Cousin Sarah. His response to Pius's generosity is to say that having a woman about will be expensive.

In reality, Cousin Sarah is anything but a financial drain. She plans to have her sons replough Pius's garden. Additionally, her ideas for improving the house after the relatives damage it are both frugal and functional. She also intends to send for her hens, which will not only increase the household income but also provide women in the community with greater access to eggs and chicken. Pius is impressed by her intelligence and capability. When she reveals that she came to Pius because she believed he would need her in the aftermath of winning the pools, he is able to see Cousin Sarah as a kind if somewhat "impetuous" woman.

Cousin Sarah's kind motivation is partially obscured by her indomitable spirit. She refuses to back down to anyone once she has decided to stay with Pius. She is not worried when she hears Salongo's insults and responds by giving the man "a look that was meant to wither him." Additionally, she dominates the crowd in Pius's home. She keeps people away from him when he becomes tired, and she limits the amount of damage that his relatives do. This strong spirit that Salongo sees as a threat is actually a boon to Pius because she uses it to benefit others.

Contrary to Salongo's opinion, Cousin Sarah's presence does not weaken Pius; it empowers him. Throughout "The Winner," Pius allows Salongo to dominate him. He is unable to speak in the BBC interview because Salongo repeatedly tells him not to say anything. Additionally, Salongo's rants serve to fuel his fear of Cousin Sarah. After Pius sets a date for his wedding, however, he finds the strength to stand up to Salongo. He does doubt his decision after Salongo warns him against marriage, but the doubt does not last long: "Then he thought of Sarah, and the wonders she had worked with his house and his *shamba* in the short time they had been together." This line of thought reinforces his belief that marrying Cousin Sarah is the best decision he can make. As a result, Pius becomes authoritative with Salongo and says that he will expect his dear friend at the wedding the next month.

The new strength that Pius exhibits surprises Salongo, who offers no further warnings or predictions of doom. Instead, he respectfully offers Pius cabbage and bananas for his "good lady." Salongo accepts Sarah as part of Pius's life and as part of the community. He concludes by admitting that she is "the real winner." This comment refers to her strength and determination, which make her an admirable feminist character who cannot be held back rather than a weak stereotype.

Cousin Sarah remains unchanged in the story, but the characters view her differently. Salongo sees a stereotype, a woman who is out to marry a wealthy man and control him. Yosefu and Miriamu, however, view her as a fine woman, which provides the reader with a clue to her true character. In the end, her strength of spirit, intelligence, and kindness becomes apparent to Pius, who sees the benefit of marrying her. The transformation does not take place within Sarah; it occurs within the mind of Pius as he takes the time to perceive her as she is rather than through Salongo's biased viewpoint.

Source: April Paris, Critical Essay on "The Winner," in *Short Stories for Students*, Gale, Cengage Learning, 2014.

Jonathan Hunt

In the following obituary, Kimenye's life and achievements are summarized.

Barbara Kimenye, who has died aged 82, was one of East Africa's most popular and best-selling children's authors. Her books sold more than a million copies, not just in Kenya, Uganda and Tanzania, but throughout English-speaking Africa. Many of her more than 50 titles are still available. Best remembered is her Moses series, about a mischievous student at a boarding school for troublesome boys. Though not always well-behaved, Moses was never malicious, possessing all the good, bad and imaginative qualities of a teenager.

His classmates at Mukibi's Educational Institute for the Sons of African Gentlemen included his closest friend, the big-for-his-age King Kong, a dedicated fan of the singer Miriam Makeba, to whom "he believed he was virtually engaged" since a secretary sent him a signed photo. Rukia, with his love of law and order,

could never keep out of anyone else's business, while Matagubya had a source of banana beer.

Perhaps the most colourful of the characters in Dorm Three was Itchy Fingers, "always very good about giving back people's belongings—even if, as occasionally happened, he absent-mindedly picked them up again later in the day." To the whole crew, Barbara brought her readable, but never patronising, style, and story-lines that gripped but never disconcerted her readers.

Barbara Clarke Holdsworth was born in Halifax, West Yorkshire, the daughter of a Jewish-born Catholic convert mother and a West Indian doctor father. She attended Keighley girls' grammar school before moving to London to train as a nurse. There she met many students from East Africa, and married Bill Kimenye, son of a chief from Bukoba in what was then Tanganyika. They settled in his home town on Lake Victoria in the mid-1950s. After the marriage broke up, she moved, with a toddler and another baby on the way, across the lake to Uganda, where she had friends. In Kampala, the capital, she was reacquainted with many people who had been some of the first Ugandan students in Britain. By now they were becoming the leaders and professionals of what would soon be an independent Uganda.

The then *kubaka* (king) of Buganda, Edward Muteesa II, invited her to work as a private secretary in his government. She lived near the palace, and her two sons, Christopher (Topha) and David (Daudi), became close to his family and other members of the royal household.

Barbara always had a gift with words (she wrote her own newspaper as a child of 11) and became a journalist on the *Uganda Nation* newspaper, possibly the first black woman in East Africa to perform such a role. She also developed a talent for storytelling, writing down the tales she told to children.

Moving to Nairobi, Kenya, in 1965 to work on the *Daily Nation*, and later the *East African Standard*, Barbara was wooed by publishers who, post-independence, sought talented authors who wrote for and about African children. However, her first book, *Kalasanda*, for OUP, was a tale of Ugandan village life, followed by *Kalasanda Revisited*. It was after this that she turned her hand to stories for children and schools.

Barbara lived in Nairobi until 1975 when, with both sons in England, she moved to London. There she worked for Brent council as a race relations adviser, while continuing to write. She assiduously followed political developments in a disrupted Uganda and played an active role supporting exile groups opposed to the rule of Idi Amin, and later the second Milton Obote regime.

In 1986, with the overthrow of Obote, she returned to Uganda. She was to spend a further three years in Kampala before deciding to relocate to Kenya where she spent the next 10 years in semi-retirement—though still writing at least one book a year. In 1998 Barbara finally settled back in London where she lived happily and was much involved in community affairs in Camden.

Shortly before her death she received the news that the Moses series was about to be relaunched by OUP and also to be translated into Kiswahili.

Christopher died in 2005. She is survived by David, and a granddaughter, Celeste.

Source: Jonathan Hunt, "Barbara Kimenye: One of East Africa's Most Popular Children's Authors," in *Guardian* (London, England), October 22, 2012, p. 32.

SOURCES

Abrams, M. H., "Point of View," in *A Glossary of Literary Terms*, 7th ed., Harcourt Brace, 1999, p. 233.

"Barbara Kimenye," in *The Companion to African Literatures*, edited by Douglas Killam and Ruth Rowe, Indiana University Press, 2000, p. 128.

Byrnes, Rita M., ed., *Uganda: A Country Study*, Federal Research Division, Library of Congress, 1992, pp. 18, 20, 81.

de Grandsaigne, Jean, and Gary Spackey, "The African Short Story Written in English: A Survey," in *Ariel*, Vol. 15, No. 2, April 1984, pp. 73–85.

"Feminism and Literature," in *The Companion to African Literatures*, edited by Douglas Killam and Ruth Rowe, Indiana University Press, 2000, p. 97.

Harmon, William, and Hugh Holman, "Foil," in *A Handbook to Literature*, 9th ed., Prentice Hall, 2003, p. 212.

Hunt, Jonathan, "Barbara Kimenye Obituary: One of East Africa's Most Popular Children's Authors," in *Guardian* (London, England) online, September 18, 2012, http://www.theguardian.com/world/2012/sep/18/barbara-kimenye (accessed September 15, 2013).

Kimenye, Barbara, "The Winner," in *African Short Stories: A Collection of Contemporary African Writing*, edited by Charles R. Lawson, Collier Books, 1970, pp. 71–83.

"Literary Criticism: East Africa," in *The Companion to African Literatures*, edited by Douglas Killam and Ruth Rowe, Indiana University Press, 2000, p. 137.

Mwaka, Victoria Miriam, "Women's Studies in Uganda," in *Women's Studies Quarterly*, Vol. 24, Nos. 1–2, Spring–Summer 1996, pp. 449–64.

"The 1966 Crisis," Buganda.com, http://www.buganda.com/crisis66.htm (accessed September 15, 2013).

Schmidt, Nancy J., "The Writer as Teacher: A Comparison of the African Adventure Stories of G. A. Henty, Rene Guillot, and Barbara Kimenye," in *African Studies Review*, Vol. 19, No. 2, September 1976, pp. 69–80.

"Uganda," in *CIA: The World Factbook*, Central Intelligence Agency website, https://www.cia.gov/library/publications/the-world-factbook/geos/ug.html (accessed September 15, 2013).

Welbourn, Hebe, "Village Gossip," in *Transition*, No. 24, 1966, p. 56.

"Women in Literature: East Africa," in *The Companion to African Literatures*, edited by Douglas Killam and Ruth Rowe, Indiana University Press, 2000, p. 302.

FURTHER READING

Davis, Caroline, *Creating Postcolonial Literature: African Writers and British Publishers*, Palgrave Macmillan, 2013.

> This book examines the literature of postcolonial Africa and how publishing shaped the expectations of authors and their audiences. Readers will appreciate Davis's use of historical context in her criticism.

Gikandi, Simon, and Evan Mwangi, *The Columbia Guide to East African Literature in English since 1945*, Columbia University Press, 2007.

> This reference book provides an overview of history, authors, and topics. The alphabetized topics make the book easy to use for students of all ages.

Krueger, Maria, *Women's Literature in Kenya and Uganda: The Trouble with Modernity*, Palgrave Macmillan, 2010.

> Krueger studies female authors in postcolonial Africa. The author examines the female role within the local community and its influence on writers and society.

Lihamba, Amadina, and Fulata L. Mayo, eds., *Women Writing Africa: The Eastern Region*, Feminist Press at the City University of New York, 2007.

> This collection provides an overview of women's literature in East Africa from 1711 to 2003.

Mwakikagile, Godfrey, *Uganda: The Land and Its People*, New Africa Press, 2009.

> Mwakikagile provides a useful introduction to the cultures and customs of Uganda. The book includes information about the history of the country as well as life in the twenty-first century.

Reid, Richard, *A History of Modern Africa: 1800 to the Present*, Wiley-Blackwell, 2012.

> This is a study of the British colonization of Africa. Reid examines how colonization has influenced African nations even after their independence. It is a valuable text for anyone interested in the history of Africa.

SUGGESTED SEARCH TERMS

Barbara Kimenye

Barbara Kimenye AND The Winner

Barbara Kimenye AND criticism

Uganda AND 1960s

Uganda AND history

Buganda AND history

Barbara Kimenye AND biography

East Africa AND literature

Uganda AND women

Glossary of Literary Terms

A

Aestheticism: A literary and artistic movement of the nineteenth century. Followers of the movement believed that art should not be mixed with social, political, or moral teaching. The statement "art for art's sake" is a good summary of aestheticism. The movement had its roots in France, but it gained widespread importance in England in the last half of the nineteenth century, where it helped change the Victorian practice of including moral lessons in literature. Oscar Wilde and Edgar Allan Poe are two of the best-known "aesthetes" of the late nineteenth century.

Allegory: A narrative technique in which characters representing things or abstract ideas are used to convey a message or teach a lesson. Allegory is typically used to teach moral, ethical, or religious lessons but is sometimes used for satiric or political purposes. Many fairy tales are allegories.

Allusion: A reference to a familiar literary or historical person or event, used to make an idea more easily understood. Joyce Carol Oates's story "Where Are You Going, Where Have You Been?" exhibits several allusions to popular music.

Analogy: A comparison of two things made to explain something unfamiliar through its similarities to something familiar, or to prove one point based on the acceptance of another. Similes and metaphors are types of analogies.

Antagonist: The major character in a narrative or drama who works against the hero or protagonist. The Misfit in Flannery O'Connor's story "A Good Man Is Hard to Find" serves as the antagonist for the Grandmother.

Anthology: A collection of similar works of literature, art, or music. Zora Neale Hurston's "The Eatonville Anthology" is a collection of stories that take place in the same town.

Anthropomorphism: The presentation of animals or objects in human shape or with human characteristics. The term is derived from the Greek word for "human form." The fur necklet in Katherine Mansfield's story "Miss Brill" has anthropomorphic characteristics.

Anti-hero: A central character in a work of literature who lacks traditional heroic qualities such as courage, physical prowess, and fortitude. Anti-heroes typically distrust conventional values and are unable to commit themselves to any ideals. They generally feel helpless in a world over which they have no control. Anti-heroes usually accept, and often celebrate, their positions as social outcasts. A well-known anti-hero is Walter Mitty in James Thurber's story "The Secret Life of Walter Mitty."

Archetype: The word archetype is commonly used to describe an original pattern or model from which all other things of the same kind are made. Archetypes are the literary images that grow out of the "collective unconscious," a theory proposed by psychologist Carl Jung. They appear in literature as incidents and plots that repeat basic patterns of life. They may also appear as stereotyped characters. The "schlemiel" of Yiddish literature is an archetype.

Autobiography: A narrative in which an individual tells his or her life story. Examples include Benjamin Franklin's *Autobiography* and Amy Hempel's story "In the Cemetery Where Al Jolson Is Buried," which has autobiographical characteristics even though it is a work of fiction.

Avant-garde: A literary term that describes new writing that rejects traditional approaches to literature in favor of innovations in style or content. Twentieth-century examples of the literary avant-garde include the modernists and the minimalists.

B

Belles-lettres: A French term meaning "fine letters" or" beautiful writing." It is often used as a synonym for literature, typically referring to imaginative and artistic rather than scientific or expository writing. Current usage sometimes restricts the meaning to light or humorous writing and appreciative essays about literature. Lewis Carroll's *Alice in Wonderland* epitomizes the realm of belles-lettres.

Bildungsroman: A German word meaning "novel of development." The *bildungsroman* is a study of the maturation of a youthful character, typically brought about through a series of social or sexual encounters that lead to self-awareness. J. D. Salinger's *Catcher in the Rye* is a *bildungsroman*, and Doris Lessing's story "Through the Tunnel" exhibits characteristics of a *bildungsroman* as well.

Black Aesthetic Movement: A period of artistic and literary development among African Americans in the 1960s and early 1970s. This was the first major African-American artistic movement since the Harlem Renaissance and was closely paralleled by the civil rights and black power movements. The black aesthetic writers attempted to produce works of art that would be meaningful to the black masses. Key figures in black aesthetics included one of its founders, poet and playwright Amiri Baraka, formerly known as Le Roi Jones; poet and essayist Haki R. Madhubuti, formerly Don L. Lee; poet and playwright Sonia Sanchez; and dramatist Ed Bullins. Works representative of the Black Aesthetic Movement include Amiri Baraka's play *Dutchman,* a 1964 Obie award-winner.

Black Humor: Writing that places grotesque elements side by side with humorous ones in an attempt to shock the reader, forcing him or her to laugh at the horrifying reality of a disordered world. "Lamb to the Slaughter," by Roald Dahl, in which a placid housewife murders her husband and serves the murder weapon to the investigating policemen, is an example of black humor.

C

Catharsis: The release or purging of unwanted emotions—specifically fear and pity—brought about by exposure to art. The term was first used by the Greek philosopher Aristotle in his *Poetics* to refer to the desired effect of tragedy on spectators.

Character: Broadly speaking, a person in a literary work. The actions of characters are what constitute the plot of a story, novel, or poem. There are numerous types of characters, ranging from simple, stereotypical figures to intricate, multifaceted ones. "Characterization" is the process by which an author creates vivid, believable characters in a work of art. This may be done in a variety of ways, including (1) direct description of the character by the narrator; (2) the direct presentation of the speech, thoughts, or actions of the character; and (3) the responses of other characters to the character. The term "character" also refers to a form originated by the ancient Greek writer Theophrastus that later became popular in the seventeenth and eighteenth centuries. It is a short essay or sketch of a person who prominently displays a specific attribute or quality, such as miserliness or ambition. "Miss Brill," a story by Katherine Mansfield, is an example of a character sketch.

Classical: In its strictest definition in literary criticism, classicism refers to works of ancient Greek or Roman literature. The term may also be used to describe a literary work of recognized importance (a "classic") from any time period or literature that exhibits the traits of classicism. Examples of later works and authors now described as classical include French literature of the seventeenth century, Western novels of the nineteenth century, and American fiction of the mid-nineteenth century such as that written by James Fenimore Cooper and Mark Twain.

Climax: The turning point in a narrative, the moment when the conflict is at its most intense. Typically, the structure of stories, novels, and plays is one of rising action, in which tension builds to the climax, followed by falling action, in which tension lessens as the story moves to its conclusion.

Comedy: One of two major types of drama, the other being tragedy. Its aim is to amuse, and it typically ends happily. Comedy assumes many forms, such as farce and burlesque, and uses a variety of techniques, from parody to satire. In a restricted sense the term comedy refers only to dramatic presentations, but in general usage it is commonly applied to nondramatic works as well.

Comic Relief: The use of humor to lighten the mood of a serious or tragic story, especially in plays. The technique is very common in Elizabethan works, and can be an integral part of the plot or simply a brief event designed to break the tension of the scene.

Conflict: The conflict in a work of fiction is the issue to be resolved in the story. It usually occurs between two characters, the protagonist and the antagonist, or between the protagonist and society or the protagonist and himself or herself. The conflict in Washington Irving's story "The Devil and Tom Walker" is that the Devil wants Tom Walker's soul but Tom does not want to go to hell.

Criticism: The systematic study and evaluation of literary works, usually based on a specific method or set of principles. An important part of literary studies since ancient times, the practice of criticism has given rise to numerous theories, methods, and "schools," sometimes producing conflicting, even contradictory, interpretations of literature in general as well as of individual works. Even such basic issues as what constitutes a poem or a novel have been the subject of much criticism over the centuries. Seminal texts of literary criticism include Plato's *Republic,* Aristotle's *Poetics,* Sir Philip Sidney's *The Defence of Poesie,* and John Dryden's *Of Dramatic Poesie.* Contemporary schools of criticism include deconstruction, feminist, psychoanalytic, poststructuralist, new historicist, postcolonialist, and reader-response.

D

Deconstruction: A method of literary criticism characterized by multiple conflicting interpretations of a given work. Deconstructionists consider the impact of the language of a work and suggest that the true meaning of the work is not necessarily the meaning that the author intended.

Deduction: The process of reaching a conclusion through reasoning from general premises to a specific premise. Arthur Conan Doyle's character Sherlock Holmes often used deductive reasoning to solve mysteries.

Denotation: The definition of a word, apart from the impressions or feelings it creates in the reader. The word "apartheid" denotes a political and economic policy of segregation by race, but its connotations—oppression, slavery, inequality—are numerous.

Denouement: A French word meaning "the unknotting." In literature, it denotes the resolution of conflict in fiction or drama. The *denouement* follows the climax and provides an outcome to the primary plot situation as well as an explanation of secondary plot complications. A well-known example of *denouement* is the last scene of the play *As You Like It* by William Shakespeare, in which couples are married, an evildoer repents, the identities of two disguised characters are revealed, and a ruler is restored to power. Also known as "falling action."

Detective Story: A narrative about the solution of a mystery or the identification of a criminal. The conventions of the detective story include the detective's scrupulous use of logic in solving the mystery; incompetent or ineffectual police; a suspect who appears guilty at first but is later proved innocent; and the detective's friend or confidant—often the narrator—whose slowness in interpreting clues emphasizes by contrast the detective's brilliance. Edgar Allan Poe's "Murders in the Rue Morgue" is commonly regarded as the earliest example of this type of story. Other practitioners are Arthur Conan Doyle, Dashiell Hammett, and Agatha Christie.

Dialogue: Dialogue is conversation between people in a literary work. In its most restricted sense, it refers specifically to the speech of characters in a drama. As a specific literary genre, a "dialogue" is a composition in which characters debate an issue or idea.

Didactic: A term used to describe works of literature that aim to teach a moral, religious, political, or practical lesson. Although didactic elements are often found inartistically pleasing works, the term "didactic" usually refers to literature in which the message is more important than the form. The term may also be used to criticize a work that the critic finds "overly didactic," that is, heavy-handed in its delivery of a lesson. An example of didactic literature is John Bunyan's *Pilgrim's Progress*.

Dramatic Irony: Occurs when the reader of a work of literature knows something that a character in the work itself does not know. The irony is in the contrast between the intended meaning of the statements or actions of a character and the additional information understood by the audience.

Dystopia: An imaginary place in a work of fiction where the characters lead dehumanized, fearful lives. George Orwell's *Nineteen Eighty-four,* and Margaret Atwood's *Handmaid's Tale* portray versions of dystopia.

E

Edwardian: Describes cultural conventions identified with the period of the reign of Edward VII of England (1901–1910). Writers of the Edwardian Age typically displayed a strong reaction against the propriety and conservatism of the Victorian Age. Their work often exhibits distrust of authority in religion, politics, and art and expresses strong doubts about the soundness of conventional values. Writers of this era include E. M. Forster, H. G. Wells, and Joseph Conrad.

Empathy: A sense of shared experience, including emotional and physical feelings, with someone or something other than oneself. Empathy is often used to describe the response of a reader to a literary character.

Epilogue: A concluding statement or section of a literary work. In dramas, particularly those of the seventeenth and eighteenth centuries, the epilogue is a closing speech, often in verse, delivered by an actor at the end of a play and spoken directly to the audience.

Epiphany: A sudden revelation of truth inspired by a seemingly trivial incident. The term was widely used by James Joyce in his critical writings, and the stories in Joyce's *Dubliners* are commonly called "epiphanies."

Epistolary Novel: A novel in the form of letters. The form was particularly popular in the eighteenth century. The form can also be applied to short stories, as in Edwidge Danticat's "Children of the Sea."

Epithet: A word or phrase, often disparaging or abusive, that expresses a character trait of someone or something. "The Napoleon of crime" is an epithet applied to Professor Moriarty, arch-rival of Sherlock Holmes in Arthur Conan Doyle's series of detective stories.

Existentialism: A predominantly twentieth-century philosophy concerned with the nature and perception of human existence. There are two major strains of existentialist thought: atheistic and Christian. Followers of atheistic existentialism believe that the individual is alone in a godless universe and that the basic human condition is one of suffering and loneliness. Nevertheless, because there are no fixed values, individuals can create their own characters—indeed, they can shape themselves—through the exercise of free will. The atheistic strain culminates in and is popularly associated with the works of Jean-Paul Sartre. The Christian existentialists, on the other hand, believe that only in God may people find freedom from life's anguish. The two strains hold certain beliefs in common: that existence cannot be fully understood or described through empirical effort; that anguish is a universal element of life; that individuals must bear responsibility for their actions; and that there is no common standard of behavior or perception for religious and ethical matters. Existentialist thought figures prominently in the works of such authors as Franz Kafka, Fyodor Dostoyevsky, and Albert Camus.

Expatriatism: The practice of leaving one's country to live for an extended period in another country. Literary expatriates include Irish author James Joyce who moved to Italy and France, American writers James Baldwin, Ernest Hemingway, Gertrude Stein, and F. Scott Fitzgerald who lived and wrote in Paris, and Polish novelist Joseph Conrad in England.

Exposition: Writing intended to explain the nature of an idea, thing, or theme. Expository writing is often combined with description, narration, or argument.

Expressionism: An indistinct literary term, originally used to describe an early twentieth-century school of German painting. The term applies to almost any mode of unconventional, highly subjective writing that distorts reality in some way. Advocates of Expressionism include Federico Garcia Lorca, Eugene O'Neill, Franz Kafka, and James Joyce.

F

Fable: A prose or verse narrative intended to convey amoral. Animals or inanimate objects with human characteristics often serve as characters in fables. A famous fable is Aesop's "The Tortoise and the Hare."

Fantasy: A literary form related to mythology and folklore. Fantasy literature is typically set in non-existent realms and features supernatural beings. Notable examples of literature with elements of fantasy are Gabriel García Márquez's story "The Handsomest Drowned Man in the World" and Ursula K. Le Guin's "The Ones Who Walk Away from Omelas."

Farce: A type of comedy characterized by broad humor, outlandish incidents, and often vulgar subject matter. Much of the comedy in film and television could more accurately be described as farce.

Fiction: Any story that is the product of imagination rather than a documentation of fact. Characters and events in such narratives may be based in real life but their ultimate form and configuration is a creation of the author.

Figurative Language: A technique in which an author uses figures of speech such as hyperbole, irony, metaphor, or simile for a particular effect. Figurative language is the opposite of literal language, in which every word is truthful, accurate, and free of exaggeration or embellishment.

Flashback: A device used in literature to present action that occurred before the beginning of the story. Flashbacks are often introduced as the dreams or recollections of one or more characters.

Foil: A character in a work of literature whose physical or psychological qualities contrast strongly with, and therefore highlight, the corresponding qualities of another character. In his Sherlock Holmes stories, Arthur Conan Doyle portrayed Dr. Watson as a man of normal habits and intelligence, making him a foil for the eccentric and unusually perceptive Sherlock Holmes.

Folklore: Traditions and myths preserved in a culture or group of people. Typically, these are passed on by word of mouth in various forms—such as legends, songs, and proverbs—or preserved in customs and ceremonies. Washington Irving, in "The Devil and Tom Walker" and many of his other stories, incorporates many elements of the folklore of New England and Germany.

Folktale: A story originating in oral tradition. Folk tales fall into a variety of categories, including legends, ghost stories, fairy tales, fables, and anecdotes based on historical figures and events.

Foreshadowing: A device used in literature to create expectation or to set up an explanation of later developments. Edgar Allan Poe uses foreshadowing to create suspense in "The Fall of the House of Usher" when the narrator comments on the crumbling state of disrepair in which he finds the house.

G

Genre: A category of literary work. Genre may refer to both the content of a given work—tragedy, comedy, horror, science fiction—and to its form, such as poetry, novel, or drama.

Gilded Age: A period in American history during the 1870s and after characterized by political corruption and materialism. A number of important novels of social and political criticism were written during this time. Henry James and Kate Chopin are two writers who were prominent during the Gilded Age.

Gothicism: In literature, works characterized by a taste for medieval or morbid characters and situations. A gothic novel prominently features elements of horror, the supernatural, gloom, and violence: clanking chains, terror, ghosts, medieval castles, and unexplained phenomena. The term "gothic novel" is also applied to novels that lack elements of the traditional Gothic setting but that create a similar atmosphere of terror or dread. The term can also be applied to stories, plays, and poems. Mary Shelley's *Frankenstein* and Joyce Carol Oates's *Belle-fleur* are both gothic novels.

Grotesque: In literature, a work that is characterized by exaggeration, deformity, freakishness, and disorder. The grotesque often includes an element of comic absurdity. Examples of the grotesque can be found in the works of Edgar Allan Poe, Flannery O'Connor, Joseph Heller, and Shirley Jackson.

H

Harlem Renaissance: The Harlem Renaissance of the 1920s is generally considered the first significant movement of black writers and artists in the United States. During this period, new and established black writers, many of whom lived in the region of New York City known as Harlem, published more fiction and poetry than ever before, the first influential black literary journals were established, and black authors and artists received their first widespread recognition and serious critical appraisal. Among the major writers associated with this period are Countee Cullen, Langston Hughes, Arna Bontemps, and Zora Neale Hurston.

Hero/Heroine: The principal sympathetic character in a literary work. Heroes and heroines typically exhibit admirable traits: idealism, courage, and integrity, for example. Famous heroes and heroines of literature include Charles Dickens's Oliver Twist, Margaret Mitchell's Scarlett O'Hara, and the anonymous narrator in Ralph Ellison's *Invisible Man*.

Hyperbole: Deliberate exaggeration used to achieve an effect. In William Shakespeare's *Macbeth*, Lady Macbeth hyperbolizes when she says, "All the perfumes of Arabia could not sweeten this little hand."

I

Image: A concrete representation of an object or sensory experience. Typically, such a representation helps evoke the feelings associated with the object or experience itself. Images are either "literal" or "figurative." Literal images are especially concrete and involve little or no extension of the obvious meaning of the words used to express them. Figurative images do not follow the literal meaning of the words exactly. Images in literature are usually visual, but the term "image" can also refer to the representation of any sensory experience.

Imagery: The array of images in a literary work. Also used to convey the author's overall use of figurative language in a work.

In medias res: A Latin term meaning "in the middle of things." It refers to the technique of beginning a story at its midpoint and then using various flashback devices to reveal previous action. This technique originated in such epics as Virgil's *Aeneid*.

Interior Monologue: A narrative technique in which characters' thoughts are revealed in a way that appears to be uncontrolled by the author. The interior monologue typically aims to reveal the inner self of a character. It portrays emotional experiences as they occur at both a conscious and unconscious level. One of the best-known interior monologues in English is the Molly Bloom section at the close of James Joyce's *Ulysses*. Katherine Anne Porter's "The Jilting of Granny Weatherall" is also told in the form of an interior monologue.

Irony: In literary criticism, the effect of language in which the intended meaning is the opposite of what is stated. The title of Jonathan Swift's "A Modest Proposal" is ironic because what Swift proposes in this essay is cannibalism—hardly "modest."

J

Jargon: Language that is used or understood only by a select group of people. Jargon may refer to terminology used in a certain profession, such as computer jargon, or it may refer to any nonsensical language that is not understood by most people. Anthony Burgess's *A Clockwork Orange* and James Thurber's "The Secret Life of Walter Mitty" both use jargon.

K

Knickerbocker Group: An indistinct group of New York writers of the first half of the nineteenth century. Members of the group were linked only by location and a common theme: New York life. Two famous members of the Knickerbocker Group were Washington Irving and William Cullen Bryant. The group's name derives from Irving's *Knickerbocker's History of New York*.

L

Literal Language: An author uses literal language when he or she writes without exaggerating or embellishing the subject matter and without any tools of figurative language. To say "He ran very quickly down the street" is to use literal language, whereas to say "He ran like a hare down the street" would be using figurative language.

Literature: Literature is broadly defined as any written or spoken material, but the term most often refers to creative works. Literature includes poetry, drama, fiction, and many kinds of nonfiction writing, as well as oral, dramatic, and broadcast compositions not necessarily preserved in a written format, such as films and television programs.

Lost Generation: A term first used by Gertrude Stein to describe the post-World War I generation of American writers: men and women haunted by a sense of betrayal and emptiness brought about by the destructiveness of the war. The term is commonly applied to Hart Crane, Ernest Hemingway, F. Scott Fitzgerald, and others.

M

Magic Realism: A form of literature that incorporates fantasy elements or supernatural occurrences into the narrative and accepts them as truth. Gabriel Gárcia Márquez and Laura Esquivel are two writers known for their works of magic realism.

Metaphor: A figure of speech that expresses an idea through the image of another object. Metaphors suggest the essence of the first object by identifying it with certain qualities of the second object. An example is "But soft, what light through yonder window breaks? / It is the east, and Juliet is the sun" in William Shakespeare's *Romeo and Juliet*. Here, Juliet, the first object, is identified with qualities of the second object, the sun.

Minimalism: A literary style characterized by spare, simple prose with few elaborations. In minimalism, the main theme of the work is often never discussed directly. Amy Hempel and Ernest Hemingway are two writers known for their works of minimalism.

Modernism: Modern literary practices. Also, the principles of a literary school that lasted from roughly the beginning of the twentieth century until the end of World War II. Modernism is defined by its rejection of the literary conventions of the nineteenth century and by its opposition to conventional morality, taste, traditions, and economic values. Many writers are associated with the concepts of modernism, including Albert Camus, D. H. Lawrence, Ernest Hemingway, William Faulkner, Eugene O'Neill, and James Joyce.

Monologue: A composition, written or oral, by a single individual. More specifically, a speech given by a single individual in a drama or other public entertainment. It has no set length, although it is usually several or more lines long. "I Stand Here Ironing" by Tillie Olsen is an example of a story written in the form of a monologue.

Mood: The prevailing emotions of a work or of the author in his or her creation of the work. The mood of a work is not always what might be expected based on its subject matter.

Motif: A theme, character type, image, metaphor, or other verbal element that recurs throughout a single work of literature or occurs in a number of different works over a period of time. For example, the color white in Herman Melville's *Moby Dick* is a "specific" motif, while the trials of star-crossed lovers is a "conventional" motif from the literature of all periods.

N

Narration: The telling of a series of events, real or invented. A narration may be either a simple narrative, in which the events are recounted chronologically, or a narrative with a plot, in which the account is given in a style reflecting the author's artistic concept of the story. Narration is sometimes used as a synonym for "storyline."

Narrative: A verse or prose accounting of an event or sequence of events, real or invented. The term is also used as an adjective in the sense "method of narration." For example, in literary criticism, the expression "narrative technique" usually refers to the way the author structures and presents his or her story. Different narrative forms include diaries, travelogues, novels, ballads, epics, short stories, and other fictional forms.

Narrator: The teller of a story. The narrator may be the author or a character in the story through whom the author speaks. Huckleberry Finn is the narrator of Mark Twain's *The Adventures of Huckleberry Finn*.

Novella: An Italian term meaning "story." This term has been especially used to describe fourteenth-century Italian tales, but it also refers to modern short novels. Modern novellas include Leo Tolstoy's *The Death of Ivan Ilich*, Fyodor Dostoyevsky's *Notes from the Underground*, and Joseph Conrad's *Heart of Darkness*.

O

Oedipus Complex: A son's romantic obsession with his mother. The phrase is derived from the story of the ancient Theban hero Oedipus, who unknowingly killed his father and married his mother, and was popularized by Sigmund Freud's theory of psychoanalysis. Literary occurrences of the Oedipus complex include Sophocles' *Oedipus Rex* and D. H. Lawrence's "The Rocking-Horse Winner."

Onomatopoeia: The use of words whose sounds express or suggest their meaning. In its simplest sense, onomatopoeia may be represented by words that mimic the sounds they denote such as "hiss" or "meow." At a more subtle level, the pattern and rhythm of sounds and rhymes of a line or poem may be onomatopoeic.

Oral Tradition: A process by which songs, ballads, folklore, and other material are transmitted by word of mouth. The tradition of oral transmission predates the written record systems of literate society. Oral transmission preserves material sometimes over generations, although often with variations. Memory plays a large part in the recitation and preservation of orally transmitted material. Native American myths and legends, and African folktales told by plantation slaves are examples of orally transmitted literature.

P

Parable: A story intended to teach a moral lesson or answer an ethical question. Examples of parables are the stories told by Jesus Christ in the New Testament, notably "The Prodigal Son," but parables also are used in Sufism, rabbinic literature, Hasidism, and Zen Buddhism. Isaac Bashevis Singer's story "Gimpel the Fool" exhibits characteristics of a parable.

Paradox: A statement that appears illogical or contradictory at first, but may actually point to an underlying truth. A literary example of a paradox is George Orwell's statement "All animals are equal, but some animals are more equal than others" in *Animal Farm*.

Parody: In literature, this term refers to an imitation of a serious literary work or the signature style of a particular author in a ridiculous manner. A typical parody adopts the style of the original and applies it to an inappropriate subject for humorous effect. Parody is a form of satire and could be considered the literary equivalent of a caricature or cartoon. Henry Fielding's *Shamela* is a parody of Samuel Richardson's *Pamela*.

Persona: A Latin term meaning "mask." Personae are the characters in a fictional work of literature. The persona generally functions as a mask through which the author tells a story in a voice other than his or her own. A persona is usually either a character in a story who acts as a narrator or an "implied author," a voice created by the author to act as the narrator for himself or herself. The persona in Charlotte Perkins Gilman's story "The Yellow Wallpaper" is the unnamed young mother experiencing a mental breakdown.

Personification: A figure of speech that gives human qualities to abstract ideas, animals, and inanimate objects. To say that "the sun is smiling" is to personify the sun.

Plot: The pattern of events in a narrative or drama. In its simplest sense, the plot guides the author in composing the work and helps the reader follow the work. Typically, plots exhibit causality and unity and have a beginning, a middle, and an end. Sometimes, however, a plot may consist of a series of disconnected events, in which case it is known as an "episodic plot."

Poetic Justice: An outcome in a literary work, not necessarily a poem, in which the good are rewarded and the evil are punished, especially in ways that particularly fit their virtues or crimes. For example, a murderer may himself be murdered, or a thief will find himself penniless.

Poetic License: Distortions of fact and literary convention made by a writer—not always a poet—for the sake of the effect gained. Poetic license is closely related to the concept of "artistic freedom." An author exercises poetic license by saying that a pile of money "reaches as high as a mountain" when the pile is actually only a foot or two high.

Point of View: The narrative perspective from which a literary work is presented to the reader. There are four traditional points of view. The "third person omniscient" gives the reader a "godlike" perspective, unrestricted by time or place, from which to see actions and look into the minds of characters. This allows the author to comment openly on characters and events in the work. The "third person" point of view presents the events of the story from outside of any single character's perception, much like the omniscient point of view, but the reader must understand the action as it takes place and without any special insight into characters' minds or motivations. The "first person" or "personal" point of view relates events as they are perceived by a single character. The main character "tells" the story and may offer opinions about the action and characters which differ from those of the author. Much less common than omniscient, third person, and first person is the

"second person" point of view, wherein the author tells the story as if it is happening to the reader. James Thurber employs the omniscient point of view in his short story "The Secret Life of Walter Mitty." Ernest Hemingway's "A Clean, Well-Lighted Place" is a short story told from the third person point of view. Mark Twain's novel *Huckleberry Finn* is presented from the first person viewpoint. Jay McInerney's *Bright Lights, Big City* is an example of a novel which uses the second person point of view.

Pornography: Writing intended to provoke feelings of lust in the reader. Such works are often condemned by critics and teachers, but those which can be shown to have literary value are viewed less harshly. Literary works that have been described as pornographic include D. H. Lawrence's *Lady Chatterley's Lover* and James Joyce's *Ulysses.*

Post-Aesthetic Movement: An artistic response made by African Americans to the black aesthetic movement of the 1960s and early 1970s. Writers since that time have adopted a somewhat different tone in their work, with less emphasis placed on the disparity between black and white in the United States. In the words of post-aesthetic authors such as Toni Morrison, John Edgar Wideman, and Kristin Hunter, African Americans are portrayed as looking inward for answers to their own questions, rather than always looking to the outside world. Two well-known examples of works produced as part of the post-aesthetic movement are the Pulitzer Prize–winning novels *The Color Purple* by Alice Walker and *Beloved* by Toni Morrison.

Postmodernism: Writing from the 1960s forward characterized by experimentation and application of modernist elements, which include existentialism and alienation. Postmodernists have gone a step further in the rejection of tradition begun with the modernists by also rejecting traditional forms, preferring the anti-novel over the novel and the anti-hero over the hero. Postmodern writers include Thomas Pynchon, Margaret Drabble, and Gabriel García Márquez.

Prologue: An introductory section of a literary work. It often contains information establishing the situation of the characters or presents information about the setting, time period, or action. In drama, the prologue is spoken by a chorus or by one of the principal characters.

Prose: A literary medium that attempts to mirror the language of everyday speech. It is distinguished from poetry by its use of unmetered, unrhymed language consisting of logically related sentences. Prose is usually grouped into paragraphs that form a cohesive whole such as an essay or a novel. The term is sometimes used to mean an author's general writing.

Protagonist: The central character of a story who serves as a focus for its themes and incidents and as the principal rationale for its development. The protagonist is sometimes referred to in discussions of modern literature as the hero or anti-hero. Well-known protagonists are Hamlet in William Shakespeare's *Hamlet* and Jay Gatsby in F. Scott Fitzgerald's *The Great Gatsby*.

R

Realism: A nineteenth-century European literary movement that sought to portray familiar characters, situations, and settings in a realistic manner. This was done primarily by using an objective narrative point of view and through the buildup of accurate detail. The standard for success of any realistic work depends on how faithfully it transfers common experience into fictional forms. The realistic method may be altered or extended, as in stream of consciousness writing, to record highly subjective experience. Contemporary authors who often write in a realistic way include Nadine Gordimer and Grace Paley.

Resolution: The portion of a story following the climax, in which the conflict is resolved. The resolution of Jane Austen's *Northanger Abbey* is neatly summed up in the following sentence: "Henry and Catherine were married, the bells rang and every body smiled."

Rising Action: The part of a drama where the plot becomes increasingly complicated. Rising action leads up to the climax, or turning point, of a drama. The final "chase scene" of an action film is generally the rising action which culminates in the film's climax.

Roman a clef: A French phrase meaning "novel with a key." It refers to a narrative in which real persons are portrayed under fictitious names. Jack Kerouac, for example, portrayed various friends under fictitious names in the novel *On the Road*. D. H. Lawrence based "The Rocking-Horse Winner" on a family he knew.

Romanticism: This term has two widely accepted meanings. In historical criticism, it refers to a European intellectual and artistic movement of the late eighteenth and early nineteenth centuries that sought greater freedom of personal expression than that allowed by the strict rules of literary form and logic of the eighteenth-century neoclassicists. The Romantics preferred emotional and imaginative expression to rational analysis. They considered the individual to be at the center of all experience and so placed him or her at the center of their art. The Romantics believed that the creative imagination reveals nobler truths—unique feelings and attitudes—than those that could be discovered by logic or by scientific examination. "Romanticism" is also used as a general term to refer to a type of sensibility found in all periods of literary history and usually considered to be in opposition to the principles of classicism. In this sense, Romanticism signifies any work or philosophy in which the exotic or dreamlike figure strongly, or that is devoted to individualistic expression, self-analysis, or a pursuit of a higher realm of knowledge than can be discovered by human reason. Prominent Romantics include Jean-Jacques Rousseau, William Wordsworth, John Keats, Lord Byron, and Johann Wolfgang von Goethe.

S

Satire: A work that uses ridicule, humor, and wit to criticize and provoke change in human nature and institutions. Voltaire's novella *Candide* and Jonathan Swift's essay "A Modest Proposal" are both satires. Flannery O'Connor's portrayal of the family in "A Good Man Is Hard to Find" is a satire of a modern, Southern, American family.

Science Fiction: A type of narrative based upon real or imagined scientific theories and technology. Science fiction is often peopled with alien creatures and set on other planets or in different dimensions. Popular writers of science fiction are Isaac Asimov, Karel Capek, Ray Bradbury, and Ursula K. Le Guin.

Setting: The time, place, and culture in which the action of a narrative takes place. The elements of setting may include geographic location, characters's physical and mental environments, prevailing cultural attitudes, or the historical time in which the action takes place.

Short Story: A fictional prose narrative shorter and more focused than a novella. The short story usually deals with a single episode and often a single character. The "tone," the author's attitude toward his or her subject and audience, is uniform throughout. The short story frequently also lacks *denouement*, ending instead at its climax.

Signifying Monkey: A popular trickster figure in black folklore, with hundreds of tales about this character documented since the 19th century. Henry Louis Gates Jr. examines the history of the signifying monkey in *The Signifying Monkey: Towards a Theory of Afro-American Literary Criticism,* published in 1988.

Simile: A comparison, usually using "like" or "as," of two essentially dissimilar things, as in "coffee as cold as ice" or "He sounded like a broken record." The title of Ernest Hemingway's "Hills Like White Elephants" contains a simile.

Socialist Realism: The Socialist Realism school of literary theory was proposed by Maxim Gorky and established as a dogma by the first Soviet Congress of Writers. It demanded adherence to a communist worldview in works of literature. Its doctrines required an objective viewpoint comprehensible to the working classes and themes of social struggle featuring strong proletarian heroes. Gabriel Gárcia Márquez's stories exhibit some characteristics of Socialist Realism.

Stereotype: A stereotype was originally the name for a duplication made during the printing process; this led to its modern definition as a person or thing that is (or is assumed to be) the same as all others of its type. Common stereotypical characters include the absentminded professor, the nagging wife, the troublemaking teenager, and the kindhearted grandmother.

Stream of Consciousness: A narrative technique for rendering the inward experience of a character. This technique is designed to give the impression of an ever-changing series of thoughts, emotions, images, and memories in the spontaneous and seemingly illogical order that they occur in life. The textbook example of stream of consciousness is the last section of James Joyce's *Ulysses*.

Structure: The form taken by a piece of literature. The structure may be made obvious for ease of understanding, as in nonfiction works, or may obscured for artistic purposes, as in some poetry or seemingly "unstructured" prose.

Style: A writer's distinctive manner of arranging words to suit his or her ideas and purpose in writing. The unique imprint of the author's personality upon his or her writing, style is the product of an author's way of arranging ideas and his or her use of diction, different sentence structures, rhythm, figures of speech, rhetorical principles, and other elements of composition.

Suspense: A literary device in which the author maintains the audience's attention through the buildup of events, the outcome of which will soon be revealed. Suspense in William Shakespeare's *Hamlet* is sustained throughout by the question of whether or not the Prince will achieve what he has been instructed to do and of what he intends to do.

Symbol: Something that suggests or stands for something else without losing its original identity. In literature, symbols combine their literal meaning with the suggestion of an abstract concept. Literary symbols are of two types: those that carry complex associations of meaning no matter what their contexts, and those that derive their suggestive meaning from their functions in specific literary works. Examples of symbols are sunshine suggesting happiness, rain suggesting sorrow, and storm clouds suggesting despair.

T

Tale: A story told by a narrator with a simple plot and little character development. Tales are usually relatively short and often carry a simple message. Examples of tales can be found in the works of Saki, Anton Chekhov, Guy de Maupassant, and O. Henry.

Tall Tale: A humorous tale told in a straightforward, credible tone but relating absolutely impossible events or feats of the characters. Such tales were commonly told of frontier adventures during the settlement of the west in the United States. Literary use of tall tales can be found in Washington Irving's *History of New York,* Mark Twain's *Life on the Mississippi,* and in the German R. F. Raspe's *Baron Munchausen's Narratives of His Marvellous Travels and Campaigns in Russia.*

Theme: The main point of a work of literature. The term is used interchangeably with thesis. Many works have multiple themes. One of the themes of Nathaniel Hawthorne's "Young Goodman Brown" is loss of faith.

Tone: The author's attitude toward his or her audience maybe deduced from the tone of the work. A formal tone may create distance or convey politeness, while an informal tone may encourage a friendly, intimate, or intrusive feeling in the reader. The author's attitude toward his or her subject matter may also be deduced from the tone of the words he or she uses in discussing it. The tone of John F. Kennedy's speech which included the appeal to "ask not what your country can do for you" was intended to instill feelings of camaraderie and national pride in listeners.

Tragedy: A drama in prose or poetry about a noble, courageous hero of excellent character who, because of some tragic character flaw, brings ruin upon him- or herself. Tragedy treats its subjects in a dignified and serious manner, using poetic language to help evoke pity and fear and bring about catharsis, a purging of these emotions. The tragic form was practiced extensively by the ancient Greeks. The classical form of tragedy was revived in the sixteenth century; it flourished especially on the Elizabethan stage. In modern times, dramatists have attempted to adapt the form to the needs of modern society by drawing their heroes from the ranks of ordinary men and women and defining the nobility of these heroes in terms of spirit rather than exalted social standing. Some contemporary works that are thought of as tragedies include *The Great Gatsby* by F. Scott Fitzgerald, and *The Sound and the Fury* by William Faulkner.

Tragic Flaw: In a tragedy, the quality within the hero or heroine which leads to his or her downfall. Examples of the tragic flaw include Othello's jealousy and Hamlet's indecisiveness, although most great tragedies defy such simple interpretation.

U

Utopia: A fictional perfect place, such as "paradise" or "heaven." An early literary utopia was described in Plato's *Republic,* and in modern literature, Ursula K. Le Guin depicts a utopia in "The Ones Who Walk Away from Omelas."

V

Victorian: Refers broadly to the reign of Queen Victoria of England (1837-1901) and to anything with qualities typical of that era. For example, the qualities of smug narrow-mindedness, bourgeois materialism, faith in social progress, and priggish morality are often considered Victorian. In literature, the Victorian Period was the great age of the English novel, and the latter part of the era saw the rise of movements such as decadence and symbolism.

Cumulative Author/Title Index

Cumulative Nationality/Ethnicity Index

Subject/Theme Index